A. C. VAN RAALTE

Albertus C. Van Raalte, official portrait with signature (*JAH*)

A. C. VAN RAALTE
Pastor by Vocation
Entrepreneur by Necessity

Robert P. Swierenga

© 2023 Van Raalte Press
All rights reserved

A. C. Van Raalte Institute, Hope College
Van Raalte Press is a division of Hope College Publishing

Theil Research Center
9 East 10th Street
Holland, MI 49423

PO Box 9000
Holland, MI 49422-9000

616.395.7678
vanraalte@hope.edu

Printed in the United States of America
Library of Congress Control Number: 2022947102

Jacob E. Nyenhuis, PhD, LittD
    Editor-in-Chief and Publisher
JoHannah Smith
    Project Editor
Russell L. Gasero, Archivist Emeritus, Reformed Church in America
    Layout and Design
Cover Design
    Willem Mineur

The cover image comes from a portrait of Albertus C. Van Raalte that hangs in the Van Raalte Institute of the Theil Research Center at Hope College (see page opposite), painted in 1896 by Joseph Warner of Holland and restored by Kenneth B. Katz of Conservation and Museum Services in Detroit, with funding from Hope College trustee, the late Peter H. Huizenga.

Dedication

Rev. Dr. Elton John Bruins, Evert J. and Hattie E. Blekkink Professor of Religion Emeritus, devoted himself to studying the life of A. C. Van Raalte and earned the epitaph, "Mr. Van Raalte." The thousands of documents he uncovered and carefully catalogued have served as the basis for this biography. (*Hope College Office of Public Relations*)

Robert P. Swierenga is the Albertus C. Van Raalte Research Professor at the A. C. Van Raalte Institute, Hope College, Holland, Michigan, and professor of history emeritus at Kent State University, Ohio. A specialist in Dutch immigration history, he is the author of fourteen books, including the widely acclaimed *Dutch Chicago: A History of the Hollanders in the Windy City* (2002), and the three-volume *Holland, Michigan: From Dutch Colony to Dynamic City* (2014). Besides a twenty-eight-year career at Kent State, Swierenga taught at Calvin College, Hope College, University of Iowa, and Catholic University Leuven. He was twice a Fulbright Fellow at Leiden University. In 2000 Swierenga was knighted by Queen Beatrix in the Order of the Netherlands Lion, and in 2003, he was named a Distinguished Alumnus by the Alumni Association of his alma mater, Calvin University.

Contents

Acknowledgments	ix
Preface	xiii
Introduction	xix
1. Father Van Raalte's Life and Ministry: "A great example to me."	1
2. Dissenter: "I followed the voice of conscience."	27
3. Apostle of Overijssel: "A partridge hunted in the mountains."	67
4. Church Struggles: "God alone can build the church."	101
5. Ommen Pastorate: "An honorable life."	113
6. Seminary Professor: "I may enjoy this work."	143
7. Fleeing the Homeland: "We must go to America."	157
8. Choosing the Site: "Michigan is the place."	185
9. Founding Holland Colony: "City on a hill."	217
10. Dauntless Dominee: "My labor is not in vain."	279
11. Public and Christian Education: "A great and difficult work."	329
12. Land and Business: "God could have made me a capitalist."	367
13. Newspaper Magnate, Political Leader, Civil War Patriot: More "worldly matters."	407
14. Retirement from First Church: "Ending a hurtful situation."	445
15. Ministry in Retirement: "May God give me strength."	483
16. Sunset of Life: "A quiet, joyous feeling."	531
17. Assessment and Evaluation: "Mighty in words and deeds."	573
Appendix	589
Bibliography	595
Index	623

Maps

"Bible Belt" region of the Netherlands, 1845	2
Van Raalte's preaching tour, 1837-38	96
Van Raalte's area of influence in Drenthe	133
Erie Canal route	189
Travel routes to Holland Colony, 1847	191
Van Raalte's hand-drawn Holland plat, 1847	226
Holland village plat, 1848	227
Holland Colony settlement, 1848	234
Third Holland plat, March 1866	439
City of Holland, 2014, with Federal District	441
Helena (Mrs. Albertus) Van Raalte farm	480
Amelia County, Virginia, settlements	491
Area of Holland Fire, October 8-9, 1871	512
Holland Colony at Van Raalte's death, 1876	588

Abbreviations

ADC	Archives and Documentation Center of the Reformed Churches, Liberated (Vrijgemaakt), Kampen, the Netherlands
BDM	Board of Domestic Missions of the RCA
HHA	Heritage Hall, Archives for the CRC, Calvin Theological Seminary, and Calvin University, in the Hekman Library at Calvin University
HMA	Holland Historical Trust Collections, Holland Museum Archives
JAH	Joint Archives of Holland, Hope College
RCA	Reformed Church in America
RPDC	Reformed Protestant Dutch Church, New Brunswick New Jersey
VRI	Van Raalte Institute, Hope College

Acknowledgments

This book is a cooperative endeavor of my colleagues at the A. C. Van Raalte Institute of Hope College. Every person has contributed in one way or another. Most important has been the dedicated work of our official translator, Nella (Mrs. Earl Wm.) Kennedy, who converted hundreds of Dutch-language, Van Raalte-related documents and news items into English with clarity and accuracy, retaining the dominee's unique style and voice. Earl Wm. "Bill" Kennedy is the sleuth who tracked down first names and other information about Van Raalte and his correspondents in genealogical websites, including Netherlands search engines. In particular, Bill searched Delpher.nl to unearth new, previously unknown information about Van Raalte, primarily from the church periodical *De Bazuin*, as well as other Dutch newspapers. All the many Delpher.nl citations in this book have been provided by Bill Kennedy, including their English translations. Bill and Nella shared their considerable knowledge of Netherlands history, the Van Raalte paternal and maternal lines, Christina de Moen's paternal lines, and father Van Raalte's pastorates. Nella Kennedy's work is evident in the early chapters; she expanded upon life in the Van Raalte manse of father and son and explained Dutch political and religious history during the tumultuous decades from 1790 to 1850. This book is far richer and more nuanced because of Bill and Nella Kennedy's diligent research in Dutch-language sources. Jan Boersma, professor of environmental sciences at Leiden University and VRI Dutch honorary research fellow and former visiting research fellow, read the penultimate draft with an eye for misspelled Dutch words and citations. My poor Dutch has now been perfected. He also drew on his vast knowledge of Netherlands church history and polity to tighten the text.

Jacob E. Nyenhuis, editor-in-chief of the Van Raalte Press, read the final copy with his usual eagle eye and saved me from embarrassing errors, misstatements, and unexplained omissions. Henk Aay, senior research fellow and historical geographer, and Donald A. Luidens, director of the Van Raalte Institute and sociologist, lent moral support and offered advice, as did Dennis N. Voskuil, professor emeritus at Western Theological Seminary, who is writing a definitive history of the seminary that grew out of the religion department of Hope College, Van Raalte's ultimate legacy. Donald J. Bruggink, general editor emeritus of the Historical Series of the Reformed Church in America, who has shepherded almost one hundred volumes to press, read selected chapters and helped me see personal biases and idiosyncrasies. I also benefitted from his knowledge of Reformed Church polity. Paul Heusinkveld read the manuscript as an "outsider" to the subject and identified names, events, and subjects that required clarification for general readers. Not one to waste an opportunity, he also spotted typos, verb tense issues, and other slip-ups early on. Most important, he touched up and arranged numerous photos, as did Henk Aay.

JoHannah Smith, our meticulous project editor, rephrased obtuse and awkward sentences, caught errors and repetition, and generally ensured that text, footnotes, and bibliography conformed to our style guide. Russell L. Gasero, retired Reformed Church archivist, laid out the text and illustrations. He and JoHannah are the essential duo in seeing this book to press. Mark Cook, Hope College cartographer, created maps of the Netherlands for American readers.

Several transnational scholars, all long-time friends and colleagues, took time from their professional duties and writing projects to read drafts of my book, for which I am grateful. Mees te Velde, professor emeritus at the Theological Seminary Kampen, marked up the first nine chapters with a sharp pen. Having written expansively on Van Raalte and knowing the literature at first hand, he sent me back to my sources to prove assertions, corrected misspelled Dutch words and book titles, and generally cleaned up the text. His colleague at Kampen, church historian George Harinck, and our mutual friend, Hans Krabbendam, my former graduate student and now director of the Catholic Documentation Center at Nijmegen, jointly offered valuable suggestions for strengthening the book. Both have published articles on Van Raalte, as has Michael Douma of Georgetown University, my former student research assistant at Hope College, who also read the text.

Gerko Warner of Ommen, the Netherlands, a local historian of note, provided copies of dozens of images from his brief but dense Van Raalte biography, written in both English and Dutch for the 2011 bicentennial of Van Raalte's birth. Warner mined local records and archives to uncover people and places and buildings where Van Raalte preached, was tried and imprisoned, and had business dealings. These fine details were priceless for an American writer who could not put boots on the ground like he could. All these colleagues and friends, of course, bear no responsibility for the final product; it is mine alone.

Translators who have worked selflessly over the past fifty years are the hidden heroes of this book. Nella Kennedy takes pride of place as the chief translator. Others, ranked generally by effort, are Nella's daughter-in-law Simone (Mrs. James) Kennedy, Earl Wm. Kennedy, Henry ten Hoor, Elizabeth (Ellie) Dekker (first secretary of the Van Raalte Institute), William (and Althea) Buursma, Harry Boonstra, William K. Reinsma, Peter T. Moerdyke, Johannes W. Visscher, Clarence L. Jalving, John VerBrugge, E. R. Post, David F. Van Vliet, Gerrit Sheeres, Richard D. Post, Seth Vander Werf, Michael Douma, Herbert Brinks, and Ralph W. Vunderink. None bears responsibility for any misquotes in this book.

Geoffrey Reynolds, former director of the Joint Archives of Holland, our sister institution in the Theil Research Center, made available digitized versions of the major local newspapers—*De Hollander*, *De Grondwet*, *De Hope*, and the *Holland City News*. He also tediously combined individual issues into annual files to ease word searches. Will Katerberg, director of the Heritage Hall Archives at Calvin University, readily provided photographs and Dutch-language books from their rich collections. Once again, these keepers of the archives have selflessly served the interests of scholars and made books such as this possible. Unless indicated otherwise, all documents or copies cited are in the files of the Van Raalte Institute and the Joint Archives of Holland, both located in the Theil Research Center of Hope College, and in the original Van Raalte Collection at Heritage Hall, archives for the Christian Reformed Church, Calvin Theological Seminary, and Calvin University, located in the Hekman Library at Calvin University.

Preface

Albertus Christiaan Van Raalte (ral′ tə) was called to preach the Gospel—to walk in the steps of his father—and for forty years, he did just that, on two continents—Europe and North America—potentially three, had his application to serve as a missionary in South Africa been accepted. His life unfolded in tumultuous times, bracketed by the French Revolutionary conquest of the Netherlands and the American Civil War. In the early nineteenth century, religious strife in the Netherlands Reformed Church, sparked by its dallying with Enlightenment thought and the subsequent Napoleonic conquest, resulted in a two-pronged reform movement—the Réveil (revival) among the upper crust and the Afscheiding (Secession) of 1834 among the lower classes. The authoritarian King Willem I tolerated reform but persecuted Seceders, especially pastors and elders, who suffered harassment by police and soldiers, crippling fines, and even imprisonment. Orthodox Calvinists rejected Enlightenment rationalism out of hand, even if it was clothed with warm feelings of happiness, progress, and liberty. They would not be reasonable, humanistic, or tolerant, nor would they subsume truth to science.

Among the Dutch, Van Raalte was customarily addressed simply as Dominee or, more formally, Dominee Van Raalte. He was truly the lord of the church and community. As founder in 1847 of the Holland colony in Michigan, he was the sole university graduate, seller of all town lots, founding pastor of the "mother church," school commissioner, newspaper proprietor, harbor promoter, and a businessman. His charismatic personality commanded attention and attracted followers. He was a natural leader in church and state—an American Moses in the eyes of his supporters, a pope in the eyes of his critics.

As a preacher's kid, Albertus in his teen years moved three times because his father had a proclivity for short pastorates, which uprooted the family and created a certain restlessness in him. But dealing with different dialects, cultures, and landscapes also made him adaptable and flexible. His religious conversion as a young adult ignited his desire to save souls and build the church on earth. After completing university studies and ordination, he joined like-minded dissidents, products of the Secession of 1834, as the "apostle of Overijssel," a circuit-riding preacher hounded by police and soldiers for conducting "illegal" (unauthorized) worship services.

From the outset, the congregation that called Van Raalte and expected his focused attention found that their pastor envisioned a wider ministry. He planted new congregations throughout the east-central region, stretching north into the provinces of Drenthe and Groningen and south into Gelderland. He logged some twenty thousand miles in his first decade (1836-46). He was always on the go, leaving his wife for weeks at a time. In short, he earned a reputation as a traveling man. When he began training men for the ministry in his parsonage, he cut back on his traveling, except to attend regional and national church assemblies and put out the "fires" among his colleagues.

In 1846 Van Raalte sought a larger stage by leading the emigration of his followers to America. Crossing the Atlantic twice (in 1846 and for a return visit in 1866) added almost sixteen thousand nautical miles to his log. In America, he traveled another sixteen thousand miles in church work, fundraising, and planting colonies. Had his hope for a missionary appointment among the Zulus borne fruit, he would have added another twenty thousand round-trip miles. His extensive travels gave him a vast knowledge of the United States, from the mid-Atlantic coast to the Kansas frontier. It also made him a household name in Dutch Reformed circles on two continents and earned him honorary doctorates from New York University and Queens College (now

Rutgers University). His primary parish in Holland suffered neglect, and worshipers often found the pulpit filled by young preachers trained at Holland Academy. In his twenty years as pastor of Holland's First Reformed Church, he was likely absent more than 10 percent of the time. In his last two years, 1866 and 1867, he spent six months in the Netherlands and on his return did not attend consistory meetings for almost a year.

The dominee "on the go" most certainly had a desk drawer full of stagecoach and railroad schedules, but none is found among his surviving papers. Given his frequent travels, he must have had these schedules mastered. In his preaching tours in the Netherlands, he normally traveled on horseback. In America, Van Raalte used stagecoaches to reach the Kalamazoo railway station that would become the New York Central Railroad and link New York to Chicago. After a small railroad reached Holland in 1870 (the Pere Marquette Railroad in 1900), Van Raalte could more easily travel to Kalamazoo, Grand Rapids, Muskegon, and points beyond by rail.

Van Raalte was the first Dutch dominee to found a colony on the Midwest frontier, and his Holland, Michigan, colony would, in time, become the largest Dutch settlement in North America. He was first among equals as a colonial leader and developer. He combined the roles of religious and economic leadership in a unique and powerful way. To help his colony thrive, he had to pinch pulpit preparations, invest in lands and businesses, develop infrastructure, foster local government, provide political and civic leadership, and, of course, plant churches and schools. His land dealings, albeit time consuming, did allow for a lifestyle above the norm, and he died a millionaire in today's dollars. But he put more on his plate than he could handle and burned out before his time. Some have likened him to Moses, who led the Israelites out of slavery in Egypt, only to be rejected by those he had rescued, was forced to wander in the desert for a generation, and then die there after gazing on the Promised Land from afar. Like Joshua, Moses' successor, Van Raalte did successfully lead his followers to their land of promise but not without their frequent rebellion and denunciation. But he was undaunted in the face of constant criticism and controversies.

My colleagues at the Van Raalte Institute have long urged me to consider the life of Holland's founding father as a writing project. Rev. Dr. Elton J. Bruins (1927-2020), professor of religion emeritus at Hope College and founding director of the Van Raalte Institute, focused his research efforts on collecting Van Raalte manuscripts in the

United States and the Netherlands. His treasure trove of six thousand documents fills six large file drawers, each document carefully cataloged, summarized, and translated by Dutch-language speakers. Bruins' lifetime quest shaved years off my research task. Bruins was also the man who invited me to join the institute in 1996 as the first A. C. Van Raalte Research Professor. The book is fittingly dedicated posthumously to Elton Bruins, rightly called the "dean of Van Raalte studies."

Bruins' files rest in large part in the Van Raalte Collection in the Heritage Hall Archives at Calvin University. This collection originated with Van Raalte heirs who safeguarded the documents, papers, financial records, and photographs of their progenitor. The family in 1946 handed the collection to Albert Hyma, professor of history at the University of Michigan, for his centennial biography of Van Raalte and the Holland colony.[1] Hyma later transferred the papers to Grand Rapids publisher William B. Eerdmans Sr., who later donated them to the Heritage Hall Archives. The Van Raalte Collection, vast as it is, suffers from Van Raalte's decision before his death to discard much of his incoming correspondence. For instance, Philip Phelps Jr., the first president of Hope College, saved nearly one hundred letters from Van Raalte, but the Dutch dominee saved nary a one from Phelps.[2]

There is no evidence that Van Raalte anticipated biographies being written about his life and work, but three have been written in the Dutch language (1877, 1893, and 1915), two in English (1947 and 1997), and a fictionalized biography (1951).[3] In 2011, as part of the Van Raalte Institute's international, bilateral conference to commemorate the bicentennial of Van Raalte's birth (Oct. 17, 1811), Elton Bruins compiled a Van Raalte bibliography of some eighty books and articles. And the published papers from that bicentennial conference[4] added fifteen additional works of the first order. The Van Raalte corpus, it would seem, had been completed.

So why another Van Raalte biography? Because the early works are incomplete. The writers lacked the voluminous Bruins' documents that have allowed for a full-length study. The Dutch-language biographies are filiopietistic (literally, ancestor worship) and rest on thin sources

---

[1] Hyma, *Van Raalte*.
[2] Bruins and Schakel, *Envisioning Hope College*.
[3] Brummelkamp, "Dr. Albertus Christiaan van Raalte"; Dosker, *Van Raalte*, 1893; Wormser, *In twee werelddeelen*, 1915; Hyma, *Albertus C. Van Raalte*, 1947; Jacobson et al., *Dutch Leader*, 1996; Schoolland, *The Story*, 1949.
[4] Nyenhuis and Harinck, *Enduring Legacy*, app. 1, 345-59.

since the Van Raalte Papers, incomplete as they are, were closely held by the family until they sold them in 1946 to Albert Hyma.[5] All the early writers drew on images first broached at the dominee's death. Anthony Brummelkamp, Van Raalte's brother-in-law and associate in ministry in the Netherlands, used the Moses motif in a lengthy obituary in the Separated Church Yearbook,[6] which in turn served as a primary source for subsequent writers. He exaggerated Van Raalte's role by claiming that "everything" depended on him, which created another common theme—that Van Raalte was indispensable.

Henry E. Dosker offered an American religious perspective for a Dutch readership in a three-hundred-page book published in the Netherlands after it was run serially in the Holland, Michigan, weekly, *De Grondwet*, for more than a year. Dosker was a second-generation immigrant pastor who served three Reformed congregations in West Michigan, interspersed with teaching at his alma mater, Western Theological Seminary. When lecturing at the seminary and in pastoring Holland's Third Reformed Church, Dosker would portray Van Raalte's life and ministry as an apologia for his denomination, the Reformed Church in America, against orthodox critics, both at home and back in the homeland. As a boy in the Netherlands, Dosker briefly met Albertus and Christina at their homecoming in 1866, which gave him a personal connection. More importantly, he interviewed family and friends in the years after Albertus and Christina's deaths. This gives his book a first-person flavor, but it smacks of hagiography and special pleading.

In 1915 Johan A. Wormser Jr., an Amsterdam legal functionary and Reformed churchman, wrote a briefer biography, also published in the Netherlands, which offers an apology for the Secession of 1834. Like Dosker, Wormser, as a young man of twenty-one in 1866, met Albertus and Christina when his widowed mother hosted the couple overnight in their Amsterdam home. These Dutch-language biographers, to some degree, had first-hand acquaintances with Van Raalte that prompted them to indulge in eulogy and uncritical praise.

Albert Hyma, a native of Holland, Michigan, and professor of history in the University of Michigan, wrote the first English-language biography at the behest of the centennial committee of Holland in 1947. Hyma was the first to use the Van Raalte Papers, having purchased them from the family under the nose of the local historical docent Willard Wichers. Hyma's book largely stitches these documents

---

[5] Bruins et al., *Albertus and Christina*, 53-62.
[6] Brummelkamp, "Van Raalte."

together chronologically and adds sparse commentary. The book has few footnotes and a woefully inadequate index, all hallmarks of a rush to publish. Hyma's book oozes ethnic pride, and in contrast to Dosker and Wormser, Hyma used his bully pulpit to defend his denomination, the Christian Reformed Church, a body born in a schism from the Reformed Church in America. Although Van Raalte was largely responsible for that schism, Hyma praises Van Raalte to the heavens, as "so great a figure that all others were dwarfed by his giant personality."

The most recent biography, written for Holland's sesquicentennial in 1997 by Jeanne M. Jacobson, Elton J. Bruins, and Larry J. Wagenaar, focuses on Van Raalte's thirty years in America at the expense of his thirty-five years in the Netherlands. Like Hyma, the book celebrates Dutch ethnicity and civic pride. Its signal contribution is to place the dominee in the broader American context, notably the Civil War era. Michael J. Douma, whose 2014 book illuminates Dutch American history and culture,[7] has in recent years published two essays that critique the writings of Van Raalte's contemporaries and biographers. In Douma's opinion, the biographers have all come up short due to bias, poor use of sources, weak analysis, and lack of a central thesis. The founder of Holland Colony, said Douma, remains "as enigmatic as his legacy is powerful."[8]

Hopefully, this book, based on the full corpus of Van Raalte documents collected on both sides of the Atlantic over the course of a century or more, will unravel that enigma. The thesis is simple: Dominee Van Raalte juggled competing roles as pastor, churchman, education promoter, social entrepreneur, opinion leader, culture manager, and community builder, first in founding the Separated[9] church at home, then in building the Midwestern wing of the Reformed Church and—his signature legacy—cofounding Hope College with Philip Phelps Jr. On a larger scale, his colony became the premier Dutch colony in North America today. Despite the tension between his life in the pulpit and his life out of the pulpit, this Dutch immigrant leader made West Michigan the center of Dutch American population and culture in the United States.

---

[7] Douma, *How Dutch Americans Stayed Dutch*.
[8] Douma, "Memory and the Myth"; Douma, "Writings about Van Raalte."
[9] Also called "Seceder."

Introduction

Albertus Christiaan Van Raalte was born in 1811, a time of extreme social and religious stress. A stagnant economy, premodern agriculture, and high population growth had led to a sense of hopelessness. Then Enlightenment rationalism and political discontent cast the Dutch Reformed Church adrift in a sea of doubt and uncertainty. This set the stage for the welcome by Dutch liberals of invading French "liberators" in 1795 and the formation of the Batavian Republic, which disestablished the public church. French dominance increased under Emperor Napoleon Bonaparte who established the Kingdom of Holland under his brother Louis in 1804 and made the nation a French vassal state in 1810. The new regime introduced the French Civil Code and modernized an antiquated bureaucracy, bringing with it new taxes and intrusive regulations, such as the first national census, universal military conscription, a civil registry, and other constraints.

By the time Albertus began elementary school in 1816, the Netherlands had regained its freedom under King Willem I (Willem Frederik), son of Willem V, the last stadtholder of the House of Orange, thanks largely to the efforts of Gijsbert Karel van Hogendorp. In hopes of creating an enlightened "Christianity above doctrinal division," Willem took control of all religious institutions and gave Catholics equal rights to Protestants. But the various legislative changes under Napoleon impeded administrative reforms, and his continental and maritime campaigns had damaged the economy.[1]

Napoleon instituted the modern French administrative state with its trappings of civil registration, new per-capita taxation, military conscription, family name requirements, school restructuring, and religious pluralism, granting equal rights for Catholics. The Netherlands Reformed Church became a department of the kingdom, micromanaged by officials, many of whom were members of the upper classes. The government paid for church buildings and pastors' salaries in exchange for high-handed rule by civil and religious authorities. Parish churches and pastors lost their former autonomy; they felt disinherited, as it were.[2]

Young Albertus received the best education the Netherlands could offer in the nineteenth century—parochial day school, Athenaeum, and university. After a religious conversion during a cholera epidemic and his subsequent ordination as a minister of the Gospel, Van Raalte became an itinerant pastor who planted congregations in the largely rural province of Overijssel. When desperate poverty drove thousands of these Separatists to emigrate to America in the 1840s, Van Raalte himself decided to emigrate and lead his followers to safer pastures. Had he remained in the homeland, as did all but a few of his colleagues, his life would have been comfortable and in familiar surroundings, within his subculture and its routines. Emigrating overseas never entered his mind until midlife, but doing so lifted him to a dynamic role in a period of change in both countries, with different speeds, directions, opportunities, and threats.

The first wave of emigration (beginning in 1846) was quelled in 1857 by the American economic crisis and subsequent Civil War (1861-65). The second wave in the postwar years was cut off by a national depression from 1873 to 1877. The Dutch agricultural crisis of the 1880s set off a third wave, which drew landless peasants by the tens of thousands to the frontier until the 1893 depression again stemmed the flow. The fourth and final wave ended in 1914 with World War I and

1   Israel, *Dutch Republic*, 1126.
2   Brummelkamp to Van Raalte, 1 April 1856 (quote), published in in *De Hollander*, 30 July 1856, trans. Henry ten Hoor; Wintle, *Pillars of Piety*, 11-20; Harinck and Winkler, "Nineteenth Century," 450; Bratt, *Abraham Kuyper*, 11; Engelsma, *Watchman on the Walls*, 25.

the immigration restriction law of 1921, which brought to an end the great century of immigration. By then, some two hundred thousand peasants and rural artisans had settled with their families in the United States.

The two major Dutch Reformed colonies in the 1840s were those of A. C. Van Raalte in Holland, Michigan, and Rev. Hendrik (Henry) P. Scholte in Pella, Iowa. Other early colonies were in Clymer, Pultneyville, East Williamson, and Palmyra, New York; Sheboygan, Oostburg, Cedar Grove, and Alto, Wisconsin; and South Holland and Roseland, Illinois. Father Theodorus Van den Broek established a Dutch Catholic settlement in Wisconsin's Fox River Valley. As these "nest" communities grew amid rising land values, some in the second generation formed daughter colonies farther west. But mother colonies continued to grow and urbanize. As a result, West Michigan, centered in Grand Rapids, has been the preeminent Dutch region, followed by northwest Iowa's Sioux County, led by Orange City, a daughter colony of Pella.

Urban Dutch clusters formed in Patterson, Passaic, and Lodi in northern New Jersey; Cleveland and Cincinnati, Ohio; Chicago; and West Michigan, bounded by the triangle of Grand Rapids, Muskegon, and Kalamazoo. Most Dutch immigrants were Protestants, but Catholics dominated in a few cities, most notably Cleveland, St. Louis, Detroit, and Minneapolis. Colonies established by secular promoters often failed or stagnated for lack of a church, such as Lafayette, Indiana; Lancaster, New York; New Amsterdam, Wisconsin; and New Paris, Indiana, to name the most prominent.

In the post-Civil War years, Van Raalte began a second colony in the war-ravaged Virginia tidewater, a humid region of plantations and slave cabins where farmland was cheap. He founded churches and a Christian academy there, as he had done in West Michigan, but the southern culture and depleted soils were problematic for Dutch farmers. He might have overcome all obstacles were it not for his failing health and, even more so, the fragile health of his wife.

Van Raalte and Scholte, erstwhile friends in the Netherlands, faced a role reversal in America, and they became rivals, competing for settlers and influence. Pella had the early advantage because Scholte had brought almost nine hundred followers, compared to Van Raalte's fewer than one hundred. But Scholte's religious independence and refusal to join the American branch of the Reformed Church, as Van Raalte did, hurt his recruitment efforts. The outgoing Van Raalte gathered many other clerics: Rev. Cornelius Van der Meulen, with four hundred congregants from the province of Zeeland; Rev. Martin Ypma, with fifty souls from the province of Friesland; Rev. Seine Bolks, with twenty families from the province of Overijssel; and other elder-led groups from the provinces of Drenthe, Groningen, Noord-Holland, and Bentheim in Germany. Within a year, Van Raalte's colony was surrounded by six villages, each with a Reformed Church, totaling two thousand souls.

Pella initially had financial and location advantages. Scholte's party had a chest full of "Gouden Willempjes" (2½-, 5-, 10-, and 20-guilder coins), enough to buy eighteen thousand acres, including tracts partially developed by squatters willing to sell their "sweat equity." These acres were rolling prairie grasslands, ready for the plow. The sixteen thousand acres Van Raalte acquired were heavily forested, and settlers had to fell trees for a generation and plow among the stumps. Pella, fortuitously, stood astride the Oregon Trail from St. Louis in 1849 and the Mormon Trail from Nauvoo, Illinois, to Salt Lake City in 1850. As the Forty-Niners and Mormons trekked west, they loaded up on foodstuffs and supplies and left Pella flush with cash.

The poverty-stricken Holland colony was isolated and twenty miles from the nearest market towns. But thanks to its harbor, wood products shipped to insatiable Chicago markets paid for provisions and supplies that were brought back on return sailings. Holland's harbor offered easy sailing to Chicago and other Great Lake ports as far away as Buffalo and even New York City via the Erie Canal. Kalamazoo, fifty-five miles southeast, provided a direct rail connection to New York. Pella in south-central Iowa lay fifty miles from Des Moines, the capitol and nearest large city, and it had no railroad service for twenty years. As a result, it remained for generations a small, market town that serviced farms within twenty miles. Holland lay astride the two most productive agricultural counties in Michigan—Ottawa and Allegan. The Holland area today has five or six times the population of the Pella area. And Holland's diverse industrial economy far surpasses that of Iowa's agricultural economy. In the rivalry with Scholte, Van Raalte's accomplishments became the embodiment of what Scholte had hoped to achieve.

CHAPTER 1

Father Van Raalte's Life and Ministry: "A great example to me."

Albertus Christiaan Van Raalte's father, Albert(us) van Raalte (1771-1833), grew up in a small-town merchant's family that gave a son to the Christian ministry, and that son did the same. An orthodox and pious pastor, Albert served six pastorates in the Netherlands Reformed Church, all located in the "Bible Belt," stretching from the province of Zeeland in the southwest to Overijssel in the northeast. These traditional congregations were well suited for the conservative dominee who, in tumultuous times, dutifully obeyed state and church authorities. As a young man, he was attracted briefly to the liberals, but in the pastorate, he was apolitical, with his loyalties set to the powers that be. Albertus and his wife, Catrina Christina Harking (1775-1837), provided the nest in which son Albertus Christiaan was nurtured and shaped and taught the scriptures. This chapter follows the life and ministry of father Van Raalte and the environment in which the son spent his first eighteen years.

Van Raalte family roots

To date, the Van Raalte family has been traced back to 1650, to the village of Zwartsluis, province of Overijssel. The upwardly mobile

"Bible Belt" region where Rev. Albertus van Raalte lived and ministered, 1845 (*Fred Hoek,* Geloven en een Nieuwe Wereld)

menfolk were respectable, small-town merchants with general stores and bakery shops; a few became clerics and city officials. Great-great-grandfather Barteld Janz van Raalte served as mayor in the second half of the seventeenth century. Albert's father Pieter, a merchant baker, left a substantial inheritance of houses and lands upon his death in 1820.

His real estate holdings had cushioned him from the economic fallout of Napoleon's trade restrictions. Pieter's prosperity allowed for Albert, his second son, born in 1771, to be a university-trained pastor in the national church. Albert's eleventh child (his third, and last, surviving son), Albertus Christiaan, in turn, also became a university-educated pastor, but family entrepreneurial genes seemingly reemerged in his life and in the lives of his sons, Petrus and Arend.[1]

Albert(us) van Raalte at University of Groningen

We know little about the childhood of Albert van Raalte before he completed the requisite Latin school and gymnasium and matriculated at age eighteen in 1789 at the University of Groningen. Curricula at that time remained very traditional and limited in scope, and lectures since medieval times had been delivered in Latin. In addition to studies in Reformed theology, students had to master classical and biblical languages. School records reveal the significant fact that Albert had changed his birth name to the Latinized "Albertus," as was common among university students of middling origin. The baker's son must have been aware that his position as a clergyman would raise his social standing above commoners, on par with notaries, mayors, physicians, and the occasional patrician. In line with Enlightenment thinking, late eighteenth-century pastors were viewed as "teachers of the population," public servants with a duty to elevate the people. On at least one occasion, in November 1794, Van Raalte displayed his education and standing by meticulously questioning a theological candidate in Hebrew and Greek, in addition to the "characteristic" dogma of "our Reformed Church."[2]

Albertus likely chose the University of Groningen because it was the alma mater of his brother-in-law, Rev. Rijnier (Reinier) Swierink, pastor at Haaften, Gelderland, who had attended from 1782 to 1786. Swierink was married to Albertus's older sister Annigje.[3] Groningen was also slightly closer to Zwartsluis than Utrecht and much closer than Leiden, the third of the Dutch universities with theological faculties. Groningen, the provincial capital, was likely a culture shock

---

[1] Bruins et al., *Albertus and Christina*, 193-200.
[2] "Kerk-Nieuws," in *Boekzaal der geleerde wereld*, 1794, 621-22.
[3] Swierink was born in Amsterdam in 1758 and married Annigje Van Raalte in 1787 at Wanneperveen. After she died of tuberculosis in 1796, Swierink in 1797 married Neeltje van Raalte, a cousin of Annigje. I am indebted for this information to Earl Wm. Kennedy who scoured the Netherlands websites genlias.nl, wiewaswie.nl, and delpher.nl.

to Albertus, a small-town boy. What he encountered there, we can only conjecture, but in all his years of ministry, he never received a call from a large city. Perhaps he remained by reputation a small-town boy.

When Albertus entered the University of Groningen, it was already in a decades-long decline, an ideological backwater, whereas the more prestigious Leiden and Utrecht universities were rising. Only forty-one students entered the school that year in all faculties, and by 1791, this number had fallen to a mere twenty-three students. Professors were said to be entrenched and uninspiring, but students received close attention, especially if they boarded with a professor who lectured in his home for rent and tuition fees. This was cheaper and far better than a university dormitory with its rigid rules and strict oversight.[4]

In revolutionary times, the Groningen faculty remained passive bystanders as the city became a battlefield between Patriots—secular reformers inspired by French Enlightenment ideals—and Orangists—supporters of Stadtholder Willem V and established oligarchies.[5] When Willem's campaign was faltering in 1787, his brother-in-law, King Frederick II of Prussia, sent twenty-six thousand soldiers to invade the Netherlands. Patriot forces melted away in the face of such overwhelming force, and Willem's office was secured. University professors feigned neutrality during the war but tended to be Patriot sympathizers. Willem required academics to sign loyalty oaths to his regime; many were elderly and had no will to resist.

Van Raalte as a young theological student would certainly have grappled with these issues. In 1897 Albertus signed a Patriot petition that gathered seventeen thousand signatures in support of the Batavian Republic and its most democratic constitution in Dutch history. Albertus, like many educated Dutch, likely viewed the French as liberators from an autocratic regime. It helped that the French allowed the Dutch a fair amount of self-government, in contrast to the more dictatorial measures imposed on other conquered countries.[6]

---

[4] Van Berkel, *Universiteit van het Noorden*, 354-55, 359. Pastor IJsbrand van Hamelsveld opined even in 1790 that there were perhaps only from forty to fifty men studying for the ministry (Israel, *Dutch Republic*, 1111).

[5] Ibid. A recent historiographical article on the Patriots is Oddens, "De Nederlandse revolutie," 565-91.

[6] Kennedy, *Concise History*, 258-62; *Naamlyst der geenen*, 143.

Renswoude—Van Raalte's first parish

As a prerequisite to parish ministry, candidates were examined by provincial synods. Van Raalte's turn came on May 14, 1793, in the presence of four deputized ministers from the provincial synod of Utrecht. The professors assessed his knowledge of Reformed doctrine and his Greek and Hebrew exegesis based on assigned texts I Peter 3:18 and Psalms 2 and 3. After passing the examination, Albertus agreed to the required ecclesiastical stipulations.[7] At age twenty-two, he was now eligible for a church to call him.

His first prospect slipped away when the Staphorst consistory in June 1793 formed a trio without him. The fact that he was single may have hurt his chances. He had to wait three months for his first call, despite a clergy shortage. In late October 1793, the Renswoude consistory chose him from a slate of four. He sustained his classical examination on the *loci* (points) of Reformed doctrine and was ordained in the sanctuary in a solemn worship service on March 2, 1794. He then preached his first sermon as minister of the Gospel. It was the beginning of a seventeen-year pastorate in Renswoude, his longest. In a sense, he had no choice since he received no calls during that span. For whatever reason, calls proved to be a rarity in his early pastorates. Eulogies after his death show that he was a faithful, dedicated pastor, but perhaps he lacked oratorical gifts or that elusive trait—charisma.

Renswoude was a picturesque village at the eastern edge of the province of Utrecht. This large and prosperous place was a good fit for the young pastor, reputedly a godly and pious young man. The church eschewed theological adventurism for solid biblical preaching, tinged with introspective, soul-searching piety. The parsonage dated from the 1640s and the church from 1639. Architect Jacob van Kampen, whose claim to fame was the Royal Palace on the Dam in Amsterdam, had designed the sanctuary, topped with an octagon-shaped cupola instead of a tower. Hence, the locals still call the church the "koepelkerk."[8]

Rev. Van Raalte's first charge stretched from the Batavian Republic to the last gasps of the Napoleonic era in 1815. This was a time of political, religious, and economic turmoil. Stadtholder Willem V went into exile in 1795 after the Dutch more or less welcomed French troops into their country. The newly formed Batavian Republic worked under the watchful eye of the French. Orangist sympathizers of the

---

[7] *Boekzaal der geleerde Wereld*, June 1793, 156; Nov. 1793, 668-69.
[8] https://www.archimon.nl/utrecht/renswoudeherv.htm, accessed, January 2021.

stadtholder were ousted from various public positions. The Dutch had to pay a heavy price for this quasi occupation because it came with a set of demands, especially heavy taxes and conscription into the French army. Understandably, as the cost of occupation became onerous, the French welcome soured.

The change in the political order had profound consequences for the Reformed Church, which for almost two centuries had enjoyed a favored status. The National Assembly in 1798 disestablished the privileged Nederduitse Gereformeerde Kerk. All churches, pastors, and professors were defunded on the grounds that "The idea of an established Calvinistic church was in radical conflict with the equalitarian ideals of the revolution."[9] Religion was to be a private, not a state, affair. God, however, was not entirely removed. Assembly rationalists addressed God as the "Supreme Being" to avoid overt religiosity.[10]

In 1801 Napoleon Bonaparte as first consul of France restructured the republic with a far less democratic constitution and reappointed many of the Orangist ruling class to positions of authority. He compelled Holland to pay ƒ100 million for its "liberation," an amount equal to 225 percent of annual national income in 1807. In 1806 he replaced the republic with a monarchy under his brother, Louis, the "King of Holland," who ruled until 1810. Then Napoleon dismissed him for being too accepting of Dutch laws and habits and turning a blind eye to the lucrative smuggling practices of Dutch traders who flouted the so-called "Continental System," a trading blockade to cripple the United Kingdom of England and Ireland. Although that strategy failed, the blockade had the secondary effect of stifling Dutch commerce and plunging the country into depression. The national debt doubled, and Amsterdam lost its place as the world's chief financial center to London.

Napoleon considered formal religion the cornerstone of civil society, but it had to be statist. Giving the Reformed church favored status came at the cost of state supervision. In 1803 the Dutch National Assembly made the Christian religion paramount in civil life but only under tight state oversight. Pastors were tasked to tout civic virtue for the good of the nation. An 1802 church manual, for example, required pastors to read the Scriptures in order to explain and derive from these admonishments improved behavior . . . [and] to affect the Christian

---

[9] Pronk, *Goodly Heritage*, 61, quoting Bratt, *Rise and Development of Calvinism*, 89.
[10] Kennedy, *Concise History*, 267-68, 274, 277-78, for this paragraph and the next.

Napoleon Bonaparte (1769-1821), Emperor of the French, 1804-14

household, and particularly morals, so members do not drift away but are drawn back by authority." A minister "must be upright himself, act rightly, and follow Jesus' teachings," in order to develop "duty and virtue for mankind, in order to get approval of God. Jesus came to reform and improve humankind."[11]

In line with Napoleon's view of the importance of the role of religion, he reinstated the salaries of pastors and theology professors, and restored congregational ownership of edifices and the right to ring church bells before worship. He made membership and tithing mandatory for everyone over age sixteen. Van Raalte received his stipend from the provincial church warden in Utrecht. But there was no guarantee. When the public purse was empty, salaries went unpaid, as happened in 1811. The next year, pastors received only one-third of their salaries, which cast some into bitter poverty. Three years later, however, under the new Dutch monarchy, all pastors were promised reimbursement for any shortages from 1811 to 1813. In return for their state salaries, clergymen were told to foster national virtue and patriotism for the good of society. They must "speak words of peace and love," not discord.[12]

---

[11] Konijnenburg, *Lessen*, 22-24.
[12] Rasker, *Nederlandse Hervormde Kerk*, 20-21; Den Ouden, *Kerk onder patriottenbewind*, 12, 24-25; Amanda Foreman, "The Original Victims of Cancel Culture," *Wall Street Journal* (Jan. 2021), C5, 30-31. Pope Pius VII was not impressed, and he excommunicated Napoleon in 1809, for which the pontiff was kidnapped and held for five years.

In Renswoude, Rev. Van Raalte encountered the long arm of the French "occupation." As the village pastor, he was responsible to catechize orphans in the Burgerweeshuis, a privately funded orphanage under church auspices. The orphans were trained for crafts suited to their abilities. In 1795 the French overlords took boys over the age of sixteen off campus for military training in the belief that soldiering was a noble calling. This clashed with the orphanage's pacifist ideals, but protests were to no avail. In 1811 Napoleon tried to soften the blow of forced recruitment by selecting some boys for the elite Imperial Guard.[13]

Van Raalte-Harking marriage

Eighteen months after Van Raalte's ordination in the Renswoude church, the bachelor dominee, then age twenty-three, on November 12, 1795, married twenty-year-old Catrina (occasionally Catharina) Christina Harking of Amsterdam, a daughter of Arend Harking and Johanna Toonk. The banns were read in Amsterdam the required three Sundays prior, and with father Pieter van Raalte's permission, the couple was wed in Renswoude by Albertus's brother-in-law, Rijnier Swierink, who had Amsterdam connections and may have introduced the two. Catrina's father, Arend Harking, assisted in the ceremony. He was a carrier of cheeses at a weigh house in Amsterdam, and at his death in 1821, at age eighty-eight, he was the oldest carrier in the Straw Hat Union (Stroohoeden-Veem). He had also achieved the status of citizen (*burger*).[14] It took fortitude for the Van Raaltes to marry on the cusp of French conquest. Albertus signed his name on the marriage document with the letters VDM (Latin for *Verbi Dei Minister*, or Minister of the Word of God), a practice he later used on official documents.[15]

After her marriage, Catrina Christina Harking left the bustling metropolis of Amsterdam for a series of remote villages. But she had gained social status through her marriage and her social inferiors now treated her with deference. Status, however, did not spare her from

---

[13] *Geschiedkundige herinneringen*, 55-63.
[14] Obit., Amsterdam, 31 Oct. 1821, placed by A. van Raalte ('s Heer Abtskerke) and C. C. Harking van Raalte (Centraal Bureau voor Genealogie). The fact that his belongings are listed shows its importance. The carriers did more than carry cheeses; they also carried out commercial transactions. The numerous times that Arend was a witness to real estate transactions indicates his solid status in Amsterdam.
[15] *Boekzaal der geleerde Wereld*, July 1793, 130; Nov. 1793, 652-53; Kennedy, *Concise History*, 266-72.

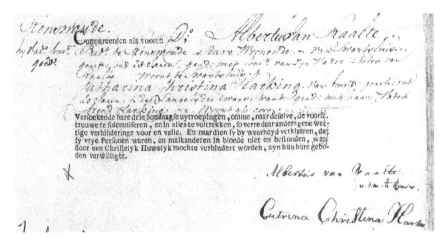

Wedding certificate of Albertus van Raalte (1771-1833) and
Catrina Christina Harking (1775-1837), Amsterdam,
12 November 1795 (*courtesy Archief Ameland*)

heartache. She lost nine of her sixteen children to death in infancy, and apart from that, we know little about her. Her parents had married in their thirties, late for this time; her father, Arend, had come to Amsterdam from the eastern Netherlands, and he married a native of that city. Of their two children, both daughters, the younger, Bartha, died in infancy.[16]

That Catrina prized her family is indicated by her following the traditional custom of naming her children after her parents' given names: for example, Arend and Johannes (or Jan) for males; Arendina and Johanna for females; and her maiden name, Harking, for both sexes. The name of her deceased sibling, Bartha, was used several times in various forms. From the Van Raalte side came Petrus, Albertus (masculine of Alberta), Roelof, and Cornelius, and for a female, Niescina, and the masculine, Niesceüs. Notably, several of these given names were Latinized versions of Dutch names, the "step up" being a mark of upward mobility.

Children of Albertus and Catrina Christina Harking van Raalte
Petrus Alberti*...1796-1797
Johanna Arendina*... 1797-1798

[16] See Bruins et al., *Albertus and Christina*, 202, for this paragraph and the next.

Petrus [Peter] Johannes Alberti 1798-1840
Arend [Arent] Johannes Christiaan.................... 1800-1837
Joan Niescie* 1802-1803
Barthus Cornelius Nisceüs*............................. 1803-1803
Roelof Barth Niesceüs* 1804-1804
Niescina Margaretha Anna 1806-1842
(married Hendrik Cornelis van der Linden, a physician and obstetrician in Scherpenisse, Zeeland)
Johanna Bartha.. 1807-1877
(married Dirk Blikman Kikkert, an Amsterdam shipbroker)
Alberta Christina 1810-1889
(married a physician)
Albertus Christiaan..1811-1876
Gerrit Jan Harking* 1813-1816
Gerrit Rademaker*... 1815-?
Anna Arendina Harking 1816-1877
(married Johannes Teessen, an Amsterdam shipbroker)
Gerrit Jan Harking* 1818-1819
Jan Harking (not recorded in civil registry)* 1821-1821

* Died in infancy or childhood

Source: Bruins et al., *Albertus and Christina*, 193-96; Warner, *Door het venster*, 102; Earl Wm. Kennedy added genealogical details.

Wanneperveen pastorate

The Renswoude church, in terms of number of members and its historic status, might have been a stepping stone to more prestigious pulpits for Van Raalte, but his second pastorate was a step down. In 1811 he accepted a call—the first in eleven years—from the Nederduitse Gereformeerde Kerk in Wanneperveen, a small village in the northern part of Overijssel that was barely six miles from Albertus's birthplace of Zwartsluis, where his elderly widowed father, Pieter, still lived. Perhaps he accepted the call in order to be near his father or maybe for the income in these meager times. He served this congregation for nine years, again with no calls.

Wanneperveen was seventy-four miles from Renswoude, and the family with five young children and a mother four months pregnant with Albertus Christiaan had to travel by carriage on rural roads, frequently impassable. Fortunately, river and canal tow boats were dependable and quite comfortable, although they barely covered four miles per hour. These narrow boats held a limited number of passengers, so family belongings would be transported by canal freighters. Years later, when Albertus Christiaan, as an itinerant pastor, traveled these same rural roads, they were still difficult, although the major arteries were much improved.[17]

Wanneperveen's population had declined markedly over the previous fifty years, from 1,058 to 600. Centuries of digging peat for fuel created shallow lakes and canals, interspersed with meadows for grazing. Poor soils meant poverty and population decline. Drinking water was polluted, and constant dampness was hazardous to one's health. The grounds around the church and parsonage were edged by canals and ditches. An eighteenth-century pastor had complained about standing in the pulpit with wet feet, a result of having to travel to church through wind and wet mud twice each Sunday. The ground was so waterlogged that two earlier sanctuaries (the first dating from 1350) had already been moved to higher ground due to encroaching water. Father Albertus had the use of a church-owned rowboat to conduct house visitation. No doubt the children entertained themselves jumping over ditches in the summer and ice skating in the winter.[18]

The historic Wanneperveen edifice dated from 1502, shortly before Martin Luther sparked the Protestant Reformation. The church that dominated the small village counted 850 souls out of a regional population of 1,400, a 60 percent rate. Given that all children in Reformed families were baptized, this percentage was standard. The village was essentially a church center that drew worshipers from a wide area.[19] What did the city-raised Catrina find in small Wanneperveen surrounded by multiple waterways? The historic 1502 church needed to be modernized, but authorities had denied the funding request. Seemingly, Albertus's lot in life was to pastor dilapidated churches.[20]

---

[17] Van Deventer, *Jaarboekje*.
[18] Wesseling, *Afscheiding van 1834, Classis Zwolle*, 271-72; Paasman, "Bestuurlijke en economische aspecten," 29, 41; Krabbendam, "Education," 2.
[19] Warner, *Door het venster*, 102. This bilingual history was published in 2011 for the commemoration of the bicentennial of Van Raalte's birth.
[20] Minutes, Wanneperveen Nederduitse Gereformeerde Kerk, 17 July 1816, Historisch Centrum Overijssel (NL-ZIHCO, 0385, I, Inv. Nr. 5); copy, VRI.

Wanneperveen Nederduitse Gereformeerde Kerk, 1810s
(*courtesy Gerko Warner*)

Albertus Christiaan's birth

Albertus Christiaan was born in the Wanneperveen parsonage on October 17, 1811. His parents named him after his father Albertus, his mother Christina (masculine, Christiaan), and his grandmother Christina Harking. His next older sibling, Alberta Christina, had the feminine form of these names. Albertus was born shortly after Napoleon promulgated the Netherlands Civil Registry, which required all inhabitants to register births, marriages, and deaths at local courthouses, instead of pastors marking these life passages in church records, as had been the practice since the Middle Ages. The civil registry served as a stalking horse for tighter government control, especially for military conscription and taxation in this still-Napoleonic era. Albertus's father duly registered his son's birth within three days in the civil registry of Wanneperveen. Older siblings had been recorded in the baptismal records of the Renswoude church. Albertus Christiaan was the first in the family to be registered in civil records, perhaps as a French citizen of sorts.[21]

---

[21] Bruins et al., *Albertus and Christina*, 188-93; Kennedy, *Concise History*, 282-83; Ten Zythoff, *Sources of Secession*, 1-9. Albertus Christiaan dropped the second "a" later in life in Michigan.

Father Van Raalte baptized his two-week-old son in the Wanneperveen church on Sunday, November 3, 1811. Around the baptistery, one can visualize Albertus's mother and older siblings—Petrus, age thirteen, and Arend, age eleven. Youngsters Niescina Margaretha Anna, age five; Johanna Bartha, age four; and Alberta Christina, age one, likely remained at home. Albertus's brothers left the house before he grew up, leaving him to be coddled by his sisters. His younger sister Anna Arendina (Mrs. Johannes Teessen), born five years later, must have cherished her older brother. Years later, she gave her first child, Alberta Christina, born in 1847, the name of her older sister, the wife of a Dutch physician, and her second child, born in 1850, the name of her renowned older brother in faraway Michigan.[22]

Van Raalte's salary was adequate at first to support his family, but then it fell short. In 1814 he was paid 572 guilders, 17 stuivers (5 cents), and 6 penningen (pennies) ($4,000 today), with the money coming from town coffers and proceeds from church-held properties. In 1816 the national government's minister of religion instructed the governor of Overijssel to have consistories review salaries annually, with the state providing a base amount and local churches responsible for the rest. The Wanneperveen consistory, however, could only pay a fraction of its share, and the dominee's pay fell to a meager ƒ224 ($1,548 today), with the rest owed. Nevertheless, Van Raalte faithfully continued his ministry.[23]

Father Van Raalte presided over consistory meetings and may have served as clerk (*scriba*), but the minutes are unsigned and sparse in the extreme. The consistory met infrequently, only every two or three months, and the pastor began each meeting with a short sermon. Surprisingly, in all his years in Wanneperveen, not one of the more than three hundred confessing members was cited or censured for ill behavior, even though elders routinely made home visits. Eyebrows are raised even more by the fact that the consistory received high marks from classical examiners whose task it was to come and assess the spiritual health of the congregation.

---

[22] All the Van Raalte, Harking, and De Moen generations from 1650 are in Bruins et al., *Albertus and Christina*, 188-210. See also, Nauta, "Leadership." Brothers Petrus and Arend and sisters Niescina and Anna died before Albertus emigrated in 1846, leaving sisters Joanna and Alberta behind.

[23] Minutes, Wanneperveen Nederduitse Gereformeerde Kerk, 29 Apr., 5 Aug. 1814, 17 July 1816, 4 Aug. 1818; Fijnaart Bevolkingsregister, 1830, in wiewaswie.nl; Rasker, *Nederlandse Hervormde Kerk*, 24. The NL monetary unit was the florin, replaced by the guilder in 1816, but still designated "f" or "fl" (worth $.40 in the 19th c.). All inflation calculations in this book are based on the value of one dollar in 2023; www.officialdata.org.

Father and son were quite different in this respect, as noted in later chapters. Son Albertus Christiaan ran a tight ship and fined consistory members for missing meetings without cause or even for being tardy. He was also a fastidious clerk who recorded the minutiae of disciplinary cases. Such scrupulous attention to discipline, according to Article 29 of the Belgic Confession, was one of the three marks of the True church, along with the "pure preaching of the Gospel" and the "pure administration of the sacraments as instituted by Christ."

An exception in father Van Raalte's usually bland recording of consistory minutes was his run-in with the *burgemeester* (mayor) of Wanneperveen in 1812 over the congregation's Christian school. The School Law of 1806 made education the responsibility of the state, and it mandated teachers to open the day with a nonsectarian prayer and read without comment from the Statenbijbel (the state-funded Protestant Bible of 1636-37) in order to inculcate "all social and Christian virtues." They could portray Jesus as a great moral teacher but not as Lord and Savior. Schools had to be strictly neutral religiously, instill good citizenship, and after 1815, foster loyalty to the Royal House. In reality, however, since clergymen comprised more than half of the school supervisors, schools often remained de facto either Reformed or Catholic.[24]

In any case, Van Raalte disapproved of the religious veneer and tolerance of error of the Wanneperveen public school. His congregation opted for a private school where the Christian faith, including the Heidelberg Catechism, could be taught unimpeded. This was permissible, though not encouraged. The sexton doubled as the teacher, since Christian schools were denied public funding.[25]

After the Wanneperveen church built its one-room schoolhouse, the mayor wanted to seize the building for lack of proper authorization. Van Raalte successfully appealed to Petrus Hofstede, the prefect of Overijssel, who decided in the church's favor in November 1812. Another problem facing the elder Van Raalte was Napoleon's conscription of some of his male congregants for his ill-fated Russian campaign when fifteen thousand Dutch conscripts were sent with his large army and only one-third came home alive.[26] And in 1813, a final difficulty was that the imperial procurator at Zwolle ordered the mayor of Wanneperveen

---

[24] Harinck and Winkler, "Nineteenth Century," 620; Sheeres, "Struggle," 36-39. The church had 364 confessing members in 1820.
[25] Ten Zythoff, *Sources of Secession*, 26-27; Reenders, "Van Raalte als leider," 189.
[26] Kennedy, *Concise History*, 281-91.

to seize the church's baptism, marriage, and burial registers (dating back to the early 17th century) and place them in the town hall as public records, as was being done throughout the Netherlands.[27]

General Regulations of 1816

The inauguration of the Dutch monarchy in 1815 brought to a head the religious declension in what was renamed in 1816 the Nederlandse Hervormde Kerk, which substituted a modern name, "Hervormde," for the historic name "Gereformeerde" (in English, both mean Reformed). Under the influence of veteran church bureaucrats like Jacobus D. Janssen and J. H. van der Palm, King Willem I (1772-1843), in January 1816, reorganized the public church as a department of the state without so much as consulting synod officers or provincial assemblies. His "Algemeen Reglement" (general regulations) authorized micromanagement of the church from above. The Reformed Church had been the privileged or public church, closely associated with the House of Orange and the Dutch state since the Netherlands declared its independence from Spain in the late sixteenth century. This was in keeping with the Constantinian idea of the heavenly and earthly kingdoms working in harmony, but the Dutch Reformed Church had never before 1816 been administered by the government.[28]

Under the new regulations, the king convened a national synod in 1816, the first in two hundred years. The heads of his religion department hand-picked delegates, rather than to allow lower assemblies to choose them, as the Church Order of Dort required. The church truly became a state church, a mere administrative arm of the government, run by appointed bureaucrats for whom matters of faith played a subordinate role. Value-free toleration gutted doctrinal integrity. Loyalty to king and country was paramount. For example, government officials chose a few select clerics and a single elder for the important gatekeeping role of examining new pastors in doctrine and life, which traditionally was the work of provincial synods.[29]

Even more significant, synod subtly revised the Dort form of subscription that all clerics and other office bearers must sign, which rendered its meaning ambiguous. Clerics could accept the Reformed

---

[27] Minutes, Wanneperveen Nederduitse Gereformeerde Kerk, 26 Nov. 1812.
[28] Bos, *Servants of the Kingdom*, 108-13; Van Lieburg, *Ramp of Redding*; Oostendorp, *Scholte*, 34.
[29] Ten Zythoff, *Sources of Secession*, 35-39, 43-45; Van den Broeke, *"Pope of the Classis,"* 11-13.

Confessions *insofar as* (in Latin *quatanus*) they agreed with scripture, rather than *because* (in Latin, *quia*) they agreed with scripture. This disingenuous wording allowed pastors and professors to interpret official doctrines as they saw fit, which emasculated church confessional standards.[30]

The king's actions aroused very little public dissent at first, and dissident voices were smothered. Dutch *burgers* were relieved that the revolutionary era had passed; they craved a time of tolerance, peace, and prosperity. Apathy was therefore understandable, and church members, 1.2 million strong in 1815, accepted the king's oversight, since he gave the public church more freedom than in the days of the Batavian Republic.[31] By tying the church to the political order, however, the king created a major problem when the Separation of 1834 led to a "free church," independent from the sanctioned public church.

Under the General Regulations, the Wanneperveen elders had to change standard confession-of-faith procedures. They were instructed to hear confessions of faith in a "solemn manner" in the consistory room, after which the new members were to make their public profession before the congregation. Father Van Raalte's sons Petrus and Arend made profession of faith in 1816 and 1817, respectively. Petrus did not have to confess publicly (but only before the consistory, the old practice), but Arend did (after confession before the consistory). Judging from the consistory minutes, Dominee Van Raalte went along with the new regime, albeit perhaps with latent unease. As a possible indication that the congregation and its pastor were adapting to the new situation is that the consistory minutes report that the congregation marked the anniversary of the Protestant Reformation (1517) but not that of the Synod of Dort (1618-19).[32]

There is no doubt that the Hervormde Kerk had become intentionally more liturgical under the 1816 church order. In Sunday worship, pastors were urged to display eloquence in the pulpit, in keeping with their lofty social standing. Church weddings were recommended as an optional supplement to the newly mandated civil marriage as the

---

[30] Acts of the Provincial Church Board, published in *Kompleete uitgave* (1884), 523-31, quote 535, trans. Nella Kennedy; Pieters, "Historical Introduction," in *Classis Holland Minutes*, 10-12. See also, Vree, "Dominating Theology"; Sinnema, "Form of Subscription."

[31] Schotel, *Geschiedenis van den oorsprong*, 355-56; statistics in De Kok, *Nederland*, 292-93.

[32] Minutes, Wanneperveen Nederduitse Gereformeerde Kerk, 19 Mar. 1816, 18 Feb., 17 June, 15 July, 5 Oct. 1817; Boot, *De kerk over de brug*, 25.

King Willem I (Willem Frederik) (1772-1843), Prince of Orange-Nassau, and Grand Duke of Luxembourg, 1814-40

only legal marriage for everyone (1811, by Napoleon); previously, the Dutch had had two legal options for marriage: civil or ecclesiastical. To make church weddings more attractive, the authorities permitted them on weekdays, and they were promoted "to strengthen mutual love" according to set formularies.[33]

There were many orthodox pulpits across the country like that of Van Raalte, but the church leadership believed that the church's role should be to promote morality; minor—and even some major—points of doctrine were anathema. For example, the highly regarded pastor G. Benthem Reddingius (1774-1844), a doctor of theology, and pastor L. Meijer Brouwer (1766-1855) wrote a pamphlet in 1833 that denied Christ's divinity and rejected the doctrine of the Trinity as rationally unbelievable. Parish pastor Johannes van der Linden of Kantens, Groningen, described the Reformed Confessions as "'worn out old shoes' no longer beneficial to the church." (The Reformed Confessions, or the Three Forms of Unity, are the Belgic Confession, the Heidelberg Catechism, and the Canons of Dort.) Van der Linden denied Christ's atoning death on the cross and labeled the doctrines of original sin and predestination as "Satan's doctrines . . . that emanate from Rome."[34] Many parishioners did not take to this "Parisian godlessness"

---

[33] Harinck and Winkler, "Nineteenth Century," 626.
[34] Quotes in Kamps, *1834*, 34, 51-52, 55-56, 59-60, 62; Ten Zythoff, *Sources of Secession*, 17-42.

that was "dressed in the religious apparel of an ecclesiastical sort."³⁵ This confirms the old adage that "fish rots from the head." As Jasper Vree noted: "A rather small circle of theologians pulled the strings" in the universities and within the church. But, he added, the "theology of the leaders was not as dominating as they liked it to be."³⁶

's-Heer Abtskerke pastorate

In 1820 father Van Raalte accepted a call from the church at 's-Heer Abtskerke, Zuid-Beveland, 165 miles distant in the far-off province of Zeeland. It was no promotion. This isolated village of 320 inhabitants was surrounded by wetlands that made it inaccessible for eight months of the year. But it was his first call after eight years at Wanneperveen. He accepted only months before his aged father died, although the decision contradicted his family-inspired move to Wanneperveen in the first place. In Reformed circles, reasons for accepting or declining calls always have an air of mystery. For Van Raalte, any call seemed to be an opportunity to move, and he had a pattern of increasingly short pastorates.³⁷

Religiously, Zeeland was experiencing a secularization in which orthodoxy was linked with ignorance. Van Raalte would have none of this; he proclaimed the Holy Scriptures. His inaugural sermon in early May set the tone: "For we preach not ourselves, but Christ Jesus the Lord" (II Cor. 4:5a, KJV). His farewell sermon pressed the same theme: "Let us hold fast the profession of our faith without wavering; for he is faithful that promised" (Hebrews 10:23, KJV).³⁸

Catrina, then forty-five years old, was again pregnant when the family moved to Zuid-Beveland. This sixteenth child lived only one month. Albertus Christiaan, age nine, and his five sisters were all in grammar school, and his older brothers were beyond school age.³⁹ Schooling was weak, and the youngsters had to learn practically another language to communicate with children in Zuid-Beveland,

---

[35] Den Ouden, *Kerk onder patriottenbewind*, 16-17; Rasker, *Nederlandse Hervormde Kerk*, 20, 22.

[36] Vree, "Dominating Theology," 34. A concise overview for the province of Overijssel is Bosch and Pereboom, "De Hervormde Kerk."

[37] Krabbendam, "Education," 3, citing Bloemhof, *Wanneperveen 700 jaar*, 16-18.

[38] Arno Neele, "Religie en cultuur," *Geschiedenis van Zeeland* 3 (2015): 221-305, esp. 228; Van Raalte's brief biography of his father's ministry, dated 2 Aug. 1866 (quote), is based on information he had obtained during his Netherlands visit, HHA.

[39] *Boekzaal der geleerde Wereld*, May 1819.

who spoke a Low Franconian Zeeuws dialect. This was quite different from the Low Saxon dialect of northwest Overijssel, which was closer to standard Dutch. Preacher's children had to be adaptable. Van Raalte cut short his tenure and departed on April 28, 1822.

Rijsoord pastorate

After the move to Rijsoord, in the province of Zuid-Holland, some sixty miles distant, Van Raalte again had a brief tenure of three years. Short pastorates broke community bonds for the family. Rijsoord was similar in size to Wanneperveen, with 880 souls, of which the church counted only 249, barely a quarter. The fine parsonage came with a scenic view of the Waal River, but the decrepit five hundred-year-old sanctuary, the oldest in the Zwijndrecht polder, was replaced eleven years after Van Raalte left.[40] Albertus, in his early teens, completed primary education in Rijsoord where Catrina's seventeenth and last child was stillborn. Father Albertus fittingly based his farewell sermon, delivered on October 23, 1825, on the Pauline benediction: "The grace of our Lord Jesus Christ be with you. My love be with you all in Christ Jesus. Amen" (I Cor. 16:23-24, KJV).[41]

Scherpenisse pastorate

The next pastorate was back in Zeeland, a forty-two-mile move. Van Raalte accepted a repeat call from the Hervormde Kerk in Scherpenisse after the congregation had received four other declines. The village was the oldest on the island of Tholen and situated directly east, across the Oosterschelde estuary from the previous pastorate at 's-Heer Abtskerke, Zuid-Beveland. Pastor Van Raalte was installed on October 30, 1825, in the medieval edifice, with gravestones in the nave dating to the 1400s. The brick building, clad with natural stone, displayed the earlier prosperity of the village. By the time Albertus came, the edifice had been truncated on the side and the east end, due to decay, though it could still seat 250 worshipers. The pulpit was two hundred years old. The pastor's family enjoyed a front-row pew atop some of the graves.[42]

Scherpenisse was a conservative church. Albertus's immediate successor denied categorically and with grief the complaint of a parishioner that he had denied and obscured the Reformed Confessions. The

---

[40] Boot, *De kerk over de brug*, 25.
[41] Van Raalte's brief biography of his father's ministry.
[42] Wesseling, *Afscheiding van 1834, Zeeland*, 263-65.

words later spoken from the pulpit by a successor upon Albertus's death indicate the kindhearted nature of the congregation. Members "with true emotion" praised their former dominee Van Raalte for "his genuine, amiable and faithful gospel labors, beloved and a blessing for many."[43]

In spite of the warm appreciation of the congregation, Van Raalte moved again in three years. After lengthy ministries of seventeen and nine years, respectively, in Renswoude (1793-1811) and Wanneperveen (1811-20) his next ones were only three years—the minimum without classical approval. Salaries would not have differed much among these congregations. Was Van Raalte burned out, disillusioned with the privileged church, or restless? Did he seek better educational opportunities for his children? These moves gave the young Albertus Christiaan a deeper understanding of life in different communities and may have whet his appetite for new experiences.[44]

Fijnaart pastorate (1828–1833)

From Scherpenisse, Van Raalte accepted a call from the Hervormde Kerk in Fijnaart in the province of Noord-Brabant, twenty-four miles distant. It was nestled in the eastern edge of the Bible Belt. The congregation, yoked with the small Heijningen church three miles to the west, was overjoyed; four previous calls had been declined.[45] Van Raalte preached his inaugural sermon on July 27, 1828, in what would be his last pastorate. Five years into his ministry in Fijnaart, he died in office on March 27, 1833, and his body was "buried before the door of the consistory chamber."[46]

> Death notice of Albertus van Raalte (likely written by son Albertus Christiaan for his mother):
> This morning, after "brief but intense suffering," to my great sadness, I announce the death of my tenderly beloved husband, the Rev. Mr. Albertus van Raalte, at the age of sixty-one years and five months, the blessed and faithful pastor, husband and father, pastor of this

---

[43] *Boekzaal der geleerde Wereld*, Jan. 1833, 527-28.
[44] Ten Zythoff, *Sources of Secession*, 41-42 (quote), citing Wanneperveen church minutes; Kuiper, *Geschiedenis*, 25 (quote), 28-29, 60-61. Van Raalte's brief biography of his father's ministry.
[45] *Verkade's Dominees Memories*. First call was extended on 7 Dec. 1827.
[46] A. C. Van Raalte, biography of father's ministry; Van Raalte family history, 25 Sept. 1871. HHA.

> congregation. The gospel's doctrine of grace, which he proclaimed so warmly for forty years, is for all of us a hope for comfort, blessing and ultimate union.
> C. C. Harking, widow of A. van Raalte
> Fijnaard [sic], North Brabant, March 28, 1833
>
> *Opregte Haarlemsche Courant*, 4 Apr. 1833, provided by Earl Wm. Kennedy, and translated by Nella Kennedy.

The ministerial periodical, *Boekzaal der geleerde wereld*, published an extensive account of Van Raalte's life, funeral service, and interment. The writer praised the deceased brother as a "zealous, faithful, and godly shepherd and teacher who proclaimed the gospel of salvation for forty years." Resolutions from former consistories heaped more words of praise on a "jewel of the church of Jesus Christ through example and pastoral work," a "worthy man whom we will not easily forget." One account singles out a son "who is preparing himself for the ministry at Leiden University, to the joy and hope of his mother."[47] Van Raalte's piety and dedication was clearly appreciated, but he had not played a major role in provincial church assemblies, and he had received very few calls, which suggests that he was not a pastor in high demand.

It was a tough blow for Albertus Christiaan at age twenty-one to lose his namesake and role model. He had never spoken a disparaging word about his father, a truly Christian parent. His father's words and life had proven him to be a devout man with a cheerful and child-like faith. Later in life, Albertus recalled "the doctrine of grace in the gospels that [his father] had proclaimed so warmly for forty years." Brummelkamp, who was closer than a blood brother, insisted that father Van Raalte had been "an example to him [and] had pointed him not to his own works but to the merits of Christ. Not only in words but in all of his life, he had allowed him to observe the man of joyful and childlike faith."[48]

It is possible that the eulogistic death announcement (in blocked text) had come from A. C. Van Raalte's hand, though signed by his mother. Catrina Christina Harking was grief-stricken at the death

---

[47] *Boekzaal der geleerde Wereld*, 1833, 527-28; Engelsma, *Watchman on the Walls*, 19; Van Gelderen, *Simon van Velzen*, 9.
[48] Brummelkamp, "Van Raalte," 93.

of her husband of thirty-eight years, and it had serious financial implications. Under King Willem I's church policy, widows of deceased pastors and their children below age twenty would receive a one-year stipend—the so-called *annus gratiae* (year of grace)—which at ƒ3,500 ($50,700 today) per annum was generous. Catrina could also stay one more year in the Fijnaart parsonage. The stipend and her husband's estate enabled her to send Albertus Christiaan to Leiden University. A comparison of her bold signature and that of son Albertus on the estate document, when compared with her husband's crabbed and timid signature in earlier documents, suggests that the namesake was not quite the mirror image of the father. He may have inherited more of his mother's genes than his father's.[49]

Van Raalte family

As youngsters, Albertus and younger sister Anna often had to deal with death and grieving. By age twelve, Albertus had lost five younger siblings and Anna had lost two—all before their first birthday. With his older brothers on their own, Albertus—the only boy still at home—became a special son to his parents. When Albertus was nine, his paternal grandfather, Pieter Van Raalte, died, and when Albertus was ten, his maternal grandfather, Arend Harking, died. Albertus's grandmothers had died a year before his birth. Death often lurked nearby before modern medicine, but Albertus Christian was providentially spared. He was said to be "cheerful and eager for life," with a good mind and a spiritual sensitivity."[50]

Brothers Petrus and Arend, both merchants, died in midlife when Albertus Christiaan was in his midtwenties. Arend passed away two weeks after his mother in April 1837, and Petrus died in 1840 in Ommen. Petrus's death notice, written by his younger brother, stated: "According to the expressed wishes of the deceased, there is to be no wearing of external signs of mourning." This request broke the usual pattern of families dressing in black for six weeks. Albertus's four surviving sisters married well and lived full lives long after their

---

[49] *Boekzaal der geleerde Wereld*, 1833, 527-28; Fijnaart Bevolkingsregister (Civil Registry), 1830, lists Catharina Christina Harking van Raalte as moving in 1834 to Amsterdam with daughters Catharina Alberta (19) and Anna Arendina (13) and her twenty-one-year-old maid.

[50] Reenders, "Van Raalte als leider," 100, trans. Dekker, citing Brummelkamp, "Van Raalte," 92 (quote). The son next younger than Albertus Christiaan died at age three, in 1816.

brother left for America. Niescina wed physician Hendrik Cornelis van der Linden at Scherpenisse during her father's ministry there. Johanna Bartha wed Dirk Blikman Kikkert, and Alberta Christina married physician Hendrik Jan van Dijk, both in Amsterdam. Youngest sister Anna Arendina married Johannes Teessen at Amsterdam. Blikman Kikkert and Teessen were ship brokers, the former became Albertus's business associate. After Van der Linden's death, Niescina wed Jan Mansier, a miller in Ommen.[51]

The senior Van Raaltes ran a tight household that valued obedience and diligence. As "PKs" (preacher's kids), Albertus Christiaan and his siblings certainly experienced life in a "fishbowl" and struggled to measure up to public expectations of being role models for village youngsters. His father, however, left virtually no reminiscences of their home life in the various parsonages.[52] He did not smoke a pipe, a habit common among clerics. Beer was likely the beverage of choice in the Van Raalte household, given the poor quality of drinking water. Albertus later in life had a standing order of a keg of beer a month delivered to the parsonage in Holland. His brother-in-law Anthony Brummelkamp had been addicted to a pipe in his younger years. He admitted later that he would have seven filled pipes next to him on his desk before studying. Van Raalte, who had been taught by his father not to smoke, admonished Brummelkamp that his addiction "was not worthy of a Christian." Brummelkamp vowed never to smoke again, and "with God's power" he kicked the habit after a year-long struggle.

---

[51] Bruins et al., *Albertus and Christina*, 192-200. I am indebted to Earl Wm. Kennedy for finding Peter's death notice, Ommen Death Records, 9 Feb. 1840. Rein Nauta hypothesized that Van Raalte suffered from a "personality syndrome," due to the frequency of death and mobility during his upbringing. His youth was "characterized by sorrow and uncertainty, by dissoluteness and distance, indeed by aimlessness. This lack of purpose may reflect an inner void," Nauta suggests. "To be a child of a suffering mother and a rather distant father may have a lasting effect" on the structure and character of one's personality." His mother was unable to give him "enough time" and his father had "no interest to sustain this child in his growing independence." The result was an "open wound," "some narcissistic injury," and a person who as an adult "will require the recognition and respect as a surrogate and substitute for the love once missed." Nauta concludes that Albertus's relationship with his father was "ambiguous"—did he want to satisfy him out of love or fear? Was he loved or ignored? Was he properly guided or overly criticized? (Nauta, "Leadership," 109-10). These questions are left hanging after Nauta's dubious attempt to psychoanalyze young Albertus. More than likely, he happily grew up in the manse, and this inclined him to follow in his father's footsteps.

[52] Wormser, *In twee werelddeelen*, 12-13, trans. Henry ten Hoor, English typescript, 7; Krabbendam, "Education," 2-3; Te Velde, "Ministerial Education."

Arend (Arent) Johannes Christiaan van Raalte (1800-1837), Albertus's older brother (*courtesy Sara Fredrickson Simmons*)

For a time, he left pipes on his desk for the aroma. Van Raalte later picked up the pipe habit himself.[53]

Father Van Raalte's character

What kind of pastor was Albertus van Raalte? Was he learned or pietistic? Yes, and yes. His university degree proved his learning, and colleagues and parishioners noted his piety and tender conscience before the Lord. His sermons had an experiential (*bevindelijk*) emphasis with stern warnings about dying in sin. He was certainly orthodox and devout, "a sincerely God-fearing man" with pastoral gifts that exceeded preaching skills. His soft voice was better suited to small sanctuaries; yet he managed for sixteen years in the large Wanneperveen sanctuary. A young pastor who met him late in life dubbed him as a "very godly greybeard."[54]

In a time of political turbulence, Rev. Van Raalte kept his head low and obeyed the regulations of church and state without questioning. "His only desire was to do his work unhindered," and to "follow the traditions of the past without questioning them." This was in keeping with the Apostle Paul's injunction: "Let every soul be subject

---

[53] Brummelkamp Jr., *Brummelkamp*, 192; Reenders, "Van Raalte als leider," 100; *Noord-Brabanter*, 8 Apr. 1837 (www.delpher.nl, accessed, June 2021), cited Scholte's periodical, *De Reformatie*, for implying that Van Raalte smoked a pipe.

[54] Brummelkamp, "Van Raalte," English typescript, 2, trans. Ten Hoor; Dosker, *Van Raalte*, 24-26, trans. Dekker.

Alberta Christina van Raalte van Dijk Mansier, Albertus's older sister (*HMA*)

unto the higher powers. For there is no power but of God: the powers that be are ordained of God (Romans 13:1, KJV). His son, Albertus Christiaan, confirmed this classic formulation. "From the cradle my father inculcated in me obedience to the powers over me, so my whole soul was permeated to obey, including ecclesiastical government. . . . Obedience, if it did not debase me, must be rendered for God's sake . . . [unless] it would run contrary to his [God's] command." After experiencing disorder in church and state, Van Raalte was thankful for King Willem I, who honored the Sabbath and brought order to the church. He was not one to interfere in larger church affairs.[55]

Van Raalte was content to serve his ministerial career as a faithful son of the public church. In remote villages he faithfully followed synodical directives and was shielded from religious apostasy and ecclesiastical turmoil. He could center his energy on his flock and be grateful for its restoration and public funding of salaries and edifices. In only one instance did he challenge local government officials; he successfully defended the Wanneperveen church's parochial school against the mayor's proposal to make it a nonsectarian public school. Albertus Christiaan attended this school until he was eight or nine years old. The father's ardent defense of that school may well explain the son's strong support for Christian education throughout his life.[56]

---

[55] Wormser, *In twee werelddeelen*, 12; Te Velde, *Brummelkamp*, 32; Van Raalte, *Kompleete uitgave* (1884), 534-35.

[56] Minutes, Wanneperveen Nederduitse Gereformeerde Kerk, 4 Nov. 1811, 26 Nov. 1812; Ten Zythoff, *Sources of Secession*, 25.

CHAPTER 2

Dissenter: "I followed the voice of conscience."

Albertus Christiaan Van Raalte was a PK and a most remarkable one at that. Although he had chosen his father's profession, he would not walk in his father's footsteps. Instead of a tranquil and traditional ministry, the "voice of conscience" took him on a radically different path as an outcast, a rebel. He broke free from the church of his parents at the cost of persecution and midcareer led persecuted followers across the ocean to the Michigan frontier, where he established the largest Dutch colony in North America. His road had far more twists and turns than even he could have ever imagined.

As a teenager, Albertus Christiaan had to cope with frequent family moves since his father's last four pastorates were unusually brief. This unsettled life may have created a sense of unrest and uncertainty; it could have hindered making close friendships with schoolmates. Resilience and parental compensation were required to avoid discontent among such children. Mother Christina likely compensated more than the busy father, who spent much of his time in the study and visiting parishioners

The decade of the 1830s was critical for shaping the course of Van Raalte's life. When he entered Leiden University, he came under the influence of the Réveil (Fr. Revival, reform), an intra-European Christian evangelical movement in the 1820s that found a strong voice in the Netherlands. At Leiden he also fell in with reform-minded theology students led by Hendrik Scholte and his student club. Albertus and his classmates also had to deal with the Belgian revolt for independence in 1830, as he watched older students volunteer to fight against the rebelling southern provinces. He, too, felt driven to volunteer and to train as a soldier, but by then the major fighting was over.

Then a cholera epidemic that claimed nearly five thousand lives in the nation almost took Albertus's life. This personal crisis led to a spiritual awakening and turned his heart fully toward the pulpit. Subsequently, he fell in with the Scholte coterie, which ultimately caused difficulties for his plans to serve in his father's denomination, due to guilt by association and his own stubborn questioning of church rules. Consequently, church authorities would not ordain him, and he turned to the "free-church" Seceders, who in 1834 began a widespread departure from the national church.

Son unlike his father

Albertus van Raalte named his eleventh child after himself, hoping perhaps that he would follow in his footsteps, unlike his two older surviving sons. But young Albertus had no such plans when he entered Leiden University; his genes, personality, and experience seemed to shape him otherwise. At Leiden he may have questioned the public church in ways his father most likely had never done, but the death of his father before he finished theological studies freed the younger Albertus to chart his own course.

Albertus Christiaan spent his infancy and early youth in the Wanneperveen parsonage. He entered elementary school under an able teacher who doubled as the church *voorzanger* (foresinger or precentor) and sexton. When he was nine, Albertus's parents moved to the smaller village of 's-Heer Abtskerke in Zeeland, where the local schoolmaster, L. J. Dorst, was poorly trained, often inebriated, and woefully inadequate.[1] The boy turned inward and took a special interest in collecting plants and animals, especially rabbits, until they overwhelmed the parsonage, which ended that venture. His brother-in-law, Anthony

---

[1] Krabbendam, "Education," 3, citing De Ruiter, *Historie*, 41-46.

Brummelkamp, noted many years later in a biographical obituary of Albertus Christiaan that he knew little about Albertus's youth but assumed he was a jolly, playful, and lively boy. At the university, Brummelkamp found Albertus to be lively and industrious, which showed that he had sat under his father's preaching and catechetical teaching and observed him in his study, all of which instilled values of diligence, duty, and obedience. Browsing in his father's library was a special delight; Albertus respected his father and aimed to please him in every way.[2]

As a young teenager, Albertus completed his primary education at Rijsoord, where his father had a brief pastorate. The family then moved to Scherpenisse in Zeeland in 1825. Recognizing the sharp mind of their fourteen-year-old son, his parents in 1826 sent him for "training in academic studies" to a classical colleague, Rev. Hermanus J. Krom, pastor of the Willemstad Hervormde Kerk, twenty-five miles distant. The private studies with Krom, who had taken his theological studies at Leiden, prepared Albertus Christiaan for higher education. Like father Van Raalte, the orthodox Krom was critical of but loyal to the public church up until his death in 1850.[3]

In 1827 Van Raalte enrolled his fifteen-year-old son in the small Latin academy in Bergen op Zoom, a large garrison town eleven miles distant, with eight hundred soldiers. Spanish troops had ravaged the city in the sixteenth century, and French troops did the same in the eighteenth century, but it retained its seventeenth-century fortification and old town gates. During the Protestant Reformation, the medieval edifice became a Reformed church. The classical academy, under the academically trained schoolmaster, Johannes Steuerwald, a Lutheran married to a Remonstrant widow, had fewer than ten students for the two-year program. The annual fee per student was $f24$ ($314 today). It was the perfect place for a promising schoolboy to prepare for university studies. Albertus likely boarded with a Hervormde Kerk pastor's family and mastered Latin, Greek, mathematics, geography, and history.[4]

In June 1829, after his family moved to Fijnaart in Noord-Brabant, Albertus Christiaan received his gymnasium diploma and his father took him to enroll at Leiden, the oldest (from 1575) and most prestigious

---

[2] Brummelkamp, "Van Raalte," 92; Van Raalte, Apr. 1862, "Naschrift," in *Kompleete uitgave* (1884), 534; Pieters, *Dutch Settlement*, 159, Warner, *Door het venster*, 102-3.

[3] *De Heraut*, 31 July 1866 (www.delpher.nl, accessed, June 2021), trans. Earl Wm. Kennedy. I am indebted to Kennedy for extensive information on Krom in *Provincie Noord-Brabant* (J. P. van den Tol, 1988).

[4] Krabbendam, "Education," 3-4.

university in the Netherlands. Father Van Raalte knew personally Leiden's renowned professor Johannes J. Clarisse. He and Clarisse became friends in the 1790s when they served neighboring churches at Renswoude and Doorn, respectively, in the Utrecht provincial synod. Clarisse began writing theological works at Doorn that hewed to the Reformed faith. He was a man to be trusted with a promising son. As explained below, Clarisse's efforts to help Albertus after his ill-fated candidate's examination indicates that his relationship with the Van Raalte family was very personal.[5]

Rev. Clarisse moved from the pulpit to the classroom, beginning as a teacher at Harderwijk Academie in 1803, where he proposed a broad theological curriculum to include modern foreign languages, history, philosophy, and natural science. His reputation and vision prompted King Willem I to appoint him to the divinity faculty at Leiden University in 1815, which professorship he held until his death in 1844. In his inaugural oration, Clarisse expressed his aim as a professor to excel in erudition, to be genuinely honest, to have modest freedom, and to be moderate and fair. This forward thinking may well have appealed to both Van Raaltes—father and son.[6]

Travel time was not a factor in the choice of Leiden. The distance from Fijnaart to Leiden or to Utrecht was almost the same, forty-eight versus fifty-five miles. The University of Groningen—father Van Raalte's alma mater—lay 165 miles away and had a lackluster reputation. All theological faculties tended to be open to theological rationalism, but Leiden stood midway between "conservative" Utrecht and "liberal" Groningen, both terms being relative. Leiden's theology department was known for its adherence to so-called supranaturalistic thinking.[7]

Réveil

At Leiden, young Van Raalte came in contact with theology classmates who introduced him to leaders of the Réveil movement. The first acquaintance he made in the fall of 1832 was Simon van Velzen (1809-1896) who introduced him to Anthony Brummelkamp

---

[5] Vree, "Dominating Theology," 36-41; *Biografisch Lexicon*, 114; Heideman, "Van Raalte," 271-72.
[6] "Johannes Clarisse (1770-1846)" in *Biografisch Lexicon*, 113; Krabbendam, "Education," 6.
[7] Te Velde, *Brummelkamp*, 40; Bos, *Servants of the Kingdom*, 223-24. Supranaturalism is a belief in an otherworldly realm or reality that in one way or another is commonly associated with all forms of religion.

(1811-1888). The three became good friends, and through them Van Raalte met Hendrik P. Scholte (1805-1868), the Réveil students' leader on campus, soon to graduate and enter the ministry.[8]

Van Raalte and his classmates at Leiden found themselves at the center of the Réveil movement, which had originated in Geneva and spread across West Europe. Jean-Henri Merle d'Aubigné (1794-1872) brought the Swiss revival to the Netherlands in 1823 when King Willem I appointed him preacher to the royal court. This movement had its American counterpart in the Second Great Awakening, led by Charles G. Finney. Finney's reform was sparked by middle class merchants and shopkeepers, whereas the Dutch Réveil attracted aristocrats and an intellectual upper class.[9]

Réveil leaders raised their voices against what they saw as apostasy in the Hervormde Kerk. Nicolaas Schotsman (1754-1822), a Leiden minister, in 1819 published a booklet of sermons lauding the two-hundredth anniversary of the Synod of Dort and its defense of Calvinism. His sermons sparked the minireformation and drew intense fire from church leaders. This prompted Willem Bilderdijk (1756-1832), a noted lawyer and private lecturer with a doctorate from Leiden University, to come to Schotsman's defense. Bilderdijk's teachings and writings in defense of orthodoxy earned him the title, "father of the Dutch Réveil."[10]

Bilderdijk recruited a bevy of students who became Réveil leaders—Isaac da Costa (1798-1860), Abraham Capadose (1795-1874), both Jewish converts, and Guillaume Groen van Prinsterer (1801-76), who became the founder of the Anti-Revolutionary Party. Da Costa's 1823 brochure, *Bezwaren tegen den geest der eeuw* (Objections to the spirit of the age), was labeled the "birth-cry of the Réveil." Capadose's 1835 pamphlet, *Ernstig en biddend woord aan de getrouwe leeraren der Hervormde Kerk van Nederland* (Earnest and prayerful word to the faithful ministers of the Reformed Church of the Netherlands), urged church leaders to stop besmirching the "honor of the King of the Church and

---

[8] Oostendorp, *Scholte*, 38-48; Engelsma, *Watchman on the Walls*, 29, 39, 53; Hyma, *Van Raalte*, 31; Brummelkamp Jr., *Brummelkamp*, 32-33.

[9] Hambrick-Stowe, *Charles G. Finney*.

[10] Ten Zythoff, *Sources of Secession*, 59-74; Wintle, *Pillars of Piety*, 21-27; Pronk, *Goodly Heritage*, 61-70; Schotsman, *Eerezuil ter gedachtenis van de voor twee hunderd jaar te Dordrecht gehouden Nationale Synode* (1819); Groen van Prinsterer, *Ongeloof en Revolutie*. For a list of authors, see Vree, "Dominating Theology," 35.

ignoring the rights of the people."[11] Groen van Prinsterer attributed the bloody French Revolution to its blatant anti-Christian spirit. No state, including the Netherlands, can survive if it rejects Truth. These learned and articulate Réveil men made resistance to confessional heterodoxy intellectually respectable, but none left the public church.[12]

It is not surprising that a number of students—whether training for the ministry or not—were affected by writings against "the spirit of the age," which criticized deviant theological views within the Hervormde Church. Scholte, who had grown up in the Lutheran Church, attended Bilderdijk's lectures and was captivated by the writings of Da Costa and Capadose. Scholte, in turn, swayed Simon van Velzen and Anthony Brummelkamp, among others, and introduced them to the wealthy Abraham J. Twent van Roosenburg, another leading evangelical light, who held forth on two evenings a week at his Leiden estate. Scholte left Leiden in November 1832 for a pastorate in three small congregations in Noord-Brabant. This was three months after Van Raalte's spiritual renewal, when he came under the teachings of the godly Johannes Le Feburé (1776-1843), a Leiden grain miller (*grein fabricant*). For many years, in the evening, at his home, Le Feburé would discourse on the Reformed faith. But it was Bilderdijk's "grave and prayerful word" that convinced Van Raalte, as he recalled many years later, that the "contemporary church government in her foundations, management, and operation was anti-Reformed and in direct opposition to the honor of the King of the Church and ignored the rights of the congregation."[13]

The Réveil leaders clearly had a direct influence on the young theological students at Leiden, although all the university-trained Réveil leaders, such as Da Costa, Capadose, Groen van Prinsterer, Van Hall, and Bilderdijk remained within the privileged public church in order to reform it from within. Capadose declared that he would not "lock out of the church as un-Christian the adherents of Socinianism [Unitarianism] and Deism." Bilderdijk stated: "Even if the visible church fades away in errors, . . . Christ still rules, and the gates of hell will not overpower his church." In short, most Réveil men called for reform but would not secede. They preached sin and grace but never

---

[11] Dosker, *Van Raalte*, 13, citing *De Reformatie*.
[12] Sweetman, "Children of the Day," 30, citing Da Costa, *Bezwaren tegen*, 5; Pronk, *Goodly Heritage*, 57-83.
[13] *Kompleete uitgave* (1884); "Naschrift" (1863), 315; Dosker, *Van Raalte*, 13.

W. Bilderdijk   Dr. A. Capadose   Issac da Costa   G. Groen van Prinsterer

Réveil leaders: Willem Bilderdijk, Abraham Capadose, Isaac da Costa, Guillaume Groen van Prinsterer (*Rullmann,* De Afscheiding)

declared the public church as false; it was only sick and would recover.[14]

Life-changing years at Leiden University

Albertus Christiaan entered Leiden University on June 16, 1829, after he had passed the examination required of all prospective students. His name that day was registered in the *Album Studiosorum*, the student registry, as a theology major. He chose this major mainly to please his father; his call to the Gospel ministry came later. The costs of a university education often dissuaded families with modest or low income. Given the great need for erudite and cultured pastors, the Crown in 1815 reserved most state scholarships and grants for theology students. The program was so successful that by 1830 six hundred students, one-third of the student body, studied theology, and almost two hundred, like Van Raalte, had a "Reverend" father.[15]

As a newcomer in Leiden, a city five times larger than Bergen op Zoom, he boarded first with the family of the paperhanger Nortier on the Langebrug and then with the Widow Van de Meij on the nearby Breestraat. He was a serious student but not a bookworm. He joined a student society (*senate*), a kind of fraternity, and perhaps fell into typical student life.[16] He worshiped at the city's famed Pieterskerk (the church of Pilgrim leader Rev. John Robinson). His conservative upbringing certainly clashed with the French revolutionary ideals he found on

---

[14] Ten Zythoff, *Sources of Secession*, 59-97; Kamps, *1834*, 22-25 (quote 23); Pronk, *Goodly Heritage*, 77-79. Kamps provided English translations of key documents.

[15] Bos, *Servants of the Kingdom*, 172-75. Van Raalte may have had no other choice than choosing theology, if he indeed had received the ministerial tuition grant.

[16] Brummelkamp, *Brummelkamp*, 32-33.

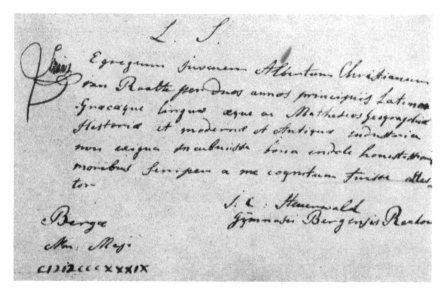

Van Raalte's gymnasium diploma (in Latin), June 1829 (HHA)

campus, guided by reason, human goodness, and virtue. By this time, Leiden's curriculum had broadened to include more subjects, with a wider aim to better the nation.

Young Van Raalte carried the normal, heavy load of ten courses, including law, logic, universal history, mathematics, theoretical philosophy and humane letters, and Dutch language and literature. The courses in theoretical philosophy and humane letters were designed to make graduates cultured members of society. Van Raalte did well in his preparatory studies in, for example, mathematics (even cum laude), in history, and in literature. He passed his core exams in May 1831 and was admitted to the department of theology, with two additional exams in September 1833.[17]

Belgian revolt

King Willem I interrupted the education of Scholte, Van Velzen, Brummelkamp and, ultimately, Van Raalte, by calling them to volun-

---

[17] Bos, *Servants of the Kingdom*, 168; Krabbendam, "Education." See also, Leiden University student almanacs, Archives of the University of Leiden, DOSA Zaal, trans. Nella Kennedy, and documents, in Latin, attesting to Van Raalte's mastery of various subjects: law, 1 May 1831; logic, 13 May 1831; mathematics, 14 May 1831; universal history, theoretical philosophy, and humane letters, 26 May 1831; philosophy and criticism, 25 Sept. 1833; Arabic and Aramaic, 27 Sept. 1833, all in HHA.

University Hall, Leiden, Rapenburg, 1581 (*Leiden University*)

teer for military service to quell the Belgian Revolution. Discontent had been brewing for some time in the southern Netherlands. Three quarters of the United Kingdom was Roman Catholic, with the majority of them in the south. The government had drawn up religious regulations for the Reformed and Lutheran churches, the Jews, and the Catholics. The king allowed Catholic monasteries to reopen under strict governmental rules, instituted a more academic and state-prescribed seminary curriculum for future priests and a more enlightened education in church schools. Catholics submitted grievance petitions with 350,000 signatures between 1828 and 1830 to no avail. The final straw was an economic recession in the textile industry and subsequent labor unrest.[18]

The southern citizens took to the streets in 1830 to demand independence. They rejected the misguided decision of the Congress of Vienna (1815) to join the Catholic provinces to the Protestant north to serve as a buffer on France's northern border against future French expansion. Belgian nationalists rejoiced when the London Conference of 1830 recognized their demands for independence, but King Willem I refused to acquiesce in losing his six most-industrialized provinces. The king then called Dutch citizens to arms to preserve the nation.[19]

---

[18] Kennedy, *Concise History*, 291-95.
[19] For this and the following paragraph, see Engelsma, *Watchman on the Walls*, 24-34.

Leidse Jager in military uniform, 1830

The Leiden University enlistees, 250 strong, comprised the Vrijwillige Jagers der Leidsche Hoogeschool (volunteer riflemen of the Leiden School of Higher Education).[20] Scholte, Brummelkamp, and Van Velzen went, but not Van Raalte, who was too young. The Jagers trained for several weeks at various sites in the city, and in mid-November 1830, they marched past cheering crowds to travel to North Brabant to fight the Belgians, clad in "crisp uniforms, high, tasseled hats, and their bayonet-tipped muskets and a saber."[21] The first mission was to defend the Dutch city of Breda near the Belgian border, but the enemy did not attack, and the winter and spring passed with little action. The war seemed to be a lark, all glory and no gore. But in late

---

[20] The large percentage of theological students in the Jagers was understandable because the king had granted a stipend and free tuition to divinity students. Added to their enthusiasm for battle was clerical hostility to the Roman Catholic south. Furthermore, loyalty among Reformed pastors toward the House of Orange had also been quite high. Bos, *Servants of the Kingdom*, 189-93.

[21] Anthony Brummelkamp's son remembered that his father, for whom the Belgian campaign had been a glorious time, kept all his life the high hat with visor and pom pom on it and crossed bandoleer (Brummelkamp Jr., *Levensbeschrijving*, 25).

summer 1831, the Jagers (riflemen) were ordered to join the regulars in a major campaign to capture Brussels, the capital.

In the so-called Ten Days' Campaign (August 2-12, 1831), Dutch forces invaded Belgium. After marching for three days, the Jagers came under heavy fire in a potato field near the village of Beringen, and one of their comrades, Lodewijk Justinus Beeckman from Kampen, was killed. Suddenly the war became personal. Two more riflemen from other universities died in the failed attempt to capture Leuven, the famed university city, after the French military intervened. Van Velzen and Brummelkamp happened to find cover in the same foxhole, which cemented their friendship. King Willem ordered a retreat in the face of overwhelming French forces. Cheering crowds welcomed the Jagers home as they passed through Dordrecht, Rotterdam, and Delft, en route to Leiden, where they arrived on September 23. The city staged an elaborate ceremony in the Pieterskerk that day and awarded a commemorative silver medal to each volunteer. A year later, in June 1832, the king personally awarded the returned students with the Metal Cross for bravery.

Van Raalte was not part of this campaign. He joined the university volunteers more than a year later, in November 1832, eleven days after his twenty-first birthday. He enlisted for an indefinite term and was not officially discharged until 1839 when King Willem I conceded and ended the financially ruinous war. Van Raalte's discharge certificate contains "boiler plate" language of "wounds sustained," "campaigns taken part in," and "exceptional exploits," none of which were filled in for him. He had continued his studies uninterrupted, except for six months of training during free time.[22]

A bonus for historians is the detailed physical description upon enlisting. It reads: "height: 1 el [sic], 6 palms, 1 thumb, 3 stripes (i.e., 1.61 meters and 3 millimeters [5' 3½"]); face, full; forehead, high; eyes, blue; nose, small; mouth, small; chin, round; hair, blonde; eyebrows, blond; visible marks: none." He was a fair-haired, blue-eyed young man of relatively short stature with a full face and high forehead. Little here distinguish him from his peers.[23]

---

[22] Te Velde, *Brummelkamp*, 38-39; Van Gelderen, *Simon van Velzen*, 12-16; Brummelkamp Jr., *Brummelkamp*, 25.

[23] Van Raalte, Discharge Certificate, 14 June 1839, trans. Nella Kennedy, HHA. The metric height measure was mandatory after 1 Jan. 1820, but the military continued to use the old nomenclature of ell, palm, thumb, and stripe, which was interpreted in metric as 1 ell equaled 1 meter, a palm 10 cm, a thumb 1 cm, and a stripe 1 mm.

The king continued the misguided resistance to Belgian independence on and off until 1839. This necessitated keeping a standing army, which ultimately depleted the nation's treasury. The war cost the king his throne, forcing him to abdicate in 1840, and taxpayers had to bear the enormous cost.[24] The secession of the South from the North and the final resolution during the 1830s coincided with another unpopular secession from the Hervormde Kerk. The same intensity of loyalty to king and kingdom can be observed in both conflicts, and objectors were hated and vilified as disloyal and unpatriotic. Van Raalte as a student lived through this turmoil.

Call to the ministry: "Spare my life, so that I can preach."

While his friends were at war, Van Raalte continued his studies and faced his own "war," a spiritual one. In August of 1832, his personal faith was tested when he became ill with cholera, ravaging Leiden. With no effective treatments available, the disease swept away almost five hundred townspeople and students. Newspapers were rife with stories of healthy people getting sick and dying in agony within hours. In Da Costa's words, it was "God with his cholera shaking the peoples!" The fearsome plague prompted Van Raalte to do some serious soul searching.[25]

The turning point came when reading the Apostle Paul's epistle to the Romans: "When I saw... that God was united with man through Jesus the crucified, I was absorbed in peace, joy, and love, and then I received the purpose in life." "A fire burned inside me, from which my first and serious prayer to God welled: 'O God, spare my life, so that I can preach to my poor fellow human beings that You are, that You care about us, and that You invite us as the fallen ones to find righteousness and eternal life in Jesus." This confession became the hallmark of his preaching: God exists, God cares, God saves.[26]

After he found the "treasure of redemption," Albertus committed himself earnestly to his divinity studies to prepare for the ministry. His life took a more serious turn and set him on a path with international

---

[24] Te Velde, *Brummelkamp*, 38-39; Van Gelderen, *Simon van Velzen*, 12-16; Brummelkamp Jr., *Brummelkamp*, 25. His second marriage with Belgian and Roman Catholic Countess Henriette d'Oultre also caused great resistance.

[25] Brummelkamp, "Van Raalte," 92, trans. Ten Hoor; Bos, *Servants of the Kingdom*, 173. A total of 1,087 out of 35,128 citizens fell ill, and 485 died by mid-November (Krabbendam, "Education," 8).

[26] Van Raalte, "Naschrift," in *Kompleete uitgave* (1884), 538; Nauta, "Leadership," 111.

consequences. The prayers of his aging father had been answered. "Purpose and responsibility developed shortly before and then right after the cholera epidemic," he later recalled, and "no worldly ambition but the service of the Gospel became from that time my prayerful aspiration.... I desired nothing but to spend my life in preaching.... The form and government of the church were rather dead notions to me."[27] This last statement shows that Albertus had been sheltered from the turmoil in the public church during the French protectorate and restoration of the Dutch monarchy. His newfound missionary zeal, however, set him on a path that was bound to clash with a church in which rules that disinterested him were prioritized at the expense of the historic Reformed faith.[28]

In preceding centuries theological studies were given separately from other university disciplines, and were funded by the Reformed Church. This privileged separateness ended in the Batavian Republic. In the new kingdom, however, theological study would have closer relationships to other academic disciplines, including general history and physics. In the first year, theological students took courses in other disciplines, in hopes of becoming cultured and learned professionals. The next years covered Old and New Testament exegesis, Christian ethics, biblical exposition and church history, doctrinal and apologetic theology, apologetics, homiletics, and pastoral theology. Church history proved to be Van Raalte's forte.[29]

Rector Magnificus C. J. van Assen in 1830-31, the second year of Van Raalte's studies at Leiden University, was a friend of Groen van Prinsterer and may have shared his Réveil sympathies. Yet the Leiden theology faculty taught "supranaturalism," a system of thought that could not be at odds with reason. In Bible courses, these professors directed students to study nature empirically, as a "particular revelation." This "mild-mannered, polished liberalism," however, did not appeal to Van Raalte.[30]

Leiden at this time had six hundred students and twenty-six professors. Theology students enjoyed lower tuition than those in

---

[27] Wormser, *In twee werelddeelen*, 17-20, trans. Ten Hoor; Hyma, *Van Raalte*, 27-29; Van Raalte to Van Velzen Jr., April 1862, in *Kompleete uitgave* (1863), 323-38, trans. Nella Kennedy, HHA.

[28] Van Raalte, *Kompleete uitgave* (1884), 534 (quote); Ten Zythoff, *Sources of Secession*, 130-31 (quote).

[29] Bos, *Servants of the Kingdom*, 183-85.

[30] Oostendorp, *Scholte*, 37 (quote). Van Raalte to Van Velzen Jr., April 1862, in *Kompleete uitgave* (1884), 534.

law or medicine, with annual fees ranging from ƒ30 to ƒ50 ($419 to $699 today). The theology major, however, was so popular that some graduates could not find pulpits due to a surplus of ministers.[31]

Scholte club rebels

Simon van Velzen met Van Raalte in the fall of 1832 and invited him to join the so-called Scholte club, which decision proved to have major repercussions. Scholte, the scion of an Amsterdam merchant family, was a natural-born leader who attracted theological students—rebels, as Van Raalte labeled the group—who were dissatisfied with the theological declension within the Reformed Church and with the 1816 regulations. The club members desultorily attended faculty lectures but enthusiastically went to informal teachings by Bilderdijk and Le Feburé. As Scholte told a friend, "I do not have to be taught lying by the professors, I already know how to do that better than they." Brummelkamp and Van Velzen were the first recruits; they and Scholte had met originally at the Amsterdam Athenaeum, a small gymnasium or Latin school. Of Van Raalte, Brummelkamp wrote: "This younger student is a lovely acquisition."[32]

Albertus fit well with these "pariahs," the "scourings at our alma mater," "dompers" (Da Costians). Brummelkamp said it well: "You had to have gone through those days to understand what it was like then. The Liberalism, the study of virtue and good deeds, personal courage, human progress, and rationality, were the gods to which men could not stop singing praises."[33]

Outside of class, the young men studied the scriptures, the Reformers Luther and Calvin, and the Dutch *Oude Schrijvers* (Old Writers) of the Nadere [later] Reformatie—Bernardus Smijtegelt, Willem Teellinck, Wilhelmus à Brakel, Jodocus van Lodenstein, Alexander Comrie, and others—and also Puritan devotional books translated into Dutch. This reformation had a kind of counterpart in the First Great Awakening of the 1740s in the English-speaking world.

---

[31] Bos, *Servants of the Kingdom*, 172-77.

[32] Oostendorp, *Scholte*, 28-29 (quote); Brummelkamp Jr., *Brummelkamp*, 32 (quote); Pronk, *Goodly Heritage*, 101-32; The Amsterdam Athenaeum was a forerunner of the present University of Amsterdam. As a young man, Scholte managed the family business, a sugar-box-making factory in Amsterdam, but the death of his parents and his only brother allowed him to sell the business, leaving him a wealthy man at age twenty-three, free to pursue higher education.

[33] Brummelkamp Jr., *Brummelkamp*, 33 (quote); Brummelkamp, "Van Raalte," English typescript, 2-3 (quote), trans. Ten Hoor; Dosker, *Van Raalte*, 3 (quote), trans. Dekker; Bos, *Servants of the Kingdom*, 223-25.

Anglican revivalist, George Whitefield (1714-1770)—the stepfather of Methodism—sparked the movement and carried it to America, where New England Puritan divine Jonathan Edwards (1703-58) joined the crusade.[34]

Besides Johannes Clarisse, the theological faculty consisted of Wessel A. van Hengel, Nicolaas C. Kist, Lucas Suringar, and J. H. van der Palm. Clarisse specialized in dogmatics, apologetics, homiletics, pastoral theology, and Old Testament exegesis; Van Hengel in New Testament exegesis; Kist in church history and historical theology; and Suringar in natural theology and the confessions. These professors understandably did not appreciate it when Scholte and friends skipped their lectures. Louis Bähler, another follower, upbraided Scholte's absences, although he and all the club members, especially Van Raalte, sat approvingly under Clarisse.[35]

A dignified man of culture and composure, Clarisse's passion was to instill in his students the cultural graces of good posture, clear speaking, eloquent preaching, mastery of fencing and dance, and playing a musical instrument. He would also be a moderating voice in the ensuing religious conflicts, initiating a circular sent to pastors, encouraging them to refrain from casting aspersions on their Reformed Confessions. He admonished church boards to pay attention to the behavior of their pastors. The strait-laced Van Velzen praised Clarisse as "a man whose colossal knowledge demanded everyone's respect, whose powerful speech controlled the minds, whose charm won all hearts, and [who] sometimes was a highly serious champion of orthodoxy and of pious people of former times." Clarisse even spoke in favor of Hendrik de Cock (1801-1842) at the 1834 Synod of the Hervormde Kerk, and he was the only delegate to do so. Perhaps too much can be made of this congenial attitude since Clarisse also defended such heretics as the presbyter Arius (250-336), Pelagius (354-418), and Jacobus Arminius (1560-1609), father of the Remonstrants.[36]

Over his career, Clarisse's theology gradually moved from orthodoxy to social engagement, as in the "Nut," the Maatschappij tot

---

[34] Pronk, *Goodly Heritage*, 27-56; Brienen et al., *Nadere Reformatie*.
[35] Oostendorp, *Scholte*, 37-39; Brummelkamp in *Kompleete uitgave* (1863), 283.
[36] In 1834 D. Hogendorp condemned Clarisse for "pleading for heretics like Arius and Pelagius, and also for the Remonstrants" (Vree, "Dominating Theology," 40, citing Van Hogendorp to Scholte, 14 July 1834, in Smits, *Afscheiding van 1834*, 6:117-18; Engelsma, *Watchman on the Walls*, 35 [Clarisse quote]). Remonstrants counted a mere 4,100 adherents in the first national census in 1809 (De Kok, *Nederland*, 292-93). Vree, "Dominating Theology," 32-47, offers the best analysis of Clarisse and his relations with Van Raalte and the Separatists.

Johannes J. Clarisse (1770-1846), Van Raalte's favorite professor at Leiden University (*Vree, "Dominating Theology"*)

Nut van 't Algemeen (Society for Public Welfare).[37] His eight-hundred-page magnum opus, *Encyclopaediae theologicae epitome* (1832), although not yet captured by German higher criticism, offered a "prudent equilibrium between the old Reformed tradition at the one hand and the 'enlightened virtue and philanthropy' at the other hand."[38] Clarisse, in contrast to his hostile colleagues, Van Hengel and Kist, remained cordial toward his nonconforming students and passed each one in their preliminary and final examinations. He recommended them to the mother church and, "with ample frankness," urged them to serve faithfully. The Zuid-Holland Provincial Church Board put these disciples of Da Costa and Le Feburé through the usual twelve-hour examination and—hoping they would mature and settle into normal routines—commended them, with misgivings, to the church for calls.[39]

Once these theological students took up their pastorates, they found it difficult, if not impossible, to work for reform within the Hervormde Kerk. They faced the realities of divided congregations and resistant members who spurned their dogged calls for theological

---

[37] The Nut, founded in 1784, is a national association with local chapters that strives to promote individual and social development, notably in education and socioeconomic development of the underprivileged, all of which aims to further the democratization of the Netherlands (https://www.nutalgemeen.nl, accessed, May 2022).

[38] Vree, "Dominating Theology," 37-40, for this and following paragraphs.

[39] Engelsma, *Watchman on the Walls*, 42-43; Vree, "Dominating Theology," 44n16, quoting Van Velzen, "Stem eens wachters op Zions muren"; Soepenberg, *Afscheiding in Amsterdam*, 48.

Van Raalte as theology student at Leiden University (*Pereboom et al.,* Afscheiding in Overijssel)

orthodoxy. Yet, some of them persisted in calling out leaders as apostates and labeling the Hervormde Kerk a false church, according to the criteria of Article 29 of the Belgic Confession. The public church, said Scholte in his mouthpiece, *De Reformatie,* "lacked the characteristics of being a church of Christ." It failed to uphold Reformed doctrines and acknowledge Christ as "the King who is nearby and coming soon... not the King of a far-off land."[40] Notably, Van Raalte and Brummelkamp were critical but never called the church false.[41]

Candidacy examinations

In the spring of 1832, Albertus finished his studies and prepared for the required "trial" sermon. He carefully wrote a full sermon text—his first—based on Romans 5:1 (KJV): "Therefore being justified by faith, we have peace with God through our Lord Jesus Christ." This text encapsulated the entire Gospel message the Apostle Paul was called to preach, and it became Van Raalte's message as well. With the sermon safely tucked into the back pocket of his coat, Albertus entered the

---

[40] Eugene P. Heideman raised this question and answers in the negative, in *Hendrik P. Scholte,* xx, 21-42. See also, Engelsma, *Watchman on the Walls,* 82-86. For a brief review of this history, see Bruins, "From Calvin to Van Raalte."*De Reformatie* began in 1837.

[41] Vree, "Dominating Theology," 35-36; Engelsma, *Watchman on the Walls,* 83, citing Van Velzen, "Apology of the Ecclesiastical Secession."

PROFESSORES THEOLOGIAE

IN ACADEMIA LUGDUNO-BATAVA

L.

S. P. D.

Praestantissimus Juvenis, *Albertus Christianus Van Raalte* inde ab anno 1829 hujus Academiae civis, in instituenda studii Theologici ratione, cum ad Legem Regiam d. 2 Augusti cIↃIↃCCCXV N°. 14. Art. 46, 47, 63, 73, 74, 75, 82, 98, 110, 116, tum ad normam, Statutis Ecclesiasticis praescriptam et Augustissimi Regis Decreto d. 30 Julii cIↃIↃCCCXVI approbatam, se composuit. Primum igitur Literis Graecis, Latinis, Belgicis et Hebraicis, nec non Mathesi, Philosophiae et Historiae Universali operam dedit, et die 26 *Maji* anni 1831 Candidatis Philosophiae Theoreticae et *Literarum Humaniorum* adscriptus est. Deinde in Theologiam Naturalem, Historiam Ecclesiasticam, Criticam Sacram et Hermeneuticam incubuit, et in utroque Codice Veteris et Novi Foederis accurate et legitime interpretando vires exercuit. Ad ipsam denique Theologiam Dogmaticam, quam vocant, et Historicam se contulit, atque omnes et singulos Doctrinae Christianae, cum Theoreticae, tum Practicae, locos tractavit: neque Homileticae artis aut Curarum Pastoralium scientiam neglexit. Nec solum requisitis, ut ad Sacrorum Antistitis munus admitti posset, Scholis biennium interfuit, sed *totos* annos in examinibus progressuum in Historicis, Dogmaticis, Moralibus ceterisque Disciplinis Theologicis factorum specimina edidit. Neque Oeconomiam ruralem intactam reliquit. Bis eum de rebus sacris concionantem audivimus.

Quam studiorum viam et rationem cum vitae integritas ornaverit, non dubitavimus, huic Juveni, *Candidatis Theologiae* die 19 *Aprilis* anni 1834 adscripto, eoque ipso, secundum Regium Decretum diei 12 Junii cIↃIↃCCCXXII, in Ecclesiasticum Ordinem recepto, hoc operae rite praestitae testimonium exhibere, Deum precantes, ut omnia ipsi ex votis et meritis succedant, in uberrimum Ecclesiae Christianae emolumentum.

Scripsimus in Academia Lugduno-Batava,
die 10 *Junii* 1834.
W. A. Van Hengel.
Fac. L. t. Dec.

Van Raalte's Leiden University Certificate in Theology,
April 19, 1834 (*Hyma*, Van Raalte)

Pieterskerk, filled with young men eager to hear their fellow student. Perhaps some knew his association in the Scholte club. Professor Clarisse led him to the pulpit. As the nervous candidate mounted the stairs to the enclosed wooden pulpit, dubbed the *houten broek* (wooden pants), Clarisse "dexterously pulled the notes out of his pocket, and now the astonished young chap was forced to speak extemporaneously." Although "terribly disconcerted" for a few moments, Albertus preached a remarkable sermon that impressed his professor and classmates. He declared afterward that he had never "spoken better than that morning." The quick-witted Albertus used this experience to master preaching without notes for his entire ministry, although he usually reviewed a note card with the main points.[42]

Years later, Albertus recalled his frame of mind as he prepared for the sermon and the subsequent oral exam for ordination:

> As a heedless youth, I had no goal in life. Examining my own heart and insufficiency, the prospect of being a pastor filled me with fears. I trembled to be the cause of the perishing of souls since I myself was a victim of unrest. Earlier, while at home during the onset of cholera, God had comforted my tense and fatigued soul with Jesus to some extent. God, having heard my cry of distress, let me find the righteousness of faith through Paul's letter to the Romans. Yes, then I had a purpose, but not through men.... I fell on my knees and did not pray for forgiveness but prayed in bliss that God would spare my life.... I desired, I dared, and I had to preach about what I learned.[43]

On April 19, 1834, Van Raalte passed his examination with flying colors, and one month later, professors Clarisse, Kist, and Van Hengel signed his official graduation certificate (written in Latin), albeit with misgivings due to his tainted association with Scholte's group. Kist told Van Raalte that some professors had brought "objections about his feelings." Kist asked the source of these "strange ideas," since they had not been taught at the university. Did they come from the lay preacher Le Féburé? Van Raalte denied this. He insisted that he had prayerfully searched the scriptures and learned, through God's Spirit, the "truth of justification by faith in Jesus." Kist cut off the

---

[42] Wormser, *In twee werelddeelen*, 22; Hyma, *Van Raalte*, 33. This story, attributed to Van Raalte himself, as related to Nicholas H. Dosker, first appeared in Dosker, *Van Raalte*, 5-6, trans. Dekker.

[43] Van Raalte, "Naschrift," *Kompleete uitgave* (1863), 323-38 (quote 334-35).

conversation with a condescending smile. This curt reaction presaged trouble for Van Raalte in the ordination process, which proved to be lengthy, laborious, and ultimately futile.[44]

Secession of 1834

Events beyond Van Raalte's control further complicated his ordination. Rev. Hendrik de Cock in the Hervormde Kerk in far off Ulrum, Groningen, had set off a religious upheaval. Although not the first pastor to protest declension in the mother church, De Cock's actions changed the course of Dutch and American church history and earned for him the title, "Father of the Secession of 1834." Van Raalte was caught up in this turmoil, although the schism was not of his doing or approval.

De Cock had studied for the ministry at the University of Groningen under the rationalist theologian, Herman Muntinghe (1752-1824), progenitor of the supranaturalistic Groninger School. James Bratt aptly summarized the theology of this school: "Christ was less a bleeding Savior than a model of fully realized humanity; the end of religion was less salvation from sin than the achievement of virtue; the human heart was less a sin-blackened seat of evil in need of radical conversion than a trustworthy organ of discernment fit to replace doctrinal standards as the ultimate measure of religious truth."[45] Petrus Hofstede de Groot (1807-1886), De Cock's classmate at Groningen, preceded him in the Ulrum pulpit from 1826 to 1829, when he was promoted to theology professor at the university. Understandably, the theological studies of De Cock and De Groot under Muntinghe and colleagues left serious gaps, notably the historic Reformed Confessions, which all candidates and office bearers pledged to uphold when they signed the form of subscription.

When De Cock in 1829 began his second charge at Ulrum, his erudite sermons stressed good works more than God's free grace, and like his predecessor, he tried to straddle the orthodox and progressive factions in the congregation. Then he experienced a spiritual awakening when a few devout parishioners brought him up short. They noticed that their pastor's sermons slighted the Confessions and the writings

---

[44] Van Raalte, *Kompleete uitgave* (1884), 537; Hyma, *Van Raalte*, 29-31.
[45] Ten Zythoff, *Sources of Secession*, 104-9; Bratt, *Dutch Calvinism in Modern America*, 5. I thank Joshua Engelsma (*van Velzen*, 36) for highlighting this quote. Besides Ten Zythoff, the best treatment of the Groninger School in English—albeit highly critical—is Kamps, *1834*, 38-41, 50-58.

Petrus Hofstede de Groot (1802-1886) as a young professor at Groningen (Bos, Servants of the Kingdom)

of Calvin and other Reformed theologians. Klaas Pieters Kuypenga, an untutored farmer, remarked to the dominee: "If I might add one sigh to my salvation, then I would be eternally lost." This off-hand comment created doubt about the merits of good works. Then a widow urged De Cock to read the Confessions. Nudged by these humble people, he took up the Canons of Dort and John Calvin's *Institutes of the Christian Religion* (available only in Latin) and became fully aware that salvation was entirely a gift of God's grace. He also saw books by the Old Writers of the seventeenth century in the library of one of his elders, as well as more recent pamphlets, notably by Baron Cornelis van Zuylen van Nijevelt (1771-1833)—*De Hervormde leer* (Reformed doctrine) and *De eenige redding* (The only salvation). These events and writings changed his thinking and his preaching.[46]

De Cock's conversion empowered his sermons, and folks flocked to Ulrum from surrounding parishes, including parents requesting baptism for their children, who mistakenly feared that their pastors, being unconverted, might render the sacrament meaningless. Baptizing children from neighboring parishes violated church rules, but De Cock obliged anyway, despite a warning from Scholte that it would cause trouble. Sure enough, the Classis of Middelstum instituted formal proceedings.[47]

De Cock was no milquetoast. One biographer described him as a "simple, unassuming, and serious man, a true son of the north, sober, and calm, with an eye for reality." He could be frank to a fault. He

---

[46] Kamps, *1834*, 77-80, 93-95; Pronk, *Goodly Heritage*, 87-100. A modern biography is Veldman, *Hendrik de Cock*.
[47] Kamps, *1834*, 157-74, for this and following paragraphs.

attacked hymns in the *Evangelische Gezangen* of 1807 as "a concoction of siren love songs [*sirenische minneliederen*] fit to draw Reformed believers away from the saving doctrine," specifically the Calvinist doctrine of predestination.[48] The singing of at least one hymn in worship was prescribed by the 1816 synodical regulations, to supplement the metrical Genevan psalms introduced by John Calvin himself. Although the Psalms were paraphrases of Holy Writ, man-made versification in hymns presumably was not.[49]

In his most controversial pamphlet, *Defense of True Reformed Doctrine and of the True Reformed Believers*, De Cock castigated fellow clerics, who had published their own pamphlets, as "wolves in the sheep-fold who can preach much better about eating and drinking, nice weather and long days, about gardening and farming, about newspapers and war, than about the Kingdom of Heaven, as they lead the way for their congregations to the markets and horse races, drinking and singing until early dawn, or attending meetings for the so-called [society for the] common good."[50] He certainly had a way with words.

The Classis of Middelstum suspended De Cock without salary for more than a year, and futile appeals for reinstatement left him no choice but to secede. The consistory and most members of the congregation of Ulrum signed a document of secession on October 13, 1834. That same month Scholte traveled to Ulrum in a show of support. When the news spread of Scholte's coming, thousands of people gathered to hear him preach. At a Friday evening service, Scholte fervently proclaimed the Reformed faith and condemned unfaithful ministers as "idolaters and prophets of deceit." The Classis of Middelstum was not pleased and barred him from the Ulrum pulpit the following Sunday. The local constabulary locked the church doors to avoid a riot by angry parishioners and rescued Scholte from hoodlums who roughed him up. That night, Scholte boldly preached in a pasture behind the parsonage and left town immediately.[51]

---

[48] Ten Zythoff, *Sources of Secession*, 117-25; Heideman, *Scholte*, 6; Engelsma, "Covenant Doctrine," 101, cited in Engelsma, *Watchman on the Walls*, 60.

[49] Kamps, *1834*, 25-30; Pieters, "Historical Foundation," in *Classis Holland Minutes*, 11-12; Jacobson et al., *Dutch Leader*, 93-98.

[50] Van Hinte, *Netherlanders*, 90; Kamps, *1834*, 315; Rullmann, *Nederlandsch Hervormde Kerk*, 101-4.

[51] Kamps, *1834*, 157-77, esp. 173 for his salary; Pronk, *Goodly Heritage*, 93-94.

The next day, October 14, 1834, the consistory signed a beautifully handwritten document, "De Akte van Afscheiding en Wedekier" (Act of secession and return), and the next night, most of the congregation followed suit. No doubt, the pastor was behind the drafting of the text, but he did not write or sign it himself. This document was crafted and signed by the consistory, to enable the congregation to restore their deposed pastor to his rightful pulpit.[52] De Cock exclaimed: "Everything now fitted together for me, as if it were an indication of the Lord what I had to do and which way I had to go." The document was signed by 137 members, both couples and single adults. The Ulrum church had thereby sparked the Secession of 1834. It was their Declaration of Independence. De Cock within a year would plant sixteen free churches throughout the provinces of Groningen and Drenthe and begin a theological school to train pastors.

Two weeks after De Cock's secession, on October 31, he was fined ƒ150 ($2,100 today) and imprisoned for three months. Two days earlier, church officials had suspended Scholte, which prompted his resignation, and several hundred members of his combined congregation of Doeveren, Genderen, and Gansoyen followed him. Scholte resigned shortly before Simon van Velzen's installation service on November 9 in the Drogeham Hervormde Kerk of Friesland. Van Velzen's and Brummelkamp's provincial synod examinations had been conducted amicably. They were subtly warned, however, that should any points of their doctrine be unclear, they "would be clearer with continued studies."[53]

Van Velzen's congregation flourished with his full-orbed doctrinal sermons that drew worshipers from miles around, but he was deposed on January 13, 1836. By then all his likeminded classmates had met the same fate. Brummelkamp was dismissed on October 7, 1835, a few months after being ordained by the Hattem, Gelderland church. George F. Gezelle Meerburg, who had served in Almkerk, Noord-Brabant since October 1833, was removed on November 24, 1835. Huibertus J. Budding at Biggekerke, Zeeland, resigned in 1836 before being expelled. The synodical board castigated these men as "snakes," charging that they had entered the ministry solely "to cause dissension and schism in the Hervormde Kerk." This was patently false; all wanted only to serve honorably in the church of their birth.

[52] Keizer, *De Afscheiding van 1834*, 578.
[53] Pronk, *Goodly Heritage*, 96; Brummelkamp Jr., *Brummelkamp*, 37.

ACT OF SECESSION OR RETURN

We the undersigned, overseers and members of the Reformed congregation of Jesus Christ at Ulrum, have observed for a considerable time the corruption in the Netherlands Reformed Church [*Nederduitsch Hervormde Kerk*], as well as the mutilation or denial of the doctrine of our fathers, based on God's word; the degeneration of the administration of the holy sacraments, according to the regulation of Christ in his word; and the almost complete neglect of ecclesiastical discipline, all of which matters are, according to our Reformed Confession, article 29, distinguishing marks of the true church. We have received through God's grace a pastor and teacher who sets forth to us according to the word of God the pure doctrine of our fathers, and who applied the same both in particular and in general. The congregation was thereby more and more awakened to direct its steps in confession and walk according to the rule of faith and of God's holy word (Gal. 6:16; Phil. 3:16), to renounce the service of God according to human commandments, because God's word tells us that this is in vain (Matt. 15:9), and at the same time to watch for the profaning of the signs and seals of God's eternal covenant of grace.

Through this the congregation lived in rest and peace; but that rest and peace was disturbed by the highly unjust and ungodly suspension of our commonly loved and esteemed pastor as a consequence of his public testimony against false doctrine and against defiled public religious services. Quietly and calmly has the congregation with their pastor and teacher conducted itself to this point; various very fair proposals were made, both by our pastor and teacher and by the rest of the overseers of the congregation; repeatedly investigation and judgment on the ground of and according to God's word were requested, but all in vain. Classical, provincial, and synodical ecclesiastical administrators have refused this most just request, and on the contrary have demanded repentance and regret without pointing out any offense from God's holy word, as well as unlimited subjection to synodical regulations and prescriptions without demonstrating that those are in all things based on God's word. Thereby these ecclesiastical administrators of the Netherlands Reformed Church have now made themselves equivalent to the popish church rejected by our fathers, because not only is the previously mentioned corruption observed, but in addition God's word is rejected or invalidated by ecclesiastical laws and decisions (Matt. 15:4; Matt. 23:4; Mark

7:7–8), and they persecute those who will live godly in Christ Jesus, according to his own prescriptions, recorded in his word (Matt. 2:13; Matt. 5:11–12; Matt. 10:23; Matt. 25:34; Luke 11:49; Luke 12:12; John 5:16; John 15:20; Acts 7:52; Acts 9:4; Acts 22:4, 7; Acts 26:11, 14–15; Rom. 12:14; 1 Cor. 15:9; Gal. 1:13, 23; Gal. 4:29; Phil. 3:6; 1 Thess. 2:15; Rev. 12:13; Matt. 5:10; Matt. 13:21; Mark 10:30; Acts 8:1, 50; Rom. 8:15; 1 Cor. 5:12; 2 Cor. 4:9, 12; Gal. 5:11; Gal. 6:12; 2 Thess. 1:4; 2 Tim. 3:11–12), and the consciences of men are bound. Finally on the authority of the provincial eccclesiastical administrators the preaching of the word of God by a publicly acknowledged minister in our midst, the Rev. H. P. Scholte, Reformed pastor at Doveren and Genderen, in the land of Heusden and Altena, province of North Brabant, was forbidden, and the mutual assemblies of the believers, which were held with open doors, were punished by fines.

Taking all of this together, it has now become more than plain that the Netherlands Reformed Church is not the true but the false church, according to God's word and article 29 of our Confession. For this reason the undersigned hereby declare that they in accordance with the office of all believers (article 28) separate themselves from those who are not of the church and therefore will have no more fellowship with the Netherlands Reformed Church until it returns to the true service of the Lord. They declare at the same time their willingness to exercise fellowship with all true Reformed members and to unite themselves with every gathering founded on God's infallible word, in whatever place God has also united the same. Hereby we testify that in all things we hold to God's holy word and to our old forms of unity in all things founded on that word, namely, the Confession of Faith, the Heidelberg Catechism, and the Canons of the Synod of Dordrecht, held in the years 1618–19; we order our public religious services according to the ancient ecclesiastical liturgy; and with respect to divine service and church government, for the present we hold to the church order instituted by the aforementioned Synod of Dordrecht.

Finally, we hereby declare that we continue to acknowledge our unjustly suspended pastor.

Ulrum, the 13th of October, 1834

J. J. Beukema, elder

K. J. Barkema, elder

K. A. van der Laan, deacon

D. P. Ritsema, deacon

Geert K. Bos, deacon

Act of Secession of 1834, signed by seventy men for their families (Keizer, De Afscheiding van 1834), document with signatures in Kamps, *1834*, 245-46, English translation. Note the name J. P. Swierenga, distant relative of this author, midway down the second column (see arrow).

All but Budding were deposed for (among other things) refusing to sing at least one hymn at each worship service.[54]

The youthfulness of these "soldiers of the cross" in 1834 is noteworthy. Except for De Cock, who was age thirty-three, the rest were in their twenties. Albertus later reflected on this: "In our youthfulness, we felt bereft of courage and strength and would have liked to have hidden ourselves, but they [church leaders] did not destroy us.... I hope that by now in the Netherlands they have discovered that a testimony for the truth is not dependent upon age."[55]

---

[54] De Jong and Kloosterman, *Reformation of 1834*, 28 (quotes); Ten Zythoff, *Sources of Secession*, 125-27, Engelsma, *Watchman on the Walls*, 55-56, 62-63, 70-71; Oostendorp, *Scholte*, 40, 57-63; Kennedy, *Commentary*, 30 April 1851, 1:148.

[55] Van Raalte to Van Velzen Jr., Apr. 1862, "Naschrift," in *Kompleete uitgave* (1884), 533, trans. Dekker; Dosker, *Van Raalte*, 14; Brinks, "Father Budding"; De Graaf, "Een Monument der Afscheiding," 5-6.

George Frans Gezelle Meerburg

Simon Van Velzen

Albertus Christiaan Van Raalte

Anthony Brummelkamp

The Scholte Club

Hendrik P. Scholte

Scholte club alumni (Heideman, *Scholte*)

Huibertus J. Budding, minister at Biggekerke, province of Zeeland (*Keizer,* Afscheiding van 1834)

Official persecution

King Willem I and other monarchs reinstated autocratic rule after Napoleon demanded religious uniformity in their kingdoms, believing that civil peace required religious unity. Willem had a distaste for doctrinal disputes and feared protest movements and disorder in the post-Napoleonic decades. He would not tolerate religious disorder and disloyalty, and deemed Separatist pastors to be "schismatics, fomenters of unrest, and secret agitators" and demanded that they submit to the "established and recognized church."

The king found legal footing for suppressing religious dissenters in Articles 291, 292, and 294 of the Napoleonic Code of 1811, which barred public assemblies of more than twenty persons for "religion, literature, politics, or other purposes, ... except by approbation of the High Government." Napoleon's major objective was to limit political rallies. But Willem seized on the word "religion," and by invoking the Code, he made unauthorized worship services illegal. Thereafter, governors and mayors ordered police to stand at the door of Separatist gatherings to ensure compliance. Stiff persecution continued until 1840, in the vain hope of containing the dissenters.[56]

---

[56] Ten Zythoff, *Sources of Secession,* 48-49, for English translations of Articles 291, 192, 294; J. Weitkamp, "De vervolgingen," 246, 255-57, 264; Lucas, *Netherlanders,* 42-53; Tris, *Sixty Years' Reminiscences,* 45.

Worship with no more than twenty persons, on pain of stiff fines, was hardly the freedom of religion guaranteed by the Constitution of 1815 (Articles 190, 191, and 193), which specifically granted that "complete freedom of religious beliefs," unhindered public worship, and "equal protection to all religious groups *existing currently* in the Kingdom." The key italicized phrase left interpretation to the discretion of judges, but neither article set aside the criminal code. In addition, Separatist services must not have the "signs, the form, and the appearance" of regular worship, that is, no sacraments, no ministerial titles, no customary clerical garb, and certainly no claim to be successors of the Gereformeerde Kerk existing in 1816. Van Raalte, when he entered in the civil registry the births of his two eldest children in the late 1830s, was described as "without occupation," since the government viewed his ordination as illegitimate until the king granted the Ommen congregation recognition in 1841 (ch. 5).[57]

Many in the Dutch upper class and Hervormde clerics either agreed with the crown or kept silent, deeming it too risky to resist. Further, the *kleine luyden* (little people) must be kept in their place. That the educated class demeaned the common people cannot be exaggerated. In humorous essays and poetry, the lives of coarse and ignorant folks amused a reading public. Ironically, when the same lower classes unleashed their fury against Seceders in acts of public violence, officials offered little restraint and even gave quiet approval.

Rejected for ordination

A year after Van Raalte passed his exams, spring 1835, he stood before the Provincial Synod of Zuid-Holland, the body to which the Renswoude church belonged. But the synod said no, even though Van Raalte had fully met the requirements: he held a faculty recommendation as a "proponent" for the ministry and a university certificate and had the recommendation of his Leiden consistory. The consistory's letter declared "our brother" to be "without blemish in beliefs and lifestyle" and worthy of being helped "on his Christian journey."[58] After months of preparation, he was ready for the candidates' rigorous oral exam,

---

[57] Paasman, "Bestuurlijke en economische aspecten," 25, 32; Bos, *Souvereiniteit en Religie*, 101-5, 133-45; Oostendorp, *Scholte*, 64-65, 88-89; Bos, *Servants of the Kingdom*, 11-14. Many such writers wrote essays in *De Nederlanden*, 1842, which led a reviewer to observe with horror that these lower-class folk represented more than half the Dutch population.

[58] Rev. Nanning Berkhout, Hervormde Kerk, Leiden, to Provincial Synod, 17 Jan. 1835, trans. Simone Kennedy, HHA.

convinced that all he needed was "a clear head, a humble disposition, and a warm heart," but he was in for a rude awakening. Put simply, "he knocked on the door at the wrong time."[59]

In May 1835 Albertus presented himself, along with a second student, H. G. van Nouhuijs, before an eight-member committee at The Hague for examination and admission to candidacy. After rigorous exams of "four full hours," the committee passed Van Nouhuijs with six votes and granted him a license to preach. Van Raalte expected the same outcome. But the committee raised a new requirement, adopted only six months previously for prospective pastors, namely, that theology students must attest to their agreement with all synodical regulations. "Do you know the regulations of the church, and do you agree with them?" the examiners asked the candidate. "I do not know those regulations," the candidate answered honestly, "but I will have to sign the form of subscription of our church, and I have no qualms about that. "Then sir," came the retort, "go and learn the regulations." "But sir, what is this?" Van Raalte asked somewhat saucily. "This was never asked of anyone and no one knows them.... Why is it that this is asked of no one else?" The examiners responded that no candidate had ever confessed to such ignorance.[60]

Van Raalte then played his trump card. He quoted a statement of one of the examiners, Johannes A. Pluiger of Leiden, who had stated that General Synod allowed office bearers to sign the form of subscription *insofar as* (*quatanus*), instead of *because* (*quia*) the Confessions agree with the Word of God. "In that case," the impudent candidate replied, "I cannot and will not utter these vows and do not desire to be a minister in your denomination." As he said later, "I was utterly dumbfounded that anyone had attached so much importance to me." The examiners backpedaled a bit by saying that Pluiger was speaking for himself, but the demand to study the regulations remained.[61]

After polite banter about procedures, one of the examiners finally admitted that the real issue was his membership in "those clubs" at Leiden that caused confusion in the church. When pressed, according to the official report on the examination, Van Raalte "agreed to study the regulations when he has time and inclination." The committee

---

[59] Van Raalte to Johannes P. Oggel, 2 Aug. 1844, quoted in Te Velde, "Ministerial Education"; Dosker, *Van Raalte*, 9 (quote).

[60] Minutes, Provincial Synod of Zuid-Holland, 1835, cited in Ten Zythoff, *Sources of Secession*, 131-32.

[61] The rationalist Pluiger was a colleague of the orthodox Lucas Egeling, both Leiden pastors. Pluiger undoubtedly knew who had been involved with the Scholte club.

accepted this conditional response, and gave him a rather unusual three-month extension to read the regulations and then stand before the provincial ecclesiastical board again.[62] He went to Brummelkamp at Hattem who had purchased "four to five volumes" of the regulations, realizing that ecclesiastical officials insisted on their importance. He had encouraged Albertus to acquaint himself with them over the winter before the exam, but the advice was ignored.[63]

Van Raalte's low view of the general regulations was strongly influenced by reading Abraham Capadose's book, *Ernstig en biddend Woord aan de getrouwe Leeraren in de Hervormde Kerk in Nederland* (Earnest and prayerful word to the faithful ministers of the Hervormde Kerk in the Netherlands) (1835), which called the church polity "undemocratic." Only reluctantly did Van Raalte read the regulations—four or five octavo volumes—in Brummelkamp's study at Hattem. "Church officials derived their authority from them," said Brummelkamp, "so I was resolved not to neglect them." And neither should you, Albertus, he might have added. Years later, Albertus admitted that as a teenager he "was not in the least attracted to that large stack of church laws that I saw in my father's study. I remained totally unenlightened of these church laws and government." This view of the laws as "dead notions" may well have echoed his father. After reading the regulations, Albertus recalled laconically many decades later, "I got to know more than I desired." It convinced him that the Hervormde Kerk was not only illiberal in its foundation, organization, and management, but also anti-Reformed in principle, direction, and practice.[64]

Dirk Molenaar, a pastor in The Hague, for example, had in 1827 published a booklet, *Adres aan al mijn Hervormde Geloofsgenooten* (Address to all my Reformed fellow believers), in which he charged that the new form "could be signed by a Christian of any persuasion, by a Roman Catholic, and even by a Jew." Molenaar called for a general synod to consider such matters in a "calm and Christian" manner

---

[62] Van Raalte's account is in *Kompleete uitgave* (1863), 315-21, and *Naschrift*, 321-38. See also, Official transcript, *Acts of the Provincial Church Council of Zuid-Holland*, 6 May 1835, 1st. sess., in Nationaal Archief, Rijksarchief, Zuid-Holland, trans. Nella Kennedy; Reenders, "Van Raalte als leider," 103-4, trans. Dekker; Vree, "Dominating Theology," 40-43.

[63] Brummelkamp, "Van Raalte," 96-97.

[64] Van Raalte to Van Velzen Jr., Apr. 1862, trans. Nella Kennedy; Van Raalte, "Naschrift," in *Kompleete uitgave* (1863), 323-38; Wormser, *In twee werelddeelen*, 33 (quote). Brummelkamp had bought the four or five columns for ƒ20, knowing that ecclesiastical bodies were strict about following its regulations (Brummelkamp, "Van Raalte," 96-97, trans. Ten Hoor).

Dirk Molenaar (1786-1865), pastor in Leiden Hervormde Kerk (*Heideman*, Scholte)

and to allow any who might disagree "to proceed in simplicity and great calm mutually to divide the church and its properties." Reaction against this call for separation was very strong. The king believed that Molenaar had attacked "his" regulations and committed treason for implicitly undermining national unity. Besieged, Molenaar apologized, but never recanted.[65]

Professor Clarisse invited his rejected student to his home and gave him a letter of appeal to Hendrik H. Donker Curtius (1778-1839), president of General Synod. Van Raalte traveled sixty-eight miles to Arnhem to meet the distinguished divine, who almost word for word repeated the provincial synod's fear that Van Raalte would, once admitted to the ministry, bring uproar (*rep en roer*) in the church. The audacious candidate then asserted his assent to the doctrine of election, Christ's atonement for sin, and the "avenging justice of God." "His Reverence protested vehemently" and revealed his true spirit. "Preach as you want, but allow us to preach what we want, but obey the regulations." Van Raalte never forgot this cold rebuff. But the Donker Curtius did accept Clarisse's appeal and sent him back to the provincial board secretary, Hermanus H. Sluiters, with a directive to follow the regular procedure.[66]

---

[65] Ten Zythoff, *Sources of Secession*, 111-13 (his translation), quoting Molenaar, *Adres*, 10, 14.

[66] Van Raalte, in *Kompleete uitgave* (1863), 316-18 (quote), trans. Nella Kennedy; Verhagen, *De geschiedenis*, 235; Ten Zythoff, *Sources of Secession*, 133; Kamps, *1834*, 62 (Donker quote).

Hendrik H. Donker Curtius, president of General Synod (*Kamps*, 1834)

After this blunt consultation, Van Raalte, in May, wrote Wolter W. Smitt, a Separatist lay leader at Zwolle, detailing his mistreatment by church leaders. He also sought the advice of members of The Hague Réveil circle. Van Raalte seemingly would follow Scholte and the club members and secede from the Reformed Church. Smitt, a week after receiving Van Raalte's letter, published a brochure containing the letter, with or without permission is not clear, and he added objections to church governance that the late Baron van Zuylen van Nijevelt had recounted in a book.[67]

Van Raalte returned to the provincial ecclesiastical body in August. When asked to speak, he declared boldly that he had examined the regulations but could not sign without reservations because he had discovered several objectionable rules. Echoing the specifics in his letter to Smitt, he named a rule that barred pastors over thirty years of age from instructing catechumens and another that opened the Lord's Table to Remonstrants, whom the Synod of Dort anathematized for teaching free will, conditional election, universal atonement, and resistible grace. This, Van Raalte declared, "refuted

---

[67] Vree, "Dominating Theology," 42; Smitt, *Nederlandsch Hervormd Kerkbestuur*, 9-12. The letter was the source, almost word for word, of Van Raalte's 1862 recollections. The letter quoted (a small portion of the main body, an imagined dialogue) was written after his first meeting. The booklet was published before Van Raalte appeared before the South Holland synod in the summer of 1835. Van Raalte most likely took the booklet with him to the United States.

what our Forefathers had accomplished . . . and is completely against my principles." At this, he was cut short. "Enough, sir. Then you cannot be admitted." The reverend gentlemen were "satisfied" that the pesky candidate had hanged himself.[68]

The laconic minutes of the interview provide the board's gloss: "Van Raalte declared . . . that he had found regulations and ordinances that could not be brought into harmony with his view and convictions; also, that the entire spirit of the ecclesiastical policy did not at all agree with the Doctrine of the Synod of Dordrecht and that he therefore would not be able to sign the said Statement and promise with a clear conscience."[69] The examiners stopped the candidate and would not allow for a further exchange when he tried to argue his case theologically. "We have enough zealots; we do not desire any more," said Rev. Van Slochteren, president of the board.[70] Clearly, Van Raalte had the misfortune to graduate last among the Scholte club members, and the board was determined to make an example of him.

In retrospect, it was not unreasonable or unexpected that candidates be acquainted with the "regulations of the church," the "Algemeen Reglement" of 1816. Disloyalty to the church threatened unity and could therefore be "treasonous." In the early years of King Willem I's reign, citizens were tired of unrest and economic decline and accepted church rule by a few administrators—albeit of a predominantly unorthodox stripe. Several church assemblies and pastors objected to being stripped of their rightful authority and bemoaned the doctrinal drift due to the weakened 1816 subscription form. It was also not unusual for candidates to be found wanting and ordered to be re-examined pending further study. Two other candidates met the same fate. So the board was technically correct when they averred that they had not singled him out.

It is remarkable that Van Raalte's recollections in an 1862 letter to nephew Simon van Velzen Jr. are more bitter and biting than in an account in 1835. He was more explicit about the vicious treatment he

---

[68] Van Raalte, *Kompleete uitgave* (1863), 319 (quote), 527-28, 536, trans. Nella Kennedy; Verhagen, *De geschiedenis*, 237; Ten Zythoff, *Sources of Secession*, 134; Brummelkamp, "Van Raalte," 96-97; Wormser, *In twee werelddeelen*, 33-34. Vree, "Dominating Theology," 41, quotes Van Raalte's words and notes that article 17 of the regulations granted national canonic recognition of religious teachers (46n).

[69] Ten Zythoff, *Sources of Secession*, 134, quoting (his translation) Minutes, Provincial Synod of Zuid-Holland, 1835, 24.

[70] Quote in *De Bazuin*, 15 June 1854 (www.delpher.nl, accessed, June 2021), trans. Nella Kennedy.

received from Donker Curtius and Sluiters, and labeled such men as "haughty and out for fame." He recalled tyranny in church and state and being branded a monster and moral leper.[71]

In summary, it would be difficult to believe that Van Raalte was not fully aware of the dissension in the Hervormde Kerk in the 1820s and early 1830s. He certainly knew the long-running controversies over polity and doctrine. He should have guarded his tongue. The most plausible explanation for his ostrich-like behavior amid the religious controversies was his fervent wish and single focus to preach the Gospel, as a Moses among sheep. He well knew that his brothers-in-law, who had become parish ministers, faced opposition in their congregations and from ecclesiastical authorities, which soon led to dismissal. The church, according to Guillaume Groen van Prinsterer's analysis, had become "administered," with the Reformed church a kind of ecclesiastical department of state, with pastors as virtual clerks and church members as subjects. The king ruled almost like a regent or chief of the church. The church had now become a vehicle to preserve national unity.[72]

In August 1835, Van Raalte and Brummelkamp traveled to consult with Van Velzen in Drogeham and De Cock in Ulrum; it was their first face-to-face meeting. The four stiffened Van Raalte's backbone, and in October, Van Raalte boldly asked the board to rescind his exclusion from the preaching office. "I have a legitimate claim to it," he declared, since "I am wholeheartedly committed to the doctrines of our Church—as based on the Word of God—and am able and willing unequivocally to sign the *normal* promise to adhere to these, and through it also to be subject to a Reformed administration and its regulations. Therefore, there is no good reason to refuse me the ministry any longer." By "normal," Gerrit ten Zythoff explained, Van Raalte meant the historic form of subscription based on the 1619 Dort church order not the gutted version adopted by the 1816 Synod referenced by Pluiger. The candidate added a second qualifier, that the doctrines must be based on the Word of God.[73]

---

[71] Van Raalte, *Kompleete uitgave* (1884), 532-33.
[72] Van der Zwaag, *Réveil en afscheiding*, 94; Barnhoorn, *Amicitia Christiana*, 21.
[73] While the sisters shared a warm reunion, the men met privately to discuss the rising secession movement and the matter of hymns. Brummelkamp gave a public lecture advocating their use in worship, and all the in-laws concurred, provided that the congregation desired it; otherwise, they refrained. The men and their wives all grew up with hymns in their parental homes and cherished them (Wormser, *Karakter en Genade*, 20; Dosker, *Van Raalte*, 109).

Expecting a rejection, Van Raalte added a final request: "If you are not willing to listen to my plea, I ask you to send me a certificate in which you declare that it is not incompetence, or sentiments, or moral misconduct that is the cause of your refusal." Less than two weeks later, on October 15, Synod replied that it found no reason to modify its decision. But they did provide a personal endorsement by reiterating the board statement at its May meeting that the candidate was not excluded on the "basis of incompetence nor because of religious convictions manifested by him in his examination."[74]

"I followed the voice of conscience"

In a defiant letter to provincial officials, Van Raalte in a Luther-like moment, took his stand and resigned from the "Hervormde denomination" and its "conscience-binding laws, which are not based on God's Word." He declared: "The voice of my conscience and the infallible sayings of the Holy Scriptures compelled me some time ago to break all ecclesiastical union with you, and to join those who by word and deed prove their desire to live according to God's ordinances, the opposite of which is taking place in the Reformed Denomination." Van Raalte later admitted that following the voice of conscience "cost me very much."[75] It closed entry into the church of his youth and heritage. Notably, he did not publish a vehement attack on the church, as De Cock, Scholte, and Van Velzen had done. But renouncing the church of his birth as renegade softened the blow of being denied ordination by that church.

Until this rejection, Van Raalte's heart was clearly in the mother church. The last thing he wanted or intended was to secede and sadden his parents. He and his brothers-in-law all hoped to remain silently in the church. The 1834 Separatists never quite fit his heart and mind. Thirty-seven years later, in 1862, in a lengthy letter from Michigan to his nephew Simon van Velzen Jr., Van Raalte stated that he did all

---

[74] Ten Zythoff, *Sources of Secession*, 134; Engelsma, *Watchman on the Walls*, 77; Van Raalte, Drogeham, to Zuid-Holland Board, 3 Oct. 1835, trans. Nella Kennedy; J. Sluiter, secretary, to Van Raalte, 15 Oct. 1835, Nationaal Archief, Rijksarchief, Zuid-Holland, in *Kompleete uitgave* (1863), 329-32.

[75] Van Raalte to Zuid-Holland Board, Dec. 1835, in *Kompleete uitgave* (1884), 529 (trans. Ten Zythoff, *Sources of Secession*, 135); Vree, "Dominating Theology," 42 (quote), p. 47 for the citation in Zuid-Holland synod records. Vree notes that Van Raalte mistakenly gave the date Dec. 1835. Van Velzen had a similar Luther moment when he wrote about seceding: "With my hand on my heart, I may not, I cannot do otherwise" (Engelsma, *Watchman on the Walls*, 86, citing Van Velzen, *Stem eens wachters op Zions muren*, 2:253).

he could to avoid an open break. "To give up the preaching" he "so fervently desired" was the "most painful sacrifice" of his life. "I was loath to see that I could no longer enter the pulpit of my father and that I had become a disgrace to my mother, who was still living, and to my generation." The only redeeming aspect was that his father had passed away two years earlier and did not have to bear this heartbreak.[76]

Hommo Reenders, who carefully studied Van Raalte's career, was correct when he concluded that Van Raalte "would never have left" his mother church "if the Provincial Synod had not pressed him to do so." For his part, Van Raalte admitted decades later, "I was young and timid and let myself be cowed." For synod's snub, Gerrit ten Zythoff concluded: "The Netherlands Reformed Church lost a loyal, capable son."[77]

Van Raalte pressed the provincial synod to accept him, but largely on his terms. Neither would yield and reconciliation became impossible. Jasper Vree placed the denouement in the larger context: "The Dutch years of Van Raalte, Clarisse's student, reflected the complexity of the relation between the dominating theology within the Netherlands Reformed Church and the Secession of 1834."[78]

Van Raalte's sympathies for the public church were evident in a remarkable step he and brother-in-law Carel de Moen took in 1842 to send to General Synod an *Adres* on behalf of their respective congregations in Ommen and Den Ham. The pair appealed for "a true linking of all upright Reformed people, Separated as well as non-Separated Christians, . . . in a reformation 'based on God's Word.' Seeing the "finger of the Almighty" in the 1834 Separation, the appeal called for "a closer bonding of their hearts and the restoration of the Christian Calvinist Church." Most remarkably, it stated: "We still feel connected to those in the Church who forever love Christ."[79]

---

[76] Van Raalte to Van Velzen Jr., Apr. 1862, *Kompleete uitgave* (1863), 323-38 (quote 325), trans. Nella Kennedy.

[77] Van Raalte, undated personal history of pre-Secession of 1834, trans. Nella Kennedy, HHA; Reenders, "Van Raalte," 279; Ten Zythoff, *Sources of Secession*, 135 (quote); Dosker, *Van Raalte*, 9-10. Van Raalte's ordination exempted him from military service (governor of Noord-Brabant to Van Raalte, 20 Nov. 1835, trans. Nella Kennedy).

[78] Vree, "Dominating Theology," 43.

[79] Van Raalte and De Moen to General Synod, 24 June 1842, handwritten cover letter, enclosing a nineteen-page booklet, *Adres aan de Algemene Synode*, Ommen, 1842, trans. Simone Kennedy; advertisement in *Opregte Haarlemsche Courant*, 14 July 1842; Vree, "Dominating Theology," 42-43; Te Velde, "Dutch Background," 87. Despite its call for unity, the *Adres* castigated the Reformed Church for "lukewarmness and

The reference here is to theologically orthodox Réveil leaders—Groen van Prinsterer, D. van Hogendorp, Capadose, Carel van der Kemp, and others. These men had also sent their own address to General Synod, which urged that body to embrace the new Reformation and resist "both Rome's Papal church dominion and unbelief within the Netherlands." These efforts to undo the secession in hopes of reforming the church came to naught; its dominating theology was entrenched. But Van Raalte's *Adres* shows that, at a time when, and perhaps because, the Separated churches were barely holding together, he and certainly Brummelkamp still hoped for reformation under the umbrella of the Hervormde Kerk.

Given his centrist church polity and abhorrence of schism, the question arises: Why was Van Raalte's ordination problematic? Why would he not accept, pro forma, the church regulations, without singling out a few relatively insignificant ones as unacceptable? Was he influenced by Capadose's book, or by the experiences of Brummelkamp and Van Velzen, who were expelled after entering pulpits in the Hervormde Kerk? Did his synodical rejection and subsequent persecution cut so deeply that it embittered him to his mother church and raised his hackles to the point that he found reasons to justify spurning that church as renegade? The answer to all these questions is affirmative. Once he joined the Separatists, Van Raalte remained loyal to them, even though he differed in outlook and spirit. He never reconciled with the Hervormde Kerk, but in America, he joined the American daughter of that church, the Dutch Reformed Church in New York, which had been under the Classis of Amsterdam until 1793.

Contrasts with ministerial colleagues

Albertus Christiaan Van Raalte differed from his colleagues in important ways. He was the only son of a cleric in the Hervormde Kerk, and his ties to that body were tight. Among theology students in the Scholte club, he was the only one denied admittance into the public church. On the plus side, he was the only one not expelled or forced to resign from a Hervormde pastorate in which he had been ordained. Throughout his career, he committed himself to the unity of the Christian church; he loathed church secessions and schisms, and on

---

indifference, conformation with the world, faithlessness and sin, . . . the vanity, the ostentatiousness, the wasteful extravagance and sinful practices," namely Sabbath desecration and impure living, besides unfaithful administration of the sacraments and lack of church discipline.

several occasions, he expressed doubts about the Secession of 1834. He preferred to speak of the Free Church—that is, free of the state—rather than the Separated Church. Two decades later, in Michigan, he fiercely opposed yet another secession among his followers, and he also never completely disentangled himself from the church of his youth.[80]

Scholte, Brummelkamp, Van Velzen, and Van Raalte expected to minister in the church of their birth and the first three did so. Van Raalte would also have served wholeheartedly in the church, especially like his father in traditional, rural congregations. He could compromise to get along; schism was not in his heart and soul. And even though rejection for ordination and persecution as a Separatist pastor had hardened his heart toward the public church, he did maintain a soft spot for it the rest of his life.

---

[80] Brummelkamp, "Van Raalte," 99-100; Wormser, *In twee werelddeelen*, 20; Reenders, "Van Raalte," 279; Wormser, *Karakter en Genade*, 24-25; Rullmann, *Een nagel in de heilige plaats*, 91-95.

CHAPTER 3

Apostle of Overijssel: "A partridge hunted in the mountains."

Official persecution was the lot of all the itinerant preachers. Van Raalte worked in Overijssel; De Cock in Groningen; Scholte in Utrecht, Noord-, and Zuid-Holland; Van Velzen in Friesland; Brummelkamp in Gelderland; Gezelle Meerburg in Noord-Brabant; and Budding, the only bachelor among the clerics, in Zeeland. Overijssel was an agrarian province, with farms on the sandy soils improving from crop rotation and better fertilization, which allowed for smaller plots and large-scale cultivation of potatoes. By 1830 Overijssel led the country in farm ownership and average population growth. A progressive governor stimulated road and bridge construction and opened and upgraded rural schools.[1]

Called to Genemuiden-Mastenbroek

Pending ordination, Van Raalte conducted worship in a half dozen of Van Velzen's Frisian churches before boarding temporarily with the Brummelkamps in Hattem, Gelderland, a city near Zwolle. There, he began leading worship in area houses, barns, and stables, in

[1] Swierenga, *Faith and Family*, 103-4.

good weather and bad, even at night. He started tentatively but gained boldness with experience. "My first sermon," he recalled, "was neither foreskin nor circumcision but only 'faith at work through love.' My second sermon was 'prayer without ceasing.' This was not surprising. I had nothing else to say . . . that gave peace and joy to my agitated and despair-tortured heart."[2]

In January 1836, the ardent preacher accepted a call from the combined Genemuiden and Mastenbroek congregations in Overijssel. The two villages stood only three miles apart. Genemuiden was the first Separated church in the province, founded in 1835 by De Cock himself. Twenty-seven families, mainly craftsmen and shopkeepers, left the large Hervormde Kerk in town because of its use of hymns. The Van der Haar family was one of those families. Teenage daughter Geesje recalled the excitement of De Cock's coming to Genemuiden.

> He preached at grandmother's home four times, and everyone enjoyed him. His sermons were so powerful, and he presented the truths of the Gospel so attractively. We had not heard anything like that for a long time. Oh, how comforting for my soul! My oldest brother was also converted through his preaching, and together we joined many others of God's people in seceding from the "State Church." My father, my uncles and my grandmother also seceded, and De Cock formed a congregation in our village as he had in many others.[3]

Brummelkamp established the Mastenbroek congregation in March 1836, bringing the number of churches in Overijssel to eleven. Mastenbroek was larger at two hundred members, and Genemuiden had about 150 members. Combining the two bodies made it feasible to call the twenty-five-year-old Van Raalte. For a parsonage, the members bought and remodeled a small house on the Hoofdstraat in Genemuiden.[4] This picturesque town in the northwestern part of Overijssel was located on the Zwartemeer, a polder protected by dykes from the nearby Zuiderzee. With the best grazing lands in the province, its seventeen hundred residents (in 1842) engaged mainly

---

[2] Dosker, *Van Raalte*, 19; Van Raalte, in *Kompleete uitgave* (1863), 334-35, quotes, trans. Nella Kennedy.
[3] "Geesje Van der Haar-Visscher Diary," 3.
[4] Reenders, "Van Raalte als leider," 106-10; Warner, *Door het venster*, 106-7; Wesseling, *Afscheiding van 1834, Classis Zwolle*, 65-70. Hattem is listed as Van Raalte's place of residence in his marriage banns and marriage certificate. The Hoofdstraat address of 1836 is today Langestraat 10.

in general farming and dairying. Mastenbroek was more prosperous than Genemuiden. Both towns had suffered a disastrous flood in 1825 that left eighty families without homes and livestock. But they were thriving again during Van Raalte's pastorate in the 1830s.[5]

Before Van Raalte's coming, Separatists worshiped either in conventicles, under lay preachers (*oefenaars*), at the Albert Roetman farm, midway between Genemuiden and IJsselmuiden, or at Jacob de Jong's house, just outside of Hasselt. The lay preachers deeply resented being sidelined by the fresh, ordained, university graduate, "a worker of the eleventh hour" or, in the American vernacular, a "Johnny come lately." Worse, they knew of Van Raalte's stated disapproval of lay preaching. He might have been more understanding if he had worshiped in conventicles and mastered the Old Writers in his father's library.[6]

Since the Later Reformation of the eighteenth century, lay preachers led house churches, known as conventicles, where experiential worship fed spiritually thirsty believers who maintained formal membership in the public church for marriages and burials, and some of whom continued to attend the public (Hervormde) church in addition to their house meetings. Such pious folks sought relief from the "dead orthodoxy" of university-trained ministers, whose highbrow sermons appealed to the head but left the heart cold. They turned in increasing numbers to prayer meetings and Bible studies taught by untutored laymen of widely varying ability.[7]

Ordained

On March 2, 1836, Van Raalte was examined for ordination at the first synod of the Christian Separated Church (Christelijke Afgescheiden Kerk), held on the upper floor of an Amsterdam sugar refinery on the Jordaan, with the gable inscription "De Drie Fonteynen" (house of three fountains), with Scholte in the chair. The building belonged to Scholte's brother-in-law Jan Daniël Brandt, a sugar refiner. It was an emotional gathering in the midst of severe persecution. Secrecy was necessary to avoid police detection.

The brothers kneeled when Scholte opened with prayer, and then they each affirmed the Dort form of subscription, meaning they

---

[5] Reenders, "Van Raalte als leider," 107-9; Wesseling, *Afscheiding van 1834, Classis Zwolle*, 64-65.
[6] Reenders, "Van Raalte," 279-80, 282; Warner, *Door het venster*, 106.
[7] Ten Zythoff, *Sources of Secession*, 45-48; Kamps, *1834*, 31; Van Hinte, *Netherlanders*, 88-89.

attested that the Three Forms of Unity were wholly biblical, and they promised to defend them against apostasy and submit to the authority of the church if they should dissent.

The first question facing the small assembly of five ministers—Scholte, De Cock, Brummelkamp, Van Velzen, and Gezelle Meerburg—and eleven elders was whether to examine candidate Van Raalte or simply admit him. The issue came up because two of the five clerics—Brummelkamp and Van Velzen—were his brothers-in-law, and others were Leiden classmates, except for De Cock, who was outside the circle. How could the examination be objective? The full body, including the elders, decided to vote on going forward, and the result was a tie. Half believed that Van Raalte was well known and had proven his loyalty to the "true Gereformeerde Kerk." The other half were sticklers for church polity, who held that he must be examined, "since he had not yet held the official position of minister and Synod must be able to justify their permission if asked to do so by the Church at any time in the future." Given the tie vote, the brothers decided to cast lots and "God showed us... that a further examination would take place." So he would be put through his paces, brother or not.[8]

Scholte handled the examination and focused on the "most important points" (Latin *loci*) of Reformed doctrine, on church discipline, and on worship, but he passed over other subjects because of Van Raalte's Leiden diploma. "After discussing the answers with the other brothers present, the examination was deemed a success by all, and this brother was accepted to be minister of the Church." Thus, Scholte alone examined Van Raalte; his in-laws and friends refrained, to avoid an appearance of impropriety. No wonder Brummelkamp went out of his way to justify the action. "From the very first moment," he declared, "it had to be firm that among each other [the synodical delegates] we could proceed in this matter in the Gereformeerde way and avoid any imputation of rashness."[9] The brothers believed that their young denomination stood upon the Gereformeerde foundation of Dort and was thus, "the true church," whereas the Hervormde Kerk, under its new administration, had failed in this respect. This logic allowed the rump assembly to regard Van Raalte's ordination as standing within the formal line of apostolic succession in the Christian church.

---

[8] Acts of Separated Church Synod, Amsterdam (*Handelingen van de Opzieners*), 2 Mar. 1836, 1st session, 8-9, trans. Simone Kennedy; Wormser, *In twee werelddeelen*, 44-50; Warner, *Door het venster*, 105; Makkinga, "Bricks for Ommen Poor."

[9] Acts of Separated Church Synod, 2 Mar. 1836, 2nd sess. Art. 12-14, 3rd sess. Art. 19, trans. Simone Kennedy.

"De Drie Fonteynen," meeting place of first synod of the Christian Separated Church, 1836 (*courtesy Gerko Warner*)

Following approval, Van Raalte signed the Dort form of subscription, took the oath against simony (selling ecclesiastical privileges), and was ordained by the laying on of hands by Simon van Velzen. Finally, he signed the pledge of allegiance to "his Majesty, our respected King," which the other delegates had signed at the opening session. The pledge included an appeal for religious freedom. Van Raalte could then accept the call from the combined Genemuiden and Mastenbroek churches for ministry in their midst and throughout the province.[10] From this point, he was a minister who, in Dutch parlance, was referred to as "Dominee" (Latin, "Dominus"), or in writing, "Ds.," seldom as "Rev.," the English title.[11] After he received his honorary doctorate(s), Van Raalte was usually called "Dr." in both Dutch and English. In time, however, the newly ordained dominee would acquire another title: "the apostle of Overijssel."

---

[10] Dosker, *Van Raalte*, 22-23; Heideman, *Scholte*, 50-65, 103-5. Acts of Synod Amsterdam 1836 are in *Handelingen en verslagen*, 13-71, portions trans. Simone Kennedy. Scholte's 1837 church order, "Regulations of the Congregation of Utrecht," was published in book form by Amsterdam publisher Henricus Höveker and serially in *De Reformatie*, 1837-40 (Heideman, *Scholte*, 105n7).

[11] Scholte and De Cock statement affirming Van Raalte's examination and ordination, 4 Mar. 1836, HHA; Te Velde, *Brummelkamp*, 80-81.

Marriage to Christina de Moen

A week after Van Raalte's ordination in the Amsterdam Separated Church at Bloemgracht No. 42, the assembly returned to the church on the evening of March 11, 1836, to solemnize the Christian marriage of Albertus Christiaan Van Raalte, age twenty-four, and Christina (Chris) Johanna de Moen, age twenty-one (born January 30, 1815), the middle De Moen sister.[12] The couple's civil ceremony had taken place that morning in the Leiden town hall under Paulus G. van Hoorn, civil registrar and city alderman. Albertus's widowed mother, Catrina Harking Van Raalte, had given her permission a week prior, and Christina's parents were deceased. Witnesses were Christina's half-brother, Johannes Benjamin de Moen, a commission agent in Leiden; her uncle, Carel Godfried Menzel, a Leiden bookseller; Israel Montagne, a Leiden solicitor and De Moen family acquaintance; and her cousin, Willem Fredrik Menzel, a theology student at Leiden University who later served Hervormde congregations for twenty years. As dictated by a notary in proper legalese, the bridegroom bequeathed to his wife "everything that the existing laws will permit at my death, both in property and well as usufruct [right of use], whichever is most advantageous and appoint her my heir or legatee."[13]

We have the colorful, and possibly apocryphal, story of the bashful Albertus, after seeing three attractive young women come to church, being drawn to the one in a purple velvet cloak. Learning that the three were the De Moen sisters, he determined to call at their home, much to the astonishment of his university friends since he never met them, and he did not even know the name of the woman of interest. He rang the bell and when the maid asked his business, he replied that he wished to see the lady who wore the purple velvet cloak. Christina agreed to see him, and the rest, as they say, is history.[14]

His classmate Gezelle Meerburg, a friend of Carel de Moen, played matchmaker; he had previously linked Van Velzen and Brummelkamp to Christina's sisters. Their parents had died, leaving the three sisters and two brothers to live together on the east side of the

---

[12] Reports of the Zuid-Holland Hervormde Classis, Mar, 1836, in Smits, *Afscheiding van 1834*, 7: 27, 29-30, trans. Nella Kennedy. For a copy of the marriage certificate and its translation, see *Origins* 19, no. 2 (2001), 25, trans. Gerrit Sheeres.

[13] Permission letter, Christina Harking van Raalte, 7 Mar. 1836; Last Will and Testament of A. C. Van Raalte, 14 Mar. 1836, trans. Gerrit Sheeres (HHA); Bruins et al., *Albertus and Christina*, 205-9.

[14] Brummelkamp Jr., *Brummelkamp*, 32; Pieters, *Dutch Settlement*, 160-61, source was "a member of the family."

𝔅urgerlijke Stand.   Provincie Zuid Holland.
Stad Leyden.   **District Leyden.**

EXTRACT.

Uit het *Trouw* Register der *Stad Leyden*
des Jaars 1836 is geëxtraheerd,

dat op den elfden Maart achttienhonderdzesendertig zyn getrouwd *Albertus Christiaan van Raalte*, jongman, oud 24 Jaren, Kandidaat in de Godgeleerdheid, geboren te Wanneperveen, wonende te Hattem — en *Christina Johanna de Moen*, jongd, oud 21 Jaren, zonder beroep, geboren te Leyden, wonende op de Heerengracht.

Ik ondergeteekende Wethouder der Stad LEYDEN, Ambtenaar van den Burgerlijken Stand, verklare dat het vorenstaande Extract is overeenkomstig met het bovengemeld Register.

Leyden, den 11 Maart 1836.

Marriage certificate, Albertus C. Van Raalte
and Christina Johanna de Moen, on
March 11, 1836, Leiden City Hall (*HHA*)

Hooigracht in Leiden. All had a fine education and could speak fluent French. In a double wedding two years earlier, between graduation and installation, on August 16, 1834, Brummelkamp had married Maria (Mietje) Wilhelmina, age twenty-six, a widow with two young children, and Van Velzen had married Johanna Maria Wilhelmina (Naatje), age seventeen. Brother Carel Godefroi de Moen had attended the Latin school and medical school and practiced medicine before becoming a Separatist minister in 1842.[15]

Chris Van Raalte occasionally visited her sister, Mietje Brummelkamp, at Hattem, fourteen miles distant, where Anthony based his itinerant ministry in Gelderland, after being dismissed as pastor of the Hattem Hervormde Kerk. When she was engaged to be married, Chris had earlier visited her younger sister, Johanna van Velzen, in the parsonage in Drogeham, Friesland, where her husband served the Separated Church. Chris likely took the long journey of 115 miles to help in the coming birth of Simon Jr. Barely two years later, Chris returned to Drogeham in May 1837 for a sadder occasion, to be with Johanna in her final weeks of life due to end-stage tuberculosis. She was only twenty years old and had been married for three years already. Six months later, in October 1837, Chris with her own baby accompanied Albertus to meetings in Amsterdam, where Van Velzen had taken a call. The Van Raaltes could then re-connect with Simon and his new wife, Johanna Alida van Voss, a sister-in-law of Carel De Moen, brother of Johanna and Christina.[16]

Christina's upbringing

Christina Johanna, born at Leiden, in 1815, was the second surviving daughter of Benjamin de Moen (1751-1824), age sixty-four years, and his third wife, Johanna Maria Wilhelmina Menzel (1780-1831), daughter of Christiaan Fredrich (Gottlieb) Menzel (1744-1794), a Lutheran from Silesia (Prussia then, Poland now), and Helena Lindermann (1751-1809) of Germany. Benjamin's first wife, Elizabeth Haak, bore no children, and his second, Sebilla Wilhelmina Lindeman, gave birth to five, of which only one, Johannes Benjamin, lived a full life. Benjamin de Moen married Johanna Maria Menzel in Leiden in 1804, and they had nine children together. Three died in infancy. Two

---

[15] Agatha S. van Voss de Moen to husband Carel de Moen, 22 Dec. 1836, trans. Nella Kennedy, ADC; National Militia Certificate, 21 July 1830; Brummelkamp to Van Raalte, 12 Jan. 1842, JAH; Te Velde, *Brummelkamp*, 48; Engelsma, *Watchman on the Walls*, 54, 97. The Zuid-Holland Provinciale Kommissie van Geneeskundig Onderzoek en Toevoorzicht, 3 July 1832, stated that he passed his examination (ADC).

[16] Van Raalte to Governor of Overijssel, 2 Feb. 1837, in Wesseling, *Afscheiding van 1834, Classis Zwolle*, 72; Van Raalte to Christina, 24, 28 Apr., 1 May, 2, 4 Oct., 28 Dec. 1837; Van Gelderen, *Simon van Velzen*, 29; Engelsma, *Watchman on the Walls*, 97, 127. Simon Jr. was born on 2 Nov. 1835.

daughters, Helena and Johanna, lived to be twenty-one and twenty, respectively, whereas only one son and two daughters lived to full maturity.[17] Helena was only two years older than Christina, and her death certainly hit her sister hard. Christina's mother died nine months later. So, as a child, she had her share of sorrows. In her marriage document, Christina Johanna listed the home of her stepbrother Johannes Benjamin on the Heerengracht as her Leiden address.[18] Later, he functioned as a witness at her wedding.[19]

> **Surviving Children of Benjamin de Moen (1751-1824) and Johanna Maria Wilhelmina Menzel (1804-1831)**
> Maria Wilhelmina.. 1808-1873
>   Wife of Anthony Brummelkamp (her 2nd marriage)
> Carel Godefroi 1811-1879
>   Physician turned Separatist pastor
> Christina Johanna... 1815-1871
>   Wife of Albertus Van Raalte
> Johanna Maria Wilhelmina................................. 1817-1837
>   Wife of Simon van Velzen
> Source: Bruins et al., *Albertus and Christina*, 205-9.

Christina grew up in a family that climbed economically more than socially, whereas Albertus enjoyed social privilege but not economic security. The De Moen family lived a simple but comfortable life. Her parent's will, drafted in 1823, included a *speeltuin* (play area) with a small pavilion on the city outskirts.[20] Father Benjamin rose from the artisan class, as a *greinwerker*, a specialist weaver of Angora goat wool and mohair, to the upper middle class (*petite bourgeoisie*) as a real estate investor. New power looms rendered his skilled craft obsolete, and Napoleon's Dutch trade blockade undermined Leiden's prosperous economy. Of twenty-eight thousand inhabitants in 1816, a staggering 50 percent (14,000) lived on the public dole.[21]

---

[17] Helena de Moen was Christina Johanna's next oldest sister who lived to be twenty-one years old. She died on 13 Jan. 1831 when Christina was nineteen. Their mother died 17 Sept. 1831, both on the Hooigracht in Leiden.

[18] It is interesting that her brother, Carel Godefroi, lived in the parental house on the Hooigracht in the 1830s.

[19] Bruins et al., *Albertus and Christina*, 205; "Testament Johanna Maria de Moen," 30 Dec. 1825; Kennedy, "Twice Torn Asunder."

[20] Inventory, 57. Regional Archives Leiden.

[21] Blok, *Geschiedenis*, 93; Posthumus, *De Geschiedenis*, 2:235, 272-73, 3:1088; Van Maanen, *De Geschiedenis*, 47, 142, 144.

The clever Benjamin turned capital from his deceased wives' estates into real estate. He purchased eight houses in his lower-class Middelstegracht and later moved up to elegant seventeenth-century houses on the *grachten*, costing from two to three times as much. But his bread and butter was dozens of small, often decrepit, workers' cottages that served as almshouses for elderly folks, funded by the city and church deaconates. At this time, 40 percent of these Leiden houses were owned by professional landlords, derisively called *huisjesmelkers* (literally, milkers of houses). In modern parlance, De Moen was a slum landlord, albeit presumably an honest one. He actually lived in one of these as city-paid steward for the elderly tenants. The parents' will of 1823 include in the list of belongings cribs, benches, blankets and sheets, all for the almshouses. Between 1797 and 1823, De Moen handled hundreds of houses and other properties. At his death in 1824, his estate of ƒ20,000 ($250,000 today) passed to his wife Wilhelmina. When she died in 1831, the will bequeathed her modest gold and silver jewelry, designating specific pieces for each daughter. Inexplicably, Johanna (Naatje), the youngest, received more valuable jewelry than her sisters. She and Maria Wilhelmina sold their jewelry to pay fines of the husbands for preaching "illegally." Christina kept her mother's ring as a keepsake.[22]

The De Moen family faithfully worshiped in the prestigious Pieterskerk, led by the orthodox and dignified Rev. Lucas Egeling (1764-1835), who had baptized both Da Costa and Capadose. Egeling taught both human depravity and God's grace in his popular pamphlet, *De weg der zaligheid* (The way to salvation), and urged confessing members to lead lives worthy of their vows. But he disapproved of sharp formulations of doctrine, such as the Canons of Dort. The De Moen sisters attended Egeling's catechism classes, which likely nurtured their evangelical faith, and he married them both. Their pious parents did their part by reading the Bible at mealtimes. This upbringing prepared the De Moen sisters to be "in harmony with their spouses, . . . helpmeets ordained by

---

[22] The De Moen family history relies on Kennedy, "Twice Torn Asunder"; last will and testament of Benjamin and Johanna Maria de Moen, 5 Jan. 1823; Testaments of Benjamin de Moen and Wilhelmina Menzel de Moen, 15 Jan 1823, no 144, folio 9, *Notariële Akten*, 1811-42, Regional Archives Leiden; Marriage document, 11 Mar 1836, HHA; Brummelkamp Jr., *Brummelkamp*, 134; Smit, *Leiden Boek*, 238; Van Maanen, *De Geschiedenis*, 51-58; Christina's ring is in the A. C. Van Raalte Collection, HMA.

Lucas Egeling, pastor of Pieterskerk, Leiden, who instructed the three De Moen sisters (*Engelsma, Watchman on the Walls*)

God for the man of their choice."[23] The sisters were characterized as rather timid, but firm in adversity. After the Secession of 1834, the De Moen siblings placed biblical truth above social status and joined the Leiden Separated Church as charter members, along with thirty others from the "lower and lowest classes."[24]

Christina's marriage to an aspiring pastor initially meant exchanging her "life of refinement, comfort, and ease" in Leiden for the "restricted means of a poor village preacher of a persecuted sect" in far-off Overijssel. Marriage for Albertus was a high point second only to his ordination, but for Christina, wedlock meant a pinched existence and submission to her husband's will on major decisions—accepting calls, going on extended preaching tours, and ultimately emigrating to America.[25]

Separatist Preacher

Life in the parsonage proved to be even more difficult than his university examinations. Van Raalte as a "well-known separatist" was targeted by both authorities and rabble rousers as the "head of this

---

[23] Kagchelland, *Van Dompers*, 172, 264n48; Brummelkamp Jr., *Brummelkamp*, 33 (quote); Te Velde, *Brummelkamp*, 48; Harinck, "'O, may the Lord,'" 76. Egeling ended his ministerial career in the Pieterskerk. A devout and humble man, he wrote a number of books to aid both young and old to a deeper spiritual life. As a pastor he taught divinity students for years, which included members of the Scholte club.

[24] Brummelkamp Jr., *Brummelkamp*, 34. Pieters, *Dutch Settlement*, 166; Kennedy, "Twice Torn Asunder," 48-49.

[25] Kennedy, "Twice Torn Asunder," 43-44.

Separatist worship service. Hendrik Valkenburg, *Een stichtelijk uurtje in den achterhoek* (a worshipful hour in the achterhoek), 1883 (oil on canvas, Museum Catharijneconvent, Utrecht). Anthony Brummelkamp has often been named as the pastor in the painting.

fanatical crowd." Hommo Reenders noted that "there was not a riot or uprising against the Separatists that did not involve him." His very presence riled village thugs and drew trouble. The Genemuiden city secretary called him "impulsive, emotional, and arrogant, someone with way too little respect for the government." As Brummelkamp put it, "Barns and stalls were his sanctuary, but God caused his preaching to be effective, and very soon, he was hauled into court like a criminal." Brummelkamp well understood the injustice because, as the "apostle of Gelderland," he too had itinerated under persecution.[26]

When Van Raalte accepted the call to the Afgescheiden congregations in March 1836, the Hervormde church under Wilhelm Scheuer had been rife with controversy since 1805. He was an avowed supranaturalist; he banned an orthodox catechism book, and obliged the singing of Evangelische songs. Using "man-made" hymns led to violent protests. Faithful members were attracted to lay leaders (*oefenaars*) from Zwolle who preached at house meetings. Scheuer, who despised "religious fanatics," had Jacob Hendrik Graaf van Rechteren, the governor of Overijssel (1830-40), prohibit those men from coming to Mastenbroek. He gloated that he had crushed fanaticism in his church. But he could not blunt a persistent desire for more doctrinal preaching, which came to a head in 1834. "Fanatics" began joining the Afgescheiden church that Brummelkamp organized in December 1835 and Van Raalte came to serve.[27] Scheuer and his consistory, in order to prevent further "disasters," appealed to the mayor of Mastenbroek to ban Van Raalte. The mayor asked the governor for the most suitable means to stop the "illegal" worship services. Scheuer also complained

---

[26] Reenders, "Van Raalte als leider," 113, 118 (quotes), trans. Dekker; Brummelkamp, "Van Raalte," 99-104, for this and the next paragraph.

[27] Wesseling, *Afscheiding van 1834 in Overijssel*, 49-52, 100. The archives of the minutes of Hervormde church of Genemuiden in the early years of the Afscheiding were lost in a fire of 1868.

to classis that his "formerly flourishing" congregation was declining rapidly due to the "intrigues" of Van Raalte, and that collections for the poor had shrunk.[28]

First charge—Genemuiden-Mastenbroek

Although Governor Van Rechteren had little sympathy for Separatists, he was said to be more tolerant than small town mayors and provincial governors, but Separatists would hardly have noticed the difference.[29] The governor ordered mayors and constables to break up services, and judges to levy fines and imprison clerics and elders who broke the law, according to the Napoleonic Code. He garrisoned soldiers in Separatist towns to stamp out religious rebellion. Van Raalte was "slandered, imprisoned, and fined" by state authorities, which made his calling stressful and taxing in the extreme. His life had the "appearance of martyrdom." These bitter experiences increased his resentment against the church of his youth and strengthened his conviction that he had been right to break with it.[30]

The young dominee ran into trouble even before his marriage and ordination. He was a marked man from the outset. While living with the Brummelkamps in Hattem in January 1836, he preached in the Separated congregation at Genemuiden. The mayor informed Van Rechteren that the church had a consistory of "decent middle class" men but the twenty-seven family heads were "unwise fanatics" who objected to smallpox vaccinations and public education. To eradicate the cancerous growth, he urged an armed response.[31]

On Sunday, January 21, Van Raalte conducted the typical three services with far more than twenty persons present. Butcher Jannes van der Haar opened his home for morning and afternoon worship, and baker Hendrik van Rees hosted evening worship. Scheuer, the Hervormde Kerk consistory, and two policemen stood by to witness the illegal meetings and then report to the provincial church bureau and governor. The upstart dominee, they charged, was "greatly exasperating well-meaning people. . . . Please take actions to prevent confusion and disagreeable clashes and consequences; and our police

---

[28] Ibid., 56.
[29] Paasman, "Bestuurlijke en economische aspecten," 25-43; Weitkamp, "De vervolgingen," 199-200.
[30] Weitkamp, "De vervolgingen," 228; Dosker, *Van Raalte*, 44 (quote), trans. Dekker; Reenders, "Van Raalte als leider," 113; Van den Broeke, *"Pope of the Classis,"* 3, 93; Lucas, *Netherlanders*, 42-53.
[31] Wesseling, *Afscheiding van 1834 in Overijssel*, 66-67.

are too few." Mastenbroek mayor L. Nijlant appealed to Van Rechteren, who asked C. F. van Maanen, minister of internal affairs, to order soldiers to the area. The hard-nosed minister called out 1,430 soldiers for use throughout Overijssel.[32]

On Wednesday March 23, 1836, eight days after Van Raalte's marriage and a very brief honeymoon, classical representatives installed him in the combined Genemuiden-Mastenbroek congregation, a body of 350 souls. The novice preacher—the first and only Separated minister in the province of Overijssel—was up to the task. The congregation worshiped in the barn of Jannes van der Haar, located in the center of town. Rev. Scheuer demanded that the mayor call in more than fifty soldiers to snuff out the renegade congregation. The mayor did so, but Governor van Rechteren dissimulated, and the troops were delayed a month.[33]

Van Raalte, who had earned the epithet "hot head," brazenly threw down the gauntlet. At the very first service, he challenged the civil authorities by preaching to more than twenty people. He stood in front of the town hall and declared that he would never comply with any rules against freedom of worship, and he would never give up his office as a servant of God. He then left in a "big huff, swinging his three corner hat," which gesture was a rebuff of civic authority. A local report stated bluntly: "The law, as well as the mayor's authority, were totally not recognized." For this insolence, a squadron of four soldiers was housed in the small parsonage, and Christina had to feed them when her husband was on his preaching circuit. In one letter to her, Van Raalte referred to the men as "our soldiers." Twenty others were placed in homes of fellow congregants. The indignity, although unconstitutional, was condoned by local authorities.[34]

Van Raalte was undeterred. In May he installed consistories of Separatist churches at Den Ham, Dedemsvaart, and Heemse and formed the Classis of Ommen. On May 15 he organized the Dedemsvaart congregation with nineteen Hervormde Kerk members who signed the Act of Secession. Two days later, twenty-nine members

---

[32] Genemuiden Town Council to Governor of Overijssel, 21 Jan. 1836; Governor of Overijssel to Minister of Internal Affairs; Report, State Secretary to Minister of Internal Affairs, 4 June 1836, in *Archiefstukken*, 3:138-39; Weitkamp, "De vervolgingen," 233, 237-38, 244, 247-48.

[33] Weitkamp, "De vervolgingen," 246-48.

[34] Ibid., 251-67 (quote 264); Van Raalte to wife, 24 Apr. 1837, in Sweetman, *From Heart to Heart*, 3-4; Warner, *Door het venster*, 106-7; Carel de Moen report, Den Ham, 17 May 1836.

of the Den Ham church seceded, followed the next day by nineteen members at Heemse. Acts of Secession, emulating that of De Cock at Ulrum in 1834, were spreading like flies across the countryside. In May 1842, Brummelkamp installed his brother-in-law Carel de Moen as the first pastor at Heemse.[35]

Persecutions continued as Van Raalte, undeterred, continued holding unauthorized services. In early June, at Varsen, a village in Ambt Ommen, he led worship in a farmhouse, with eighty people one day and forty the next. Ommen mayor Jan Dikkers, forewarned, forbid the "self-proclaimed pastor of the Seceded congregation" from holding any services. Van Raalte ignored the warning, after Dikkers came in person and ordered everyone to go home. No one got up to leave. Dikkers immediately reported the infractions to Overijssel governor Van Rechteren. Three days later, Van Raalte preached at Varsen for over five hundred people. Dikkers then sent an urgent appeal to the governor for soldiers to stop the illegal services. Several hundred soldiers arrived in July and were billeted with Seceder families. Van Raalte was fined ƒ20 ($262 today) and the Varsen farm owner ƒ10 ($131 today). With a salary of only one guilder per week, Van Raalte's fine equaled almost five months of salary.[36]

In August 1836, the Van Raaltes and seventy-one members of the Ommen congregation signed a petition to Mayor Dikkers asking permission to meet four times on the Sabbath for worship. He denied the request on the grounds that a royal resolution of July 1836 forbade gatherings that have the "signs, form, and appearance" of official church services. This meant no garb, sacraments, marriages, or professions of faith. Understandably, Van Raalte criticized the king's decree in a "fiery and insolent" manner. Dikkers then charged the dominee with violating Article 291 of the Napoleonic Code—unlawfully gathering for worship with more than twenty persons. He levied the maximum fine of ƒ100, plus court costs (over $1,300 today). The young dominee was destined to serve months in prison before wealthy congregants paid his fine.[37]

---

[35] Warner, *Door het venster*, 110-11.
[36] Ibid., 112-13. The meager salary is noted in De Haas, *Van Dominees*, 46, cited in Pronk, *Goodly Heritage*, 131-32.
[37] Weitkamp, "De vervolgingen," 256-67 (quote 264); Petition, Genemuiden Separated Church to Mayor, August 1836; Van Raalte to Governor of Overijssel, 8 Aug. 1836; Zwolle judgment, 26 Oct. 1836; Groen van Prinsterer to King's commissioner M. J. Koenen, 29 Jan. 1837, trans. Nella Kennedy.

Genemuiden Afgescheiden Kerk on the Drecht
dedicated 1840 (Pereboom et al. *Afscheiding van 1834*)

A few days earlier, the congregation had purchased a site for a sanctuary on the outskirts of Genemuiden on the Drecht, a small river linked to the Zwarte Waterway and the national water transport system. The energetic members built the small building themselves and dedicated it a year later, on March 22, 1840. Families by the dozens walked to church on the waterway towpath that horses trod on weekdays pulling canal boats. The dominee and his consistory continued to worship boldly and incur fines of hundreds of guilders. In early 1837, the governor again billeted twelve soldiers in Genemuiden and Mastenbroek and charged them to persecute the pastor and disperse worshipers every time they tried to gather. The soldiers were so zealous in Mastenbroek that they even dispersed members on rumors of a gathering. They once harassed Van Raalte at breakfast as he smoked his pipe.[38]

The pastor complained to the governor by letter about the daily indignity and expressed concerns about safety in his home. Scoundrels were banging on the door and pulling the bell, which greatly alarmed his wife, who was "exposed to harmful terror." During their visit to

---

[38] Report in *Noord-Brabander*, 8 Apr. 1837 (www.delpher.nl, accessed, June 2021); Warner, *Door het venster*, 106.

Genemuiden, the Brummelkamps were hounded and smeared with mud and manure. The Van Raalte maid was grabbed and hit, and the rabble tore her clothing. The complaint fell on deaf ears.[39]

Geesje Van der Haar, a teenager in the Genemuiden church, whose family followed Van Raalte to Michigan in 1846, recorded in her memoirs the impact of his preaching. The extended Van der Haar families were bulwarks of the congregation. Geesje was in church on the inaugural Sunday. She recalled the day:

> Dominee Van Raalte exhorted us to lay aside the cloak of sin and unbelief and to look to Jesus as the chief leader and finisher of our faith. I felt greatly comforted by this sermon, and then we sang from the 16th Psalm. Oh, how refreshing for me. I myself could also believe that such would be my heritage. . . . Shortly after that, Van Raalte preached on Romans 12, about the cloud of witnesses we had round about us. . . . For a long time, we met in grandmother's barn, but the burgomaster and the soldiers broke up the meeting there while we were singing Psalm 46:1: "God is a refuge for His people," etc. The people felt strengthened in their faith. After the dominee prayed they all went home. . . . The government sent soldiers who were quartered in the homes of the seceders, in one home three, in another four, etc. This caused great confusion. Four were stationed in father's home.[40]

Van Raalte quickly won the hearts of parishioners in the Genemuiden-Mastenbroek church. His extemporaneous sermons, preached from scribbled notes, lived. He was "fervent of spirit and mighty in speech, and proclaimed an active, not passive, faith. He stressed so strongly that sinners must take responsibility for their sins and repent that some critics claimed he preached works righteousness over God's grace to unworthy sinners."[41] "Life is a shadow, and the world parishes," he told a bereaved friend. "'Soul lost, everything lost; soul saved, everything saved.' It must become for us the most serious, the most important, yes, the only necessary matter."[42]

This devout language echoed the Old Writers. As Separatist lawyer, Anne M. C. Van Hall, noted critically, "old pious people"

---

[39] Brummelkamp Jr., *Brummelkamp*, 194 (quote); Wesseling, *Afscheiding van 1834*, *Classis Zwolle*, 72-73; Reenders, "Van Raalte," 291.
[40] "Diary of Geesje Van der Haar-Visscher," 3-4.
[41] Spykman, *Pioneer Preacher*; Reenders, "Van Raalte," 281-82.
[42] Van Raalte to Paulus Den Bleyker, 22 June 1859, trans. Ten Hoor, BHL, copy JAH.

Separatist lawyer Anne M. C. van Hall (1809-1838) (*Rullmann*, De Afscheiding)

stress "experiential work and fall into the extreme boasting . . . and uncharitable condemnation of people," whereas young converts emphasize "sins by presumption and arrogance." It would be more useful, Van Hall concluded, if the two factions "did not bite and devour each other."[43] The extreme piety was both a curse and a blessing to the Separatists and caused many schisms.

Persecuted preacher

The itinerant preacher faced more persecution in small towns than large cities, where authorities were less stringent in enforcing nuisance laws. For example, in the Amsterdam church at Bloemgracht No. 42—the seminal body from October 1835—local authorities looked the other way. Although Van Raalte did not qualify under the royal proclamation of July 1836 as a resident minister, he did conduct services without incident on two Sundays in August. On the fourteenth, 325 worshipers attended in the morning, 188 in the afternoon, and 251 in the evening, and "no unrest took place." On the twenty-first, 373 gathered for the morning service, 180 in the afternoon, and 329 in the evening. With prayer, singing, preaching, and a love offering for the poor, everything remained peaceful. Van Velzen enjoyed the same peace when he preached the following Sunday. In September, however, the king, at the request of justice minister Van Maanen, agreed to

---

[43] A. M. C. van Hall to H. J. Budding, 1837, quoted in English translation in Reenders, "Van Raalte," 280.

send troops, levy fines, and force the sale of the Amsterdam edifice, "whenever the law fell short." Governor Van Rechteren, however, did not take such drastic action, but fines for unauthorized worship at Amsterdam did mount to more than ƒ2,000 ($31,400 today).[44]

Van Maanen's charge that Van Raalte "seems to be even more indifferent to the stipulations of His Majesty" than other Separatist pastors was hardly the case. Leiden's mayor also told the king that Separatists "do not pay the least attention to legal persecution." He pleaded for more tools "to disband the illegal gatherings." No wonder that the authorities billeted dragoons in villages to prevent Van Raalte from preaching.[45] Rural mayors and police were more diligent in face-to-face administration of justice against neighbors.

Illegal worship services mounted in late September 1836, and authorities took drastic action. On September 25, Staphorst mayor Frederik Ebbinge Wubben and two constables trekked to the farm of Hendrik Egberts Dunnink where, according to a tip-off, an illegal worship service was to be held. The mayor found Van Raalte, dressed in a black coat of tails with a three-quarter hat, leading some five hundred people in worship. The standard garb, which he was not entitled to wear, was as much an affront as his brazen ministry.[46]

Mayor Ebbinge Wubben rudely approached Van Raalte, who was reading of Psalm 33. "What is the purpose of your coming, sir?" asked Van Raalte respectfully. "I have come in the name of the King, and I order you to end this meeting," Wubben replied. The dominee retorted: "But I have a mandate from the King of Kings to preach the gospel to these people. My mandate is higher than yours. And therefore, I inform you that I cannot respond to your command." At this, Wubben blurted out, according to a young boy: "Van Raalte, shut your trap."[47]

At this Van Raalte became more aggressive, interrupting the mayor's orders repeatedly and snapped: "You are the craftiest of mayors

---

[44] Report of Noord-Holland Governor to Minister of Internal Affairs, 16, 19 Aug. 1836; Police of Amsterdam to Minister of Justice, 18, 22 Aug. 1836, in *Archiefstukken*, 3:364-66; Weitkamp, "De vervolgingen," 255-57; Wormser, *Karakter en Genade*, 34. See also, *Iowa Letters*, 17-18.

[45] Report of Minister of Justice, to Attorney General, 18 Aug., 1 Sept. 1836, in *Archiefstukken*, 3:364, 367.

[46] Wesseling, *Afscheiding van 1834, Classis Zwolle*, 211, 215.

[47] Lammert J. Hulst, a likely eyewitness, relates this story in his autobiography, *Drie en zestig jaren prediker*, 12. The distance between Staphorst and Dalfsen, Hulst's parental village, was eleven miles. In other accounts, the mayor's language is not recorded as quite that crude. For a blow-by-blow account of events from June to Dec. 1836, see Weitkamp, "De vervolgingen," 267-301.

Farmhouse of Hendrik E. Dunnink, Staphorst, where Van Raalte often preached (*courtesy Gerko Warner*)

I have ever met." He then declared the mayor to be an enemy of God, a profane man who refused to take off his hat during the singing. At this the mayor threatened: "I will initiate judicial process against you." "Go your way," Van Raalte replied flippantly, as he went outside, climbed on a farm wagon, and blithely preached his sermon, using a turned-over churn for his pulpit. The mayor then left "with his tail between his legs." With the dominee's "serious, fiery nature, he had a way of getting what he wanted."[48]

A week later, Governor Van Rechteren sent more than one-hundred soldiers to Staphorst and neighboring Rouveen, and remarkably, he ordered them billeted equitably—two in large houses and one in smaller ones, including those of Hervormde citizens, much to their chagrin, although families were reimbursed thirty-five cents per soldier per diem. He stipulated that no military actions could be taken unless illegal services were conducted. The quartering did not last long; the troops were withdrawn within ten days. The governor tended to be less militant than the mayors.[49]

On November 14, 1836, Van Raalte returned to Ommen and conducted the first consistory meeting of the small congregation in

---

[48] Wesseling, *Afscheiding van 1834, Classis Zwolle*, 210.
[49] Ibid., 214.

Egbertus ten Tooren's bakery, located on the Bouwstraat in Ommen, where Van Raalte preached, boarded, and met with the consistory (*courtesy Gerko Warner*)

the home of baker Egbertus ten Tooren and wife Martha Konijnenbelt. As was his practice, he had office-bearers sign the form of subscription and then exhorted elders to begin family visitation (*huisbezoek*) and catechism lessons, and warned them about "godless amusements at the horse fairs [races]." The next day being Sunday, he preached and administered the Lord's Supper. On Monday evening, he baptized three children. Early that evening, while the consistory was in session at the bakery, a riot broke out. Rabble-rousers, who had imbibed at the café Het Zwarte Paard (the Black Horse), damaged the homes of twenty-five families, tearing off roof tiles, breaking cobblestone facades, and smashing windows. The mayor stood by and made no attempt to stop the riot, which he minimized as youthful mischief. The families spent the next day cleaning up the damage. Van Raalte left the following day for Heemse. The rioters were acquitted but for a total fine of ƒ10.[50]

After Van Raalte led a worship service in Heemse, a hamlet near Hardenberg, some twenty men armed with sticks came looking for him. Some even talked of killing him, but in God's providence, Van Raalte

---

[50] *Groninger Courant*, 22 Nov. 1836 (www.delpher.nl, accessed, June 2021); minutes, Ommen consistory, 14 Nov. 1836, in De Graaf, "Een afgescheiden dominee"; Mayor of Ommen to Governor of Overijssel, 9 Nov. 1836; Governor to Minister of Internal Affairs, 21 Nov. 1836; Minister of Internal Affairs to King, 23 Nov. 1836, in *Archiefstukken*, 4:100-3; Warner, *Door het venster*, 116.

Van Raalte arrested at Den Ham
(*courtesy Gerko Warner*)

left town before they found him. Undeterred, at week's end, Van Raalte led a worship service and performed a baptism in Den Ham for eight to ten families at the farm of Mannes Boers, ignoring a warning from the local constable. For this, Ommen mayor Jansen Smit had seven deputies armed with piker and guns go to Den Ham to bring Van Raalte back to Ommen, where the mayor held him in the town house, "shut up in a little hole, where he was treated as a criminal," with a vagabond for a cellmate. The mayor "complained bitterly" about Separatists "who stay away from normal worship services . . . [and] blindly hold fast to 'old-rooted ideas,'" based on "superstition and fanaticism . . . instead of enlightenment ideas." Townsfolk deemed them disloyal for breaking with "their" Hervormde church and for disturbing civic peace. Several lynching mobs talked of a hanging. To safeguard the prisoner, the mayor had thirty soldiers billeted in Ommen, and locals, regardless of church affiliation, again had to house and feed them[51]

In the morning, Van Raalte was marched to Deventer on foot for seven hours by an armed military squadron to stand before a justice of the peace. The kindly judge immediately released him, declaring: "Mr. Van Raalte, I release you because there are no legal grounds upon

---

[51] Minister of Justice to Department of Internal Affairs, 2 Dec. 1836, in *Archiefstukken*, 4:105-6; Warner, *Door het venster*, 113-14; Reenders, "Van Raalte also leider," 138 (quotes); Warner, *Door het venster*, 113-16.

which I can detain you." Meanwhile, the governor, at the mayor's request, dispatched a detachment of fifty-six soldiers to keep the peace. The persecution in Ommen resulted in two dozen people joining the congregation. "Much opposition, much blessing," Brummelkamp noted.[52]

Dominee Van Raalte won the battle of wills, but it was a pyrrhic victory. In February 1837, he was arrested and sent to prison in Zwolle for three months for having insulted Mayor Ebbinge Wubben of Staphorst many months earlier. According to the court record, he had used "abusive language," accusing the mayor of being the "craftiest and most evil of all mayors he had ever met and an enemy of God and his service."[53]

Christina Van Raalte, staying with the Brummelkamps in nearby Hattem, came with Anthony to visit Albertus in prison. When she saw the massive gates and locks being opened and shut, she thought of the Apostle Paul and Silas, imprisoned in Ephesus and singing Psalms during the night. Just before Christmas 1836, Van Raalte appealed to a higher court at Arnhem, where Anne Maurits van Hall, the highly respected Amsterdam lawyer, successfully defended him, pleading religious freedom. The judge who, like the Deventer judge, was sympathetic, reduced the sentence to eight days because the defendant had not insulted the mayor, according to the law of *animus laedendi* (intending to insult).[54] For Van Raalte, paying Van Hall for his legal prowess and eighty-four-mile round trip from Amsterdam was well worth the expense. After eight days in prison, Van Raalte was freed and hurried home to Genemuiden to be with Christina and their nine-week-old firstborn son, Albertus.[55]

---

[52] Reenders, "Van Raalte als leider," 113-25; Wormser, *In twee werelddeelen*, 54-62; Brummelkamp, "Van Raalte," 102, trans. Ten Hoor. See also, Petition, Citizens of Ommen to Overijssel Governor J. H. van Rechteren, 19 Nov. 1836; Report of Minister of Internal Affairs Vollenhoven to King, 23 Nov. 1836; Report of Minister of Justice to Department of Internal Affairs, 26 Nov. 1836; in *Archiefstukken*, 4:101-5. For a transcript of the court case, translated into English, see "Van Raalte and the Law," 14.

[53] Van Raalte to wife, 7 Dec. 1836, in Sweetman, *From Heart to Heart*, 40-41; Agatha Sophia de Moen to Carel de Moen, 22 Dec. 1836; Brummelkamp, "Van Raalte," 103; Warner, *Door het venster*, 109-10, 117.

[54] *Noord-Brabanter*, 8 Apr. 1837 (www.delpher.nl, accessed June 2021); Report of Minister of Internal Affairs to King, 12 Sept. 1838; Report of Minister of Religion to King, 19 Sept. 1838, in *Archiefstukken*, 4:324-28, trans. Nella Kennedy.

[55] Sweetman, *From Heart to Heart*, 1. The church officers, all farmers, were each fined ƒ50 plus ƒ9 court costs ($772 today). Van Hall died young in 1838, costing the Separatists their major legal defender.

Huis van Verzekering, Zwolle, where Van Raalte was imprisoned from February 27 to March 7, 1837 (*courtesy Gerko Warner*)

The Separatist congregation in Amsterdam was the next place of confrontation for Van Raalte in March 1837. Elder Diedrich A. Budde informed the city council that the Separatists expected to meet without hindrance in his house on the Nieuwe Zijds Achterburgwal, but police put the house under surveillance. With Henricus Höveker, the Separatist bookdealer at his side, Van Raalte preached before one hundred worshipers at noon and two hundred in the afternoon. When the chief of police came to the afternoon service and demanded that the people disperse and the dominee show his permit, he was told that the dominee had a permit from the Lord. When the officer asked who he meant, the dominee replied: "Christ," to which the officer said a permit was needed from secular authorities. Van Raalte then appealed to the Constitution of 1815.[56]

With the congregation backing the dominee, the commissioner declared that they were in violation of the law and would be arrested. Van Raalte had the congregation sing a psalm, and the flummoxed officer left. Following the afternoon service, fifty people remained for a psalm service of singing, which continued to eight o'clock that evening. The police chief came again, this time, with two witnesses,

---

[56] For this and the following two paragraphs, see Report of Amsterdam City Council to Governor of Province of Noord-Holland, 20 Mar. 1837, in *Archiefstukken*, 4:149-51; Verhagen, *Oude David*, 38-43, trans. Nella Kennedy.

knocked on the door, and served Budde a warrant and demanded a halt to the meeting. This time, Van Raalte read scripture passages and began preaching, declaring that he would not stop preaching unless "compelled to do so by force." The officer again declared that he and Budde were disobeying the law, the king, and public authorities. He then left, and the service ended without a disturbance of the peace, although a crowd had gathered in front of the house.

Thereafter, the governor ordered the Amsterdam police to disperse any further services "with a strong arm," if necessary. So the congregation stayed within the law by meeting the next Sunday in different houses with fewer than twenty persons each. Police stationed officers at every house to count the worshippers. In four houses, the police broke up the services anyway to "protect the people from the assaults of riotous rabble lurking about." This police action thus became a rationale for denying freedom of worship, but the authorities recognized that they met lawfully and there was no violence. Before leaving Amsterdam, Van Raalte, in late March, preached in a house from nine o'clock in the evening until two in the morning, including celebrating the Lord's Supper. Fines for these Amsterdam services totaled ƒ345 ($4,400 today), with another ƒ209 ($2,650 today) levied on Van Raalte. Scholte helped arrange payments by wealthier Separatists.

That Van Raalte's ministry in Mastenbroek was bearing fruit is evident in a frank report of the Overijssel provincial church board to the central administration of the Hervormde Kerk. It read:

> The village is experiencing a sad decline in the flowering of the congregation by the intrigues of Van Raalte, who spares no opportunity to persuade innocent and simple souls to leave the Hervormde Kerk and join the Separatists. Already forty members are Separatists who, with their children and housemates, total 150 people. Many others, although not leaving the church, already band with the Separatists and neglect public worship entirely.[57]

Van Raalte had a peak moment in April 1837, when he preached to more than a thousand people in Ommen at the cost of a "troublesome sore throat." Then he was cast into the depths when he heard the news that his widowed mother, Catrina Christina, at age sixty-two, had died in Amsterdam, on April 15, following an illness. Albertus, whom

---

[57] Overijssel Provincial Church Board to Minister of Religion, 28 June 1837, in *Archiefstukken*, 4:279-81.

the mayor described as a "mischief-maker and instigator of schisms," was then in Deventer facing yet another day in court while his wife Christina was in Leeuwarden, Friesland, tending to her younger sister, Johanna van Velzen, dying of consumption (tuberculosis) at age nineteen. Albertus came to Leeuwarden later, but he could not stay. He made a solo journey back to all the churches in Overijssel and was away nearly a month. In a letter to his wife, he reported that he had learned from a Genemuiden parishioner that "soldiers are lodged with Jannes Van der Haar [who later followed Van Raalte to Michigan], and that a notification of our fine has arrived. This must be paid by the fourth of May. I have requested him to take care of that for us."[58]

Albertus reassured his beloved Christine (Chrissie), "Dear Wife, I hope that you do not become discouraged because of these persecutions. Dear wife, it is my calling to preach, and if it costs money that belongs to God . . . He will not leave us. For a short time, it will be bad here, and then we shall have to leave everything behind, and what would happen then if we did not have a treasure in heaven?" For conscience sake, he wrote Scholte, "I personally feel like a hunted partridge on the mountains, an outlaw and tramp," an embarrassment to my family and scorned by "respected citizenry."[59]

Persecution did not deter Van Raalte from his itinerant ministry. In Hellendoorn, on Ascension Day, in 1837, the Ommen mayor and a constable rudely interrupted Van Raalte's worship service on the farm of Gerrit Jan Immink and ordered him to dismiss the people. Van Raalte replied that the mayor had no jurisdiction, since they were in a neighboring village. The mayor than asked the homeowner to comply and he responded with a firm "NO." The dominee then proceeded to baptize a child, administer the Lord's Supper, and organize the congregation. Afterward, he installed an elder and a deacon. For his actions, he was fined ƒ100, plus ƒ25 in court costs, and Immink had to pay ƒ20.[60]

---

[58] *Opregte Haarlemsche Courant*, 20 Apr. 1837, announced by Dirk Blikman Kikkert on behalf of the family; Reenders, "Van Raalte als leider," 124; Albertus to Christina, 24 Apr., 28 Apr., 1, 7 May 1837, in Sweetman, *From Heart to Heart*, 3-4, 7-8, 10-13; Van Raalte to Governor of Overijssel, 2 Feb. 1837, in Wesseling, *Afscheiding van 1834, Classis Zwolle*, 71.

[59] Albertus to Christina, 1 May 1837, in Sweetman, *From Heart to Heart*, 10-11; Van Raalte to Scholte, 18 Feb. 1839, Smits, *Afscheiding van 1834*, 3:169-71, trans. Nella Kennedy; Hyma, *Van Raalte*, 36; Reenders, "Van Raalte," 285 (quote).

[60] Kraker, *Overisel, Michigan*, 7-8; Warner, *Door het venster*, 117-18.

Widow Woertink's barn, where Van Raalte led worship
(*Warner,* Van Raalte)

Van Raalte's last unauthorized worship service in the Ommen area took place on September 10, 1837, when he preached and conducted a baptism before three hundred people at the farm of Widow Hendrikje Woertink-Gerrits. While he was preaching, the mayor, the constable, and a civil officer came and ordered him to stop. He refused and was fined *f*100, and the widow was fined *f*8.[61]

Van Raalte was not dissuaded by brushes with the law or bouts of rheumatism and upper respiratory ailments. He carried on, unless forced to stop by armed soldiers. He kept riding the circuit and sending reassuring letters home. He reported to Scholte in May 1839:

> Thursday, I arrived in good health at Hellendoorn and spent the night there because the trip to Rijssen was too long. Friday morning, I was able to accomplish something there, so that I did not reach Rijssen until Friday evening. On Saturday, I went to Enter, and I preached there and accepted some new members. This all happened without disturbance, thanks to God's goodness. On Sunday morning, I preached in a hamlet near Rijssen, and in the evening, I taught catechism at Rijssen without interference.

---

[61] Warner, *Door het venster,* 107-8. Reenders, "Van Raalte als leider," 167. The fine was equal to his annual salary at Arnhem.

This morning (being Monday), I went to Deventer to accomplish that which is needed there.[62]

Travel schedule

The young minister's reputation grew as he rode the circuit of some twenty congregations within a radius of forty miles. By all accounts, he was an excellent speaker, a "virtuoso orator," who had the ability to touch the hearts of his hearers. His parish also stretched into southern Drenthe province. He and his fellow Separatist clerics, each in their own region, cared for thousands of people who were prone to squabbling. The work involved leading worship, administering sacraments, teaching catechism, organizing churches, installing consistories, and starting Christian schools. All this while keeping one step ahead of the law and facing arrests and fines that would break lesser men.[63]

Van Raalte's letters to his wife in May 1837 provide a window to his traveling schedule over several weeks. He preached in Den Ham on Saturday, in Ommen on Sunday and Monday, in Dedemsvaart on Tuesday, in Hellendoorn on Wednesday, and in Rijssen on Thursday. On Friday and Saturday he conducted *huisbezoek* (family visiting) in the sizeable Ommen congregation. On Saturday afternoon, he set out for the Hofwijk House near Dalfsen to conduct two Sunday services for a "very large crowd" of one thousand worshipers. He stayed there overnight to conduct a communion service on Monday. On Tuesday, he traveled to Hattem to have his tattered vest and trousers mended. He preached in Mastenbroek on Wednesday, in his hometown of Genemuiden on Thursday, in Nieuwleusen on Friday, in Meppel on Saturday, and in Steenwijk on Pentecost Sunday. He then returned to the parsonage in Genemuiden. Altogether, he covered 155 miles in sixteen days. He usually traveled on horseback or with his buggy, but occasionally he rented a carriage or caught a canal or river boat (*trekschuit*) in the national waterway system that linked virtually every town and city with scheduled passenger service.

An extended twenty-seven-day tour, from December 1837 to January 1838, took Van Raalte on a 182-mile circuit from his

---

[62] Van Raalte to Scholte, 7 May 1839, in Smits, *Afscheiding van 1834*, 3:173-74; Van Raalte to Widow Helena Suzanna van Hall, 23 May 1839, trans. Nella Kennedy; Hyma, *Van Raalte*, 37-38 (quotes).

[63] Reenders, "Van Raalte als leider," 98, trans. Dekker; Jacobson et al., *Dutch Leader*, 207 (quote); Dosker, *Van Raalte*, 1.

parsonage in Genemuiden to Germany by way of Hellendoorn, Rijssen, Enter, Deventer, Almelo, Ommen, Stegeren, Den Ham, Heemse, Uelsen/Itterbeek (County Bentheim), Dedemsvaart, and back to Genemuiden.[64] In Uelsen on New Year's Day 1838, he established the congregation founded by elder Harm Schoemaker and forty-three Seceders from the Bentheim Hervormde Kerk. Sensing trouble from local authorities, Van Raalte left Itterbeek that same evening. In the morning, soldiers arrived to arrest the Separatist, so his premonition had spared him a long imprisonment in Germany. En route home, in a rented carriage, with several friends, Van Raalte survived a serious accident. The horse "strayed off the road in the heavy darkness into the meadow. Every minute we were in danger of tipping over," he wrote his wife, and added, "During my life, I've ridden much but never have gone from bad to worse in this way."[65]

Traveling on horseback had its difficulties. "The horse is fresh and spirited," Van Raalte wrote Christina from Stegeren shortly after Christmas 1837, but "every now and then, he coughs quite a bit. . . . I am glad I took the riding cushion with me since the water from the Vecht [River] is so high in this region that I have to do everything on the horse." On occasions when his horse went lame, parishioners were reluctant to lend him a horse because the animal might be badly injured on the way. A fellow itinerant wrote of roads that were "pools of mud, a strip kneaded by hundreds of horse hoofs and wagon wheels."[66] Itinerating also took a toll on Van Raalte's body. He mentioned being fatigued and complained at times of a "troublesome sore throat," a "bad cold" that lingered, and a "heavy chest cold." Christina at home had to deal by herself with the hostile population of Genemuiden.[67]

Encounters with the law during Van Raalte's years of itinerant ministry in Overijssel show various aspects of his personality. When ordered to stop meetings on pain of fines or imprisonment, his ripostes were blunt and even cheeky, a "go ahead and do it" dare. His cause

---

[64] Reenders, "Van Raalte als leider," 134-35; Wormser, *Karakter en Genade*, 76-78. For the itinerary, see Van den Broeke, *"Pope of the Classis,"* 43, or his "Van Raalte and Ecclesiastical Organization," 242-43. Mileage calculated by author.

[65] Reenders, "Van Raalte als leider," 124; Albertus to wife, 18, 28 Dec. 1837, in Sweetman, *From Heart to Heart*, 3-14; Warner, *Door het venster*, 119-21.

[66] Albertus to wife, 28 Dec. 1837 (quote), in Sweetman, *From Heart to Heart*, 25-26; Van Koetsveld, *Schetsen*, 116-17; Van Raalte to De Moen, 23 Nov. 1838, ADC.

[67] Albertus to wife, 28 Apr., 2 Oct., 28 Dec. 1837, in Sweetman, *From Heart to Heart*, 7, 15, 25; Van Raalte to Budding, 9 Jan. 1839, in Gunning, *Budding*, 575-79, trans. Ten Hoor.

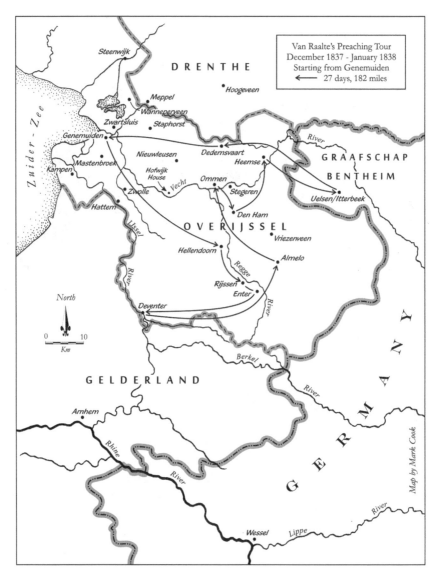

Van Raalte's twenty-seven-day preaching tour from December 11, 1837, to January 6, 1838

was righteous and he would obey God rather than men. At times he expressed himself too strongly, tactlessly, and even rudely. Officials described him as a scofflaw who undermined lawful authority and demeaned officials, who were also God's servants. When Genemuiden authorities asked him to meet in "quiet seclusion" and during specified hours, he reportedly reacted in a most severe and highly abusive way, declaring that he would never obey such instructions, and left "in a great temper, while waving his three-cornered hat." He insulted the mayor of Staphorst by calling him an enemy of God for offending the Almighty by keeping his hat on during the singing of a psalm. When soldiers dissolved a meeting in a Genemuiden barn, the worshipers complied but not the dominee; soldiers had to remove him forcibly. He did not seek conflict with officials, but he also did not shy away from it.[68]

Looking back on what happened, Van Raalte recalled in 1862, "It still hurts me to be fined in my own fatherland, . . . encouraged by the Hervormde Kerk Synod and local governments, suppressed by quartering [soldiers], cast into prison, mocked for years, pelted with mud and stones, and chased and plagued like an outcast." The government treated us as "monsters, prey to the rage of the populace, and branded as moral lepers of the land." In the "bombardment" with stones, Van Velzen who was with him, was hit directly, but Van Raalte, "small as he was," escaped the worst.[69]

The campaign to silence the Separatists was doomed. A police informer in 1837 estimated that eighty thousand devout people were gathering for worship in groups small and large all over the country. It was impossible for civil authorities to stop them.[70] In spite of crippling fines and deploying thousands of troops to break up the illegal services, which the government defined as riots, Separatist clerics and elders carried on, preaching to as many as a thousand spiritually thirsty people in open-air worship services. Preachers gathered surreptitiously and tried, often not successfully, to keep one step ahead of the law. Sometimes they even spread false information to frustrate authorities. It is no wonder that in America Van Raalte cherished freedom of religion as such a precious right.

The persecution was relatively short lived, as one would expect in the generally tolerant Netherlands, and the intensity varied from province to province and even in cities or villages. The government

---

[68] Weitkamp, "De vervolgingen," 264-68, 277.
[69] Van Raalte to nephew Van Velzen, Apr. 1862, Wormser, *In twee werelddeelen*, 62-63; Roelof Pieters' report, *Acts of Synod of the Christelijke Gereformeerde Kerk* (Kampen, 1875), 70-72, trans. Nella Kennedy.
[70] Report of Director of Police, Den Haag, to Attorney General, 4 Feb. 1837, in *Archiefstukken*, 4:125-26.

learned that it was not only costly but also impossible to stifle devout believers, who were willing to be banished from the fatherland or beheaded for the faith. The policy of quartering soldiers in homes of dissidents ended in 1837. No Separatists were jailed after 1839, and soldiers did not break up Separatist meetings after 1840. But fines continued to be levied in scattered places until 1846, particularly in the province of Utrecht.

Persecution of dissenters in the Netherlands did not go unnoticed in other European counties. Several Swiss cantons, meeting at Lausanne in 1837, sent a letter of support to "Christians in Holland who are suffering persecution for the sake of our great God and Savior, Jesus Christ." Swiss Christians at Geneva urgently petitioned the Dutch government to "allow freedom of conscience and religion on behalf of all Christians in that country." The Canton of Waadland sent a letter, addressed to all pastors, directly to the Hervormde Kerk synodical committee, and it was curtly dismissed: "You have been wrongly informed; you would have been better off keeping silent."[71]

Fines levied on clerics and laymen for illegal worship totaled in the tens of thousands of guilders, but many provinces did not tally them. By 1837 Van Velzen's fines in the province of Friesland amounted to $f6,860$ ($87,000 today), and in Zuid-Holland and Lower Gelderland, fines totaled $f11,323$ ($143,500 today). Budding, in the Zuid-Holland islands, accumulated fines of $f5,000$ ($63,400 today). Van Raalte's fines in Overijssel likely were similar, but they remain untallied. Van Raalte allowed wealthy followers to pay his fines, but Budding refused this option and spent seven months in jail for unpaid fines, until King Willem II pardoned him. He counted it joy to suffer for Christ, but Van Raalte scolded him. No minister should "consider himself more useful sitting locked up, while the progress of the Word is stopped, while being free he can be busy in his service."[72]

Fines impoverished Separatist leaders, but followers suffered social ostracism, economic boycotts, and job blacklists. They heard epithets like Cocksianen (De Cock ones), *knikkers* (bald heads), *fijnen* (sanctimonious ones), Pharisaic pietists, and Geuzen Beggars

---

[71] Wormser, *Karakter en Genade*, 147-52.
[72] Van Raalte to Budding, Oct. 1838, 9 Jan. 1839 (quote), in Gunning, *Budding*, 575-79, trans. Ten Hoor; Brummelkamp to Van Raalte, 17 Mar. 1842, JAH; *Algemeen Handelsblad*, 29 June 1840 (www.delpher.nl, accessed July 2021); also Beets, *Life and Times*, 10; Van Hinte, *Netherlanders*, 127. On Budding's checkered career, see Brinks, "Father Budding," and De Rijcke, *Huibert Jacobus Budding*, 61.

(nickname of Calvinist pirates in the Dutch Revolt against Spain, 1568-1648). They were also denied the right to establish Christian schools without government interference. Many remained lukewarm members of the Hervormde Kerk to avoid public ridicule and discrimination.[73]

---

[73] Van Hinte, *Netherlanders*, 127; Sheeres, "Struggle," 34-47.

CHAPTER 4

Church Struggles:
"God alone can build the church."

The nascent Christian Separated Church struggled with schism in its seminal years. Fissures were apparent at the first synod in 1836 and they came to a head in 1840. Geesje Van der Haar-Visscher described the sad story. "Dissension had become rife among God's people. One was a follower of Van Raalte, another of Budding, another of Lambertus Ledeboer. Differences of opinion were aired, and further separation occurred, although the majority stuck with Revs. De Cock, Van Raalte, Brummelkamp and Van Velzen." The Christian Separated Church had a "crisis of youth."[1] Could they accept one another in love and forbearance and work together to build up congregations? Or would they fight over polity and cause schisms? Provincial synods sometimes suspended elders and deacons for being spiritually unfit or for holding unorthodox views.

Van Raalte became entangled in the tussles because he faithfully attended church assemblies. In twenty-three meetings of the regional classes of Zwolle, Ommen, and Apeldoorn, he was present nineteen

---

[1] "Geesje Van der Haar-Visscher Diary," 6; Bouwman, *Crisis der jeugd*; Engelsma, *Watchman on the Walls*, 128-29.

times—the best attendance record of all. No wonder he often served as president and/or clerk and opened with prayer. Likewise, in twenty-two meetings of the provincial synod of Overijssel, he was elected either president or clerk all but seven times. Van Raalte was a devoted churchman who consistently tried to mediate between factions and bring peace. For this, he faced bitter opposition from the traditionalists, much to his chagrin and anguish.[2]

Van Raalte learned that reformation is difficult to channel into constructive paths. Clerics differed over church polity, lay preachers, royal recognition, sacraments, and even vestments. Traditionalists De Cock and Van Velzen were determined to restore the Dortian folk traditions of historic Dutch Calvinism, whereas the radical Scholte wanted a free congregational model akin to the primitive New Testament church. Van Raalte and Brummelkamp held the middle ground by striving for reconciliation and wider evangelical preaching. Scholte had the "bully pulpit" after the denomination adopted his periodical, *De Reformatie*, as its official mouthpiece. He also had the best mind and a forceful personality, but he was expelled by the 1840 synod. A small fringe element, the Cross followers led by Budding and Ledeboer, resented any lordship by higher bodies and seceded to uphold the "pure" Dort doctrines and church order. They had considerable influence in Zeeland

Synod Utrecht 1837

A week before Synod Utrecht 1837 convened, Van Raalte, Van Velzen, and Brummelkamp called for a church-wide day of prayer for peace and unity. At synod, delegates sequestered for the two-week assembly, guarded by an armed sentry at the door day and night since they numbered more than the statutory limit of twenty. The major issues were the authority of the Dort church order, the status of lay preachers, and the question of *who* at infant baptism could make covenant promises—confessing parents, grandparents, an elder, nonconfessing parents, or other relatives.[3]

Church order issues bedeviled Separatists from the beginning. Was the Dort church order a foundational document, like the American Constitution, to be accepted as is, or was it a living document, to be

---

[2] Van den Broeke, *"Pope of the Classis,"* 29-40.
[3] Wormser, *In twee werelddeelen*, 65-66; Engelsma, *Watchman on the Walls*, 110-12; Acts of Synod Utrecht 1837, in *Handelingen en verslagen*, 73-176.

modified as circumstances changed? Originalists, such as De Cock and Van Velzen, viewed the Dort order as a document written by spirit-filled delegates. Scholte, on the other extreme, rejected Dort in favor of his own version, the so-called Utrecht church order, which he put on the table at Synod 1837.

Van Raalte feared the worst since many of his Overijssel congregations were strong Dortians. After the opening session, before the main discussion had begun, he captured the tense atmosphere in a letter to his wife. "The differing points of view that come to expression are numerous and frequently voiced. I cannot disguise the fact that the difficulties often make me depressed. I feel that God alone can guard, protect, and build the churches.... The Lord's finger must be revealed in this because, humanly speaking, it is impossible."[4]

Van Velzen, the synod president, held a firm gavel. He had the delegates consider each of the one hundred articles in Scholte's church order, compared to the eighty-six in the Dort order. In the end, the delegates modified forty-two articles in the Dort order, rejected eight, and accepted thirty-six as is. Van Velzen demanded that everyone adhere to the revised order, but De Cock rejected the document out of hand and threatened to leave the infant denomination. Van Velzen then added six solidly Reformed doctrinal articles as a preface, which temporarily mollified De Cock and his northern allies.[5]

Credentialing lay preachers was a major stumbling block. Scholte's proposal, backed by Van Raalte and Brummelkamp, to deny lay preachers ordination, struck at the heart of the Separatist movement. Since the eighteenth century, conventicle worship under lay preachers was treasured by pietists. De Cock considered these faithful servants a "beneficial gift from God to the church" and a major reason that the Separated churches were flourishing. Most delegates agreed with Scholte, that laymen should not be ordained and that they must read approved sermons and not write their own. The issue, which pitted university-trained clerics against unordained preachers, embroiled every classical and synodical gathering from 1836 to 1845. Van Raalte yielded on many points for the sake of unity and not, as Scholte supposed, that he "fell for the truth."[6]

---

[4] "Van Raalte to Dearly Beloved Wife," 2 Oct. 1837, in Sweetman, *From Heart to Heart*, 15.
[5] Te Velde, *Brummelkamp*, 96-97; Oostendorp, *Scholte*, 112-15; *Handelingen en verslagen*, 111-12, text of Utrecht church order, 122-57.
[6] De Graaf, "Een Monument der Afscheiding," 6 (quote); Te Velde, "Ministerial Education," 197-99; Wesseling, *Afscheiding van 1834, Classis Zwolle*, 150-51, 198.

Kruisgezinden schism

Kruisgezinden (literally "cross-minded," referring to the "Churches under the Cross," i.e., the suffering churches[7]) were an ultrapietist contingent, prominent in Van Raalte's congregations. Eventually, they either withdrew or seceded, despite Van Raalte's "undeniably fearful wrestling against the seeds of secession." Unity was more important than any church order. The very survival of the Separated Church was at stake, he believed. His willingness to compromise on church polity opened him to charges of being "internally divided, uncommitted on all his paths," "weak" "a child."[8] He was even charged with sacrificing truth for unity. When he and De Cock met with a contingent of elders at the Zwolle congregation in November 1838, they faced such a storm of protest that Van Raalte "wearied of his life."[9]

The critics revered the Old Writers of the Later Reformation. They wanted experiential preaching and objected to changing Dort rules on baptism, church membership, and even the minor matter of limiting terms of office of elders and deacons to two years. Van Raalte favored life-time tenure, believing that it was "unprofitable for the church" to force seasoned officers to resign so soon. Such a policy, he argued, would undermine the office of elder, remove experienced leaders, and add a qualification "not written anywhere."[10]

Having De Cock's endorsement on church order issues did not spare Van Raalte from schism. In 1838 hundreds of ultrapietists withdrew from his congregations, including two dozen from Ommen who bolted after he put them under discipline. All objected to any weakening of the Dort church order. Wolter W. Smitt, a lay preacher at Zwolle, accused Van Raalte of "unorthodoxy." Smitt was a manufacturer who actually served as a lieutenant in the citizen militia. Because of Smitt's high-handed demeanor in church affairs, Van Raalte derided him as "Lieutenant Smitt." Elder Derk Hoksbergen at Kampen and Rev. Lambertus Ledeboer in Zeeland were equally as critical, as was

---

[7] They were suffering for their refusal to let the state govern the church, for their insistence on "Gereformeerd" in their name (prohibited by the state), and for their adherence to the Dort church order.

[8] Classis Nieuwleusen, minutes, 25 May 1842; Reenders, "Van Raalte als leider," 129-32, trans. Dekker, citing Scholte's letter to A. M. C. van Hall, 28 Oct. 1839, in Smits, *Afscheiding van 1834*, 5:394, and Helenius de Cock, *De Cock*, 58-81.

[9] Classis Nieuwleusen, minutes, 1 Nov. 1838, trans. Nella Kennedy, VRI; Reenders, "Van Raalte als leider," 129-32, trans. Dekker.

[10] Wormser, *In twee werelddeelen*, 71-72, 75-77.

Wolter W. Smitt, elder in the Gereformeerde Kerken onder 't Kruis and Van Raalte antagonist (Wesseling, Afscheiding, Classis Zwolle)

Douwe Van der Werp, a soon-to-be minister Van Raalte would meet again in the Holland colony. The controversy caused his "throat to tighten up." Lighten up, wrote Brummelkamp: "You take that matter too seriously.... It might be better to cut the ecclesiastical ties."[11]

The upshot was a split in Van Raalte's Ommen congregation, caused by a mass exodus of the Kruisgezinden who joined the Gereformeerde Gemeenten (Reformed Congregations), consisting of ten congregations mainly in the North, all committed to the Dort church order. The Separatists were now split into two distinct denominations.[12]

Scholte was blamed for the schism, but the roots went deeper, harkening back to the experiential Later Reformation. Van Raalte felt this when he first itinerated across Overijssel. The Kruisgezinden

---

[11] Minutes, Ommen consistory, 14 May, 20 Nov. 1838; Brummelkamp to Van Raalte, 17 Mar. 1842 (quotes), trans. Simone Kennedy, JAH; Dosker, *Van Raalte*, 52-55; Wormser, *In twee werelddeelen*, 81; Te Velde, *Brummelkamp*, 126-28. For Van Raalte's leadership in classical meetings, see Van den Broeke, "Pope of the Classis," 29-49. Douwe Van der Werp (1811-1876), student of De Cock, led the breakaway group briefly in 1841-42. In 1864 he accepted a call as pastor of the Graafschap CRC in the Holland colony and became a leader in the True Holland Reformed denomination (Sheeres, *Son of Secession*, 56-60).

[12] *Handelingen en verslagen*, 1158. The Kruisgezinden in 1845 adopted the name "Gereformeerde Kerken onder 't Kruis." In 1869, after being independent for twenty-five years, most congregations reunited with the Christelijke Afgescheiden Kerk to form the Christelijke Gereformeerde Kerk.

Douwe Van der Werp (1811-1876), Christian school teacher and Separatist pastor trained by Hendrik de Cock (*Pereboom et al., Afscheiding in Overijssel*)

were *bevindelijk* (literally, "experiential"), pursuing inward peace and emotional experiences. Van Raalte could not win them over. He later called the Overijssel secession "a frightening, tearful, and heartbreaking hurt," far worse than all the persecution he had endured. It caused him to doubt the seminal Secession of 1834.[13] "If the Lord had not prevented it," he wrote Budding in 1839, "I would have left the narrow path to seek my carnal desires." This was clearly the low point of his entire ministry in the Netherlands. Little did he know that he would face schism in America that would again test him to his limits.[14]

Sacraments

The subject of the sacraments also roiled Synod 1837, superficially, the question of who belongs to the church of Jesus Christ. Was Christianity the religion of the nation (Corpus Christianum, i.e., body of the christened), in which case everyone belonged? Or was it limited to Christ's elect (Corpus Christi, i.e., the Body of Christ)? Were sacraments signs (pictures) preferred by the body of Corpus

---

[13] Van Raalte to Budding, Oct. 1838; Te Velde, *Brummelkamp*, 86-89; Reenders, "Van Raalte als leider," 125-27 (quotes), trans. Dekker, citing letter of 1 Sept. 1839. A general history is Bos, *Kruisdominees*.

[14] Van Raalte to Budding, 9 Jan. 1839, quoted in English by Reenders, "Van Raalte," 279, citing Gunning, *Budding*, 587.

Christianum adherents, or seals (redemptive actions), preferred by adherents of the Corpus Christi view? The Hervormde Kerk clearly was a *volkskerk*, but most Separatists limited membership to baptized or confessing believers.[15]

This question affected the administration of the sacraments. Should the Lord's Supper be limited to confessing believers (the Body of Christ) or open to all? Who may make the vows on behalf of children in the sacrament of baptism? Confessing parents (Body of Christ adherents) only? Or may nonconfessing parents, themselves baptized as infants but seldom attending (*volkskerk*), also make these vows? And what about confessing grandparents?

De Cock followed the standard *volkskerk* practice, which likened infant baptism to the Old Testament ceremony of circumcision required of all Jewish males. The promises of baptism are for all children who sprang from "attendance in her bosom," said De Cock (meaning essentially all children in the community). Baptism is an outward covenant for the *visible* church, not the "seal of the righteousness of faith." If neither parent was a professing member, grandparents or other family members, who were professing believers, could step in and present children of the covenant promise. "We must baptize not only the children of 'nearest' believing parents, but also the infant children of unregenerate, unconverted, worldly, and wicked confessors are proper recipients of baptism," De Cock declared. His practice was therefore public christening rather than covenant baptism. Van Velzen allowed an elder or other confessing member to present children, but not nonconfessing parents.[16] Scholte, Brummelkamp, Gezelle Meerburg, and Budding insisted that only confessing believers could present their children for the sacrament since they alone were members of the church of Christ. They maintained that this was the teaching of the Reformed Confessions.

Synod ended without settling the baptism question, but the stricter view won general acceptance and was adopted by Synod Groningen 1846. Initially, Van Raalte stood with the majority, but he wavered and eventually adopted De Cock's position, as did Van Velzen

---

[15] Leonard Verduin, "CRC: Hewn from the Rock," *Banner*, 8 Oct. 1984, 9; Oostendorp, *Scholte*, 101-10, and Heideman, *Scholte*, 67-80.

[16] Oostendorp, *Scholte*, 105 (quote); Kamps, *1834*, 210-13, citing Deddens et al., *Hendrik de Cock*, 2:350. De Cock's practice was akin to the "half-way covenant" practiced by Congregational churches in colonial New England, which permitted baptized, but non-confessing, members of moral life and orthodox faith to present their children for baptism and become church members.

and Brummelkamp. All children of the congregation "by virtue of the Covenant of Grace . . . must be baptized," Van Raalte declared. He followed the same practice in America for much of his ministry (ch. 14), as did the Reformed Protestant Dutch Church that he joined.[17]

Clerical garb—the "cocked hat" controversy

The seemingly silly matter of clerical garb further embroiled Synod Utrecht. Some months before the gathering, Scholte set off an uproar by casting off the garb as unbiblical and popish. Clothing that set ministers apart was deemed a symbol of liturgical orthodoxy, tradition, and authority in Reformed churches; it must be distinct from Catholic priestly attire. Protestant pastors were not priests. The attire consisted of a black cloak of swallow tails with bands, knickerbockers, and a three-cornered (or cocked) hat, which some argued symbolized the Three Forms of Unity or the Holy Trinity. Many clerics also wore this attire when visiting the sick and during informal tea visits. The Batavian Republic banned the garb in 1798, but King Willem restored it in his General Regulations of 1816, only to see this provision disregarded over time. The king's aim was to use the garb to help bind church and state and to intimidate professors, lawyers, and other professionals who had had their distinctive garb for centuries.[18]

Scholte's rejection of the garb led De Cock and Budding to charge him with "modernism" and confusing the faithful. Budding broke off friendship with Scholte over this issue, which caused Van Velzen to ask Budding, "Are you crazy? Or do you want to be the Pope completely?"[19] Synod Amsterdam 1840 tried unsuccessfully to resolve the matter, and it festered for nearly a decade. For underpaid pastors, many of whom could not afford expensive suits worn by *burgers*, clerical garb was convenient and conveyed authority and status. In time, fashions changed, and the coat of tails, breeches, and cocked hat gave way to a Prince Albert frock coat and trousers. In 1853 the traditional attire was banned in the Hervormde Kerk, and by 1868, it was also done in the Christelijke Afgescheiden Kerk.[20]

Van Raalte, Brummelkamp, and Gezelle Meerburg followed

---

[17] Scholte to Van Hall, 23 Aug. 1837, in Oostendorp, *Scholte*, 107-10. See also Kennedy, *Commentary*, 13 Sept. 1854, 1:461-63; Heideman, *Scholte*, 69-74, 77-80 (quote 77n). The RCA did not ban the practice until 1979, long after the CRC did so in 1902.

[18] *Handelingen en verslagen*, 36, 45-48, 54.

[19] Van Raalte to Budding, 1 Sept. 1839, in Gunning, *Budding*, 552, trans. Ten Hoor; Reenders, " Van Raalte," 295-97; Reenders, "Van Raalte als leider," 169-75.

[20] Aalders, *Toga*, 40-51.

Traditional clerical garb in the nineteenth century, with black cloak of tails with bands, knickerbockers, three-cornered hat, and buckle shoes (*Aalders, De komst van de toga*)

Scholte in discarding the special attire. They acted out of conscience, not out of a need to dispense with expensive clothing they could ill afford. After all, Jesus' disciples never wore priestly garments, and the Apostle Paul urged believers to dress modestly. "Many simple people are dragged into this through ignorance," Van Raalte declared in exasperation.[21] When Carel de Moen urged his brother-in-law not to discard the garb, Van Raalte replied: "I find your advice to continue to wear that Jewish, popish, Pharisaic priestly garment sinful.... We come to the Father through Christ, not the high priest Levi."[22]

Despite drawing a line in the sand, Van Raalte sometimes reluctantly yielded to the demands of individual congregations so as not to give offense. Like the Apostle Paul, the Gospel was more important than externals and traditions. He wore the garb in Genemuiden, but not in Ommen, where early in his tenure he "emphatically" and "tersely" informed the consistory of his deep conviction against the "priestly attire." Only one elder dared to disagree with the dominee. The rest conceded, provided he "teach the congregation in order to prevent problems." To this, he readily agreed and did so within a week. Brummelkamp, more rigid than Van Raalte, would not concede, at the cost of being isolated from many congregations in Gelderland.[23]

---

[21] Van Raalte, Groningen, to wife, 26 Oct. 1837, JAH; Scholte to A. M. C. van Hall, 10 Oct. 1837, in Smits, *Afscheiding van 1834*, 5:395; Heideman, *Scholte*, 128.

[22] Van Raalte to De Moen, 26 July 1839, trans. Nella Kennedy, ADC.

[23] Van Raalte to Scholte, 5 Sept. 1839, in Smits, *Afscheiding van 1834*, 3:176-78;

As presiding officer (moderator) of the Classis of Gelderland in 1843, Van Raalte had the body make an official decision to leave the matter of clerical dress to pastors and congregations. In 1847, after he left for America, Van Raalte's moderating influence was gone. Then, for five years (1847-52), the Gelderland and Overijssel provincial synods, now led by Brummelkamp, set opposing rules—Gelderland would be the synod *without* the cocked hat, and Overijssel would be the synod *with* the cocked hat.[24] In Michigan, Van Raalte mounted the pulpit with the traditional Prince Albert frock coat with tails, but no cocked hat.

Official church recognition

Separatists could have ended persecution by requesting recognition from the king, but only on his terms. On July 5, 1836, Willem I issued a royal decree that permitted "illegal" churches to apply for recognition under stringent conditions. They must submit a petition for freedom of assembly that would admit to their former illegal behavior, thus making them confess to being a false church. They must renounce their rights in the Hervormde Kerk and not use the title "Gereformeerde Kerk," the historic name since the sixteenth century. (Both names translate as "Reformed.") Churches must agree to take care of their own poor and be entirely self-supporting. They must also formulate a church order other than that of Dort and promise to submit to the government. Accepting these terms meant complete surrender of their rights, name, property, salaries, and most important, their hope of restoring the historic Gereformeerde church.[25]

Synod 1836 commissioned Scholte to appeal to King Willem I on behalf of the newly organized denomination for recognition as the Christelijke Gereformeerde Kerk (Christian Reformed Church). The appeal noted that the Hervormde Kerk was not faithfully administering the sacraments or disciplining those with heretical teachings, such as the denial of the Trinity, of Jesus' divinity, and of original sin, all taught as truth in the Reformed Confessions. Brummelkamp and two elders hand delivered the letter to the palace. Recognition would have brought an end to persecution. But the request had a thinly

---

minutes, Ommen consistory, 28 Aug., 31 Oct. 1839, trans. Nella Kennedy, VRI.

[24] Reenders, "Van Raalte," 295-97; Reenders, "Van Raalte als leider," 169-75.

[25] Minutes, Provincial Classis of Overijssel, Dalfsen, 4 July 1844, in Bouwman, *Crisis der jeugd*, 91-94; Dosker, *Van Raalte*, 18-19. King Willem III in 1870 recognized the Christelijke Afgescheiden Kerk and granted the right to adopt the name Gereformeerde Kerk.

veiled trap. By asking for the name "Gereformeerde," the Separatists were claiming to be a continuation of the True church confessed at the Synod of Dort and recognized by the states-general in 1619. Left unsaid was the assertion that the Hervormde Kerk, having tolerated an "enlightened" Christian rationalism, was no longer a True church. The king and his church officials rejected the request for recognition out of hand.[26] Unofficially, the Separated brothers had been using the name Gereformeerde as early as 1843 in minutes of their provincial assemblies.

Scholte in 1838 broke the united front and, without consulting colleagues, unilaterally bent to the king's demands and petitioned on behalf of his Utrecht congregation "to be recognized in civil society" as a Christelijke Afgescheiden Kerk. The Ministry of Religion granted the request in early 1839 and "admitted and recognized [the congregation] in civil society." Scholte had explicitly asked for recognition in *civil*, not *ecclesiastical*, terms because he believed in a church free of government control. He willingly gave up "Gereformeerde" for the larger goal of restoring the sovereignty of Christ over the church. Unlike the Dortian defenders, Scholte had no desire to restore the old Gereformeerde church. Scholte's concession ended crushing fines and harassment. Separatist congregations in Amsterdam, Rotterdam, and Groningen followed suit.[27]

"Separatist pinks"

Van Raalte was an economic activist who combined an interest in business with philanthropy, providing jobs for Separatist laborers blacklisted for employment. His first business venture gave work to some fishermen at the North Sea port of Scheveningen, who had been fired for honoring the Sabbath. In 1837 the young dominee at Genemuiden joined with Scholte, lawyer Van Hall, financier H. J. Koenen, and political leader Groen van Prinsterer to invest ƒ6,000 ($76,000 today) in two fishing boats, dubbed "Separatist pinks,"[28] one of which was christened *Sara Johanna* (after Scholte's daughter). In two weeks at sea in 1838, *Sara Johanna* returned with a large catch worth ƒ250 ($3,170

---

[26] Te Velde, *Brummelkamp*, 86-108, 194; Heideman, *Scholte*, 67-80, 105-14.
[27] Oostendorp, *Scholte*, 97-98, contains document in English; Reenders, "Van Raalte," 285-86; Heideman, *Scholte*, 124.
[28] A pink (French "pinque") is a small flat-bottomed sailing ship with a very narrow stem. Scholte and Van Raalte paid ƒ1000 and Van Hall ƒ500. The fishermen included Arie de Lange, Matthijs Taal, Klaas van den Dijk, Maarten Plokker, and Cornelis Roeleveld and son.

today). The Separatists honored the Sabbath, but they caused tongues to wag by going to sea on the Second Pentecost (the Monday holiday after Pentecost Sunday) in May 1844. Most North Sea fishermen would not work on holidays, but Separatists preferred to fish on holidays. Jasper de Maas managed the business and kept the books from 1837 to 1840, and P. Varkevisser took over from 1840 to 1845. The firm was liquidated in 1846 when Van Raalte and Scholte prepared to immigrate to America. It is unlikely the investors earned large profits; the venture was more benevolent than profit driven.[29]

Van Raalte as the "apostle of Overijssel" established many congregations in the rural heartland. He served three congregations as resident pastor—Genemuiden/Mastenbroek (1836-39), Ommen (1839-44), and Arnhem/Velp (1844-46)—all founded by De Cock and Brummelkamp. These steady pulpits provided a measure of financial security, although his salary was often in arrears. As a first generation cleric in the Christian Separated Church, Van Raalte became the leader and spokesperson in the provinces of Overijssel and Gelderland, with eighty congregations and twenty thousand souls. He created polity *de novo*—in the pastorate, catechism, consistory, diaconate, benevolence, church discipline, and adult education—but all according to Reformed principles, guided by the Dort church order. Bringing unity and order to Separatists was like herding cats. Many were headstrong, strong willed, unyielding, cantankerous, and convinced they had the correct view of scripture and Reformed doctrine. What left the deepest scars on Van Raalte, however, was the persecution and harassment he had suffered at the hands of the authorities.[30]

---

[29] Reenders, "Van Raalte als leider," 193n573, citing Van Raalte's letter to Scholte, 26 Oct. 1840, in Smits, *Afscheiding van 1834*, 3:181, trans. Dekker. See also, Report of Director of Police to Attorney General, 27 May 1837, in *Archiefstukken*, 4: 130; Van Hall to Scholte, 20 Feb., 4 Mar., 8 May 1837; Van Hall to Budding, 11 Feb. 1837; Van Hall to Scholte, 13, 19 Jan., 13 Feb., 19 May 1838; Scholte to Van Hall, 16 May 1838, all in Smits, *Afscheiding van 1834*, 5:467-70.

[30] Reenders, "Van Raalte als leider," 98; Reenders, "Van Raalte," 278-80; Van Raalte to Van Velzen Jr., Apr. 1862, in *Kompleete uitgave* (1884), 533, trans. Dekker.

CHAPTER 5

Ommen Pastorate: "An honorable life."

Parish ministers had favorites among the churches they served, and Ommen held pride of place for both Albertus and Christina, but for different reasons. Van Raalte thrived in preaching, teaching seminarians, and church administration, and he plunged into business partnerships. Christina relished the stability of her one remaining sister nearby and a welcoming congregation. Ommen was the epitome for both, and Albertus left with sincere regrets, under pressure from Anthony Brummelkamp to combine their respective seminaries at Arnhem. Van Raalte's life, however, was not all harmony and peace. He was pained by the Kruisgezinden schism, and he learned to his chagrin that royal recognition had a downside. As a churchman, he was driven to despair by conflicts among his colleagues and elders as the nascent Separatist church experienced its crisis of youth.[1]

In 1839 Van Raalte had accepted the Ommen call at the urging of the Provincial Classes of Gelderland and Overijssel after previously declining a call from the Amsterdam congregation. Church leaders believed that Ommen was better situated for an itinerant minister than

[1] Bouwman, *Crisis der jeugd*.

was Genemuiden, in the northwestern corner of Overijssel. Ommen was centrally located twenty miles east of Genemuiden at the nexus of several main roads in an area of Separatist strength.[2]

The Genemuiden-Mastenbroek church regretted losing its beloved dominee. As Geesje Van der Haar-Visscher noted: "We loved him, and his ministry had been richly blest and many people had become converted." Van Raalte offered a mixed self-assessment of his ministry there in a letter to Budding. "In a backward glance on my now finished path, I find many shameful and humiliating memories that bring my own weakness and sorrow into the daylight, but I also find very many earthly interventions from the Lord that accomplished much good that brings me to adoringly confess: 'God is good.'" Most disappointing were suspicions about his orthodoxy and the lack of spiritual awakening in his congregants. But it was not for lack of trying.[3]

A congregation of modest means, the sixty-five families in Ommen and environs provided a sizable house on Bouweind (presently Van Raaltestraat) for their dominee's growing family, thanks to the largess of elder Derk Jans Kleinjan. The young congregation could not own a parsonage until the king granted recognition. Van Raalte's meager salary of ƒ600 ($7,860 today) was, however, enough for his family to have two maids and a gardener. The growing city with twelve hundred residents had a municipal building, a public school, and a dominating 550-member Hervormde Kerk.[4]

Church life

The Van Raaltes found their five years in the Ommen church to be a time of "surprising peace and unforgettably sweet bonds," but the tranquility the dominee sought was broken by the Kruisgezinden

---

[2] Reenders, "Van Raalte als leider," 136-39, 178, citing Dosker, *Van Raalte*, 43 (quote), trans. Dekker; "Geesje Van der Haar-Visscher diary," 5; Warner, *Door het venster*, 122. Van Raalte married the couple in Genemuiden on 2 May 1841.

[3] Van Raalte to Budding, 9 Jan. 1839, in Gunning, *Budding*, 586-92; Reenders, "Van Raalte als leider," 133.

[4] Reenders, "Van Raalte als leider," 136-38; Warner, *Door het venster*, 122-23. Martin Makkinga, a local Ommen historian, in several publications between 1970 and 1990, stated that the Van Raalte family and servants lived on Lagen Oordt Street, immediately behind the seminary building, used for classes and student housing. See Te Velde, "Ministerial Education," 201. This building, long abandoned and in disrepair, was demolished on 15 Dec. 2020 by the owner of an adjacent property (Gerko Warner, email to author, 18 Dec. 2020).

Van Raalte's Ommen parsonage and theological school in the 1840s, what is now Dr. A. C. Van Raaltestraat 24-25, demolished in 2020 (*courtesy Gerko Warner*)

schism. Some thirty-five "divisionists" complained of elders being intrusive and sermons being unbiblical. Van Raalte tolerated the dissidents, believing that they were simply untutored in the faith.[5] He went on to more productive tasks—finding jobs for blacklisted Separatists, gaining royal recognition, establishing a Christian school, and training preachers in the parsonage (ch. 6)

Dominee Van Raalte was installed on March 21, 1839, but he had already been guiding the young Ommen congregation for four years, worshiping at the farmstead of Hendrik Wolterink's widow. As president and clerk, he ran consistory meetings according to the Dort church order and equipped elders to serve for life, whether in specific terms of office or not. He demanded high personal standards—no winebibbers, quarrelers, money grubbers, or skinflints. Elders must rule their own households well. He demanded annual family visitation (*huisbezoek*) and punctiliousness. Weekly consistory meetings began on the hour, with ten-cent fines for latecomers after thirty minutes, though he would bow to the seasonal demands of farmers. He also

[5] Reenders, "Van Raalte als leider," 142-43, 184-85.

called the consistory together on alternate weeknights for an hour of prayer.[6]

The dominee and his elders set high standards of conduct for the congregation. Lukewarm Christians who spent their time visiting fairs, markets, and taverns were not welcome at the Communion table, nor were drunkards, fornicators, and unfaithful Sabbath observers. Teenagers and young adults with bad habits also drew a warning that they would hurt their marriage prospects by such behavior. Those guilty of premarital sexual relations had to make public confession before the congregation. Van Raalte also would not perform "mixed marriages," that is, between Separatists and Hervormden. Couples had to conform beforehand.[7]

Van Raalte also dealt with budget matters and regularized worship services. He supported the lottery system for pew rental, believing that "then there were no differences between the people." Yet women were charged barely half that of men. Opposition to the lottery was so strong that the consistory fell back to the customary auction system, in which seats were rented by bidding every three years, with the choicest seats going to the highest bidders. The consistory assigned seats for the poor, charging a minimal seventy-five Dutch cents for a chair and sixty cents for a pew. Men and women sat separately; mixed seating was unthinkable in Reformed churches until the twentieth century.[8]

Worldly behavior among young people greatly concerned the dominee and his consistory. Youth were censured for Sabbath desecration, cursing, blasphemy, premarital intimacy, frequenting taverns, drunkenness, and "sinful and impious" behavior at the hugely popular Ommen market day. Couples were told to date only within the church. The pursuit of a sanctified life was as challenging at Ommen as elsewhere in Christ's church, both then and even more so now.[9]

Worship services were plagued with talking before the service, which interrupted prayerful preparation. To prevent such "church talk which hinders the scattered seeds of the Word," *voorzangers* were told to lead the congregation in several Psalms. But the biggest problem

---

[6] Minutes, Ommen consistory, 14 Nov. 1836, 28 Apr. 1837, 2 Nov. 1842; Reenders, "Van Raalte als leider," 183-85. Consistory minutes begin in April 1837, when Van Raalte took charge from Genemuiden.

[7] Te Velde, *Brummelkamp*, 153-54.

[8] Minutes, Ommen consistory, 1, 16 Apr. 1842; Reenders, "Van Raalte als leider," 180.

[9] Minutes, Ommen consistory, 15 June, 10 Dec. 1840. 1 Apr. 1841.

was worshipers, including elders and deacons, nodding off during lengthy sermons, despite the sexton (*koster*) opening the windows. The consistory sat in front, elders on one side, deacons on the other. And the youths took note. When several were admonished for visiting a local tavern, they replied that falling asleep in church was equally condemnable. The dominee was upset at the tit-for-tat banter and warned the elders that their "admonishing word" would "lose its strength" if they did not stay awake.[10]

Perhaps the dominee's preaching was the problem, although it was said that he spoke with "emotion and deep seriousness." Only three years into his ministry and overburdened by preaching throughout the province, training ministers in the parsonage, and engaging in business matters, Van Raalte had likely short changed his sermon preparation. He left his pulpit vacant so often that the consistory urged him not to miss two Sundays in a row. This pattern continued throughout his thirty years of active ministry.[11]

Christian education

The education of covenant youth was essential for the dominee. He followed Brummelkamp in instituting catechism classes for all ages, including adults, with three months of study required before public confessions of faith. Texts for weekly classes for children followed Jacobus Borstius's *Korte Historische Vragen uit de Heilige Schriftuur . . . voor de kleine kinderen* (Short historical questions from Holy Scripture for small children), which they had to memorize. Older youth and adults mastered the *Compendium of the Heidelberg Catechism, Kort Begrip der Christelijke Religie* (Short summary of the Christian religion) (1609), and the Bible itself. Van Raalte called his approach "biblical catechization," believing that the Bible itself must be the congregation's *lees en leerboek* (reading and study book) to increase knowledge of the scriptures.[12]

Catechism was essential but insufficient. Children needed a three-legged stool—church, home, and school—to become mature believers. Van Raalte was a firm believer in Christian day schools, and he condemned his Ommen congregation for "faithlessly neglecting" Christian education. Since 1836 the congregation had conducted an unauthorized school under the guise of catechism. Parents paid a

---

[10] Oggel to Brummelkamp, 8 July 1856, published in *De Bazuin*, 5 Sept. 1856 (www.delpher.nl, accessed June 2021).
[11] Minutes, Ommen consistory, 25 Jan. 1843.
[12] Te Velde, *Brummelkamp*, 151.

pittance for tuition—fifty Dutch cents per year, per child, with deficits covered by the congregation. E. van Elburg taught the youth until 1838, when he was found drunk at a local café. Van Raalte then took over, using as his textbook, Herman Faukelius's *Kort begrijp der Christelijke Christian Religie* (Brief understanding of the Heidelberg Catechism, 1810).[13] City authorities threatened to stop the illegal school, but Van Raalte claimed that the school law of 1806 permitted Bible reading under its "social and Christian virtues" rubric. The city denied not only this request but also three more petitions in the next five years, all due to strong opposition by the district school supervisor.[14]

Following the 1843 rejection, the dominee cited the recent shift in governmental policy that opened the door for the legal creation of special diaconal schools, with permission by local authorities. He noted that Amsterdam city leaders in 1841 had granted the Separatist Church a permit for its diaconal school, and the Ommen consistory asked for the same consideration. The request was rejected, ostensibly because the public school would suffer financially if Separatist parents channeled school payments to their own school.[15]

In deep frustration, Van Raalte and five Ommen citizens petitioned again for a Christian school in January 1844, after they learned from Justinus J. L. van der Brugghen (1804-1863), a non-Separatist friend of the Réveil, that he had won the right from the Nijmegen city council to found a parent-run, Christian school—the first in the Netherlands. The petitioners cited the Nijmegen precedent and pledged to continue paying communal taxes for the public school and also to bear the full cost of the Christian school, aided by "certain private persons."[16]

The curriculum would include the three Rs (reading, writing, and arithmetic), as well as geography, national history, and Bible history. They would hire "an able and articulate teacher" and construct "a most suitable building." This petition, too, was rejected. In October 1845, after Van Raalte had moved to Arnhem, his successor in the Ommen pulpit, Jan W. ten Bokkel, and the same five citizens petitioned once

---

[13] Minutes, Ommen consistory, 14, 28 May, 8 Sept. 1838; Kennedy, "Van Raalte and Parochial Schools," 174-76; Te Velde, *Brummelkamp*, 151-52; Warner, *Door het venster*, 127-28; Kennedy, *Concise History*, 277.
[14] Minutes, Ommen consistory, 14, 28 May, 3 Sept. 1838; Sheeres, "Struggle."
[15] Reenders, "Van Raalte," 190; minutes, Ommen consistory, 16 May, 14 June 1843.
[16] The first Christian elementary school, De Klokkenberg (1843-76), added a pedagogical school for teacher training in 1846.

more without success.[17] Ommen would not obtain a Christian school until 1849, after the 1848 Constitution granted more religious and educational freedom.[18]

Van Raalte, Brummelkamp, and Ten Bokkel wrote a pamphlet at the behest of the Classis of Gelderland, *Nog is er hulpe! Een woord aan al het godvreezend volk* (There is still help! A word to all God-fearing people) (1844). It set forth their demands for Christian schools and voiced their indignation at the government's refusal to grant permits. Since government schools no longer allowed the "main elements of Christ's teachings," the authors contended, parents had a right to establish private schools that honored "God's Word and the laws of the land." Breaking free of public education was more urgent than ecclesiastical separation because the faith of the children was at stake. Separatist leaders founded Christian schools in obedience to the Church Order of Dort, which required every congregation to provide "good Schoolmasters" to teach not only the three Rs but also "the catechism and the first principles of religion." This was in obedience to the biblical mandate to raise their children in the fear and understanding of the Lord. Dutch authorities routinely suppressed these Christian schools on the grounds that education was the prerogative of the state, not the church.[19]

Many Christian school teachers immigrated to America after being thwarted by the government and expelled from the profession. Egbert Dunnewind and Alexander Hartgerink joined the Holland colony in 1847, and Douwe Van der Werp followed in 1864, but he came in the elevated position of preacher.[20]

---

[17] Schram, "Raalte," *Biografisch Lexicon*, 1:271; Albertus C. Van Raalte et al., petition to Ommen City Council, 16 Jan. 1844, 21 Oct. 1845, Gemeentearchief Ommen, VRI, trans. Nella Kennedy; "Justinus van der Brugghen," wikipedia.org/wiki/Justinus_van_der_Brugghen, accessed 1 Dec. 2021. I am indebted to Earl Wm. Kennedy for the Van der Brugghen citation.

[18] Reenders, "Van Raalte als leider," 190; Report of Minister of Internal Affairs to King, 21 July 1838; Report of Minister of Justice to Minister of Religion, 12 Oct. 1837, both in *Archiefstukken*, 4:282-84, 288-89.

[19] Wesseling, *Afscheiding van 1834, Classis Zwolle*, 186-88; Brummelkamp and Van Raalte, "Landverhuizing," 35, 50; Reenders, "Van Raalte als leider," 189, trans. Dekker, citing Brummelkamp et al., "Nog is er hulpe," 13-17. Acts, Classis of Gelderland, 3 July 1844, noting Brummelkamp's letter to Van Raalte, Aug. 1844, cited in Te Velde, *Brummelkamp*, 390. See also, Petition, Van Raalte et al., to Ommen City Council, 16 Jan. 1844, requesting permission for a Christian school, and the opposing letter of district school supervisor, 21 Jan. 1844.

[20] Reenders, "Van Raalte als leider," 190; Wesseling, *Afscheiding van 1834, Classis Zwolle*, 226-28, 240-41; Sheeres, *Son of Secession*; Kennedy, "Van Raalte and Parochial Schools," 173-76.

Legal recognition for Ommen Church

Van Raalte initially applauded Scholte's requesting and obtaining royal recognition for his Utrecht church as "good tidings from a far-away land" and a mark of "God's undeserved... goodness." On Van Raalte's recommendation, the Classis of Ommen and his congregations at Den Ham, Genemuiden, Heemse, Hellendoorn, Ommen, and Steenwijk all applied for legal recognition in March 1839, but the king made the process more arduous by requiring churches to have a building and to care for their poor. This was reasonable but beyond the reach of small churches. Benevolence came first. The Genemuiden and Ommen congregations promised to take care of their poor "as His Majesty's clearly stated," and the diaconate stepped up to the task. They designated one offering in the morning service for the poor, and the monies were distributed immediately afterward. But able-bodied poor could expect no help. Operating expenses were met by annual pew rentals, which had been standard congregational practice for many centuries.[21]

Van Raalte donated ƒ350 ($4,875 today) to buy a plot of land from member Harm Timmerman for an edifice on the Bouwstraat, and he added ƒ2,200 ($28,800 today) for the building. The monies likely were part of Christina's inheritance. The hostile mayor, with the backing of the provincial governor, made the application process for the building harrowing because the pastor was a proven troublemaker. When the building was nearing completion, the mayor deemed it a "criminal deed" and threatened fines if it was used for worship before receiving permission from the king. Despite several urgent letters from the consistory, written in Van Raalte's hand, fall stretched into winter without a response from the king. Meanwhile, while Ommen waited, the Seceder churches in the towns of Groningen and Amsterdam received recognition. Van Raalte complained to the governor about the double standard, and he urged the king to ask local officials to provide a temporary permit to end the "painful" situation.[22]

When relief did not come, the frustrated congregation decided to break the law and worship in the new edifice anyway, which they

---

[21] Van Raalte to Scholte, 7, 24 May 1839, in Smits, *Afscheiding van 1834*, 3:173-76; minutes, Ommen consistory, 4, 17 Apr., 26 July, 28 Aug., 31 Oct. 1839, 29 Jan. 1840; Reenders, "Van Raalte als leider," 112-13, 120, 145-46, 175-78, 180-81; Wesseling, *Afscheiding van 1834, Classis Zwolle*, 204-6.

[22] Petition, Ommen Separated Church to King, 31 Oct., 6 Dec. 1839; Van Raalte to Governor of Overijssel, 13 Jan. 1840, trans. Nella Kennedy.

Oude Gereformeerde Kerk, Ommen, 1840. The congregation, with 633 souls by 1856, was the largest in the province of Overijssel. (*Wesseling*, Afscheiding, Classis Zwolle)

did in January 1840. The troublesome mayor came to the service and demanded that Van Raalte send the 150 worshipers home. The pastor called the mayor's bluff and continued the service, all without incurring any new fines or police action. The mayor was stymied by a lenient governor who ordered him not to close the church without consulting him first. The status quo continued for another year. Then, in January 1841, King Willem II issued a decree that granted recognition to all Separated churches, provided they did not use the historic name "Gereformeerde," and that they operated "without burdening the state." They had to cover expenses for buildings, salaries, and relief for the poor.[23]

Nearly fifty members of the congregation signed a petition to the king, promising to meet the stipulations of self-funding. Receiving no response, they sent another petition signed by more than fifty members, plus more than one hundred townspeople. The governor wrote the Ommen congregation on April 15 that he had no objection to their receiving royal recognition. The king finally granted the coveted recognition on April 28, 1841, thus ending a two-year quest that was frustrating in the extreme. One can imagine the joy when

---

[23] Statement of Ommen mayor Hendrik Jansen Smit, 5 Feb. 1841, trans. Nella Kennedy; Wesseling, *Afscheiding van 1834, Classis Zwolle*, 204-6.

Van Raalte read the king's decree from the pulpit, although decorum dictated no outward exclamations, except perhaps a few amens. Van Raalte's reputation grew with this act. Legal status freed him from the fear of being harassed or fined. He could now preach openly with a free conscience and live the "honorable life" befitting a privileged son of the cloth. Best of all, he could seek the communion of the saints under the Lordship of Christ, instead of contending with hostile government officials.[24]

Van Raalte preached freely in Ommen during the hiatus before recognition, but when he led worship in his former congregations at Genemuiden and Vriezenveen, both with new buildings and also awaiting recognition, he was heavily fined, up to half his annual salary, that is, ƒ255 ($3,325 today), which a sympathetic judge in Zwolle reduced to "only" ƒ55 ($720 today), still a heavy burden. Decades later, Van Raalte dubbed the Vriezenveen congregation, which he had organized in December 1838, his "persecution house" (*verdrukkingshuis*).[25]

Downside of recognition

What Van Raalte did not anticipate was the negative fallout from the disjointed recognition process. Congregations were not on the same page, and the result was inequality and fragmentation. In a very short time, Van Raalte had second thoughts. The problem was that churches that refused to ask for recognition continued to be fined and harassed, most notably the Genemuiden and Vriezenveen churches in Overijssel and the Baambrugge church in Noord-Holland. This upset the dominee to the point that he questioned his decision to ask for recognition at Ommen. In his 1846 "Letter to the Faithful in the United States of America," he returned to the subject. By asking for royal recognition, Van Raalte vowed that he had not bowed to the high-handedness of the king.[26] Looking back from America sixteen years later, in 1862, his regret was even more intense. To sell one's soul for peace had been a mistake, he then declared. Giving up the honorable

---

[24] Petition of Ommen church to king, 11 Feb. 1841; Van Raalte and Carel de Moen to king, 27 Mar. 1841; governor's letter to Ommen church, 15 Apr. 1841; governor's recognition letter, 28 Apr. 1839, trans. Nella Kennedy; *Overijsselsche Courant*, 9 July 1841 (www.delpher.nl, accessed, June 2021). Governor's letters are in Nationaal Archief, The Hague.

[25] Reenders, "Van Raalte als leider," 175-78 (quotes), trans. Dekker; *De Bazuin*, 18 Dec. 1868 (quote) (www.delpher.nl, accessed June 2021), trans. Earl Wm. Kennedy.

[26] Brummelkamp and Van Raalte, *Landverhuizing*, "Appeal to the Faithful in the United States of North America, May 25, 1846," 31, in English translation in Lucas, *Dutch Immigrant Memoirs*, 1:15.

title of "Gereformeerd" for rights was a bad bargain. He should have sent the Ommen recognition document back to the king. Better to openly oppose the government than silently to accept discrimination.[27]

Van Raalte and Scholte's deposition by Synod Amsterdam 1840

Van Raalte was one of only twenty-seven pastors and elders who attended Synod Amsterdam 1840, which was boycotted by all Scholte-leaning congregations. The Christian Separated Church was being torn apart by issues of church polity and internecine conflict. Scholte had set the agenda by stating beforehand that he would not accept the Dort church order. This led the rump assembly to defrock their only leader, which marked a turning point in Scholte's ministry and in the Separated church as a whole. Hence, the synod became known as the *"eerste Amsterdamsche twist"* (first Amsterdam dispute).[28]

The break with Scholte began in a contest with Van Velzen for the Amsterdam pulpit, the flagship church in the denomination, which Scholte had organized in 1835 and served whenever he could be away from his home churches in Utrecht and Noord-Brabant. The Amsterdam pulpit for three years was filled, variously, by Scholte, Van Velzen, Van Raalte, and Brummelkamp, among others. In 1837 Scholte, Van Velzen, and Van Raalte had all declined calls from the congregation, but in 1838 Van Velzen accepted their call, and the members rejoiced in finally securing a regular pastor.[29] But Van Velzen was reluctant to leave the Friesland congregations he had fathered. He and the Amsterdam congregation, after a year of back and forth, finally agreed to a shared ministry between Amsterdam and Leeuwarden. In mid-1839, Van Velzen finally moved his family to Amsterdam, and Hendrik de Cock installed him. He was home again; the Amsterdam church literally occupied his boyhood home.[30]

Scholte, however, instead of fostering peace, picked a fight, known as the *tweede Amsterdamsche twist* (second Amsterdam dispute).

---

[27] Van Raalte to Simon van Velzen Jr., 1862, in *Kompleete uitgave* (1884), 541-44.
[28] *Verslag van de Vergadering van Opzieners*, published in *Handelingen en verslagen*, 177-266.
[29] Engelsma, *Watchman on the Walls*, 122-23; Wormser, *Karakter en Genade*, 40-42, trans. Buursma, JAH. It should be noted that Johan A. Wormser Jr. was a son of elder Johan A. Wormser. Scholte received 27 out of 108 votes in the first casting; he had the most votes but was far from a majority.
[30] Wormser, *Karakter en Genade*, 42-44; Engelsma, *Watchman on the Walls*, 123-24; Soepenberg, *Afscheiding in Amsterdam*, 296-328, for the 1840 synod. Owner Judith van IJsseldijk-Zeelt lent the house to the congregation (Wormser, *Karakter en Genade*, 5; Engelsma, *Watchman on the Walls*, 9-10).

He accused Van Velzen of teaching "a conglomeration of theoretical truths without the living Christ, without a regenerating Spirit, and without the living and active faith." Scholte's objections were with the doctrines of election and predestination. He charged Van Velzen with preaching "how a sinner *cannot* be saved," rather than proclaiming the so-called "well-meant offer of the Gospel," that is, that God sincerely desires that all who hear may respond and be saved. This Van Velzen considered "free grace" universalism. In his preaching, Van Velzen believed that God gives His Spirit to the elect only, not the reprobate. They remained dead in their sins.[31]

The dispute involved historic differences regarding the doctrine of election and human responsibility that had stirred the Reformed churches since the Synod of Dort. Scholte, Brummelkamp, and Van Raalte agreed on the need for God's grace but not on the fallenness of humankind in heart, mind, and will. Brummelkamp and Van Raalte promoted the "well-meant offer of salvation," that preachers must declare "to all people in general the need of faith for all creatures," so they can respond and be saved. To this, Van Velzen thundered in the synodical sermon: "Man *can do nothing*, yea, *may not* do anything" to attain salvation, "because this would be one's own work, and that such work is condemned before God."[32] Only the Holy Spirit's quickening can enable a hearer to respond to the Gospel.

To carry the fight to Van Velzen, Scholte traveled to Amsterdam and appeared at a consistory meeting from which, to his chagrin, his Nemesis was absent, having returned to Friesland to preach in his former churches. Scholte, nonetheless, read his explosive letter aloud. When asked about the source of the charges, Scholte said he had personally heard Van Velzen preach in November 1838 and found

---

[31] For an extensive discussion of this theological issue from the predestination side, see Herman Hoeksema, *The Clark-Van Til Controversy*, ed. John W. Robbins (The Trinity Foundation, 1995), 33-49. For Van Velzen, the word "offer" was problematic. If it meant that "God promised to bestow grace and salvation upon all who come under the preaching of the gospel," then "absolutely not!" But if it meant eternal life for all who hear the gospel and "come to Him and believe," then "absolutely yes" (Engelsma, *Watchman on the Walls*, 178-80, quoting Van Velzen article in *De Bazuin*, 21 May 1858). Van Velzen had the Canons of Dort and John Calvin on his side. Calvin wrote in his *Institutes of the Christian Religion*, book 2, v. 17: "There is no will or running by which we can prepare the way for our salvation; it is wholly of the Divine Mercy."

[32] Van Raalte, handwritten essay on the doctrine of the covenant and grace (undated), trans. Nella Kennedy. Oostendorp, *Scholte*, 123; Wormser, *Karakter en Genade*, 99; Brinks, "Afscheiding," 26; Engelsma, *Watchman on the Walls*, 132.

many objectionable points, and he had so informed his Utrecht consistory. Scholte had to admit that he had failed to follow Matthew 18:15, KJV: "If thy brother shall trespass against thee, go and tell him his fault between thee and him alone." When Van Velzen learned of Scholte's charges, he cried "Slander!"[33] Brummelkamp, hoping to prevent an open church split, had Scholte come to Amsterdam to prove his charges against Van Velzen before an assembly of elders and pastors. Scholte failed to convince the body and refused to retract the charges, so Synod Amsterdam 1840 had the impossible task of dealing with the issue and restoring a semblance of peace.[34]

Van Raalte was praying for reconciliation between the two when he went to Synod, but even though Scholte had come to the city, he refused to attend the meetings. With Brummelkamp in the chair, the delegates first made the major decision of adopting the historic Dort church order over Scholte's new Utrecht church order. After a lengthy discussion, and without discussing Van Velzen's theology, the delegates demanded that Scholte retract his slander of the brother and unconditionally accept the Dort church order. Despite the urgings of De Cock, his dear friend since 1834, Scholte refused to comply, and synod suspended him from the ministry.[35]

The four brothers-in-law—Van Raalte, Van Velzen, Brummelkamp, and De Moen—plus De Cock were the main voting bloc that deposed Scholte. Van Velzen was a thoroughly Dort man, and Van Raalte and De Moen could live with Scholte's church order but not his individualistic and independent spirit, which they believed harmed the church and undermined the communion of the saints. For Van Raalte, Dort rules were of secondary importance. He would concede nonessentials, even church orders, for the sake of church unity and peace. Brummelkamp believed that removing the "terrible, indecisive soul" (Scholte) would bring peace to the young church. In the end, it was Scholte's rather imperialist personality that caused the break.[36] The deposition shocked Scholte's congregation and indeed the whole denomination. The Christian Separated Church lost one of its "most capable leaders," as one biographer wrote. Actually, the denomination

---

[33] Oostendorp, *Scholte*, 118-28, quote 122; Wormser, *Karakter en Genade*, 44-45.
[34] Engelsma, *Watchman on the Walls*, 131-33; Wormser, *Karakter en Genade*, 46-48.
[35] *Handelingen en verslagen*, 188.
[36] Brummelkamp's Report of Synod Amsterdam, 6-7 Mar 1840, trans. Ten Hoor; Te Velde, *Brummelkamp*, 126, 131, 136; Dosker, *Van Raalte*, 51 (quote); Engelsma, *Watchman on the Walls*, 108-10, 121-22.

lost its top leader, brightest mind, and chief moving force, but it gained a semblance of peace.[37]

Van Velzen also castigated Van Raalte's situational approach to wearing clerical garb and his lukewarm defense of the Dort documents at the 1837 and 1840 synods. At Synod Groningen 1846, which Van Raalte did not attend because he was preparing to emigrate, Van Velzen derided his brother-in-law for refusing to wear the "regular clothing of ministers." He did not deign to mention Van Raalte by name but only as *"that minister* [italics mine] . . . who departed for North America." Brummelkamp derided Scholte as the "fifth wheel on the wagon." Van Velzen's long-standing bond with Van Raalte and Brummelkamp was badly fractured for a time. Since Van Velzen's first wife, Johanna de Moen, was deceased, this lessened the anguish for the remaining sisters, Christina Van Raalte and Maria Brummelkamp. The rift between Brummelkamp and Van Velzen was healed when they were appointed as professors at the theological school in Kampen in 1854. Van Raalte made his peace with Van Velzen in person when he returned to the Netherlands in 1866 and lectured at Kampen (ch. 14).[38]

In the Acts of Synod 1840, Van Raalte added a "Clarification" of his views on the church order. Appealing to Article 32 of the Belgic Confession, the so-called "Calvinistic principle of government," Van Raalte posited that no church order stood on par with Holy Scripture ("they cannot bind where God does not bind"), but rules are necessary for good governance. "Agreements among brothers should be respected, and nobody is allowed to depart from them, except for the compelling reason of saving the core of our religion." In short, members must submit to the Dort church order for the sake of unity, but there must be room for conscientious objection. Whereas Van Raalte placed himself under Dort, Brummelkamp and De Moen were more open minded and reserved the right of conscience. When Brummelkamp chaired the provincial assembly in 1842 that examined and ordained De Moen, he pointedly did not ask him to sign the Dort church order. "We live in freedom and joy," his wife Maria wrote her sister Christina. Although Van Raalte would not "deify" Dort and "make it into a shibboleth of orthodoxy," he honored synodical decisions based on Dort more

---

[37] Oostendorp, *Scholte*, 126 (quote); Cornelius Van der Meulen to Brothers in Christ, 11 Dec. 1840, in Van der Meulen, *Ter Nagedachtenis*, 47-49, trans. Ten Hoor. VRI.

[38] Dosker, *Van Raalte*, 55, quoting 1840 synod minutes; Engelsma, *Watchman on the Walls*, 145 (quote).

so than the other two. On this issue, he actually stood closer to Van Velzen, his other brother-in-law.[39]

Before adjourning, Synod Amsterdam commissioned Van Raalte, Brummelkamp, and Van Velzen to publish a new edition of the *Ecclesiastical Manual*, the standard guide for pastors and consistories. The 1841 manual guided elders and congregations in proper church polity, often sorely lacking, as evident in the chaotic assemblies.[40]

Afterward, Van Raalte traveled to Scholte in Utrecht to attempt a reconciliation. Scholte had strongly influenced him since Leiden days, even to accepting Scholte's church order. Unity trumped polity. "I believe this [visit] has benefited me," he wrote his wife, "and in this way our discussion served to revive brotherly love." But it actually led to a parting of the ways. He could not change Scholte's mind about the church order or reconciling with Van Velzen. Scholte's free church independentism was more than he could tolerate. After 1840 Van Raalte accepted the Dort church order and the synodical examinations of candidates, even with conservative examiners like Frederik A. Kok, a concession Brummelkamp would not make.[41]

Others saw two sides in the dispute. Gezelle Meerburg's congregations in Noord-Brabant followed Scholte's Utrecht church order. Van der Meulen, who had studied for the ministry under Scholte, implored his teacher to turn back. "Your beginning was good and just . . . but you went too far." But Van der Meulen told Brummelkamp that, in his view, Van Velzen "is definitely guilty as well" for not giving Scholte an opportunity to confront him at synod. "His [Van Velzen's] character is tolerated and the other [Scholte's] is kindled [like a fire]." But Brummelkamp, who presided at synod, noted that Scholte had rejected an invitation prior to synod to defend himself before a commission of clerics. After Scholte's deposition, the churches in Utrecht, Zuid-Holland, and Lower Gelderland formed one group, but they continued to recognize him as a brother, if not a leader.[42]

[39] Van Raalte, "Clarification," in *Handelingen en verslagen*, 25-27; Reenders, "Van Raalte," 290 (quote), trans. Dekker; Wormser, *In twee werelddeelen*, 92-94. Engelsma, *Watchman on the Walls*, states that Brummelkamp and Van Raalte were upset with the decision, believing that synod had acted "out of a slavish sense of traditionalism" (139).

[40] Te Velde, *Brummelkamp*, 78-79, 84; Reenders, "Van Raalte," 290n50.

[41] Albertus to Christina, 20 July 1838, in Sweetman, *From Heart to Heart*, 28-29; Reenders, "Van Raalte," 288-95.

[42] Van der Meulen to Scholte, 9 Mar. 1841; Van der Meulen to Brummelkamp, 22 Feb. 1841, in Smits, *Afscheiding van 1834*, 5:207-10, trans. Nella Kennedy; Rullmann, *Gezelle Meerburg*, 198-99; Engelsma, *Watchman on the Walls*, 146.

Synod Amsterdam 1843—the *"rovers"* (robbers) synod

When Synod 1843 met in Amsterdam, Van Raalte was still frustrated by controversies over all the major issues—lay preachers, elders' terms of office, classical examinations of candidates, acceptance of ordained preachers from other assemblies, and more. He again tried to mediate between "divisionists" and "unionist." Scholte came in person, despite his deposition, and the forty-three delegates worshiped together. But reconciliation did not follow. After two days of fruitless debate, Van Raalte offered a resolution asking everyone to accept Dort's church order as "binding." He and Van Velzen voted yes, but Scholte and Brummelkamp said no. Van Raalte then proposed adjourning in order to consult the constituent assemblies, but that motion failed. At this point, Brummelkamp and half the delegates walked out, but not before Van Raalte read Ezekiel 34, which warns against unfaithful shepherds. Consistency was a hobgoblin for Van Raalte. His centrist views required flexibility and compromise.[43]

The remaining delegates elected Van Velzen as president and continued the business of synod as a rump body, which the Brummelkamp contingent declared to be illegal, hence the "robbers" allegation. From this point, the Christian Separated Church was split between the Van Velzen and Brummelkamp factions for a decade before making peace (at Synod Amsterdam 1854). Each congregation had decided for itself what rules to follow. In Overijssel, for example, the congregation at Dalfsen had accepted the Groningen church order, Ommen the Utrecht church order, and Steenwijk had written its own rules.

Regarding Scholte, Brummelkamp befriended him after he was deposed, but Van Raalte did not. Brummelkamp opened his Arnhem pulpit to Scholte in 1844 and presided in 1845 at Scholte's second marriage to Maria (Mareah) Kranz. Scholte's growing embrace of premillennialism, however, barred further reconciliation. In 1838 Scholte had begun corresponding with John N. Darby, a major figure in the Plymouth Brethren movement in England. Scholte promulgated Darby's teachings in his periodical, *De Reformatie*, and translated into the Dutch language Darby's 1842 book on the millennial reign of Christ in Jerusalem. Scholte also adopted Darby's anticlerical view that ordination was a sin against the Holy Spirit since the Spirit could work through any believer. Scholte's biographer, Lubbertus Oostendorp,

---

[43] Acts of Synod Amsterdam 1843, in *Handelingen en verslagen*, 267-380; Bouwman, *Crisis der jeugd*.

says Darby "pretty well indoctrinated his Dutch admirer." Scholte faded into insignificance in the Netherlands after his immigration to America in 1846, where he never rejoined a Reformed denomination. Van Raalte's fallout with Scholte presaged later discord and rivalry in America.[44]

"Center" Overijssels-Gelders party, "right" Gronings-Drents party, and "left" Utrechts party

The salience of the Church Order of Dort was the crux of the brothers' quarrels (*broedertwisten*) at Synods 1837, 1840, and 1843. Three main blocs emerged. The Gronings-Drents party made this historic document absolutely authoritative, even of eternal value, but the independent-minded Scholte group could jettison it entirely. The Overijssels-Gelders party stood in the middle; they could take or leave the Dort Order, according to circumstances. Practice was more important than procedure. Related questions revolved around closed or "close" communion, the use of hymns in worship, regard for "feast days," terms of office bearers, preaching the Lord's Days of the catechism, and similar matters. The Gronings brothers accused the Gelders brothers of polluting the Lord's Table, ignoring the catechism, allowing "perennial elders," and other Dortian laxities.[45]

The centrist Brummelkamp-Van Raalte party was concentrated in Gelderland and Overijssel, with lesser contingents in the Randstad (Noord- and Zuid-Holland and Utrecht), and Zeeland. Carel de Moen, Helenius de Cock, Seine Bolks, and Cornelius Van der Meulen were other clerics in the Overijssels-Gelders party. Van Raalte was open minded and would accept revisions to Dort if it brought harmony and unity. Like the Apostle Paul, on church-order matters he would be "all things to all men." He was a man of compromise, who would not raise church rules to the level of godly principles.[46]

The orthodox Gronings-Drents party, led by Van Velzen and Tamme F. de Haan, was concentrated in the provinces of Drenthe, Groningen, and Friesland; with related groups, led by Budding, in Zuid-Holland, Zeeland, and Amsterdam; and many others from Graafschap

---

[44] Oostendorp, *Scholte*, 128-31; Heideman, *Scholte*, 186-87; Engelsma, *Watchman on the Walls*, 141-42; Wormser, *Karakter en Genade*, 98-117; Swierenga, "Van Raalte and Scholte."

[45] Te Velde, "Dutch Background," 90-91. Closed communion was limited to confessing members of a particular congregation; close communion limits communion to other churches in the same denomination.

[46] Reenders, "Van Raalte," 291-92, 297-98.

Wolter Alberts Kok (1805-1891), leading Gronings-Drents preacher and teacher

Bentheim, led by Jan Barend Sundag, who had studied for the ministry with Scholte.[47] The pietist Drenthe party (Drents *richting*), led by Wolter Alberts Kok, who following the Old Writers stressed the doctrines of election and regeneration, at the expense of assurance of salvation.

Scholte's Utrecht congregations, as an independent party with strong Réveil roots, weak ties to Dortian polity, and a stress on personal faith, Kingdom building, and biblical eschatology, were a third strand. This group lost their leader when Synod 1840 expelled Scholte for "ecclesiastical anarchy"—to use Van Raalte's words. Scholte also espoused a premillennial, nonconfessional Christianity—"no creed but the Bible." Most of Scholte's followers joined the Overijssels-Gelders party of Brummelkamp, Van Raalte, and De Moen.[48]

Issues of dispute

The same issues of dogma, polity, mentality, and culture resurfaced in Michigan and bedeviled Van Raalte for the remainder of his life. The doctrinal differences centered on the nature of the church and the well-meant offer of the Gospel. The first generation of Separatists were conflicted between seeking truth or unity, orthodoxy or catholicity. The dominant Gronings-Drents party of Van Velzen and De Haan was untouched by the international Réveil movement; they valued orthodoxy above unity. They closed their pulpits and the Lord's Table to the Overijssels-Gelders party, which was sympathetic to the

---

[47] Beets, *De Chr. Geref. Kerk*, 34-36, 45-48. The factions were also called Van Velzianen and Brummelkampianen. Cf. Kromminga, *Christian Reformed Church*, 30-31.

[48] Oostendorp, *Scholte*, 134-44; Heideman, *Scholte*, 185-203; Reenders, "Van Raalte," 283; Kennedy, *Commentary*, 1:644.

Réveil and valued unity, even at the risk of relativism. Their dominees "were more inclined to practice patience with aberrations and to cooperate freely with other-minded people."[49] Brummelkamp in 1845 participated in the first Réveil meetings with "Christian Friends," and Van Raalte in January 1846 sent a letter to the second Réveil meeting of the same "Friends," expressing unity with them. No wonder the Gronings-Drents party accused the pair of not having "really seceded" and of being not "solidly Reformed."[50]

Doctrinally, Gelders dominees preached revival, whereas Gronings dominees preached predestination, human depravity, and the mystery of saving faith. Gronings followers partook of the Lord's Supper when they *felt* worthy not because they *were* worthy in Christ. Sin was preached to the neglect of grace, and although most worshiped faithfully, they were never fully assured of salvation.[51]

The rival parties also differed in temperament and spirit. The Overijssels-Gelders party was culturally more modern; they welcomed change over tradition, as for example, in rejecting clerical garb. They did not glory in secession but rather longed to return to the Hervormde Kerk in the belief that it could be restored to its old status. They were inclusive and nondoctrinaire, with Réveil leanings, hence willing to compromise on Dortian theological and church order issues. They stood solid on a doctrine of predestination, but waffled on the doctrine of election.[52] The Gronings-Drents faction, in contrast, condemned the Hervormde Kerk as a false church and defended the doctrine, liturgy, and polity of Dort as biblically grounded. They were traditional Calvinists who stressed the need for Christian schools and catechetical instruction of the youth, given the "Godless influence" in the public schools. The Gronings-Drents men had steel in their bones, and the Overijssels-Gelders men had pewter, a malleable metal.

Overijssel, the province geographically in the middle, was hurt the most by the division. It was bisected by a diagonal line between southeastern and northwestern halves. The southeastern party drew ministers tutored by Van Raalte and Brummelkamp at Ommen and Arnhem, namely, lay pastor Hendrik Wormser at Hellendoorn and Rev. Carel de Moen at Den Ham. A few congregations in Zeeland and

---

[49] Te Velde, "Dutch Background," 87-98 (quotes, 88); Vree, "Dominating Theology," 43.
[50] Te Velde, "Dutch Background," 87 (quote); Te Velde, *Brummelkamp*, 181-92, 226-45; Kluit, *Het protestantse réveil*, 454.
[51] Te Velde, "Dutch Background," 88-89.
[52] *De Afgescheidenen van 1834 en hun nageslacht*, 25.

elsewhere had close contact with the Gelderse churches. Van Raalte's influence stretched to Graafschap Bentheim across the German border and to southeastern Drenthe, called the Zuidenveld.[53] Churches in the northwestern half of Drenthe called parsonage-trained ministers, taught by De Cock and Tamme de Haan. By late 1835, the Separatist movement counted twenty thousand souls in eighty congregations.[54]

Ministerial training and clerical garb remained flash points between the blocs. Ultimately, differences were determined largely by whether they were impacted by the Old Writers. Gronings-Drents preachers De Haan in Groningen and brothers Wolter and Frederik Kok in Drenthe read the Old Writers, whereas Van Velzen in Friesland and Noord-Holland harkened back to the Synod of Dort. Van Raalte and Brummelkamp downplayed the Old Writers, and Scholte was not impacted at all. The distinction between the two parties was the best predictor of affiliation in America, although kinship relations, social dependency, and rate of assimilation must also be considered. Immigrant followers of the Overijssel-Gelders party primarily joined the Reformed Church, and followers of the Gronings-Drents party joined the Christian Reformed Church.[55]

Throughout the years of turmoil in the infant Christian Separated Church, Van Raalte stood as the "man in the middle," the *homo ecumenicus* (ecumenical man), as Hommo Reenders characterized him, a man who sought the "middle road between the liberty of the children of God, on the one hand, and the unity and order in the church, on the other hand." He was not a separatist by temperament or at heart. His own secession was forced on him by the rejection of his

---

[53] Prakke, *Drenthe in Michigan*, 19-23; Beuker, "'The Area beyond'"; Eglington, *Bavinck*, 8-12.

[54] Engelsma, *Watchman on the Walls*, 90, for the statistic. Reenders, "Van Raalte," 291-92, makes the case for this division in Overijssel. Van Raalte's student Wormser served as pastor at Hellendoorn from 1838 for almost forty years. When most of the congregation emigrated to Michigan under Rev. Seine Bolks, Wormser stayed behind because of his wife's ill health (Roelofs, "Hendrik Wormser," 57-65; Roelofs, "Carel Godefroi de Moen, 142-51).

[55] Te Velde, "Dutch Background," 92-98; Swierenga, "True Brothers," 72-73. For an earlier, less robust analysis, see Swierenga, "Local-Cosmopolitan Theory." Te Velde, "Dutch Background," 99n10, found that, of Separatist clerics in the Reformed Church, nine were trained by the Gelderse party of Brummelkamp and Van Raalte, five by Scholte, four by De Haan at Groningen, and only one by the Koks at Hoogeveen. In contrast, the CRC attracted six Separatist pastors from Hoogeveen, five from Groningen, four from Bentheim in Germany, and *none* from either Overijssel, Gelderland, or Utrecht, based on Te Velde, *Brummelkamp*, 290-92, 370-72.

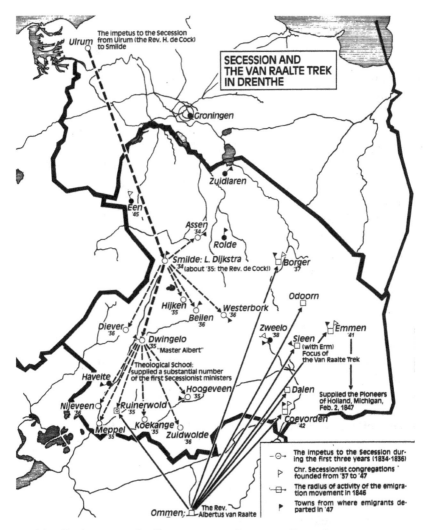

Van Raalte area of influence in southeastern Drenthe province, in villages of Borger, Odoorn, Sleen, Emmen, Dalen, and Coevorden (*Pereboom et al., Afscheiding van 1834*)

professors and church authorities. In his eyes, the Secession of 1834 "was not 'a good thing' but at best a necessary evil." Yet, he remained loyal to the Separated Church through thick and thin, always holding to the ideal of unity, even though it remained beyond his grasp.[56]

---

[56] Reenders, "Van Raalte," 288-89 (quote), 297-98 (quote); Kennedy, *Commentary*, 1:153 (quote), citing Te Velde, *Brummelkamp*, 236.

Van Raalte called for brotherly love, not brothers' quarrels. When the dispute over clerical garb broke out, he followed the wishes of his congregation, despite being personally opposed. When schism seemed inevitable at Synod Utrecht 1837 over church order matters, he fearfully wrestled "against the seeds of dissension" to save the day. He wrote his wife: "To our human eyes, it is dark, yes, very dark!" But he trusted that the Lord would not forsake his church.[57] He even traveled to Amsterdam after Scholte's deposition in hopes of healing his rift with Van Velzen. Years later, Van Raalte recalled that the bickering was "harder to bear than the persecution; it deprived me of all enjoyment of life and made me afraid of life."[58]

One of Van Raalte's frequent sermon texts was I John 4:7a (KJV): "Beloved, let us love one another, for love is of God." The dissensions that wracked Separatists saddened him. He hoped to restrain the "ignorant dissension and narrow sectarian spirit" that corrupted "otherwise splendid people." His irenic spirit was shaped by the Kruisgezinden schism of 1838 that rent his twenty-one Overijssel congregations. He lamented the dispute between Scholte and Van Velzen that led to Scholte's deposition, which deprived the Christian Separated Church of its seminal leader.[59] Despite his forbearing spirit, Van Raalte lived his entire life with controversy, both religious and secular, sometimes due to his own actions and sometimes caused by narrow-minded critics.

"Work relieves poverty": Ommen and Lemele factories

In Ommen, Van Raalte truly became a social entrepreneur, mixing ministry and business on a larger scale than in Genemuiden. His model was Ottho Heldring's renowned social experiment in Nijverdal, a town in the Twente district of Overijssel, where the nation's textile industry was centered. Heldring developed a Christian community to employ poor adults in Nijverdal's textile factories. This was the social-action wing of the Réveil at its best. Van Raalte certainly knew the Nijverdal social program at first hand, and he developed his own version in Ommen for unemployed Separatists, who were cut off from diaconal funds by the Hervormde church.[60]

---

[57] Reenders, "Van Raalte," 277-98.
[58] Hyma, *Van Raalte*, 38-39.
[59] Reenders, "Van Raalte," 297 (quote); Van Raalte to Scholte, 10 Dec. 1837, in Smits, *Afscheiding van 1834*, 3:168, trans. Dekker.
[60] O. W. Dubois, "Ottho Gerhard Heldring," *Biographisch Woordenboek Gelderland* (Verloren, 2002); Makkinga, "Bricks for Ommen Poor"; Gunning, *Budding*, 43.

Work was the answer for robust men blacklisted by employers. Any kind of manual labor was preferable to idleness. In Van Raalte's words, "work relieves poverty" and builds "moral character." The Lord Himself in the Ten Commandments enjoined his people to work: "Six days shalt thou labor and do all thy work" (Ex. 20:9, KJV), and the Apostle Paul added: "If any would not work, neither should he eat" (II Thess. 3:10, KJV). In short, Van Raalte believed that it was a diaconal duty to provide work for the poor, so they could earn their bread.[61]

In April 1840, Van Raalte ventured into manufacturing businesses for the same purpose as the Scheveningen fishing boats, to employ Separatists. But this time, profit took priority, with philanthropy as a side benefit. He recruited Carel de Moen and Cornelis Dros, a Leiden soap manufacturer, to partner with him in a business to manufacture earthenware in Lemele (or Lemelerveld), a village three miles south of Ommen rich in clay deposits. Dros was related to Brummelkamp's wife, Maria Wilhelmina de Moen, through her first husband, Casper Tieleman, who operated a soap factory in Leiden that he made available on Sunday for Separatist services.[62] De Moen moved to Ommen to manage operations, although he lacked business-management skills.

De Moen & Co. began operations in March 1841 with thirty employees—men, women, and children—making earthenware, shingles, and tiles—all clay products that could be "made with a profit." The operations included two brick kilns, three houses for workers, an office, and a barn for horses and wagons. The pottery factory was located on the Varsenerdijk in Ommen, and the brick works stood on the Ledeboerweg in Lemele. The buildings and lands were valued at the princely sum of ƒ50,000 ($699,000 today).[63]

---

[61] Minutes, Ommen consistory, 10 July 1844, in Van Raalte's hand; Smits, *Afscheiding van 1834*, 6:295-95, trans. Nella Kennedy.
[62] Nella Kennedy, "Twice Torn Asunder," 52n47. The De Moen and Tieleman inheritances enabled Maria Wilhelmina and fellow heirs, Maria Elisabet Tieleman-Dros and Adrien Tieleman, to provide funds for a Christian kindergarten and for the Christian Separated Church in Leiden. In 1840 Van Velzen sold to his brother-in-law Carel de Moen a small portion of his inheritance, consisting of seventeen acres located in Grambergen, Overijssel, valued for tax purposes at ƒ2,390 ($33,400 today); Van Velzen to De Moen, sales contract, 5 Feb. 1839, ADC.
[63] De Graaf, "Een afgescheiden dominee," trans. Ralph W. Vunderink; Warner, *Door het venster*, 125- 27; Bruins, "Funding His Vision." De Graaf was able to interview descendents of Van Raalte's former Ommen congregation who knew about his local business affairs.

De Tichelarij (former De Moen & Co. brickworks), Ledeboerweg, Lemele (*courtesy Gerko Warner*)

Profits were to be divided annually among the partners at 5 percent, based on the amounts invested. Unfortunately, the documents do not state the capital that each invested. Benjamin and Johanna de Moen's children—Maria, Carel, Christina, and Johanna—had each inherited ƒ5,000 ($64,000 today) of their parent's estate of ƒ20,000 ($255,000 today). As true entrepreneurs, the aim of the partnership was profit.[64] Yet they paid "exceptionally high" wages that dented the bottom line. Elias Ravenshorst, an Ommen merchant, may have been a silent partner since he allowed De Moen & Co. to dig clay from his pits in Lemele. Van Raalte was to receive "ten percent in advance, as an honorarium."[65]

The partners were obligated to raise the necessary capital, but Van Raalte had the steepest hill to climb. He first solicited Scholte, his friend and colleague, who had inherited a successful business in Amsterdam from his father. Van Raalte requested a loan "for de Moen and me" of from ƒ5,000 to ƒ10,000 ($65,400 to $130,800 today) at 5 or 6 percent interest. He noted that ƒ15,000 ($196,000 today) "of our own

---

[64] Contract, Van Raalte and Carel de Moen, 13 Apr. 1840, ADC. Father Benjamin de Moen's estate at his death in 1824 was valued at ƒ20,000 ($250,800 today). When his wife died in 1831, his four children each presumably inherited ƒ5,000 ($62,700 today) (*Notariële Akten*, Benjamin de Moen's estate, 11 Feb. 1824, Inventory no. 141, 51-58, Regional Archives Leiden).

[65] Elias Ravenshorst, Ommen, to Van Raalte, 19 Nov. 1860, original owned by Barbara Nugent, a Van Raalte descendant.

Pottenbakkerij (former De Moen & Co. pottery factory), Varsenerdijk 2, Ommen
(*courtesy Gerko Warner*)

money is out of our reach, and we cannot invest in the business." Van Raalte had provided $f2,550$ ($35,700 today) for the Ommen church building project and other monies for the fishing vessels. Finally, should Scholte be disinclined to invest, Albertus asked if he would intercede with Judith van IJsseldijk-Zeelt, a wealthy widow friend of Scholte and a Separatist benefactor living on a country estate in Baambrugge, Utrecht. In the end, both declined to invest. Scholte was likely miffed that Van Raalte only a few months earlier had joined in the vote at Synod 1840 to oust him from the denomination.[66]

Van Raalte's problems were compounded when De Moen indicated his decision to enter the Gospel ministry, a step Albertus had encouraged. De Moen needed to sell his half ownership to finance his schooling, so Van Raalte turned to another brother-in-law, his sister Johanna's husband, Dirk Blikman Kikkert (1813-1868), a prosperous shipbroker, who lived along the prestigious Amsterdam Singel, the innermost canal. Blikman Kikkert agreed to buy in. In March 1841, the Ommen mayor and councilmen allowed the new partnership to begin production. De Moen managed the business until Blikman

---

[66] Van Raalte to Scholte, 26 Oct. 1840, in Smits, *Afscheiding van 1834*, 3:179-81, trans. Dekker. For Judith Zeelt, see *Iowa Letters*, 11, 223-24.

Carel Godefroi de Moen (1811-1879) (*Rullmann*, De Afscheiding)

Kikkert moved to Ommen in mid-September 1841 to assume direct management. "Thanks be to God," Van Raalte declared when the leadership transition was complete.[67]

It was a major career decision for Blikman Kikkert to leave Amsterdam for the small town of Ommen, but his wife, Johanna Bartha Van Raalte, and three daughters certainly applauded it since it brought Johanna and her brother Albertus together again. Blikman Kikkert built for his family the first brick house in the Heidepark of Lemelerveld.[68]

Under Blikman Kikkert, the bottom line improved markedly. De Moen sold his half ownership to Blikman Kikkert on December 7, 1841, for ƒ12,446 ($174,000 today). The sale included three pieces of property. First was a former farm in Lemele, purchased in September 1840 from the farmer's widow, which contained a brick-shingle-tile factory, three laborers' cottages, an office, horse barn and wagons, two brick kilns, a shingle oven, and two barns to store bricks. Second was property acquired in December 1840 from Elias Ravenshorst that included a Frisian ceramics factory, earthenware factory, and another barn and office next door, all located on the market grounds in Lemele. Third

[67] Van Raalte to De Moen, 15 Sept. 1841, Deventer Gemeente Archief, ADC. See also, letters of Ommen mayor and city council to De Moen, 9 Mar. 1841, Ommen Gemeente Archives.

[68] Makkinga, "Bricks for Ommen Poor." A monument stands in Lemele for Blikman Kikkert.

were seven lots in Lemele, purchased from a Zwolle lawyer in December 1840. The sellers took back mortgages, then standard practice. De Moen agreed to leave his capital in the business at 5 percent interest for at least half a year. The agreement specifically released De Moen from his obligations and responsibilities and also from all profits. The new partners obligated themselves to pay annual interest of ƒ662 ($9,230 today). Prior to this contract, Van Raalte and De Moen had bought out Dros.[69]

On December 27, 1841, Van Raalte and Blikman Kikkert signed a contract to form a new partnership named Blikman Kikkert & Co. to begin on January 1, 1842, and run for fourteen years. The value of the firm, secured by mortgage, was set at ƒ50,000 ($699,000 today), 60 percent for buildings, 40 percent for operations. This notarized document was registered in Amsterdam. On February 1, the partners agreed to stipulations additional to the December 7, 1841 contract involving De Moen. First, Van Raalte granted Blikman Kikkert the right to dig peat and raise grains on a thirty-hectare parcel he had purchased from local farmer Albertus Wilpshaar on June 2, 1840. Second, the pair agreed to split profits of the partnership, even though Blikman Kikkert paid in a larger share of the capital, with Van Raalte receiving an extra 5 percent for "care, execution, and administration of the affairs of the partnership." Third, both partners shared equally in the "rights of possessing buildings, land, and proper wares" purchased from De Moen, namely the buildings and lands in Ommen and in Lemele. The contract does not mention the capital each partner invested, except that Van Raalte's capital was less than half, that is, under ƒ25,000.[70]

The contract in Article 8 wisely specified a detailed succession plan. In the event of Van Raalte's death, Blikman Kikkert would receive within a year ƒ25,000 ($350,000 today), and if Blikman Kikkert died first, the same amount would be paid to his heirs but over a longer period of time since Blikman Kikkert had not made a contract with Van Raalte's heirs. They "will have adequate funds of their own or will obtain them from other sources, but in the application of Article 8, one must not be unfair and deprive Van Raalte of the capital with which to operate his factory."[71] Given the large sums of money involved,

---

[69] Sale Contract, De Moen to Blikman Kikkert, 7 Dec. 1841, ADC; De Graaf, "Een afgescheiden dominee," 8-9; Warner, *Door het venster*, 125-27.
[70] Sale Contract, De Moen to Blikman Kikkert, 27 Dec. 1841, Van Raalte Collection, HHA; *Deventer Courant*, 21 Jan. 1842.
[71] Hyma, *Van Raalte*, 121-24.

more than half a million in today's dollars, for Van Raalte to assume such a significant financial obligation was no easy decision, but he had confidence that Blikman Kikkert could manage the businesses profitably. When Van Raalte in 1844 accepted the call to Arnhem, Blikman Kikkert closed the declining brick works and relocated the tile works to a new factory on the south side of Lemelerberg, which he continued to 1862.[72]

There are no known documents indicating that Van Raalte sold his interest in Blikman Kikkert & Co., either before or after he left for Michigan in 1846. This is in sharp contrast to the five extant documents that carefully detail the founding of the firm and the ownership change in 1841-42. The likelihood, therefore, is that he did not sell his interest but, rather, left the firm in Blikman Kikkert's hands and took very little money, if any, out of the company. Dirk and Johanna Blikman Kikkert remained in Lemele for the remainder of their lives and were charter members in 1862 of the Lemele-Archem Hervormde Kerk, not having joined the Ommen Separated Church of his brother-in-law.

Brummelkamp calculated that Van Raalte would earn more interest if he sold his share of the company to Blikman Kikkert and put his money in the bank, and he advised Van Raalte to sell before he lost any more money. The Bentheim Separatist preacher, Jan Barend Sundag, a Van Raalte critic, surmised that "by establishing a brick factory, he lost most of his money." Van Raalte himself admitted years later that the project had been "unhappy for me."[73] Johan A. Wormser Jr., in his biography of Van Raalte, remarks that he "did not win his spurs in finance." Wormser's son Andries surmised that Van Raalte emigrated to "restore his lost fortune."[74] All these off-hand comments suggest that Albertus did not profit from these manufacturing ventures.

W. De Graaf studied the financial history of Van Raalte's Ommen businesses and concluded more positively: "There are sound reasons to accept that the financial basis for the American undertaking was laid to a great extent during Van Raalte's stay in Ommen, where he was a

---

[72] Arnold Huijsmans, Ommen, email to Elton Bruins, 29 Aug. 2017; Ravenshorst to Van Raalte, 19 Nov. 1860.

[73] Brummelkamp to Van Raalte, 8 Aug. 1844; Jan Barend Sundag to brother in Ostfriesland, 18 Mar. 1847, both cited in Reenders, "Van Raalte als leider," 193n578, 194n579; Andries N. Wormser, quoted in Pieters, *Dutch Settlement*, 95; Van Raalte to Brummelkamp, 11 Sept. 1852, HHA. Blikman Kikkert's role is described in Hyma, *Van Raalte*, and in Wesseling, *Afscheiding van 1834, Classis Zwolle*, 202-3.

[74] Wormser, *In twee werelddeelen*, 103, trans. Ten Hoor.

pastor and 'businessman' who knew how to gain interest from money he already possessed. He would not be entirely impecunious" when he departed for America. But Van Raalte's business dealings in America (ch. 12) suggest that he carried less money than De Graaf assumed.[75]

The joint commercial and philanthropic ventures in Ommen helped several dozen hapless Separatists, but Van Raalte opined that his jobs program was largely fruitless. As he and Brummelkamp noted in their *Landverhuizing* pamphlet of May 1846:

> We are driven to this [emigration] even more after several years of fruitlessly trying to give work to many in order to provide bread, and by the conviction that public welfare for the poor will become too heavy a burden, given rising unemployment, misery, destruction, and higher taxes. It brings pain and inward strife even to those who receive aid. And the very destructive competition is a fruitful breeding ground for many sins.[76]

A growing household

Albertus was a solicitous and caring husband, and he and Christina became the parents of many children. In Genemuiden, Albertus was born in 1837 and Johanna Maria in 1838; in Ommen, Benjamin was born in 1840 and Christina's namesake (who died at fifteen months), Christina Catherina (Christine or Chris), in 1842; and Dirk Blikman Kikkert as born in 1844 and the second Christina Catharina (Christine) in 1846. The birth of Christine, the sixth child in nine years, was the lull before the storm of emigration. She brought pure joy, even three decades later, when her father looked back on her birth and wrote her:

> Oh, that hour of your birth was such an unforgettable moment for me because of your mother's joy. We thanked God when He gave you to us. This brightening, the loving care and responsibility, once again cheered mother's difficult path. I see you in her arms. I see you as the comfort on the ship, on the journey, and as a stranger in this land. To remember this sweetening of her cup of life is continually a refreshment for me. And we still have you, thank God.[77]

---

[75] De Graaf, "Een afgescheiden dominee," 8.
[76] Brummelkamp and Van Raalte, *Landverhuizing*, 34 (freely translated).
[77] Van Raalte to daughter Christina Gilmore, Apr. 1875, trans. Nella Kennedy (Charles Vander Broek).

Four adult siblings also settled in Ommen—Christina's brother, Carel de Moen (an elder in the Ommen church), and wife Agatha Sophia van Voss; and Albertus's sisters, Alberta Christina, who kept a boarding house, and Johanna Bartha and husband Dirk Blikman Kikkert. Albertus's brother Petrus, a widower and physician in the final stages of tuberculosis lived in the parsonage for his final year, before dying at age forty-one on February 2, 1840. Joy followed sorrow, providentially, for Albertus and Christina, with the birth of Benjamin (Ben) on May 8. In addition to managing a growing congregation and winning the struggle for recognition and Christian education, Van Raalte began training ministers in the parsonage, which would prove to be his most rewarding and significant work.

Van Raalte solidified the Ommen congregation in his five-year pastorate. Besides training the consistory and building a cohesive congregation, he organized a Christian school despite recalcitrant government officials, began training seminarians, and launched several factories to bring in extra income and provide work for Separatists. He won legal recognition for the congregation on the king's terms, again after several frustrating years of royal resistance. But he chafed under church regulations and later came to regret giving up the beloved "Gereformeerd" name as a price too steep to pay. These years also coincided with the contentious 1840 and 1843 synods of the infant Christian Separated Church that expelled Scholte and led his brother-in-law Van Velzen to berate Van Raalte for being a conciliator who tried to maintain unity at all costs. In Ommen, Van Raalte's social entrepreneurship came to fruition in the factories he opened to employ Seceders, but the results were mixed. His partners, most notably Blikman Kikkert, succeeded where he had failed. The challenges in Ommen were many; yet this was his most rewarding and significant pastorate in the Netherlands.

CHAPTER 6

Seminary Professor: "I may enjoy this work."

Van Raalte became a seminary professor in a wholly unexpected way. It came about at Brummelkamp's encouragement in 1839 when three lay preachers (*oefenaars*) from the Drenthe contingent requested Van Raalte to train them for the ministry. Van Raalte, however, was not keen on the idea, having himself been a minister for only three years, but he "dared not refuse them." The dominee was a doer, not an intellectual. He believed he had an obligation to train laymen properly for ordination, given that he had opposed ordaining untrained laymen. Besides, these men were forbidden to attend universities because they had not completed classical studies at gymnasiums, a prerequisite for admission.[1]

Brummelkamp's suggestion meshed with Van Raalte's expressed view that Separatist pastors must come from "those within their midst, those who have grown up during the Secession," not from clerics ordained in the Hervormde Kerk who wanted to come over. Such men, he wrote Carel de Moen, "who have lived in the Babel of the Hervormden for years bring confusion in our midst.... [They] do not comprehend

---

[1] Te Velde, "Ministerial Education."

church, sacraments, discipline, and government." To train their own men suited Van Raalte's disciplined, diligent, energetic, and directive personality. There was enough dissension among the Afgescheidenen themselves, complicated further by the addition of former Hervormde pastors. Perhaps the Afgescheidenen were resentful that some of those pastors had not participated in the suffering of the 1830s. Further, the minimally educated pastors may have been fearful that university-trained ministers would either question their legitimacy or "upstage" them.[2]

Four centers developed for training Seceder ministers. All were essentially apprenticeship programs since the training was mainly tutorial. Candidates for examination had to present statements from their home congregation that attested to their piety, humility, moral behavior, modesty, knowledge of Greek and Hebrew, and church history. Those with "extraordinary gifts of the Spirit" could bypass the languages, provided they had a "thorough knowledge of the inner and immediate knowledge of God, a good understanding of the pastor's work, and were a capable preacher."[3]

Beginning in May 1839, Van Raalte's ministry focus shifted to instructing, examining, and ordaining seminarians. "I may enjoy this work through the Lord's goodness, notwithstanding that I looked upon it with trepidation," he confessed. He had joined Scholte, De Cock, and Brummelkamp, the "fathers of the Secession," who one by one had begun training ministers. De Cock taught at the city of Groningen until his early death in 1842 when Tamme F. de Haan stepped in. The Kok brothers, Wolter and Frederik, trained men at Hoogeveen, Drenthe. Van Raalte trained men in Ommen and Brummelkamp in Hattem and Schiedam. Scholte at Utrecht trained a number of ministers until Synod Amsterdam 1840 expelled him. Later, Van Raalte and Brummelkamp joined together at Arnhem and set the highest training standards. Given the open disdain from university professors of these renegade preachers who began rump seminaries, it took considerable courage to begin such parsonage apprenticeships. Courage was buttressed by need, which at first dictated only brief, one-year training programs. The Christian Separated Church had just seven ordained ministers to serve some two hundred congregations. Even by

---

[2] Van Raalte to De Moen, 26 July 1839, trans. Nella Kennedy, ADC; Te Velde, "Ministerial Education," 203.

[3] Te Velde, "Dutch Background," 85-87; De Graaf, "Een Monument der Afscheiding," 20.

itinerating and holding weekday services, it was not possible to cover that many churches. Lay preachers and reading services (*leesdiensten*) by elders had to fill the gap.[4]

Van Raalte's first students were Poppe Rykens de Wit from Wildervank, Groningen; Klaas Marinus Wildeboer from Midwolda, Groningen; and IJsbrand Jans Veenstra from Joure, Friesland. De Wit, nine years older than Van Raalte, was an authorized catechism teacher in the Hervormde Kerk, who on occasion was asked by Separatist and Mennonite (Doopsgezinden) pastors to fill in for them. Wildeboer was a baker who had demonstrated preaching gifts in the Midwolda congregation. Veenstra was an elder in Friesland, a province under De Cock and Van Velzen. These laymen met the dominee's initial qualifications: "a clear head, a humble attitude, and a warm heart."[5] But these criteria soon proved inadequate.

Theological School at Ommen

Training seminarians (also elders and deacons) proved rewarding for Van Raalte, and it came to take precedence over all his pastoral work, except sermon preparation. During his Ommen pastorate of five-and-a-half years, Van Raalte trained at least twenty men and took great satisfaction that by 1844 every church in the province of Overijssel had its own minister, even though their support was often a financial struggle. Some married men had stipends from congregations they were serving, and others, single or married, were supported either by diaconal funds or faithful believers. The training stressed learning by observation. Students gathered on Mondays to analyze the sermons of the previous day. The dominee questioned them carefully on the content. At the Friday "sermon classes," students had to present their own sermons without notes or even an outline. Van Raalte's critique could be "sharp, almost too sharp."[6]

How the young Van Raalte couple, soon with three children, plus two domestics and a handyman, could give up several rooms in the modest parsonage for classrooms and student study rooms is a puzzle. But there is good evidence that the Van Raalte family lived on

---

[4] Van Raalte to Scholte, 18 Feb., 24 May 1839, in Smits, *Afscheiding van 1834*, 3:170, 175-76, trans. Nella Kennedy; Reenders, "Van Raalte," 292-94; Te Velde, "Ministerial Education," 197; Reenders, "Van Raalte als leider," 185.

[5] Reenders, "Van Raalte als leider," 187n544 (quote), citing Pieter Jan Oggel's letter to his father, 24 Aug. 1844, in Bouma, *Woord des Geloofs*, 34, trans. Dekker.

[6] Reenders, "Van Raalte als leider," 187.

Den Lagen Oordt directly behind the historic Van Raalte house on the current Van Raaltestraat, which served as the seminary.[7]

The theological curriculum included biblical history, content, and exposition; dogmatics (doctrinal and apologetic theology); church history (Van Raalte's forte); homiletics; and practical theology. Textbooks were the Statenbijbel, with marginal commentary; Old Writers: Wilhelmus à Brakel, *Redelijke Godsdienst* (Reasonable religion), and Aegidius Francken, *Kern der Christelijke leer* (Heart of Christian doctrine); Calvin's *Institutes of the Christian Religion*; church histories; Anglican cleric Joseph Milner's ten-volume *History of the Church of Christ* (London, 1794-1809), recently available in Dutch translation; church polity by Dirk Molenaar; Latin-, Greek-, and Dutch-language texts; and the Reformed Confessions and dogmatic works. Molenaar was a highly positioned pastor in the Hervormde Kerk in The Hague who befriended and advised De Cock. His call for reform, *Adres aan alle mijne Hervormde geloofsgenooten* (Address to all my Reformed coreligionists) (1827), reprinted eight times in six months, caused consternation in the church.[8]

Van Raalte's workload at Ommen was eased after the first years by hiring additional faculty in 1843. Adriaan Zweedijk, a boarding-school teacher, taught general subjects and the Dutch language, and Albertus Bernardus Veenhuizen (soon to marry Brummelkamp's sister), who had studied at the Theological School in Geneva (founded in 1559 by John Calvin), taught Latin, Greek, and Hebrew languages, all nontheological subjects. The congregation paid ƒ100 toward Veenhuizen's salary, with an additional ƒ50 coming from tuition. Veenhuizen's appointment was heavily criticized by the congregations in the Drenthe party because he was not ordained and had not joined the Secession movement. In short, strict Separatists did not trust him. Brummelkamp presided at the Zwolle provincial meeting where Veenhuizen's appointment was hotly debated. In the end, because Veenhuizen would not join the Separated Church, he was appointed as a "foreign brother."[9]

Student Abraham C. Tris described a typical week at the seminary in Ommen, where professors and fellow students welcomed him "with great esteem and love." The eager students were industrious

---

[7] Ibid., 179; Te Velde, "Ministerial Education," 201, citing Makkinga, "Bricks for Ommen Poor." Chapter 5 pictures the house and notes its demolition in 2020.

[8] Te Velde, "Ministerial Education," 203-4.

[9] Ibid., 204-6; Reenders, "Van Raalte als leider," 166-67, 187-88; Wesseling, *Afscheiding van 1834, Classis Zwolle*, 210-14.

to a fault. "Every hour, yea every minute, was counted." Classes began at 8:00 a.m. and went as late as 8:00 p.m. in Van Raalte's home. On Monday, Zweedijk gave two hours of Dutch-language instruction. Van Raalte followed with an hour of church history. After a two-hour break, Veenhuizen taught two hours of Greek and Hebrew. In the evening, Van Raalte taught two hours of dogmatics and apologetics. On Tuesday morning, Zweedijk taught an hour of geography, and in midafternoon, Veenhuizen taught two hours of Latin, followed by four hours of dogmatics, apologetics, and symbolism with Van Raalte. No classes were scheduled on Wednesday and Thursday. On Friday morning, Zweedijk taught general history and Dutch language for an hour each, followed in the afternoon by Veenhuizen's two-hour Greek and Hebrew lessons, and Van Raalte taught two hours of dogmatics, exegesis, and Bible in the evening. On Saturday, Zweedijk began with two hours of general history and Dutch language, with Veenhuizen in the afternoon giving Latin and Hebrew lessons, and Van Raalte in the early evening teaching preaching skills (homiletics) for two hours, including practice preaching. He ended the long day and week with an exposition of a Bible chapter. This was education up close and personal: teachers and students formed special bonds.[10]

Van Raalte's church history lectures, in chronology, periodization, and focus, likely followed those of his Leiden professor Nicolaas Kist, although filtered through his own experiences in the quest for religious reform. Van Raalte saw church history as the unfolding of God's plan to preserve the church in the face of declension and decay. The Reformation was the fulcrum of church history against the despotic bishop of Rome and the superstition and false authority of the Catholic Church. Reformers, especially Martin Luther (Calvin's role is downplayed), and the great Synod of Dort paved the way for modern Dutch Protestantism. Van Raalte ignored the great Catholic theologian Thomas Aquinas. By this time, he had made his peace with the Secession of 1834 and its goal of restoring the True church. Van Raalte and his in-laws, Brummelkamp and Van Velzen, coedited in 1841 the *Kerkelyk Handboekje* (church handbook) for the separated churches, which grounded their doctrines and polity in Dutch synods since 1568, especially Dort in 1618-19.[11]

[10] Tris, *Sixty Years' Reminiscences*; Tris to Van der Meulen, 16 Jan. 1844, VRI; and Te Velde, "Ministerial Education," 205-6, for the weekly schedule in detail. Van Raalte's church history lessons are preserved at the Archives of the Theological University of the Reformed Churches, Kampen.

[11] Van Raalte left these notes behind when he emigrated in 1846. Henri W. van Baalen

Pastoral training had quality-control problems at first. When provincial assemblies examined the first candidates for ordination, as per a decision of Synod Utrecht 1837, they found them wanting. By failing to bring attestations from their churches that they were suitably gifted for ministry, the seminarians had not followed Article 8 of the church order. And candidates were not given sufficient preaching opportunities. Van Raalte caught it in the neck first. In October 1839, the Overijssel Provincial Classis raised objections to both candidates De Wit and Wildeboer, calling their training "an arbitrary penetration of the two men into the church." The pair had studied for less than six months and were rushed into ministry. It was said that the men lacked the "singular talents of godliness and humbleness." Van Raalte strongly defended the two as sound in training, gifts, and experience. He insisted that they met the biblical qualifications for ministry, citing several dozen scripture passages from Paul's letters and epistles to prove his case.[12]

Both men were ordained and accepted calls—Wildeboer from the Rijssen church and De Wit from the Apeldoorn church—but their ministries were both cut short by death—De Wit within a year, and Wildeboer within three years. IJsbrand Jans Veenstra was sent packing after having had an affair with his housekeeper, but he eventually completed his training under Wolter A. Kok in Hoogeveen, Drenthe. The rebuke from the provincial assembly, however, led Van Raalte and other teaching pastors to raise their standards and increase the training period to two and three years.[13]

Synod Amsterdam 1840 regularized the examination of seminarians. The body required every province to appoint a preacher-professor and set a rigorous course of study. Seminarians must pass exams in Hebrew, Greek, church history, theology, dogma, ethics, and pastoral knowledge. (The Old and New Testaments must have

---

copied them, and Adriaan de Bruijne signed them. See Van Raalte et al., *Kerkelijk Handboekje*; Te Velde, "Ministerial Education," 204n16; Douma, "Rediscovering"; Brummelkamp to De Moen, 7 June 1842, requesting Van Raalte to return the church history notes of Kist to Gezelle Meerburg who had lent them and wanted them returned, trans. Nella Kennedy, JAH; Wormser, *In twee werelddeelen*, 27, trans. Ten Hoor; and Douma, "Writings about Van Raalte." Douma transcribed and translated into English Van Raalte's 434-page, handwritten lecture notes in the Archives of the Theological University of the Reformed Churches, Kampen (email to author, 6 June 2013).

[12] Reenders, "Van Raalte als leider," 160-64 (161, quote), trans. Dekker.
[13] Van Raalte to De Moen, 10 Dec. 1839, trans. Nella Kennedy.

been covered in one of these fields.)[14] Examinations must take place in Provincial Classis meetings, with two of the six examiners being synodical appointees, prepared to screen out weak candidates. But the very system was inherently flawed because the candidates reflected their teachers in preaching style, garb, lifestyle, choice of church order, and other matters.

Scholte trained Hendrik G. Klyn (Klijn) and Cornelius Van der Meulen, and then he examined both men by himself. No wonder the Amsterdam consistory would not accept them. When Carel de Moen was ready for ordination in 1842, Van Raalte and Brummelkamp, his brothers-in-law, could not agree on who should examine him. Van Raalte did not want Scholte, and Brummelkamp did not want either Budding or Ledeboer. De Cock was sick unto death; Gezelle Meerburg was unwilling, and De Haan was tied up training students in Friesland. This left only De Moen's two brothers-in-law. The roster of dominees in Separated churches was thin. Nevertheless, between 1840 and 1842, forty candidates were admitted to the ministry, thirty from the northern provinces.[15]

Van Raalte and Brummelkamp rode herd in the Overijssels-Gelders congregations, Van Raalte even more so. They determined to raise standards and require churches in their bailiwick to call pastors they alone had trained. Van Raalte insisted that students master preaching without notes, as he had learned to do the hard way as a seminarian. These demanding professors stretched some exams into a second day, and Van Raalte would pose as many as 170 questions. Candidates who trained under more traditional (and presumably less demanding) pastors in the provinces of Groningen and Drenthe, such as De Cock in the town of Groningen and Wolter Kok in Hoogeveen, were free to serve congregations in the northwest of Overijssel. In 1843, at Van Raalte's instigation, the classis of Overijssel declared that candidates not trained at Ommen or Arnhem who took calls in the province must submit to a peremptory examination to confirm their readiness before being installed. In fact, this happened only once because Van Raalte did not want to alienate churches in the North.[16]

Of the twenty men trained at Ommen, from 80 to 90 percent became ministers, and several had significant careers: De Moen and Ten Bokkel in the Christelijke Afgescheiden Kerk; Seine Bolks and

---

[14] Minutes, Synod of Christelijke Separatist Kerk, 3 Dec. 1840.
[15] Te Velde, *Brummelkamp*, 157-58, for the statistics.
[16] Reenders, "Van Raalte als leider," 165-66.

Pieter (Peter) J. Oggel, Van Raalte's future son-in-law, in the Reformed Church in America; and Abraham Tris in the Christian Reformed Church. Jannes Van de Luyster Jr. and Mannes Mensink immigrated but were never ordained. Vande Luyster became a successful merchant in the Holland colony, and Mensink farmed and served as a Reformed Church elder in Alto, Wisconsin, and Greenleafton, Minnesota. Willem Van Leeuwen served as an independent minister in Wisconsin and New Jersey churches. That so many men followed Van Raalte overseas testifies to his charisma. In terms of the number of ministers supplied to the churches, Ommen was a distant second to the Groningen and Hoogeveen seminaries that turned out most of the 164 men ordained from 1839 to 1854.[17]

Oggel's fine mind caught Van Raalte's attention. Van Raalte wrote Oggel's father, J. P. Oggel, "He is a joy to me, and not only to me but also my brother Brummelkamp. He is faithful in his use of time and makes good progress so that I trust, if the Lord spares him, that he will be, after further development, a very useful instrument for the Kingdom of God."[18]

Settling in at Arnhem

Brummelkamp and Van Raalte had each begun training pastors in their parsonages—in Hattem and Schiedam for Brummelkamp, and in Ommen for Van Raalte. As early as 1839, they had spoken of a cooperative effort, but where? Both Zwolle, the provincial capital of Overijssel, and Amsterdam would be ideal central locations, but the infant denomination could not fund a seminary. The two men must serve churches in the same city. Arnhem, a city with forty-two thousand inhabitants, was that place; it was preferable to "backward" Ommen. In 1844 the United Provincial Classis of Gelderland and Overijssel put its authority behind Arnhem. Brummelkamp had organized the first Arnhem Separatist congregation in late 1842 after leaving a pastorate

---

[17] Van Raalte's twenty students at Ommen included Klaas M. Wildeboer, Ijsbrand J. Veenstra, Poppe R de Wit, Seine Bolks, Hendrikus de Vries, Carel de Moen, Anton Herman Veenhuizen, Jan Schuurman, Mannes Mensink, Willem van Leeuwen, Abraham C. Tris, and Jan W. ten Bokkel, among others. Three students died after short careers; six had troubled careers, and four took calls from American churches (see Te Velde, "Ministerial Education," 210-39, for a brief biography of each). See also, for Tris, his *Sixty Years' Reminiscences*; for Mensink, his letter in *Iowa Letters*, 51-54, and for Van Leeuwen, Sheeres, *Minutes*, 573.

[18] Van Raalte to J. P. Oggel, 28 Feb. 1845, in D. J. Oggel, Jzn, "The History of the Oggel Family and Other Related Families," manuscript, JAH.

at Schiedam, near Rotterdam. Now Van Raalte had to come to Arnhem, much to the disquiet of his Ommen consistory. The theological school would supply pastors for some twenty-five congregations in Gelderland and Overijssel, representing the Gelderse party, plus a few congregations in Zeeland and elsewhere who remained in close contact.[19]

The door was opened for Van Raalte when the small congregation of Velp, near Arnhem, called him in 1844. His former student Klaas Wildeboer had organized the congregation in 1841 but left after six months for a church in Groningen. Classis urged Van Raalte to accept the call to the vacant pulpit. He agreed reluctantly, preferring to remain in Ommen. That congregation was dear to his heart and had shared many of his trials. Above all, Van Raalte feared that the congregation might call a Kruisgezinde minister and undo his work.

Brummelkamp tried to pull Van Raalte's heart toward Arnhem by sending five strongly worded letters within fifteen days that applied heavy moral and spiritual pressure. "It is a calling that you come here," Brumelkamp declared. He urged Van Raalte to pray about it but to not consult anyone, especially Van Velzen and Gezelle Meerburg, who would only "cause confusion." The Arnhem school, he added, was the best way to "build a dam against the Groningers," meaning the school of De Haan and the Kok brothers. Anthony also mentioned the sore point—Albertus's losing partnership with Blikman Kikkert, which he insisted was high time to end.[20] To counter Van Raalte's financial concerns, Brummelkamp nudged the small Arnhem and Velp congregations, with a combined membership of 125 souls, to raise the proffered annual salary from ƒ925 to ƒ1,000 ($15,000–$16,220 today). Brummelkamp needed no salary, thanks to his wife's inheritance, but Van Raalte did because he had invested his wife's inheritance in struggling businesses.[21]

When Van Raalte informed the Ommen consistory that he would accept the Arnhem call, he confessed that "his life had become like a blank piece of paper to the Lord, even though, for many reasons, he would rather have continued to work in his own congregation." Van Raalte struggled with the Arnhem call more than any other in his entire ministry. He asked the consistory for advice but realized that, ultimately, he alone would have to make the decision. The need in the

---

[19] Te Velde, "Ministerial Education," 206-7; Te Velde, *Brummelkamp*, 156-60 (quote 159); Brummelkamp Jr., *Brummelkamp*, 193-94; Warner, *Door het venster*, 127-28.
[20] Brummelkamp to Van Raalte, 1, 8, 10, 15 Aug. 1844, JAH.
[21] Reenders, "Van Raalte als leider," 168-69, 372n430; Te Velde, *Brummelkamp*, 159.

churches of Overijssel and Gelderland for the seminary finally tipped the scales.[22]

The Van Raalte family traveled the fifty-seven miles to Arnhem by canal boat and stagecoach, arriving on November 20, 1844. They found housing in a newly renovated tannery named De Nieuwe Vlijt (the new diligence), located on the Buitensingel (the outer canal). The former factory, a two-story building, could not compare with the homey "simple villa" at Ommen. At high water, the lower level would sometimes flood. It also stood outside the city wall at the Sabelspoort (sable gate, also known as the Eusebius Gate), where an iron gate closed nightly at eleven. After that hour, one had to pay "gate money" at the guardhouse to enter or leave. Typically, upper-class families had breakfast at eight, coffee at eleven, dinner at two, tea at five, and supper at ten. As Anthony Brummelkamp Jr. recalled, the Van Raaltes had to hasten home after supper at the Brummelkamp's city home to beat the gate clock, except in winter, when they could walk over the frozen canal and bypass the gate. As Anthony added: "They considered gate money a kind of fine and preferred not to pay it."[23]

Poor living conditions in Arnhem for the Van Raaltes were outweighed by being near the Brummelkamps for the first time since their marriages in the mid-1830s. It pleased Christina greatly to experience *gezelligheid* (coziness) with her dear sister Maria, whom she had sorely missed. Sister Johanna Maria, who had married Simon van Velzen, died in 1837. The Brummelkamps lived in a large, stately home on the Bakkerstraat, near the River Rhine, which they had purchased in January 1845. The large home hosted daily seminary lectures.

At Velp, Van Raalte's first assignment was to direct construction of a church building on a donated lot at the corner of Bergweg and Wilhelminastraat. He also successfully applied for royal recognition for the Velp congregation in late 1845.[24] He and Brummelkamp preached on alternate Sundays at the Arnhem Separated Church on the Varkensstraat. Worship services were held in the spacious upper room of a barn, where up to 250 worshipers, divided by gender, sat on benches astride a center aisle. Near the rather imposing pulpit sat

---

[22] Minutes, Ommen consistory, 8 Apr., 6, 14 Aug. 1844, trans. Nella Kennedy.

[23] Brummelkamp Jr., *Brummelkamp*, 194, trans. Nella Kennedy.

[24] Van Raalte to Budding, 9 Jan. 1837, Gunning, *Budding*, trans. Ten Hoor; *Arnhemsche Courant*, 23 Dec. 1845 (www.delpher.nl, accessed, June 2021); Wormser, *In twee werelddeelen*, 103; Warner, *Door het venster*, 128-29; Te Velde, "Ministerial Education," 206-10; Te Velde, *Brummelkamp*, 160; De Graaf, "Een Monument der Afscheiding," 23.

the *voorlezer*, who read scripture and announced the Psalms (and also pitched the tunes in the absence of an organ). This important layman often also taught school and catechism. The Arnhem building was sold after a substantial number of members emigrated to the United States.[25]

Arnhem seminary

Van Raalte's six Ommen students found rooms in a boarding house near the Arnhem theological school, which met in Brummelkamp's large parsonage, and there they joined Brummelkamp's ten students. The faculty complemented one another. Brummelkamp taught exegesis, Old and New Testament, and pastoral subjects, often using the Socratic method of posing questions. Van Raalte taught church history, the Reformed Confessions (dogmatics), Bible exposition, apologetics, and homiletics (the art of preaching). Veenhuizen, who had also moved to Arnhem, ran the preparatory Latin school and taught Hebrew and Greek. For a long time, Israël Waterman, a Jewish teacher of the Israelite school in Arnhem, taught Hebrew. The daily and weekly schedule was similar to that at Ommen: lectures from nine to two and three to five, then continued in the evening, with practice preaching on Friday. The full program was three years (five, if it included two prior years of preparation).

The Velp congregation paid Van Raalte's salary, supplemented by provincial assemblies, but Veenhuizen's salary was paid with difficulty out of tuition. Brummelkamp considered asking the talented Scholte to join them; he was independently wealthy and needed no salary, but Van Raalte put his foot down. Other than this disagreement, the brothers-in-law were closely knit and fed off each other.

Van Raalte continued placing stringent demands on students, some of whom found it "deadly." He had high expectations and insisted on preparation and competence. He was far more demanding than Brummelkamp, who took the sharp edges off his dear brother-in-law. Both held high standards and sought excellence in preaching. Brummelkamp was the theologian and educator and Van Raalte the practitioner, who also taught dogmatics. Both were pastors by training and ordination, not professors. Scholarship and creative thinking were not their forté. They were, however, confessional-biblical in their teaching and preaching. Brummelkamp decried the customary preaching tone (*preektoon*), and both he and Van Raalte insisted that,

[25] Brummelkamp Jr., *Brummelkamp*, 183.

after solid preparation in biblical and other sources, students preach with voice inflection and without notes, using short sentences and simple, practical examples, speaking in a lively manner. Van Raalte's evaluations could be sharp, almost crushing, as students honed their skills at Friday-evening preaching classes.[26]

When the Provincial Classis of Zuid-Holland examined two candidates in 1844 and invited Van Raalte and Brummelkamp to participate, Harmen Hendriks Middel, a blacksmith by trade, did not impress the body. Van Raalte summed up the general feeling when he declared that Middel "had gathered many matters in his mind ... and demonstrated in the preaching and in further examination that he is somewhat slow in understanding, incorrect in judgment, and has confusion in language, so that ... his confusion and darkness makes his presentation unintelligible." But Middel passed his examination a year later at the Provincial Classis of Groningen, Friesland, and Drenthe, with Van Raalte and Brummelkamp present as examiners, and he turned out to be a good pastor. In 1856 he led the Middelburg, Zeeland, congregation of 635 souls. Clearly, Middel's lack of education made him stumble when learned men asked theoretical and philosophical questions, such as: "One speaks much about reason, the preciousness of it, and its authority. What is reason?" The professors aimed for an educated and articulate clergy, but they failed to ground their expectations in reality. Most parishioners in Separated churches were uneducated.[27]

Willem Van Leeuwen's classical examination offers yet another example of candidacy issues, specifically, which church body had the right to examine candidates. The provincial synod of Overijssel and Gelderland resolved in 1844 that they as a higher body must *re*-examine candidates admitted by the Overijssel classical examiners on the ground that this assembly lacked rigorous standards. When the provincial synod of sixteen pastors, together with elders and deacons, gathered for their 1845 meeting, they had to face the fact that Middel and Van

---

[26] De Graaf, "Een Monument der Afscheiding," 23; Reenders, "Van Raalte als leider," 169n443; citing Brummelkamp's letter to Van Raalte, 8 Oct. 1844; Van Raalte to seminarian Dirk Broek, 30 Nov. 1863, trans. Ten Hoor; Te Velde, *Brummelkamp*, 155-71; Te Velde, "Ministerial Education," 206-7. Scholte's wife, Sara Brand, had died on Jan. 23, 1844, and he was left to care for five daughters. On 13 June 1845, he married Maria Hendrika Kranz, an artistic and cultured younger woman, unsuited for life in a frontier Iowa manse (Oostendorp, *Scholte*, 131-34).

[27] Smits, *Afscheiding van 1834*, 1:338-44; Te Velde, *Brummelkamp*, 163; De Graaf, "Een Monument der Afscheiding," 24; Soepenberg, *Afscheiding in Amsterdam*, 293-95; *Jaarboekje voor de Christelijk Afgescheidene Gereformeerde Kerk*, 26.

Leeuwen had been rejected by one school but accepted by another. The differing standards and religious emphases understandably caused dissension. Synod 1845 was slated to examine Van Leeuwen and Apolonius G. de Waal. Van Leeuwen had trained under Van Raalte at Ommen, and De Waal sat under Brummelkamp and Van Raalte at Arnhem. Neither had been examined by the Classis of Overijssel. The question was: If they successfully passed the synodical exam, would they have to stand a second time for a classical exam?

Van Raalte argued, successfully, to rescind the resolution of the previous synod and allow classis to have the final say. At this, his brother-in-law, Carel de Moen, objected vociferously, believing that the classical examiners had admitted too many incapable pastors. "May God prevent this," De Moen cried. But classis stuck to its decision, and the examination proceeded. But it quickly became apparent that the candidates' sermon exegeses were confused, so Brummelkamp, the president, stopped the examination. All agreed with this decision, yet the body acknowledged that both men were fully capable of pastoring congregations, as they did after later passing classical examinations. Van Leeuwen served four churches in the Christian Separated body before leaving for America, and De Waal labored in eight congregations in the homeland for more than four decades.[28]

The Arnhem "school of the prophets" of the Gelderse *richting* (Gelderland party) was competing against the Drentse *richting* (Drenthe party) schools of De Haan in the city of Groningen and the Kok brothers in Hoogeveen. Brummelkamp and Van Raalte claimed their training was far superior to that of the old fashioned De Haan and the brothers Kok. The protégés of De Haan and the Koks, however, charged the Arnhem men with doctrinal errors and their graduates with ineptness in the pulpit. Although excellence is in the eye of the beholder, the Arnhem school likely had the edge, but the Northern schools carried the day. They trained three-quarters of all Separatist ministers prior to the founding of the seminary at Kampen in 1854. Their conservative stamp shaped the young denomination.[29]

[28] De Haas, *Gedenkt uw voorgangers*, 180; minutes, Provincial Classis of Overijssel, 1848; *Honderd Veertig Jaar Gemeenten* (Oct. 1974), 233, 262. The founding of the theological school at Kampen in 1854 brought greater unity. In 1856, according to the first denominational directory, the seminary had 4 professors and 42 students. The school served the denomination, which had 234 congregations with 50,000 communicants (Van Raalte letter to editor, 9 July 1856, in *De Hollander*, 16 July 1856).

[29] Te Velde, "Dutch Background," 85-87; Engelsma, *Watchman on the Walls*, 172-73.

Little did Van Raalte know that his fruitful ministry in church and school in Arnhem would end abruptly. The Velp church that had committed to pay his annual salary of ƒ1000 was unable in early 1846 to fulfill its pledge; all they could contribute was house rental. Crop failures had devastated the economy, and the Overijssel and Gelderland congregations, including those in Velp-Arnhem, could no longer support the seminary. As a result, the consistory gave Van Raalte "his freedom to look elsewhere" for a position. This was the crisis that pushed him to emigrate to America. After he left, most of the students seriously considered going to America as well. They all learned English industriously. Veenhuizen, the language teacher, emigrated in March 1847, and half of the fourteen students soon followed. Brummelkamp worried that the seminary might have to close, but he carried on, at first with only seven tuition-paying students. In 1854 he was appointed to the new school at Kampen, where he remained until retirement in 1882. Van Raalte, for his part, never lost his drive for good schooling. One of his first acts in the Holland colony was to found a school to prepare ministers and teachers for immigrant communities.[30]

---

[30] Brummelkamp, "Van Raalte," 110-11, trans. Ten Hoor; Reenders, "Van Raalte als leider," 169, trans. Dekker; Te Velde, *Brummelkamp*, 163; Kennedy, *Commentary*, 2:1260-61.

CHAPTER 7

Fleeing the Homeland: "We must go to America."

Life was not going well for Van Raalte in Arnhem in 1844-46. The joys he had experienced teaching with Brummelkamp and the close familial contacts that Christina had treasured had all come crashing down. A national economic downturn and penury among Separatists had left him without church support. His decade-long ministry as the "apostle of Overijssel," though dogged by persecution, had, however, strengthened the Reformed faith in the southeastern heartland, and this itinerant ministry was "his finest hour." But he suffered permanent wounds from disputes among his colleagues over church polity and practice. Even his brother-in-law and clerical colleague, Simon van Velzen, had derided him. Schisms by Kruisgezinden and other like-minded groups had rent his congregations. Then typhoid fever ravaged him. In agony, Van Raalte cried to God: "All thy waves and all thy billows have washed over me" (Psalm 42:7b, KJV). His prayer was answered by another raging epidemic—America fever. The cure was emigration with his family and followers to the land of opportunity.[1]

---

[1] Dosker, *Van Raalte*, 55-59, trans. Dekker; Brummelkamp, "Van Raalte," 109-10; Kennedy, *Concise History*, 305.

"Malaise"

Van Raalte's biographers took their cue from the dominee that religious oppression was his primary motive for emigrating. Later in life, as he reflected on his decision, Van Raalte emphasized persecution all the more. And he was half right. Although overt police repression had ended five years before his emigration, harassment had continued with fines for worship, blacklists of employees, and boycotts of craftsmen and shopkeepers. Separatists in the villages had remained *personae non gratae* for decades. Some have equated the persecution of the Dutch Separatists with that of the English Puritans and even with the hardships experienced by the Israelites in Egypt. Nevertheless, even during these conflicts, Van Raalte's star had shone brightly. He had countered opposing mayors and constables as a soldier without a sword, a warrior fighting for a righteous cause.

The future of the Netherlands at that time was as clouded as Van Raalte's personal future. The *Landverhuizing* pamphlet that Brummelkamp and Van Raalte had published in 1846 cited the economic crisis and forebodings of a dark future. The country was in a state of deep depression and malaise and in the throes of political protests that climaxed in the revolutions of 1848 across Europe. God's hand of judgment lay heavy on the nations, including the Netherlands.[2]

Brummelkamp and Van Raalte put their stake in the ground in the much-quoted pamphlet, *Landverhuizing, of waarom bevorderen wij de volksverhuizing en wel naar Noord Amerika en niet naar Java?* (Emigration, or why do we advocate emigration to North America and not to Java):

> Let us rather plumb the depths of our misery, even though this might cause our hair to stand on end.... The future of the land of our Fathers is most pitiable! No, our pen is not dipped in gall.... We have to write the truth, the plain truth to brethren elsewhere; because we may not say that misery and distress are glory and joy.... The cry of the laboring man ascends to the ears of the Lord.... Oh, observe that the common people, the salt and backbone of the nation, are being made ready to leave you![3]

The pair decried the fact that able-bodied men had to rely on charity. "Among those who we supported from the deacons' chest, there

---

[2] Brummelkamp and Van Raalte, *Landverhuizing*; Krabbendam, *Freedom on the Horizon*, 10-16; Swierenga, "By the Sweat of our Brow," 1-6; Swierenga, "The Dutch," 285.

[3] Brummelkamp and Van Raalte, *Landverhuizing*, 4-7, 27.

were those in the full strength of their lives," they declared. "Didn't they want to work? Oh, so much; of this, we were convinced, but there isn't any work or not enough to sustain a living." The clerics continued: "When a farmstead was for rent or came up for sale, there were twenty or forty people speculating on it. If a house had to be built, twenty carpenters wanted the work; otherwise, they would be without work." Breadwinners could not fulfill the biblical injunction "By the sweat of your face, you shall eat bread" (Gen. 3:19, NASB), which contains both a promise and a duty. "We need a place where work waits for workers, not where workers wait for work." When critics charged that the clerics were being too materialistic, Brummelkamp softened the rhetoric: "We have indicated the material aspect as the cause why many *must* move, but we have also pressed the point that this is to be achieved in a religious and God-glorifying manner."[4]

That the clerics were describing real problems is clear from a review of setbacks the Netherlands had been facing since the French occupation. The nine-year Belgian war of independence (1830-39) cost the Netherlands the most industrialized half of its kingdom, lowered Dutch national prestige, and prompted the king to abdicate the throne in 1840. These years were marked by persistent poverty and pauperism, with high population growth, handcraft workers undercut by cheap factory imports, and farm laborers supplanted by machines. The Dutch economy was working at a low level of productivity, and industrial modernization was lagging. The government levied high taxes and heavy regulation, whereas Great Britain and the United States were moving toward low taxes and free trade. The industrial revolution in the Netherlands began late in comparison to other countries, more than one hundred years after England and fifty years after the United States.[5] Industry began in the mid-nineteenth century in various isolated spots in the Netherlands but was not full blown until the new century.

Farming in the Netherlands had too many laborers working small and inefficient plots. Wheat had become an international commodity, and to compete, Dutch farmers had to consolidate farms and mechanize routine tasks. Grain farmers in the sea-clay regions led the way in modernization, and redundant farm workers were cast adrift.

---

[4] Ibid., 7, 34 (quotes), trans. Nella Kennedy; Brummelkamp Jr., *Brummelkamp*, 201-2; Van Raalte, Detroit, to Brummelkamp, 30 Jan. 1847, a lengthy report published in Brummelkamp, *Holland in Amerika*, 5-43, trans. Ten Hoor, Nella Kennedy.
[5] Griffiths, *Industrial Retardation in the Netherlands*.

They could not find factory work because of lagging industrialization. In short, political and religious turmoil, lackluster economic growth, and agricultural change created a climate of despair that left landless workers destitute.

In the mid-1840s, the failure of the potato and rye crops—mainstays in the diet of the lower class—pushed many over the edge. The Dutch lived on potatoes, sometimes three meals a day. They were second only to Ireland in potato consumption. For fifty years, potatoes were cheap and abundant, but in 1845, a fungus blight wiped out three-quarters of the crop, and two-thirds were lost the next year. Potato prices shot up 250 percent. Rye, the cheap grain of the poor, had rust disease, and rye prices doubled in 1846. Losing these crops was a double whammy for the poor. Day laborers fortunate to find work earned thirty Dutch cents per day (12 US cents), compared to one dollar per day in America.[6] The Netherlands was in the throes of a depression akin to Great Depression of the 1930s in the United States.

This was a wake-up call for Van Raalte and Brummelkamp who proclaimed a day of prayer and fasting in August 1845 for all Separatist churches. Provincial assemblies announced the event in local newspapers, such as *Drentsche Courant*, reporting potato fields "stand dying" from a "powerful pestilence," and grain crops "are still threatened." Everyone "who still believes that God blesses a nation or chastises it... must confess their sins and the nation's... [and] submit to the mighty hand of God."[7]

Six months later, in February 1846, Rev. Cornelius Van der Meulen, who served twelve congregations in the province of Zeeland from his mother church at Goes, called believers together for another day of fasting and prayer. The state of the country and the church is deplorable, he declared. There is "general misery," and people are "given over to complete destruction and callousness." Sin is "openly indulged as in Sodom, and expertly practiced as in Nineveh." People must repent to gain God's blessings.[8]

---

[6] Hein Van der Haar, a Holland Colony pioneer, recalled this wage at a gathering of old timers, "Our Old Settlers," *Holland City News*, 23 Mar. 1878.

[7] Van Raalte and Brummelkamp to Mr. Smedes, Assen, 15 Aug. 1845, Rijksarchief Gelderland, trans. Ten Hoor; Brummelkamp and Van Raalte, *Landverhuizing*; *Provinciale Overijsselsche en Zwolsche Courant*, 19 Aug. 1845 (www.delpher.nl, accessed, June 2021); *Drentsche Courant*, 1845.

[8] Van der Meulen, *Opwekking tot het houden van eenen algemeenen Dank-, Vast- en Bededag* (25 Feb. 1846), 3, 5 (quotes), trans. Ten Hoor.

King Willem II proclaimed a national day of prayer to ask God to deliver the people from their "deep suffering." Food riots broke out in cities. By 1850 more than one quarter of the population needed food and fuel handouts. Taxes were crushing those still employed. Workingmen paid one-seventh of their income in taxes, including license fees on all trades. Worse, said the Separatist dominees, tax monies went "to support the State Church and Roman Catholic superstition." Sharply dropping birth rates also indicated hard times; the number of live births declined in the 1840s by nearly 20 percent.[9]

Social conditions in Van Raalte's Arnhem congregation at the turn of the year 1845-46 reflected the national situation in microcosm. In the face of "bitter poverty," the consistory, under the terms of its royal recognition, was duty bound to care for its poor, yet the potato famine was overwhelming. Should the deacons give money or food? They chose the latter. Needy families were given a barrel of cabbage, four barrels of rye to grind and bake into bread, and coal dust for the cook stove. Clothing was also distributed. Van Raalte insisted on giving alms for as short a time as possible, to pressure men to find work. He did not want to create dependency, "permanent almsmen," he called them. Widows and the infirm were exempted. The dominee himself was a victim of the economic crisis when in 1845 the Arnhem-Velp congregation had to release him. That many of its members were leaving for America added to the tight purse.[10]

Hendrik Scholte reinforced calls for emigration among the *kleine luijden* (literally, "little people") in the Separatist periodical, *De Reformatie*. Hans Krabbendam calls Scholte the "crowbar," whose skillful editorials pried loose folks of all classes, especially those who were wavering. Newspaper reports on Scholte's recruitment efforts labeled his followers simpletons for listening to him. Emigration was unpatriotic and hurtful.[11]

What God wills

Guided by the Bible for faith and life, the immigrants lived by the credo: "What God wills, not what I will." They believed that God had called them to leave the fatherland, and they explained (some

---

[9] Lucas, *Netherlanders*, 54-55.
[10] Minutes, Arnhem Separated Church, 6 Nov. 1845, 20 Aug. 1846, art. 7, copied and translated into English by H. Hafkamp, Arnhem, 12 Aug. 1847; Lucas, *Dutch Immigrant Memoirs*, 1:14-20, 23-27.
[11] Krabbendam, *Freedom on the Horizon*, 342.

would say rationalized) their decision by an appeal to the scriptures. Barring repentance like Nineveh of old, the Lord will "spew out of his mouth . . . the hardened Netherlands." Its public sins rivaled the immorality of Sodom and the "lukewarm" Laodicean church in Asia Minor (modern Turkey) that boasted of its wealth while neglecting the poor. It was a modern Babylon. Van Raalte also had a foreboding sense of dread over the rising political unrest of liberal democrats to bring down monarchs. "Rebellion and betrayal" were in the air. "The entire social structure [is] suffering from oppression," and "laboring men [are] crying to the Lord for relief."[12]

Scholte preached even more strongly that Europe was a decadent, doomed civilization, ripe for God's judgment. Believers must escape the wrath to come, quoting the Apostle John's apocalyptic warning: "Come out of her, my people, that ye be not partakers of her sins, and that ye receive not of her plagues" (Revelation 18:4, KJV). In this conviction, Scholte later named his Iowa colony "Pella" (city of refuge), after a town in the district of Decapolis (east of the Sea of Galilee in the mountains of Gilead), where Christians had fled in 70 AD following the Roman destruction of Jerusalem. The revolutions of 1848, barely a year after the first Separatist groups emigrated, lent credence to Scholte's prophecy. Erupting first in France and spreading quickly to Germany, Austria, the Netherlands, and elsewhere, mob violence and street fighting behind barricades seemed to presage the breakup of European civilization.[13]

Rev. Van der Meulen, in a widely circulated letter for prospective immigrants, also urged believers to consider fleeing to America because the fatherland was "going under. . . . God is just and chastises sin." Europe was Sodom and Gomorrah, and the emigrants should leave immediately and not look back. "Remember Lot's wife" (Luke 17:32, KJV), declared Rev. Gerrit Baay, who led his followers to Alto, Wisconsin.[14]

[12] Swierenga, "Pioneers for Jesus Christ," and Brummelkamp and Van Raalte, *Landverhuizing*, 7-11.
[13] Oostendorp, *Scholte*, 147-52. The Dutch "revolution" deserves asterisks, according to James C. Kennedy, because "unrest remained limited." A liberal constitution in 1848, written by Leiden professor Johan Rudolph Thorbeke, was passed in 1848. Technically, but not actually, it separated church and state and granted parliamentary governance, popular sovereignty, and property suffrage for the most wealthy 10 percent (Kennedy, *Concise History*, 304-9, quote, 307).
[14] C. Van der Meulen to church community in Goes, 8 Oct. 1847, in De Jonge, *Aan al mijne geliefde vrienden in Nederland*; Gerrit Baay, 4 Jan. 1849, to "Dear Friends in Holland." The letter was published in pamphlet form in Amsterdam in 1849. An

And they did flee, but fear of the sea was very real for Dutch landlubbers. When a young man from Uithuizen, Groningen, bade farewell to his church family before setting out on the ocean, the pastor's wife insisted on reading aloud:

> They that go down to the sea in ships, that do business in great waters; these see the works of the LORD, and his wonders in the deep. For he commandeth, and raiseth the stormy wind, which lifteth up the waves thereof. . . . Their soul is melted because of trouble. They reel to and fro, and stagger like a drunken man, and are at their wits' end. Then they cry unto the LORD in their trouble, and he bringeth them out of their distresses. He maketh the storm a calm, so that the waves thereof are still. Then they are glad because they be quiet; so he bringeth them unto their desired haven. (Psalm 107: 23-30, KJV)

Derk Natelborg noted in his memoirs, written years later, that God had answered this prayer. When the storm was at its height, and the passengers at their wits' end, they cried to the Lord and he "brought them to their desired haven."[15]

The Separatists were steeped in the Bible and turned to it in every crisis in life. It was said of them that a Bible always lay close at hand. And when facing death, it provided a solace. In a last letter to her children, a widow wrote: "Dear Children, oh, pray to God daily and do not let a day pass without reading his Word. Let nothing keep you from doing that, it alone remains when all else fails."[16]

Christian education

Dire economic circumstances forced the Seceders to look overseas for a better life, but there was another factor that occupied them for many years: educational freedom. For Van Raalte, this was of equal importance to religious freedom. In the appeal for Christian schools that Van Raalte, Brummelkamp, and Ten Bokkel published in 1844, *Nog is er hulpe! Een woord aan al het godvreezend volk* (There is still help! A word to all God-fearing people), they pressed parents to honor vows made at baptism to support Christian schools. "Home, school, and

---

English translation, "Dear Friends Back Home," was published in *Delta* (Sept. 1959): 26-35 (quote 34).

[15] Derk Natelborg, "Memoirs," Chicago, 23 Dec. 1890, provided to the author by great-great-grandson Robert Zwiers.

[16] H. S. (Mrs. Anne M.) Van Hall-Schermbeek letter, 20 Dec. 1843, in *Iowa Letters*, 31.

church must be one; otherwise, the lack of principle and the confusion of tongues of this age will characterize our children."[17]

The *Landverhuizing* pamphlet of 1846 continued the theme:

> The heavy hand of government . . . encroaches on the most sensitive rights of a father, compelling him to choose between two extremes, both leading to a state of wretchedness; either to let his children grow up in ignorance, or send them to a school, where, according to the father's deepest convictions, their minds will be corrupted, and where the Bible, the Word of God . . . is banned at the request of a third party, who bows down to images or teaches that children must not be encumbered with the Word of God. . . . And does not proof abound that the well-meaning teacher is regarded as a lawbreaker for his biblical teaching and educating and must inevitably lose his job?[18]

Van Raalte brought the matter home when he confessed that Christian education for his growing family was one of his strongest motives for going to America.[19]

American pull factors

Though he had never been there, Dutch poet Everhardus Johannes Potgieter idealized life in the United States. In one of his poems, he encouraged the Dutch to go to the United States, copying the title of Emanuel Gottlieb Leuze's 1861 mural, *Westward the Course of Empire Takes Its Way*, which now hangs in the US Capitol. Holland was in decline, and America was a place of rising expectations.[20] Its economy was booming, and the newly opened midwestern frontier offered cheap and abundant farmland. Wages of one dollar a day (equivalent to the Dutch *rijksdaalder*, or f2.50) were double and triple that of the Netherlands; food was better, including meat and bacon; social class distinctions were minimal; most male citizens could vote; and everyone could worship freely and open Christian schools without government hindrance. The $1.00 wage, coupled with the $1.25 per acre price of public lands, meant that fifty days of work could fund forty acres of virgin land. For Dutch tenant farmers, day laborers, and small

---

[17] A. Brummelkamp, ten Bokkel, and Van Raalte, *Nog is er hulpe!* 14 (quote); Reenders, "Van Raalte als leider," 189, 376n552.
[18] Brummelkamp and Van Raalte, *Landverhuizing*, 16-17, trans. Nella Kennedy.
[19] Te Velde, *Brummelkamp*, 178.
[20] Potgieter, "Landverhuizing."

landowners, whose plots upon death had to be sold to pay siblings their inheritance, owning a farm was unthinkable, but in America, it was easily within reach. What was there not to like about the land of opportunity and freedom, where nobody was called master?[21]

Sparking colonization

As early as 1844, poor families from the Achterhoek region in southeastern Gelderland began emigrating to America, prompted by tens of thousands of Germans moving down the Rhine for a better life in America. In the next decades, more than thirty-six hundred Hollanders left the Achterhoek, the most overseas emigrants from any region of the Netherlands. Soon return mail brought a steady flow of glowing "America letters" about abundant food, cheap farmland, low taxes, and social equality. The euphoria was so great that it motivated half the inhabitants of Winterswijk—the epicenter of the early emigration. Separatists were in the vanguard. More than half of all emigrants from Gelderland in the 1840s were Separatists, and they comprised fully two-thirds of all Separatists in the province. Churches were hollowed out, and many closed.[22]

News of the movement reached Van Raalte and Brummelkamp at Arnhem in the fall of 1845, and for the first time, they gave serious thought to emigrating. But most Separatist clerics strongly condemned emigration as desertion of the fatherland, disrespectful of government authority, and the worship of Mammon. Even though the future of the Netherlands looked dark, emigrating was still a sinful act. Van der Meulen, the "apostle of Zeeland" and later cofounder of the Zeeland, Michigan, colony, opposed Van Raalte to his face. "We pray that the Lord may spare his children from leaving the land of their birth because of worldly mindedness and go to foreign lands to find a roomier existence." Those who left for America risked losing their Christian faith, and they put heavier burdens on those staying behind to maintain churches and communities.[23]

Debate among Separatist leaders continued as emigration became a "great moving force," with "thousands ... ready to go." Many

---

[21] B. W. A. E. Baron Sloet tot Oldhuis, "The Cause of Dutch Emigration to America: An 1866 Account," Robert P. Swierenga, ed., Dirk Hoogeveen, trans., *Michigan*, 24 (nos. 1-2), 1979.

[22] Swierenga, *Faith and Family*, 104-5; Ligterink, *De landverhuizers*, 31-32; Lucas, *Netherlanders*, 53-55, 62.

[23] Van der Meulen, *Opwekking*, 8. A brief biographical sketch is Krabbendam, "Cornelius van der Meulen," 315-32.

a congregational meeting was devoted to discussing the issue. For a generally "stay put" people, America was far away, across a feared ocean, and leaving loved ones was like a deathbed goodbye, to be reunited only in Heaven. Deserting the fatherland also made emigrants a despised lot among kith and kin. Nevertheless, more and more believers became convinced that going to America was a God-given opportunity. In May Scholte reported in *De Reformatie* that colonization would go forward, whether in large or small groups.[24]

Van Raalte considers emigration

Van Raalte was also convinced: "Look at the children," he told his wife. "We must go to America." The tipping point came when Alexander Hartgerink, a Separatist schoolmaster in the Achterhoek (the "back corner" of the province of Gelderland, near the German border) made a farewell call on Brummelkamp in the fall of 1845 and showed him glowing letters from Separatists who were already prospering in America. Hartgerink agreed to send back a report after a year, but he was so amazed by what he found in Toledo, Ohio, that he penned a letter after six months, in May 1846. "You cannot imagine how beautiful this country looks in summer and in autumn," he wrote. "Commerce and shipping, both internal and foreign, thrive abundantly. The mills and many other industries are better than in the Netherlands." Instead of a "savage land for riff-raff," America was a place for Separatists to thrive. Hartgerink told of living like a king in a boarding house. "I have a private room, receive three times a day sweetened coffee or tea, bread, butter, meat, fish, potatoes, vegetables, and since Easter, many eggs. A family of three or four can live on those for fourteen shillings [$2 US], and daily wages are six to eight shillings [75 cents to $1, or $30 to $40 today]."[25]

Hartgerink's report, which was too good to be believed, was backed up by Arnoldus Hallerdyk's letter from Milwaukee, in which he reported eating pork and beef three times a day, and Jan Arend Beukenhorst's letter from Decatur, Illinois: "The poor here are as good as the rich, and no one needs to doff his hat to anyone, as in Holland." These three Separatist families, sent out as scouts with

---

[24] Scholte to Groen van Prinsterer, 15 May, 9 Oct. 1846, trans. Dekker; "*Aanmerkingen betrekkelijk,*" *De Reformatie* (June 1846), 355-59, trans. Ten Hoor.

[25] Van Hinte, *Netherlanders*, 128; Hartgerink (Toledo, OH) to Brummelkamp and Van Raalte, 3 May 1846, in De Jonge, *Reglement der Zeeuwsche Vereeniging*, 47-55; Brummelkamp, "Van Raalte," 107-8.

financial help from the dominees, spoke in glowing terms of life in the heartland. Hartgerink later homesteaded in Noordeloos, Michigan; Hallerdyk found work as a carpenter in Milwaukee, and Beukenhorst farmed in Decatur, Illinois.[26] Roelof Sleyster, a deacon from the Velp congregation, reported from Waupun, Wisconsin, in August 1846, that the ten Dutch families there were thriving on land costing from $1.25 to $2 per acre. Best of all, the influence of Christianity is strong, the Sabbath is "faithfully observed," and people lived in peace. Brummelkamp was dumbfounded:

> I read, was amazed, and full of emotion, I sent for Van Raalte. We both knew the writers of these letters had been poor as church mice; but these lines spoke of an abundance such as was no longer imaginable in the Fatherland. We were speechless. A light dawned on us in the darkness of the diaconate's welfare program. God opened our eyes. . . . Now we saw that on God's earth, there was plenty of room, one only had to move over a bit![28]

America, not Java

As the leaders looked to plant a colony overseas, the island of Java in the Netherlands East Indies (now Indonesia) was an attractive possibility because it was under the Dutch flag and settlers would not have to renounce the Dutch monarch and be demonized for deserting the fatherland. Scholte took the lead in considering Java, and Van Raalte and Brummelkamp went along, until government officials squashed the idea.

In April 1846, in a meeting in deacon Johannes Donner's house in Arnhem, some prospective emigrants, hesitant about going to North America, pushed for Java.[29] This was a naïve aspiration from the outset; the hurdles were far too high. Decades earlier, in 1819 and

---

[26] A. Hallerdyk (Milwaukee, Wisconsin) to My Dear Father (Sept. 1845), 40-43; J. A. Beukenhorst (Decatur, Illinois), 16 June 1845, 44-46. The letters of A. Hallerdyk (Milwaukee), Sept. 1845; Beukenhorst (Decatur), 16 June 1845; Hartgerink (Toledo), 3 May 1845, are published in *Reglement der Zeeuwsche Vereeniging*, 40-56. Hartgerink served in the Mexican War and then settled on a farm in North Holland, Michigan. For his life course and tragic death, see *Holland City News*, 28 Sept. 1874.

[27] Sleyster to Brummelkamp, 25 Aug. 1846, in Brummelkamp, *Stemmen uit Noord-Amerika*, trans. Ten Hoor; Scholte, "Amerika," *De Reformatie* (1846), 276-91, trans. Ten Hoor; Ottho G. Heldring, "*Eenige Gedachten over Colonizatie*," *De Reformatie* (1846), 260-64, trans. Ten Hoor; Lucas, *Netherlanders*, 58.

[28] Brummelkamp, "Van Raalte," 107-8; Brummelkamp Jr., *Brummelkamp*, 202-3.

[29] Lucas, "Landverhuizing Memoriaal, 1846," 103.

1825, the Dutch government had restricted East Indies emigration to technical and trained men. Then, in 1830, King Willem I established the Cultivation System, which, among other things, stipulated that native farmers must produce only staple crops for export, that is, sugar, indigo, tea, coffee, and tobacco. How could Separatist farmers successfully grow these unfamiliar crops in a climate much hotter than their own? Moreover, Java's mostly Muslim population was prone to rebel, so government policy toned down Christianity to appease them.[30] How could devout Protestants have managed in such an environment?

Rev. Ottho Heldring, a friend of Separatists, persuaded Scholte to ask the minister of colonies in The Hague to allow Separatists to set up a colony on the island of Java. Heldring agreed to accompany him. A fervent royalist, Scholte also found attractive the idea of remaining a subject of the king. But their request fell on deaf ears. The minister had, some years earlier, sent four hundred Dutch settlers to plant a colony in Surinam, but many died, and most survivors returned.[31] This failed experiment was reason enough to turn Scholte down. He did the leaders a favor, but they did not recognize it at the time.

Brummelkamp and Van Raalte wrote bitterly in their *Landverhuizing* pamphlet:

> We have come to the conclusion that this government is completely unwilling to promote any kind of emigration to Java, even though the Minister admitted that vast land regions were lying unused. . . . The stubborn opposition of the government against freedom of religion and education encourages the wish to leave.[32]

In an address in 1872, Van Raalte still maintained that the Netherlands "did not dare to permit liberty to flourish on Java."[33] This thinking indicates that Van Raalte had never grasped the complexities of colonial life in the Indies, the stringent farming regulations, and the emigration restrictions. In short, Brummelkamp and Van Raalte were as naïve as the prospective emigrants at Deacon Donner's house.

The *Landverhuizing* pamphlet went through three printings and prompted families to depart in droves. Amsterdam newspapers,

---

[30] Burgers, *De garoeda*, 266.
[31] Lucas, "Beginnings of Dutch Immigration," 498-99.
[32] Brummelkamp and Van Raalte, *Landverhuizing*, 22-25, 35.
[33] Van Raalte "Commemoration Address, 1872," 2:484.

Johan A. Wormser (1807-1862), Amsterdam educator, law partner of F. A. van Hall (*Wesseling, De Afscheiding van 1834*)

the *Amsterdamsche Courant* and *Handelsblad*, reported on groups of Separatists sailing from Dutch ports throughout the fall of 1846. Johan A. Wormser told Groen van Prinsterer that as many as six thousand Separatists "have decided to go to America." This turned out to be a gross exaggeration. The pamphlet also sparked criticism from Separatists opposed to emigration as morally unjustified—even a "sickness"—and economically unnecessary.[34]

Arnhem Emigration Society

The May 14, 1846, meeting showed that Van Raalte and Brummelkamp were resolved to go to North America. Emigration fervor "like a breath of God ... ripened simultaneously [and] moved over the entire country," Van Raalte noted. "It can be stopped no more than the course of the Rhine [River] can be changed." Some "shepherds of the flock" had to step up and "prevent scattering and the intrusion of strangers," he told Groen van Prinsterer, since it would "be fruitless work to give direction to the stream after the dike has been broken."[35] This was a metaphor every Hollander could understand.

---

[34] Wormser, *Door kwaad gerucht*, 196-201, citing letters between Wormser and Groen van Prinsterer, 15 May, 9, 29 Oct., 12 Dec. 1846, trans. Buursma; *Algemeen Handelsblad* (Amsterdam), 23 Sept. 1846, 12 Jan. 1847; *Leydsche Courant*, 9 Oct. 1846 (www.delpher.nl, accessed, June 2021).

[35] Van Raalte to Groen van Prinsterer, 17 Apr. 1846, trans. Ten Hoor (quote); Brummelkamp and Van Raalte, *Landverhuizing*; *De Bazuin*, 15 Nov. 1872 (www.delpher.nl, accessed June 2021).

In mid-April 1846, Brummelkamp and Van Raalte organized an emigration society of congregants from Arnhem, Velp, and Oosterbeek, plus a few from Genemuiden, Van Raalte's first charge. The fledgling society adopted a constitution, known as the *Landverhuizing Memoriaal 1846*, which stated that its purpose was to plant a colony based on God's commandments and salted by a majority of true believers.[36]

The Arnhem Emigration Society was governed democratically by a ten-member commission, elected by male members, who would "subject themselves to the Word of God," serve "out of love for God and the Brethren," and act as a "Christian government to maintain the enforcement of God's law in every situation." Total travel expenses were estimated at ƒ100 per person ($1,580 today). Wealthy members lent passage money to the able bodied and donated the funds for the needy, notably widows and orphans. Van Raalte contributed ƒ500, and Brummelkamp doubled that with ƒ1,000; Derk Van de Wal gave ƒ300 and Jan Binnekant ƒ100. Altogether, the society raised ƒ3,000 ($47,400 today) in "Gouden Willempjes" to purchase land in America. Members who borrowed passage fare and monies for land in America from the society pledged to devote one-fifth of their income or profits in America to pay it back, with 5 percent interest added. Only when the loans were repaid would they obtain land titles. They owed only the purchase price, plus expenses. Society funds were also given to buy land. These provisions enabled many poor people to emigrate and succeed.

Beginning in May 1846, the Arnhem society sent some thirty families (more than 100 souls) who were "knowledgeable in agriculture and the trades and able to earn their living." They were told to "unite with those living in Wisconsin, and in this way to seek one district to which the emigrants who follow can go." Wisconsin was specified because Separatists from the Winterswijk area of Gelderland and the province of Zeeland since 1844 had settled in and around Milwaukee. The group was tasked to report on land prices and soil fertility. If the news was favorable, the society would send "capable individuals" to purchase land in a bloc "for a community or village."[37]

---

[36] "Constitution for the Society for Dutch Emigration to North America," 16 articles, published in Wormser, *In twee werelddeelen*, 109-12; Lucas, "Landverhuizing Memoriaal 1846," 101-11; "Aanmerkingen betrekkelijk," *De Reformatie* (June 1846), 355-59, trans. Ten Hoor.

[37] Brummelkamp and Van Raalte, *Landverhuizing*, 38, 40-41; Swierenga and Krabbendam, "Dutch Catholics and Protestants," 48-49; Krabbendam, *Freedom on the Horizon*, 32-33; Lucas, *Netherlanders*, 59-61, 196-97; Van Hinte, *Netherlanders*, 123-24.

"Gouden Willempje," 2½ guilder coin (*Fred Hoek, Geloven in een Nieuwe Wereld*)

The Arnhem society is remarkable for its careful planning and for sending scouts in order to make intelligent decisions for a group migration to Wisconsin or Illinois. The Arnhem constitution mirrored that of Hendrik Scholte's Utrecht society. The expectation was for the two groups to settle together in one large colony, but this was never clearly spelled out.[38]

Scholte informed all Separatists in *De Reformatie* about the scouting party and advised anyone contemplating emigration to notify either him at Utrecht or Brummelkamp at Arnhem, and provide personal information, financial status, and willingness to help the poor. He specified that only sincere Christians need apply, in order to provide "a quiet and undisturbed life in godliness and decency . . . [where] folks can properly attend to social, moral, and religious development of the coming generation."[39] A consecrated Christian colony was the goal.

The appeal

In May 1846, Van Raalte and Brummelkamp wrote an appeal "to the Believers in the United States of North America" seeking their help. The emotional tract plucked at the heartstrings of the Old Dutch:

---

[38] Van Raalte "Commemoration Address, 1872," 2:484-85. The constitution of the Zeeland Emigration Association is reprinted in Beets, *Life and Times*, 24-30.

[39] Scholte, "Opmerking in Betrekking tot de Landverhuizing naar Noord-Amerika," *De Reformatie* (May 1846), 296-99, trans. Ten Hoor.

> Our heart's desire and prayer to God is, that in one of those uninhabited regions in America there may be a spot where our people ... may find their temporal subsistence secured. ... We would desire that they, settling in the same villages and neighborhoods, may enjoy the privilege of seeing their little ones educated in a Christian school.[40]

This appeal included a bill of indictment against the Netherlands. Every statement began with the question:

> Is it not true: that unequal taxes oppress the middle class, that laborers are often unemployed or underemployed, that greedy employers exploit their workers, that public welfare of *f*20 million is yet not enough, that Christian schools and religious worship are not allowed, that the fatherland is under God's imminent hand of judgment because of injustice and worldliness?[41]

The immigrant leaders had every expectation that their appeal would be heard. What they could not have known was that their timing was auspicious. Dutch New Yorkers by the mid-nineteenth century were experiencing a revival of ethnic pride, and those who could still speak the mother tongue were again looked on with favor.[42]

Van Raalte enlisted Roelof Sleyster, his ministerial student, and Jan Brusse to travel to America and personally deliver the appeal to Dutch New Yorkers in hopes of winning their support and advice about possible sites for a colony. The duo, with ten families in tow, fifty in number, all from the Gelderland Achterhoek and the province of Zeeland, sailed from Rotterdam on June 1, 1846, for the port of Boston. After disembarking, they took the train to Albany and found lodging at the Germania Hotel. Providentially, Rev. Isaac Wyckoff, pastor of the Second Reformed Protestant Dutch Church, happened to walk by and stopped short at hearing the Dutch tongue. After brief introductions, he invited Sleyster and Brusse to his home. This was Sleyster's perfect opportunity to deliver the appeal, which alerted Wyckoff to the coming Separatist immigration. A member of Wyckoff's congregation translated the document, and Wyckoff published it in the *Christian*

---

[40] Brummelkamp and Van Raalte, *Aan de Geloovigen*, published in *Christian Intelligencer*, 15 Oct. 1846; and in Lucas, *Dutch Immigrant Memoirs*, 1:14-20; Van Raalte to Brummelkamp, 27 Nov. 1846, in *Voices from America*, 11.
[41] "To the Believers," in Lucas, *Dutch Immigrant Memoirs*, 1:14-20.
[42] Fabend, "The Synod of Dort," 273-300.

Intelligencer, the denominational weekly based in New York City that reached every pastor in the denomination.[43]

News spread quickly in the Netherlands about Van Raalte's plans, especially among farm laborers, and the issue of emigrating became one of "serious spiritual and temporal concern," as Jan Hendriks Stegink recalled. "We approached the Lord for light in this weighty undertaking and came to the decision that we could leave the land of our fathers with a clear conscience." Evert Zagers and Egbert Frederiks from Emmen, Drenthe, traveled to Arnhem to consult with the trusted dominee and were convinced. The pair recruited six families and four unmarried adults, plus two families from Graafschap Bentheim. "It is remarkable," said Stegink, that "people totally unaccustomed to travel were bold enough to undertake such a long voyage. Most of us had never seen a ship. . . . But when the Lord inclines men and makes them willing, there is nothing to stop them," not even mockers who derided them as they left town. Crossing the feared ocean was God's will for them.[44]

Why did relatively few Separatists emigrate?

The secession from the Hervormde Kerk never became a mass movement. The 1849 population census counted only 40,300 Separatists—2.3 percent of Reformed believers—compared to 1.67 million (97.7 percent) in the Hervormde Kerk.[45] Of the 40,300 Separatists, one-fifth (7,600) emigrated at the height of America fever from 1846 to 1856. In those few years, they comprised nearly half of all emigrants, which gave them an outsized impact on the pioneer colonies. Over the entire period, to 1880, Separatists made up one-fourth of Dutch Protestant emigrants. In the 1840s, most emigrants were either followers of Van Raalte and Brummelkamp in Gelderland and Overijssel or Scholte in Utrecht, Zuid-Holland, and Zeeland. Considerably fewer came from Drenthe, Friesland, and Groningen. The outpouring from the North—Drenthe, Friesland, and Groningen—came after the Civil War, particularly during the agricultural crisis of the 1880s.[46]

---

[43] "Arend Jan Brusse's Reminiscences," in Lucas, *Dutch Immigrant Memoirs*, 1:46. Arend Jan was the eldest son of Jan and Grada Brusse.
[44] Jan Hendriks Stegink, "My Journey to America," in Lucas, *Dutch Immigrant Memoirs*, 1:135.
[45] De Kok, *Nederland*, 292; Swierenga, "Pioneers for Jesus Christ."
[46] Swierenga, "Pioneers for Jesus Christ," 40-43; Bruins and Swierenga, *Family Quarrels*, 6-7; Stokvis, *Nederlandse Trek naar Amerika*, 53-57.

Why did most Separatists stay home? One answer Hans Krabbendam suggests is that Separatists were divided in their ideas about the relation between church and state and their future prospects in the homeland. Van Raalte's brother-in-law Simon van Velzen, for instance, rebuked the Hervormde Kerk for its apostasy, but he also strongly opposed the emigration plans of Van Raalte, Brummelkamp, and Scholte. They stood on one extreme and Van Velzen on the other. He believed in law and order and submission to God's anointed rulers (Romans 13:1) and opposed "everything leading to disorder and agitation." He would settle for recognition of Separatist churches under the authority of a Christian monarch and an established church. Like Hendrik de Cock, Van Velzen trusted that Dutch monarchs would uphold Article 36 of the Belgic Confession, which charged righteous rulers with defending true religion against falsehood. Most Separatists embraced Dutch royalty and the Constitution of 1848. Scholte, at the other end of the spectrum, believed in separation of church and state—the American model—although he had welcomed King Willem II in 1840.[47]

Van Raalte and Brummelkamp stood in the middle; they accepted the conjoining of church and state but demanded freedom of worship and education for free churches. Their mentor was Groen van Prinsterer, the foremost proponent of a theocratic church-and-state regime, who remained loyal to both. Where one stood on church-state issues and their expectations, or not, for national moral improvement, strongly influenced their desire to emigrate. Yet, individual factors also came into play, and most ministers did not see their way clear to go to America.

By 1879, after many thousands of Separatists had emigrated to the United States, the Netherlands denomination numbered 140,000 souls, or 6 percent of Reformed believers. This total was a whopping 350 percent increase over thirty years. There were more than 350 congregations and about 250 ministers. This was no insignificant body, but it paled in comparison with nearly two million souls in the Hervormde Kerk. The Secession of 1834 cost the national church an estimated 5 percent of its membership by 1849, and not a single

---

[47] Simon van Velzen to King Willem II, 29 Jan. 1847; Baron Zuylen van Nyenvelt, secretary of religion, to King Willem II, 17 Feb. 1847, in *Archiefstukken*, 4:481-86, cited in Krabbendam, "Emigration as Protest?" 61-70 (quote 62); Heideman, *Scholte*, 143-62.

minister seceded after 1834. From the viewpoint of church leaders, the secession of 1834 was merely a blip on the screen of time.[48]

Final decisions

Van Raalte hovered near death from typhoid fever in the summer of 1846. It was his second health crisis after contracting cholera at Leiden fourteen years earlier. Soon after his recovery, his stressed congregation at Velp-Arnhem told him to "look elsewhere" for a position. For a minister to lose his pulpit due to penury was rare indeed, but Separatist clerics were at such a risk after breaking with the national church. Had he kept his position, he might well have continued to teach with Brummelkamp, and in 1854, the pair would likely have moved to the new seminary at Kampen.[49]

In September 1846, Van Raalte stunned Brummelkamp with a letter:

> So then I am thinking of leaving my fatherland! The voice and the needs of the brethren departing for North America urge me to do so. The hope that in this way many of our brethren in oppressed and straightened circumstances may find relief cheers me in my chosen path. And the needs of my family and especially the need of school instruction give me, besides other urgent reasons, keen incentive for this.[50]

He must go to shepherd the people and lessen the risk of their being scattered and lost to the faith. Brummelkamp was stunned and could hardly imagine losing his soulmate. He obviously expected other clerics to lead the way, perhaps younger men, without family obligations and church commitments.

It was a done deal. Van Raalte added that he had already purchased tickets from Rotterdam ship brokers Hudig & Blokhuizen to sail

---

[48] Van Gelderen, "Scheuring en Vereniging," 100-146; De Kok, *Nederland*, 292-93, reports that the Hervormde Kerk counted 60 percent of the population in 1839 and 55 percent in 1849, a 5 percent decline. Sweetman, "Children of the Day," 33, estimates a 10 percent decline, which may be closer to the mark than census statistics because a great number of Separatists remained officially registered as Hervormd (Te Velde, "Dutch Background," 92-93).

[49] Reenders, "Van Raalte als leider," 188; *Handelingen, Provinciale Vergadering Gelderland/Overijssel*, at Deventer, 14 Aug., 5 Sept. 1844; minutes, Arnhem Afgescheiden Kerk, 20 Aug. 1846, cited in Stokvis, *Nederlandse Trek naar Amerika*, 65; Scholte to Groen Van Prinsterer, 29 Oct. 1846, trans. Dekker.

[50] Van Raalte to Brummelkamp, 21 Sept. 1846, in Lucas, *Dutch Immigrant Memoirs*, 1:22-23.

on the SS *Southerner* on September 25. His party of 110 hailed mainly from Overijssel, with lesser contingents from Drenthe, Groningen, and Friesland. Albertus concluded his letter with lament for "the schisms, the estrangement, yes, even the embitterment among God's people." What he did not anticipate was that his followers would carry the controversies in their "baggage," and make his life in America even more fraught than in the homeland.[51]

Some months before this point of critical decision making, the General Synod of the Reformed Protestant Dutch Church commissioned Rev. Thomas De Witt of New York's Collegiate Church to visit the Netherlands and gather information on the Hervormde Kerk. That very year of 1844 saw the last Dutch-language worship service in New York at the Middle Dutch Church. Upon arrival, De Witt, to his surprise, learned about the emigration fever. He went to Utrecht to meet with Scholte in July 1846, who told him about the emigration societies and handed him a copy of the *Landverhuizing* pamphlet. De Witt, to his credit, promised to enlist his congregation and classis to help when immigrants arrived at New York harbor. He even formed a society that employed an agent to meet the ships, and he wrote numerous articles in the *Christian Intelligencer* to inform the faithful of the desperate needs of their Dutch cousins.[52]

In August of 1846, before his party was ready to embark, eleven members of Van Raalte's Genemuiden congregation decided to go ahead by way of Baltimore to St. Louis. The dominee gave them his blessing. They left Rotterdam on October 4, 1846, disembarked at Baltimore on December 18, took the train to Pittsburgh, boarded an Ohio River steamer, and arrived at St. Louis in February 1847. Later, six weeks after Van Raalte had established his Michigan colony, he urged them to come. They did and became vital members of the Holland colony. The group included siblings Wouter, Hein, and Elizabeth Van der Haar; Jannes Vrieze; and brothers Evert Jans and Jan Jans Visscher, with wives and children.[53]

Jan Jans Visscher's wife, Geesje (Grace) Van der Haar, sister of Hein and Wouter, described the emotional decision to emigrate:

[51] Ibid. Van Raalte's party, according to a newspaper report from Zwolle, included 18 from Heerde in Overijssel, 17 from Staphorst in Overijssel, and 9 from Noordbarge in Drenthe; 8 from Stadskanaal in Groningen, and 9 from Franeker and Sneek in Friesland (*Groninger Courant*, 2 Oct. 1846, report from Zwolle, 29 Sept. 1844, www.delpher.nl, accessed, June 2021). This is not the complete list.

[52] Demarest, *History and Characteristics*, 83; Lucas, *Netherlanders*, 70.

[53] Van Raalte commendation letter, 28 Aug. 1846, trans. Ten Hoor, HHA.

Then came the rumor that Van Raalte wished to go to America. My husband and brother wished to verify this and so made a trip to Arnhem where Van Raalte was then living. I was so against going to America that I warned them not to give any indication that they wanted to go too. I felt so firmly attached to our home in the Netherlands that I would rather die than go to America. But look what happened! The men came back and were of the opinion that we should go if God would show the way. Now we prayed about it and asked God for His light and counsel. We had a good living, and it seemed there was no reason why we should go to America. But the Lord wanted us to go. I prayed much that God might give us light. . . . Then it pleased God to make me realize it was His will that we should leave the oppressive atmosphere of the Netherlands with other people and emigrate to free and roomy America, where people, with God's help, could enjoy more freedom and better their economic condition.[54]

One of Van Raalte's last thoughts was to write a sort of apology to Groen van Prinsterer, who disapproved of the emigration: "You have not been ashamed of us, despite differing points of view. I found in you in the midst of scorn and rejection a warm brotherly love. One has to tread the path of scorn in order to discern who is a truly a brother. May God strengthen you and be a strength and bonding with the brethren."[55]

Van Raalte preached his farewell sermons on Sunday, September 20, 1846, based on the text: "Beloved, let us love one another: for love is of God; and every one that loveth is born of God, and knoweth God" (1 John 4:7, KJV). In the morning, he mounted the Velp pulpit and in the evening the Arnhem pulpit. Emotions were close to the surface in both congregations. After evening worship, the Velp-Arnhem elders released their pastor for greater service among those going to America. On Monday evening, the Arnhem congregation gathered again; Brummelkamp thanked his beloved brother for his ministry and commended him to the care of the Almighty. It was an irredeemable loss for the Brummelkamps. Albertus was his "beloved brother-in-law," and the feelings were mutual. For Brummelkamp to lose his seminary partner and fellow fighter for the future of the Separatist denomination cast

---

[54] "Geesje Van der Haar-Visscher Diary," 6-7.
[55] Brummelkamp Jr., *Brummelkamp*, 105, citing the letter in the Groen van Prinsterer archives. The entire letter can be found, in translation, in Lucas, *Dutch Immigrant Memoirs*, 22-23.

a dark shadow. As his parting gift, Van Raalte gave Brummelkamp a beautifully bound, five-volume set of the *Letters of Bilderdijk*.[56]

On Tuesday, Anthony and Maria Brummelkamp, along with members of their respective congregations, comprised a "praying and heart-rending escort" for the Van Raalte family as they all boated down the Rhine River to Rotterdam. Scholte awaited them at the steamship docks to say his goodbyes and perhaps to plan a joint venture. His departure was delayed by the illness of his wife. The Brummelkamps bade the group godspeed, and Anthony handed Van Raalte a purse with ƒ1,890 ($30,000 today). The money was prepayment for land in America from Jan Binnekant, Gerrit Ter Vree, Albert De Weerd, and Seth Nibbelink, plus ƒ500 ($7,900 today) for general expenses. The entire leave-taking was "unforgettable," Van Raalte recalled.

The farewell was essentially a funeral. Overseas travel was rare and much feared, and all but a few emigrants ever again saw the family they had left behind. Young son Anthony Brumelkamp Jr. remembered that his father fought tears during the congregational prayer on the first Sunday afterward. "My strength forsook me," his father confessed. His wife "having just arisen from childbirth, was ill for weeks due to the departure" of her only living sister.[57]

An unexpected, week-long delay made the leave-taking worse for the Van Raaltes. Two days after their ship left Rotterdam and traversed the Voorne Canal to Hellevoetsluis, the last port before the North Sea, a fire in the cook's galley on September 24 forced a delay for repairs. This gave Van Raalte the opportunity to preach in the packed Hellevoetsluis Separated church on September 27; the attendees were so crowded that everyone had to stand tightly packed.[58]

Christina hoped the Brummelkamps would follow them to America, but this was not to be, even though they had been practicing English. Albertus even bought property in Holland for the Brummelkamps, so certain was he that Anthony would come. But Anthony and Christina's brother Carel turned down repeated calls to Michigan congregations. De Moen declined five calls, one at Kalamazoo after his wife Agatha Sophia had died.[59] Why pastors accept or decline calls often remains inscrutable. Brummelkamp and

---

[56] Brummelkamp Jr., *Brummelkamp*, 579.
[57] Ibid., 219-20.
[58] Brummelkamp, "Van Raalte," 110; Dosker, *Van Raalte*, 66, trans. Dekker; Lucas, *Netherlanders*, 69-70. There was no direct entrance to the North Sea from Rotterdam until the Nieuwe Waterweg (the New Waterway) was completely finished in 1885.
[59] Wesseling, *Afscheiding van 1834, Classis Zwolle*, 268-69.

Anthony Brummelkamp (1811-1888), middle age (*JAH*)

Maria Wilhelmina de Moen Brummelkamp (1808-1873), middle age (*Rullmann, De Afscheiding*)

De Moen never lost their positions, as Van Raalte did, and neither one shared Albertus's restless and adventurous spirit. Brummelkamp's son described Van Raalte as a "man of energetic and short deliberation." He made up his mind quickly and went into action. Brummelkamp lacked this drive, this spirit of "go."[60]

Once in America, Christina reported later, Albertus "dreams regularly" about a trip to see Carel in Kalamazoo, and to visit with Anthony. "I often meet you in a dream," Albertus wrote Anthony, "and I embrace you while crying in joy." Christina was "consumed by the need to enjoy relationships with blood relatives," Albertus admitted. Christina spoke often of the trial of leaving but always added: "It is the Lord."[61]

The sense of separation deepened in America since letters from the homeland were infrequent and could only partially compensate for the loss of close familial connections. Albertus confided to Carel de Moen that they might hear from family only once a year and then only to announce a birth or death. "It irritated my wife," he noted, that "strangers had informed them of the upcoming wedding of Wilhelmina, a daughter of Maria de Moen's first marriage to Casper

---

[60] Brummelkamp Jr., *Brummelkamp*, 219.
[61] Van Raalte to De Moen, 25 March 1857; Brummelkamp Jr., *Brummelkamp*, 202, 219-20, 242; Anna (Mrs. Henry D.) Post, "The Van Raalte Colony," *Holland City News*, 30 Jan. 1903 (quote).

The Emigrants, oil on canvas, by Frans Breuhaus de Groot (1824-1872)

Tieleman. A postscript by Christina came from her heart: "Please write all the time, for my thoughts are always with you all; I wished that the way may be paved that we would see each other.... The absence of my cherished family torments me very much."[62] She had moved three times in the Netherlands, bore six children in the first ten years of her marriage, and then experienced agonizing family goodbyes before crossing the feared ocean.

Ocean passage

The party boarded the *Southerner*, a barque registered in Boston, under Captain Tully Crosby, bound for New York. The Van Raalte family of eight, with berths befitting their high status, traveled in first class with Captain Crosby, with meals prepared by the ship's cook. Mevrouw Van Raalte insisted on traveling first class, fearing that bunking among the common folks "would be the death of her." The household included Albertus, age thirty-five; Christina Johanna, age thirty-two; Albertus Christiaan, age nine; Johanna, age seven; Ben, age five; Dirk, age two; Christine, five months; and maid Fennegje Lasker, age forty. Between decks (steerage) were 102 Separatists who had to provide their own provisions for the voyage. On October 3, the ship headed into the North Sea. Van Raalte was in his prime but burdened

---

[62] Van Raalte to De Moen, 23 May 1851.

A model of the SS *Southerner*, a three-mast barque (model)

with the heavy responsibility of leading an unprepared people into an unimaginable future.⁶³

The dominee had taught himself only a rudimentary reading knowledge of English, so he spent much of his time at sea studying the language, and by the time he had landed in New York, he could speak some broken English. Mastering the language, of course, took years, and he did not preach in English until his final years, and then only in informal settings or far from Holland.⁶⁴ He always used the Dutch *ij* instead of the English *y* in his letters.

---

⁶³ A photostat copy of the *Southerner* manifest is in the Holland Museum and also printed in Lucas, *Netherlanders*, 644-45. One passenger had left the ship before sailing, and two died at sea, leaving one hundred on arrival.

⁶⁴ Van Raalte to Brummelkamp, 27 Nov. 1846, in *Voices from North America*, 19; Van Raalte to Phelps, 18 Nov. 1869, in Bruins and Schakel, *Envisioning Hope College*, 222-23; Hyma, "When the Dutch Came to Michigan," 52. Van Koevering, *Legends of the Dutch*, 145, misjudged that Van Raalte gained "quite apt facility" in English on the voyage.

Captain Tully Crosby
(*courtesy Gerko Warner*)

Unfortunately, the *Southerner* and several other vessels with Dutch immigrants aboard left late in the shipping season, when voyages were long and stormy. The passage of the *Southerner* was far from a lark. Hendrik De Kruif's account is hair-raising. The second day on the open Atlantic, the barque encountered a severe storm lasting a week that brought rampant seasickness. Worst of all, Van Raalte was thrown about his cabin so severely that his head and hands were injured; he stayed out of sight for most of the voyage. One passenger died, and the dominee committed his body to the sea. The believers took comfort in the angel's promise to the Apostle John: "And the sea gave up the dead which were in it" (Rev. 20:13, KJV). The trans-Atlantic crossing took forty-five days, until November 17.[65]

Why did Van Raalte emigrate?

What induced Van Raalte to emigrate? Was the motivation of it religious? A diaconal concern for black-listed Separatists? A desire to gain a competence and satisfy his entrepreneurial instincts? A promise to God in a near-death illness? Was it a craving for leadership or personal ambition? Frustration after struggling for ten years with meager and unsatisfying results? Was it a personal sense of failure and grave financial concerns? Should he be his people's Moses or Joshua, their Napoleon, their pope, their commander? The Separated church

---

[65] Hendrik De Kruif memoir, partly published in Jacobson et al., *Dutch Leader*, 26.

was also in disarray. At the Groningen Synod in the fall of 1846, which Van Raalte had helped plan but could not attend, the leaders were badly fragmented over much-contended issues. The nation was in the throes of a potato famine and extreme economic hardship.

In short, Van Raalte's world had fallen apart. The loss of his ministerial and seminary posts, his failing businesses, petty church squabbles, and his mental and physical health were all tipping points. He was tired of carrying heavy burdens with unsatisfying results, especially the hurtful secessions in his congregations.[66] This confluence of events brought clarity to Van Raalte's quest for a career change.

Of the Separatist leaders, only Van Raalte and Scholte had left for America, not Brummelkamp, Van Velzen, Gezelle Meerburg, or the rest.[67] Budding, a wealthy man who emigrated a year after Van Raalte and Scholte, soon returned to the Netherlands and eventually broke with his associates in the Reformed faith. He was all talk and no conviction. In 1846 he had praised emigrating dominees for not wanting to "breathe in the midst of dead orthodoxy" in the fatherland, who rather "gasped for fresh air" in America, where people were born free and "grow up, marrying, dying, being buried, travel, moving, keeping horses, slaughtering cattle," all with no commissions and license fees to pay. But religious life in immigrant communities in West Michigan and the Sheboygan area disgusted him, and he returned to the Netherlands completely disillusioned.[68]

Van Raalte *was* willing to breathe the dead orthodoxy, until church leaders summarily turned him away. Then, after a decade, he wholeheartedly committed to emigration and never looked back. His promise to God was genuine, and his sense of obligation was strong. Henry Dosker, Van Raalte's first biographer, said simply: "The Father of the colonization plan," was "compelled" to lead the emigration. This became the explanation for subsequent biographers Johan Wormser Jr. and Albert Hyma who stated that Van Raalte "felt obliged" to be "responsible for the fate of thousands." Then Dosker added a personal reason—the future of "his own boys."[69] Dosker opined that Van Raalte might have wanted to leave before Scholte to gain the upper hand in

---

[66] Dosker, *Van Raalte*, 64.
[67] Wormser, *In twee werelddeelen*, 125-29; Dosker, *Van Raalte*, 64-66.
[68] Gunning, *Budding*, 212, trans. Ten Hoor; Lucas, *Netherlanders*, 501. Gezelle Meerburg in 1856 led the large Almkerk, Gelderland, congregation of 800 souls (*Jaarboekje voor de Christelijk Afgescheidene Gereformeerde Kerk*, 16).
[69] Dosker, *Van Raalte*, 67; Wormser, *In twee werelddeelen*, 128; Hyma, *Van Raalte*, 53.

founding the first colony and recruiting settlers. As Dosker stated bluntly: "The relationship between them was not of a kind that made living and working together desirable." Put simply, Van Raalte was a go-getter, an adventurer, a risk-taker, willing to take the plunge.[70]

---

[70] Swierenga, "Van Raalte and Scholte," and Dosker, *Van Raalte*, 66 (quote), trans. Dekker.

CHAPTER 8

Choosing the Site: "Michigan is the place."

Albertus C. Van Raalte's momentous decision in January of 1847 to locate his colony in West Michigan was an unexpected reversal of the plan to settle in the Milwaukee area, where Separatists from the Arnhem Society had settled in 1846. The choice of Michigan, made at the last moment and under great pressure, was his alone. His emigrant band wintering in Detroit trusted their pastor and leader implicitly and accepted his abrupt change of plans.[1] His decision rested on an intriguing blend of personal faith, risk-taking, and Michigan boosterism. In looking back on the crucial months of migrating, the dominee, then beardless and in his prime at thirty-six years of age, saw God's hand of providence at work: "Man proposes, but God disposes," he declared.[2] But human agency, especially the efforts of early Michigan leaders, is clearly evident in the historical record.

What Michigan promoters could not do, however, was to prepare the dominee and his followers for life on the frontier. The Dutch were not aware of the hardships that awaited them in the dense forests

---

[1] Hyma, *Van Raalte*, 63-100; Hyma, "When the Dutch Came to Michigan," 49-57.
[2] Hyma, *Van Raalte*, 75.

with no food and shelter, no roads, and no stores and businesses. The nearest towns lay twenty miles distant. It was survival of the fittest by people who had never experienced such privation. And empty purses only compounded the problems. Van Raalte could have settled in Milwaukee or another rising urban center and avoided the raw frontier, but his followers wanted cheap farmland in an ethnic enclave, and that dictated a hard beginning.

The state of Michigan was only a decade old, and its institutions were immature and unstructured. Like other frontier regions, native tribes still lived in the state, and the settlers were Jacksonian Democrats, eager to remove the natives. Divisiveness, partisanship, and harsh and abrasive rhetoric was standard fare, with violence, fighting, and raw justice commonplace, all fueled by hard liquor. A primitive economy, subsistence agriculture, small shops and factories, and "wildcat" banking made existence hand to mouth.[3] Paying for goods with bank notes of varying cash value was problematic, and bartering was common. There was little shame in going bankrupt and starting over again. Immigrants had to master the land survey system, laws of citizenship and inheritance, local and state property taxes, elections at three levels—local, state, and federal—and a host of other activities not allowed or required in the Old Country.

Inland travel

The *Southerner* cast anchor offshore in New York harbor on November 17, 1846, after an arduous forty-five days at sea. The temperature in the city that late fall day was a mild fifty degrees, cloudy with a weak offshore wind.[4] The captain dutifully handed over his passenger manifest to US immigration officials, as required by an 1820 law. Prior to the opening in 1855 of the Castle Garden immigrant reception center at the tip of Manhattan Island, docking was chaotic and frightful. "Runners" swarmed ships and haggled to offload trunks, book hotel rooms, and sell tickets for inland travel by steamboat, canal boat, and railroad, all at inflated prices. The rail line was completed from New

---

[3] So-called "wildcat" banks, common on the cash-starved Michigan frontier, issued bank notes redeemable in specie (gold or silver coins) but then did not hold sufficient specie in their vaults to redeem their notes on demand. The worst offenders located their offices in deep woods or far-off places like Michigan's Upper Peninsula, where note holders wanting to redeem their worthless notes could not find them.

[4] Weather data provided by Huug van den Dool, email, 14 Oct. 2020, National Oceanic and Atmospheric Administration, Washington, DC.

York City to Detroit and Kalamazoo but had not yet reached Chicago. This would have been the most convenient way to travel inland, but the Van Raalte party could not afford that luxury, and they lacked reliable information and letters of introduction to ease the way.

Van Raalte was upset at "swindlers, both German and, sadly, Dutch, too," but God protected the people in the person of Rev. Thomas De Witt of New York's Collegiate Reformed Church, who had preached his last Dutch-language sermon barely two years earlier in August 1844. "Hitherto hath the LORD helped us" (I Samuel 7:12, KJV), he exclaimed, quoting King David's praise when he reclaimed the Ark of the Covenant. De Witt understood the need and "spared no pains" in helping the distraught newcomers at the dock, assisting them with lodging, tickets, and exchanging guilders for US gold coins. He alerted churches to be ready with charity for fellow Reformed believers. He also informed Scholte by letter after Van Raalte arrived that he was anxious to "proceed immediately on the way to Wisconsin as navigation on the [Erie] canal and on the lakes was drawing to a close."[5]

Happily, the "Young Dutch" influx coincided with a push by De Witt's denomination to plant mission churches on the frontier to serve both "Old Dutch" migrants and "Young Dutch" immigrants. What better way to grow churches than with the newcomers who might otherwise "be swallowed up by men of every name and creed."[6]

Van Raalte was eager to leave New York before the hard winter set in. After one night in a hotel, his party boarded an overnight steamer for Albany, where the genial Rev. Isaac Wyckoff of Second Albany Reformed Church, who was fluent in Dutch, welcomed them. He housed the dominee's family and provided breakfast and lunch. "His generous, homelike, and relaxed American hospitality was a delight," Van Raalte reported. It was the beginning of a long and fruitful friendship.

Wyckoff offered to send three men to help find a prime location in Wisconsin, but Van Raalte politely demurred; he would be his own scout. Wyckoff then provided letters of recommendation to anyone

---

[5] *Leeuwarder Courant*, 29 Sept. 1846; Demarest, *History and Characteristics*, 83; De Witt, "Emigrants from Holland," *Christian Intelligencer*, 31 Dec. 1846, Lucas, *Netherlanders*, 645.

[6] Van Raalte's account, written to Brummelkamp aboard the *Great Western*, in Buffalo, 27 Nov. 1846, in Brummelkamp, *Stemmen uit Noord-Amerika*; De Witt to Scholte, 27 Nov. 1846, trans. Ten Hoor, CCA. *Reports of the Board of Domestic Missions*, Western Department, in *Acts and Proceedings*, 1846, 28-29, 88-89; 1847, 133-34, 191-96; 1848, 424-27 (quote, 425); 1849, 503. Jacob van Hinte coined the phrases "Old Dutch" and "Young Dutch" in his monumental work, *Netherlanders*, 39, 75.

Thomas De Witt, Collegiate
Reformed Church. New York City
(JAH)

Isaac N. Wyckoff, Second
Reformed Church, Albany
(JAH)

willing to help the newcomers along the way. Detroit, unfortunately, had no Reformed Protestant Dutch Church for another twenty-five years, but some Yankee Dutch had settled there, and they opened their hands. And it was a bonus that Detroit was then the capitol of Michigan. The enthusiastic welcome led Van Raalte to see God's hand in his decision to emigrate.[7]

De Witt and Wyckoff stayed busy during the next weeks as more ships with Dutch immigrants landed in New York. It was a boon that these clerics had formed societies to aid the bewildered Hollanders. Those who embarked for Baltimore and New Orleans found no aid societies to greet them.[8]

To save precious time, Van Raalte bought train tickets for his family to travel from Albany to Buffalo, the eastern terminus of the Erie Canal, whereas his followers took the cheaper canal boat from Troy, which, with eighty-three locks and the gait of plodding mules, took a week to cover 383 miles. The boats were long and narrow, forty feet by eight feet, with benches running full length on both sides. At night, the benches were converted into very tight upper and lower beds. The usual sixty passengers were "packed like herring in a vat." Men occupied the upper deck, and women sat among the luggage below.

---

[7] Van Raalte (Detroit) to Brummelkamp, in *Voices from North America*, 21-34.
[8] *Christian Intelligencer*, 8 Oct., 31 Dec. 1846; Wyckoff to Van Raalte, 18 Oct. 1846, in *Voices from North America*, 60-62; De Witt to Scholte, 27 Nov. 1846.

Erie Canal route

Erie Canal boat

Arend Jan Brusse described the journey: "The horses go nearly always on a walk. In the daytime, I walked a good deal of the time by the side of the boat [on the towpath]. It was a slow and tedious way of traveling. Our daily fare on the boat was bread and milk, which we bought along the route of the canal."

The trip took a week. The train trip of the Van Raaltes also had its difficulties. Christina complained that her family was "pushed into a miserable leaky cab, although there were good carriages." This and the "arbitrary stops" made the trip "very disagreeable." In the rising city of Rochester, Van Raalte was surprised to find several hundred Hollanders, mainly Zeelanders. Their apparent worldliness strengthened his conviction that a frontier colony would best safeguard the spiritual life of the Separatists.[9]

[9] "Arend Jan Brusse's Reminiscences," in Lucas, *Dutch Immigrant Memoirs*, 1:46; T. D. W. [Thomas De Witt], "Emigrants from Holland," *Christian Intelligencer*, 31 Dec. 1846; Versteeg, *Pelgrim-Vaders*, 36, trans. Reinsma.

Steamship *Great Western*, Captain Eber Brock Ward, that carried the Van Raalte party from Buffalo to Detroit, November 1846 (*C. J. Dow Collection, Historical Collections of the Great Lakes, Bowling Green State University*)

Detroit winter layover

At Buffalo, thirty penniless members of Van Raalte's party decided to stay and seek work. Others settled among Dutch immigrants at Clymer and Williamson (Pultneyville), New York. The rest, numbering about seventy, on November 27, took passage on the SS *Great Western* bound for Detroit, under Captain Eber B. Ward. "The cold weather is becoming very severe, and the Lake looks angry and turbulent," a Buffalo newspaper reported.[10] The fare was three dollars ($119 today) with meals. Before leaving, Van Raalte wrote Brummelkamp that he would decide in Detroit whether to winter there or proceed on Lake Huron through the Mackinac Straits to Milwaukee. Christina picked Detroit; Van Raalte preferred Milwaukee. The weather settled the matter in her favor. A three-day winter storm held them in Detroit, and then Captain Ward learned that the straits had iced over, and the shipping season had closed. As Albert Hyma aptly put it: "Only the icy hand of winter prevented them from executing their plan."[11] If the party had left the Netherlands earlier, or if they had crossed the Atlantic in the normal four or five weeks, instead of six weeks, they would have continued directly to Wisconsin.

---

[10] *Buffalo Morning Express*, 28, 30 Nov. 1846, quoted in Lucas, *Netherlanders*, 73.

[11] Hyma, "When the Dutch Came to Michigan," 53 (quote); Van Raalte to Brummelkamp, 27 Nov. 1846, and 16 Dec. 1846, in *Voices from North America*.

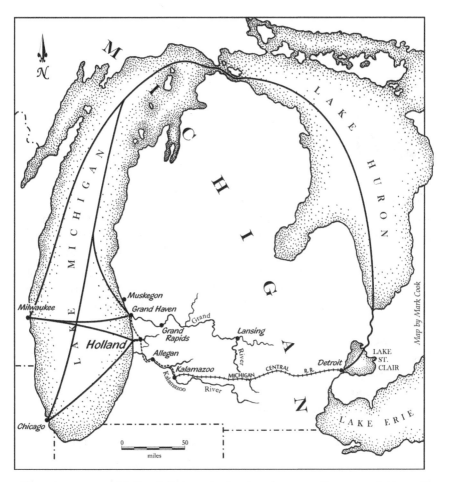

Travel routes to Holland Colony by land and water after completion of Michigan Central Railroad from Detroit to Kalamazoo in 1847

As the *Great Western* traversed a calm Lake Erie, with a stop in Cleveland, Van Raalte had four days to reflect on crossing his personal Rubicon. He would be bold and confident, no matter the difficulties. "We must seek freedom for worship and education and also room to live. In this country, God gives these things . . . I am happy that I crossed the ocean because my soul is tranquil."[12]

Finding the right place for the colony and then establishing it was hardly effortless. The full responsibility fell on the shoulders of Van Raalte, with the willing and able assistance of the capable

---

[12] Van Raalte to Brummelkamp, 16 Dec. 1846, in *Voices from North America*, 17.

Eber Brock Ward (1811-1875), captain of the *Great Western*, and "the richest man in Michigan" as a shipping and steel magnate (*Burton Historical Collection, Detroit Public Library*)

Bernardus Grootenhuis. "The rest were good for nothing on the trip," Van Raalte wrote, and added, "I feel that I am living at a tremendous point in time."[13] If not for lack of money, they would have continued to Wisconsin, taking the Grand Central train to Kalamazoo (the end of the line at that time), then a stagecoach to St. Joseph, where a lake steamer would have taken them to Milwaukee, on the still ice-free southern Lake Michigan. But Van Raalte's little band could not afford the fares; they must winter in Detroit.

The kindly Captain Ward provided work for ten families at his shipyard at St. Clair, fifty miles north on the St. Clair River. He housed them in an old warehouse and paid the men in food, shelter, and firewood for their stoves. Rev. Oren C. Thompson, a Princeton Seminary graduate and pastor of the St. Clair Congregational [formerly Presbyterian] Church, offered his sanctuary for worship services. The rest of the group spent the winter in Detroit. Meanwhile, Rev. De Witt used the pages of the *Christian Intelligencer* to urge local employers to hire mechanics and farmers from among the group and to send alms for the few "entirely destitute" families. Two women from his own congregation in New York City were among the first to help "Christ's little ones."[14]

With Ward employing most of the men, Van Raalte was relieved of the pressure and could assess his options, but time was of the essence. He settled his family in a two-room upstairs apartment with a kitchenette and a small attic room above for the Grootenhuis family. The rent was $4 per month, but he spent $26.50 for a table, six chairs, a child's chair, pots and pans, and bedsteads.[15]

[13] Van Hinte, *Netherlanders*, 133, 136.
[14] "Oren Cook Thompson," Princeton Seminary Necrology Report, 1890, 78-79; *Christian Intelligencer*, 5 Jan. (quote), 4 Feb. 1847.
[15] Versteeg, *Pelgrim-Vaders*, 24-25.

The crucial weeks of decision were in January 1847. Van Raalte labored under serious handicaps. He could speak only broken English and knew little about American geography and culture; yet he must act quickly, or his followers would scatter. He had to explore flora and fauna, judge soil quality and transportation routes, master the methods of buying lands at federal and state land offices, comprehend the rectangular land survey system that mapped them out, and assess prospects for agriculture. He had to become a "geographical engineer," in the apt words of Jacob van Hinte, a social geographer and first Netherlands historian of American immigration. Clearly, the dominee must rely on new friends he could trust.[16]

Van Raalte's plan was to seek out "the faithful believers in these parts, . . . [and] through God's providence, I found those believers."[17] By "believers," Van Raalte had in mind fellow Calvinists, either Dutch or English. At Wyckoff's direction, Van Raalte received from a Presbyterian minister near Buffalo letters of recommendation to Presbyterian and Congregational clerics in Detroit, Milwaukee, St. Louis, and elsewhere. Van Raalte felt most comfortable with these denominations, although in West Michigan, he also relied on Methodist and Baptist men.

Van Raalte wrote Brummelkamp about plans for his solo scouting trip west. Chicago was first, to meet Robert Stuart, a Scottish Presbyterian land investor, based in Detroit, but in the Windy City as secretary of the Illinois-Michigan Canal project. He might hire the Hollanders. Stuart until 1834 was chief trader at John Jacob Astor's American Fur Company fort on Mackinac Island, Michigan, and later, he settled in Grand Haven and dealt with the Odawa (Ottawa) bands in the area. Stuart recommended the Black Lake watershed to the Dutch dominee, the first American to do so.[18]

Michigan boosters

One of the first Detroiters Van Raalte came to trust was the prominent attorney Theodore Romeyn (1810-1880) of Hackensack, New Jersey, whose son and brother were both clerics in the Reformed Protestant Dutch Church. Romeyn was expecting the immigrants

---

[16] Van Hinte, *Netherlanders*, 133.
[17] Hyma, *Van Raalte*, 95.
[18] www.findagrave.com/memorial/7253704/robert-stuart; www.oregonencyclopedia .org/articles/stuart_robert/; Barendregt (St. Louis) to Scholte, 14 Dec. 1846, in Lucas, *Dutch Immigrant Memoirs*, 2:514-19; Van Raalte to Brummelkamp, 16 Dec. 1846, in *Voices from North America*, 25- 29; Lucas, *Netherlanders*, 75; Anna (Mrs. Henry D.) C. Post, "A History Making Event," 1897 semicentennial address, JAH.

Robert Stuart (1785-1848), Scottish Presbyterian fur trader, explorer, Indian agent, and Illinois-Michigan Canal official, who later helped Van Raalte secure Holland harbor funding

because his brother had written to alert him. After meeting Van Raalte, George Duffield confided to his diary: "I have been exceedingly pleased with him and his spirit . . . I have felt a deep interest in him and his people." Duffield, of Scottish Irish heritage, could speak a little Dutch, and he took Van Raalte to meet Romeyn at his home on Monroe Avenue. Duffield was open to Van Raalte because he equated the Free Church Dutch with the Free Kirk Scots who in 1843 broke with the Church of Scotland.[19] William Witherspoon, a commercial baker, hosted the Van Raalte family on the second floor of his home. He was another friend of Romeyn and likely a fellow member of Duffield's First Presbyterian Church.

That Romeyn could understand a few Dutch words was a bonus, especially for Christina. Romeyn went one better; he found a lady in Detroit sufficiently fluent in Dutch to be an interpreter so Christina could talk with his wife Anna. This boosted her spirits. "At times, her soul's barometer is too low," Albertus noted with concern. Wintering in Detroit afforded several months for Mevrouw Van Raalte and the other wives to enjoy "woman time."[20] It was a pleasant interlude before leaving civilization for the wilds.

---

[19] Duffield was a New School Presbyterian, once pro-Finney but now anti-Finney; he was also a premillennialist. New School Presbyterians were a bit less "conservative" than the Old School Presbyterians (split 1837). George Duffield diary, entries of 21 Dec. 1846, 22 Jan., 1 Feb. 1847 (Duffield Papers, Burton Historical Collection, Detroit Public Library); Romeyn interview, 1883 or 1884, Moerdyke Papers; Van Raalte to Brummelkamp, 16 Dec. 1846, in *Voices from North America*, 28.

[20] Van Raalte to Brummelkamp, 16 Dec. 1846; in *Voices from North America*, 9 (quote), 21, 27 (quote), 32.

Van Raalte told Brummelkamp that Romeyn "often opens the way for me to the highest and most respectable people in the State."[21] Romeyn introduced Van Raalte to such dignitaries as "the agent and pioneer of this movement, and whom we cheerfully recommend as a gentleman of energy, talent, piety, and disinterested zeal." When these dignitaries learned that Van Raalte was the vanguard of a huge stream of devout Hollanders, they were determined to snare him for Michigan. The Dutch leader also showed his mettle by winning the confidence of these prominent men. The relationship was mutually beneficial.[22]

The influential coterie of "grey heads," as Van Raalte dubbed them, included Rev. George Duffield, Romeyn's pastor at the First Presbyterian Church, Judge Shubael Conant, railroad magnate Chester C. Trowbridge, commercial baker William Witherspoon, Detroit mayor and attorney Ezra C. Seamon, US Senator Augustus S. Porter, developer Eurotas P. Hastings, and railroad entrepreneur John W. Brooks. Witherspoon, Trowbridge, and Hastings also belonged to Duffield's church. Hastings developed the city of Hastings and many other town sites. This seven-person committee recruited a wider body of influential men in western Michigan.

In Kalamazoo were Rev. Ova P. Hoyt of First Presbyterian Church and attorney M. L. Colt, both friends of Duffield and Romeyn, and state senator and attorney Nathaniel A. Balch. In Grand Rapids were Rev. Andrew B. Taylor and elder George Young of First Reformed Protestant Dutch Church, and John Ball, attorney, land dealer, and state representative. Taylor and Young were Reformed bedfellows, and when Young introduced himself in the Dutch tongue, he created an immediate ethnic bond as well.

In Allegan were county officials John R. Kellogg and Elisha Bourne Bassett. In Grand Haven were Rev. William Montague Ferry (1796-1867) of First Presbyterian Church and fellow parishioner Henry Pennoyer, Ottawa County treasurer. Ferry had studied at New Brunswick Theological Seminary, the only RPDC seminary, and that drew Van Raalte to him. Besides being tied religiously and politically, these Michigan boosters served on the boards of directors of banks, canals, and railroads. Van Raalte could hardly have imagined such a group of supporters and advisors for his colonial venture.[23]

---

[21] Van Raalte to Brummelkamp, 30 Jan. 1847, in Brummelkamp, *Holland in Amerika*, 7.
[22] Lucas, *Netherlanders*, 80.
[23] George Young, *American Biographical History of Eminent and Self-Made Men of the State of Michigan* (Western Biographical Publishing Co., 1878); ancestry.com., Michigan

Michigan's reputation had suffered in the 1830s because of the activities of land speculators and the bankruptcy of several canal projects. The word among immigrants was to avoid Michigan. Van Raalte himself confessed to harboring "many a bias against Michigan." But already in New York, he had heard otherwise. A well-traveled Zeelander advised him to consider Michigan because it had already passed the early stages of development and had roads, railroads, and navigable waterways to "tie us to New York's markets." Van Raalte later wrote Brummelkamp:

> I had many prejudices against the state of Michigan, and in my heart I had chosen another dwelling place, but in many respects I have come to a different conclusion about conditions here. From the first moment of my arrival in America I began to have doubts about my choice, namely Wisconsin. And certain hints from friends whom I met caused me to think hard about the geographical location of these states and awakened in me the need to get the opinion of informed, pious and prominent people. By God's mercy I found Dutch people.[24]

At a meeting in Judge Conant's office in Detroit, Van Raalte reiterated that he had been "predisposed" against Michigan and "inclined to go elsewhere," but the pledge of help by the boosters, fellow Calvinists all, "disposed [him] to commence his colonization here." These men had won the dominee's trust. They were "God-fearing, upright gentlemen," Van Raalte wrote his wife. "I don't believe that immigrants were ever before welcomed in America with such love and distinction as we enjoy," he told Brummelkamp. For their part, the promoters claimed to be acting from "disinterested and philanthropic motives" and without any "selfish impulse."[25]

Biographies, 1878 database online. Young later helped the colonists buy supplies and sell surplus grain in Grand Rapids. First RPDC in Grand Rapids had only 33 members in 1846 (Ballast, *Then, Now, Always*, 47). Until 1834, Wm. M. Ferry directed the Michigan Indian Agency at Mackinac Island when Stuart headed the fur-trading post. The two became close friends, and Ferry considered himself Stuart's spiritual son ("Our Neighbors," *De Grondwet*, 9 Sept. 1913).

[24] Van Raalte to Brummelkamp, 16 Dec. 1846, in *Voices from North America*, 6 (quote), 32-33; Van Raalte to Brummelkamp, 30 Jan. 1847, in Brummelkamp, *Holland in Amerika*, 9-11.

[25] Hyma, *Van Raalte*, 94-95.

Scouting trip

On December 21, 1846, Van Raalte took the train to Kalamazoo for what turned out to be a month-long scouting trip. He had planned to meet Stuart in Chicago and then sail to Milwaukee to visit Sleyster, who had settled at Alto (near Waupun), and learn of possibilities in Wisconsin. Next, he would ride horseback to La Crosse to catch a Mississippi River steamer to St. Louis to meet Barendregt, leader of Scholte's advance party, about settling in Iowa. Michigan still did not figure prominently in his plans. He carried letters of introduction from Duffield to Presbyterian clerics in Kalamazoo, Chicago, Milwaukee, and St. Louis. "Pray fervently and earnestly," Van Raalte wrote Brummelkamp, "for the Lord's leading in this matter. . . . A great deal depends on our choice."[26] The Lord answered his prayer before his letter reached the Netherlands. He never got farther than Kalamazoo, which spared him an arduous, and possibly fatal, journey westward. He had no idea of the great distances involved, especially riding a pony in the bitter winter through virgin forests across the entire state of Wisconsin.

In Kalamazoo, Van Raalte's host, Rev. Hoyt, impressed the Hollander as "a man of influence with deep interest in the Dutch emigration." Hoyt seconded Stuart's suggestion to investigate western Michigan along the Grand River, where government land was still available in large blocks. Attorney Colt, to whom Romeyn had given Van Raalte a letter of reference, cordially welcomed the visitor and invited him for supper. He then introduced him to Judge John Kellogg (1893-1868) of Allegan, a large land investor in northern Allegan County who happened to be in Kalamazoo. Kellogg, a Presbyterian from Connecticut, eighteen years Van Raalte's senior, immediately promised to help him find suitable government lands for the colony. Kellogg had settled in Michigan a decade earlier and quickly gained political prominence as a Michigan legislator and Allegan County judge. Kellogg was an intimate friend of US Senator Lewis Cass, Michigan's former territorial governor, soon to be Democrat candidate for the American presidency and one of Detroit's most renowned politicians.

---

[26] Van Raalte to Brummelkamp, 16 Dec. 1846, in *Voices from North America*, 29. Hyma, *Van Raalte*, 70, notes that this letter rendered inaccurate the statement of Gerrit Van Schelven ("Michigan and the Holland Immigration of 1847," *Michigan Historical Magazine* 1 [1917]: 75) that Van Raalte in early Dec. 1846 returned to New York to consult with Wyckoff, De Witt, and other friends, and that he also went to Washington and met Michigan Senator Lewis Cass.

Michigan Boosters

Theodore Romeyn   George Duffield   Shubael Conant

Ova Hoyt   John R. Kellog   Lewis Cass

Michigan boosters: attorney Theodore Romeyn, Detroit; Rev. George Duffield, First Presbyterian Church, Detroit; Judge Shubael Conant, Detroit; Rev. Ova Hoyt, First Presbyterian Church, Kalamazoo; Judge John R. Kellogg, Presbyterian elder, businessman, Allegan; Lewis Cass (1782-1866), Michigan's second territorial governor (1813-31), secretary of war in President Andrew Jackson's cabinet (1831-36), US ambassador to France (1836-42), and US Senator (1845-48, 1849-57) (*JAH*)

This put Kellogg in high company since Cass shared the national stage with such titans as John Calhoun, Henry Clay, and Daniel Webster. Kellogg later introduced Van Raalte to Cass in Detroit.[27]

---

[27] Swierenga, *Holland, Michigan*, 1:64; Van Raalte, "Commemoration Address, 1872," 2:486 (quote).

Kellogg took Van Raalte to his Allegan home and suggested potential sites for his colony along the Kalamazoo, Rabbit, Black, and Grand Rivers, including a block of six townships in Allegan County. The old judge became a "father to me," Van Raalte said. "He is constantly with me when I purchase land."[28] Kellogg proved to be the critical intermediary. Gerrit Van Schelven called Kellogg the dominee's "able and faithful counselor and right hand man in the selection of the site for the Holland colony and the acquirement of lands." Van Raalte years later called him "my never-to-be-forgotten friend."[29]

That Kellogg was persuasive is evident from Van Raalte's letter to his wife, written on Christmas Eve, in which he opined that the judge was a "faithful, upright, and understanding man." To have "fallen into such good hands" was gratifying, Van Raalte noted. "More and more, I think that the state of Michigan is the place in which we shall make our home," he confided. "So I have every reason for thanksgiving to God for the treatment I received. . . . You may be very happy for all the good that I have experienced. You must not be sad and discontent; you must thank God, for really, we have enjoyed many privileges in this strange land."[30]

New Year's Eve welcome

On Christmas Day, Kellogg, Van Raalte, and a native guide set out from Allegan for the Old Wing Mission of Rev. George N. Smith (1807-1881), the first Congregational cleric in Michigan, and his associate, Isaac Fairbanks (1818-1903), who came in 1844 to erect Smith's house and was then appointed agricultural agent to teach the Odawa natives to farm. The threesome arrived at the mission on New Year's Eve and were greeted by George and Arvilla Smith and Isaac and Ann Woodruff Fairbanks, whose houses stood fifty feet apart. Fairbanks, a soft-spoken man with a twinkle in his eye and a smile, vividly recalled the evening.

> I heard a rap on my cabin door and for the first time met the Rev. A. C. Van Raalte and, if I mistake not, J. R. Kellogg from Allegan, and learned from them that a colony from Holland, Europe, were about to locate in Fillmore and vicinity for a home. It was a joy that I gave them a warm welcome to my humble cabin.

---

[28] Van Raalte to Brummelkamp, 30 Jan. 1847, in Brummelkamp, *Holland in Amerika*, 34.
[29] Van Schelven, undated "Addenda," Van Schelven Papers.
[30] Van Raalte to wife, 24 Dec. 1846, in Sweetman, *From Heart to Heart*, 32-33.

George N. Smith,
Congregational cleric and
teacher, Old Wing Mission
(JAH)

Arvilla (Mrs. George) Smith,
host of Van Raalte family
(JAH)

Fairbanks offered the pair a cozy place to sleep on the floor by the fireplace in their ten-by-twelve-foot cabin, which also housed Ann's brother, Henry S. Woodruff, and wife Harriet Sherburne, all Yankee Methodists.[31]

At midnight, the exhausted dominee's sleep was shattered by the sound of musket fire from the natives' huts. Smith's diary entry for January 1, 1847, tells the reason: "Last evening the Ind[ian]s fired 3 salutes in very fine order, most of the young men. This is their invariable custom [at midnight to welcome the New Year], and they give us the first compliment." Van Raalte likely did not share this sanguine opinion.[32]

The Smiths, both Vermont natives, had arrived in the Kalamazoo area in 1833 and established congregations in Plainwell and Otsego. In 1838 Smith agreed to be the missionary teacher and preacher of Chief Joseph Wakazoo's Odawa band, a mission under the auspices of the Allegan-based West Michigan Society to Benefit the Indians that Judge Kellogg and other Protestant leaders had founded "to civilize" native peoples. The society was an arm of the American Home Missionary

---

[31] Isaac Fairbanks, "Incidents in the History of the First Settlement of the Holland Colony"; William E. Welmers, "Family of Stephen and Nancy (Briggs) Fairbanks, with special reference to the history of Holland," both in Fairbanks Papers; Henry S. Woodruff, "Here before Van Raalte," newspaper clipping, Moerdyke Papers.

[32] Smith diary, 1 Jan. 1847, in Swierenga and Van Appledorn, *Old Wing Mission*, 297.

George and Arvilla Smith home, Old Wing Mission, where Van Raalte was sheltered (*JAH*)

Society, one of the joint Congregational-Presbyterian agencies formed in the Plan of Union of 1801.

Several dozen mission natives held patent titles to 1,380 acres, ranging over three square miles of present-day Fillmore Township in Allegan County, centered at the Smith and Fairbanks homes and schoolhouse on present-day 147th Avenue (east Fortieth Street). The Odawas raised corn, pumpkins, squash, and other crops on their land, but the braves left tending the crops to the women. Wakazoo's band also owned sixteen acres at the Indian Village, or Landing, on the north bank of Black Lake at the narrows (the present site of the Heinz plant), where they had a chapel, burial ground, and about twenty primitive log houses.[33]

Fairbanks, who served as justice of the peace, threw in his lot with the Dutch and proved to be a great help for the colonists. He built Van Raalte's house and tried to learn Dutch but admitted that the Algonquin language he had picked up working with the mission band was "easier." His descendants live in the Holland area to the present day. In his honor, Van Raalte named the street in front of his house Fairbanks Avenue.[34]

---

[33] Swierenga and Van Appledorn, *Old Wing Mission*, 18-20.
[34] "Interview with Isaac Fairbanks," typescript by Barbara Lampen, Fairbanks Papers.

Tramping Black Lake watershed

On New Year's Day 1847, Van Raalte, Smith, George Harrington, and a native guide set off to explore the Black Lake watershed between the Kalamazoo and Grand Rivers. The men had easy going the first day because heavy rains had melted all the snow. But winter storms soon brought more snow, with two-foot drifts that required Van Raalte to don unfamiliar snowshoes. He tired quickly and finally cried out in bad English (but typical Dutch): "I can no more!" (*Ik kan niet meer*). Years later, the dominee recalled the day. The guide "let me stand on his snowshoes in the snow, which thus made my travels easier." Another day scouting land with Smith, the pair became lost, with the dominee totally exhausted. At his request, Smith left Van Raalte in the snow and went for help. "The bark of the dogs brought him back to the right place, but it was with much labor that he was able to assist me to his house. In that unforgettable night, I rejoiced being especially in God's care, although I could sleep but little on account of excessive exertions." Smith may be the one who recalled finding the Dutchman kneeling in the snow praying for guidance and strength.[35]

The wiry dominee soon adapted, and for ten days, he tramped on snowshoes over the future site of Holland. He also trekked to Grand Rapids to consult with Rev. Taylor, following blazes notched in trees to find his way, a trick he mastered quickly. He returned to Old Wing Mission on January 11 and the next day went back to Allegan on Kellogg's borrowed pony.[36]

The dominee saw the advantages of the Black River watershed between the Kalamazoo and Grand Rivers with the country-seat towns of Allegan and Grand Haven, respectively. As he explained at Holland's twenty-fifth anniversary celebration, his object was "to secure the advantages of both these rivers—for we could not get along without the settled regions—and at the same time to establish a center for a united and spiritual life and labor for God's kingdom." The virgin hardwoods were ideal for lumbering, Lake Michigan for shipping, and the temperate climate for fruit growing. This was the ideal place for the colony, despite some swampy, low-lying areas.

The eclectic dominee dug under the snow to check soil qualities. He knew something about soils and farming, as well as medicine,

---

[35] Van Raalte "Commemoration Address, 1872," 2:486; Van Raalte to Brummelkamp, 30 Jan. 1847, in *Holland in Amerika*, 18; Smith diary entry, 31 Dec. 1846, in *Old Wing Mission*, 297; Wilson, "Life and Work," in *Old Wing Mission*, 484 (quote).

[36] "Anna C. Post Reminiscences [1911]," in Lucas, *Dutch Immigrant Memoirs*, 1:402.

law, and business. Missionary Smith, in the apt words of William O. Van Eyck, initiated Van Raalte into the "mysteries" of townships and sections. "What designing and crafty real estate dealers would have done to the ignorant and less informed Hollanders, may be imagined." But in "the hands of the gentle and unassuming Rev. Smith, they were safe."[37]

In Allegan, Van Raalte had time to write his wife about his reconnaissance. "Michigan attracts me more than Wisconsin," was the key sentence. To support this conclusion, he enclosed positive comments of his Michigan friends. Albertus asked Christina to pass his letter to Romeyn, who must have rejoiced that his boosterism had borne fruit.[38]

Before returning to Detroit, Van Raalte traveled back to the Ottawa County Courthouse in Grand Haven, where he completed a most incredible feat. He spent a week with county treasurer Henry Pennoyer, who identified choice tracts of land in the Black Lake watershed that were about to be sold at the annual tax sale for back taxes—that is, for pennies on the dollar. The Hollander was able to buy forty-three parcels, totaling 2,750 acres, plus three "water lots" on Black Lake (Lake Macatawa), all for only $252 ($9,350 today). This was truly "acres for cents." This plunge at the tax auction by the novice land investor during his first month on Michigan soil gave him a leg up on the road to financial success. Putting money on the line also cemented his decision to choose Michigan.

Van Raalte focused his land purchases in and around the neck of Black Lake. Rev. Ferry hosted Van Raalte for a week and welcomed him for worship at First Presbyterian Church, probably on January 17. Ferry's son, William M. Jr., recalled years later: "I well remember the eager manner of this worthy gentleman, his limited use of the English language, and the long interviews with my father concerning his proposed enterprise and a suitable location for it." Ferry was the kind of cleric-capitalist that Van Raalte could emulate. He opened the Hollander's eyes to the economic possibilities in Michigan. Rev. Ferry had founded Grand Haven and Ferrysburg while engaging with his sons in lumbering, shipping, and mercantile pursuits. At his death in 1867, Ferry was worth more than $1 million.[39]

---

[37] Van Eyck, "A Story That is Filled With Indian Lore," undated newspaper clipping, Van Eyck Papers.
[38] Albertus to Christina, 13 Jan. 1847, in Sweetman, *From Heart to Heart*, 36-37.
[39] Swierenga, "Albertus C. Van Raalte," 286; "Our Neighbors," *De Grondwet*, 9 Sept.

Henry Pennoyer, Ottawa County treasurer who helped Van Raalte buy tax delinquent land (*JAH*)

Detroit working committee

By January 20, Van Raalte was back in Detroit, accompanied by Revs. Hoyt and Taylor who, at the dominee's request, had traveled a considerable distance to endorse his decision.[40] They met in Judge Conant's office, together with Theodore Romeyn, Rev. George Duffield, and other citizens, to draft resolutions to be presented to a mass meeting at Duffield's church on January 22, 1847. Those attending were Senator Augustus S. Porter, banker Eurotas P. Hastings, attorney Ezra C. Seaman, and developer John Ball of Grand Rapids. Conant chaired the meeting, and Nathaniel Balch as secretary kept the minutes.

Romeyn explained that Van Raalte's band was the first of a large stream of persecuted Dutch Separatists that would "bring a most valuable class among us" if they could be persuaded to select Michigan over Wisconsin. The punch line for the boosters was: "A little sacrifice by individuals, a little advice and attention to the emigrants, might be of inestimable advantage."[41]

1913. "The Ferrys," *Historical and Business Compendium, Ottawa County, Michigan* (Grand Haven, 1892), 1:197-98.

[40] Van Raalte's expense ledger for the scouting trip totaled $53 for fares, food, lodging, maps, ax handles, cloth, and other items (financial ledger, 13 Feb. 1847, signed by Judge Kellogg), HMA.

[41] "Detroit Committee minutes, 22 Jan. 1847," *Christian Intelligencer*, 11 Feb. 1847, reprinted in Lucas, *Dutch Immigrant Memoirs*, 1:31-33; "Emigration from Holland,"

That such an impressive group of prominent men would help Van Raalte settle in Michigan is a testament to his prowess. He left his mark wherever he went. Secretary Balch described the leader of the "persecuted Puritans" as a "gentleman of energy, talent, piety, and disinterested zeal." Van Raalte responded briefly but warmly in broken English, as paraphrased by secretary Balch for posterity: "In a most touching and impressive manner," he expressed his gratitude "for the sympathy and aid proffered to his countrymen, and his gratification at having thus far succeeded in the preparatory steps for the settlement in a land where labor would meet with its reward, and civil and religious freedom would be secure." John Ball of Grand Rapids made an appropriate reply and the meeting was adjourned.[42]

The assembly pledged to aid Van Raalte and "invite, encourage, and direct the settlement of these emigrants within our state." Snaring the Dutch colony for Michigan was a coup. The men put teeth in their resolve by appointing a seven-man Detroit committee and six regional committees to assist the Dutch immigrants. The Detroit body included Romeyn, Duffield, Conant, Seaman, Porter, Hastings, and Brooks. Committees were also appointed in Marshall, Kalamazoo, Grand Rapids, Grand Haven, Allegan, and Saugatuck.[43]

The Detroit committee allied themselves with the New York-based Netherlands Society for the Protection of Immigrants from Holland that De Witt had formed on January 23, 1847, to solicit aid from the Old Dutch for the Young Dutch "strangers in a strange land." In February the society hired as general agent Pieter Hodenpyl, an 1840 immigrant who taught modern languages at Rutgers College, the denominational college in New Brunswick, New Jersey. Hodenpyl met ships at the docks and assisted untold Hollanders with guidance, lodging, and tickets for travel inland. He also arranged labor contracts for the men with Knickerbocker farmers and factory owners in the West. Subsequently, Hodenpyl became a real-estate promoter, which

---

Detroit Free Press, 23 Jan. 1847; "Emigration from Holland," *Kalamazoo Gazette*, 29 Jan. 1847; Van Raalte to Brummelkamp, 30 Jan. 1847, in *Holland in Amerika*, 26-27. Regional committees were Ova Hoyt, Senator Balch, and William Denison in Kalamazoo; Andrew B. Taylor, George Young, and John Ball in Grand Rapids; Ferry, Pennoyer, and Thomas W. White in Grand Haven; Judge Kellogg, Judge Elisha B. Bassett, Ezra C. Southworth, and Michigan legislator Flavius J. Littlejohn in Allegan; S. D. Nichols, William Carley, and William G. Britton in Saugatuck: Congregational cleric John D. Pearce, Michigan legislator and lawyer Henry W. Taylor, and Samuel Hall in Marshall.

[42] Minutes of 22 Jan. 1847 meeting, quoted in Van Schelven Papers.
[43] Lucas, *Netherlanders*, 81.

George Young, founding elder in 1840 of First Reformed Protestant Dutch Church, Grand Rapids (*Ballast, Then, Now, Always*)

Rev. Andrew B. Taylor, pastor (1843-48), First Reformed Protestant Dutch Church, Grand Rapids (*JAH*)

raised conflict-of-interest concerns. But many immigrants found the personal attention of De Witt and especially of Wyckoff more valuable than the efforts of the Netherlands Society.[44]

Romeyn sent a detailed report of the decisions to his friend Wyckoff in Albany and requested him to direct new arrivals to Michigan where helpful committees awaited. Van Raalte's followers attended the Detroit meetings, but they could not speak a word of English and did not know enough to contribute, so the dominee made the decisions. His rudimentary knowledge of English proved to be

---

[44] *Christian Intelligencer*, 31 Dec. 1846, 4, 11 Feb., 11, 17 (quote), 25 Mar., 6, 13 May 1847, all reprinted in Lucas, *Dutch Immigrant Memoirs*, 1:27-44. On Hodenpyl and the Netherlands Society, see Lucas, *Netherlanders*, 84-85, 268-69. Jannes Van de Luyster Jr. urged family members anticipating emigrating to have nothing to do with De Wit[t] in New York, but in Albany "Look up the old, God-fearing and kind Rev. Wyckoff. You can bring all your problems to him, and he will treat you well" (Van de Luyster Jr. to parents, 15 Dec. 1847, in Van Malsen, *Achttal Brieven Mijner Kinderen*, published in English by Yzenbaard, "'America' Letters," 65). Vande Luyster Sr. apparently had a falling out with De Witt and his ally Hendrik Scholte, who met the ship in New York and tried to induce the Zeelanders to settle in his Pella, Iowa, colony.

of vital importance. The whirlwind pace of January 1847 shows Van Raalte at his best in making the critical decision of where to locate his colony. His stamina, determination, and decisiveness were remarkable.

Under extreme pressure, he had to find his way as a stranger in a strange land. Unexpected obstacles faced him from the time he set foot in Detroit. First was the closing of the Straits at Mackinaw, which forced his group to winter over. That the ship's captain offered to employ most of the men in his shipyard was a godsend. Even more providential was that the Michigan capitol, then located in Detroit, was in session. Wyckoff sent Van Raalte to Theodore Romeyn who opened doors to dozens of leading politicos and boosters. They took the dominee seriously and convinced him to change plans and choose Michigan instead of Wisconsin. Meeting John Kellogg at Rev. Hoyt's parsonage in Kalamazoo was the final critical event. Kellogg's personal tour of the Black Lake region clinched the matter. Van Raalte clearly saw the Lord's hand in these critical weeks. For a clergyman with minimal knowledge of the English language and American geography and a purse much too meager, Van Raalte came through unscathed and in a strong position. It was a tour de force.

"Reasonable reasons"

Should the question be *what* convinced Van Raalte to choose Michigan, or *who* convinced him? It is clear that the Michigan boosters who had gained his trust were persuasive. He did not personally explore Illinois, Wisconsin, or Iowa. Indeed, he did not even go to Ada and Ionia in Michigan, areas also suggested to him. He limited his search to Allegan and Ottawa Counties. Time and money were running out, and the distances and travel difficulties in America were much greater than any Hollander could have imagined. Van Raalte had convinced himself that it was not necessary to investigate other locales. His trustworthy friends had sealed the deal. Kellogg deserves most of the credit, but Duffield boasted in a letter to Governor Epaphroditus Ransom: "I may say I was particularly instrumental in directing & determining their choice to settle in Michigan."[45] Kellogg persuaded Van Raalte to select the Black River watershed, but John Ball urged him to settle upriver from Grand Haven along the Grand River, which had few settlers and cheap land. The dominee, however, rejected Ball's advice, saying there were "too many settlers" on that river.[46]

---

[45] George Duffield to Governor E. Ransom, 12 Nov. 1847, folder 1, box 155, RG 44, E. Ransom Papers, State Archives of Michigan, Lansing.
[46] Ball Powers, *Born to Wander*, 109.

Arguments against more westward states were often spurious. Stuart warned Van Raalte that the climate south of the Milwaukee area, in states like Illinois, Iowa, and Missouri, was "mortally unhealthful" and rife with "malignant fevers, dysentery, and infections." The "unanimous opinions" of his advisors "turned me away from Iowa," Van Raalte noted.[47] Unlike Wisconsin, no specific reasons were given, leaving one to think that the Michigan promoters had little or no first-hand knowledge of the Hawkeye State. Van Raalte himself noted that Iowa lacked access to markets, except via the unhealthful port of New Orleans. He soon learned to his sorrow that West Michigan wetlands were also unhealthful.

But the location was ideal. The Black River watershed was virtually unpopulated, except for a small Odawa band. It offered "space enough for settlements of thousands and thousands," Van Raalte declared. Besides the Smith and Fairbanks families at the mission, the only whites farming in the future Fillmore Township were Anton Shorno, a German American, and Gilbert Cranmer, a Yankee. To be near Americans and yet live in a Dutch Reformed enclave was the object. "It is of first importance to us to live together," Van Raalte stated, quoting the Dutch motto, *eendragt maakt magt* (unity makes strength).[48]

The harbor at the mouth of Black Lake opened Van Raalte's newly founded colony to booming Chicago and Milwaukee markets and also to New York City via the Great Lakes and the Erie Canal. Holland "is and remains dear to me above Wisconsin," Van Raalte averred, "because I am here near the great inland waterway of America; transportation and shipping mean much to me." The harbor was essential; it was the "cornerstone of our whole building," the dominee declared, using biblical imagery. Black Lake, like every other body of water emptying into Lake Michigan's western shore, was formed by the mouths of rivers dammed by sand blown in fierce storms that turned river outlets into cigar-shaped lakes. When the Dutch arrived in the spring of 1847, the channel was barely two feet deep. Yet Van Raalte envisioned Holland harbor being the "most beautiful and safest" on the entire west side of the state. Little could he know that perennial siltation would thwart his harbor hopes for twenty years.[49]

[47] Van Raalte to Brummelkamp, 30 Jan. 1847, in *Holland in Amerika*, English typescript, 8.
[48] Ibid., 22.
[49] Van Raalte to De Moen, 11 Feb. 1849, in *Der toestand*, 7-8; Van Raalte to Brummelkamp, 30 Jan. 1847, in *Holland in Amerika*, 23; Van Raalte letter of 1848 reprinted in *Holland City News*, 16 Mar. 1872; Van Raalte to Paulus Den

Cultural factors also impinged on Van Raalte's thinking. Lower Michigan was populated by Yankees of Old Dutch and Presbyterian stock, whereas Wisconsin, especially Milwaukee, was thick with German Catholics, and the Fox River Valley was sprinkled with Dutch Catholic settlements. In Van Raalte's words, Michigan was

> less populated by foreigners, . . . the mixed multitude from Europe, . . . and this is exactly why Michigan recommends itself to me. . . . The people here are more knowledgeable, God-fearing, and enterprising, and are related in many ways to the old states. . . . The Old Dutch families have great influence and respect among Americans, and to a certain extent, these advantages accrue to us in this state.[50]

These comments suggest that the Michigan boosters, mainly Presbyterians, played on the traditional Dutch Reformed prejudice against Catholics. Van Raalte accepted their stereotypic view of Wisconsin. Antipathy toward Catholics was deep in the bones of Dutch Calvinists. Students studied the Eighty Years' War for Independence against Catholic Spain and how Prince Willem of Orange finally broke the starvation siege of Leiden on October 3, 1574, a date that is commemorated every year. Had the Michigan boosters been Catholics, Van Raalte might well have settled in Fond du Lac, Wisconsin.

Pros and cons of Holland

When critics derided his choice of Michigan, Van Raalte explained his reasoning in detail in an 1849 letter to his wife's brother, Carel de Moen, then serving the Separatist church in Den Ham, Overijssel. "The choice of this area was not the result of deception . . . by speculators," he declared. "Amid sincere wrestling before God, I was led by reasonable reasons gathered from the geographical location, from earlier settlements, from the advice of unselfish ministers and Christians, and from farmers during my roaming through prairies and forests."[51]

Bleyker, 9 Jan. 1851, HHA. Detailed histories of harbor developments, shipping, and shipbuilding, to 1870, are in Swierenga, *Holland, Michigan*, 1:681-721, and Douma, "Struggle Against the Sand."

[50] Van Raalte to Brummelkamp, 29 Jan. 1847, in *Holland in Amerika*, 11. For Dutch Catholic settlements in Wisconsin, see Lucas, *Netherlanders*, 217-25; Swierenga and Krabbendam, "Dutch Catholics and Protestants," 39-64.

[51] Van Raalte to De Moen, 11 Feb. 1849, in *Der toestand*, 6.

The dense woodlands, scary as they were to the settlers, would become money in the bank, a gift of God waiting to be exploited. The trees would furnish free firewood and building materials for houses and barns that prairie settlers must buy at great cost. Forests can become fertile prairies after logging, but prairies cannot grow trees. Harvesting trees was cheaper than custom sod-busting with three-yoke of oxen at $1.25 per acre, costing as much as the land itself. Although the forests would cause problems for farming and road building, their trees would yield logs for homes, roof shingles, tar, pitch, potash (pearlash), tannin, lumber, and maple sugar, all marketable commodities in Chicago. Wood would provide income for lumbermen, coopers, tanners, carpenters, joiners, and cabinetmakers. Businessmen could open sawmills and tanneries, and shipbuilders could ply their craft. Cornelius Van der Meulen said it best: "I have made more from the sale of seven trees than I have paid on twenty acres upon which I now live [$25], and simply to have shingles made for my roof." Since he paid $25 ($927 today) for his raw land, each tree was worth $3.57 ($139 today).[52]

The milder climate near the lake would produce excellent fruits and cranberries. Pigs could root among the acorns in the woods, and cattle could graze on grasses in the small openings, even in the winter. "It is possible immediately to start large dairy farms," Van Raalte added, and "it would be a good thing for the rich to buy many young cattle immediately."[53] Moreover, forest work requires heavy manual labor, so there would always be work for newcomers "who have capable hands." Learning to use the ax and adze, however, was no mean feat for Dutchmen who had little prior experience with these tools. Many an errant blow injured feet and legs, and many a girdled tree fell in the wrong direction, until Americans and natives could instruct the Dutch in the skills of ax and saw. "We were a wretched, ignorant, small group," Van Raalte acknowledged, "but God heard our prayer, and we were not destroyed."[54]

Forest lands would have other advantages as well, Van Raalte believed. The soil was guaranteed to be fertile; the presence of many huge trees proved it. Farmers could plant Indian corn and potatoes

---

[52] Van der Meulen to De Moen, 20 Jan. 1849, in *Der toestand*, 20, trans. E. R. Post and D. F. Van Vliet.

[53] Van Raalte to Brummelkamp, 30 Jan. 1847, *Holland in Amerika*, 16, 19-23 (quotes); Van Raalte to De Moen, 11 Feb. 1849, *Der toestand*, 5-6.

[54] Van Raalte to De Moen, 11 Feb. 1849, *Der toestand*, English typescript, 6.

among the stumps as soon as the trees were felled in windrows. Forest lands, Van Raalte added, were also healthier and better served with water supplies than the semiarid prairies where the rotting of turned-over prairie sod produced a vapor, a miasma, that could cause sickness in the first years.[55] On the issue of soil quality and bad vapors, Van Raalte cannot be faulted for accepting misguided frontier folk wisdom that favored woodlands over prairies, but he soon learned to his chagrin that damp forests and swamps could also be very unhealthful, and cut-over lands had thin soils. Soon farmers had to spread to the north and east of Holland in search of fertile clay soil.

Native and Dutch relations

One issue never mentioned in any extant source is Van Raalte's thinking about planting his Dutch colony among Chief Wakazoo's Odawa band. Did he ever consider that the colonists would disrupt the hunting, fishing, and trapping lifestyle of the natives by slashing the forests to farm and letting their hogs and cattle forage in the woods? Had he heard from his Michigan friends that the days were numbered before the natives were forced to move to Indian Territory in the West? Did he assume that white famers had a higher right to the land than hunters and gatherers who lived off the land but did not develop it as God had intended? After all, Adam was told to "replenish the earth, and subdue it" (Gen. 1:28, KJV). Did Van Raalte ever think of intermarriage between the Dutch and the natives? No Dutch ever married a native, but Rev. Smith's daughter, who had grown up among the natives, married a nephew of Chief Wakazoo.

Rev. Smith recorded a premonition in his diary. The Odawas "are not prepared to defend their fields against the large number of cattle and hogs the Dutch are bringing in, especially as they [the natives] have to be absent and cannot watch them [the crops]. Considerable damage is already done." Smith's granddaughter, Etta Smith Wilson, many years later voiced a more jarring complaint that the Dutch were so "filthy" that the natives "could not live near them." Dutch women polluted the wells when they drew water and had no compunction about using "night vessels" to cook porridge in the morning. The smallpox epidemic that raged the first summer in the Dutch colony also frightened the natives, who were very susceptible. "They fear it as

---

[55] Van Raalte to Brummelkamp, 30 Jan. 1847, in *Holland in Amerika*, 13. Appraisals of the two immigrant leaders are Swierenga, "Van Raalte and Scholte," and Aay and Ester, "Immigration Leaders."

they do death," said Smith. The natives quickly went to Grand Haven to be vaccinated. The Dutch, for their part, were frightened when drunken Odawa men came by their cabins. What the Dutch "influence will be on our mission, the future must determine," Smith opined. "We hope it may be good eventually." It was not, and within two years, Wakazoo's band and Smith relocated the mission two hundred miles north to Northport overlooking Grand Traverse Bay.[56]

In retrospect, Dutch-Odawa relations were generally peaceful, and no violent acts marred the few years of joint occupation. Both groups were Christian, with clerical leaders who counseled peace. But the cultural gulf was great, especially in the first months when the desperate Dutch found maple sugar-making equipment seemingly abandoned. They took the cast-iron kettles, sap buckets, and axes, and used the wood troughs to slop hogs or for cooking. When the natives returned in the fall from spending summers up north, Chief Wakazoo complained bitterly to Rev. Smith who informed Van Raalte of the offense. He took immediate action, according to Engbertus Van der Veen. "One Sunday, our dominee announced from the pulpit that a chief had complained that some settlers had taken away their sugar troughs and that the natives were revengeful. He demanded that we punish the guilty persons and that the troughs be returned." The dominee feebly explained that this had happened "perhaps by mistake or through ignorance," but he made the four offenders pay $40 ($1,484 today) for the stolen property. So the sticky matter was resolved honorably.[57]

Years later, after the Indian Rights movement had emerged, descendants of Wakazoo's band at Northport in the Leelanau Peninsula, charged the Dutch with having driven them away and seizing their lands. Isaac Fairbanks' son Austin, no Indian lover, decried the saying among the band: "The Bad Spirit says shoot every Dutchman, but the Good Spirit says, go away, let Dutchman be." Chief Wakazoo made the decision to relocate in order to preserve the hunting and gathering way

---

[56] Smith report to Indian Superintendent William A. Richmond, 31 Aug. 1847, in Swierenga and Van Appledorn, *Old Wing Mission*, 586; "Evert Zagers' Account," Lucas, *Dutch Immigrant Memoirs*, 1:85; Smith to Rev. William M. Ferry, 23 Mar. 1840; Smith Memoranda, 3 Mar. 1848; Wilson, "Life and Work," quote 204.

[57] Van der Veen, "Life Reminiscences," 1:511; Smith Memoranda, 22, 24 Jan., 10, 23 Feb. 1848, both in Swierenga and Van Appledorn, *Old Wing Mission*, 44-45, 305, 309. The account of Van Hinte, *Netherlanders*, 261, does not square with Van der Veen, an eyewitness. The natives did not complain to Van Raalte in a morning worship service, and the dominee did not shout angrily and derisively that the guilty men must "leave *De Kolonie* and the sooner the better."

of life.⁵⁸ And the Dutch and American buyers paid a fair price to the Odawa families for their partially improved lands. The average price was five dollars per acre, a fourfold increase over the purchase price a decade earlier. Austin's father, Isaac Fairbanks in his "Recollections," succinctly wrote: The natives "were not forced to give up their lands, but sold them for a good price."⁵⁹

Scholte breaks ranks

Newspaper reports of Van Raalte's departure for America set group migration in motion among Seceders. In late September, a group of sixteen Separatists from the Zwolle church departed from Rotterdam. On October 3, the same day the SS *Southerner* dropped anchor at Hellevoetsluis, Scholte's advance party of eight families and five single men, led by Hendrik Barendregt, sailed for New Orleans, bound via a Mississippi River steamboat for St. Louis, where they arrived in late November. Barendregt expected to meet Van Raalte in St. Louis and then decide on the best location, likely in Iowa, where Scholte had his eye.⁶⁰ Van Raalte desired a joint colony, but it is doubtful that he and Scholte had a pre-agreement. "I hope that Brother Scholte will not go to Iowa," Van Raalte wrote. "I believe that he cannot do any better than to settle in Michigan." Scholte rejected that idea. Michigan, he said, was an "unfortunate choice." It was unhealthy, isolated, without good roads, and controlled by land speculators. "In Albany, as well as in New York, the general opinion is that things will turn out badly [for Van Raalte]." And, in the short run, they did.⁶¹

Once in America, Van Raalte ruled out the isolated frontier state of Iowa in favor of either eastern Wisconsin or western Michigan, both with Lake Michigan ports and vast woodlands. He urged Scholte to join him. He wrote Brummelkamp in late January 1847:

---

58   This negative view came from "Arvilla Powers Smith's Memoirs" (1892) and granddaughter Wilson's, "Life and Work," both reprinted in Swierenga and Van Appledorn, *Old Wing Mission*, 443-70, and 471-93. William O. Van Eyck repeated the complaints of both Smith and Wilson in a lengthy, front-page account in *Holland City News*, 3 July 1930, "A Story is Filled With Indian Lore: Strife between Holland Settlers and Red Men was Constantly Rife."
59   Isaac Fairbanks, "Recollections," in Lucas, *Dutch Immigrant Memoirs*, 1:382. Henry Fairbanks, Isaac's son, stated that "The Indians were lazy and, rather than work on a farm, they stole food from the Hollanders," see "Holland Man Was Indian Boys' Playmate" and "Isaac Fairbanks Was First White Man in These Parts," *Holland City News*, 1 Apr. 1937.
60   "H. Barendregt's Letter from St. Louis, Missouri, Dec. 14, 1846," in Lucas, *Dutch Immigrant Memoirs*, 2:514-19.
61   Swierenga, "Van Raalte and Scholte."

It is most important for us all that we live together. "In unity there is strength." . . . For whenever a couple of thousand souls unite for one purpose, . . . they will have an unbelievably great influence and can accomplish much. I hope God will grant this, but may His will be done.[62]

Scholte had planned to follow Barendregt immediately, but his pregnant young bride, Maria Kranz, was late in a difficult pregnancy. The newborn's death and her illness rendered this plan moot. The "painful event," as Scholte phrased it, pushed their departure date back to May 1847. In the meantime, after receiving favorable word from Barendregt, Scholte used *De Reformatie* to recruit prospective emigrants. On Christmas Day of 1846, Scholte organized at Utrecht his Christian Association for Emigration, with thirteen hundred members. In April 1847, he chartered four three-masters for seventy families with nine hundred souls who were ready to go. His party, mainly from Zuid-Holland and Utrecht, departed Rotterdam for Baltimore, bound for St. Louis via the Pennsylvania Railroad and Ohio and Mississippi River steamboats.[63]

The fertile Iowa prairies beckoned Scholte after he had read some German travel guides. He embellished the ease of farming the prairies, where wood was scarce, and thick sod had to be broken with special plows, but dismissed the positives of woodlands.[64] His assessment, however, was correct that Michigan's thin soils could not hold a candle to the thick black loam in Iowa, whose acreage of Class I soils exceeded that of any other state. Near Lake Michigan, Holland's sandy soils amid thick forests were thin. Only the upland clay soils farther inland provided excellent farmland. Holland's fevered shanties in the woods had no counterpart in Pella's healthy "strawtown" on high ground.[65] Over time, however, it became clear that Holland had the locational advantage, situated near Grand Rapids and accessible by water to Chicago and Milwaukee. Holland had a harbor on the Great Lakes and after 1871 rail links to Chicago and New York. Pella had a road link

---

[62] Van Raalte to Brummelkamp, 30 Jan. 1847, in *Holland in Amerika*, 35.

[63] *Groninger Courant*, 2, 13 Oct. 1846; *Provinciale Overijsselsche en Zwolsche Courant*, 9 Oct. 1846 (www.delpher.nl, accessed, June 2021); Lucas, *Netherlanders*, 160-65. A listing of the passengers on the four vessels is in *Souvenir History of Pella, Iowa*, 35-44.

[64] For appraisals of the two immigrant leaders, see Swierenga, "Van Raalte and Scholte," and Aay and Ester, "Immigration Leaders."

[65] The phrase comes from Sara E. Gosselink's historical novel, *Roofs over Strawtown* (Eerdmans, 1945).

to Des Moines and after the railroad came in 1866, a link to Chicago markets, three hundred miles away. In Van Raalte's mind, this was divine providence at work; Holland was preordained.

That Van Raalte and Scholte chose different locations was understandable. Van Raalte's people hailed from the sandy and forested eastern Netherlands, and Scholte's group came mainly from the flat, clay soil southwestern region. Scholte's group had money; Van Raalte's did not. This dictated the choice. Van Raalte saw the advantage of exploiting forest resources, and Scholte wanted rolling prairies, ready for the plow. Going separate ways meant that the titans became rivals in recruiting settlers. Scholte chastised Van Raalte for being "thoroughly American" in this regard, but he did the same.[66] Recruitment was the name of the game. The breakdown in cooperation between the two men was due to their personalities. Both were strong-willed, but Scholte was more independent and less irenic of spirit. In equestrian terms, both men were stallions who would not share a stable.

From 1846 through 1850, more than six thousand Separatists entered the United States, with thirty-two hundred in 1847, the high point. Census marshals in 1850 counted almost five thousand Dutch-born immigrants in Michigan, Iowa, Wisconsin, and Illinois. Most of these folks were either Separatists or sympathizers willing to live among them. They came first and put their orthodox, conservative stamp on all the colonies. By 1857, after seventy-six hundred Separatists had emigrated, their wave was over. From 1850 to 1880, three-fourths of Protestant emigrants were members of the Hervormde Kerk, and only one-fourth were Separatists.[67]

Over those same decades, from 1850 to 1880, Dutch Reformed immigrants experienced a major falling away from the Reformed faith. I estimate that only one-third (15,000 out of 50,000) of Dutch Reformed immigrants joined similar congregations in America. Up to two-thirds of adult immigrants either joined American churches or discarded formal religious practice. This latter fact is telling because Netherlands religious censuses show almost 100 percent church affiliation. In 1880 the immigrant wing of the Reformed Church in America had 18,000 souls (baptized and confessing members), and the Christian Reformed Church had 12,300. Of these, children born in America made up nearly half this number. Many adult members, of course, had died by then.

[66] Lucas, *Netherlanders*, 166-68; Van Hinte, *Netherlanders*, 141-42; Scholte (Boston) to Andries Wormser (Amsterdam), 14 May 1847, in *Iowa Letters*, 63.
[67] Bruins and Swierenga, *Family Quarrels*, 6-7.

In the diverse, American religious environment, the joining of culture and faith, as the term "Dutch Reformed" implies, was problematic. The forces of Americanization were strong and not fully understood.[68]

---

[68] Swierenga, "True Brothers," 72-73; De Kok, *Nederland*, 292-93.

CHAPTER 9

Founding Holland Colony: "City on a hill."

In Detroit, in late January 1847, on the cusp of planting his colony, Van Raalte's "greatest hope" was that it would be "a city set on a hill" (Matt. 5:14), like Boston, the well-known Puritan beacon. At Holland's twenty-fifth anniversary, the preacher returned to that theme. Speaking directly to young people, he prayed: "May Holland shine in your hands like the city of God on the earth."[1] But Van Raalte had set the bar too high. Although Holland thrived economically, it was no utopia. The dominee had only a brief respite from serious trouble. He experienced school squabbles, harbor failures, a church schism, bad press, and a business failure. The Dutch have a penchant for cutting off leaders at the knees, and Van Raalte was no exception.

Advance party

Before leaving Detroit, Van Raalte suggested a name for his colony. "I could think of no better name than Holland," he stated,

---

[1] Van Raalte to Brummelkamp, 30 Jan. 1847, in Brummelkamp, *Holland in Amerika*, 35; Van Raalte's Ebenezer speech, "Eendragt maakt magt," 17 Sept. 1872, in Lucas, *1847–Ebenezer–1947*, 21-30.

but his was only a proposal. "What we call the village can be decided later by the people." Few ever questioned the name for the township or the city.[2]

The next step was to send off an advance party. On January 30, 1847, the dominee delegated his right-hand man, Bernardus Grootenhuis, to go to Allegan to arrange with John Kellogg to erect several log cabins at the Holland site. A week before Grootenhuis and his wife Janna departed, Van Raalte directed the ten families at St. Clair to meet him in Allegan. Given that southern Michigan was still in the grip of winter, only six families decided to come immediately, led by Widow Geesje Schutte (Mrs. Jan) Laarman—the only one with means. The others were Harm Kok, Willem Notting, Egbert Frederiks (Fredriks), Evert Zagers, and Hermanus Lankheet, forty-three souls in all. The remnant followed in March.[3]

These bold families traveled by sleigh the sixty miles from St. Clair to Detroit, where Theodore Romeyn treated them kindly and put them on the Michigan Central train to Kalamazoo with a letter of introduction to Rev. Ova Hoyt, whose Presbyterian Church families hosted them. The next day, the party rode an ox-drawn sleigh to Otsego, where a kindly tavern-keeper fed them *gratis*. The following day, they reached the home of John and Mary Otterson Kellogg in Allegan. Local families housed and fed them, including Elisha and Lydia Baxter (Mrs. Elisha) Ely, a woman of Knickerbocker parents, who spoke some Dutch. She gave special attention to the ladies. Van Raalte paid fifty-three dollars for rail fares ($2 for adults, $1 for children), meals, maps, axe handles, and winter clothes. The Van Raaltes reached the Kelloggs the same day as the St. Clair families, Saturday, February 6. On Sunday, they worshiped and rested.[4]

After conferring with Kellogg and his hired hand, George S. Harrington, Van Raalte decided to join the work party at the Holland site, namely Grootenhuis, Fredriks, Lankheet, Jan Laarman (eldest son of Widow Laarman), Zagers, and Notting, plus Notting's wife

---

[2] Van Raalte to Brummelkamp, 30 Jan. 1847, in Brummelkamp, *Holland in Amerika*, 37; Swierenga, "Changes and Complications." A Netherlands newspaper took notice of the naming, which shows the interest in Van Raalte's venture (*Utrechtsche Provinciale en Stads-Courant*, 30 Apr. 1847).

[3] "Dagboek," Apr. 1847-15 Dec. 1849, Eerste stuk, HMA; Lucas, *Netherlanders*, 87-88.

[4] Frederiks, "Egbert Frederiks' Pioneer Memories," 1:66; Van Raalte financial ledger, signed by Kellogg, 13 Feb. 1847; Romeyn to Van Raalte, 5 Mar. 1847, HHA; "Our Old Settlers," *Holland City News*, 23 Mar. 1878, lists the "original forty-seven," instead of forty-three.

Macheldtje. She agreed to join Janna Grootenhuis as helper and cook. Harrington, a "trustworthy and capable American" in Van Raalte's words, was a New York Englishman, whose wife was also of Old Dutch stock.[5]

On February 9, Harrington transported the men on his ox-drawn sleigh through deep snow the twenty-four miles from Allegan to Old Wing Mission. For the last five miles from Richmond (now Fennville), the oxen followed the road that Chief Wakazoo's men had "chopped" through the virgin forest to link the mission to New Richmond on the Kalamazoo River. Kellogg paid Harrington two dollars per day for his team and time. Van Raalte paid the six volunteers in kind; he reduced the cost of their quarter-acre lots in Holland from forty dollars to fifteen dollars, making their "sweat equity" worth twenty-five dollars.[6]

George and Arvilla Smith, the hospitable missionary couple, graciously gave Van Raalte, the Grootenhuis couple, and Macheldtje Notting the parlor, the best room in their new frame house. Isaac and Ann Fairbanks hosted the other five men in their crude cabin; they slept on the floor in front of a roaring fireplace. Christina and the five children stayed for three months with the Kelloggs and then spent several weeks with the Smiths while their house in Holland was being built.[7] But the Van Raaltes may have overstayed their welcome. The children left "many unacceptable and irreparable marks" behind on the parlor walls. Arvilla had some hard feelings about this but was ultimately pacified, and for the two years that the Smiths remained in the area, the two couples shared several "pleasant" visits.[8]

Setting the date for the founding of Holland Colony is rather arbitrary, but February 9, 1847, the day the work party began erecting shelters, is by tradition the official date. Half the crew felled trees, and the other half chopped a road from the mission to the head of Black Lake. It took them eighteen days to open a clearing wide enough for an oxteam. The road ran west from the mission on present-day Fortieth Street to Waverly Avenue and north to Eighth Street, where

---

[5] "Emigration from Holland," *Christian Intelligencer*, 11 Feb. 1847; "Evert Zagers' Account," in Lucas, *Dutch Immigrant Memoirs*, 1:85. Lucas, *Netherlanders*, 87-89, cites memoirs of five pioneers in HMA. Five weeks later, Macheldtje Notting was the first to be buried in the new homeland.

[6] Isaac Fairbank's address at Holland's 25th anniversary in *Holland City News*, 21 Sept. 1872.

[7] Swierenga and Van Appledorn, *Old Wing Mission*, 463-64.

[8] Van Raalte to Brummelkamp, 11 Sept. 1852, HHA; Sheeres, "Six Names; Six Stories."

George S. and Margaret
Van Alstyne Harrington (JAH)

Isaac Fairbanks in later life
(JAH)

the impenetrable Cedar Swamp stopped them. The shelter crew erected two, sixteen-by-thirty-foot log shanties with brush roofs on the hill above Waverly Avenue, entering today's Holland Heights—the site of the future Wouter Van der Haar family farm on the northeast corner. Not one of the work party had ever cut down a tree before and, like beavers, they were wont to girdle the trunk and let gravity fell it, sometimes with grave consequences. No doubt, Fairbanks, Harrington, and the natives taught them how to fell trees safely. In two weeks, on February 23, the first shanty was finished, and the men sent word to Allegan for their families.[9]

Meanwhile, Van Raalte, who had remained at the Smith home, barely escaped a watery grave when he went out with five colonists to scout farm sites north of the ice-covered Black River. On their return, they found the river ice breaking up because of "a heavy, warm rain." They were "cut off from all help and could have succumbed from cold and want, and by night our clothes were frozen." In the morning, the group discovered a "bridge" on today's Paw Paw Drive near 112th Avenue where "Indians had felled a long, slender tree that was held in place by trees and supported by cakes of ice." The slippery tree trunk

---

[9] Frederiks, "Egbert Frederiks' Pioneer Memories," 1:67; Lucas, *Netherlanders*, 89-92; *Christian Intelligencer*, 11 Mar. 1847, 84; Van Koevering, *Legends of the Dutch*, 222-24.

was the "only means to save us from death. For me, it was a bridge," the dominee reported, "but some of our group cried and wept for fear when I began to cross. Contrary to every expectation, we all escaped death."[10]

More arrivals

While the advance party was still at work on the second shanty, fifteen families, led by Jan Rabbers, arrived unexpectedly on March 10. They had embarked from Hellevoetsluis on October 13, ten days after Van Raalte's party had sailed, and docked in New York on December 21. They stayed in the city for two months until, at Van Raalte's urging, they set out in mid-February for Holland. When they arrived by sleigh from Allegan, Van Raalte assigned them to the second shelter. Rabbers chose as their village the knoll at the bend of present-day 106th Street at Perry Avenue and named it Groningen, after the home province of many of them.[11]

On March 16, Teunis Keppel, Hein Van der Haar, and Jan Binnekant, arrived in Holland at Van Raalte's behest, having walked all the way from St. Louis by way of Chicago and the southern shoreline of Lake Michigan. They had sailed three weeks after Van Raalte and came by way of Baltimore to St. Louis. Some two hundred Hollanders, mainly followers of Scholte, had gathered at St. Louis after an arduous trip via the Ohio and Mississippi Rivers from the port of Baltimore. The threesome spurned Scholte for Holland; their arrival raised the settlement to forty-three souls, the original pioneers. Van Raalte immediately put Keppel to work shingling his cabin. The rest of the party, with women and children and all the baggage, followed more slowly, also on foot. But in Chicago, they boarded a schooner to Grand Haven and went by wagon via Port Sheldon to Holland, arriving March 17.[12]

Battling winter weather with little food, the "shanty-dwelling brothers" formed a special bond. Grootenhuis years later recalled the dire situation the so-called "icebreakers" had faced.

---

[10] Van Raalte "Commemoration Address, 1872," 2:488. The men were Johannes Hellenthal, Arend Kamper, Hendrik Van Duren, Wouter Van der Haar, and Edward J. Harrington.
[11] Lucas, *Netherlanders*, 91.
[12] *Christian Intelligencer*, 25 Mar. 1847 (quote); newspaper clipping, Van Schelven Papers; Teunis Keppel recollections, *De Hope*, 24 Mar. 1886; Lucas, *Netherlanders*, 92.

Lokkers' log cabin (*JAH*)

One evening, when we were still together as one family in the shanties, the women (who were the cooks) reported that the entire supply of food stuff had been used up, and that there was not anything left for breakfast the next morning.... But how did the Lord provide? Without any expectation, late in the evening, a wagon arrived before the doors of the shanties, loaded with all kinds of victuals: bacon, corn meal, flour, etc. brought by a Quaker or Friend (as they call themselves) from Otsego. Imagine how one still remembers the moment.

Judge Kellogg was the kindly man responsible for the food. He used all his available money to buy bran, some middlings, beans, and "a little corn for the pigs," which Harrington delivered by wagon. Kellogg had given sacrificially; "I am about out of money," he confessed.[13] Forty-three years later, in 1890, Keppel invited to his home the nine surviving pioneers to commemorate their feat in the forest. He claimed the honor of being one of the original forty-three pioneers, which

---

[13] *Christian Intelligencer*, 26 Apr., 1847; Kellogg to Van Raalte, 25 Mar. 1847, HHA. Harrington taught the colonists how to clear land, handle oxteams, and open roads. Margaret (Mrs. George) Van Alstyne helped bond with the Young Dutch. In April 1847, Harrington entered 160 acres of public land near Old Wing Mission in the future Fillmore Township.

First citizenship papers filed by Van Raalte April 6, 1847, at Allegan, and refiled in Grand Haven, on October 11, 1851 (*HHA*)

Grootenhuis disputed. "I really regret that we old settlers must quarrel about such small things, but we are human," he declared. Grootenhuis could claim priority of place since he was in the work party that arrived on February 9, 1847, but Keppel was correct to count himself in the original forty-three of March 17, 1847.[14]

Before leaving Allegan, Van Raalte filed his "declaration of intention" to apply for citizenship. Under oath, before Allegan County

[14] Teunis Keppel, *Holland City News*, 21 Mar. 1874, *De Grondwet*, 17 Mar. 1890, 14 June 1892; Bernardus Grootenhuis, "A bit more with reference to the first settlers," *De Hope*, 22 June 1892, trans. Nella Kennedy; Anonymous, "Honor to whom deserves honor," *De Hope*, Dec. 1892.

Van Raalte in his late forties (*JAH*)

clerk Nathan Manson Jr., Van Raalte declared his "bona fide intention" to become a citizen and "to renounce all allegiance and fidelity to every foreign prince, potentate, state and sovereignty whatever, and particularly to Willem II, King of the Netherlands." The Dutch cleric had no love lost for his monarch. Under federal and state law, free, white male aliens, after one year's residency, could file their "declaration of intent to naturalize," the so-called "First Papers." After two years, they could vote in local elections and in national elections after five years, upon gaining full citizenship. Van Raalte "jumped the gun" in Allegan and had to refile later in Grand Haven.[15]

Founding Holland Colony

On April 9, 1847, after two months of hard work, the primitive log shanties, without windows and doors, were ready to shelter the women and children. Early that morning, Harrington brought the families by wagon from Allegan. The Van Raalte family had contracted with George and Arvilla Smith to use their parlor while their frame house was under construction. The weather that day was a typical mix of sun and clouds, with temperatures below normal—near freezing at dawn and rising to forty-eight degrees in midafternoon—with a stiff breeze from the northwest.[16] The remnant of Van Raalte's group that had

---

[15] Eileen Bolger, "Naturalization Process in U.S.: Early History," citing Congressional Acts of 29 Jan. 1795 (1 Stat. 414) and 14 Apr. 1802 (2 Stat. 153)

[16] Weather data provided by Huug van den Dool, email, 14 Oct. 2020, National Oceanic and Atmospheric Administration, Washington, DC.

remained in Detroit arrived that same evening. The fifteen founding families and singles, including the Van Raalte household, numbered sixty, a little over half of the original group of 110 on the *Southerner*. The others had peeled off in Buffalo or Detroit, and a few settled on better farmland southeast of Holland in the future Fillmore Township. These sixty people comprise the founders of Holland.[17]

Dominee Van Raalte laid out his vision for the colony. "My fellow countrymen, unite, inform, and elevate yourselves; aim at a lofty standard of life, cultivate knowledge, lay an adequate foundation for your colony according to a well-developed plan, that you may be a great people among the other groups of this land. Be diligent in educating your children; don't hold a calf in higher esteem than your own child."[18]

First plat, Village of Holland

In late summer of 1847, Van Raalte hired Elisha Bourne Bassett, the Allegan County surveyor, to lay out the first plat of Holland with compass and chain in a grid pattern. Bassett used the model of Allegan and laid out thirty blocks, containing 139 lots large enough for a house, a milk cow, and a garden. Self-sufficiency and bartering were common, and only absolute necessities were store bought.[19] Bassett and his assistants completed this initial survey in eighteen days, and he went home sick. The north end of the village was hemmed in on the west by Black Lake and on the east by Black River, largely a swamp. East-west streets ran from First Street south to Eighth Street, with three north-south axis streets—Lake (now Pine), River, and Market (now Central). In 1848 Van Raalte transferred to the village the rights to build piers into the lake at the foot of Second, Third, Fourth, and Fifth Streets for shipping.

In late 1847, Bassett sent John Dumont of Allegan to complete the survey from Ninth Street to Sixteenth Street and east to Cedar (later Central) and Fish (later Columbia) Streets. Dumont laid out the blocks and then sold the compass and chain to Bernardus Grootenhuis

---

[17] Theodore Romeyn to Van Raalte, 5 Mar. 1847, HHA. Holland's founding families include Hendrik De Kruif, Egbert Dunnewind, Egbert Frederiks (Fredriks), Bernardus Grootenhuis, Gerrit Jan Hofman, Harm Kok, Jan Kolvoord, Hermanus Lankheet, Widow Laarman, Jan Laarman, Willem Notting, Hendrik Oldemeyer, Dirk Plasman, Abraham Slaghuis, Frans Smit, Jan Van den Boogard, Albertus C. Van Raalte, and Evert Zagers

[18] Quoted by Van der Veen, "Life Reminiscences," 1:500-501.

[19] Swierenga, *Holland, Michigan*, 1:95; Jacob Harms Dunnink, 20 May 1856, HMA; 1848 Holland City plat, HMA.

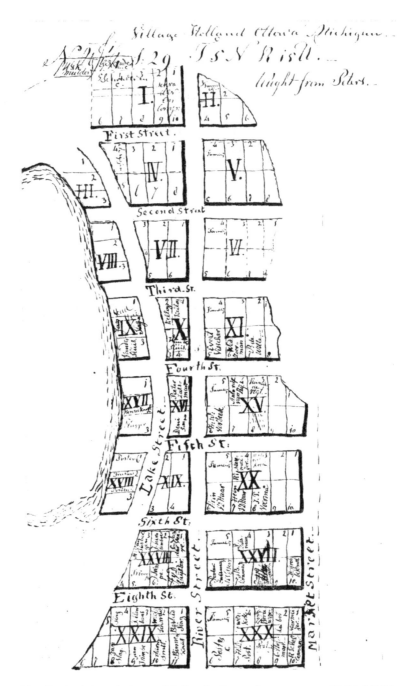

Van Raalte's hand-drawn Holland village plat, summer 1847 (*HHA*)

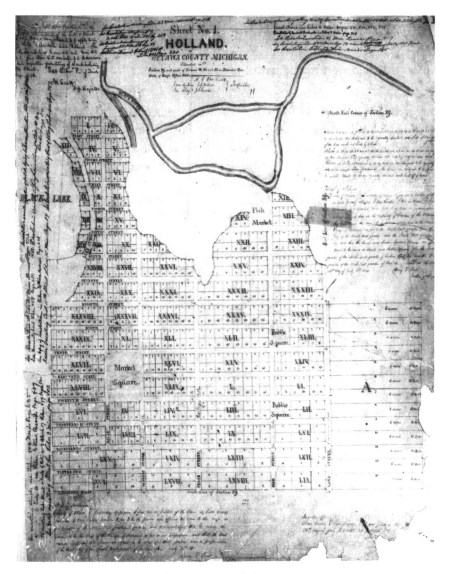

Holland plat, filed July 21, 1848, by E. Bourne Bassett, completed by John Dumont and James Brayton (*HMA*)

who, with the help of Adrianus Van Dam, laid out the lots, bringing the total to 687. The village then covered six hundred acres. Inaccuracies in this first official survey led to a second survey in 1866, and by then, the village had grown to 1,625 acres. That Van Raalte chose no Dutch street names signaled his desire to conform to American ways, but he did follow the Dutch practice of setting aside public squares for a central market and a fish market.[20]

Van Raalte house and garden

In early March, Van Raalte ordered a "plain board shanty" erected for his family on what would become Fairbanks Avenue beyond the east border of *de stad* (the town, as the immigrants referred to the village). Money was tight, and Van Raalte had only $400 in hand, but he stretched it to the limit. His property covered 160 acres from present-day Eighth Street south to Sixteenth Street and from Fairbanks Avenue east to Waverly Avenue. The homestead faced Fairbanks Avenue midway between Ninth and Tenth Streets. No log cabin for Albertus and Christina; they deserved a frame house. He contracted with Joseph Maksabe, a Potawatomi chief at the mission, for 4,200 board feet of lumber, including flooring and siding, for $29.90. He put $15 down and paid the remainder three months later. Maksabe had the building supplies shipped to Isaac Fairbanks, who had recently completed Rev. Smith's frame house at the mission and would now build one for the Dutch dominee. Fairbanks' brothers-in-law, Henry and Milton Woodruff, likely assisted in the construction. The family moved into the unfinished house in late May, and it soon became the "headquarters for everything."[21]

From his meager purse, Van Raalte gave Kellogg three hundred dollars to purchase for the colony eighteen cows and two oxteams, with yokes and whips. The price included pay for men to drive the animals from Allegan. The oxen responded to "Buck" and "Broad" and "Pete" and "Bill." Van Raalte kept the first pair—brindle breeds, marked by dark brown coats. Every farmer had oxen; they were far cheaper and stronger than horses of that day and could eventually be used for food. The dominee's oxen, cows, pigs, and small animals were housed in Van Raalte's barn, north of the house. The cows calved, which boosted the

---

[20] Van der Veen, "Life Reminiscences," 1:499-500; Cornelia Van Malsen to parents, 12 July 1847, in Yzenbaard, "'America' Letters," 42; "Dorpslands Dagboek," 3 Aug., 2 Dec. 1847, 22 June 1848, 15 Dec. 1850; Van Raalte Account Book with Post & Co., 22 June 1850, HHA; Van Raalte to Brummelkamp, 11 Sept. 1852, HHA.

[21] Van der Veen, "Life Reminiscences," 1:496; Edward J. Harrington, "Early Reminiscences," 1:383, both in Lucas, *Dutch Immigrant Memoirs*. Van Raalte himself dated the arrival of the family in Holland at the end of May. See "Biographical Sketch of Christina Van Raalte," July 1871, trans. Boonstra, HHA. Van Schelven reported that Van Raalte's house was built by "Fenn of Richmond," but he gives no source ("Van Schelven's Historical Notes"), Moerdyke Papers.

milk supply and built the herd. When feed grain prices were high, work animals were let out to pasture; pigs could root in the woods.²²

Among other tasks, the dominee's hired hand, Cornelius Van Herwynen, pulled logs with the oxteam to lay a firm road from Holland to Zeeland (present-day Paw Paw Drive). He directed the animals by oral commands and a whip or goad if necessary—"get up" (go), "haw" (turn left), "gee" (turn right), and "whoa" (stop). After a few years, when roads were improved and his purse fattened, the dominee exchanged his oxen for a span of horses and a mule. Hired hands worked his land with the animals. Van Raalte's favorite horse, Frank, pulled his buggy and sleigh, but he rode horseback on house calls out to the country. The dominee was an excellent horseman and could control Frank, who was sometimes ornery. A hired hand once beat Frank, leaving him temporarily crippled. No doubt, that man was fired. In the 1850s, Adrian Moes tended the plot fronting Sixteenth Street that later became part of Pilgrim Home Cemetery. Hendrik J. Van Os, who immigrated in the 1870s, spent six years clearing and cultivating the acreage behind the Van Raalte homestead that stretched to Waverly Avenue, which gave the family "plenty of meadow land for horses and cows." In 1862 Van Raalte sold two small horses and his mule, leaving him with a span of horses.²³

In May 1847, Van Raalte ordered from a Buffalo, New York, hardware merchant, twenty-seven dollars worth of items for his house and garden, including silverware, cutlery, doors and locks, garden tools, two cowbells, a manure fork, hemp rope, nails, and other items. Visitors could often find him puttering in his garden, a quiet place, shaded by fruit trees.²⁴

Van Raalte did watch his purse when it came to his home, but he did not cut corners. In early June, he ordered a large quantity of lumber through his agent, colonist Harmen Jan Hesselink, on consignment from three merchants at Newark (Saugatuck, in 1868), from mills on the Kalamazoo River. From Mehetable Field, he ordered 10,711 board

---

²² Bill of sale, George Young, Allegan, 26 Mar. 1847, HHA; Ben Van Raalte to father, 4 Mar. 1859; Van der Veen, "Life Reminiscences," 1:509; P. Huyser's "From Soetermeer to Soetermeer [1912]," in *Dutch Immigrant Memoirs*, 2:471-72.

²³ Dirk Van Raalte to father, 19 Feb. 1861; Ben Van Raalte to father, 4 Mar. 1859, Dec. 1862, 4 Feb. 1863; Van Raalte to Den Bleyker, 8 May 1851; Van Os obit., *Holland City News*, 18 July 1940; Adrian Moes obit., *Holland City News*, 5 Dec. 1918. The 1850 federal census of agriculture for Ottawa County reported seventy oxen but no horses.

²⁴ Bill of Sale, John Patterson, Hardware Importer, Buffalo, NY, 6 May 1847, HHA.

feet, from Artemus Carter 1,852, and from Henry Fisher 5,084, totaling 17,647 board feet. The lumber was loaded on a scow, floated down the Kalamazoo River to Lake Michigan, towed to Holland harbor, and poled or sailed across Black Lake to the village of Holland.

Remarkably, Van Raalte wrote the letter in crude English after barely six months in America. This letter, the first we have from his pen in English, merits printing in full.[25]

> The subscriber want 15 M [thousand] feet lumber. He wil paij at last 1 October. Because he not can look after the matter, send he the Bearer of this Mr. Hesselink to the dealers in lumber along the Kalamazoo. He must ascertain bij whom he cane get this lumber cheapest. He must look out that the lumber have a good measure and not is spoiled; likewise we very sad have get. The Dealer in lumber must him only help to make a raft, but Mr. Hesselink wil self the lumber bring to the Blacklake. Mr. Hesselink know the kind of lumber. The Subscriber demand the lumber to get for the cheapest rate it cane be; that he will paij after some weeks already in cash.
>
> Your Neighbor,
A. C. Van Raalte
Holland, Ottawa, Michigan
4 June 1847

The dominee demanded the "cheapest rate," and he received it. He paid the merchants $5.50 per board foot—$1.50 less than Maksabe's rate two months before. And somehow Van Raalte came up with the funds to pay for these materials. Over the next years, he bought more lumber and other building materials—nails, glass, door knobs and locks, sashes, slate, plaster, and other items.

Van Raalte also spent lavishly for furniture, supplies, equipment, and food for his household. He purchased in Detroit a bedstead and feathers for bedding and pillows, which must have pleased Christina greatly. He also ordered household items for his "Lady" and furniture from Chicago. J. Saunders Coates of Grand Haven opened the first store in Holland in May 1847, and soon Jan Binnekant and Henry D. Post also

---

[25] Van Raalte letter "To the Merchants in Lumber on the Kalamazoo River," 4 June 1847, HHA. The merchants were Mehetable Field and and Henry Fisher at Newark (Saugatuck), and Artemus Carter at Singapore. See Van Raalte account book with Post & Co., 1848-50 entries, for additional expenditures, HHA.

Van Raalte's letter, written with beautiful penmanship in crude English, ordering lumber from Newark merchants, June 4, 1847 (HHA)

> To the Merchants in lumber an the Kalamazoo River.
>
> The Subscriber want 15 m. feet lumber, He will pay at last *illegible*. Because He not cane look after that matter Send he the Bearer of this Mr. Hesselink to the dealers in lumber along the Kalamazoo. He must ascertain by Whom he Cane get this lumber cheapest. He must look out of that the lumber have a good meashure and not is Spoiled, likewise we very bad have get. The Dealer in lumber must Him only help to made a raft, but Mr. Hesselink wil the lumber bring to the Blacklake. Mr. Hesselink know the Kind of lumber. The Subscriber the lumber to get for the cheapest rate, it cane be, that He wile pay after some few weeks already in cash.
>
> Your Neighbour
> A.C. Van Raalte
>
> Holland Ottawa
> Michigan
> 4 June 1847.

opened general stores. Van Raalte patronized them to buy a tea kettle, a mustard pot, a coffee can, a pail, candlesticks (for lighting), bowls, a wash kettle, a garbage can, a milk bowl, and other utensils. The cost of these items easily exceeded one hundred dollars. Van Raalte's food bills were also high, including flour and meal by the barrel, potatoes by the bushel, sugar (including white sugar) and molasses, pork by the barrel, butter and coffee by the pound, soap, starch, brandy, and other foodstuffs. Pints of brandy were "for my wife," as well as for himself, and, of course, tobacco for his pipe. Tailor Willem Brouwer filled orders for bedding, linen padding, buttons, clasps, thread, cotton goods, a silk waistcoat, and other articles of clothing for the family. Diapers were another matter. Christina missed the sturdy Dutch cloth to sew them and asked her brother Carel de Moen, then serving the Den Ham church, to take some along if he accepted the nearly unanimous call to the First Reformed Church in Kalamazoo. But he declined the call, and she never got the good cloth.[26]

Holland Colony grows by leaps and bounds

More immigrants arrived over the next eighteen months from Protestant parts of the Netherlands and bordering German regions. Group migration was the norm the first summer and this induced "chain migration" of family and friends over the next years. The flow varied by region, with concentrations in areas dominated by the seminal leaders. In April 1847, Scholte's main group of eight hundred persons traveled on four ships from Rotterdam to Baltimore, and then by train and canal (with one hundred locks) to traverse the Allegheny Mountains, to Pittsburgh, where Ohio River steamboats brought them to St. Louis. It was a laborious and costly inland passage.[27]

That same month, 430 Zeelanders, comprising the congregation of Rev. Van der Meulen from Goes, embarked for New York on three ships under Jannes Van de Luyster, Jan Steketee, and Van der Meulen. Scholte, who traveled to Boston by fast steamship, met Vande Luyster's party at Buffalo and tried unsuccessfully to persuade them to go to Iowa. Van der Meulen had studied for the ministry under Scholte and respected him highly, but his ship, which had departed first, arrived second behind that of Van de Luyster, the moneyman of the Zeelanders. Scholte apparently rubbed Vande Luyster the wrong way, and he declared that his group was going to Van Raalte in Michigan. They exchanged St. Louis tickets for Holland.[28] The arrival of the Zeelanders

[26] Van Raalte account with Post & Co. 1847-51, 1 Apr. 1848, 12 Feb. 1851 (tobacco); Van Raalte account with Jacob Van der Veen, 20 Nov. 1850, 1 Jan. 1851, 1 Jan. 1852, HHA; Van Raalte to De Moen, 25 March 1857; *De Bazuin*, 20 Feb. 1857 (www.delpher.nl, accessed, June 2021).

[27] Lucas, *Netherlanders, in America*, 122-27, 167-71; Van Koevering, *Legends of the Dutch*, 606-10, lists passenger manifests of the three vessels.

[28] Cornelius Van der Meulen to Friends in the Netherlands, 8 Oct. 1847; Cornelia M. Van Malsen (fiancée of Jannes Van de Luyster Jr.) to Parents, 11 July, 22 Sept. 1847, in Van Malsen, *Achttal Brieven Mijner Kinderen*, published in English by Yzenbaard, "'America' Letters," 46, 50; Den Herder, "Brief History"; Lucas, *Netherlanders*, 127-35.

ensured the success of the Holland colony, much to Van Raalte's relief and Scholte's chagrin.

At the same time, Rev. Marten Ypma's congregation of one hundred souls from Hallum, Friesland, formed the Vriesland colony on fertile clay-soil land ten miles east of Holland. A group of thirty-four from the province of Drenthe and nearby Staphorst in Overijssel settled on clay-soil land a few miles south of Vriesland to form the Drenthe colony. Some seventy members of Rev. Jan Barend Sundag's German-speaking congregation at Graafschap Bentheim (county of Bentheim), just over the German border, settled five miles southwest of Holland in the Graafschap colony. Other groups formed the colonies of North Holland and Noordeloos, both north of Zeeland. Many smaller family groups and individuals arrived almost daily. Van Raalte out competed Scholte in recruiting immigrants. In September 1847, Van Raalte returned to New York to personally arrange transportation for immigrants to Michigan, in cooperation with volunteers from De Witt's church who worked the docks. Van Raalte founded Reformed churches wherever possible, which Scholte declined to do, and churches ensured the success of every new colony. Those lacking a church died.[29]

To prepare for the new groups heading eastward, Van Raalte had a work party erect a large log hut, dubbed the Little Water House (*het Waterhuisje*), at the Y in the Black River, where the main branch flows south, and Frenchman's Creek (later Noordeloos Creek) flows north. The Y was the end of navigation for scows to transport people and goods from Holland harbor to Zeeland, Vriesland, Noordeloos, Zoetermeer, and other points to the northeast.[30]

By October 1847, the Holland colony had two thousand inhabitants, centered around nine villages that dotted the countryside. Each area had its unique dialect—Fries, Gronings, Drents, Zeeuws, Low German, and so forth—and colonists could barely understand one another. The educated class, not common folk, spoke High Dutch, the language of the pulpit.[31]

---

[29] *De Reformatie*, May 1846, 190-93; Aug. 1846, 14; *Leydsche Courant*, 4 Oct. 1847 (www.delpher.nl, accessed, June 2021); Lucas, *Netherlanders*, 104-87; Van Koevering, *Legends of the Dutch*, 253-58.

[30] Abraham Stegeman, "Historical Sketch of Groningen," in Lucas, *Dutch Immigrant Memoirs*, 1:159-63. For "Plymouth Rock," see *Holland City News*, 16 June 1921. Today the site has a Michigan Historical Marker in Paw Paw Park—formerly the Holland Country Club. Nearby on Paw Paw Drive is the original marker, a giant rock dubbed the "Plymouth Rock of Michigan."

[31] Lucas, *Netherlanders*, 135-50.

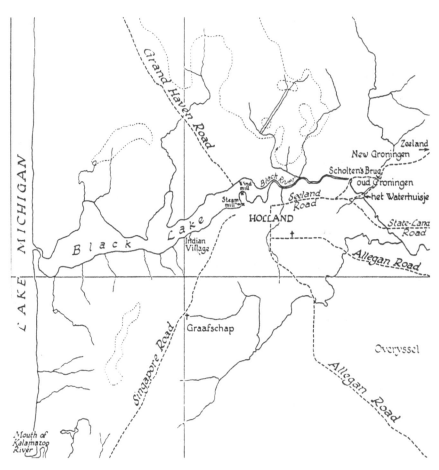

Holland Colony settlement, 1848

In 1848 Rev. Seine Bolks' congregation of twenty families from Hellendoorn, Overijssel, settled on high ground to the south in Fillmore Township. They had emigrated in 1847 but spent a year in Syracuse, New York. Bolks was a protégé of Van Raalte and founded the Overisel Reformed Church. The nearby village of Bentheim collected some of Sundag's group. Immigrants from the province of Zuid-Holland settled in three places—at Soetermeer, south at present-day Thirty-Second Street, and southwest at Collendoorn (now East Saugatuck).[32]

[32] De Witt, "Holland Emigrants," *Christian Intelligencer*, 28 Oct. 1847; Gerrit J. Kroon to Mother, Sister, and Brothers, 11 Aug. 1847, in *Pillar Postscripts* 25, no. 2 (2001): 14-15; Van der Veen, "Life Reminiscences," 1:494; *Provinciale Overijsselsche en Zwolsche Courant*, 13 July 1847 (www.delpher.nl, accessed, June 2021); Kraker, *Overisel, Michigan*, 25-30; Sytsma, *Our Blessed Heritage*, 7-8.

No foretaste of heaven

Clearing the forests in the cold, wet spring and in the stifling summer heat was difficult work. Settlers had to deal with mosquitoes, deerflies, and horseflies; poison ivy, oak, and sumac; snakes (some poisonous); and bears, cougars, and mountain lions. All were strange and fearsome. And the desperate need for food and shelter was unimaginable. "Meal, potatoes, meat and fat were not to be had," Frederiks reported. Fortunately, some fresh immigrants came with provisions, such as Jan Kolvoord's younger brother, Lambertus (Bert), who brought flour and pork. But the need far surpassed the supply.[33]

The newcomers had to live on buckwheat, bran, and corn, all cooked on open wood fires. The natives had introduced corn to the Dutch and shown them how to cook it. But even though, to immigrants, corn was "pig feed," it quickly became the mainstay of their diet. The natives also taught the newcomers how to make "coffee" from burnt corn, a beverage no Hollander could do without. Allegan was the go-to city for provisions, but it required scarce currency and carrying everything home on one's back. In spring, the priority was to plant potatoes, corn, and buckwheat in every natural clearing within ten miles. Pigs were the first livestock; they foraged for themselves, multiplied rapidly, and provided meat.[34]

"Many of us imagined the journey to be a foretaste of heaven," Rev. Van der Meulen wrote to friends back home, "but you must not count on that. . . . We shout to those who follow: Do not take this journey unprepared or without the Lord!" As a result of poor food and housing, "Many sick folk suffered a long time, many [were] painfully lost, and very many in poverty." But Van der Meulen, who was a doer, added hopefully, "This is also a land of plenty."[35] Van Raalte, another doer, blamed failure on laziness and faintheartedness. "Some do not care to work or think the pay is not high enough. Others cannot get accustomed to bartering, or they isolate themselves by the attitude:

---

[33] Cornelius Van der Veere obit., *Holland City News*, 24 Mar. 1899; Cornelia (Mrs. Kommer) Schaddelee née Slag, "Historical Reminiscences," box 15, Moerdyke Papers.

[34] Frederiks, "Egbert Frederiks' Pioneer Memories," 1:68; Michael Duyser, "Recollections of the Life of the First Settlers of Holland and Zeeland During the Years 1847-1848"; "Pioneer Memories," box 9, Van Schelven Papers.

[35] Van der Meulen letter, Oct. 1847, published in *Ter nagedachtenis*, 56-57, trans. Ten Hoor.

'I can't do that. I never did that before.' Not everyone has the right attitude to savor the freedom we have here."[36]

The first months were a time of dying, never to be forgotten. Everyone shook from mosquito-borne ague (malaria), dubbed "next-day fever," which could be cured by quinine. The pointed rhyme about Michigan that circulated in the East said it all: "Don't go to Michigan, that land of ills. The word means ague, fever, and chills."[37] Dysentery (aptly called rotten bowel disease) resulted from drinking foul surface water. Typhoid and diphtheria also took a toll, given overwork, poor hygiene, and inadequate food and shelter. Van Raalte downplayed the risk of malaria. Shortly after returning to Detroit from his Black Lake scouting trip, he wrote Brummelkamp: "Here the land is high, and the people enjoy the best health," except for the nonacclimatized Europeans. Either he did not learn that fever and ague had struck one in ten people at Old Wing Mission the previous summer and autumn, including the Smith and Fairbanks families, or he did not want to hear negative reports about his chosen region.[38]

The number of deaths in 1847 is not recorded, but the Grim Reaper was busy. The first death was that of Macheldtje (Mrs. Willem) Notting, the cook for the vanguard, followed by seven others in the shanties. In July a smallpox epidemic broke out. Some had immunity, having survived smallpox in the Netherlands, but most were susceptible because Separatists, following the lead of Hendrik de Cock, had generally spurned vaccination on the medical and religious advice of Dr. Abraham Capadose. This revered Réveil leader likened the procedure to rejecting God's fatherly hand.[39] Jan Slag, a ship carpenter, made crude coffins without charge. Many fathers had to bury children with their own hands. Others were buried "promiscuously throughout the forests," at the harbor mouth, in a small plot near River Avenue, and at the Van der Haar farm on Paw Paw Road. It was said of many immigrants that their success rested on the "bones of the settlers."[40]

---

[36] Van Raalte to De Moen, 11 Feb. 1849, in *Der toestand*, 13, trans. Nella Kennedy.
[37] "The Settlement of Michigan," http://geo.msu.edu/extra/geogmich/settlement_of_mi.html.
[38] Van Raalte to Brummelkamp, 30 Jan. 1847, in *Holland in Amerika*, 9; Verhave, *Disease and Death*, 9-32; Frederiks, "Egbert Frederiks' Pioneer Memories," 1:68.
[39] Report of Rev. Smith in William A. Richmond's Report, in Swierenga and Van Appledorn, *Old Wing Mission*, 584; Cornelia Slag Schaddelee, "Historical Recollections, XIX," *De Grondwet*, 2 May 1911; Verhave, *Disease and Death*, 13n21; Ten Zythoff, *Sources of Secession*, 91-94.
[40] Van Koevering, *Legends of the Dutch*, 244 (quote); Verhave, *Disease and Death*, 33-37 (quote).

Watercolor drawing of oxcart loaded with bodies being taken for burial, by Anneus J. Hillebrands, signed "JH," school teacher in Old Groningen, 1848-52 (*HMA*)

Rev. Andrew Taylor in Grand Rapids and De Witt in New York City recognized the crisis and urged their congregants to help the "devoted brethren ... that a kind providence has cast on our shores." Taylor reported a "most painful state of want.... Their provisions have failed them, and some have been subsisting on bran, despite the best efforts of their self-denying leader." Without generous aid, Taylor wrote, "Black River must afford them only a resting place for their bones."[41]

Van Raalte, the only university-trained man in the colony, practiced medicine as best he could. Grootenhuis saw him hold daily office hours and be ready to go out

> night and day, in all kinds of weather ... to the house of suffering and death, to comfort and aid in the preparation for the burial and conduct funeral services. Every morning, the sick lined up at his house, with the kitchen as the waiting room. His medicine chest held quinine [for malaria], which he administered with a tablespoon, opium, blue pills [mercury, for consumption],

---

[41] A. B. Taylor, "The Holland Emigration," *Christian Intelligencer*, 9 May 1847, in Lucas, *Dutch Immigrant Memoirs*, 1:41-42; Van Schelven, "Historical Sketch of Holland City and Colony," 466-69.

rhubarb root extract [a purgative for bowel complaints], morphine, whiskey, alcohol, camphor, and other nostrums.⁴²

While preaching one Sunday from a stump in front of his home, Van Raalte broke down and blurted out: "O Lord, must we all die then?" The hyperbole stemmed from his fear for the future of the colony. Many years later, he recalled the crisis vividly:

> Never had I been so near collapse as when in those crowded log houses ... I saw how all sorts of family activities—housekeeping, being sick, dying, and the care of the dead—had to be discharged. Small wonder that in that hour of trial, there appeared traces of despair and indifference. But God granted a change!

Another time, the dominee remembered the fear of failure. "I feared that I would go down to the grave having accomplished nothing at all." But Cornelis Van Malsen noted his resolve: "Van Raalte has much courage." By fall the sufferers had recovered, and newborn infants and fresh immigrants had more than replaced those who had perished. "Few, if any, sick here at present," sister Cornelia Van Malsen reported. "The Lord has spared our lives, despite severe illnesses"⁴³

The flurry of deaths may have abated after the first months, but during the first two years, approximately four hundred settlers died. Calculating the death rate is problematic because the population was fluid, with new immigrants arriving daily and others, particularly young people, leaving to work in nearby cities. By mid-1849, the population in the colony was about three thousand, which puts the death rate at a frightful 13 percent (400 divided by 3000).⁴⁴

To provide for orphans, Van Raalte had a small, two-story frame house erected, funded by donations of precious gold and silver jewelry brought from the Netherlands. But the Orphan House was not needed

---

⁴² Bernardus Grootenhuis, "Our History," De Hope, 24 Mar. 1888, typescript, trans. Moerdyke, Moerdyke Papers; Van Raalte Account Book, Post & Co., 1848-50, HHA.

⁴³ Dosker, *Van Raalte*, 103 (quote), English typescript, 41; "Van Raalte's Commemoration Address, 1872," in Lucas, *Dutch Immigrant Memoirs*, 2:490 (block quote); Van Raalte to Wormser, Amsterdam, 7 Jan. 1848, for similar comments; Cornelis R. Van Malsen to Parents, 12 July 1847, and Cornelia M. Van Malsen to Parents, 16 Nov., 16 Dec. 1847, all in Yzenbaard, "America' Letters," 44 (quote), 54, 55 (final quote).

⁴⁴ These figures come from J. P. Verhave, an epidemiologist, who carefully weighed all the available evidence. See his "Disease and Death," 20-23.

because other families took in the children and raised them as their own. The building later became the first schoolhouse.[45]

Settlers took comfort in the assurance that sickness and death were in God's hands. "Blessed are the dead which die in the Lord" (Rev. 14:13) were the dominee's customary words at funeral services. By July 1847, Johannes J. M. C. Van Nus, a trained physician, had arrived with the Zeeland immigrants and lifted a heavy burden from Van Raalte. In 1848 Dr. Charles Shenick of New York settled in Groningen and developed a large practice. When Van Nus left for Pella in 1853, the Marsh brothers, Wells and Charles, moved their practice from Kalamazoo to Holland. Van Raalte's doctoring days outside the family circle were finally over.[46]

Death and graves went unrecorded until the second year when Van Raalte had Het Kerkhof van [cemetery of] Holland marked out behind the Log Church on 3.5 acres, set aside in 1848. By then, the death rate had dropped sharply; food was more plentiful, and settlers had dug wells for drinking water and built houses on higher ground. But sickness remained rampant. Hendrik Van Eyck, who arrived in late August 1848, found "sick people in nearly every house I entered, sometimes as many as five of six in one dwelling." But he happily noted that the death rate was "in no way comparable" to that of the first year. Van Raalte agreed. By early 1849, "The ice is broken; we are accustomed to the climate," he noted. Van der Meulen reported only four deaths among his eight hundred Zeeland congregants during all of 1848.[47]

One of the deaths in October 1849 was of the Van Raaltes' infant daughter, Maria Wilhelmina (1848-1849), who died of dysentery at thirteen months. Her father conducted her funeral in English for the benefit of Henry Post and teacher Elvira Langdon, the only Americans present. Maria bore the name of Christina's sister Maria Wilhelmina de Moen (wife of Brummelkamp). The next daughter, born in 1851, was again named Maria Wilhelmina, and she lived to a ripe old age, which ensured that her namesakes would not be forgotten. The first

---

[45] Van Zwaluwenburg, "Life Sketch," 1:423; Lucas, *Netherlanders*, 103-4.
[46] R. T. Kuiper, "In Memoriam" [for Egbert Frederiks], *De Grondwet*, 16 Oct. 1888 (quote), trans. Buursma; Van der Veen, "Life Reminiscences," 1:497-98; Yzenbaard, "'America' Letters," 55.
[47] Van Zwaluwenburg, "Life Sketch," 1:423-28; "Hendrik Van Eyck Diary," in Lucas, *Netherlanders*, 1:474; Van Raalte to De Moen, 11 Feb. 1849, in *Der toestand*, 7, and Van der Meulen to De Moen, 20 Jan. 1849, in ibid., 20.

Maria was the second of four children that mother Christina had lost in infancy, one in the Netherlands and two others in Michigan.[48]

A "plague" in 1851 caused a second food crisis. Rats, squirrels, raccoons, and deer were the culprits, and they ravaged ripe crops. Some farmers were ruined and gave up. But most hung on and bought cats and dogs to ward off the critters. The grasshopper plagues in Sioux County, Iowa, in the early 1870s were far worse; the large, winged insects left nothing behind.[49]

Log Church of Holland

Freedom of worship was the primary objective of the immigrants, with a decent livelihood a close second. "There is much joy among the people at being free of the persecutions found in the Netherlands," Cornelis Van Malsen reported.[50] Van Raalte began worship services outdoors in front of his house, standing on a box, with worshipers seated on logs. He preached from the Statenbijbel, the authorized Dutch Bible, with its massive clasps, that he had carried carefully from the Netherlands. "Those Sundays were an inspiration for us because of the spiritually pithy sermons we were privileged to hear," Frederiks recalled. "His preaching and prayers were so excellent that it gave us renewed courage," Geesje Van der Haar-Visscher noted. "His sermons were so lively that we were strengthened."[51]

Henry Pennoyer of Grand Haven happened to be in Holland in late May 1847 and heard Van Raalte's first sermon. "It was at a place near where Dr. Van Raalte's house now stands," he recalled, "a place cleared by fallen trees and forming a hollow square." Although he could not understand a word of it, he described it as "the most eloquent and impressive sermon he ever heard."[52]

---

[48] Bruins et al., *Albertus and Christina*, 65, 159-60, 192-200; Albertus C. Van Raalte family history, 25 Sept. 1871 (quote); "Deaths in Ottawa and Allegan Counties, June 1, 1849-June 1, 1850," Ralph Haan, comp., Herrick District Library; Elvira H. Langdon, "An Interesting Reminiscence," *Holland City News*, 18 Dec. 1898.

[49] Versteeg, *Pelgrim-Vaders*, 136-39.

[50] Cornelis R. Van Malsen to Parents, Brothers and Sisters, etc., 12 July 1847, in Yzenbaard, "'America' Letters," 39.

[51] Frederiks, "Egbert Frederiks' Pioneer Memories," 1:70 (quote); Cornelia Slag Schaddelee, "Historical Recollections," *De Grondwet*, 2 May 1911; Versteeg, *Pelgrim-Vaders*, 180-81; "Geesje Van der Haar-Visscher Diary," 6-7. The large pulpit Bible is preserved and on display in Pillar Church.

[52] Summary in *Holland City News*, 21 Sept. 1872, of Henry Pennoyer's speech at Holland 25th anniversary celebration on 17 Sept. 1872.

After Van Raalte's barn was raised, he preached and conducted catechism classes there. Morning services ran three hours, from nine o'clock to noon. In November 1847, the dominee conducted the first communion service "under the blue skies—a large crowd was present." Worshipers stood in a circle to receive the elements from the pastor and elders. "It was a solemn sight," recalled Engbertus Van der Veen, then a nineteen-year-old. "The Lord is doing great things for us; everything needed for administering the sacraments and baptism were given as a gift by American Christians in Buffalo." The wine pitcher, two common cups, and a baptism basin, all essential vessels for the sacraments, were treasured and used for decades. Holy Communion was "a real feast for us, and we thanked God for it," noted Geesje Van der Haar.[53]

Engbertus Van der Veen's younger brother Christian, then only nine years of age, recalled that first communion service three decades later.

> It was in the fall of '47, upon a pleasant Sabbath morning, that my father took me to the first church service.... To a considerable gathering, scattered upon the felled trees and under the shadow of the untouched forest, the pastor preached the word of life and distributed the bread and wine.

Looking on was the pastor's "faithful wife, tending, while she listened, the cradled babe [Albertus, her firstborn]."[54]

The first child born in the colony was Hermina Laarman, daughter of Jan and Geesje Laarman. The dominee baptized the boy in front of the parsonage. And Van Raalte performed the first marriage, that of Lambert Floris and Jantjen Meyerink, on July 25, 1847, at a "church meeting in the woods," near his house. Two Sundays previous, the minister had announced from the pulpit the couple's intention to marry. The so-called "banns" enabled anyone who might object to come forward and state the reasons.[55] As a matter of convenience, Christina stood in as one of the two witnesses in many early marriages, signing her name—"C. J. Van Raalte." The August 8 wedding of Hendrik

---

[53] Cornelia M. Van Malsen, to Dear Parents and Relatives, 16 Nov. 1847, in Yzenbaard, "'America' Letters," 54; Van der Veen, "Life Reminiscences," 1:502-3; "Geesje van der Haar-Visscher Diary," 9.

[54] Christian Van der Veen, "Mrs. Christina De Moen Van Raalte" (funeral sermon, 3 July 1871), JAH; De Vries and Boonstra, *Pillar Church*, 102 (quote).

[55] Van Hinte, *Netherlanders*, 245; Van Koevering, *Legends of the Dutch*, 222; Keppel, *Trees to Tulips*, 16; Van der Veen, "Life Reminiscences," 1:492; "First Holland White Child is Made Known," *Holland Sentinel*, 12 May 1938.

Grijpmoet Michmerhuizen and Hendrika Johanna Rozendom was especially memorable. The wedding certificate in Van Raalte's hand notes that the couple "are joined in marriage by me in a Church meeting held in the great temple of God's creation, in the woods of Michigan, near the village of Holland." After the ceremony, the dominee took the newlyweds to his house and prophesied to the bride: "Rozendom! Rozendom! There is a rose tree under the window of my home, but there are sharp thorns on it." It was a clever play on words—Rozendom and *rozenboom*—a rose tree bearing thorns. The bridal pair never forgot this exhortation, that their married life would be a mix of joys and sorrows.[56]

As soon as families had crude shelters, Van Raalte had a log church constructed on the cemetery plot he had donated on the future Fairbanks Avenue at Sixteenth Street. The site was readily accessible from farmsteads and villages springing up all around. "There's nothing like a church and worship to set off a settlement and make it into a little village," recalled a parishioner. "Well, we started all of us cutting and hauling logs for the church. It was to be the best building of its kind in this part of Michigan." Wags, however, dubbed it "Van Raalte's woodshed."[57] In the fall, settlers squared the hemlock logs with "much difficulty, labor, and expense." Van Raalte purchased a compass for twenty dollars from Bassett to survey the road running from his house to the church site (present-day Fairbanks Avenue).[58] Architect Gerrit J. Kroon designed the thirty-five-foot-by-sixty-foot building, with a partition to separate the sanctuary from a smaller consistory room and classroom. His fee was fifty dollars ($1,854 today); he did not come cheap. The sanctuary was enclosed before snow fell and used for services, despite the dirt floor. Three windows on each side provided natural light. "We were proud of it," declared an old timer.

Dominee Van Raalte stood on a small platform in front of the partition, flanked by two communion tables. He baptized infants in front of the pulpit. Adult baptism was rare since all adults had been

---

[56] "Record of Marriages Solemnized by A. C. Van Raalte, Minister of the Gospel," Van Raalte Papers; Versteeg, *Pelgrim-Vaders*, 178-79; Van der Veen, "Life Reminiscences," 1:501-3; Jacob Van der Veen, obit., *Holland City News*, 26 May 1937.

[57] J. A. Van de Luyster, "A History of Holland City," *Excelsiora* (Hope College student periodical), 24 Mar. 1876.

[58] *Holland City News*, 28 July 1921 (quotes); Hyma, *Van Raalte*, 245; minutes, First Holland, 18 Dec. 1851, 21 Mar. 1853, trans. Buursma, JAH; minutes, People's Assembly (Volksvergadering), 7 Mar. 1849; "Dorpslands Dagboek," 1, 13 Mar., 29 Sept. 1848.

Van Raalte's list of baptisms, 1847 (HHA)

baptized as infants. The Lord's Supper was celebrated quarterly. The church had no musical instruments. Choirmaster Frederick J. Van Lente, a cooper by trade with a trained voice, was the *voorzanger* for

Log Church, a painting with Van Raalte (*on right*) and his wife, Christina (*on left*) (*JAH*). The Log Church was razed in 1856 after the dedication of a new edifice and its four corners marked off for posterity.

twenty-five years, until he became stone deaf, and his son Johannes took the honored position. Voorzangers led the congregation in singing the Psalms, just as in the Old Country.[59]

With winter coming on, the members assessed themselves forty cents per family to buy two old cook stoves, one for each side of the church. Stovepipes vented the smoke out through the walls, yet the room was often filled with smoke. But it "was warm, and the smoke mattered little," recalled Van der Veen. Sexton Kees (Cornelius) De Wit kept everything in good order. Firstcomers took "seats nearest the stoves, hugging the stove between their legs and remaining in that position throughout the sermon." The building was finished in the summer of 1848, complete with pulpit and pews, glass windows, and a wood roof, thanks to the new shingle factory. The plank floor had to wait until the completion of Holland's first sawmill.[60]

[59] John Van Lente obit., *Holland City News*, 14 Feb. 1874; De Vries and Boonstra, *Pillar Church*, 74; "Anniversary Recalls Old Colony Singing Society," *Holland City News*, 19 Oct. 1922.

[60] Van der Veen, "Life Reminiscences," 1:502-3. Van Raalte donated a city lot to De Wit (1780-1872) for his faithful service of five years, and church members built a small house for the old man (*Holland City News*, 9 Nov. 1872).

Families sat together in their assigned pew, determined by an auction and later by lot following the New Year's Day service. Pew fees were essentially a tithe for upkeep and for the pastor's salary. The deacons took up the weekly collections with black velvet "penny bags" (*zakjes*) on long poles that they passed along each row as parishioners deposited their coins in clenched fists, so only the Lord would know the amount. Consistory members took up the back rows, where they could observe worshipers. If anyone fell asleep, as some men were wont to do, the pastor would order a deacon to nudge the offender with an empty *zakje* pole.

A pail of water with a dipper stood ready near the door for thirsty worshipers. Once during the sermon, "A man went for a drink and, looking angrily at the dipper, grabbed the pail and was about to drink, when the dominee stopped preaching and said in a loud voice: 'You stupid ox, take the dipper.'" The embarrassed "ox" set the bucket down and never did that again. Jannes Van de Luyster Jr. filled the pulpit occasionally when his mentor was out of town, "which happens often and sometimes for long periods," reported Cornelia Van Malsen.[61] The pioneers looked back fondly on the intense religious emotions of the first years: "Religion was a service of the heart, of which the mouth overflowed steadily," Jacob Den Herder recalled. "It was indisputable," he continued, "that songs of thanksgiving rose up to heaven, even though the second purpose of immigration, i.e., a more comfortable existence, had not been reached yet."[62]

Indian missionary George Smith and family worshiped at the Log Church for the first time in July 1848, before the building had doors or windows. "The church was full," Smith noted in his diary, "and it was indeed interesting to witness the scene, where about a year ago, all was wilderness. Good order prevailed, and eager attention was paid, while Mr. Van Raalte preached 1¾ hours and baptized 3 children. I agreed to preach there next Sabb[ath], 4 o'cl[oc]k P.M." Smith conducted services in English for five successive Sunday afternoons in the fall of 1848 for thirteen American families living in the vicinity who had no other option but to attend the Dutch church, even though they could barely understand a word.[63]

---

[61] "Dorpslands Dagboek," 27 Sept. 1848, 20 Feb. 1850; "Old Settler Tells of the Old Log Church," *Holland City News*, 2 Dec. 1923; Dosker, *Van Raalte*, 156, for dipper story; Cornelia M. Van Malsen, 11 July, 16 Nov. 1847, in Yzenbaard, "'America' Letters," 44, 47, 54 (quote).

[62] Den Herder, "Brief History"; Kennedy, *Commentary*, 1:268-69.

[63] Henry Griffin, 10 July 1848, published in *Detroit Free Press*, 17 July 1848; minutes,

Decorum was lacking, according to Hoyt Post, one of the Americans who picked up enough Dutch to get the gist of the sermons and sing the Dutch Psalms. Post penned his disgust in 1850:

> It really annoys me to see in the house of God, that sacred place where, above all others, order and decorum are to be preserved, men sit, lie, or stand, as convenience dictates, with their hats on or off when the minister rises to give the benediction, to have the invocation of the Trinity in solemn tones nearly drowned out by the scramble after hats and the buttoning up of coats, and, more disgusting of all, the rattle of pipes and tobacco boxes.

Post obviously viewed tobacco as a vice unbecoming to Christians.[64]

Contrary to standard Reformed church polity, Van Raalte and his followers did not organize a church, issue a formal letter of call, or elect a consistory. Van Raalte simply began preaching and dispensing the sacraments, and the pioneers who had been elders and deacons in the Old Country simply continued in their offices. Neither First Reformed Church nor any other congregation in the colony was formally organized by a regional assembly as required by the Dort church order. The pastors—Van Raalte at Holland, Van der Meulen at Zeeland, Marten Ypma at Vriesland, and Seine Bolks at Overisel—and the elders at Graafschap simply installed consistories without a vote of members. This was the same way the Separatists in 1835 formed congregations and classes de novo, without official ecclesiastical authorization.[65]

A year later, on April 23, 1848, Van Raalte organized the congregations into the Classis of Holland to provide ecclesiastical oversight. Again contrary to standard Reformed polity, classis did not affiliate with the Reformed Protestant Dutch Church in New York, its natural partner. They could have joined the First Grand Rapids congregation in the English-speaking Classis of Michigan. But language, cultural barriers, and distance stood in the way. Rather, they formed an independent Dutch-language body.

Classis also faced the 1849 deadline for the mandatory rotation of the initial elders and deacons after two years, according to the Dort church order. Given the "difficulty about the temporal [need]," the body decided that office bearers "must serve as long as our bodily powers and

---

People's Assembly, 11, 18 Oct., 8, 29 Nov. 1848; Swierenga and Van Appledorn, *Old Wing Mission*, 329-31.

[64] Hoyt G. Post Diary, 13 Jan. 1850, HMA.

[65] Kennedy, *Commentary*, 23 Apr. 1848, 1:3-6.

Seine Bolks   Hendrik Klijn   A. C. VanRaalte

C. Vander Meulen   Martin Ypma

Ministers of
the Classis
of Holland

Clerics in the Classis of Holland, 1848: Seine Bolks, Hendrik Klijn, Albertus C. Van Raalte, Cornelius Van der Meulen, and Marten Ypma (*JAH*)

spiritual capacity are equal to the task, unless someone make himself unworthy of the ministry." "Once an elder, always an elder," was the mantra. Van Raalte's consistory first addressed the retirement of office bearers in November 1851 and decided against it. The assembly judged that it was neither good nor necessary that they should retire, unless the congregation should "decide it to be necessary." This did not happen until 1860 (ch. 14).[66]

The Log Church was the largest congregation that Van Raalte had ever served in his ministry. The congregation in 1849 had 500

---

[66] Ibid., 1:15-16; Minutes, First Holland, 24 Nov. 1851, trans. Buursma.

worshipers and the rolls in 1852 numbered 624 souls. This for a building that could seat 225 people. Not even the formation of congregations in the villages of Zeeland, Graafschap, Overisel, Drenthe, and Vriesland relieved the pressure. When these congregations were joined in the first classis in April 1848, the delegates sang a versification of Psalm 103 from the *Psalmboek*. In English, the text is: "Bless the Lord, O my soul; and all that is within me, bless His holy name" (Ps. 103:1, KJV).[67]

In 1849 the Holland church consistory took the legal step of incorporation under an 1846 state statute. The document, dated August 25, 1849, was signed by "A. C. Van Raalte, DM" (short for VDM, "*Verbi Dei Minister*," i.e., minister of the word of God), seven elders and four deacons, and witnesses Henry D. Post, Hoyt Post, and James Westveer. This was the official birthday of the congregation. The signatories declared: "We and our successors in office shall be a body corporate forever... under the name of the consistory of the First Dutch Reformed Church of Holland." To make the document official, the twelve subscribers had to appear in person before Holland justice of the peace Henry Post, affix their signatures, and "acknowledge the same to be their own act and deed." Running their farms took precedence, and sixteen months passed before all the men had signed the document, filed at the courthouse on New Year's Day, January 1, 1851.[68]

The consistory made several key decisions. First, they agreed that it was "neither good nor necessary" for elders and deacons to retire; they could serve indefinitely, provided they consented and were re-elected. The Dort church order recommended two-year terms, with half retiring each year. But a dearth of qualified men led Van Raalte to allow consistory members to serve for life. This semiclosed system aroused conflict for twelve years, and the consistory finally allowed the membership a choice to elect half the consistory each year.[69] Second, elders committed themselves to institute regular family visits on the pragmatic grounds that "parents are to be admonished that children attend school and catechism." Third, they decided to commit all loose offerings to missions: 15 percent for the American Tract Society, 15 percent for the American Bible Society, 20 percent

---

[67] Kennedy, *Commentary*, 23 Apr. 1848, 1:xvii-xviii, 3-30.
[68] Incorporation document, First Holland church, 25 Aug. 1849, HHA. I am indebted to Earl Wm. Kennedy for interpreting Van Raalte's "DM" designation.
[69] Dosker, *Van Raalte*, 159, trans. Dekker; Wormser, *In twee werelddeelen*, 187-88; Pieters, "First Reformed Church."

First Reformed Church in Holland, incorporation document, August 25, 1849 (HHA)

for the denomination's foreign missions, and 50 percent for domestic missions. That the congregation placed such a high priority on missions outreach stemmed from Van Raalte's evangelical outlook. The American Bible and Tract Societies, founded in New York City in 1816 and 1825, respectively, were arms of the Plan of Union in 1801, formed by the Presbyterian and Congregational denominations, which English Reformed bodies of the Dutch Reformed Church wholeheartedly supported.[70]

The consistory was also responsible for the cemetery and, as usual, Van Raalte took the lead for nearly thirty years. When the graveyard had become rundown in 1850, Van Raalte decried its "desolate condition" as shameful and demanded the consistory "improve the situation," or he would assume personal ownership. This threat

[70] Van Raalte to Garretson, 10 Dec. 1851, BDM.

induced the consistory to act. They raised funds for upkeep by setting grave prices at one dollar. Most families bought just enough for their needs, but some wealthy individuals acquired entire blocks of thirty to forty gravesites. The consistory donated to the dominee thirty choice graves adjacent to the Log Church, along what is now Dr. Van Raalte Drive.[71] In 1855 the congregation, under a new state law that cemeteries be incorporated, formed the Holland Cemetery Association, which made the cemetery a separate legal entity. All adult male church members were named as owners of the Pioneer Plots, as the original section of the cemetery came to be called. Pilgrim Home Cemetery is truly a miniature city of the dead.[72]

Volksvergadering (People's Assembly)

Dutch immigrants had no experience in democratic governance, but they did recognize consistorial authority. The dominee and his consistory meted out justice in both religious and civil matters, following the scriptural injunction that believers should settle disputes among themselves, without going to law against one another. The consistory settled disputes among members over land dealings, business contracts, wages, livestock and woodlands, schooling, and domestic troubles. The elders, as spiritual overseers, had the power to bar wayward members from the Lord's Table or, worse, to excommunicate them. With only one church in the village for the first fifteen years, the threat of ecclesiastical discipline was severe. It meant being ostracized as an outcast.

Civic matters fell to the Volksvergadering, a New England-type town meeting of adult males that Van Raalte formed in mid-March 1847. The extra-legal body met weekly either in homes of members or at the Log Church and by common consent levied per capita assessments for roads and bridges, a school, and a pier at the mouth of Black Lake. Bridges were needed to cross the Black River and its tributaries—on the north to the county seat at Grand Haven, on the east via Zeeland to Grandville, and on the south via Overisel to Allegan. Creeks in and around the village also needed to be bridged—Tannery Creek on the west and Maple Creek on the south. The assembly also set rules for fire protection, elementary education, livestock penning regulations, and

---

[71] Minutes, First Holland, 28 Nov. 1850, 30 July 1852, 16, 29 Mar., 9 Apr., 7 May, 25 June, 2 Aug., 22 Oct. 1855, trans. Buursma.

[72] Ibid., 2, 20 Nov. 1855, 5 Jan. 1856; "Cemeteries—Holland," HMA; *Holland City News*, 17 July 1875.

securing a village bell to call worshipers, warn of fires, and announce daily work times.[73]

At the first meeting, Hein Ter Haar, the first president, gave the floor to Bernardus Grootenhuis, Van Raalte's respected lieutenant, who made an impassioned speech that recounted the religious persecution and dire poverty that prompted immigration under Dominee Van Raalte. The humble farmer and surveyor then spoke of a promising future for thousands more immigrants wanting freedom of worship and free enterprise. "Never were spiritual concerns lost from view, nor were they supplanted by material concerns," Grootenhuis declared. The speech reminded the desperate settlers why they had come and encouraged them to persevere. With cold weather, little food, and no warm place to lay their heads, they would face the future, "no matter how dark," with "cheerful hearts" and a firm trust in God's "providential leading." Grootenhuis's speech, in the pattern of Joshua's speech at the Jordan River when the Israelites faced giants in the Promised Land, was exactly what these desperate pioneers needed to hear.[74]

The assembly appointed constables to keep law and order, with a special emphasis on honoring the Lord's Day: no business in factories and shops on Sunday and no offloading of merchandise from schooners anchored offshore, even if storms threatened. The body chastised Henry Post, the leading American merchant in the colony, for allowing his oxteam to haul corn for his animals on the Sabbath. Making and selling spirituous liquors—but not beer—was also proscribed. Merchant Jan Binnekant complained that Jacobus "Koos" Vinke was selling liquor on the "lands of Rev. Van Raalte," thus violating the proviso in his town lot deeds that proscribed the sale of "strong drink" on the premises. The dominee allowed hard liquor only for "medicinal purposes." Most cupboards included wine, *jenever* (Dutch gin), and the homemade concoction of brandy with raisins (*boerenjongens*, or "farmers' boys"). But "not one grog shop" opened in the village if Van Raalte had anything to say about it. He even frowned on social drinking (*gezelligi drankgebruik*).[75]

---

[73] Minutes, People's Assembly, 2 Apr. 1848; 4 Apr. 1849, Moerdyke Papers.
[74] "Meeting of First Settlers of Holland, Michigan," *De Hollander*, 26 Mar. 1878, Moerdyke Papers; Lucas, *Netherlanders*, 506.
[75] Swierenga, *Holland, Michigan*, 1:181, citing minutes, People's Assembly, 23 Oct., 8 Nov., 27 Dec. 1848, 24 Jan., 7 Feb. 1849, HMA; letter of E. H. L (Langdon) in *Grand River Eagle*, 16 Sept. 1850; Pieters, *Dutch Settlement*, 155-56; Hyma, *Van Raalte*, 248; Van Hinte, *Netherlanders*, 239. The comment on social drinking is by H. P. Oggel, editor, *De Volksvriend*, 13 July 1911 (www.delpher.nl, accessed July 2021).

Thou may'st call intoxication
"Just a little recreation",
But its right name's Ruination,
A fiend who brings
Disgrace, and blights the reputation,
Ay, e'en of kings. —
She maketh beggars of the wealthy;
She brings disease upon the healthy;
And sometimes 'neath her steps so stealthy
The great, the clever,
Sink, sink ulas! So very low, their
Are lost for ever.
Of crime she is the fruitful source;
Of darkest deeds she is the nurse;
The basest are by her made worse;
She's the best friend
Of Satan; She is the bane, the curse
Of our fair land.
Myriads in misery have died;
Myriads committed suicide;
Myriads upon a scaffold tied
Have met their end,
That might have lived their country's pride
But for this fiend.
Whatever may be thy occupation,
Genius, talent, rank or station,
If given to intoxication,
Thus saith heaven.
Thou'lt sink low in the estimation
Of God and men. —
Oh could poor erring mortals see
One half of her deformity,
Methinks they'd quit her company;
For I am sure
They'd then lose half the misery
They now endure.

Van Raalte's poem deploring the evils of intoxication (HHA)

Constables dealt with civil crimes, such as theft. In the first months, a young couple, living in a log shed, was caught with some stolen goods. Van Raalte and two constables took the couple to the jail in Grand Haven to be held for trial by a justice of the peace. The trip was memorable. The party hugged the lakeshore in a crude flatboat rowed by the constables, which proved unequal to a storm that came up. The rowers out of fear had ignored the dominee's order to stay safely offshore, and the raft ran aground and broke up. Van Raalte jumped ashore and stayed reasonably dry. He then "laughed at the courageous crew" that had gotten wet. Walking the rest of the way, they came to Pigeon Creek, and the dominee said: "You are wet anyway; just carry me across as well. . . . Hold me tight!" he commanded the constable carrying him. At midstream, the packman deliberately stumbled and dunked the dominee, who replied dryly: "I figured this would happen." He said nothing more. Clearly, he was already becoming an American.[76]

In 1848 the People's Assembly, at Van Raalte's directive, established primitive fire protection after lightning set a house on fire and "No one had any protection against it, except shovel and axe." Signal bells and cisterns were placed around the village for bucket brigades. Every home was required to have a fire hook, shovel, pails of water, and a twenty-foot ladder, on pain of a fine up to $1,000 for "wantonness or carelessness" in regard to fire safety. The exorbitant maximum fine was more than three years' wages of common laborers.[77] For twenty years, the village had no regular fire force and paid for it dearly with frequent loss of lives and property. When Holland Township was organized in 1847, informal justice gave way to county constables and justices of the peace, with jury trials in the Grand Haven courthouse.

Alongside the consistory and assembly stood the board of trustees (a colonial executive committee), also led by Van Raalte. The trusteeship was formed early in 1848 at a special meeting of the male settlers to manage the financial affairs of the colony, sell communal town lots, manage a communal store, and set priorities for public improvements. But one major problem was that it had no defined structure, no lines of accountability, and no terms of tenure; it was an unaccountable governing body. And it did not limit actions to lands and finances but

---

[76] P. Schut, "Account of my Journey," in Lucas, *Dutch Immigrant Memoirs*, 2:474-75, trans. Henry De Mots.
[77] Swierenga, *Holland, Michigan*, 3:1831-34, 1850; minutes, People's Assembly, 7, 21 Feb. 1849; Den Uyl, *Holland Fire Department*, 3-7 (quotes 4).

it also meddled in legal matters. Trustees, for example, forbade selling liquor, butchering cattle, or erecting shoddy fences in the village.[78]

From 1847 to 1849, the trustees sold lots with small down payments and three years to pay the remainder; almost half, however, ended up in default. By 1849 debts on lots ballooned to several thousand dollars, and payments on lands purchased in 1847 were due, plus money owned on goods for the communal store. The trustees asked Van Raalte to assume all debts and take personal ownership of some six hundred town lots. New additions to the city doubled and tripled his eventual inventory of lots. Van Raalte accepted this huge responsibility with some reluctance, but the decision proved to be the foundation of his wealth (ch. 12).[79]

Opening main roads

If Van Raalte's itinerating in Overijssel on horseback and buggy was difficult and time consuming, travel on the Michigan frontier was far worse, given the Indian trails and narrow paths through the woods. Van Raalte wrote Ottawa County treasurer Henry Pennoyer in April 1847 asking for help to improve the primitive road from Grand Haven via Port Sheldon, which required bridging Pigeon Creek and the Black River, including two large swamps. "How difficult it is for us to come to Grand Haven," Van Raalte lamented. "I pray you will do what you can to get a road from Port Sheldon to the head of Black Lake. Every moment we feel that difficulty, and it will get worse in wintertime. Our people can do nothing about it; they are too sick, too feeble, and the few men of good health are too occupied in the care of buildings." With a state appropriation of four hundred acres of public land to provide funds for a bridge over the Black River, Van Raalte and Jan Binnekant were able to hire men to construct the first primitive bridge.[80]

Grand Haven came to Holland's aid in the construction of the road, but patches of it were still not ready for wagons when a stagecoach and mail connection was proposed in 1850. A plank road was started in March of that year on what has become today's Butternut Drive.[81]

---

[78] Van Hinte, *Netherlanders*, 240, citing Van Schelven, "Historical Sketches," *De Grondwet*, 15 June 1915.

[79] Compiled from "Dorpslands Dagboek," vols. 1 and 2; Van Raalte to Brummelkamp, 11 Sept. 1852 (quote), HHA; Swierenga, "Albertus C. Van Raalte," 295-97.

[80] Van Raalte to Henry Pennoyer, 30 Sept. 1847 (quote) and 22 Nov. 1847, both reprinted in *Holland City News*, 10 Jan. 1891.

[81] *Holland Historical Review and Service Book*, 1936; Louis and Henry Naberhuis Collection, HMA.

A preaching assignment in Grand Haven—a twenty-two-mile round trip—in 1854 meant a long day on horseback through swampy terrain. "The ride really gets to me," the dominee complained. The editor of *De Hollander* had reported that the Grand Haven road was a "good road."[82]

Ready access to Allegan, twenty-two miles distant, also demanded Van Raalte's attention. Allegan was the major market town upriver on the Kalamazoo River, about twenty miles northwest of Kalamazoo. Van Raalte sought road and bridge funding from the Michigan legislature, but the best the lawmakers could do was appropriate four thousand acres from the Michigan portion of the Congressional Internal Improvement Land Grant of 1841. Allegan merchants that desired to tap the Dutch trade hired John B. Dumont in early 1847 to survey Dumont Road, which ran north out of Allegan before bending northwest through Heath Township via Overisel to Holland. A second road farther west ran through a corner of Valley Township into Fillmore Township, crossing the Rabbit River at present-day Hamilton on its way to Holland. The current highway M-40 essentially follows this second route after entering Heath Township. The Allegan stage in 1854 served the colony regularly.[83]

Governor Epaphroditus Ransom appointed Flavius T. Littlejohn of Allegan and John A. Brooks as road commissioners, but strangely, they neglected the gap in the Dutch Road between Zeeland and Georgetown Road. In March 1849, Hollanders themselves funded a bridge over the south branch of the Black River at present-day Twenty-Fourth Street. In mid-1850, Gerrit J. Havekate managed with his team and wagon to use the primitive Allegan road to haul mail, freight, and passengers.[84]

Van Raalte personally experienced the travel risk in February 1851 when he rode Havekate's wagon home from Allegan. He described the scene vividly:

> The streams were flowing with water everywhere. A couple of miles on this side of the mill [the Colony Mill at Twenty-Fourth

---

[82] Van Raalte to Garretson, 14 June 1854, BDM; *De Hollander*, 11 May 1854.
[83] Van Schelven, "Our Nearest Neighbors," Van Schelven Papers; "Van Schelven Gives Some Interesting History of Holland," *Holland City News*, 19 Aug. 1915, quoting *Christian Intelligencer*, 3 Feb. 1848; *De Hollander*, 11 May 1854.
[84] *Grand River Eagle*, 23 Apr., 22 July 1850; Cornelia (Mrs. Kommer) Schaddelee, "Historical Reminiscences," in Moerdyke Papers; Petition from Allegan County to Governor John S. Barry, 23 Apr. 1850, Archives of the State of Michigan, Lansing, RG 44, box 223, folder 8.

Street] was a creek; the under-planks of the bridge had floated away, and the top logs were still in order, so that we did not see any danger until both horses were struggling in the water. Havekate himself fell in and was completely soaked. With a lot of effort, we got both of them [the horses] out by God's goodness without any injuries. Yet, we had to leave the wagon behind. . . . The trip from there was difficult and exhausting. Even so, I received double payment when I returned home and was allowed to see my entire family healthy and well.[85]

Allegan merchants were well aware of the Dutch colony, three thousand strong in 1849, far more numerous than Americans in the region. "Why," asked Kellogg, "is flour now retailing there [at Holland] at $9 and upwards a barrel, when here [Allegan] it can be bought for $5.75 only 23 miles away? It is the state of the roads and nothing else." As late as 1860, the link from Holland into Allegan County was still incomplete because of "factious opposition."[86]

More vital for the Holland colony than links to Grand Haven and Allegan was a good road to Grandville and beyond to the bustling city of Grand Rapids in Kent County, whose commercial markets and industries were essential to the Dutch. By the 1840s, Grand Rapids mines produced salt and gypsum; its flour mills ground grain and sawmills supplied lumber, and its iron works and metal shops made machines of all kinds, including woodworking tools, hand saws, and steam boilers. Grand Rapids factories turned out wagons, carriages, and ships for the Great Lakes and inland waterways, as well as all kinds of building products.[87]

Already in July 1847, barely five months after the founding of the Holland colony, a sympathetic group of Grand Rapids businessmen, led by Edmund B. Bostwick, formed a committee to help the Dutch colonists. This blue-ribbon group noticed the growing Dutch colony and determined to compete with Allegan merchants for the Dutch trade. They named committees: (1) to "wait upon our neighbors, the Hollanders, and inform them of our interest in their welfare," and (2) to "acquaint them with the best and shortest route to the settlements of the colonists" and let contracts for the road. When three committee

---

[85] Van Raalte to Paulus Den Bleyker, 28 Feb. 1851, Den Bleyker Papers, trans. Dekker.
[86] *De Hollander*, 4 Jan., 16 May 1855; *Allegan Journal*, citing *Ottawa Register*, 6 Feb. 1860; *Grand River Eagle*, 28 Sept. 1849 (quote), 22 July 1850. Havekate was the first colonist to own a yoke of oxen.
[87] Swierenga, "Better Prospects for Work."

Early Holland roads, ca. 1850

members set out for Holland, they encountered the first Dutch immigrants about nine miles east of Holland, deep in the woods, and they all arrived at Van Raalte's home at 5:30 p.m. No doubt, Christina prepared food for the tired travelers. Van Raalte, thankful for the visit, spoke for the immigrants who were "necessarily dependent" on the Americans "for all their provisions . . . until the almost unbroken forest shall be turned into fruitful fields." Boarder Cornelis Van Malsen, who could speak a smattering of English, likely translated for the men. All agreed that a road linking Holland and Grand Rapids was a top priority.[88]

---

[88] *Grand River Eagle*, 28 July 1847, for this and next paragraph.

Van Raalte pledged that the Dutch would chop a primitive road eastward about ten miles, following present-day Paw Paw Road, and build the Paw Paw bridge. Hiram Jenison agreed to chop the road southwestward for six miles from Jenison to Hudsonville, crossing Quincy Street and Seventy-Second Avenue, with a link-up to Riley Street and Seventy-Sixth Avenue. In early August 1848, crews directed by Zeeland merchant Marinus De Putter chopped the three-mile Paw Paw Road segment, but the Dutch Road project remained unfinished, much to the disgust of Rev. Van der Meulen, who charged: "There is not alone a slow progress, but it seems as if it is not cared for at all." By fall 1847, a primitive road to Grandville was usable after men cleared stumps and crossed creeks, bogs, and swamps. They threw logs over streams and laid them side by side over bogs and swamps, creating a "corduroy" path. In early October 1847, to buy land warrants from dealer John Ball, Van Raalte had to walk the thirty-five miles since the road was still impassable either on horseback or by wagon or oxcart.[89]

An 1851 report on the so-called Dutch Road showed little progress. The Georgetown portion required several costly bridges over the Black [Macatawa] River. It was 1854 before the Dutch Road allowed Havekate's stage to provide twice-a-week service. It ran twenty-nine miles, from Zeeland, north of the swamp, through Beaverdam and Blendon to Jenison, with the Half-Way House run by Aaltje (Mrs. Reiner [Ryne]) De Regt located south of Blendon. Van Raalte's efforts to link Holland to its neighboring cities did eventually pay off, but it took years, rather than months.[90]

Van Raalte homestead

The small Van Raalte home was crowded with five children and three boarders, including maid Cornelia Van Malsen, her brother Cornelis, and her fiancé, Jannes Van de Luyster Jr., son of the Zeeland capitalist. Van Raalte performed the wedding ceremony for Cornelia and Jannes in September 1847 in his home—his third wedding—and

---

[89] James Walker, in *Grand River Eagle*, 13 Oct. 1848; Report, Nelson Bliss and Andrew Fries, Commissioners of Highway, to Georgetown Township Board, 24 Mar. 1849, in Georgetown Township Board Record Book. Hiram and his twin brothers, Lucius and Luman, were the pioneer settlers in Jenison; *Jenison History*, no. 2014-3 (July 2014), Jenison Historical Association.

[90] Minutes, First Zeeland, 29 Mar. 1849; minutes, Holland Township, 2 Apr. 1849, reprinted *Holland City News*, 25 Mar. 1909; Report, Freeman Burton and Holden Lowing, Highway Commissioners, to Georgetown Township Board Record Book, 12 July 1851.

The Half-Way House on Dutch Road (later, 5301 Barry St.) (*courtesy Robert Essenburg*)

the newlyweds continued to live there. "Mrs. Van Raalte would not let us go," Cornelia wrote her parents. "We live here bound by ties of love.... She is a dear friend and sister in the Lord." Two months later, Cornelia added: "Mrs. Van Raalte and I have progressed about equally well [in speaking English]. We are often asked to go to Allegan and other places." In 1848 six-year-old Klaas Wildeboer, son and namesake of Van Raalte's former student at Ommen, was taken in after his widowed mother died.[91] In addition to a wedding venue, the homestead doubled as a doctor's office and an apothecary, a meeting place for the People's Assembly and church assemblies, and a catechism classroom.[92]

Mother Christina usually had domestics to help with household tasks. Household servants set the Van Raaltes apart. There were only a few families of similar social standing in the colony. Occasionally, however, Christina would have to do without. In late 1850, her husband placed an ad in *De Sheboygan Nieuwsbode* for a "servant girl for his family who is a capable cook, for $1.00 a week." Perhaps the salary was inadequate, given the great demand by American families for "upright" Dutch maids, prized for their work ethic and cleanliness. A few months later, Van Raalte told Paulus Den Bleyker, a Kalamazoo friend, that he and his wife could not visit them, ostensibly because Christina was without a maid. That same spring, Albertus wrote Carel de Moen that, although Christina was very weak, she "works hard; rather, she has too much to do and this exhausts her." In 1857 Jannemieke Verbeek,

---

[91] Record of Marriages Solemnized by A. C. Van Raalte, Minister of the Gospel, 1, HHA; Cornelia to parents, 22 Sept., 16 Nov. 1847, in Yzenbaard, "'America' Letters," 50, 53-54; Van Raalte to Garretson, 10 May 1855, BDM.

[92] Religious ceremonies took place in church during a worship service, often two at a time. The celebration would take place on the next day in the evening. See Parr, *Hope Church*, 33-34.

age seventeen, was Christina's maid.⁹³ In 1858 Dirk remarked that his parents had a handyman for gardening, Cornelius Van Herwynen, and a maid, Effie, from the Overisel colony, for *huiswerk*. In 1859 Ben informed his father in New York that the hired hand had "run off angry, so I have not been able to do anything about the fence." Periodically, Christina would hire someone to do laundry, iron, and sew. In mid-1860, her maids were Magdelene De Vries, age twenty-two, and Jacoba Van Fasen, age seventeen.⁹⁴

Van Raalte complained in the spring of 1851 that his home was "too small for my numerous family, . . . [yet] I am not considering adding to it." In 1855 he could afford to have the house enlarged, the first of many expansions, and a red brick façade added. An out-of-town visitor in 1859 described it as a "very pleasant farm and homestead." It was at that time the finest home in the village.

Forming Holland Township governance

Van Raalte and his family were still living in Allegan when, on March 6, 1847, he requested the state legislature to set off Holland Township from Ottawa Township. Legal matters moved slowly in those days. It was 1849 before the Ottawa County Board of Supervisors formally organized the new township that included what is now Holland, Zeeland, and Park Townships and the cities of Holland and Zeeland (Township 5 North and Ranges 14, 15 and 16 West).⁹⁵ Township governance rendered moot the ad hoc bodies—the People's Assembly and board of trustees.

Civil governance required that voters be citizens, and Van Raalte as the political tutor moved to make that happen "by way of our own smartest citizens."⁹⁶ But that was a tall order. As local American Henry Post opined: "The prospect of making anything more than raw Dutchmen out of this generation is poor indeed. . . . They have no idea of a [democratic] government or a people's capacity to govern themselves. . . . They are not fit to elect their public officers, being on

---

⁹³   Van Raalte notice in *Sheboygan Nieuwsbode*, 27 Dec. 1850; Van Raalte to Paulus Den Bleyker, 21 April 1851; Van Raalte to De Moen, 23 May 1851.

⁹⁴   Van Raalte to De Moen, 1 May 1858; Ben Van Raalte to father, 4 Mar. 1859, trans. Nella Kennedy; Dirk Van Raalte to father, 19, 28 Feb 1861; Swierenga, *Dutch Households in U.S. Population Census*, 1140. In mid-1870 Christina did not have a maid, but she could rely on Helena, age 32, wife of the absconded Albertus, and her five children, who were living with them.

⁹⁵   Kit Lane, ed., *Ottawa County Historical Atlas and Gazeteer* (Pavilion Press, 1999), 13.

⁹⁶   Van Raalte to Brummelkamp, 30 Jan. 1847, in *Holland in Amerika*, English typescript, 76.

those points they are entirely destitute of judgment."[97] He was correct that the Dutch were unfit; virtually no one had ever cast a vote in the Netherlands, except the wealthy Jannes Van de Luyster, since only the richest 2 percent could vote. In the United States, every free white male could vote already in the 1820s, when the Andrew Jackson administration ended all property qualifications.

In July 1848, Van Raalte persuaded Ottawa County clerk Henry Griffin to come from Grand Haven for a wholesale naturalization at half his normal fifty-cent fee. After walking the twenty-two miles on Saturday, Griffin worshiped on Sunday at the Log Church. After the service, the dominee announced Griffin's presence and purpose and asked the men to gather Monday at Jan Binnekant's hotel to file First Papers. The next day, Griffin went to Zeeland, Vriesland, and Drenthe. Van de Luyster paid the fee for the Zeeland townsmen. Griffin was impressed that only six of the 309 men had to sign their name with an X. He went home whistling through the forest with $77.25 jingling in his pockets and his ears ringing from Hollanders who had gladly taken their oaths. These men comprised the first citizenship class, which fulfilled a "fundamental understanding" that Van Raalte had made in the Netherlands, that all adult male emigrants would have equal rights and a full voice in governance.[98]

Although the Dutch had to wait to vote in local elections, they could not be "undisputed lords in their own castle," as Van Hinte put it. They had to rely on the few Americans in the township—stalwart Democrats all—to run the local government. On March 31, 1849, ten Americans caucused at Henry Post's store to nominate themselves for the several offices—Henry D. Post, supervisor (mayor); William Bronson, clerk and assessor; Hoyt G. Post, treasurer and school inspector; and others for justices of the peace, school inspectors, highway commissioners, directors of the poor, and constables. The first

---

[97] Scheffer, *Short History*, 116-20, 135.

[98] H. Griffin Report, 10 July 1848, in Detroit *Daily Free Press*, 17 July 1848; Pieters, *Dutch Settlement*, 157-58. To keep abreast of current events, the dominee ordered newspaper subscriptions from the Netherlands and the United States—the *Rotterdamsche Weeklijksche Courant*, *De Nederlander*, *De Handwijzer*, the *Christian Intelligencer*, the *American Messenger*, the *New York Observer*, *Harper's Weekly*, the *Detroit Advertiser*, the *Detroit Free Democrat*, the *Grand River Eagle*, the *Grand River Enquirer*, and the *Allegan Record*. He paid subscriptions with cash earned on the sale of lots and profits from business ventures. In 1848, his account book with Post & Co. listed $1,000 in cash income, but by 30 Dec. 1851, he was short by $1,357 ($53,800 today). See Van Raalte account with Post & Co., 1847-51; Van Raalte Account, Holland Post Office, Jan-Mar. 1853, HHA.

election took place two days later, on April 2, at Van Raalte's home, when the same qualified voters elected themselves to their respective offices. The ten, comprising the township board, then ordered a twenty-five-dollar tax levy for expenses—their salaries. Taxes were soon increased for schools and operating expenses.[99]

The 1850 township election followed the same script, according to Hoyt Post. "Held a town meeting, polled three votes, and Henry [Post], Mr. [William] Bronson, and myself voted ourselves into office with hardly enough opposition to make it interesting. Our townsmen took very little interest in town matters. But two or three were there, and they were too busy quarreling among themselves to give attention to town matters."[100]

Interestingly, in the midterm general election in November 1850, the Michigan ballot included a referendum to grant "free suffrage to colored persons." Of the fourteen townships in the Ottawa County canvass, only Holland Township voters, five in number, including the Post brothers, supported black suffrage, and their vote was unanimous. Why only five of the dozen or so eligible Americans cast votes speaks to political indifference. County wide, the referendum failed by a vote of 381 to 75. Although the local vote was largely symbolic, since no blacks were known to be living in Holland Township, it did show that Van Raalte's American friends, notably the Posts, and likely the dominee himself, favored black suffrage.[101]

The first Dutch citizenship class was eligible to vote in state and local elections in spring 1851 and in presidential elections in November 1852. The practice in the nineteenth century was for voters to caucus in person to nominate candidates for township offices. The 1851 Holland Township caucus was held in the large Zeeland log church on April 14. It was a near disaster, which might have been expected, given that the immigrants were political novices, and the typical American-style caucus was raucous. The fight was over the spoils of office and the distribution of tax dollars for roads and bridges. In cash-starved settlements like Holland and Zeeland, government jobs were coveted because they paid a regular salary in hard currency. The low tax base meant that public funds were never enough, and politicos who set priorities had power. Settlers in the villages on the east side were

---

[99] Van Hinte, *Netherlanders*, 242-43 (quote); "A Holland Election," *Holland City News*, 30 Mar. 1889.
[100] Quote in Hoyt G. Post Diary, 1 Apr. 1850, typescript, 27.
[101] *De Hollander*, 10 Nov. 1850, for the official canvass.

frustrated from the outset that township trustees had given priority to the North River Avenue Bridge to Grand Haven over the Black River Bridge on Paw Paw Road to Zeeland and Vriesland, and the Statesland (later Adams) Road Bridge to Drenthe.

Holland postmaster William Van Eyck called the 1851 caucus the "most boisterous and disorderly ever held hereabout." A huge crowd of 264 men came to cast ballots, but a brawl broke out inside and later outside with shoving and some fisticuffs. The caucus was in the Zeeland church, the largest building in the colony, with Rev. Van der Meulen in the chair and pastors Van Raalte, Marten Ypma of Vriesland, and Roelof Smit of Drenthe in the pews. The dispute went deeper than jobs and dollars. The event aroused latent rivalries and animosities between the people of *de stad* (the town) and *de dorpen* (the villages), which had age-old roots in the Old Country. Zeelanders and their compatriots from Drenthe—Staphorsters all—had reputations for being headstrong and stubborn. No wonder these villagers often spit out *"de stad"* in a "venomous tone," as pioneer settler Engbertus Van der Veen had noted. The animosity between *stad* and *dorpen*, like a "prickly little thorn," persisted for more than fifty years in the Holland colony. Beside the historic issues, the outlying villagers resented Van Raalte's perceived autocracy and theocracy.[102]

Van der Veen, an eyewitness, recalled the scene vividly in his *Reminiscences*. The meeting clearly made an indelible impression:

> Early in the morning of the day of the caucus, Dominee Van Raalte, accompanied by such as had the right to vote, and also by some friends and boys, went to Zeeland, walking the entire distance, climbing over fallen trees, and wading through water. They arrived in time for the meeting. Dominee Van der Meulen was in the pulpit, acting as chairman. Soon there was great excitement, and Dominee Van Raalte stood on the pews appealing to the men, saying "Brothers! Brothers!" The Zeelanders, supported by their friends from Statesland [West Drenthe], wanted all the offices to the exclusion of the men from Holland. The dominee's exhortations calmed the spirits just in time to prevent hard blows. After the caucus, we went home in a body. Some of the office seekers were angry and jealous, complaining that the

---

[102] Swierenga, *Holland, Michigan*, 2:1668-71, citing Van der Veen, "Life Reminiscences," 1:512-13; William O. Van Eyck, "The Three Town Halls," *Holland City News*, 23 Jan. 1930; Van Hinte, *Netherlanders*, 243.

Watercolor drawing of brawl in Zeeland church, April 14, 1851, by Anneus J. Hillebrands, signed JH, school teacher in Old Groningen, 1847-1852 (*HMA*)

Zeelanders had captured the best offices. Pieter Van den Burg said: "Holland is ignored." Others said: "Well! Well! That old Jan Hulst from Statesland, justice of the peace. That man was such a rebellious character! He is more for war than peace!" [Hulst, a native of Staphorst, in June 8, 1847, was the first white settler in what would become Zeeland Township.]

Van der Veen then explained the background of the conflict:

> The Zeelanders and Stateslanders were angry with the men from Holland. They declared that the Pope and his Cardinals of Holland [Van Raalte and the consistory] had come to Zeeland to impose their rule, and they were selfish. The expression "'Pope and his Cardinals' was frequently employed by malcontented spirits ... who gloried in publishing vicious articles."[103]

For the Dutch, calling a leader "Pope" was the ultimate insult. After the Protestant Reformation, militant Calvinists in the Low

---

[103] Van der Veen, "Life Reminiscences," 1:512.

Founding Holland Colony   265

Holland Township election, likely May 12, 1851, watercolor by Anneus J. Hillebrands (signed JH) (*HMA*).

Counties, under rebel leader William of Orange (William the Silent), revolted in 1568 against the Catholic King Philip II of Spain and his brutal warlord, the Duke of Alva, and won their freedom as a Protestant Republic in the Eighty Years' War (1568-1648), actually the Dutch War for Independence. The two-year siege of Leiden early in the war (1573-75) that caused thousands to starve to death is still celebrated on the Third of October after nearly 450 years.

Zeeland's population in the early years was three times that of Holland, but Holland was the kingpin. It was founded first and soon had the harbor, the first mills and factories, a post office, a newspaper, an academy, and a small professional class. Zeelanders determined to challenge Holland's dominance. After the testy 1851 caucus, Jannes Van de Luyster, who had platted the Zeeland village, petitioned the state legislature to set Zeeland Township off from Holland Township. The Michigan legislature readily obliged.[104]

Although the Dutch fought among themselves over the nominations, at the election, held on or about April 15, 1851, they dominated the township election, taking all the offices except supervisor (town-

---

[104] *Grand River Times*, 2 July 1851. The Ottawa Township board appointed Van Raalte as school inspector on 8 May 1851 (minutes, Holland Township Board, book 1, p. 9), HMA.

ship mayor). They reelected Henry Post; they needed his leadership and understanding of the American political system.[105]

Hillebrands' political cartoon portrays the veiled hostility between the Dutch and the Americans in the 1851 minirevolution. The Dutch (on the left) stand ready to "Replace!" (old Dutch, *afgeloest*) the Americans (on the right) in the offices of supervisor, clerk, justice of the peace, and director of the poor. The Dutch look spiffy, and the Americans look scruffy. At the top are the words "time pass" and "one year," with the wind goddess blowing the Americans away over a flashing lightning bolt. Above the heads of the Dutch is the word "majority" and the number of votes, viz., 38, 62, 33, and 76 2/3 (the 2/3rds is a joke). Over the heads of the Americans is the phrase "Nothing to do for us, etc., etc.," and four zeroes, to suggest that they had nary a vote. Hoyt Post, the outgoing treasurer, is pictured with a moneybag on his shoulder containing $1500. Bronson, the clerk, has an ink quill stuck between his ear and glass frame. The structure in the middle tells the same story, with a small gold case hanging on the left and a white towel of surrender on the right. Although the cartoon does not show it, Henry Post, as already explained, retained the office of supervisor.

At the state and national level, Van Raalte led his people into the pro-immigrant Democrat Party. Frontier Michigan, like western states generally, had been a Democrat stronghold since the rise of President Jackson (1829-37). Democratic politicians had befriended the dominee at his arrival in Detroit, including Lewis Cass, Jackson's secretary of war, and Robert Stuart. The Dutch also strongly opposed Whig prohibition referenda and legislative efforts to stretch the naturalization period from five to fourteen years.[106]

Van Raalte became a full-fledged citizen of the United States on April 16, 1853, twelve days after appearing before Circuit Judge George Martin of Ottawa County to give his oath to "support the Constitution of the United States . . . absolutely and entirely renounce, and abjure all allegiance to William, King of the Netherlands, whose subject he had hitherto been." County clerk Hermanus Doesburg signed the certificate. Why the dominee waited a full year after he was legally permitted to become a citizen is not clear. Perhaps he had his hands

---

[105] *De Hollander*, 17 Apr. 1851.
[106] Krabbendam, *Freedom on the Horizon*, 287; William O. Van Eyck, "Old History on Sheriff-ship in Ottawa County," *Holland City News*, 25 Sept. 1930; and "When Holland Was Democratic," *Holland City News*, 23 Feb. 1911.

STATE OF MICHIGAN, } ss
County of Ottawa.

THE Circuit Court for said County. At a session of said Circuit Court, holden at Grand Haven, on the _____ day of _____ A. D. 185_. Present the Hon. _____ Circuit Judge.

_____ having appeared in open Court, and having made application to become a citizen of the UNITED STATES, and having introduced the testimony of two witnesses, by which it appears to the satisfaction of the Court, that the said _____ has resided in the United States, for five years, and in the State of Michigan, for one year previous to the date hereof, and having made oath in open Court, (which oath signed by said _____ is now on file,) that he would support the CONSTITUTION of the UNITED STATES, and that he would **ABSOLUTELY AND ENTIRELY, RENOUNCE AND ABJURE, ALL** ALLEGIANCE AND FIDELITY TO EVERY FOREIGN PRINCE, POTENTATE, STATE, OR SOVEREIGNTY, whereof he was before a citizen or subject, and particularly _____ of _____ whose subject he has hitherto been.

The said _____ is hereby now declared a CITIZEN OF THE UNITED STATES OF AMERICA, from and after the date hereof.

STATE OF MICHIGAN, } ss
County of Ottawa.

I hereby certify the foregoing to be a true copy of record, in witness whereof I have hereunto set my hand, and affixed the seal of the Circuit Court for said County, at the Clerks Office, in Grand Haven, this ___ day of _____ A. D. 185_.

_____ Clerk.

Van Raalte's certificate of citizenship, October 17, 1853 (HHA)

full with business dealings and church affairs. But this meant that he did not vote in the 1852 presidential election that pitted Democrat Franklin Pierce against Whig Winfield Scott, which Pierce won handily. In that election, Holland Township voters cast 123 of 127 votes for Pierce, a 24:1 ratio, whereas Zeeland Township voters gave Pierce 128 of 141 votes, a 12:1 ratio.[107]

American friends

New England natives George Harrington and Isaac Fairbanks cast their lot with the Dutch. Van Raalte's closest friend was the able, young American, Henry D. Post, who became a lifelong confidant and business associate. Post and his bride, Anna Coatsworth Post, natives of Vermont, were the first American couple to join the Dutch colony.

---

[107] Van Raalte's Certificate of Citizenship, 17 Oct. 1853, HHA.

Henry Post, merchant, business associate of Van Raalte (*courtesy Randall P. Vande Water*)

Anna (Mrs. Henry) Coatsworth Post, of Dutch ancestry (*JAH*)

They learned the Dutch language, adopted the Reformed faith, and often exchanged coffee visits with the Van Raaltes. Albertus "looked so young and with no beard," Anna recalled. After Sunday worship services at the Log Church, Christina hosted the Posts for tea at the parsonage. Anna Post, one of Holland's social pillars, made her home the center of social life in Holland. It stood on the northwest corner of what would become the main intersection at Eighth and River Streets (later the Waverly Stone bank building). Post's store was across the street from it on the northeast corner (later Model Drug store). Post bought the choice lots from the dominee in September 1847 for ninety-six dollars ($3,560 today), on a one-year mortgage contract.[108]

Post moved from Allegan after listening to Van Raalte's

> glowing prophecies of the future city on the eastern shore, based on his keen judgment of its great advantages and future resources. I caught the infection of his enthusiasm, and when

---

[108] "Isaac Fairbanks," *Holland City News*, 1 Feb. 1890; "Interview with Isaac Fairbanks," typescript by Barbara Lampen, Fairbanks Papers; "Anna C. Post Reminiscences [1911]," in Lucas, *Dutch Immigrant Memoirs*, 1:402; Post & Co. one year note, $96, 23 Sept. 1847, Van Raalte Account book with H. D. Post & Co., HHA. In 1854 the Posts and a few other Yankees from the East began meeting for worship, and in 1862, they organized the English-speaking Hope Reformed Church.

he asked me to come and help him lay the foundations of the future commonwealth, I enlisted with him, heart and hand, in the service.[109]

Post had his hand in everything from business to civic affairs. He helped Van Raalte organize township government, establish schools, lay out roads, notarize legal transactions, open a general store, and establish mills and other businesses. Post held the offices of justice of the peace, highway commissioner, school inspector, city supervisor, and postmaster. He was also the founding editor of the *Ottawa Register*, a Democratic sheet in Holland for English-speaking residents. No wonder he earned the distinguished title of squire. In 1848 thirteen Americans sat with five hundred Dutch under Van Raalte's pulpit. They learned a smattering of "street Dutch," adapted to clannish Dutch ways, and saw their children marry Hollanders. By 1854 sixteen American families lived in the village.[110]

Christina formed a loose relationship with Arvilla Smith, who considered her to be "a good and noble woman" with a "heart open to every good work." Anna Post became her dearest American friend and confidant. Christina obviously picked up enough conversational English to get by. But her dearest friends were among the Dutch. Geesje Van der Haar-Visscher recalls frequent visits of the Van Raaltes to her parents' farmhouse. Christina also called on Geesje on her own, and she and other women passed the time discussing church and religion, in Dutch, of course.[111]

Class distinctions that governed in the Netherlands were virtually nonexistent in America. Manners, no; companionship with equals, yes. "My children do not have the need for a feverish state of enforced and artificial set of manners," Van Raalte explained. But some Americans found the Dutch uncouth. Henry Post's immature younger brother Hoyt was one such Dutchman. In 1848 Hoyt found refuge from a blinding snowstorm in the log cabin of the Jacobus Vinke family. The

---

[109] "Henry D. Post," *Holland City News*, 1 Aug. 1896.
[110] Minutes, People's Assembly, 25 Oct. 1848, art. 11; 8 Nov. 1848, art. 10; Henry D. Post, obit., *Holland City News*, 24 July 1897; "Reminiscences of Anna C. Post," in Lucas, *Dutch Immigrant Memoirs*, 1:399; David McNeish to Van Raalte, Apr. 1854, BDM; Swierenga, *Holland, Michigan*, 1:161.
[111] Swierenga and Van Appledorn, *Old Wing Mission*, 464; Anna Post, "The Van Raalte Colony," *Holland City News*, 30 Jan. 1903; "Anna C. Post Reminiscences [1911]," in Lucas, *Dutch Immigrant Memoirs*, 1:403; Van Raalte to Helenius de Cock, 26 Sept. 1851, AGK; Brummelkamp, *Stemmen uit Noord-Amerika*, in *Voices from America*, 84, 90; "Geesje Van der Haar-Visscher diary," 10; Yzenbaard, "'America' Letters," 53.

three-day experience was unnerving. With acid dripping from his pen, Hoyt described the family in his diary. Vinke's "boy" (hired hand) was "a thick-headed, fat, stout lump of mortality, who seems to have two visible objects in view for which he cares; these are sufficiency of potatoes and pork to supply his wonderfully capacious belly, and his pipe." Vinke's six-year-old daughter was a "dirty, lazy, ragged, saucy little imp, who seems to have a large portion of the spirit of evil for so small a body." Father Jacobus was "loutish," and the kitchen of "buxom" Vrouw Wilhelmina was unkempt. Eating pork with "the bristles on lessens materially one's relish for the food spread before him." But eat the food Post did; it was that or go hungry. The class-conscious American despised the crude Vinkes but not the educated dominee. "The more I see Mr. Van Raalte, the more I see to admire.... He is so determined to succeed in everything he undertakes that he will carry everything through that he thinks ought to be done."[112]

Van Raalte welcomed Americans like the Posts. As businessmen, teachers, and doctors, they were necessary since few immigrants had these skills and training. Within a decade, three of the seven stores in the village of Holland were American owned, and by 1860, fifty-two households of "outsiders" made up one-sixth of Holland Township residents. After the city was set off from Holland Township in 1867, the number of non-Dutch households increased to ninety-five (18 percent) in 1870 and seven hundred (35 percent) in 1880—a doubling in a decade. Besides Americans, the city attracted other immigrant groups—Germans, English, Irish, Norwegians, and Swedes. Thus, within three decades of its founding, one in three households in Holland was non-Dutch. Van Raalte, as we will see, grudgingly watched his Christian Dutch colony morph into a diverse, multiethnic city.[113]

Guiding the harbor project

Priority no. 1 was the harbor project, which turned out to be a costly, twenty-year effort, completed by the Army Corps of Engineers. The first effort of the colonists to open the shallow channel were pitiful. The People's Assembly sent men with picks and shovels to remove sand bars and line the banks with skinned tree trunks. Smallpox and

---

[112] Postma, "Isaac Fairbanks," iv; Hoyt G. Post Diary, 4 Dec. 1848, 25 Feb., 3 July 1850, Post Family Papers. Hoyt Post never intended his diary to be read by others, as he stated in the opening and closing pages. He moved to Grand Rapids in 1853.

[113] Compiled from federal manuscript population census lists in Herrick District Library.

malaria sickened many and halted the work. Van Raalte wasted no time bringing pressure to bear on Congress for appropriations, using contacts he had established with Senator Lewis Cass and Charles Stuart, a Michigan House member. After a frustrating wait, Stuart dashed Van Raalte's hopes for federal dollars but promised to send topographical engineers to survey the harbor, a necessary first step. Van Raalte also petitioned Governor Ransom, state representative Silas F. Littlejohn, and other lawmakers. In lieu of cash, the state donated forty thousand acres (worth $50,000, or $1.9 million today) under the 1841 Congressional Internal Improvements Act, the sale of which would fund a "suitable and substantial wharf or pier . . . at the mouth of the Black River."[114]

With this encouraging news and a successful subscription campaign, the assembly in October 1848 established a harbor board and a joint stock company, which issued shares at ten dollars each, to be paid in either cash, material, or labor. Within a month, ninety-three men subscribed, and only one colonist reportedly refused. Van Raalte secured an additional $1,000 loan from Wyckoff in June 1849, secured by a mortgage on two thousand acres of the Internal Improvement lands dedicated to the harbor.[115]

A pier was the best option initially since the shallow outlet would not permit lake schooners to enter the harbor. Van Raalte and Jan Binnekant took the construction job in the spring of 1849 in exchange for $300 ($11,500 today) of Internal Improvement lands. The pier allowed for goods to be transferred from lake vessels to flatboats for transport up Black Lake to Holland. But the next winter storm destroyed the pier. It would take a much stronger structure to withstand the pounding waves of an angry lake.[116]

Stuart made good on his promise for a survey. In June 1849, Major John R. Bowes of the topographical engineers and two associates arrived unannounced on a Sunday morning. They found the village deserted but followed the sound of singing to the Log Church, where the morning worship service was underway. That afternoon, Bowes and his crew attended the second service after they learned that Rev.

---

[114] Minutes, People's Assembly (Volksvergadering), 21 Nov. (quote), 29 Dec. 1848, 7 Mar. 1849 (quote), HMA; Van Raalte to Henry Pennoyer, 22 Nov. 1847, published in *Holland City News*, 10 Jan. 1891; Act No. 32, 3 Feb. 1848, Laws of Michigan 1848 (quote), 5.

[115] *Holland City News*, 19 Aug. 1915; minutes, People's Assembly, 23 Oct., 15 Nov. 1848, HMA; "Dorpslands Dagboek," 23 Apr., 25 June 1850.

[116] Hoyt G. Post Diary, 3 May 1849, typescript, 17, Post Family Papers.

Wyckoff was in town and would preach in English for the benefit of the Americans. After the service, Van Raalte invited the men to the parsonage for tea. The congregation rejoiced at the arrival of the government crew; "They now felt prosperity was near."[117]

Bowes and his small surveying party spent six weeks preparing a full-fledged plan for a channel. His report spoke highly of the harbor's promise as the "best on Lake Michigan." Bowes recommended that a deep channel be cut between the twin hills of Mt. Pisgah on the north and Old Baldhead (not to be confused with Saugatuck's Mt. Baldhead) on the south, with piers extending far into the lake, to cost an estimated $106,000 ($4.1 million today).[118] The plan was solid, but the price tag was far beyond the colonists' means, even with revenue from the sale of the Internal Improvement lands. But Bowes' plan did eventually become the route of the channel.

With Bowes' report in hand, Van Raalte pushed Congress in 1850 for an appropriation of $45,000 ($1.7 million today) to make Black Lake "one of the safest, most accessible, and capacious harbors on the whole chain of lakes." In a letter to Alpheus Felch, the junior Democratic US senator from Michigan, the Dutch cleric declared: "The whole population . . . is now entirely depending on shipping off the products of their labor. . . . An abundance of riches is here in staves, shingles, bark, ship timber, etc., but it wants an outlet." When the lawmakers balked, Van Raalte wrote directly to Vice President Millard Fillmore on behalf of the Holland colony, which he claimed was the largest settlement on the west side of Lake Michigan. He "humbly" begged for $10,000 ($385,000 today) in harbor funding, so that "our hopes may not end in disappointment and despair."[119] Neither letter bore fruit.

The problem was a political logjam in Washington, which mystified the Dutch and delayed federal funding until 1852 when Congress finally appropriated $8,000 ($308,000 today) to erect the first of twin breakwaters. This grant induced Holland Township trustees to create a harbor board, headed by Van Raalte, which issued $20,000

---

[117] "Elvira H. Langdon's School Reminiscences," Aug. 1897 (quote), published in *De Grondwet*, 17 Dec. 1910, and reprinted in Lucas, *Dutch Immigrant Memoirs*, 1:395; Post Diary, 1 July 1849, 18-20; "Dorpslands Dagboek," 1 Dec. 1849.

[118] Official Report of Major J. R. Bowes, 31 Jan. 1850, reprinted in *Grand Rapids Enquirer*, 25 Dec. 1850.

[119] Petition, Harbor Committee, to US Senate and House of Representatives, 12 Dec. 1849; Hoyt Post Diary, 6 Oct. 1850, 77; Van Raalte to Felch, 31 Jan. 1850; Van Raalte to Vice President Millard Fillmore, 5 Feb. 1850, HMA.

($790,000 today) in harbor bonds. Many men went to work rebuilding the pier and dredging the channel. They were paid in kind—a reduction on payments for their village lots at a rate of fifty cents per day. Van Raalte donated a village lot to pay for the first lighthouse at the harbor.[120]

Shippers appreciated the improvement, and hundreds of ships called at Holland annually in the 1850s. In 1852 alone, ninety-one vessels cleared the port and carried twenty-four hundred cords of bark, nine hundred thousand staves, three hundred and fifty thousand feet of lumber, two hundred thousand wood shingles, twenty-seven hundred leather hides, and fifty-one barrels of potash. But the battle against wind and sand was constant. A winter storm in late 1855 destroyed two hundred feet of the pier, as well as the expensive pile driver.[121]

Van Raalte unsuccessfully petitioned the Democrat Congress for emergency funding. "Complete our harbor, and Holland and the entire colony will begin a new life." By that fall, the entrance to Black Lake was again completely blocked by a sand bar, and the water level had risen by five feet until the pressure broke the bar and rushing water carved a new channel.[122]

The editor of the *Grand River Eagle* got it right when he declared that the Dutch would build a harbor themselves to "shame our parsimonious, niggardly stepmother government, which has millions to expend in building useless hulks for epaulette [ceremonial] drones [e.g., retired military brass] to strut over, but not one cent for a harbor for the protection of our commerce."[123]

Van Raalte demanded "action without any delay" at a town meeting in November 1857. The men agreed to dig a new channel, from eight to ten feet deep, between the two high dunes that Lt. Col. John D. Graham had recommended—the shortest route across. To fund the project, they floated additional harbor bonds and reached out to all the surrounding townships to broaden the tax base. The goal was to

---

[120] "Dorpslands Dagboek," 1850-51; Van Raalte to Brummelkamp, 11 Sept. 1852, HMA; Van Raalte donation for lighthouse, 24 Oct. 1853, HHA.

[121] *De Hollander*, 4 May, 8 June, 24 Aug., 2 Nov. 1853, 8 Feb., 27 Apr., 11 May, 23 Nov. 1854, 1 Feb., 14 Nov. 1855; Van Raalte to Brummelkamp, 11 Sept. 1852, HMA; Swierenga, *Holland, Michigan*, 1:705, 716n79.

[122] *De Hollander*, 11 Nov. 1857; Petition, Holland Harbor Commission, Dec. 1857, HMA.

[123] For epaulette drones, see *Friend's Review: A Religious, Literary and Miscellaneous Journal* 4 (1851), 326.

Jan Roost, harbor bond salesman, Republican leader, Van Raalte understudy (*HMA*)

complete the project before the 1858 shipping season opened.[124]

Van Raalte recruited John Roost (Jan Roest) to go to New York to sell harbor bonds to Old Dutch businessmen, but Roost found donors tapped out by earlier appeals on behalf of Van Vleck Hall and First Reformed Church. Roost lacked a salesman's natural bent and fluency in English. "I find it verry [sic] hard to sell bonds. I have not sold any in New York or Brooklyn, notwithstanding I tried verry [sic] hard," he told Van Raalte. But with "indefatigable perseverance," and the critical backing of De Witt and Wyckoff, Roost peddled $5,000 worth of bonds.[125] Homesick for his wife and children, he was ready to quit. "If there is a person of ambition, he might have mine place, and I shall be glad to go home and leave the hardworking of begging for somebody else." That person of ambition was Van Raalte, a master fundraiser, but he did manage to sell an additional $1,000 worth of bonds. The well was indeed dry, especially in the face of the national depression triggered by a financial crisis in 1857. It is remarkable that the two men raised $6,000 ($220,000 today) in that environment.[126]

Back home again, Van Raalte wrote Governor Kinsley Bingham, asking the state to cover the $25,000 ($916,000 today) shortfall to complete the new channel and provide a "highway of transportation" for our isolated colony. "If you would enter our houses and see our tables, you would be astonished at the burden that we are determined

---

[124] *Grand Rapids Eagle*, 24 Nov. 1857; *De Hollander*, 11 Nov. 1857; *Ottawa Register*, 16 Nov. 1857.

[125] Van Raalte to Samuel B. Schieffelin, 8 July 1858; Van Raalte to Samuel Pruyn, NYC, 8 July 1858; Van Raalte to Roost, 15 July 1858; Roost to Van Raalte, 11 Sept. 1858, HMA; *Grand Rapids Eagle*, 6 Sept, 4, 12 Oct. 1858, *De Hollander*, 30 Dec. 1858.

[126] Roost (Albany, NY) to Van Raalte, 11 July 1859, HMA; Van Raalte to Philip Phelps Jr., 19 Nov. 1859, in Bruins and Schakel, *Envisioning Hope College*, 28-29; *De Hollander*, 19 Nov. 1859. In August 1859, Wyckoff and De Witt separately visited Holland (*De Hollander*, 4 Aug. 1859; *Christian Intelligencer*, 22 Sept. 1859).

to bear." A second letter was even more emotional. "A man will resist being murdered, and so we shall. We must be aided in some way. We cannot stop, and therefore we cannot give up."[127] The Dutch leader also sent another petition to Congress with 269 signatures, titled: "A few words from the Hollander in Michigan." All these efforts for public funding fell on deaf ears.[128]

Discouraged by tight purses within both public and private sources and squabbles among settlers over how to complete the work, Van Raalte resigned as president of the harbor board in 1860, having served nearly a decade. "Harbor quarrels [are] at an end," he noted optimistically. But he was wrong. Work progressed slowly with the extension of piers and breakwaters. But then Fillmore, Overisel, and Zeeland Townships refused to pay taxes assessed for harbor improvements, and Holland Township unsuccessfully filed a lawsuit to compel them in 1862.[129]

In 1870, after twenty years of the colonists fighting the lake, the Army Corps of Engineers took over the management of harbors nationwide, including Holland. Already in the 1850s, the estimated value of exports and imports to Chicago and other lake ports totaled $1.2 million ($42 million today). The harbor increased Holland's trade fourfold, and the city's population soon doubled. Holland became a major lake port for all kinds of forest and farm products. The Army Corps placed red and green lights at the pier heads in 1870 and in 1872 erected a wooden lighthouse on stilts, with an oil lamp beacon, magnified by a mirror, to guide ships into safe harbor. In 1874 the Corps added a raised catwalk to enable the lighthouse keeper to reach his station when waves crashed over the pier. The persistent dominee lived to see his hopes for the harbor fulfilled, but he could hardly imagine a future in which millions of tons of oil, slag, scrap metal, and other products would transit the harbor every year.[130]

---

[127] *De Hollander*, 3 Feb. (quote), 24 Feb. (quote), 24 Mar. 1858, trans. Nella Kennedy; Van Raalte to Governor Bingham, 3 Dec. 1857; Record of Harbor Committee of the Township of Holland, Van Raalte chair and clerk, 6 May 1858, HMA.

[128] Petition to Michigan Governor Bingham, *Allegan Journal*, 31 Jan., 7 Feb. 1859; *Grand Rapids Eagle*, 26 Jan. 1859; *De Hollander*, 1, 22, 29 Sept., 8 Dec. 1859; Michigan House of Representatives, Act of 5 Mar. 1858, amended Act No. 169 of 4 Feb. 1869.

[129] *De Hollander*, 12 Dec. 1860; minutes, Holland Harbor Board, 1 Aug. 1860, HMA; Bruins and Schakel, *Envisioning Hope College*, 66; Van Raalte to Giles Van de Wall, 29 June 1860, HMA.

[130] "Letter from the West," *Christian Intelligencer*, 10 Jan. 1867; *Holland City News*, 30 Mar. 1872, 7 June 1886, 7 Mar. 1902, 11 May 1922, 5 Apr., 5 July, 23 Aug. 1923. In 1867 the Harbor Commission became the Holland Harbor Board.

Agricultural promoter

Van Raalte promoted Dutch-style market days, which brought farmers to town for "exchanges and purchases of cattle, sheep, hogs, horses, etc." He also called for agricultural fairs to encourage improved farming techniques and livestock breeding that would "enlighten the whole by precept and example."[131] He often touted the well-being of farmers in the colony in the Dutch press. In 1854, when he learned that Ottho Heldring, a renowned Netherlands social reformer, was planning a colony near Cape Town, Van Raalte published a letter in a major Utrecht newspaper that asserted that his colony ranked above Cape Town; it was even preferable to the Afrikaans-speaking Orange Free State and Transvaal. America had more cheap farmland, and white laborers had a stronger work ethic than nonwhites—a typical stereotype of that day.[132]

Van Raalte's sanguine tone changed when adverse weather threatened the 1858 harvest. Rumors about a major crop failure in Holland, with "untold distress, and even starvation," set off a public relations nightmare for colony leaders. The "s" word spread among the Old Dutch and reached the front page of New York newspapers, including the *Christian Intelligencer*. Understandably, the news set off alarm bells. Church folks began sending old clothes and money for "our suffering brethren" to keep the "deserving poor" from dying of hunger.

These well-intentioned acts of charity did not set well in Holland. The *Intelligencer* article "did us much mischief," Van Raalte declared. He flatly denied the report. "There is no starvation here, nor is there any danger of it, I trust." The harvest was better than expected, despite early rains and a brief summer drought. The settlers are not "a miserable, thriftless set of paupers." "Wealthy Americans may look with pity on our simple mode of life, but the majority of us never enjoyed in the Netherlands such rich tables as they do here." For his American friends in Michigan, the Dutch leader published "The truth of the case" in the *Grand Rapids Eagle*, the *Detroit Advertiser*, and the *Allegan Journal*. He admitted that crops "failed partly"—this they could see with their own

---

[131] *De Hollander*, 28 Dec. 1850 (quote); Vande Water, "Holland Fairs Date Back to 1851."

[132] *Utrechtsche Provinciale en Stads-Courant*, 18 Aug., 1 Sept. 1854; *De Bazuin*, 8 Nov. 1854; *Rotterdamsche Courant*, 6 Dec. 1854 (all www.delpher.nl, accessed, June 2021).

eyes—but the colony was "covered with farms, mills, schoolhouses, and churches," and all was well.[133]

Van Raalte was "the man" in this pioneering period. From morning to night, he had his hand in everything: land dealings, building infrastructure (roads, bridges, and the harbor), establishing civil government, attending to legal and medical concerns, and directing public and Christian schools and Hope College. Newspaperman Gerrit Van Schelven, the first historian of the colony, aptly described the situation: "The People's Assembly at Holland was Van Raalte, the consistory at Holland was Van Raalte, and the Classis of Holland was Van Raalte." One might add "unofficial mayor of the village" to Van Raalte's titles. His leadership was necessary, given the circumstances, and "It was the best way," said Van Schelven. Jacob van Hinte observed wryly that "Not everyone was in favor of this theocracy, and many saw in the 'democracy' of Van Raalte actually his 'autocracy.'" Despite this negative comment, Van Hinte idolized Van Raalte, his hero. He dedicated his *Netherlanders in America* tome to Van Raalte and used Van Raalte's iconic photograph as the frontispiece.[134] Founding a colony of destitute immigrants in the forests of West Michigan had required a strong hand, and Van Raalte had provided that hand. Holland would became the premier town in Ottawa County, despite not being the county seat. And West Michigan would eventually became the national center of Dutch American life and influence.[135]

---

[133] *Christian Intelligencer*, 9, 23 Sept., 7 Oct. 1858; *Detroit Advertiser*, 23 Sept. 1858; *Grand Rapids Eagle*, 23 Sept. 1858; *New York Courier and Enquirer*, copied by *Allegan Journal*, 28 Oct. 1858; Henry D. Post to Christian Van der Veen, 19 Oct. 1858, Christian Van der Veen Papers.

[134] Van Schelven, "The Classis Holland: Social Relations and the Schism Following in 1857," *De Grondwet*, 9 Feb. 1915, trans. Seth Vander Werf, box 9, Van Schelven Papers; Van Hinte, *Netherlanders*, 241. Van Schelven obit., *Holland City News*, 4 Apr. 1927; eulogies, ibid., 14 Apr. 1927.

[135] Van Schelven, "Early Historical Data: Political," Van Schelven Papers; Den Herder, "Brief History"; Swierenga, "Dutch Imprint" and "Dutch in West Michigan."

CHAPTER 10

Dauntless Dominee: "My labor is not in vain."

Dominee Van Raalte took his marching orders from Jesus' High Priestly Prayer, that "all may be one" (John 17:21, KJV). In church struggles, he abhorred schism and sought compromise and unity. But this goal slipped from his grasp in 1850 when he led the independent Classis of Holland—an assembly of seven congregations in the Holland colony—into union with the Reformed Protestant Dutch Church, the longest Protestant ministry in North America, founded in New Amsterdam in 1628. This decision reverberated for decades and caused both immediate and long-term disharmony in immigrant settlements across the county. The peace and harmony that Van Raalte so much desired by immigrating to a free country had been lost. To some extent, conflict rode in the baggage of the immigrants. Dutch Separatists, like the English Pilgrims, to whom they are often compared, came to America for religious liberty. But that very liberty freed them to fight among themselves and prepare the way to secede again. As Van Hinte noted, they placed a "higher value on faith than on love."[1]

---

[1] Van Hinte, *Netherlanders*, 262 (quote). Versteeg, *Pelgrim-Vaders*, first linked 1846 Dutch immigrants with 1620 English Pilgrims. Dosker reinforced the comparison

The dominee's honeymoon was brief, three years at best, from 1847 to 1850. In the fifties, he had to deal with biting personal attacks in the press, rising religious unrest that came to a head in 1857, a failed milling venture, a national financial crisis in 1857, and growing political division between north and south over slavery. Withal, the settlers had to deal with the inevitable process of Americanization. Some wanted to assimilate faster than others and adopt the English language in school and church. Others wanted to keep the Dutch tongue and culture. Van Raalte, for his part, favored assimilation but not absorption.

The Overijssels-Gelders and Gronings-Drents factions in the Netherlands carried over to Michigan and resulted in a second schism in 1857 and the founding of the True Holland Reformed Church (the future CRC). The leaders of the True church hailed from the Gronings-Drents party. As Herbert Brinks explains: "Though the general lines of descent display astounding complexities, it is clear that the Christian Reformed Church . . . originated from De Cock's adherents, while the Reformed Church in America attracted Van Raalte and his disciples."[2] In time, every neighborhood and rural hamlet had both churches, often facing each other, and were divided into rival camps.

Most immigrants settled in hamlets of their heritage, where they accepted, at least tacitly, the social contract of the community. Those who prized individual liberty and freedom from peering eyes found anonymity in cities like Paterson, Cleveland, Chicago, Grand Rapids, Kalamazoo, Muskegon, Milwaukee, and St. Louis. There they could either worship in small Reformed congregations, or affiliate with a plethora of American churches, or drop out of church entirely. After the 1857 schism, those of the Reformed faith could "church shop" between the rapidly acculturating Reformed Church and the "Dutchy" True church. This winnowing process strengthened cultural bonds and made for a tight, in-group mentality. In a perverse way, the immigrants demonstrated the Reformed doctrine of human depravity.[3]

Van Raalte's flock, though winnowed, was no different. As he said:

> Worldliness and worry, ignorance, unbelief, pride are rumbling here too. A few are right with God; word and conduct are evidence of this. Missing delight in God's commandments,

---

with the term, "pilgrim fathers of 1846," in *Van Raalte*, introduction, v, 215, trans. Dekker.

[2] Brinks, "Afscheiding," 26.
[3] Taylor, *Dutchmen on the Bay*, 15-16, 120-21, 135-36, 173-74.

they feel uncomfortable here. Others are in adversity because of missteps, ignorance, carelessness, or sickness. These are suffering especially when they consider neither themselves nor God's hand as responsible, but circumstances.[4]

Denominational courtship

As noted earlier, Reformed Church leaders, notably De Witt and Wyckoff, took an early interest in the Dutch immigration. At General Synod 1847 and 1848, the Board of Domestic Missions spoke pointedly about the newcomers:

> A new body of Pilgrims has reached our shores from Holland, the land of our Fathers. . . . We will be recreant to the power of our principles, to the name we are honored to bear, and to the descent we may warrantably boost, if we fail to welcome them, to cheer them in their enterprise, and to express our love, not in word and tongue, but in deed and truth. Providence has cast the lot of the first detachment in the immediate vicinity of our Western churches [Classis of Michigan]; a second wave has arrived, and thousands more are on their way—and now we have brought within our reach an opportunity for securing the accession of a people, poor and afflicted, it is true, yet possessed of a faith precious, tried and true.[5]

The merger initiative with the Holland colony came from the East. General Synod 1848 instructed the missions board to look to the needs of the immigrants, with a "view to bring them into connection with our own Church . . . to which they are most nearly assimilated." The intent was clear, but the assumption of being nearly assimilated was ludicrous.[6] The Young Dutch could be the nucleus of the denominational initiative to plant new congregations on the frontier. Indeed, the newcomers were considered essential to "sustaining our enterprise" in the West. The new Classis of Holland in 1849 counted 922 communicants and 3,000 souls in seven congregations, whereas the older American Classis of Michigan had only 153 communicants and 805 souls in six congregations.[7]

---

[4] Van Raalte to De Moen, 11 Feb. 1849, in *Der toestand*, 13, trans. Nella Kennedy.
[5] *Acts and Proceedings*, 1847, 191-92.
[6] Ibid., 1848, 424-28 (quote, 427); Kennedy, *Commentary*, 27 Sept. 1848, 1:43-44.
[7] Wyckoff, "Official Report" (to Board of Domestic Missions), in Lucas, *Dutch Immigrant Memoirs*, esp. 1:451, 453; *Acts and Proceedings*, Classis of Michigan, June

General Synod 1849 invited the Classis of Holland to their gathering, but no clerics could be spared, and distances were great and finances few. There was also the language barrier—all church assemblies were conducted in English. The missions board then commissioned Wyckoff to carry synod's merger invitation to Holland. On arrival, Wyckoff marveled at the determination of the "very industrious and frugal" immigrants "to tame the wilderness." Wyckoff was the perfect choice. He was Van Raalte's friend and had earned deep gratitude for helping the desperate immigrants when they first arrived.[8]

Union of 1850

In the first years, Van Raalte thanked God for peace and harmony among the colonists. Common struggles to survive brought unity. In 1849 he wrote Carel de Moen in the Netherlands:

> God is good and merciful! I love my field of labor, a distinct pleasure, preaching is an unspeakable delight. I am deeply concerned about the rising generation. I love the people. I am convinced that my labor is not in vain. I witness the conversion of those who do not know God, yes, my position is enviable! But not my sinful heart, my temper, and moods![9]

The harmony that Van Raalte craved ended in 1850 when he and his fellow clerics made a crucial decision that had lasting repercussions. They merged the independent Classis of Holland with the RPDC, headquartered in New York City, which until the American Revolution was an arm of what would become in 1816 the Hervormde Kerk. The colonists welcomed Wyckoff "literally with a shout of joy," he reported to his board. "With the exception of a few individual brethren, they mourned that the Dutch Church counted them strangers and had no word of encouragement, no hand of help for them. The reaction, therefore, was electrical." Wyckoff continued: They feel "one with those churches that possess the expression of the same faith, the same liturgy

---

1850, 2:66 (no report in 1849); Janssen, "Perfect Agreement?" 54-58. Classis of Holland in 1849 comprised seven churches with 625 families—Holland 225, Zeeland 175, Vriesland 6, Graafschap 50, Drenthe 45, Overisel 35, and Groningen 30. Classis of Michigan in 1849 comprised six churches with 185 families—Mason (ca. 28), Centreville 45, Constantine 40, Ridgeway 30, Medina 20, and Mottville 12.

[8] Wyckoff, "Official Report," 1:454-55; Kennedy, *Commentary*, Apr. 1850, 1:99-100.
[9] Van Raalte to De Moen, 11 Feb. 1849, in *De toestand*, 6, trans. Nella Kennedy.

and church order, and defend God's truth against untruth."¹⁰ Wyckoff was too glib, and he soon had to backtrack.

Wyckoff carried a donation from the missions board of $300 ($11,900 today). Van Raalte declared the gift "most acceptable to us, and a source of thanksgiving to God." He and his colleagues believed that the RPDC was a true Reformed body and that church unity was proper and good. The basis for the former belief was slim since few settlers had firsthand knowledge of the church in the East, and none, including Van Raalte, had attended a regional or national synod. The language barrier was huge. But money talked; the East was rich, the West poor. Wyckoff buttressed his backing in a material way; his congregation provided a $1,000 loan ($39,500 today) to fund a pier at Holland harbor.

Riding Dr. Charles Shenick's horse (the only horse in the colony), without a saddle, Wyckoff for five days visited the six other villages of the Holland colony. On June 4, 1849, he met with church leaders and a smattering of consistory members who could assemble on short notice. But before Wyckoff could complete the rounds, Van Raalte hastily called a special classis meeting, and Wyckoff presented the union plan to the four ministers in the colony—Van Raalte, Van der Meulen, Ypma, and Bolks—and several dozen elders. This was not quite the "large company" that Wyckoff reported. Given the initial reluctance of some to see him, he was probably not surprised to find the brethren "a little afraid of entering into ecclesiastical connection with us. . . . They have so felt to the quick the galling chain of ecclesiastical domination and have seen with sorrow how . . . [this] leads to the oppression of tender consciences . . . that they hardly knew what to say." Their desire was that "Each church and consistory should direct and manage its own concerns, and . . . that an appellate jurisdiction of superior judicatories is not so." Fraternal relations, yes; synods, no, especially synods of the church in the Netherlands that had recently persecuted them.¹¹

Seeing the resistance, Wyckoff changed tactics. "Ecclesiastical tyranny . . . was the farthest from our thoughts," he declared. Then he made a fateful promise—that should any congregations be unhappy with union, they "would be perfectly free, at any time . . . to bid us a fraternal adieu and be by themselves again." Amazingly, after hearing

---

10   For this and following paragraphs, see Wyckoff, "Official Report," 1:450. Kennedy, *Commentary*, Apr. 1850, 1:99, describes this report as "extensive, perceptive, and enthusiastic."
11   Wyckoff, "Official Report," 1:454-55, for this paragraph and the next.

these honest views opposing union, Wyckoff reported to his superiors the exact opposite. "As a result, they agreed with these explanations to join our Synod." Perhaps a few minds were changed after Wyckoff offered another $200 from the domestic missions board to fund the salary of a missionary pastor for vacant churches in classis. The $500 was worth $19,750 in today's money.

Over the next five weeks, only three of seven consistories brought the 922 communicant members into the discussion. Leaders in the other four churches may have consulted members informally, but there is no record of congregational meetings. In any case, on July 10, Van Raalte convened a meeting in his home with the four clerics and twenty elders from the three churches, and this rump assembly approved a report in Van Raalte's hand of the June 4 meeting, which committed classis "to live in communion" with the RPDC. The signatories included twelve elders from Zeeland, six from Vriesland, and two from Overisel. It is puzzling that *no* elders from the Holland, Drenthe, Graafschap, and Groningen churches signed the document. As it stands, the critical document does not appear to speak for the colony as a whole.[12]

Why Van Raalte's own elders or deacons did not attend is incomprehensible. Perhaps they assumed that their dominee would carry the day, and they could attend to more pressing duties. The absence of the Drenthe, Graafschap, and Groningen consistories is easier to explain. They were from the Gronings-Drents party and did not share the centrist, ecumenical views of the Overijssels-Gelders party. The Grand Rapids (Second) Church was just forming in 1849 under elders Frans Van Driele and Geert (Gerrit) Dalman and could not participate in the decision.

Wyckoff's rhetoric and concrete offers at the parsonage won over the Zeelanders and the Frisians. There was no need for further discussion. According to Tede Ulberg, an eyewitness who caught the spirit of the day. "We *must* accept," they said, "and it is not necessary to ask the congregations about this matter." Van Raalte, however, urged caution: "Brethren this is wrong, I warn you. If this thing later appears wrong, then it will be our fault. Let us place it before the congregations for decision. Should it be wrong, then the congregations will

---

[12] Bruins and Swierenga, *Family Quarrels*, 50-56, 63-64; "Dorpslands Dagboek," 16 Dec. 1849. Wyckoff, "Official Report," records that "quite a large company" of church members were present, but only church officers had signed the document, 453.

have to share part of the guilt."[13] The leaders heeded this warning and consulted with the individual consistories. The Vriesland consistory met and voted to approve the union proposal, but a majority of the Graafschap consistory voted against it. The early minutes of the Zeeland, Overisel, Groningen, and Holland churches are lost, but it is likely that these consistories were consulted. Further evidence of official malfeasance is the fact that the topic of union never came up in the October 1849 meeting of the Classis of Holland, the first following Wyckoff's visit.[14]

It appears that the clerics drove the decision and not the elders or parishioners, except for the Zeeland and Vriesland consistories. "Most immigrants had little sympathy with that American church, or 'the East' as it was usually called," according to Grootenhuis. Already in 1840, General Synod was considering dropping "Dutch" from the name of the Reformed Church, a move Van Raalte opposed for disowning history, provided one was not a hypernationalist. (He changed his mind thirteen years later.) No wonder that the union of 1850 became the source of trouble that Van Raalte had feared. Some believed that "If it had been a matter of congregational or consistorial concern, there would have been more time and discussion about it." Van Raalte had clearly misjudged the situation. Months after the fact, he insisted in a private letter to his brother-in-law in the Netherlands that all the "congregations are glad with the ecclesiastical union with the Old Dutch Church."[15]

Most amazing, the Classis of Holland never voted on a motion to merge. Hence, the "legality" of the decision has been debated. That the procedure did not go "by the book" is understandable, given the extenuating circumstances. Earl Wm. Kennedy notes that the minutes "do not prepare the reader for the apparently precipitous move to affiliate with the RPDC, . . . [but] much had been going on 'behind

---

[13] The Van Raalte quote is from Ulberg, "Notes," in Lucas, *Dutch Immigrant Memoirs*, 1:287 (italics added).

[14] Kennedy, *Commentary*, 31 Oct. 1849, 1:103-17; Beets, *De Chr. Geref. Kerk*, 70-71, HHA; Bruins and Swierenga, *Family Quarrels*, 64-65; Van Eyck, *Union of 1850*, 32-33.

[15] Van Raalte to De Moen, 23 May 1851, trans. Nella Kennedy; "Proposed Name Change of the Reformed Dutch Church," *De Hollander*, 23 Mar. 1854; Van Raalte, "Name change of Dutch Reformed Church," *De Hollander*, 8 June 1854, trans. Nella Kennedy; J. A. De Peyster, "A Friendly Request," *De Grondwet*, 18 Mar. 1884, trans. Buursma; Bernardus Grootenhuis, "Our History," 24 Mar. 1888, published in serial form in *De Hope*, 1889, English typescript 7-8, trans. Moerdyke, HMA. On the name change, see De Jong, "Dropping the Word Dutch," 158-70.

the scenes.'" From mid-1849 to mid-1850, Kennedy continues, the relationship "could be likened to a courtship or perhaps even a trial marriage, in which couples live together before becoming legally wed." Union made sense to the clerics. The Classis of Holland was an orphan body, ecclesiastically, and poor in resources. Moreover, the immigrants and the Eastern church shared the Reformed Confessions and had cultural ties, albeit very distant.

At the April 1850 classis meeting, the brothers delegated Van Raalte to attend the Particular Synod of Albany meeting at Schenectady and "facilitate the desired union." He carried a statement from his pen, endorsed by classis:

> In consideration of the precious and blessed unity of the church of God, and the clearly declared will of our Saviour that they all should be one, as well as the need which the particular parts of the whole have of one another—especially we, who feel our weakness and insignificance—our hearts thirst for fellowship with the beloved Zion of God. Since the day that we stepped ashore in this new world, our hearts have been strengthened and encouraged by meeting the people of God [in the East].... It was gratifying to us to experience from the other side no narrow exclusiveness but open, hearty, brotherly love. This awakens in us a definite desire to make manifest our fellowship and to ask for the hand of brotherly fellowship in return. For these reasons, we have resolved to send as our representative to your church assembly ...A. C. Van Raalte,... instructing him in our name to ask for all necessary information which may facilitate the desired union.[16]

With train tickets supplied by synod, Van Raalte carried the letter to Schenectady in early May 1850. He insisted on joining as a special Dutch-language classis and not under the American Classis of Michigan. Wyckoff had conceded this point, and synod concurred, but not without a vigorous debate, given the rump nature of the immigrant classis. The resolution reads: "Under the peculiar circumstances of the case, this Synod gives its sanction to the action of said Classis of Holland, relating to the mode of its organization, and refer to the General Synod the matter of its reception." General Synod, meeting in

---

[16] Kennedy, *Commentary*, Apr. 1850, 1:95-98. Because of the sudden death of clerk Johannes A. Terhorst before he could turn his rough minutes into the official minutes, Van Raalte composed "fragment minutes" to the best of his recollection, including the lengthy quote.

June 1850 at Poughkeepsie, rubber stamped the decision and resolved "that the Classis of Holland be received under the care of General Synod, and that it be connected with the Particular Synod of Albany."[17]

With these actions, the Classis of Holland and its by-then nine congregations was accepted into the RPDC. Unfortunately, the vote totals are not recorded. General Synod then passed a second resolution that placed the Classis of Holland under the "particular attention" of the domestic missions board. Van Raalte's brief letter expressed the "feelings cherished by the Classis of Holland towards the General Synod." Synod replied that it was "highly gratified" by the dominee's letter and reciprocated "the kind feelings expressed." The marriage was consummated with warm feelings by all. Van Raalte understood that synod's promises would pay rich dividends for his schools, church, and settlement in general.[18]

A year after the Union of 1850, Van Raalte defended his decision in a letter to Helenius de Cock, then serving the church in 's-Hertogenbosch, Noord-Brabant, who had in-hand a call from the local Graafschap congregation. Van Raalte urgently appealed for De Cock to accept the call to this orthodox congregation and made certain to remind him of Van Raalte's strong personal ties with his late father, Hendrik, and with the parents of his wife, Anna van Andel.[19]

> Our principles are deliberately Reformed [Gereformeerd], not from habit or by compulsion from the outside, but from complete and heartfelt conviction. I feel a determined and strong call to do everything possible to keep the Hollanders to their standards of faith. I heartily detest vagueness, ignorance, indifference and neglect of them, and consider it one of my dear callings to promote and help to maintain firmness and order of the Reformed Church. If I were not to do so, I would sin before God, and violate the most sensitive concerns of this people. . . .

[17] *Acts and Proceedings*, convened at Poughkeepsie, June 1850, 68-69.
[18] *Minutes of the Particular Synod of Albany*, convened at Schenectady, 1 May 1850, 22-23; *Acts and Proceedings*, 1850, 68-69; 1871, 131, 149; Kennedy, *Commentary*, Apr. 1850, 1:96-101. The minutes of the crucial April 1850 classis meeting were lost in clerk Johannes A. Terhorst's house fire and death. Van Raalte later wrote brief "Fragments" based on memory, which make no mention of a formal union vote, so one can assume none took place.
[19] Van Raalte to Helenius de Cock, 26 Sept. 1851, AGK. For the debate at Albany and the "pragmatic" American decision, see Kennedy, *Commentary*, 30 Oct. 1850, 1:111, Sept. 1851, original in Archief de Cock, Gemeentearchief Kampen; Wesseling, *Afscheiding van 1834, Classis Zwolle*, 25.

Rev. Helenius de Cock (1824-1894), Van Raalte correspondent, son of Hendrik de Cock

We are united with the Reformed Church of this country, which has remained firm in its truth, and loves us for our attachment to Reformed doctrine. We act as a distinct classis for linguistic reasons and have communicated through our representatives. The pastors and congregations are deliberately and heartily of one mind in this. There is also a warm and agreeable relationship between pastors . . . who have brotherly meetings four times a year, usually in my house as the most central point.

In the last sentence, Van Raalte was referring to the informal gathering of pastors in the classis, known in Reformed circles as *inter nos* (literally, between us), which allowed the men and their wives to let their hair down. To Van Raalte's chagrin, De Cock declined the call, on the counter negative advice of Van Raalte's brother-in-law, Simon van Velzen, a member of the Gronings-Drents party.[20]

Pros and cons of union

The case can be made that patience might have forestalled yet another church schism in America. If Van Raalte and his clerical colleagues had waited at least a decade before joining the RPDC, they might have maintained unity. In time, immigrant leaders would have learned rudimentary English and gained more familiarity with their Old Dutch cousins. By the early 1860s, the young men in the colony were already being trained for ministry at New Brunswick Seminary and returning with an American flavor to pastor immigrant churches.

---

[20] Kennedy, *Commentary*, 14 Oct. 1851, 1:174-75.

Freedom of religion in America and its pervasive Judeo-Christian culture were so different from the Netherlands, with its privileged public church, autocratic royal house, and stratified society, that new ways of thinking would soon emerge. Immigrants who returned to the Old Country after a few decades found that they could not go home again. They had changed, and so had the Netherlands. Time may heal all wounds, but three years was simply not enough for the persecuted Separatists to make the momentous decision of church union. Informal ties, yes; formal merger, not so fast.

Within a year of the Union of 1850, questions were raised. That the process was rushed seems clear in retrospect, at least from the settlers' side. What motivated the two parties? The RPDC was eager to plant congregations on the frontier, and the nine congregations with three thousand souls was a big boost. John Garretson's goal, as corresponding secretary of the Board of Domestic Missions in the 1850s, was to plant "a line of churches between East and West." In 1851 he put flesh on the bones of union. He offered to send a teacher to instruct children in the English language and prepare boys in Latin and Greek to be future ministers. This was the right button to push: higher education in the West was Van Raalte's passion. The advantages of union were obvious to the Dutch dominee—linkage with a denomination that held the same confessions—the Three Forms of Unity—and whose affluent members stood ready to help the "needy and stressed" immigrants.[21]

As the clerk who wrote the minutes of classical meetings for many years, Van Raalte used his "second 'pulpit,'" as Earl Wm. Kennedy delicately phrased it, to stress the theological orthodoxy of the RPDC but ignore the real concerns expressed at classis meetings. As wags are wont to say, he "gilded the lily" by attesting to that denomination's "strong attachment" to the Reformed Confessions. The union of 1850, he gushed, was a "source of joy and gratitude," and "It is our duty to take a tender and hearty attitude towards it."[22]

But how well did Van Raalte know the American denomination, which was well integrated into mainstream American Protestantism—"evangelical, ecumenical-minded, and increasingly less interested in doctrinal questions?" Its congregations worshiped in the English language; promulgated revivalist beliefs and practices of the Second

---

[21] Ibid., 30 Apr. 1851, 1:141-44 (quote, 141); Van Koevering, *Legends of the Dutch*, 506-20 (quote 514).
[22] Kennedy, *Commentary*, 30 Apr. 1851, 1:126 (quote), 1:145-46 (pulpit quotes).

Great Awakening; sang "man-made" hymns, tainted with Arminianism; neglected the Heidelberg Catechism (Van Raalte was also so charged), family visitation, and church discipline; and had evangelical Sunday schools. Although a few New Yorkers still spoke the mother tongue, it stung that they had little appreciation for the persecution the Young Dutch had suffered for the faith.[23]

But the Old Dutch did reveal vestiges of ethnic pride in a brief nostalgic revival in the early nineteenth century. Dutch speakers, albeit a rarity, took pride in giving speeches in the mother tongue. And residents of Albany and Schenectady, the heart of Dutch New York, memorialized the birth of the Dutch Republic in 1588.[24] Nevertheless, the Knickerbocker Hollanders in theology and practice were more American than Dutch. Indeed, in 1867, after three decades of debate, they dropped *Dutch* from their denominational name, with the yea vote of Van Raalte, a delegate from the Classis of Holland. Separatists in West Michigan, on the other hand, wished to remain tied to the Dutch mother church.[25]

Fissures in the fellowship

Given the spirit of disquiet in the Holland colony over linking with the Old Dutch Church, the decision was fraught with difficulty. Even before synod finalized the union, a secession movement had begun in the outlying congregations that disturbed Van Raalte no end. "The disputes of God's children lead to darkness and ruin.... I loathe that fighting and suppressed anger, that making of factions, that sectarian spirit."[26]

Old Groningen church and Rev. Jacob R. Schepers

The hamlet of Old Groningen, founded by Jan Rabbers in 1848, three miles southwest of Zeeland, was stymied in organizing a church by the Classis of Holland. Rabbers, an elder in the Sleen congregation in

---

[23] The theological critique is in Fabend, *Zion on the Hudson*, 16, 38-39, 214-16 (quote), 224-27; Janssen, "Perfect Agreement?" 49-55, for Americanization; and Bruins and Swierenga, *Family Quarrels*, 47-52, 58-60, 63-67, for detailed complaints.

[24] Fabend, "The Synod of Dort," 273-300. In an email to the author, dated 21 Dec. 2020, Michael Douma notes examples of Dutch nostalgia in the *Buffalo Gazette*, 8 Mar. 1814, and speeches in Dutch by Arent A. Vedder, president of the St. Nicholas Society (Schenectady Cabinet report of 23 Mar. 1823).

[25] *Acts and Proceedings*, 1868, 458; De Jong, "Dropping the Word Dutch," 169.

[26] Van Raalte to De Moen, 23 May 1851; Bruins and Swierenga, *Family Quarrels*, 67-82.

the province of Drenthe, shared Van Raalte's energetic and enterprising nature and cast his lot with him. His group of fifteen families left a month after Van Raalte's party did, wintered in New York City, and arrived in Holland on March 10, 1847. Rabbers located his hamlet on a promontory above the head of navigation on the Black River (at present-day 106th Ave. and Perry St.). He platted a village, laid out a cemetery, erected a schoolhouse, built a bridge over the Black River, and installed a water-driven sawmill on the river.

Rabbers, initially an elder in the Zeeland church, wanted a church for his followers, who spoke a dialect akin to Gronings, which was quite different from the Zeeuws dialect. Van der Meulen's Zeeland consistory in 1850 allowed these settlers to call Jacob R. Schepers as a lay preacher, or exhorter. A Drenthe native, Schepers had studied for the ministry under Wolter A. Kok, a disciple of De Cock.[27] Van Raalte as a matter of conscience stood against "lightly organizing small churches . . . no matter what the decision of the Classical Assembly might be." Classis in 1851 denied the Groningen request on the ground that it was too small and the children could easily walk for catechism to the Holland, Zeeland, or Drenthe churches up to six miles distant. "His will is not God's will," Van Raalte declared in spurning Rabbers' request. But classis was not consistent in its nonproliferation policy.[28]

In 1852 classis permitted the equally small North Holland church to split off from the Zeeland church on the ground of *distance*. This congregation had no pastor until 1856 and was served by classical appointment. The distance from Zeeland to North Holland was 6.4 miles, and from Zeeland to Drenthe, 6.2 miles. Families and catechumens could presumably walk to one but not the other. The disparate decisions likely turned on the pastor involved. North Holland was "regular," Groningen was "irregular," and its lay preacher, Schepers, opposed the union of 1850. Van Raalte's view prevailed, and the denial of a church doomed the Old Groningen settlement—no church, no town. In 1857 its residents relocated a mile north to New Groningen.[29]

---

[27] Kennedy, *Commentary*, 25 Apr. 1849, 1:52-53 (Schepers); 30 Apr. 1851, 1:123-25 (Rabbers).
[28] Kennedy, *Commentary*, 30 Apr. 1851, 1:138-41.
[29] Swierenga, *Holland, Michigan*, 1:70, 80, 607, 762, 769.

South Holland and Harm Jan Smit and Rev. Jacob R. Schepers

A request to classis from the South Holland church set off secession. South Holland was a Dutch-speaking faction from the provinces of Drenthe and Overijssel that in 1848 broke away from the German-language Graafschap church. Led by Harm Jan Smit, a wealthy landowner and Graafschap elder, the dissidents erected a log church in the hamlet of South Holland about three miles northeast of Graafschap. (The site today is the northeast corner of present-day Michigan Avenue and Thirty-Second Street.) Classis reluctantly allowed Rev. Koenraad S. Van der Schuur, a lay Separatist pastor, from the province of Drenthe, to serve the congregation, although that body had not officially recognized him. When Van der Schuur in 1851 took a call to Oostburg, Wisconsin, Van Raalte, who disfavored the schismatic South Holland congregation, breathed a sigh of relief. But his hopes were dashed when the local congregation called the obstreperous Jacob Schepers.[30]

Classis, led by Van Raalte, reluctantly granted Schepers written permission "to exhort" and exercise his gifts for ministry in the South Holland congregation, but he would not submit to an ordination examination by the Classis of Holland. The South Holland elders asked classis for permission simply to install him. But classis summarily dismissed this unorthodox request; the church order gave classis alone the right to examine and admit ministers of the Word. That the South Holland church was born in schism also set the teeth of the clerics on edge; they demanded that members return to the Graafschap church. Their refusal infuriated Van Raalte.

At being rebuffed by classis, Schepers in 1852 turned to the Michigan Presbytery of the Associate Reformed Church, a conservative, psalm-singing, Scots-Irish Calvinist body, where his brother was ministering at Gun Plains. This body readily ordained Schepers, and his small congregation affiliated with the Scotse Kerk, as it was popularly known. Van Raalte, normally quite tolerant, condemned the sectarian spirit of the Presbytery. The South Holland church membership topped out at fourteen families in 1858 and declined to five families by 1865. By then, Schepers had joined the "twice separatists," the Christian Reformed Church.[31]

---

[30] Minutes, Classis of Holland, 18 Feb., 28-29 Apr. 1852, trans. Buursma, JAH; Kennedy, *Commentary*, 14 Oct. 1851, 1:174-75.

[31] Kennedy, *Commentary*, 15 Oct. 1851, 1:224-29; 29 Apr. 1852, 1:258-64, 281 (quote); Harms, "Other Reformed"; Harms, "Fissures in the Fellowship"; Harms, "South Holland."

Drenthe and Rev. Roelof Smit

The Drenthe congregation was the second to secede, in 1853, after the Classis of Holland deposed its pastor, Rev. Roelof Smit of Rouveen, Overijssel, who had also trained under Wolter Kok and served two congregations in Friesland. The Michigan hamlet of Drenthe and its congregation had a history of factiousness and strife in the Old Country that had entangled Van Raalte. The Drenthe consistory in 1848 had deposed elder Jan Hulst of Staphorst for "his stubborn and clannish spirit." Smit accepted the Drenthe call in 1851 and aligned himself with the Hulst faction. Both strongly opposed the union of 1850. Van Raalte questioned Smit's credentials and was predisposed against him.[32]

One issue that Smit and Hulst harped on was celebrating the festival days—Christmas, Easter, and Pentecost—as mandated by the Dort church order, as well as the day after, the so-called "second feast days." The Classis of Holland, however, made weekday worship optional, on the ground that it was impractical to force busy farmers to assemble on work days. Smit even celebrated the Lord's Supper on such days, which did not set well with those members who objected and thus missed out on the sacrament.[33]

A real feast day, Thanksgiving Day, became an issue in 1849, when the Classis of Holland, at the request of Van Raalte and Ypma, unanimously approved celebrating the American Thanksgiving Day on the last Thursday in November. In this, the Dutch were simply following the practice of their Michigan neighbors who had adopted the holiday years before President Abraham Lincoln made it a national holiday in 1863. The Log Church was full that morning, but family dinners were of "ordinary fare." Thanksgiving Day and the Fourth of July helped bind the Dutch to their new country. Some years later, Reformed churches held worship services on Thanksgiving after presidents called for citizens to assemble and give thanks to God for His blessings.[34]

In April 1853, five Drenthe church members brought a complaint to classis that their minister, Roelof Smit, "promotes factions, acts arbitrarily [and] . . . tries to make the church secede, under pretext that we were sold to the Old Dutch Church by Van Raalte for a good purse of

---

[32] Kennedy, *Commentary*, 31 Oct. 1849, 1: 91-92 (Hulst); 14 Oct. 1851, 1:175-76; 25 May 1853, 350-51 (Smit); Prakke, *Drenthe in Michigan*, 55-58.
[33] Kennedy, *Commentary*, 27 Apr. 1853, 1:332-33.
[34] Ibid., 31 Oct. 1849, 1:89.

money." This sparked the "longest and best-documented disciplinary case" at classis till then. Smit's supporters turned out in force. Classis ended up rebuking Smit for his "carnal and worldly manner" and demanded that he confess his sin. He, in turn, condemned classis for its "papist lust for lordship" and refused to confess, lest his congregation say: "See, he is already swallowing another of Van Raalte's pills." Within days, Smit advocated secession for his followers in a raucous public meeting attended by elders from every church in classis. Van Raalte attended uninvited, to catcalls of "baassie" (little boss) and "profiteur."[35]

A month later, classis reassembled and unanimously deposed Smit from the ministry, "on the grounds of incompetence, insincerity, arbitrariness, partisanship, abuse of discipline, lording it over the heritage of the Lord, vilification of church discipline, and schism." Van Raalte was the clerk who wrote the minutes of this last classical disposition of an ordained minister in his lifetime.[36] In May 1853, Smit and two-thirds of his Drenthe church seceded, and like Schepers at South Holland, they joined the Associate Reformed Church. "Hereby we certify and declare that we discontinue fellowship with you because we can no longer be in union with you," the majority party declared by letter to classis. "Our church is pure and in agreement with the Separatists among you," a member wrote family in the Netherlands. A modern churchman called Smit "an impossibly arbitrary and self-centered character." Yet Smit led a very faithful congregation at Drenthe for thirty-three years, until his death in 1886, when the body joined the Christian Reformed Church on his recommendation.[37] Smit had an alter ego in Van Raalte's home church, farmer Coenraad (Conrad) Hoffman, who for more than year bandied about Smit's complaint that Van Raalte "had brought the congregation into an impure church for money." He repented after the elders "earnestly admonished" him.[38]

---

[35] Ibid., 27 Apr. 1853, 1:328-37; 25 May 1853, 1:348-350. Smit's octogenarian grandson, John J. Brouwer, a Holland dentist, in the 1970s defended his grandfather's actions in the May 15, 1853, meeting, in which he "butted heads with Van Raalte" on a discipline issue involving Seine Bolks (John J. Brouwer Papers, HMA).

[36] Kennedy, *Commentary*, 25 May 1853, 1:332; 25 May 1853, 1:340-56 (quotes 350, 356).

[37] David McNeish, Constantine, MI, to Garretson, 11 Dec. 1853, BDM; Kromminga, "What Happened in 1857," 115; Adrian Keizer, "Drenthe's History to the Present," in Lucas, *Dutch Immigrant Memoirs*, 1:263.

[38] Minutes, First Holland, 22 Aug. 1853; Hendrik Lanning to nephew Hendrikus Lanning, 11 Sept. 1860, HMA.

Vriesland and Gysbert Haan, the "father" of the 1857 secession

Van Raalte's greatest nemesis was Gysbert Haan, a highly opinionated elder in the Vriesland church and after 1853 in the Grand Rapids church. After worshiping for a time in RPDC congregations in Albany and Rochester, Haan moved in 1850 to West Michigan, where he brought reports of purported irregularities in Classis Holland. He charged that ministers and elders held membership in "evil" secret societies (Masonic lodges) and that churches practiced open (i.e., unregulated) communion, used choirs in worship services, sang evangelical hymns rather than Davidic psalms, and neglected catechism preaching. In short, they were Americanized.[39] Freemasonry was an oath-bound, deistic, works-based society, founded in England in 1717, with flamboyant initiation and funeral rites. Jesus himself had condemned such groups: "No man can serve two masters." But in America, the quasi-religious society was more benign, and American Protestant churches found it quite acceptable, even among clerics.[40]

Freemasonry first came up at classis in 1853 when Jannes Vande Luyster Jr., a member of Van Raalte's congregation, sought advice from classis, "whether or not it was lawful for a member of the church to be a Freemason." Haan, who was present, reported the dialogue. President Van der Meulen asked: "'What is your purpose in bringing this matter to Classis?' 'None other,' he replied, 'than to hear the opinion of the brethren.' 'No,' was the response, 'you want to throw a bomb into the Dutch Reformed Church.'" At this, Haan took the floor and said: "Brethren, this evil, Freemasonry, is so prevalent in America that even many ministers are members of this order." He added: this "makes it desirable, in my opinion, to exist here as a separate body, but connected with the Separatist church in the Netherlands, and to abandon the tie with the church in the East. What need do we have of it?" Haan may have known that Wyckoff in 1851 had conducted a funeral at which twenty-four Freemasons in full regalia were active participants. Classis, Haan continued, admitted strangers to the Lord's Supper who are "unknown to the minister or consistory," and even those "known

---

[39] Kennedy, *Commentary*, 25 Apr. 1849, 14 Oct. 1851, 1:165-71 (Haan biography); 1:69 (quote), 28 Apr. 1852, 241-42, 30 Oct. 1850, 107 (lodge), 14 Oct. 1851, 165-58 (Haan); Gysbert Haan, *Stem van een Belasterde*, summarized by De Jager, "History of Our Church." For apologia articles by Christian Reformed clerics on behalf of Haan in *Reformed Journal*, see William Van den Bosch, Nov. 1962; and George Stob, Dec. 1956 and Mar. 1964.

[40] Boonstra, *Dutch Equation*; Stevenson, *Origins of Freemasonry*.

to be wicked," if they brought confession on their lips. Haan's polemics "fed the fires of discontent."[41]

The pastors objected to Haan's polemic, including Van Raalte, who stood rock solid against Freemasonry at this time. "All look upon it as works of darkness," classis declared, and the brothers judged it unlawful for a church member to belong. This first official statement of the Classis of Holland expressed traditional European and Dutch attitudes against Freemasonry, but the issue would not die and eventually led to a major schism in the 1880s.[42]

In 1853 Haan protested to classis on a second major issue, the popular evangelical book of English theologian Richard Baxter, *Call to the Unconverted*, which Haan claimed contained Arminian sentiments of universal grace. Baxter's book stood next to John Bunyan's *Pilgrim's Progress* as one of the most popular books. Van Raalte and Van der Meulen, Haan declared, recommended Baxter's book to their colleagues. This prompted Van Raalte's elder Abraham Krabshuis, Jannes Van de Luyster Jr., and nine like-minded men to publish a broadside against Baxter's book in *De Hollander*. The explosive article charged Van Raalte with being "unreformed," by denying the doctrine of election.[43] Baxter's book inevitably reached the agenda of the Classis of Holland, but rather than condemn it, the clerics praised it in an off-handed way. The minutes state: "There are a few expressions in the little work of Baxter that they themselves do not dare to defend or to employ." No heresy there. Haan, Krabshuis, and their cohorts were dismissed out of hand.[44]

---

[41] Kennedy, *Commentary*, 26 Sept. 1853, 1:383 (quote); Haan, *Stem van een Belasterde*, 5; and Haan, "The Story as Told by Gysbert Haan Himself," in *One Hundredth Anniversary, 1857-1957*, 7-8 (quote). Apologists for the Reformed Church are Van Eyck, *Landmarks*, and Dosker, *Van Raalte*, 240-58, typescript 102-10, trans. Dekker; minutes, Graafschap CRC, Feb. 1857.

[42] Kennedy, *Commentary*, 28 Sept. 1853, 1:384. The controversy is best covered by Boonstra, *Dutch Equation*.

[43] *De Hollander*, 4, 12 Jan. 1854. Krabshuis's missive is no longer extant, but it was read publicly at the 11 April 1855 meeting of classis (Kennedy, *Commentary*, 70-73, 87-88). For a condemnatory account of Krabshuis, see Dosker, *Van Raalte*, 245-58, echoed in De Vries and Boonstra, *Pillar Church*, 44-45. In 1865 Krabshuis became a charter member and elder in the Holland [later, Market Street, now Central Avenue] CRC, the first body in the city proper to result from the secession of 1857 in West Michigan. By local standards, he may have been a curmudgeon, but in church life, he was clearly no "liberal," unless one takes the view of the Reformed Church minister Peter Moerdyke that the 1882 secession "swept him from his moorings" (Swierenga, *Faithful Witness*, 4-6, 8-9, 17-18).

[44] Minutes, First Holland, 26 Sept. 1853; *De Hollander*, 24 Nov. 1853. For a thorough discussion of Baxter's booklet and its critics and defenders, see Kennedy,

Krabshuis and Zeeland elder Jan H. Boes brought up a third complaint. Van Raalte had failed to preach the catechism in the second service as prescribed by the Church Order of Dort. Van Raalte as clerk defended himself in the minutes, but his logic was questionable. His catechism service was more like an adult class. He used the Socratic method of posing questions and answers interactively but did not preach on the scriptural references. This was hardly the historic practice of preaching from the biblical underpinnings of the fifty-two Lord's Days, but it did keep people on their toes.[45]

Underlying these grievances was the suspicion that the Old Dutch church was tainted with heresy, a charge classis considered baseless. Dominees Van der Meulen and Van Raalte tried and failed to dissuade Haan, who manifested a "wrongness in his attitude of heart," they concluded. In 1856, when classis moved to discipline him, Haan withdrew from the denomination.[46] Despite his strident personality, Haan had posed the critical questions: Why not cut the tie to the RPDC and remain linked to the Christian Separated Church in the Netherlands? Why not remain true to the Separatist heritage?

In 1855 Krabshuis was again elected elder at First Reformed Church in Holland, a congregation then numbering almost seven hundred souls, but within a year, he resigned both his office and his membership, as did his wife. They "would return to the old path of the Fathers" and become Separatists once again. In 1857 the family joined the Graafschap True [later Christian] Reformed Church where he served as elder. With his nemesis gone, Van Raalte held his flock together and prevented a mass exodus in 1857 and in the years following. It was 1865 before the Separatists, including Krabshuis, established the True [later Market Street, now Central Avenue] Christian Reformed Church of Holland. The True church stood on Market [Central] Avenue in full sight of Van Raalte's church, just one block away.[47]

North Holland and Rev. Jacob Duin

Jacob Duin, a lay exhorter and disciple of De Cock in the North Holland church, was a Separatist from Noordeloos in the Bible Belt of Zuid-Holland province, a region with a tradition of religious conven-

---

Commentary, 26 Sept. 1853, 1:387-91.
[45] Kennedy, Commentary, 15 Oct. 1851, 1:200; Egbert Winter in De Grondwet, 22 Aug. 1911.
[46] Kennedy, Commentary, 2 Apr. 1856, 1:580.
[47] Minutes, First Holland, 12 Apr. 1854, 5, 19 Mar., 22 Oct., 2 Nov. 1855, Jan. 1856.

ticle worship and distrust of the public church. He accused Van Raalte of preaching the false doctrines of Arminius, making him one of the "Baal-leaders and not [true] leaders, but deceivers." Arminius taught that believers who "accepted Christ" were saved, but Duin insisted that these people had never truly "received him." In 1855 Duin induced a part of the North Holland congregation to secede with him and become an independent body. His congregation flourished for a time and then dwindled to nothing. Classis assigned Van Raalte to counsel the remnant, who were a "prey to confusion."[48]

Noordeloos and Koene Van den Bosch

The arrival in the mid-1850s of fresh Separatists from the Gronings-Drents party brought reinforcements for critics who opposed the union of 1850. These latecomers had not experienced the crucial help in the early years from the Reformed church in the East. A prime example is Rev. Koene Van den Bosch of Noordeloos, province of Zuid-Holland, who had studied under Wolter Kok, the same docent who had trained Schepers and Smit. In 1856 Kok was pastor of the fifteen-hundred-member Hoogeveen congregation in Drenthe, the largest in the entire Christian Seceded denomination.[49]

When Van den Bosch stood for his candidacy examination at the 1840 Overijssel Synod at Zwolle, along with five other students, he was caught between the Gelders and Drents parties. After reading the text of Van den Bosch's sermon, Brummelkamp, speaking for Van Raalte and the other Gelders men, agreed to sign his forms. But the next day, before Van den Bosch could stand to preach, the Gelders men withdrew their promise. All five candidates then said they refused to be examined by the Gelders men, at which the Drents men said they would examine the men. "We will close the church" to stop this, said the Gelders men. At this, the candidates and Drents delegates paraded a few hours north to Rouveen (Gemeente Staphorst). There they heard the sermons and signed the forms. At the 1847 Synod, after Van Raalte had emigrated, Brummelkamp and De Moen clashed with Van den Bosch.[50]

Before emigrating in 1856, Van den Bosch had heard by letter from dissatisfied brothers in Graafschap and Holland about the 1850

---

[48] Kennedy, *Commentary*, 8 Oct. 1856, 1:656-58; Pieter G. "Van Tongeren's 'North Holland,'" in Lucas, *Dutch Immigrant Memoirs*, 2:467; Bruins and Swierenga, *Family Quarrels*, 74-77.
[49] *Jaarboekje voor de Christelijk Afgescheidene Gereformeerde Kerk*, 14.
[50] *De Saaminbinder*, 1967. https://www.digibron.nl.

Van Raalte antagonists Koene Van den Bosch, Jacob R. Schepers, Gysbert Haan, Roelof Smit (*HHA*)

Koene Vanden Bosch   Jacob Schepers

Gysbert Haan   Roelof Smit

union, and he was particularly taken with Haan's charges against the Old Dutch church. Van den Bosch brought members of his congregation, including his extended family, and they founded the Noordeloos congregation, but Van den Bosch also served the vacant Graafschap congregation, which was also looking askance at the 1850 union. At a Noordeloos congregational meeting in March 1856, Van den Bosch and his members with virtually one voice spoke against "affiliation with the church in the East." Despite his agitation, classis elected him president of its October 1856 meeting since it was his turn by rotation. When he voiced his concerns about the Eastern church, he was told: "We will not act on these matters, and in no way will you be able to get us to bring these matters to Synod."[51]

---

[51] Kennedy, *Commentary*, 2 Apr. 1856, 1:578-81; 30 Aug. 1856, 1:607-8; 8 Oct. 1856, 1:630; *Noordeloos Christian Reformed Church, Centennial, 1857-1957*, 11 (quote); Van den Dool, "Noordeloos on Two Continents," 57.

Secession of 1857

These church tempests on the periphery of the colony from 1849 to 1856 presaged the withdrawal in 1857 of the Grand Rapids, Noordeloos, Graafschap, Vriesland, and Polkton (later Coopersville) congregations from the Classis of Holland. The leaders were all trained in Hoogeveen or Groningen: Hendrik Klyn (Kleyn) of Grand Rapids, Van den Bosch of Noordeloos and Graafschap, plus elders Haan and Jan Gelok at Grand Rapids, Hendrik Dam and Tede Ulberg at Vriesland, Krabshuis and Johannes Van Anrooy at Graafschap, and Hendrik Vinkemulder and Lucas Elbers at Polkton (Coopersville), assisted by Revs. Klyn and Van den Bosch. Deacon Johannes Van Haitsma at Vriesland joined the elders in seceding. The weak Polkton flock with no shepherd remained separate barely a year, when the tiny group returned with its one elder to the RPDC. These leaders held to a stricter interpretation of the Dort church order than did Van Raalte and his fellow clerics. Despite Van Raalte's strenuous arguments and pleadings, 10 percent of the Classis of Holland withdrew, comprising 150 families with 250 communicants and 750 souls. But only a few came from Van Raalte's church, proving again the strength of his personality and the Overijssels-Gelders character of his flock. The official birth date of the True Holland Reformed Church is April 22, 1857.[52]

Rev. Van den Bosch's letter of withdrawal was bitter, whereas Rev. Klyn's letter was irenic. Van den Bosch declared: "I cannot hold all of you who have joined the Reformed Protestant Dutch Church to be the true church of Jesus Christ, and consequently, I renounce all fellowship with you. . . . I am more constrained to do this . . . on account of the abominable and church-corrupting heresy and sins rampant among you." The Graafschap church withdrawal letter, penned by Haan and signed by Van den Bosch, levied six charges: singing hymns in defiance of the church order; allowing "open" communion; neglecting catechism preaching, teaching, and family visitation; recommending the Arminian teachings of Baxter's *Call to the Unconverted*; and, most grievous, dismissing the 1834 secession as "not strictly necessary." Van den Bosch also specified a tepid adherence to the doctrines of

---

[52] Kennedy, *Commentary*, 8 Oct. 1856, 1:631-32; 8 Apr. 1857, 2:725-28; 6-7 Apr. 1859, 2:842; *De Hollander*, 15 Apr. 1857; Lemmen, "The Early Church"; Boer, *God's Deacon*. Statistics calculated by the author from emigration, census, and church records, Bruins and Swierenga, *Family Quarrels*, 89-90. For the birth of the "True" denomination, see Sheeres, *Minutes*, xxii-xxiv, 3-4.

predestination and preservation of the saints, two of the five points defended by the Synod of Dort, and two lesser complaints of failing to practice church discipline and allowing Freemasons to be confessing members. For his withdrawal, Van Raalte saw to it that Van den Bosch paid the price by having the denomination cut off his subsidized salary as missionary in the West.[53]

In his letter of withdrawal, Klyn noted his fraternal friendship for the brethren who stood together in the secession of 1834. He reminded them of the conviction that the Church, the bride of Christ, is a "garden enclosed, . . . a spring shut up, a fountain sealed" (Song of Solomon 4:12, KJV). *Enclosed*, *shut up*, and *sealed* capture the essence of the Separatist fortress mentality espoused by Groen van Prinsterer in his motto: "In isolation is our strength." Klyn's concern, as he told Van Raalte privately, was that the Old Dutch church had become "liberal." Klyn recanted within three months and was taken back into the fold of the Classis of Holland, leaving Van den Bosch as the sole minister in the new denomination.[54]

Van Raalte condemns secession

The schism both grieved and angered Van Raalte, but the dissenters gloated. "Apparently the 'Pope' in Holland [Van Raalte] has never won the field entirely," crowed Kalamazoo capitalist Paulus Den Bleyker (ch. 12). Van Raalte blamed the "perverted uncharitable spirit" of a "few leaders," who "trample under foot" the ministers of classis and the whole denomination, in "gross ignorance, and palpable slanders . . . [and] fan the fires of distrust and suspicion." Good riddance to closed-minded men, immune to reasonable arguments. In a voice dripping with sarcasm, Van Raalte wished that those "who fancy that they can bring about a holier and purer church than the Dutch Reformed [Church] of this country may serve to put us to shame and to be a blessing to us by spiritual prosperity and an active fruit-bearing Christianity."[55]

One can sympathize with Van Raalte. His gratitude to the church in the East ran deep for its many kindnesses and gifts. Many colonists shared this sentiment, but skittish Separatists feared any ties

---

[53] Bruins and Swierenga, *Family Quarrels*, 82-84; Kennedy, *Commentary*, 8 Apr. 1857, 2:704, 712-20; 26 Sept. 1853, 1:386-91 (for Baxter book), 1:384 (Freemasonry).
[54] Kennedy, *Commentary*, 8 Apr. 1857, 2:706-12 (2:710 quote), 9 Sept. 1857, 2:754-57.
[55] Ibid., 8 Apr. 1857, 2:731-43 (731, 732, 741 quotes); Brinks, "Church History via Kalamazoo," 38.

with the former American branch of the hated Netherlands public church. These ultraorthodox, conventicle folks wanted to remain free of formal ties to any American denomination, especially one at such a great distance, with a different language, and pastors trained at New Brunswick Seminary. They wanted to remain Dutch and call pastors trained in Separatist schools back home. Except for a few, such as Haan, these Separatists lacked firsthand knowledge about the church in the East and could barely either speak or read English in order to become better informed. This made them even more dependent on forceful leaders and susceptible to rumormongers.[56]

The people in the pew also understood from their experience in the Old Country that although the spirit and life of a church might be heterodox, the formal doctrines might seem orthodox. They had seen and heard enough since arriving in the United States to be uneasy about various practices in the increasingly Americanized RPDC. Three of the four documents of secession pleaded with the Classis of Holland to remain tied to the mother church in the Netherlands, rather than the American church. Van Raalte would have none of this. His resolve was firm to remain in the Reformed Church. He had helped organize the Particular Synod of Chicago in 1856, which represented the Classes of Holland and Wisconsin, and in 1857, as synod president, he attended General Synod in Ithaca, New York. He was elected president of the Particular Synod of Chicago again in 1863.[57]

President John Kromminga of Calvin Theological Seminary opined that the 1857 Separatists did not have a "schismatic intent"; they were simply "expressing the true character of the church in the colony." As elder Krabshuis said: "It was a sin for us to unite with a people we did not know" and give up the "sweet and harmonious fellowship" among the immigrants that "lingers as the taste of honey on my lips."[58] Despite this common attitude, 90 percent of the members in the Classis of Holland did not join the secession. Rather, they accepted (or acquiesced in) the new fellowship. They either trusted their dominees, valued the

---

[56] Kennedy, *Commentary*, 8 Apr. 1857, 2:738, concluded after discussing the letters of secession and Van Raalte's response that the RPDC was "not as bad" as dissidents charged, or "as good as" defenders claimed.

[57] Van Raalte to children, 25 May 1857; *Acts and Proceedings*, 1857; *125 Years of the Particular Synod of Chicago, Reformed Church in America, 1856-1981* (Chicago, 1981), 52-53.

[58] Kromminga, "What Happened in 1857," 115; Brinks, "Another Look at 1857"; Brinks, "Church History via Kalamazoo," 40.

visible unity of the church, were too busy earning their daily bread to get involved in church controversies, or they went along to get along.[59]

Impact of the 1857 secession

As a result of the secession, the Reformed and True Holland [later Christian] Reformed churches soon faced one another in nearly every city, town, and rural hamlet inhabited by Dutch Reformed believers. The True Brothers delayed Americanization for several generations by clinging to their Separatist roots. From 1857 until 1900, *every one* of its pastors was trained in the Christian Separated Church. Many had apprenticed in Separatist parsonages or, after 1854, studied in the Theological School at Kampen. Even more significantly, three-fourths of these clerics hailed from the Gronings-Drents wing of the Separatist Church.

Conversely, in immigrant Reformed churches in the years before 1900, fewer than half of the pastors were ordained in the Netherlands, and of these, three-fourths were affiliated with the Overijssels-Gelders party of Brummelkamp-Van Raalte. Until 1869 most graduated from New Brunswick Theological Seminary and thereafter from Western Theological Seminary in Holland, staffed by English-speaking faculty from the East. Whereas Christian Reformed dominees looked to their Netherlands theological roots, Reformed Church ministers, mainly sons of immigrants, looked more to American Christianity, although they did serve immigrant churches in the native tongue until the turn of the twentieth century. Van Raalte, on the other hand, preached in Dutch until he was bedridden, shortly before his death.[60]

Church planter

Van Raalte was wholly committed to his new allegiance and devoted himself to planting congregations among the scattered immigrants. He traveled throughout Michigan, Illinois, Wisconsin, and Iowa, planting churches, ordaining elders and deacons, and bringing the sacraments. In 1850, when traveling to the Particular Synod in Albany, Van Raalte went by way of Milwaukee to encourage Separatist families there who had formed the First Milwaukee Church.

---

[59] The Christian Reformed Church in North America (CRCNA) was previously the Hollandsche Gereformeerde Kerk (Holland Reformed Church) (1857-64), the Ware Hollandsche Gereformeerde Kerk (True Holland Reformed Church) (1864-80), the Hollandsche Christelijke Gereformeerde Kerk (1880-90), and the Christelijke Gereformeerde Kerk (1890-ca. 1930).

[60] Swierenga, "True Brothers," 62.

He sent the elderly Hendrik Klyn to conduct regular services there. In 1851 a donor in New York sent Van Raalte ten dollars ($395 today) to pay his way to plant churches in Sheboygan and Fond du Lac Counties in southeastern Wisconsin.[61] He also founded First Reformed Church in Chicago and First Reformed Church in High Prairie (Roseland). In Chicago, sadly, he found the "ravages wrought by error, worldliness, and quarrels to be great" among the isolated Reformed families living in "that rapidly growing city." In 1853 he returned to bring the First Chicago and High Prairie churches into the Classis of Holland.[62]

In 1852 classis sent Van Raalte and Van der Meulen as "church visitors" to struggling churches in Grand Rapids, Grand Haven, Kalamazoo, Muskegon, and Milwaukee. Their missionary hearts went out to fellow believers in need of shepherding. The brothers made several trips to Kalamazoo in 1853 to contact young people from the colony who went there for work and neglected divine worship. Van Raalte reported: "I was there for three weeks and after admonishing them, many have now been converted." Van der Meulen went next and reported that twenty had responded positively. "Good news from a far country is like cold water for a thirsty soul," Van Raalte noted, paraphrasing Proverbs 25:25. In 1856 Van Raalte installed Peter J. Oggel in the Grand Haven church and preached on the text: "Brethren, pray for us" (1 Thess. 5:25, KJV). Oggel had studied for the ministry under Van Raalte at Ommen and served the Separated church at Utrecht.[63]

Given the great need for preachers in the immigrant communities, Van Raalte was also called on to write recruitment letters when congregations called pastors from the Netherlands. He could be blunt. A letter to Rev. Dirk P. Postma in Zwolle in 1851 is typical. "The brethren of the Classis have voted to call you, respected Reverend.... We cannot supply enough ministers ourselves, the workload is weightier than any congregation in the Netherlands, and there is also more opportunity in the Netherlands to have vacancies filled than here." The letter closed with the assurance of salary support from the Reformed Church Board of Domestic Missions.[64]

---

[61] Kennedy, *Commentary*, 15 Oct. 1851, 1:186; 27 Apr. 1853, 1:313.

[62] Ibid., 30 Oct. 1850, 1:107; 30 Apr. 1851, 1:130-31; 15 Oct. 1851, 1:186; 28 Apr. 1852, 1:237; 1 Sept. 1852, 1:297. In 1865 these congregations joined the Classis of Wisconsin.

[63] Van Raalte, "Announcement," *De Bazuin*, 11 Apr. 1853, trans. Dekker; Swierenga, "Better Prospects for Work."

[64] Isaac Wyckoff to John Garretson, 18 Oct. 1851; George Young to Garretson, 20 Jan. 1852; Van Raalte to Postma, Nov. 1851, English translation, ADC.

The spiritual welfare of American families living in Holland was another mission field for Van Raalte. There were sixteen families by 1854 who needed English-language worship services. He implored the domestic missions board to send a missionary. Rev. David McNeish of the Constantine church seconded his request: "Our Holland brethren are deeply interested in this." Van Raalte happily announced in *De Hollander* that the Classis of Michigan scheduled "pulpit supply" for two Sabbaths a month at the Holland district schoolhouse throughout the summer.[65]

Sermons: "He that hath the Son hath life"

Van Raalte was a gifted preacher whose sermons and prayers could lift hearers above their mundane lives to the glories of heaven. Earthly cares fled under his charismatic preaching, and the congregation went home refreshed. "This was his gift," said Henry Dosker, Van Raalte's first biographer in the early 1890s, after interviewing several of his elderly parishioners. One commented, "He was not a lark who inspired his hearers," but an eagle "who carried them upward into skies that are high and fresh and free." Withal, his preaching gifts were "rooted in the power of the Word."[66] The dominee preached three sermons a week as well as special occasions (e. g., Prayer Day and various commemorations). In three decades of active ministry, he must have delivered at least three thousand sermons. But only three hundred are extant, half being catechism sermons. Gordon Spykman, who analyzed these sermons, suggested that Van Raalte likely destroyed his other sermons. "Most of them apparently died with him."[67]

But did they? Spykman and Eugene Heideman, who also carefully studied the sermons, found that Van Raalte repeated favorite sermons numerous times. He preached on 1 John 5:18: "He that hath the Son hath life," twenty-six times in the Netherlands and again and again in America. He preached a Christmas sermon on the birth of Jesus (Luke 2:1-7) eighteen times—ten in the Netherlands and eight in America. He chose the text: "He that seeketh findeth" (Luke 11:10, KJV) fifteen times—nine in the Netherlands and six in America. Some favorite sermons on the beloved Psalms he preached more than ten times.[68]

---

[65] David McNeish to Van Raalte, Apr. 1854; Van Raalte to Garretson, 14 June 1854, in BDM; Notice, *De Hollander*, 27 Apr., 4 May 1854.
[66] Dosker, *Van Raalte*, 1, 299.
[67] Spykman, *Pioneer Preacher*, 22.
[68] Ibid., 22-25, 37; Heideman, "Van Raalte," 264-65, 269; Spykman, "Van Raalte Sermons."

Repeating sermons was necessary during Van Raalte's early itinerating years in Overijssel, but he continued the practice in every congregation he served, recycling sermons every two or three years. Preaching through the Lord's Days of the catechism annually would tempt any cleric to turn to old files. Some sermons he spread over two Sundays. He was also out of his pulpit regularly for weeks at a time, both on church assignments and for fundraising. Hence, the three hundred sermons may be nearly his full corpus.

Van Raalte's practice was to write out detailed sermon notes, but he spoke freely, often leaving the notes in his pocket, as he was taught at Leiden. He scribbled the notes on scraps of paper in "extremely fine letters and tightly crowded lines." Scholars have wondered how he could decode his own handwriting "in the dimly lit meeting places of his day." Obviously, the main points underlined in the notes kept him on message. Spykman noted that the sermons always had two parts: exposition of the truth and application to the life of the congregation, the *toepassing* in Dutch Reformed parlance. Most Separatist ministers— Van Raalte included—emphasized exposition at the expense of application. Van Raalte's sermons shared a uniform structure with common subdivisions: history, meaning, significance, teachings, motivation, and so forth. Over the years, however, he adopted a "looser, freer, more spontaneous" construct.[69]

Surprisingly, Van Raalte seldom chose texts that applied to pressing needs of the congregation in times of persecution, poverty, disease, and death. He did not use the pulpit to help parishioners face problems or for general social concerns, except in the Civil War (ch. 13). In Spykman's words: "There was no explicit word of comfort and encouragement, no call for perseverance." Exceptions were catechism sermons on the Ten Commandments, in which he made personal applications. Old Testament sermons focused on the spiritual life of individuals in the face of adversity, rather than on God's dealings with His covenant people. Eugene Heideman noticed that Van Raalte seldom preached on Jesus' discourses in the Gospel of Matthew or on his parables and miracles in the Gospel of Luke. Nor did Van Raalte mention either the postmillennial beliefs of social progress, preached by Presbyterian and Congregational clerics, or the premillennial ideas of Seventh Day Adventists.[70]

---

[69] Spykman, *Pioneer Preacher*, 31-35.
[70] Ibid., 34-35, 38, 42; Heideman, "Van Raalte," 272-73.

Spykman characterized the sermon texts as "general truths—timeless, placeless, nameless, faceless." This allowed Van Raalte to preach the same sermon in Ommen in the 1830s and in Michigan in the 1850s, despite differences in time and place. He simply expounded the Word of God within the Reformed faith, and instructed his people concerning the will of God, the need for repentance, a life of obedience, and the assurance of salvation. For pietists anxious about their divine election, he counseled keeping their eyes on Christ and his salvation "out of pure grace" and warned against probing into the secret counsel of God. In every case, the sermon was the focal point of worship, as in all Reformed churches since the Protestant Reformation.[71]

Van Raalte once delivered an address on the art of sermon construction, titled De Oratione Sacra (on sermons). Every sermon, he said, must have three parts—unity, coherence, and simplicity—and one purpose. "A sermon must converge like the rays of a circle upon one central point." Yet it must also allow for "some slight excursion for the sake of listener appeal." Humor was unthinkable, but heresy was fair game, notably the apparent undermining of Christ's divinity by the Groninger School and its leading theologian Petrus Hofstede de Groot. The motto of this school was: "Not doctrine, but the Lord." As a student of Latin and the early Greek and Roman fathers, Van Raalte followed the common method of breaking down the text into its various elements and covering each in turn.[72]

Van Raalte's rhetorical style was a blend of the "universal logic of human reason" and Réveil pietism, built on the nature/grace dualism typical of medieval theology the Protestant Reformers condemned, with its dichotomies of body/soul, church/world, law/Gospel, and reason/faith. In a Hope College lecture in 1875, Van Raalte spoke of wisdom as the key to knowledge, which includes "true wisdom" and "worldly wisdom": one based on reason, the other on faith, with both equally necessary. He did not integrate the two, as some Calvinists did, but he was thoroughly Reformed and kept John Calvin's *Institutes of the Christian Religion* at his fingertips.[73]

Morning sermons were "free texts," followed by catechism sermons in the afternoon service. This structure gave him a "wider vision" and militated against riding hobby horses. He also preached

---

[71] Spykman, *Pioneer Preacher*, 37-38; Heideman, "Van Raalte," 276.
[72] Spykman, *Pioneer Preacher*, 65-71, 129-40.
[73] Ibid., 44-48, 53-60, 65-66; Heideman, "Van Raalte," 262-63, 270; van Dijk, *De Preektrant*, 7-8; Kamps, *1834*, 56 (quote).

Van Raalte sermon notes on I Peter 1:22-25 (*Spykman*, Pioneer Preacher)

Van Raalte's desk and chair (*Pillar Church, Holland, Michigan*)

on festival (feast) days, but even in these, said Spykman, "The down-to-earth realism which fills biblical revelation finds only a faint echo in Van Raalte's sermons."[74]

Van Raalte's free sermons greatly favored the Psalms and the New Testament, emphasizing central truths at the heart of the Gospel. He avoided "obscure passages, isolated truths, peripheral ideas, or fragmented bits of revelation." He treated the Bible as an organic whole. He taught obedience to those in authority in both church and state and stressed male headship, with wives the "weaker vessels" to be protected, supported, and loved. He taught that Christians must be stewards of creation. Henry Dosker described Van Raalte's sermons as "practical and evangelical, his tone critical, and his spirit full of meaning and fire. . . . He colored and toned, comforted and attracted, but also crushed and wounded." He was as eloquent as he was pious.[75]

---

[74] Spykman, "Van Raalte Sermons," 38 (quote); Heideman, "Van Raalte," 274.

[75] Heideman, "Van Raalte," 274-76; Van Raalte, "Sabbath School and Family," in Spykman, *Pioneer Preacher*, 118 (quote); Dosker, *Van Raalte*, 300, trans. Dekker; Egbert Winter, "Rev. Albertus Christian Van Raalte D.D." Holland semicentennial, 19 Aug. 1897, printed in the *Anchor* (Oct. 1903), 202-9; *Holland Sentinel*, 2 May 1911; Van der Veen, "Life Reminiscences," 1:513. In America, Van Raalte dropped one *a* in his baptized middle name.

Van Raalte was an evangelist, in the style of Second Great Awakening preachers, like Charles G. Finney, of Rochester, New York. The sermon embedded in his heart, "Whoever has the Son has life," always closed with a warning of judgment and a call to repentance, which theologians refer to as the free (or well-meant) offer of the Gospel. The offer was close to an altar call. Van Raalte preached experientially. Personal faith and inner piety were paramount. Life was short and brutish, and only a strong faith would suffice. "Life is a shadow, and the world perishes," he wrote a bereaved friend. No wonder that some pastors in the Drenthe party protested to Synod Amsterdam 1843 that, in Van Raalte, "the teachings of [Jacobus] Arminius have arisen out of its forgotten corner by the Gereformeerden."[76]

Personal letters that Albertus wrote to Christina are replete with revivalist language. Although Christina had been a sincere Christian from her youth, Van Raalte assured her, "[I] pray always for your salvation," that the Lord would "grant much illumination so that with a humbled spirit you should appear before him," and "grant you the instruction of his Holy Spirit." He asked her to pray for the same assurance for him. "In walking along painful roads, when I reject and grieve God's Spirit as he knocks, I experience my blindness, darkness, spiritual darkness, and also my obstinate existence. . . . Wrestle with God in your prayers on my behalf." Albertus often expressed fear he had sinned too much to be accepted by God and that the Evil One whispered doubts about the Bible. Such pious language belied God's grace and undercut the assurance of salvation for believers, promised in the Dort doctrine of perseverance of the saints.[77]

If one could compare Van Raalte's sermons with those of his father, it is highly likely that the apple did not fall far from the tree. His father preached in the Reformed tradition, and so did he. Both men were doctrinally orthodox and taught the sovereignty of the triune God, Christ's divine and human nature, human depravity, salvation by faith, Christ's imminent return, and the organized church as the "dominant, all-pervading agency for shaping a Christian culture within a Christian community." In the church as an institute, the office of the dominee "looms largest in the life of the congregation," Spykman concluded. In

---

[76] Van Raalte to Paulus Den Bleyker (Kalamazoo), 22 June 1859, trans. Ten Hoor; Heideman, "Van Raalte," 264-65, 272-73; Reenders, "Van Raalte als leider," 192, trans. Dekker.

[77] Albertus to Christina, 24 Apr., 28 Apr., 1 May 1837, in Sweetman, *From Heart to Heart*, 3-4, 7-8, 10-11.

his view, the institutional church "exercises a kind of paternalistic care over the total life of the believing community." The dominee castigated places of temptation, such as circuses and saloons, and condemned deeds of wickedness, such as drunkenness, covetousness, and thievery. Above all, he upheld solid biblical standards, and not the lax hand of the public church of his youth and seminary days.[78]

Church with the pillars building project

The unfolding schism in rural churches in the 1850s did not directly affect the mother church in Holland, which had ambitious building plans. Six years in the Log Church was enough, Van Raalte told his consistory in March 1853. It was time to build a "real" church in the center of the growing village of seven hundred residents. The log building on the periphery "is musty and uncomfortable for the preacher," he argued, and "impossible [for parishioners] to find rest or refreshment between services. As a result, many go home and cannot be present for the afternoon service." A church in town would encourage greater attendance at that service and at the midweek prayer service. But the members themselves must come to a "decision and clarity," lest the issue "become a source of disunity." The pastor had learned that church building projects can be problematic. Happily, the minutes state: "Everyone present shares the same sentiment." After "many and long discussions," the consistory called a congregational meeting to discuss a proposal to raise $2,500 ($98,250 today). Van Raalte had decided on the location already a year earlier, when he donated four choice lots kitty-corner from the future Hope College campus on Ninth Street at Cedar [now College] Avenue.[79]

But the dominee had misread his congregation; everyone did not share the same sentiment. The building project quickly degenerated into an attack on the dominee for allegedly not performing his pastoral duties. The consistory minutes read: "Some of the brethren are of the opinion that the Rev. Van Raalte should lay aside some other activities," because "in the last few years, the power of his preaching seems to have disappeared." One would have expected their criticism to

---

[78] Spykman, *Pioneer Preacher*, 53-60.
[79] Minutes, First Holland, 21 Mar. 1853, trans. Buursma; Albertus and Christina Van Raalte conveyance of Lots 1, 2, 15, and 16, 4 Feb. 1852, book E, 406, Ottawa County deed registers. A delightful early history of First Holland church is De Vries and Boonstra, *Pillar Church*, 56-58. A detailed account that abstracts 150 years of consistory minutes is Bredeweg, *Rooster's Tail*.

focus on his "worldly activities," but their main complaint concerned his vacant pulpit—their dominee was "preaching too often in other congregations—and his writings" (likely, as editor of his newspaper, *De Hollander*).[80]

Some of the absences were legitimate, such as the standard Reformed practice of classical assignments to fill "vacant" pulpits. Van Raalte's turn came up from six to eight times a year, and some assignments required overnight trips to Chicago and Wisconsin congregations. He also was assigned to ordain candidates in their calling churches at Sunday morning services and to be a synodical deputy in candidate examinations. He represented the Classis of Holland eight times at General Synod and six times at Particular Synods.[81] Van Raalte's missionary heart to serve Dutch immigrant churches across the Midwest also took him from his own pulpit. So the complaint about frequent absences was understandable, if not fully justified.

The issue of Van Raalte's writings is puzzling and off the mark. His only writings involved lengthy reports on the progress of the colony for newspapers and periodicals, such as the *Christian Intelligencer*, all to promote the colony, defend it from criticism, and to solicit help in the East. Equally necessary was his wide correspondence with family, friends, business contacts, and public officials. Such writings merited praise, not criticism.

The unexpected attacks caught the dominee off guard. He explained that the heavy demand "to visit sick and depressed members" often forced him to work into the night to the point of exhaustion, and he was often unable to spend enough time in his study. He was fully aware "that there will be many who dislike him, no matter what." The stinging criticism was a low point in his ministry and hardly the thanks he deserved for successfully planting the colony in the wilderness. It also coincided with his business failure described in chapter 12. Against the gloom, Van Raalte learned that he had been re-elected as public school inspector by a vote of 135 to 1. His standing in the community far exceeded his standing in his congregation. At

---

[80] Minutes, First Holland, 28 Mar. 1853, for this and next two paragraphs, trans. Buursma.

[81] Van Raalte attended General Synod in 1853, 1854, 1856, 1857, 1859, 1863, 1868, 1869; Particular Synods in Albany once (1853) and Chicago three times (1857, 1859, 1863); Classis of Michigan once (1854); and Classis of Wisconsin once (1859).

this time, he and Christina also rejoiced in the birth of Anna Arendina Harking, but their joy was brief; the baby died before her first birthday.[82]

At the consistory meeting following the demoralizing charges, Teunis Keppel, the elder who had voiced the harsh complaint, back peddled. He claimed that he did not assert that the dominee's preaching had become powerless but that he had given family visiting a higher priority than sermon preparation. Van Raalte explained that he had visited nearly all the homes within the last three months because many "have fallen into sin and disputations." At this, Van Raalte as clerk was allowed to correct the minutes of the previous meeting. He then asked the brothers to "inform him of complaints and the persons making them, so that it will be possible for him to labor with a blessing." No hiding behind anonymity; they must name names. The consistory in turn requested that he notify them of upcoming absences so they could arrange for "good reading services." On the main issue of the new building, the consistory judged that the "majority lack sacrificial involvement." On family visiting, the dominee had the elders commit a half day a week to this work, which freed him to spend more time in his study. They visited from three to four hundred homes that year.[83]

For the next Sunday worship service, the dominee selected from his sermon file a favorite that he had preached at least a dozen times in the Netherlands: "He that hath the Son hath life" (II John 5:12, KJV). It was time to go back to the foundational doctrine of saving faith.[84] "Ministry in some respects is a hard business," he confided to his good friend, John Garretson. After "nearly twenty years of laboring for the people, we do not find that Love and Zeal that there ought to be." Every pastor back then and even now can echo these words.[85] Visiting minister Rev. John Schultz of Centreville received an entirely positive impression, which he reported to Garretson. "I had a pleasant and instructive visit with Dom. Van Raalte. He is a wonderful man in intellect, efficiency, and piety. May God long preserve him to the Colony and to our Church!" Garretson happily shared the praise with Van Raalte to boost his spirits.[86]

---

[82] *De Hollander*, 6 Apr. 1853.
[83] Minutes, First Holland, 28 Mar., 18 July 1853, 3 Sept. 1854; Van Raalte's report on his congregation, in Twenty-Third Annual Report of BDM, 1855, 90-92.
[84] Minutes, First Holland, 28 Mar., 22 Apr. 1853; Van Raalte Sermon, 24 Apr. 1853, trans. Ten Hoor, HHA.
[85] Van Raalte to John Garretson, 17 May 1853.
[86] Schultz to Garretson, 19 Sept. 1854, BDM.

In the middle of Van Raalte's pity party, the perennial problem resurfaced of the congregation shorting the minister's annual salary of $600 ($23,700 today). Van Raalte had received barely one-fourth of the promised amount in prior years. His debts from business ventures were pinching severely. He acknowledged that it was his responsibility to pay debts incurred in connection with the colony and lands, but it was improper to expect him to do so at the expense of meeting his family's needs. At a congregational meeting called to deal with this problem, the member families agreed "nearly unanimously" to contribute $7.50 per year ($296 today). If this promise was met, Van Raalte declared, "It would be a reason for hearty thanksgiving on his part."[87] The next year, he received half his salary, which was better than before, but still inadequate. "Some in the congregation are unwilling or are unavailable for church discipline," the consistory noted. At this, the brothers played hardball and demanded that every family provide a written account of their giving for the last three years. But the dominee's salary was still in arrears four years later.

Van Raalte as clerk had to record the excuses. "One reason for the arrears some felt was that so much of the offerings went to outside causes." A member, who later recanted, declared his intent to sever his ties because "For a long time, he finds many defects in the congregation, consistory, and pastor." The dominee agreed to accept donated labor in lieu of salary, but attempts to organize work crews fell flat. In the end, he "was forced to sell property needlessly and at a lower price to satisfy his creditors."[88] Reading between the lines, many of the parishioners disapproved of his business affairs and land dealings; some doubtless believed he needed the money less than they did.

Construction issues

Many months passed before the consistory in January 1854 unanimously agreed to proceed on the building project, provided "that no bitterness and division arise." At the February meeting, after pro- and-con positions were developed, the body decided to build a "large, new and very efficient church in this town." Elder Teunis Keppel, hired as solicitor, within a week had in hand $1,707 in cash and pledges from 145 members, averaging $12 per person. Aldert Plugger, the leading lumber merchant, gave $100 ($3,950 today), which topped by far a

---

[87] Minutes, First Holland, 22, 28 Nov. 1853, 2 Jan. 1854, 21 Sept. 1858, for this and following paragraph.

[88] Ibid., 9 Oct. 1854 (quote); 18 Jan. (quote), 14 May, 4 June 1855.

number of $30 gifts, including that of the dominee himself. Christina gave 25 cents ($9 today), likely her egg money. In two weeks, giving reached $2,500 ($90,500 today), with more coming from Reformed churches in the East. Fundraising surpassed expectations, crowed the editor of *De Hollander*. It was time to hire a contractor and make architectural blueprints. The dominee could not have been more pleased at the radical change of heart and newfound unity in his flock.[89]

Jacobus Schrader, a mill builder, was hired as architect. Why he chose the Greek-Revival style is unknown, but it was popular at the time. Van Raalte undoubtedly had a hand in the decision. Schrader likely copied the plans from Asher Benjamin's popular *Builders Guide* (1839). The low bid for the imposing edifice was $1,790. The craftsmen, "with vigor and without stopping," had the tower skeleton atop the building and the roof finished by October, and the target completion date of January 1855 seemed feasible. But many of the pledges made enthusiastically in the spring were not forthcoming in the fall. And the contractors belatedly realized that they had grossly underbid the project. Worse, the money had run out. The consistory demanded that the contractors finish the exterior work by January 1855, but they refused without getting paid. Work stopped for months, and Dominee Van Raalte declared that his health would suffer if he had to preach in such a large sanctuary before the vault and plasterwork were completed.[90]

In June 1855, the consistory mounted a second appeal to fund interior flooring, walls, ceiling, pews, a pulpit platform, plastering, and painting, estimated to cost $2,000. But the money dribbled in, and only $600 was raised. Van Raalte in desperation turned to his friends in the East, particularly Thomas De Witt of the Collegiate Church for a $1,000 loan, which was not forthcoming. The Jacob Van Putten family supplied forty thousand feet of lumber for pews, taking back a three-year loan at interest for the $394 bill.[91] A third and final fund drive took place in December 1855 when the building was nearing completion, except for the pillars. But the intense appeals and loans from suppliers were still insufficient. In the nick of time, in January 1856, the Collegiate Church, "by God's goodness," made a

---

[89] Ibid., 2 Jan., 13, 24 Feb. (quote) 1854; *De Hollander*, 23 Feb. (quote), 2, 23 Mar., 25 May 1854, trans. Simone Kennedy.
[90] Minutes, First Holland, 20 Apr., 5, 20 Oct., 28 Nov., 29 Dec. 1854; *De Hollander*, 22 Apr., 19 May 1854; De Vries and Boonstra, *Pillar Church*, 57.
[91] Minutes, First Holland, 7, 14 May, 25 June, 10 July, 2 Aug. 1855.

love gift of $1,000 ($35,800 today), which allowed for the completion of the edifice, including the pillars. The generosity of this wealthy New York congregation completely overwhelmed the poor immigrants and made them forever grateful. At a minimum, First Reformed Church cost $5,000 ($179,000 today), which exceeded original estimates by 25 percent.[92]

Christina Van Raalte chaired a committee of the Ladies Society, which agreed to decorate the sanctuary "fittingly and respectfully, preventing any impropriety," and have hanging oil lamps installed. Her committee also was responsible for cleaning the church, and at their request, a well was dug to provide fresh water. The ladies earned kudos for "their excellent work and their ongoing concern for cleanliness."[93]

The sixty-foot steeple housed the five-hundred-pound working bell that Van Raalte had ordered and paid for out of his own pocket. Initially, it stood on the ground at College Avenue and Tenth Street and announced Sunday services and weekday work hours, sounded fire alarms, and tolled for deaths. The fire alarm was six peals in rapid succession without a pause and, for deaths, six slow peals with a pause between each peal. Later, the sexton would toll the number of years of the deceased, with stately pauses between each pull.[94] To this day, the melodious bell continues to call congregants to worship. The weathervane atop the steeple, adorned with a large rooster, was crafted by Engbertus Van der Veen, the town hardware merchant and a skilled coppersmith. Roosters were customary figures on Reformed church weathervanes in the Netherlands; Catholic churches typically displayed the cross.[95]

Dedication Sunday

On Sunday morning, June 29, 1856, Van Raalte led a celebratory service of dedication, choosing as his text: "My soul longeth, yea, even fainteth for the courts of the LORD. Yea, the sparrow hath found an house, and the swallow a nest for herself, where she may lay her young,

---

[92] Ibid., 18, 27 Dec. 1855, 25 Jan., 26 Feb. 1856.
[93] Ibid., 6 Oct. 1856, 15 Dec. 1857, 25 Nov. 1858, 20 Sept. (quote), 14 Oct. 1859; *De Hollander*, 13 Jan. 1858.
[94] Minutes, People's Assembly, 29 Nov., 13 Dec. 1848, 26 Aug. 1852, 7 May 1855; *De Hollander*, 16 Oct. 1851; Minutes, First Holland, 26 Aug. 1852, 7 May 1855, 26 Feb., 29 Apr. 1856; Van der Veen, "Life Reminiscences," 1:488, 506. The story of the bell and its provenance is told by Tanis, *Bell at Pillar Church*.
[95] "Engbertus Van der Veen Interview," *Holland City News*, 1 Apr. 1915; David McNeish to Van Raalte, Apr. 1854, BDM.

even thine altars, O LORD of hosts, my King, and my God" (Psalm 84:2-3, KJV). In the afternoon service, he exposited on the third petition of the Lord's Prayer, "Thy will be done in earth, as it is in heaven" (Heidelberg Catechism, Lord's Day 49), and witnessed the confessions of faith of four young people, which "increased the celebrative spirit not a little." The rainy weather did not dampen the enthusiasm for the spacious and beautiful edifice. "It was a festive day here," reported the editor of *De Hollander*, "which we hope will long remain fresh in our memory, for minister and congregation."[96]

At the dominee's suggestion, the communion table from the Log Church was doubled from twenty to forty feet to seat more celebrants. Pews were numbered for annual pew rental at auction, as in the homeland, and arranged, again following tradition, with two aisles framing a large center section for women and children and smaller side sections for men and boys. The consistory and preseminary students of the Holland Academy sat in pews flanking the pulpit platform on both sides. Older boys and young men sat in the balcony and were often unruly, causing the pastor to interrupt his sermon and admonish them. Elders, to their chagrin, were routinely assigned to sit in the balcony to keep order among the young blades.[97]

Rev. De Witt in retirement visited Holland in 1859 and praised the edifice as Van Raalte's pride and joy. After the morning service, Van Raalte invited his guest to say a few words in Dutch. The aged New York cleric gave a fitting biblical admonition, "You may forget me, but never forget the words from the general letter from Jude 20-21: 'But ye, beloved, building up yourselves on your most holy faith, praying in the Holy Ghost. Keep yourselves in the love of God, looking for the mercy of our LORD Jesus Christ unto eternal life'" (KJV).[98] The large sanctuary was normally filled to capacity. As a visitor's report in *De Hollander* noted: "All *wish* to hear the minister." Nearly sixty years later, Van der Veen fondly recalled the edifice: "Good, old church, blessed house of the Lord, you remind us old settlers of our cash offerings, our united labors, our perseverance in building you, also the comfort

---

[96] Minutes, First Holland, note appended to book 1; *De Hollander*, 2 July 1856; *Sheboygan Nieuwsbode*, 25 July 1856. First Church Holland in 1855 counted 151 families with 669 souls, somewhat fewer than Van der Meulen's First Church, Zeeland, with 170 families and 758 souls (*Acts and Proceedings*, 1855, 570).

[97] Minutes, First Church, 29 Apr., 2 June 1856; De Vries and Boonstra, *Pillar Church*, 75.

[98] *De Hollander*, 4 Aug. 1859, trans. Simone Kennedy.

First Reformed Church, dedicated June 25, 1856. Oldest known image from 1874, on stereoptic card, with parochial school in back on Tenth Street (*JAH*)

and Christian fellowship we enjoyed in those good old days."[99] Pillar Church truly was then and remains today the city's premier public building, and its value is priceless.

Catechism

Van Raalte's heavy workload could be overwhelming. "Think of it," he said.

> Three sermons a week, six catechism classes, pastoral work, community and church meetings, correspondence, seven boisterous and disorderly children, and then only six days in a week. I am swallowed up in my work! ... Sometimes I feel that my end is rapidly approaching, and soon, I will be no more.[100]

Youngsters from age five to adulthood were catechized. On Saturday morning, Van Raalte taught children up to age fifteen in three classes, from ten to forty pupils each. They studied and memorized the *Kort Begrip*, a compendium of the Heidelberg Catechism, and Theodor Zahn's *Bijbelen kerkgeschiedenis* (Bible and church history). Catechumens sixteen years and above met at eight o'clock on Wednesday evenings and studied Zahn's book and the Confession of Faith in preparation for making public professions. In the early years, the young people's catechism class met in the parsonage on Saturday evenings. "Mevrouw" Van Raalte entertained the catechumens with chocolate and cookies and led them in singing. She was a proficient

---

[99] Van der Veen, "Life Reminiscences," 1:506; *De Hollander*, 30 Dec. 1857, trans. Nella Kennedy.
[100] Van Raalte to De Moen, 11 Feb. 1849, in *Der toestand*, 5-6, trans. Nella Kennedy.

Van Raalte's senior catechism class attendance record from Nov. 18, 1851, to July 8, 1852. Attendance was noted by 1 (yes) or 0 (no) (JAH). This list includes future clerics Egbert Winter and Christian Van der Veen.

singer and musician, thanks to lessons in singing and playing the keyboard in her Leiden upbringing.[101]

The dominee, always systematic, kept detailed records of every class, listing students by name and marking their weekly attendance. In 1855, for example, he taught four classes, totaling 145 students. Some students had perfect attendance, and others had spotty records. His own children sat at his feet, and attendance was mandatory. It was obvious that the dominee relished catechism classes. Many students fondly recalled the "treasured lessons" in Van Raalte's home and his vine-covered barn and carriage house on the north. By 1858 catechism classes were held on Thursday afternoons and all day Friday, but locations and times changed frequently.[102]

---

[101] "Diary of Geesje Van der Haar-Visscher," 9; Pieters, *Dutch Settlement*, 166, 104.
[102] Sunday school attendance reports, Van Raalte Papers, trans. Nella Kennedy; "Dr. A. C. Van Raalte," by Anoki (Van Raalte himself), *De Hope*, 22 Nov. 1876 (quote);

Van Raalte's (church) library

During the construction of the church edifice, an anonymous donor gave $15 for the church library. Van Raalte personally doubled the gift, bringing the total designated funds to $45 ($1,610 today), and ordered from a New York dealer some twenty-eight sets of books—all in English. He clearly aimed at books he could consult for sermon preparation, not books for parishioners who could barely read the language.

The order included *Webster's 4th Dictionary* (1st ed., 1828), Mathew Henry's ten-volume *Commentaries*, Alexander Cruden's *Concordance*, John Calvin's *Institutes of the Christian Religion*, John Kitto's *Cyclopedia of Biblical Literature* (2 vols., 1845) and *Illustrated History of the Bible*, Jean Henri Merle d'Aubigné's eight-volume *History of the Reformation in Europe in the Time of Calvin*, Synod of Dort documents, Jonathan Edwards' *Letters* and *Redemption*, John Newton's *Works*, Samuel Rutherford's *Letters*, Thomas Chalmers' *Commentary on Romans*, Richard Cecil's *Remains* (1825), Stephen Charnock's *Doctrine of Redemption* (1840), Alexander Campbell's *Sermons*, John Owen's *Holy Spirit* and *Forgiveness of Sin* (1669), Alexander Keith's *The Evidence of Prophecy*, John Angell James' *Christian Professor* (1836) and *Course of Faith* (1852), John Flavel's *Christ Knocking at the Door of Sinners' Hearts* (American Tract Society), and other evangelical and Puritan works.[103]

This concordance and these classic Bible commentaries, theological works, and writings of famous preachers were Van Raalte's basic sermon tools. He also kept abreast of Reformed church life by subscribing to key periodicals—the *Christian Intelligencer* and the *United Presbyterian* and, more broadly, the *Christian Observer*, the *Missionary Herald*, the *Prophetic Times*, and the Dutch *De Bezuin*.

Consistory work

Most elders and deacons had been officeholders in the Old Country and put that experience to good use in the colony. The men were usually not highly educated; they had to focus on developing farms and businesses to feed their families. Church work was squeezed into evenings. Many served consecutive terms, if willing, but some "rested"

"Diary of Geesje Van der Haar-Visscher," Feb. 1854. Merchant Jan Binnekant printed the Zahn book, a standard text in the Netherlands.

[103] Van Raalte's book order from Robert Carter & Brothers, Publishers and Booksellers, 285 Broadway Ave., NY, 7 Aug. 1854, HHA.

between terms. Harm Broek served forty years and Jacob Labots twenty years, all consecutively.

Van Raalte was the boss of the consistory (*kerkenraad*), serving for the first decade as both president and clerk (*scriba*). He kept the minutes in elegant Dutch, with a clear, firm script that bespoke his superior education. His notes detailed issues, complaints, decisions, and actions. He was a master at catching nuances and summarizing main points. He also took advantage of his pen and put his personal slant on matters, especially when the matter at hand involved him personally or was critical of church policies.[104]

Parishioners took complaints and petty grievances to the consistory, following the biblical injunction not to go to law against a brother. Besides, the nearest courts were twenty miles away in Grand Haven or Allegan. So the pastor and elders were judge and jury in countless civil infractions. For example, Brother S. was accused of pilfering trees from a neighbor's property and building his house with the lumber. His defense was that his sons may have done it without his knowledge. The elders admonished him to control his sons and stop stealing. In another case, Brother P. accused Deacon De W. of slaughtering his pig and refusing to pay four dollars for it. De W. denied it but offered to pay, in obedience to God's word. The consistory decided that Brother P.'s demand was unreasonable. Van Raalte proposed that if De W. gave Brother P. two dollars, he would give De W. one dollar, if the other brothers would make it four. They agreed, and the matter of the pig was settled.[105]

The consistory also judged matters of public entertainment. When the Holland Township Board, led by Henry Post, invited a circus to set up tents in Holland in 1859, Van Raalte voiced the general displeasure of the "good people of Holland," and the circus left after a one night stand. Most customers were Americans, and a "rush of people came in by Steamer from the mouth of Kalamazoo" (Newark).[106] Other common problems involved alcohol abuse, visiting saloons, gossiping neighbors, young couples having "untimely physical union" (*ontijdige vleeslijke verenigen*), and widows and widowers remarrying after the

---

[104] Minutes, First Holland, 4 June 1858; Kennedy, *Commentary*, 7 Apr. 1858, 2:799; 10 Oct. 1861, 2:1066.

[105] Minutes, First Holland, 26 Dec. 1850, 18 Dec. 1851; De Vries and Boonstra, *Pillar Church*, 51-55, 62-64.

[106] Van Raalte to Phelps, 8 Sept. 1859, in Bruins and Schakel, *Envisioning Hope College*, 19; Van der Veen, "Life Reminiscences," 1:504.

death of a spouse in "indelicate haste." The consistory considered it poor judgment "if a death bed is speedily changed into a wedding bed." They arbitrarily decided that widowers must wait three months and widows nine months, to "avoid mingling of the seed." In a concession to widows with children who needed a husband's support, they halved the wait to four-and-a-half months, in keeping with the decisions of two Dutch synods. But such marriages "must be performed under the stigma of disapproval."[107]

Van Raalte preached obedience to consistorial authority. He chose as his sermon text to open the semiannual meeting of the Classis of Holland in 1859: "Obey them that have the rule over you, and submit yourselves" (Hebrews 13:17a, KJV). It stirred up a hornet's nest among freethinkers, especially when he declared that "The rule of God's house was an indispensable gift of God's grace . . . [that] will enable people to be godly, and gratefully obedient, and submissive to them."[108]

First revival 1858

One bright spot for Van Raalte in the spring of 1858 was a spiritual quickening among the young people in his congregation that, in his words, opened the portal of heaven. The portal opened wide when Van Raalte was in New York over the winter of 1858, fundraising for the academy building. There he witnessed first-hand the remarkable New York City revival of 1857-58 that had sprung unexpectedly from daily prayer services in the North Reformed Protestant Dutch Church on Fulton Street. The national economic crisis of 1857 had driven many desperate people to turn to God in their extremity. People from all walks of life came to prayer meetings that had spread across the city, even in uptown Manhattan churches among the notables. Some penitents met in the late afternoon, others in the evening. The Fulton Street Revival, known as the "businessmen's revival," spread to Brooklyn, Boston, Philadelphia, and all along the East Coast. "How

---

[107] Minutes, First Holland, 10 Oct., 22 Nov. 1853 (the minutes mask the identities); De Vries and Boonstra, *Pillar Church*, 54. A woman who "fell into drunkenness" was given the choice to either confess her sin before the congregation or be censured publicly, presumably in *De Hollander* (minutes, First Holland, 21 Oct. 1856).

[108] Sermon, "The Duty of the Congregation to its Ministers," 27 Sept. 1859, trans. Ten Hoor, HMA. Van den Broek, *"Pope of the Classis,"* 61-62, 93, notes that Van Raalte's text was the same one that he and Hendrik de Cock had preached in 1838.

pleasant it is to see the crowds gather together for prayer," Van Raalte noted. "I often attend these meetings . . . where thousands are being converted in a modern-day Pentecost." The revival brought to Christ an estimated 3 percent of the total US population.[109]

On returning home, Van Raalte organized prayer meetings in Holland. He placed a notice in *De Hollander* announcing a day of prayer at his church. "Our welfare is in the Lord's hand," the notice read. To his great joy, the meeting sparked noon-time prayer meetings for several weeks. It was a bold move in the conservative colony. One of his consistory members complained: "The trouble with you, dominee, is that you are always so far ahead of the people." That nine young people in the congregation made profession of faith clinched the issue for him. They were singing Charlotte Elliot's new evangelical hymn (published 1849): "Just as I am without one plea."[110] The "extraordinary quickening" proved that "The Lord's arm may be manifested powerfully among us also."

But not everyone would take that arm. The dominee urged Henry Post, his business partner and friend, to make a public confession of sin and be saved. But Post, a typical New Englander, demurred. He kept his religious beliefs private, hid in a napkin, as he put it. But he did put pen to paper in a mea culpa.

> I am not excitable, and what would move most people to deep feelings does not affect me in the least. For this reason, my most serious feelings have been in solitary communion with my own conscience. The necessity of coming out, and standing alone and unsupported seems a great difficulty to overcome. But it is position I occupy, and I cannot change it by vain regrets.

Post was not about to step forward in a prayer meeting.[111]

---

[109] Van Raalte, NY, "To my dear congregation in Holland," 18 Mar. 1858, published in *De Hollander*, 24 Mar. 1858, and in Kennedy, *Commentary*, 29 Sept. 1858, 2:805n8; https://leben.us/fulton-street-revival/ accessed, 10 Oct. 2020 A brief, perceptive description of the New York revival is Kennedy, "Summer of Dominie Winter's Discontent," 230-31.

[110] As reported in *De Bazuin*, 30 Apr. 1858 (www.delpher.nl, accessed, June 2021).

[111] Minutes, First Holland, 8 Feb., 12 Apr. 1858; *"Kennisgeving"* (notice), *De Hollander*, 21 Apr. 1858; *De Bazuin*, 11 May 1858; Post to Van Raalte, 9 May 1858; HHA; Van Schelven, "The First Revival, 1857," *De Grondwet*, 18 Mar. 1913 (quote), trans. Nella Kennedy. For a full treatment, see Fabend, *Zion on the Hudson*, 216-23.

Albertus Van Raalte and bride Helena Hofman, February 1859 (HHA)

A pleasant interlude

Van Raalte's enlarged home was perfectly suited for the wedding reception of the decade following the marriage on February 2, 1859, of eldest son and namesake, Albertus, called Bertus (the suffix "Jr." was not typically used then). Albertus married Helena Hofman, daughter of Klaas Jans and Anje Hofman, a farm couple who had emigrated in 1848. The proud father of the groom "had the privilege and joy" to conduct the "public and solemn marriage service" before a full house of friends and old settlers in the new church. The mother of the groom was in her glory. *De Hollander* gave the event front-page coverage. "Many people, married and unmarried, hurried to the church after hearing the church bells ringing. . . . After the service, everyone—American and Dutch—went outside to see the newlywed couple and their parents off at their sleigh." The bride's side of the family went largely unnoticed.[112]

Festivities continued into the evening at the Van Raalte residence with a wedding feast hosted by the First Couple. Hundreds came to share in their generous hospitality, with tables overflowing. The bride and groom occupied the seat of honor, flanked on each side by their

---

[112] *De Hollander*, 3, 10 Feb. 1859; *Allegan Journal*, 14 Feb. 1859, from *Ottawa Register*, 8 Feb. 1859; Van Raalte to Phelps, 4, 17 Aug. 1859, in Bruins and Schakel, *Envisioning Hope College*, 9, 13; Christina Catherina Van Raalte to Helena Van Raalte, Jan. 1863, HHA.

parents. So many people came that the tables had to be replenished three and four times. Wedding gifts, both "tasteful and valuable," were stacked on another table. The Hofmans apparently contributed little to the affair. It was a Van Raalte show, and cost was no consideration for the dominee, even though his finances were tight. "I am in need, in a close corner rather," he told a friend.

Van Raalte opened the feast with appropriate remarks and words of wisdom for the newlyweds and closed with a poem he had composed for the occasion. He could not refrain from reflecting on the persecution in the Netherlands: when the groom, Bertus, was only sixteen days old Van Raalte was "torn from his family and cast into prison for holding religious meetings." The pain of that time repeatedly came to the fore for the dominee. Elder Gerrit Wakker spoke on behalf of the guests, and Rev. Giles Van de Wall closed in prayer. Then everyone moved from the dining room to the parlor for more informal events, "with guests and family members alternatively reciting appropriate verses, giving warm speeches, singing hymns and songs of joy, and saying prayers of thanksgiving and supplication." The local newspaper gushed: "It was literally a true wedding feast that will not easily be forgotten."[113]

Later that same year, Albertus and Christina rejoiced in the birth of their first grandchild, Albertus Christiaan, called Allie, son of Albertus, born December 12, 1859, and named after the paternal grandfather, as was the Dutch naming custom. The proud grandfather, however, was not home; he was in New York begging again. He felt guilty for leaving home with the grandbaby coming. As he told a friend: "You must give your allowance to a man who came to be grandpa without seeing the little fellow who places him in such a dignified position." Van Raalte made up for his absence later.[114]

Ill health

Van Raalte was always the man in front, and every malcontent targeted him. The dominee was troubled on every hand. Leading a congregation of nearly eight hundred souls was beyond his strength, especially when his preaching was criticized amid the church building project, and congregations in the surrounding villages were seceding one by one from the Classis of Holland on his watch. Barely a decade

---

[113] *De Hollander*, 10 Feb. 1859, trans. Simone Kennedy. Van de Wall, a New Brunswick Seminary graduate in 1856, taught at the Holland Academy from 1858 to 1861.
[114] Van Raalte to Phelps, 26 Dec. 1859, in Bruins and Schakel, *Envisioning Hope College*, 43.

in America, and in his midforties, his health failed. The first sign was dyspepsia, but indigestion was only the beginning. In spring 1857, he admitted to John Garretson: "Still I cannot perform the half of my duties around me. If I am to work 3 or 4 days, then the fifth I am unwell. The half of my work is being unfinished." In August, after returning from a fundraising tour in the East, he put on a stiff upper lip. He told Rev. Philip Phelps Jr., whom he had met for the first time in New York, that "My life's cup is very well sweetened by a great delight in my work. I am glad that I am allowed again to preach to my people. I feel richer than a Prince or King."[115] A year later, his tune changed. "I always have a kind of Monday sickness on Mondays," he wrote Carel de Moen. "I feel sick to my stomach, as if I had vomited."[116]

Depression overwhelmed him, and in 1858, he feared a total physical and mental collapse under the strain of his "multifaceted pastoral responsibilities." His doctor advised taking a six-month sabbatical, but Van Raalte dismissed this as impractical. Instead, he asked the consistory for a period of rest and relaxation and said he would greatly appreciate an expression of thanks for his pastoral leadership. The body did both and promptly relieved him of being clerk but only because elder Gerrit Wakker had admonished him for holding the office for eleven years. Van Raalte did continue to take his turn as president—a one-year commitment—and holding the gavel required no paperwork. Ill health or not, he traveled to Albany in 1859 to attend General Synod, as he often did (ch. 17). The day after his return, he was again in the pulpit before a full house.[117]

Albertus suffered from rheumatism, nerve pain, toothaches, irregular heartbeats, exhaustion, and often, he was just "not at all well." "Toothache is bad business," he noted at age forty, and the complaint of being "troubled with toothache" continued into his sixties. Very likely, infected teeth contributed to his many ailments. He sought treatment, but good dental care was scarce before the first trained dentist, William W. Nichols, put up his shingle in 1869, after Van Raalte had retired from his pulpit. Christina also had dental problems, which led in 1868 to having all her upper teeth replaced with dentures. Poor dental care

---

[115] Van Raalte to Garretson, 16 Apr. 1857, BDM: Van Raalte to Phelps, 26 Aug. 1857, in Bruins and Schakel, *Envisioning Hope College*, 4; Kennedy, *Commentary*, 29-30 Sept. 1858, 2:807; *De Hollander*, 30 July 1856.

[116] Van Raalte to De Moen, 1 June 1858, trans. Ten Hoor, ADC.

[117] Minutes, First Holland, 27 Aug. 1855, 14 Dec. 1858; *Acts and Proceedings*, 1855, 570-71; *De Hollander*, 16 June 1859.

was common before the mid-twentieth century.[118]

The position of pastor was Van Raalte's primary calling and his strong suit. His sermons inspired his flock and sustained them. But he spread himself too thin with church work and school and business concerns. As leader of the colony, he had to take charge of church administration, schooling, land dealings, business and industry, harbor and road infrastructure, public administration, political life, civil affairs, journalism, medical care, fire and police safety, and whatever else required his attention. The many hats he wore cost him physically and emotionally and led to misunderstandings and conflict.

The hardships of the first three years were actually the most satisfying, but the honeymoon was brief. The union of 1850 unexpectedly brought an end to the peaceful times in the churches. Then schism in the church, harsh criticism of his preaching, and the cares of life caused personal depression, which made his life miserable. He had to deal with bankruptcy in business, harassment by the press, and rejection as a political leader. Critics called him a pope, an autocrat, and other similar epithets. But there were also refreshing times of revival at home and abroad that enabled him to carry on faithfully for a second decade. His stellar efforts to establish Christian schools also buoyed his spirits and in the end brought the greatest satisfaction.

---

[118] Christina Catherina to mother, 8, 19 Nov. 1862; Van Raalte to daughter Christina, 13 July 1868, HHA; Van Raalte to Phelps, 2, 9 Jan. 1850, HHA; Van Raalte to Phelps, 19 Nov. 1859, 2, 9 Jan. 1860, 24 Aug. 1862, in Bruins and Schakel, *Envisioning Hope College*, 28, 50, 53, 93; Van Raalte to Phelps, 29 Aug. 1862, HHA; Swierenga, *Holland, Michigan*, 2:1195, 1198-1201.

CHAPTER 11

Public and Christian Education: "A great and difficult work."

Dominee Van Raalte, true to his upbringing and Separatist heritage, believed in Christian schools at all levels—primary, secondary, and college.[1] He was a champion of education, and this was a key motivation for immigrating. As he wrote Groen van Prinsterer, "The needs of my family, especially the need for Christian schooling and other urgent reasons, give me strong reasons to do this."[2] Settlers of a more ultrabent agreed with him, provided the schools were taught in Dutch, not English, as the dominee demanded. The Classis of Holland, true to its birthright, required consistories to establish such schools as "an important part of the Christian calling of God's church on earth. All lukewarmness and coldness toward that cause must be condemned and rebuked."[3]

---

[1] This chapter draws on Swierenga, *Holland, Michigan*, 1:529-87; and Kennedy, "Van Raalte and Parochial Schools."
[2] Te Velde, *Brummelkamp*, 172-73; Van Raalte to Groen van Prinsterer, 21 Sept. 1846, cited in Reenders, "Van Raalte als leider," 195, 378n587.
[3] Van Raalte to John Garretson, Jan. (or Feb.) 1852; Kennedy, *Commentary*, 23 Apr. 1848, 1:29; 30 Oct. 1850, 1:40; "A Friend of Truth," *Sheboygan Nieuwsbode*, 3 Jan. 1851.

Pocketbooks, however, pinched principles when it came to Christian schools. Money talked. Property taxes, not church tithes, paid for public schools, and as long as the colony was homogeneous and Reformed, what was the danger? Besides, Americans in the colony, few in number but very influential, wanted public schools. For fifteen years, the dominee served on the local public school board, all the while pushing Christian education. Over time, his suspicion of the inherent secularism of public education was proven correct, much to his chagrin, and he turned his attention to Christian day schools.[4]

Public education

Van Raalte's heart was in Christian education, given his struggle to found the Christian school in Ommen over the mayor's stiff resistance. But in America, the "little red schoolhouse," the symbol of the common school system, was ubiquitous. Holland would be no exception. Practicality governed. The Land Ordinance of 1785 designated Section 16 (one square mile) in the center of every township to fund public schools. And in the colony, common schools would mirror their communities. Moreover, many immigrants saw no need for schooling beyond the three Rs; their children were needed on the farm. "It is a great and difficult work to educate an ignorant mass of people, a people out of the lower class, filled with European prejudices," the dominee declared. Our youth must be more than "'hewers of wood and drawers of water'" (Josh. 9:23). In the end, he not only accepted but also led public education for the first decade while also founding Christian schools. To his great disappointment, however, most of his parishioners eschewed Christian education in favor of public schooling.[5]

---

[4] For an opposing view, see *De Hope*, 8 Jan. 1896, which reprinted the letter of Van Raalte to Brummelkamp, 27 Nov. 1846, in Brummelkamp, *Stemmen uit Noord-Amerika*, 71, and *Voices from North America*, 14. Rev. Engelbert C. Oggel, a Reformed Church cleric and younger brother of Van Raalte's deceased son-in-law Peter Oggel, added his editorial comment in this 1895 reprint, namely, that Van Raalte "showed by his deeds that it was both his calling and his privilege to support the public school by advice and deed. After all, he was for many years a member of the school board here and, if we are correctly informed, the land on which the public school was built for the upbringing of the children was given by him to the public as a gift. The tree is known by its fruits" (trans. Earl Wm. Kennedy). Kennedy added his telling comment to Oggel's statement. "Although factually correct, [it] reveals as much about the midwest RCA's 'turn-of-the-century' patriotic commitment to the ideal of the American public school system as it does about Van Raalte's early suspicion of it" (Kennedy, "Van Raalte and Parochial Schools," 178n21).

[5] The apt phrase is in Kennedy, "Van Raalte and Parochial Schools," 170 (quote); Dosker, *Van Raalte*, 183, trans. Dekker.

Van Raalte pushed instruction in English, in the village of Holland, but public schools in all the outlying villages were taught in the Dutch language by immigrant teachers. Holland public school was bedeviled by issues of gender, faith, language, and finances. Parents wanted instruction by male teachers who were Christians, as in the Netherlands, and they insisted on Dutch-language classes, the language spoken in church and catechism. Because no teachers had come with Van Raalte, the first hires had to be Americans. This helped Van Raalte's English-only crusade, but left parents unhappy.

In September 1847, Van Raalte established the first day school, an English school, under Ova Hoyt, a young Yankee Methodist from Kalamazoo, a cousin of Rev. Ova Hoyt and brother-in-law of Isaac Fairbanks. Ovid Hoyt taught adults and children at night—they had to work during the daytime to put food on the table. Parents had to pay tuition for his salary. Very creatively, he contrived a New Testament primer that set Dutch and English texts in parallel columns. As Engbertus Van der Veen recalled: "We had to read in English, and by looking on the other column, tell the meaning of what we were reading." In a few months, Hoyt managed to recruit enough younger children to add day classes, with Webster's Elementary Speller as the main textbook. Van Raalte came once a week after school to teach catechism. In spring 1848, classes moved to the half-finished Log Church, and by July, Hoyt had seventy students.[6]

In June 1848, at Van Raalte's request, the Ottawa County board of school inspectors set off the southern half of Ottawa County—the Dutch colony—as its own district—Holland District No. 1. But no public taxing authority existed to fund the school until Holland Township was organized and could levy real estate taxes. In the interim, the People's Assembly, against Van Raalte's wishes, voted for bilingual Dutch-English classes. They also voted against renting the Log Church to Hoyt, a non-Dutch speaker. Since this was the only suitable building, Hoyt had to step down.[7]

With Hoyt gone, Van Raalte and Henry Post, heads of the school board, hired another English-speaker, Elvira H. Langdon of Allegan, a native of Vermont, who taught the advanced classes. As a female,

---

[6] Van der Veen, "Life Reminiscences," 1:501 (quote); Cornelis M. Van Malsen to parents, 11 July 1847, in Yzenbaard, "'America' Letters," 39-44; Ancestry.com.

[7] "Our Pioneer School District," *Holland City News*, 25 July 1874; Isaac Marsilje, "A Historical Sketch of Public Schools of the City of Holland," *Holland Sentinel*, 11 May 1914; minutes, People's Assembly, 11 Oct. 1848; School Board Journal, 8 Aug. 1851, HMA.

she came cheaper, Van Raalte noted. He praised the schoolmarm, but enrollment plummeted to only twenty-seven students, barely 14 percent of the 191 youngsters registered in the annual school census. Many immigrants objected to female teachers, following the Apostle Paul's dictum for New Testament churches: "But I suffer not a woman to teach, nor to usurp authority over the man, but to be in silence" (1 Tim. 2:12, KJV). Van Raalte could not win; the colonists objected to female teachers and to all-English classes. The tuition charge of $1.52 ($60 today) per student was also beyond the reach of many parents. Van Raalte created a church poor fund for tuition help, which continued until voters passed the first school levy in 1851. Classes were held in the never-needed Orphan House.[8]

Van Raalte gave Langdon his full support in maintaining school discipline. When two boisterous youngsters disrupted the class with "frivolity and laughter" and received "very bad" marks on their report card, the dominee stepped in. After *catecatie* (Dutch slang for catechism), the dominee took the boys to the parsonage. He sent one— Peter— upstairs and had the other sit at the table next to the Mrs., a seat that boys viewed with dread. The dinner was *hutspot* (hodge-podge), a common Dutch dish composed of mashed potatoes, cabbage, and perhaps some bacon or pork. The dominee had the servant girl take up a heaping plate for the boy upstairs, but he refused it and threw the plate of food on the floor with a loud bang. "That's nothing," said the dominee, "I'll attend to him later." After dinner, the boy who had shared the meal received only a reprimand, but years later, he noted that the boy upstairs had gotten his comeuppance. "Judging from the noise and crying that followed, we decided that Peter got something different than hutspot for dinner." Then he added the punch line: "Peter and I never fell into the hands of the dominee again."[9]

For a few years, parents had the Christian school they desired when Hermanus Doesburg, a respected schoolmaster from Den Hitzert, province of Zuid-Holland, emigrated in 1848 and opened a private school taught in Dutch and from a Reformed perspective.

---

[8] Van Raalte to Helenius de Cock, 26 Sept. 1851, AGK; Langdon, "School Reminiscences," 1:395-96 (quote); minutes, People's Assembly, 29 Nov., 13, 27 Dec. 1848; Marsilje, "Historical Sketch."

[9] James Van der Sluis to Van Schelven, 19 Dec. 1898, "Early Punishment by an Old Scholar," Van Schelven Papers; "Reminiscences of Elvira H. Cooper, née Langdon," *Holland City News*, 16 Dec. 1898; Elvira H. Cooper obit., clipping from *Hastings* [NE] *Evening Record* in *Holland City News*, 9 Dec. 1898; Stegenga, *Anchor of Hope*, 36.

This fit the bill for many parents and justified his tuition charges. He quickly enrolled one-fourth of all students in the village. Nevertheless, half of school-aged youngsters did not attend at all; they were needed on the farm, and parents could not afford tuition. Doesburg added a night school to teach adult immigrants rudimentary English during the long winter months. When Doesburg took up the editorship of Van Raalte's newspaper, *De Hollander*, in 1852, his school closed.[10]

Antipathy to public schooling frustrated the dominee. Tight-fisted taxpayers even "blocked the wheels" when the state legislature approved a $1,200 bond issue for a building. The bonding offer got some people's blood boiling, and the "discussion thereabout was hot," the minutes reported. Van Raalte had all he could do to maintain order at school board meetings. The upshot was that, at the crucial September 1850 meeting, voters refused to approve the tax levy to support the bonds. After board head Henry Post warned that the district might "lose their organization or [have to] pay for a law suit," the meeting voted $25 for rent, $20 for wood, and $50 for debt repayment—but nothing for the teacher's salary.[11]

In early 1851, the board scaled back the building project to a $300 frame structure, and Van Raalte donated six lots on East Tenth Street for the site (now Van Zoeren Hall). The schoolhouse, later named Union School, was funded by a property tax levy to yield $1 ($39.50 today) per student per year. This proved to be woefully inadequate to cover Miss Langdon's modest salary. She was relieved of her job midterm, after voters, over Van Raalte's strong objections, rejected any levy for school or town purposes. School was closed for six months as trustees sought another female teacher.[12]

When Walter T. Taylor came from New York in October 1851 to lead the Pioneer School, he solved the staffing problem at the district school by volunteering his three adult children—Hugh, Margaret, and Anna—all experienced teachers. None, however, could speak Dutch, and younger children could not speak English. The district school occupied

---

[10] Swierenga, *Holland, Michigan*, 1:375, 382, 535; "Pioneer Education," *De Hollander*, 15 Dec. 1853; Isaac Marsilje, "A Historical Sketch of Public Schools of the City of Holland," *Holland Sentinel*, 11 May 1914.

[11] "Our Pioneer School District"; Randall P. Vande Water, "Continuing to Fulfill the Mission, Our District: About HPS—A Rich History," Holland Public Schools, 6 Aug. 2007 (quote); Wichers, *Century of Hope*, 31.

[12] Langdon, "School Reminiscences," 1:397 (quote); "Our Pioneer School District"; Van Raalte to Helenius de Cock, 26 Sept. 1851 (quote), AGK, trans. Boonstra and Nella Kennedy.

the first floor of the new schoolhouse, and the Pioneer School had the second floor. The Taylor siblings taught a wide variety of subjects in all grades, including multiplication tables and rudimentary Latin, and English. When daughter Margaret died in 1852, her father had to take on her classes. A stiff authoritarian, he demeaned grammar school boys as rough and uncouth and seemed to dislike girls. Many parents rebelled and no longer sent their children to Taylor. They could accept his mediocre Dutch but not his classroom demeanor. In 1854 Taylor returned to New York in a huff.[13]

The fall 1854 term began late for want of a teacher for the growing student body. Hiring one fell to Van Raalte since Post had resigned, disgruntled over a disputed reimbursement request. From then until 1860, the dominee was directly responsible for both public and Christian education in the village. His desire to hire a Christian teacher for the public school ran amuck. In October, long past the fall semester opening date, his candidate, Rev. Cornelius Crispell of Geneva, New York, declined. "Christian teachers are very hard to find," the dominee lamented.[14]

In desperation, Van Raalte hired a teacher before obtaining specific authorization from the board and the man proved to be a disaster. George A. Seaver, a recent graduate of Kalamazoo Literary and Theological Institute (Kalamazoo College in 1855), began teaching, but his religious views were questionable. Van Raalte advised him to keep "his peculiar notions" to himself. What these notions were is not clear. In any case, school inspector Post arranged a board examination for Seaver, and Van Raalte, the "senior inspector," failed to show up, so the board adjourned after waiting ninety minutes.[15]

Meanwhile, the immature Seaver publicly lambasted the school board for the deplorable conditions at the school. Webster's spellers were the "poorest books extant," there were very few arithmetic books and no grammar, geography, or history books. The only other textbook was the New Testament. "How can I earn my wages and do good if

---

[13] Kennedy, *Commentary*, 14 Oct. 1851, 179-81; Van Raalte to Garretson, 18 Apr. 1854; Giles Van de Wall to Garretson, 28 Dec. 1858, all in BDM; Wichers, *Century of Hope*, 35-36.

[14] Crispell to Garretson, 6 Aug. 1854; Schultz to Garretson, 11 Sept. 1854, Crispell to Garretson, 12, 18 Sept. 1854, Van Raalte to Garretson, 19 Oct. 1854, all in BDM.

[15] For this and the next paragraphs, see Van Raalte to Doesburg, 6 May 1854; Seaver to "the Public," 8 May 1854; Holland District School board to Seaver, 16 May 1854; all correspondence in *De Hollander*, 8 June 1854.

I cannot find tools to work with?" Seaver declared. The board played hardball and insisted that the teacher stand for a formal examination. To everyone's surprise, Seaver failed the examination, particularly in arithmetic. A majority of the board then decided it would be improper to certify him. Van Raalte dissented strongly and insisted that the examiners reverse themselves, but the majority overruled him, finding his reasons unsatisfactory. Van Raalte's consistory at First Church backed him and officially disapproved of the board's actions. The board wrote Seaver a softly worded dismissal letter to "spare his feelings as much as possible."[16] But the damage was done to both men.

Van Raalte, like a bulldog, would not let the matter drop. In Kalamazoo, on his way to New York, he contacted Seaver's three professors and secured a ringing letter of recommendation that would attest to his competence and Christian character. Post dismissed the letter out of hand and criticized Van Raalte in the press for trying to "browbeat" the examiners and "cast popular odium upon them, when they dare to do their duty." Clearly, in Post's mind Seaver did not measure up. For Van Raalte and Post to disagree so publicly was remarkable since they were such close friends.[17] In desperation, Van Raalte gave a one-year appointment to E. P. Pitcher, an eighteen-year-old from the Reformed Church in New York City, for the 1854-55 school year, but he barely met the qualifications. The district and Pioneer schools continued to share the building.[18]

The Reformed Church in the East then came to the rescue again by sending John Van Vleck to lead the Pioneer Academy in 1855. His wife Elizabeth and sister Cornelia Falconer agreed to staff the public school, and they stayed several years, until 1857. For children living east of the city, Ottawa County school inspectors established Holland Township School District No. 4 in the virgin forest on East Eighth Street behind Van Raalte's home. A small schoolhouse, named appropriately Van Raalte [later Federal] School, opened in June 1856 and had 236 students a year later.[19]

In 1860 Holland voters by an 80 percent majority agreed to add a high school, which required enlarging the elementary building. Launching Holland High School indicated that Hollanders were

---

[16] Minutes, First Holland, 19 May 1854.
[17] *De Hollander*, 8 June 1854.
[18] *Holland City News*, 29 July 1893.
[19] "Van Raalte School House District No. 4," *Holland Sentinel*, 2 June 1906; *De Hollander*, 30 Dec. 1857, 4 Nov. 1858.

beginning to appreciate the importance of education. The growing population and rising economy also made the expansion feasible. The population census of 1860 counted nearly two thousand inhabitants in Holland Township. This was Van Raalte's last year as a trustee. He declined re-election in 1861 and urged the election of two Americans instead. "Common sense and justice requires it," the dominee noted. Americans were coming in, and they deserved representation. The truth was that the dominee was disgusted with the lowest-common-denominator moralism that was being taught in Holland's public schools.[20]

Pioneer School—Christian secondary education under Taylor

In 1850, when Van Raalte attended the Particular Synod of Albany, he seized the moment to beg the Eastern church: "Take in hand the education of our youth, which for years we shall not be able to do ourselves."[21] The colony needed a Christian secondary school to prepare preachers and teachers for the new settlements. When John Garretson, secretary of the domestic missions board, visited the colony, Van Raalte prevailed on him to endorse his Pioneer School, an English-Dutch classical academy in the tradition of preparatory schools in the Netherlands. Garretson's missions board named Theodore Frelinghuysen, president of Rutgers College, and Revs. Wyckoff and De Witt, all strong friends of the immigrants, to a fundraising committee. With these initial steps, the eastern Reformed church endorsed the Pioneer School.[22]

The colonists received the news with mixed feelings. For some, the news "aroused rejoicing" but many considered the school to be wholly unnecessary and a "mere 'Wildcat Scheme.'" (Wildcat banks were rife in Michigan's Upper Peninsula at the time and considered the worst examples of fraudulent schemes.)[23] Leaders of the church in the East, for their part, were also skeptical of Van Raalte's vision of a "school of the prophets." Easterners already supported Rutgers College in New Brunswick and Union College in Schenectady, New York, both liberal

---

[20] "Our Pioneer School District"; Van Raalte to Philip Phelps, 16 Aug. 1861 (quote), in Bruins and Schakel, *Envisioning Hope College*, 87.
[21] Kennedy, *Commentary*, 30 Oct. 1850, 1:108-9.
[22] Garretson to Van Raalte, 1851, BDM; Voskuil, "Vexed Question," 341-44.
[23] "Our Pioneer School District" (quote), *Holland City News*, 25 July 1874; Lucas, *Netherlanders*, 399 (quote); Bruins, "Hope College," 4-13; Kennedy, *Commentary*, 30 Oct. 1850, 1:109; 30 Apr. 1851, 1:143-44; 29 Apr. 1852, 1:93; Stegenga, *Anchor of Hope*, 37.

arts colleges, to train Christian leaders in all fields. Graduates desiring to enter the Gospel ministry could then enroll in the denomination's New Brunswick Seminary.[24]

Van Raalte insisted on the need for Dutch-speaking higher education. His vision was far beyond the limited horizons of immigrants struggling to survive. His ideal won out, and eventually Hope College and Western Theological Seminary were established to serve the western immigrant wing of the denomination. Van Raalte donated five choice lots for a campus and then used his bully pulpit as clerk of the Classis of Holland to declare that higher education was of "supreme importance" for "the character, the destiny, and the prosperity of the people." Classis voted in April 1851 to begin classes in the vacant Orphan House. Each congregation promised to recruit students, and the Holland church promised to provide room and board for them, with assistance from parents and friends. "Such an arrangement need cost the parents little or no money," the dominee opined.[25]

Garretson persuaded Walter T. Taylor, an experienced educator and church elder who had founded a Christian academy in New York, to come west and head the Pioneer School under the aegis of the Committee on Education of the Reformed Church, which paid his salary. Taylor had taught himself some Dutch but could not teach in that language. He was thoroughly American. Yet Van Raalte touted him as a "zealous advocate of the doctrine of free grace and was for that reason considered to be exceptionally well fitted for this important position." Van Raalte donated to Taylor five city lots for a home site and eight additional lots as an inducement, valued at $100 each, or $1,300 in all ($51,300 today). The dominee even found a carpenter to build a house for the large Taylor family of ten.[26]

Taylor made the sacrificial move in the conviction that his teaching experience would benefit the new immigrants. "May the Lord make you a blessing among this newly planted people," the dominee prayed. The prayer was needed because Taylor's reputation would become that of a "demanding, stern, irritable, overworked, and underpaid teacher, beloved by a few but certainly not by all." Very likely, the dominee did

---

[24] Kennedy and Simon, *Can Hope Endure?* 31-34.
[25] Kennedy, *Commentary*, 30 Apr. 1851, 1:143-44 (quotes); Voskuil, "When East Meets West," 201-28.
[26] Taylor to Van Raalte, 4 Oct. 1851; Dosker, *Van Raalte*, 128; Wichers, *Century of Hope*, 35.

Walter T. Taylor, first principal of Pioneer School (*JAH*)

not know that Taylor belonged to the Masonic Order in New York, which would have disqualified him on the spot. His Episcopalian tendencies would not set well either.[27]

Taylor accepted the position, in his words, "to save these Hollander people from aimlessness." He could double up because the Christian and public schools shared a building, and his three adult children could staff the grade school. Heading both schools led to trouble. Most of the tax revenue went to fund the district school, and worse, Taylor had three bosses, each demanding a say in running the schools. For the Pioneer School, he answered to Synod's Committee on Education, which had appointed and funded him. For the district school, he was subject to an elected school board. And he also answered to the Classis of Holland, which held his credentials. As one of his students recalled years later: "All had a high opinion of their general prerogatives and were never hampered in the assertion of them." Taylor was stretched thin by the many demands and frustrated by inadequate funding.[28] Regardless of the difficulties, he had a good beginning. He and his eldest daughter, Anna, began in October 1851 with eighteen male students. In the first decade, congregations donated over $7,000 for student support, often in the form of crops or produce.[29]

For the first time, young men in the colony could study Latin. Classical education was welcome in Holland but not the exclusive use of English at the expense of Dutch. The main purpose of Pioneer School was to tutor preministerial candidates, "in order that the preaching

---

[27] Kennedy, *Commentary*, 30 Apr. 1851, 1:143-44; 14 Oct. 1851, 1:176-81 (quote 181n 211); 26 Sept. 1853, 1:384.

[28] Walter Taylor to Van Raalte, 4 Oct. 1851 (quote), HHA; *De Hollander*, 16 Oct. 1851; Kennedy, *Commentary*, 1 Sept. 1852, 1:290; 27 Apr. 1853, 1:316-17; Wichers, *Century of Hope*, 35-41.

[29] Kennedy, *Commentary*, 27 Apr. 1853, 1:315-17; Wichers, *Century of Hope*, 37-38, 49.

Pioneer School, 1856 (formerly Orphan House, 1847); Adrian Zwemer House, 1857 (on right), later used for theology classes (JAH)

may not become ridiculous by reason of the mixture of languages, and also that the people shall know how to use the pen properly in the mother tongue." At the April 1852 meeting of the Classis of Holland, Rev. Martin Ypma proposed that Pioneer School hire a minister fluent in the mother tongue, preferably Anthony Brummelkamp, professor in the seminary in Arnhem. Van Raalte sent his brother-in-law a letter of call and urged him to accept, but to no avail. Though conscience stricken that he had urged others to emigrate and would not do so himself, Brummelkamp declined the call. His *bedankje* (thanks, but no thanks) ended attempts to "Hollandize" the academy.[30]

By 1853 the synodical committee on education realized that the colonists could not sustain Pioneer School financially. "They have shown an interest and earnest desire to promote the cause of Christian education among themselves," and "out of their poverty they have done what they could." But their means were limited, and the academy needed support from the denomination. So the committee proposed "to make an entire transfer of the Academy to the General Synod." The Classis of Holland scraped up the money to send Van Raalte as its sole

---

[30] Kennedy, *Commentary*, 29 Apr. 1852, 1:264-67; 1 Sept. 1852, 1:297-98; Van Hinte, *Netherlanders*, 257-58, citing Brummelkamp Jr., *Brummelkamp*, 221.

delegate to the 1853 General Synod in Philadelphia to plead the case and save the "school of the prophets." In broken English, Van Raalte pleaded eloquently for the "moral and religious welfare of his people." Learning of his words, the colonists said that his "powerful and persuasive" speech "opened the fountains of blessing" for the colony. Synod approved their committee's recommendation and agreed to pay the operational costs of Pioneer School for a five-year trial period, but Taylor's salary fell on the colonists. The Philadelphia synod was one of the highlights of Van Raalte's life. His precious school would continue, thanks to the church in the East.[31]

But the colonists did not, or could not, keep up with Taylor's salary. After three turbulent years, Taylor's pay was $3,000 ($108,600 today) behind. He told the Classis of Holland in April 1854 that he would resign on condition that he receive the back pay. Classis readily acquiesced, believing that the financial burden and rising indebtedness had become a "source of unpleasantness." Classis then asked General Synod to help resolve the issue of back pay. Synod instructed its boards of education and missions to pay the shortfall, and the Taylor family returned to New York. Taylor's Latin class had grown to thirty students, and he sent four students on to Rutgers College, two of whom entered the Reformed Church ministry.[32]

Back pay, however, was the surface issue. Underneath was the fact that the professor and the dominee had had a severe falling out. Parents and pupils had complained that Taylor's teaching was ineffective, and Van Raalte declared that Taylor had "failed to convey heart religion to his charges." This likely stemmed from Taylor's high-brow attitude. "He is a crooked stick," Van Raalte declared. Taylor's daughter Anna alluded to the hard feelings when two years later she wrote a kindly letter to Van Raalte to inform him of her father's death. She grieved that the "pleasant social intercourse" between the two families had been marred and hoped that the "misunderstandings which have crept in between you and father destroying your friendship for one another would pass away.... Only the night before he died he was wishing that he could see you."[33]

---

[31] Wichers, *Century of Hope*, 37-39, citing 1853 synod's committee on education; *Holland City News*, 14 June 1884; *Acts and Proceedings*, 1854, 454-55.

[32] Kennedy, *Commentary*, 12 Apr. 1854, 1:418.

[33] Rev. John Schultz, Centreville, MI, to Garretson, quoting Van Raalte, 19 Sept. 1854; Anna Taylor to Van Raalte, 21 Dec. 1856, HHA.

Taylor's son-in-law and former student, Christian Van der Veen, laid the blame squarely on the dominee.

> He [Taylor] was sent out for only one purpose, in which he believed. He soon found himself thwarted in that purpose by evil influences in Holland. He did not find in Holland what he had been taught [told] to expect, nor was he permitted to do the work which he had come to carry out. He was left to fight the battle alone, and he was crushed. He went away and died of a broken heart.[34]

Taylor did actually die of a pulmonary aneurysm.[35]

Van der Veen's comments about evil influences and being left to fight the battle alone were clear to contemporaries but vague to historians. Was the evil that Taylor noted due to carping over his poor Dutch, or was it the burden of school finances? Was his complaint about being left to fight alone a veiled criticism of Van Raalte for siding with the critics? Whether Taylor resigned due to finances, criticism, illness, or a broken relationship with Van Raalte, Holland did lose a dedicated educator.

To fill Taylor's shoes, the Classis of Holland again turned to General Synod for help to provide an *ordained* man. The situation was delicate. The humble scholar sent by the denomination was run off, and now they wanted to be rescued, and with a cleric no less. Classis couched its case carefully to match the missionary thrust of the denomination and asked the board of missions to partner with the board of education and send an ordained man who could both teach and preach.[36] Synod complied with this request and appointed Frederick (Fred) P. Beidler for the 1854-55 academic year. Beidler also began regular English-language worship in the schoolhouse under the auspices of the domestic missions board, but he left after only a year.[37]

Holland Academy—Rev. John Van Vleck and Dominee Van Raalte

The denomination next appointed John Van Vleck, a fresh graduate of New Brunswick Theological Seminary, to take charge of

---

[34] Van Raalte to John Garretson, 18 Apr. 1854, BDM; Van der Veen, "Genetic History of Hope College," quoted in Wichers, *Century of Hope*, 40.
[35] Anna Taylor to Van Raalte, 21 Dec. 1856, HHA.
[36] Kennedy, *Commentary*, 12 Apr. 1854, 1:417-18; 13 Sept. 1854, 1:453.
[37] Hope Reformed Church, 80th Anniversary booklet (Holland, 1942), 5, cited in Parr, *Hope Church*, 405.

the newly named Holland Academy. Van Vleck's appointment was a "three-fer." His wife Elizabeth (née Falconer) and her sister Cornelia Falconer took over District School No. 1, which then enrolled about two hundred students. Van Vleck also carried on English-language worship services in the Orphan House for Americans. Van Raalte again sold the new teacher ten city lots at half the going price as a financial inducement. Van Vleck was examined at a special December 1856 session of the Classis of Holland and ordained. His larger role, he asserted, was to win the confidence of the immigrants in "our common church," the Reformed Protestant Dutch Church in the face of critics who charged it with errors (ch. 10).[38]

For the academy to thrive, it needed its own building and campus. The former Orphan House would not do. Van Raalte had worked since 1853 toward this goal. With the synod's endorsement, he had made three trips to New York City to tap wealthy benefactors at Collegiate Church, notably Samuel B. Schieffelin and James Suydam. Samuel Schieffelin and his brothers, James L. and Philip, owned the wholesale drug firm Schieffelin Brothers & Co.[39] Suydam and Schieffelin responded generously, but Van Raalte was frustrated by the lack of commitment in Holland. Van Raalte had donated six acres for the campus, and it was time to have a suitable building. In 1856 he gave a challenge gift of $500 ($17,900 today) and demanded that either his congregants follow suit within twelve days, or he would accept an urgent call from the Pella congregation. Recently, after having attended the Particular Synod of Chicago, he had traveled west for the first time to organize Pella's First Reformed Church. He had taken the train to its terminus at Rock Island—the rail bridge over the Mississippi River was still under construction. Proceeding overland, he had visited the newly established Reformed Church in Burlington, Iowa, and the neighboring cities of Muscatine and Keokuk. He warned his consistory that his "mission to Pella" bore "weighty significance."[40]

The brethren immediately called a congregational meeting, at which the dominee read a lengthy pastoral letter to all the congregations

---

[38] Van Vleck to Garretson, 27 Dec. 1856, BDM.
[39] This wealthy New York family stems from their grandfather, Jacob Schieffelin, who had founded the family firm in 1780. See Bruins and Schakel, *Envisioning Hope College*, 23n, 276n, citing *National Encyclopedia*, 521, and *Prominent Families of New York*, 496; Kennedy, *Commentary*, 12 Apr. 1854, 1:429; Lucas, *Netherlanders*, 309-11.
[40] Minutes, First Holland, 26 Aug., 12 Nov. 1856; Kennedy, *Commentary*, 8 Oct. 1856, 1:645; 17 Dec. 1856, 2:680.

Samuel B. Schieffelin (1811-1900), Collegiate Reformed Church elder, wholesale drug distributor, and major donor to Holland Academy and Hope College (*JAH*)

of the Classis of Holland. The Pella call "weighs heavier than my congregational connections in Holland," he declared in the letter.

> I cannot disguise the fact that my efforts have been futile in attempting to provide both for women and men an education. The lack of a response in the hearts of our people concerning this common cause was the last straw... that loosened my attachment and cooled my ardor concerning my so-called general calling for this people.[41]

The threat had the desired effect. Monies came in for the building, with more pledged, even though the congregation still lacked funds to complete the large pillars on the new church. How it would have worked for Van Raalte to live in Pella under the nose of Henry Scholte is unknowable, but it would likely have been unpleasant for both. Many of the members of First Pella Church were disgruntled colonists who had left the independent Scholte Church.

Several weeks after the congregational meeting in Holland, following the morning service on December 3, 1856, Van Raalte informed his anxious congregation that "after much and serious consideration, he had come to the conclusion to decline the call to Pella." He then

---

[41] Van Raalte to "Honorable Brethren," a three-page letter regarding the Pella call, in minutes, First Holland, 18 Nov. 1856, trans. Buursma.

"pledged himself anew to the congregation."[42] But the flock was still not out of the woods. A month later, the dominee received a second call from Pella; repeat calls were customary in those days. This call came as he was about to leave on a fundraising trip in the East on behalf of the academy. He declined the second call but made no mention of it in consistory minutes. Before leaving town, he reported that academy donations totaled $3,600 ($128,800 today); the school was flourishing with twenty-seven students and already had fourteen graduates. In an overstatement, he declared it to be "one of the best schools in the United States."[43]

When the Great Western (later Grand Trunk Western) Railroad from Kalamazoo pulled into the station at New York City, Van Raalte immediately went to meet his friend De Witt, of Collegiate Church, who had pledged $120 a year and penned an endorsement of the academy that the dominee put on page one of his unpublished, forty-page, handwritten, "Traveling & Begging Guide." Van Raalte's robust "ask" technique was to have donors sign a pledge and list the amount paid or donated. "We the undersigned promise to pay to Rev. A. C. Van Raalte the sum affixed to our names to aid in erecting a building for the accommodation of the students of the Holland Academy."[44] This meant that each donor could see what everyone else had donated. Nothing like public pressure or shaming to open pocketbooks, and the seemingly small act of signing one's pledge elevated it to a firm commitment.

The begging dominee went from one Old Dutch church to another, starting with the Collegiate Church in New York City then on to Brooklyn, Albany (where Wyckoff gave $10), Hastings-on-Hudson (to see Philip Phelps Jr., the future academy director), and dozens of other churches across upstate New York, Long Island, and northern New Jersey. Samuel Schieffelin, a leading layman in the denomination and generous contributor to Christian schools, signed first after De Witt. His pledge read: "Paid $50, more if the building be made of brick." It was brick, and Schieffelin later gave $430 for the building, furnishings, and insurance, bringing his total contribution to $480 ($17,200 today). James Suydam signed next with $82.50. Theodore Frelinghuysen

[42] Minutes, First Holland, 5, 23 Dec. 1856; *De Hollander*, 3 Dec. 1856.
[43] *De Hollander*, 7 Jan. 1857; minutes, First Holland, 6 Mar. 1857; minutes, Classis of Wisconsin, 10 Sept. 1857, art. 24 (quote); Van Schelven, "Van Vleck Hall," in *De Grondwet*, 6 Aug. 1912; Van Vleck to Garretson, 11 Mar. 1857, BDM.
[44] A. C. Van Raalte, "Traveling & Begging Guide, 1857-1860," HMA. The list gives amounts by congregation and individual contributors.

(president of Rutgers College) gave $50, William T. Kunk $100, and so it went. In each church, Van Raalte contacted the pastor first and asked for the privilege to share the pulpit and thus introduce himself and his cause to generally well-off worshipers. "Strike while the iron is hot," was his dictum. He followed up on every lead and played hardball. For example, he told Rev. Edward Livingston of the Griggstown [NJ] Reformed Church that he would "haunt him if he does not make a strong effort for us."[45]

With every contact, Van Raalte also asked for book donations for the "school library" and requested direct shipment by rail to Kalamazoo, care of John Van Vleck. Another aim was to meet John B. Thompson at New Brunswick Seminary, the denomination's state agent for New Jersey, and recruit a teacher for the parochial day school he planned to begin. The dominee also purchased hard-to-find fittings for the academy building—porcelain doorknobs and locks, handles and latches, door hinges and screws, window pulleys and sash, kegs of siding and roofing nails, paints and oils, and sheets of glass. Van Raalte knew how to shake the money tree, turn pockets inside out, and fill several key objectives simultaneously.

When Van Raalte returned, he confidently laid the cornerstone of the academy building. Everything was a "go." In June the begging dominee went east again, this time for eleven weeks. His first stop was as a delegate to General Synod; hence his trip to New York was reimbursed. His "burning words" on behalf of his beloved academy made such a "big impression" that his speech was reported in the Holland newspaper and picked up by the Netherlands Separatist periodical, *De Bazuin* (the trumpet).[46] But grubbing for money could be most discouraging. As he told Van Vleck, he had "poor success in getting the 'tin.' ... My strength did fail, and on advice of the Doctor, I did hurry homeward." Yes, Van Vleck replied, begging was an "arduous and irksome business." In the two forays, however, the persistent canvasser had signed up 712 donors for a total of $6,565 ($229,500 today), mostly in gifts of five dollars ($160 today) and less, even twenty-five cents ($8.25 today).[47]

[45] "Traveling & Begging Guide"; Van Raalte to Phelps, 26 Dec. 1859, in Bruins and Schakel, *Envisioning Hope College*, 43.
[46] Brummelkamp, Van Raalte, and De Moen began *De Bazuin* in the 1840s; it was later edited by Van Velzen, then a professor at the Separatist seminary in Kampen.
[47] "Holland Academy building account"; Van Vleck to Van Raalte, 18, 27 June 1857; Van Raalte to Van Vleck, 27 July 1857, HHA; Van Raalte to Phelps, 26 Aug. 1857, in Bruins and Schakel, *Envisioning Hope College*, 3; *De Hollander*, 3 June 1857; *De Bazuin*, 31 July 1857 (quote) (www.delpher.nl, accessed June 2021); Bruins, "Funding His Vision."

Van Raalte returned to his pulpit in mid-August on a rainy and cold day, but his sermon on Psalm 78 was warm and powerful. It stressed the calling of Christians in the world to good effect, as the report in *De Hollander* stated: "Many of the listeners, young and old, fathers, mothers, and children, were not only visibly touched and admonished, but also encouraged and inspired to start this highly important task or to doubly increase their efforts."[48] The sermon belied his exhaustion, as he confided in Phelps.

> Really, I want rest, my system is exhausted, but it is here not the place of rest, a flood of cares and duties goes over my head. I am tired of the Bussiness [sic], but my feeble body makes it rather onerous. My strength however by good nursing and slow hasting begins to gain. But I suspect, looking at circumstances, that I will soon be used up. Yet I know that we have our existence in God's will.[49]

The Lord gave him another nineteen years of life.

By 1858 Van Raalte had raised most of the needed $7,000 ($260,000 today) for the four-story brick building, later named Van Vleck Hall. With Van Raalte's strong support, General Synod promised an annual appropriation, which ensured the future of the academy. Every family in the Classis of Holland was asked to tithe one dollar annually for the academy; the Holland congregation's contribution came to $107 the first year. Unfortunately, by 1861, the tithe was not working well, and the ministers were urged to preach on the "imperative duty of our churches to sustain that institution."[50]

In February 1859, Van Vleck resigned, unhappy and disillusioned for many of the same reasons that Taylor had resigned. His salary was in arrears by $956 ($35,000 today); he and his wife were both ill from tuberculosis, and he was deeply estranged from Van Raalte.[51] This breakdown, however, had developed over time. The dominee had

---

[48] *De Hollander*, 19 Aug. 1857, trans. Simone Kennedy.
[49] Van Raalte to Phelps, 26 Aug. 1857, in Bruins and Schakel, *Envisioning Hope College*, 3.
[50] Minutes, First Holland, 6 Mar. 1857, trans. Buursma; Mr. and Mrs. Abner Hasbrouck to John Van Vleck, 22 July 1858, printed in *Holland Sentinel* (29 Mar. 1879), 26; Wichers, *Century of Hope*, 42-44, 49; Kennedy, *Commentary*, 7 Apr. 1858, 1:792; 29-30 Sept. 1858, 2:832-34; 27-28 Sept. 1859, 2:907; 3 Apr. 1860, 2:925-26; Van Raalte to Phelps, 26 June 1861, JAH.
[51] Van Vleck to Garretson, 10 Feb. 1858, BDM; Van Vleck to Van Raalte, 19 Aug. 1859, HHA.

John Van Vleck, third principal
of Holland Academy (*JAH*)

charged Van Vleck with several indiscretions: faulting Hollanders in his public writings, questionable financial accounting, discussing with the synodical board of education a plan to relocate the Holland Academy to Chicago or some other large western city, and trying to persuade two young men to accompany him back east to enroll at Rutgers College.

But Van Vleck defended himself and his reputation in a frank letter to Van Raalte. Yes, he had criticized Hollanders, but he loved them nonetheless. Recruiting young men for Rutgers College was done openly, albeit without the board's prior approval. To have his financial accounting questioned cut Van Vleck the deepest of all since his honesty and good name were at stake. He attributed the accounting problem to Van Raalte's lack of oversight. "While in Holland, my books were continuously open to inspection. I never made any effort to keep anything in the dark. Further, I am honest. I have my failings, but the love of money is not one of them." Van Vleck closed with the Aaronic blessing: "The LORD bless you and keep you; the LORD make his face to shine upon you and be gracious to you; the LORD lift up his countenance upon you and give you peace" (Numbers 6:23-26, KJV).[52]

Van Vleck's legacy was large, and the academic building erected during his tenure still adorns the center of Hope College's campus and

---

[52] Wichers, *Century of Hope*, 50-52.

Van Vleck Hall, erected 1857-59, with Van Raalte the primary fundraiser (JAH)

aptly bears his name. Van Vleck expanded the curriculum to include Greek and Hebrew and prepared several theological students for study at New Brunswick Seminary. His biblical-language instruction presaged the future Western Theological Seminary. In parting, he donated $300 of his back salary to the academy. It was a generous act.[53] That both academy principals ran afoul of Van Raalte suggests that Van Raalte himself was too ready to assert his own prerogatives as the founder and leading citizen in Holland. The dominee was a demanding man who jealously guarded the interests of his colony, right or wrong, as he saw them.

From Holland Academy to Hope College—Rev. Philip Phelps Jr. and Dominee Van Raalte

With Van Vleck gone, the dominee lost no time recruiting Rev. Philip Phelps Jr., a former member of Wyckoff's Second Albany Reformed Church. Phelps, a graduate of Union College and New Brunswick Seminary, had ministered for nine years in two Reformed congregations in New York. "I belief [sic] you are the man for it," Van Raalte told Phelps, who accepted. Phelps got along famously with Van Raalte, although he could not speak Dutch. The lower level of the academic building was fitted for the president's residence. For twenty

---

[53] Kennedy, *Commentary*, 6-7 Apr. 1858, 2:856, 865; Van Vleck to Van Raalte, 4 Aug. 1859, JAH; 19 Aug. 1859, HHA; "Our Pioneer School District"; Charles Scott, "Rev. John Van Vleck," Hope College *Anchor* (Nov. 1888): 6-7.

Philip Phelps Jr., fourth
principal of Holland
Academy, 1859-78 (JAH)

years, Phelps led the academy and fashioned its transition into Hope College as the first college president. The two men formed a tight bond, shared the same vision for Christian education, and complemented each other. Phelps was bold, persistent, and even tempered, in contrast to the Dutch dominee, who was visionary and mercurial, depending on his state of health.[54]

Van Raalte returned to the East in October 1859 on a three-month fundraising trip to pay off the remaining debt on Van Vleck Hall and build a house for a second teacher, Giles Van de Wall. Van Raalte's son-in-law Peter Oggel and wife Mina Van Raalte later occupied the house when he was appointed at a teacher. Hence, it became known as the Oggel House. "Begging journeys" were distasteful for the dominee, a "tooth-pulling business," he told Phelps. "I find everywhere an excuse." Clergymen in the East were "sick of bringing begging affairs [sic] before their people.... Kindness and sympathy enough, but money is difficult to be had.... They are all over Dutchdom used up." Wealthy benefactors were tapped out supporting church building projects, missionaries, benevolent projects, New Brunswick Seminary, and

[54] Van Raalte to Phelps, 17 Feb. 1859, in Bruins and Schakel, *Envisioning Hope College*, 9 (quote); *De Hollander*, 7 Mar. 1860; Kennedy, *Commentary*, 6-7 April 1857, 1:73-74, 2:864-65; *Hope College at 150*, 2:873-75. Bruins compares and contrasts the two men with keen insight, and he assigned Phelps the lead role and Van Raalte the supporting role in founding Hope College (*Envisioning Hope College*, xvii, xxiii-xxv).

Christian schools in the West.⁵⁵ Understandably, they "feel sour when they see or hear someone from the Academy." To make matters worse, a whistleblower, named W., had charged in the *Christian Intelligencer* that the academy was being mismanaged. Van Raalte immediately published a trenchant rebuttal to counter the charge, but the damage was done.⁵⁶

Being on the go every day also took its toll on Van Raalte physically. "Two times I have been chilled sitting on open wagons, and was unwell, cough, rheumatism, etc., but I am nearly well again. The last time, I did take timely medicines. They took good care of me." A week later he reported being "very miserable and exceedingly exhausted.... I am not strong and soon used up. Cold, rheumatism, and neuralgia are my troubles," and toothache, a "troublesome companion." Yet he decided to continue canvassing for another six weeks, despite "homesickness and despair." His friend Schieffelin finally offered a matching gift of $100 if Van Raalte could come up with *twelve* more donors within sixty days. The dominee disliked the squeeze play but did find more than twelve and came home with $3,000 ($110,000 today), enough to make Van Vleck Hall debt free. On the way home, he preached in the Rochester (NY) church.⁵⁷

Van Raalte noted that a friendly wag called "the Holland Academy my first wife and Mrs. Van Raalte my second wife." That was close to the truth; he had sacrificed her well-being for the school, as he admitted in a letter to Phelps in Holland, when he decided to extend his stay. "Do your utmost to convince my wife about the necessity of my staying so long. I pray you convince her, and if her mind is quiet, I shall feel relieved very much. I feel that this bitter piece will do a great deal of mischief in my family."⁵⁸ This was the dominee's third and last begging trip in the East.

In 1860 Van Raalte more than doubled the academy campus to sixteen acres by donating twenty-two more lots to the ten he had given initially. In addition, he obtained a court decree to close Eleventh

---

⁵⁵ Van Raalte to Phelps, 8 Sept., 2, 19 Nov., 17 Dec. 1859, in *Envisioning Hope College*, 22, 28-29, 39-40; *De Hollander*, 20 Oct. 1859.

⁵⁶ See *Envisioning Hope College*, 346-69, for all relevant documents in English translation.

⁵⁷ Van Raalte to Phelps, 19 Nov. 10, 17 (quote), 26 Dec. 1859, 2, 9 Jan., 2 Feb. 1860, in *Envisioning Hope College* 28, 36-44, 49-53.

⁵⁸ Van Raalte to Phelps, 1 (quote), 10 Dec. (quote) 1859, in *Envisioning Hope College*, 32, 36; Ottawa County Deed Records, Book M, 537, Book Q, 318, in Swierenga, "Real Estate Sales by Albertus C. Van Raalte; First Catalogue and Circular of Hope College" (Albany, NY: 1866), 45.

Public and Christian Education 351

Hope College gymnasium/chapel, dedicated July 17, 1862
(JAH)

Street from Cedar (College) to Fish (Columbia) Avenues, which created Pine Grove, now the center of the Hope College campus. In October 1862, the academy board approved Phelps' proposal to create the Collegiate Department, primarily to train those intending to become ministers, and the seminal Class of 1866 began its journey.[59] That summer, students handy with tools gave up vacation time to construct a combined gymnasium/chapel building, dedicated a day after the annual academy examinations in mid-July. Van Raalte offered the opening prayer at the dedication, and students then took over the lengthy program with singing, dialogues, and readings. It was a joyful occasion for all, especially after the stressful exams. Van Raalte was commended for his untiring efforts on behalf of the school, then with forty-two students.[60]

Phelps and Van Raalte together had transformed Holland Academy into Hope College, thanks to the endorsement of General Synod 1863 ("Lords of the East" in Van Raalte's sarcastic words). Phelps and Van Raalte, as classical delegates to the Albany gathering, made the case for a western college to stand beside the RPDC's revered Rutgers College. Seine Bolks, an eyewitness, years later recalled Van Raalte's

---

[59] Minutes, Holland Academy Board, 14-15 Oct. 1862, JAH.
[60] "Annual Public Exercises of the Holland Academy, Held at the Opening of the New Gymnasium, July 17, 1862," Philip Phelps Scrapbook, Phelps Collection, JAH; Phelps, "Holland Academy," *Christian Intelligencer*, 22 July 1862.

impassioned speech on the floor of Synod. "He stood and spoke for more than half an hour at that meeting while tears trickled down his cheeks. And when the motion of support passed, he called out: 'Now I can die, now I have a place of education for my children that is joined to that precious church in which I suffered in the old Fatherland.'" Bolks continued: "Van Raalte was a man of prayer," and many others joined him in prayer for this institution and "loved and struggled for it. I know this. Van Raalte had a broad vision." Van Raalte's hand was strengthened in that his congregation had raised $117.50 for Rutgers College, $100 ($2,400 today) of which coming from Van Raalte's own purse. With Synod's blessing, the pair now had to raise an $80,000 endowment that the state of Michigan required to charter a college.[61]

Synod authorized Phelps to solicit in Eastern churches for the money. Van Raalte gave Phelps his marching orders.

> If I was placed in your position, I would think it to be my clear duty by the necessity of the case . . . to go over the whole field and to work patiently with each Church, even if I had to stay 2 or 3 days in each church. I would entirely depend on my own exertions. I would divide the amount over the whole Church and stay until I had it in each Church.

In sum, "Church by Church will accomplish it, but nothing less. Nobody besides you can or will do it for the present." He added: "It is well, but you must paddle your own boat." The news that Schieffelin had contributed $25,000 ($466,500 today) for scholarships led Van Raalte to liken the gift to "messengers from Heaven to cheer you on."[62]

With Van Raalte's constant encouragement and advice, Phelps in two years raised $40,000 in the East, while Peter Oggel canvassed Western churches for $10,000. The denomination donated $30,000. With the minimum endowment in hand of $80,000 ($1.5 million today), Hope College received its official charter on May 14, 1866. At the first college commencement in July, Phelps gave the inaugural address, and eight students stood to receive diplomas; one was William "Will" Gilmore, Van Raalte's future son-in-law. He and six (of seven)

---

[61] *Acts and Proceedings*, 1863, 246; minutes, First Holland, 5 Oct. 1863; Bolks' address at installation of Prof. Nicholas M. Steffens, in *De Hope*, 16 Dec. 1884; Voskuil, "Continuity and Change," 148-49. Neither Van Raalte nor the denomination could have foreseen Rutgers College's abandonment of the Christian faith within fifty years.

[62] Van Raalte to Phelps, 8, 18 Mar. (quote), 17 Apr. 1865, in *Envisioning Hope College*, 139-40, 125-26, 130.

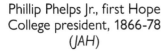

Phillip Phelps Jr., first Hope College president, 1866-78 (*JAH*)

classmates' admission to Hope's new graduate department in theology required special synodical approval since they had not matriculated at Rutgers College. Van Raalte missed the significant occasion because he and Christina were enjoying a homecoming in the Netherlands.[63]

Van Raalte and Phelps were the dynamic duo that gave birth to Hope College, but Phelps deserves pride of place for leading the institution from an academy to a college and raising the necessary monies to establish the college. Van Raalte stood by him at every turn and coined the college epigraph: "This is my anchor of hope for this people in the future," paraphrasing Heb. 6:19a (KJV): "Which hope we have as an anchor of the soul," thus connecting God's promise of faithfulness to the college itself. Phelps added theological education to the college curriculum, which eventually in 1884 led to the establishment of Western Theological Seminary on the campus.[64]

Advanced education of the Van Raalte children

The two eldest Van Raalte daughters, Mina and Christine, in 1857 went to New Jersey to study under the able sisters of John Van

---

[63] *Grand Haven News*, 23 Nov. 1864; Van Raalte to Phelps, 23 Sept. 1868, in *Envisioning Hope College*, 190-91; Voskuil, "When East Meets West," 208.

[64] Nyenhuis, "Striving for Excellence," 72-73; Wichers, *Century of Hope*, 78-79, 82-84, 99; *Hope College Catalogue*, 1891-92; *Fiftieth Anniversary Catalog of Hope College, May 1916*, 189; Voskuil, "Vexed Question."

Hope College campus in 1865 (*l-r*): Oggel House, laboratory, Van Vleck Hall (*JAH*)

Vleck. Christine, it was later said, spoke "flawless English," thanks "to her Eastern education." In 1858 the girls were called home and enrolled in the all-male Holland Academy, thus breaking a gender barrier. They gained permission, perhaps, because they attended part time.

Mina married in 1860, and Christine became an apprentice dressmaker in Kalamazoo. Her father had prepared her by buying a new-fangled sewing machine, now coming into vogue. When Van Raalte was in New York fundraising, friends donated five sewing machines for his colony, and he took lessons there so he could teach his wife and daughter, but he was inept. "Clumsy fellow that I am," he noted. "I have to suffer their jokes.... My oldest daughter [Christine], now at home, sixteen years of age, works the machine. It's a blessing. My wife cannot do it on account of her broken nervous system." Christine made shirts, underwear, and handkerchiefs for her brothers fighting in the Civil War (ch. 13). Dirk had to gently tell his mother and sister to desist since it was all too much to carry on long marches.[65]

During the war, in 1863, Christine enrolled at Olivet College in the "Ladies prep," four-year degree course; she graduated in 1867 and married in 1869. Youngest daughter, Anna Sophia, born in 1856, may have attended the Primary and Female Department of Hope College around 1873. In any event, Van Raalte's four daughters all married professional men—two married preachers, and two married professors.

---

[65] *Christian Intelligencer*, 22 May 1862; Christina Catherina, Kalamazoo, to mother, 1, 8 Nov. 1862; Dirk Van Raalte to mother, 25 July 1864.

Only Dirk, the youngest of the three sons, graduated from Hope College, in 1867.[66]

Denominational and classical support for Christian day schools

The Reformed Church backed public schools at midcentury but did allow individual congregations to conduct Christian schools. This concession prompted Samuel Schieffelin to subsidize RPDC parochial schools in immigrant churches, and a dozen congregations founded schools. To Schieffelin's disappointment, however, most of the schools proved to be short lived.[67]

Van Raalte welcomed this initiative, but the Classis of Holland demurred. He recorded the rationale in his classical report to the 1853 Particular Synod of Albany. Classis judged that Christian day schools were necessary *only* where "public schools, by being a mixed multitude, take on the character of a colorless Protestantism, which opens the way for Catholicism." In such cases, no effort would be too much "to educate the children of the church in the spirit of the positive, biblically based Protestantism of the Reformation." But in homogeneous settlements like Holland, classis "judges that it is better to use the state organization [public school] to benefit our society's children."[68] In short, public schools were fine in little Holland but not in large, diverse cities like Kalamazoo, Grand Rapids, and Muskegon, with their diverse populations, including Catholics. Actually, Schieffelin-funded schools sprouted in eighteen Dutch settlements across the Midwest, many in towns smaller than Holland.[69]

General Synod 1853 was even less Christian-school minded than the Particular Synod. The highest church tribunal spurned Schieffelin's offer. Public education was acceptable if teachers simply read the Bible daily "without note or comment." As for the freedom of individual congregations to establish parochial schools, synod opined that western congregations might better donate their money to Holland Academy. Schieffelin disagreed, stating that Reformed churches since the Reformation, including old-school Presbyterians,

---

[66] Christina Van Raalte, "Dear Children," 22 Dec. 1857, HHA; Van Vleck to Van Raalte, 5 July 1859, HHA; Bruins et al., *Albertus and Christina*, 64-65, 128, 147-48, 167; Kennedy, *Commentary*, 1 Sept. 1852, 1:284.
[67] This section relies on Kennedy, "Van Raalte and Parochial Schools." See also, Corwin, *Digest*, 478-83.
[68] Dosker, *Van Raalte*, 189, trans. Dekker. Contrary to Dosker, Kennedy, *Commentary*, 27 April 1853, 1:320, says that Van Raalte was delegated but did not attend.
[69] Aay, "Present from the Beginning," 13-15.

had established Christian schools for covenant youth. He feared that Reformed children were being corrupted in nonsectarian, minimally Christian public schools.[70]

In early 1854, the erstwhile benefactor sent a passionate letter to all pastors in the denomination that urged them to found congregational schools. Van Raalte, on the same page as Schieffelin, brought up the letter at the April 1854 meeting of the Classis of Holland, but the brothers were lukewarm. Clerk Van Raalte's minutes read:

> With respect to Parochial Schools, it is the judgment of the assembly that the churches ought to take care that their children are taught in schools where they are brought under definitely Christian influence, and that consequently wherever there is an overwhelming influence of unbelief and superstition, it is emphatically a duty to establish congregational schools.

In short, parochial schools were advisable only where public schools were under the "overwhelming influence of unbelief and superstition"—a high bar indeed.[71]

Van Raalte included this weak statement of classis in his report to Synod 1854, which he again delivered in person as a delegate. That body, along with several other regional assemblies that had extoled Schieffelin's plan, induced the senior body to reverse course and approve parochial schools, provided consistories did not belabor parents who continued to favor public schools. Synod tasked the board of education to manage the monies. Synod at first was reluctant to support parochial schools, fearing that they "might interfere with our public school system." But "after reflection and discussion," and upon the strong advocacy of the board of education, the brethren concluded "that Christian schools under the patronage influence of the Church can only exert a wholesome influence on our public schools... [and they] will keep before the public eye a model for Christian training."[72] This is one of the rare times when General Synod commended Christian day schools. Schieffelin's generous financial support temporarily won the day. Besides money and time, he wrote a history textbook chronicling

---

[70] Ibid., 15-18, citing Corwin, *Digest*, 478-79.
[71] Kennedy, *Commentary*, 12 April 1854, 1:428-29; Aay, "Present from the Beginning," 15-16.
[72] Samuel B. Schieffelin, "A Letter on Parochial Schools," 1 Mar. 1854, in General Synod Papers 1849-59; *Acts and Proceedings*, 1854, 454-55; Bruins, "Educational Endeavors," 179-81; Corwin, *Digest*, 477-83.

from Creation to Christ that Hope College adopted for sophomore classes during Van Raalte's lifetime.[73]

In April 1855, First Kalamazoo Reformed Church, not Van Raalte's church, was the first to tap Schieffelin funds for a parochial school. The school, according to the rules laid down by General Synod 1855, would be under classical supervision and taught in the Dutch language, with a gradual transition to English. Van Raalte personally, and the Classis of Holland collectively, approved the Kalamazoo request enthusiastically, believing that parochial schools "are so necessary in places where the overwhelming stream of unbelief and superstition dilutes or wipes out the color of positive Christianity." Classis then resolved to "heartily pray for the Lord's blessing upon this first attempt, not only for the sake of the flock at Kalamazoo but also as an example to the other churches." Despite Van Raalte's obvious approval of Kalamazoo's school, he did not bring up the Schieffelin plan at his own consistory meetings for a year and a half, until December 1856. The congregation had a full plate already to pay for the new church dedicated in June 1856.[74]

Parochial and female education at Holland

Van Raalte's first experience with American public schools came when his followers spent the winter of 1846-47 in Detroit, and he visited several public schools before enrolling his two eldest children, Albertus, aged nine, and Mina, aged eight. He was generally displeased with what he found. "The piety of the teachers does not provide good direction, and the schools become worldly," he told Brummelkamp. Only one schoolmaster met with his approval. Given the "worldly" public schools in Detroit, the dominee relished the freedom of education in America and determined to establish Christian day schools in his colony as nurseries of the churches. But such schools had to wait until the brutal first years of the colony had passed.[75]

---

[73] Kennedy, *Commentary*, 29-30 Sept. 1858, 2:833. The title of the 292-page textbook was *The Foundations of History, A Series of the First Things* (Board of Publication, 1855).

[74] Kennedy, *Commentary*, 11 Apr. 1855, 1:477-79; minutes, First Holland, 5 Dec. 1856. Van Raalte considered the Kalamazoo parochial school for the "scattered sheep of the house of Israel" as an example to others. It lasted at least twelve years, longer than those in Pella, Grand Haven, and Muskegon, and sixteen others in the Midwest.

[75] *De Hope*, 8 Jan. 1896 (trans. Earl Wm. Kennedy); Brummelkamp, *Stemmen uit Noord-Amerika* in *Voices from America*, 28. For a fuller discussion of the parochial school, see Swierenga, *Holland, Michigan*, 1:531-43.

The Van Raaltes were progressive in pushing for female education at the secondary and college levels. Albertus envisioned higher education for young women at his Pioneer School in 1851, and in 1858, he and Christina enrolled two daughters in Holland Academy. They were far ahead of their time. Only three years earlier, in 1848, the Seneca Falls [NY] Convention had launched the women's rights movement with a manifesto that "Education of the woman has as much weight as that of the man." Women at that time had no legal rights, no right to own property, vote, or enter the professions, except as elementary teachers.

In late 1856, the time was ripe. Van Raalte had in his pocket a call from First Reformed Church in Pella, which he used as leverage for his price to remain in Holland, to press his own congregation to establish a parochial school as a feeder to the academy. The school would also "more powerfully advance" religious instruction for younger children, especially girls, with a female teacher who could teach them "specifically feminine tasks.... Up to now, the girls, alas, have been neglected," he said. Teachers were biased in favor of boys, and parents often kept daughters home after the third or fourth grade. The dominee was also concerned about safeguarding the morals of maturing girls from teenage boys. Besides, the district school could not provide a "good Christian" education since its board was at risk of falling into the hands of non-Christians. His rationale, backed by the threat to leave for Pella, had the desired effect. The congregation approved the dominee's proposal for a parochial school, which positive response had "a great influence as to his decision." Van Raalte then had the Classis of Holland send an urgent appeal to the denomination's board of education for support.[76]

As a delegate to General Synod 1857, Van Raalte personally carried the campaign for his parochial school with an impassioned speech. Synod unanimously approved the $100 Schieffelin subsidy, which covered half the operating costs. His congregation promised to take a monthly collection for the rest. Deacon Derk Te Roller agreed to be the administrator. He opened his home for classes and boarded the teacher, twenty-year-old Hendrikje (Hendrika or Rika) Van Zwaluwenburg, an 1850 immigrant from Gelderland. For $2.50 per week ($87 today) plus board, she taught the three Rs in Dutch, using textbooks either from

---

[76] Minutes, First Holland, 6 Oct., 12, 18, 20 Nov., 5, 23 Dec. 1856; Kennedy, *Commentary*, 8 Apr. 1857, 2:746.

Derk Te Roller home, southeast corner of Ninth and Market (Central) Streets, erected 1851, destroyed in the Holland Fire of 1871 (HHA)

Christian schools in the Netherlands or reprinted in Michigan, plus the Bible and Heidelberg Catechism as mandated by Synod.[77]

Te Roller enrolled girls to age twelve and boys to age seven. The middle Van Raalte daughters, Christine, and Mary (Maria), likely attended at some point. Classes began in March 1857 and continued year round, with a three-week summer break. The response was so overwhelming that the consistory had to cap enrollment and hire a second teacher, Cornelia Falconer, sister-in-law of the new academy principal, John Van Vleck. She agreed for only the 1858-59 school year and taught English grammar and spelling since she knew little or no Dutch. Both women earned $8 per month ($296 today), plus room and board, which was a reduction in pay for Van Zwaluwenburg of $2 per month, about which she complained.[78]

The consistory in April 1857 named a building committee of Van Raalte, Te Roller, and deacon Jan De Vries to plan for a schoolhouse. In a letter to Van Vleck, Van Raalte, then fundraising in New York, noted that a building was "absolutely necessary," but "we cannot raise the

---

[77] Minutes, First Holland, 6 Mar., 8, 10 Apr. 1857, 8 Apr. 1858; Kennedy, *Commentary*, 6-7 Apr. 1859, 2:865; 9 Sept. 1860, 2:1004; *Acts and Proceedings*, 1858, 334. Dosker contends that Van Raalte objected to including the catechism, convinced that this was properly the duty of the pastor (Dosker, *Van Raalte*, 188-89, trans. Dekker).

[78] Minutes, First Holland, 6, 17 Mar., 10 Apr. 1857, 12 Apr., 19 Aug., 25 Nov. 1858.

money because of simple poverty." Although this caused him "great distress," he said he would not borrow money backed by a mortgage on his real estate. This statement is surprising. The land-rich dominee had borrowed money many times against his real estate holding. Why was he unwilling to do so in August 1857 for the parochial school? An unstated reason is surely the national financial panic at that time, triggered by the failure of a major Ohio bank. Van Raalte saw at first hand in New York City how the crisis "caused many ravages and pressing needs." This so-called Panic of 1857 set off the first worldwide economic crisis, thanks to Samuel F. B. Morse's newly invented telegraph that allowed the bad news to spread rapidly across the country and in Europe.[79]

Van Raalte's early enthusiasm for his school faded in the 1858-59 academic year when it did not achieve the "goals envisioned." The quality of education was poor, and classrooms in the Orphan House were ill-equipped. Prior to the 1859-60 school year, the dominee declared that he could not in good conscience ask the denomination's education committee to continue its annual subsidy. An unspoken factor in the dominee's change of heart was a decision of the district school to establish a high school separate from the elementary school. Younger girls would no longer be corrupted by older boys. Van Raalte threw down the gauntlet to his congregation; either improve the congregational school, or close it.[80]

His assessment read like a jeremiad. He was thoroughly disappointed that his "good intentions were either not understood or misinterpreted." The congregation, and especially the consistory, had backed off in the face of opposition or "fear of difficult circumstances." The church covered half the budget and without its full support, the dominee threatened to "shed his responsibility" for the school. No longer could he excuse the "blameworthy lukewarm attitude" of his parishioners for a "godly education."[81] This biting indictment was part of a larger falling out and came immediately upon Van Raalte's return from the three-month Pella sojourn. His congregants were not

---

[79] Ibid., 12 Apr. 1857; Van Raalte "To my dear congregation in Holland," *De Hollander*, 18 Mar. 1857; Van Vleck to Garretson, 18 Aug. 1857, BDM; wikipedia.org/wiki/Panic_of_1857. *De Bazuin*, 31 July 1857, reported that Van Raalte at synod spoke "very extensively, from a full heart. His burning words and passionate plea touched the hearts deeply" (www.delpher.nl, accessed, June 2021).

[80] Minutes, First Holland, 2 Sept. 1859; Van Brummelen, *Telling the Next Generation*, 57-58.

[81] Minutes, First Holland, 2, 20 Sept. 1859.

giving sacrificially, in his view, for either the Holland Academy or the parochial school. Christian education was not their highest priority; they were content with public schooling.

Van Raalte was too harsh in his indictment. The consistory reiterated its commitment to the parochial school and noted that fully one-fourth of the church budget was committed to the school and the Holland Academy. Supporting both schools was asking too much of the congregants, whose giving in 1858 totaled $1,100, or $6.55 per family. The expensive church pillars were still unfinished; the dominee's salary was still in arrears, and the financial panic and ensuing three-year national depression prompted those with money to hold it tight.

Then General Synod of 1859 turned down Van Raalte's request on behalf of the congregation for the annual subsidy, which left the budget short barely three months into the school year. The rejection "has a significance that will become apparent in the future," opined the consistory ominously. Van Raalte's harsh criticism of the school's shortcomings may have given cover to Synod's board of education. The next telling blow came at a congregational meeting later that month, when the membership, due to the "financial need of the times," voted down by a small majority the consistory's proposal to improve the school building. Despite the difficulty "to advance this cause among our people," the consistory declared its continuing commitment to the school. The synodical rejection so grated on Van Raalte that he vowed never again to be a delegate to that august body.[82]

In a further disappointment, Van Zwaluwenburg in April 1860 announced her resignation at the end of the term. She had remained one additional year after receiving a teaching offer from another school, and the congregation pled penury in not granting her request for a raise. The consistory made immediate work of finding a "competent and God-fearing" replacement, and the elders launched a pledge drive to continue the school and cover the debts. In one month, they had pledges from twenty members totaling $117 ($4,300 today), and the canvass was ongoing. This gave the consistory the courage to recruit Marietta (later Mary) (Mrs. Owen) Van Olinda, a Normal School graduate, to replace Van Zwaluwenburg. The consistory also appointed a committee to administer the school, one-half from its body, led by Van Raalte, and the other half from the congregation.

---

[82] Ibid., 25 Nov. 1858, 2, 20 Sept., 24 Nov. 1859; Van Raalte to Giles Van de Wall, summer 1861, trans. Jalving, HMA.

Marietta Van Olinda, teacher at Holland parochial school 1860-61 (HHA)

One appointee from the congregation disapproved of the school and recommended merging it with the district school. Van Raalte feared that the opposition to Van Olinda was "on account of me." He had hired her, even though she could not speak Dutch.[83]

Van Raalte and the consistory brought the school issue to a head at the annual congregational meeting in November 1860 with the question: Should it cease or continue? After much discussion, the tally by secret ballot was a resounding yes, continue, with only one negative vote. The annual financial report that day showed an $87 contribution for the school, double the $48 donated the previous year, plus $120 in special pledges for the current year. But the school was $630 ($23,000 today) in debt.[84] Mrs. Van Olinda bravely carried on, promising that "all studies and handwork (sewing) essential for a good-bringing up will be taught," as well as music for interested pupils.[85]

During the 1860-61 school year, attendance declined to the point that classes could meet in a home. Van Olinda's salary was $151 in arrears at the end of the school year, and she resigned to take a position

---

[83] Minutes, First Holland, 30 Mar., 9, 16, 27 Apr., 15 June, 6 July 1860; Van Raalte to Phelps, 17 July, 16 Aug. 1861, in Bruins and Schakel, *Envisioning Hope College*, 84-85, 86-87; Van Koevering, *Legends of the Dutch*, 252; statistical report, *Acts and Proceedings*, 1858, 425.

[84] Minutes, First Holland, 24 Nov. 1859, 29 Nov. 1860, 11 Oct. 1862.

[85] "Pioneer Schools," *De Hollander*, 9 Dec. 1858, 8, 25 Aug. 1859.

in the district school. This brought the parochial school board close to the point of quitting, unless the congregation would provide the necessary monies.

Van Raalte confronted the issue at the congregational meeting that same month, and the members again reacted positively, committing themselves to raise academic standards, build an "appropriate building," canvass the congregation for pledges, and hire a teacher who would "give instruction in the Holland language, so dearly desired by so many." This person was Cornelius Doesburg, an experienced district school teacher who had previously opposed the parochial school. (This can be explained by the fact that in his native Zuid-Holland, Cornelius Doesburg, an 1855 immigrant, belonged to the Hervormde Kerk, not the Christian Separated Church). That very evening, twenty-four members pledged $297 for his salary, plus $197 for the building, and two businessmen donated ten thousand board feet of lumber and a thousand shingles.[86]

But a second congregational meeting only one month later had a far different outcome. The financial drive for the school raised only $15, plus $11 for the building. A motion that all members present make an additional pledge was voted down. The lengthy discussion that followed revealed "sharply differing principles" on whether the school was even necessary, as well as all the problems involved. Not only was there no unity, but some members "actively worked in public against the program." The upshot was a compromise plan to raise $600 ($20,700 today) to continue the school on a smaller scale; it passed by a vote of thirty-five for, seven against, and two blank. The unusually low attendance greatly concerned Van Raalte and depreciated the 80 percent yes vote. After one more year, in April 1862, the school closed for good. For many, the spirit was willing, but the flesh was weak.[87]

Evaluating Van Raalte's ideals of Christian education

"Parochial education lies buried here," Van Raalte lamented to his colleague, Giles Van de Wall. "But I am following the advice you gave me. I am doing nothing at all." On this vital issue, Van Raalte stood alone. His congregation, like the Reformed denomination generally, was satisfied with public elementary education. "It is a shame that the Reformed Church should leave the whole field of Christian education for children to mere chance, or in general, to Providence."

[86] Minutes, First Holland, 23 June 1861.
[87] Ibid., 1 July 1861.

The dominee's true feelings spilled out in a remarkable postscript to the Van de Wall letter.

> Here are a few more lines, but I beg you to bury them with you. I am longing for a call, for I am very anxious to take up a different position. Do not show this composition to anybody else, and do not let any of its contents be known in the Netherlands.... It is impossible for me to continue my work amidst this dissension, for my labors are rendered fruitless by it, and my heart turns sour.

He voiced four reasons for his disillusionment.

> The public school system is extinguishing the parochial schools, and now I am called upon to promote the cause of the public schools. In the second place, our congregation has become completely indifferent to the Holland Academy. Moreover, there is always trouble with the members of the consistory over the acceptance of persons for the administration of the sacraments [Specifically, the issue of "closed" or "close" communion. Van Raalte favored "close" communion.] The elders have caused me to become estranged from them.... Above all, the immersion in worldly affairs is galling to me, and I am unable to tear myself loose from them, so that this cause alone is enough to make me leave the country.[88]

Earl Wm. Kennedy, in his masterful history of Van Raalte's experiences with Christian education on both sides of the Atlantic, attributed the closing of the parochial school to the "realities of the American situation." Families could have "Christian education for nothing" at Union School, if they were satisfied with the teachers and a brief Bible reading to open the day. Besides, attending the common schools was "a patriotic thing to do."[89] As a result, the dominee had "to reconcile himself with the fact that his financially hard-pressed parishioners had other priorities than a tuition-based free school, when they could obtain education from Christian teachers in the local tax-supported public schools.... Practicality triumphed over ideology

---

[88] Van Raalte to Van de Wall, 29 June 1862, translated in Hyma, *Van Raalte*, 259-60, 270-71. The postscript to this letter has been lost, but fortunately Hyma printed it, *Van Raalte*, 225-26.

[89] Kennedy, "Van Raalte and Parochial Schools," 190, 195; Wichers, *Century of Hope*, 88-89.

and history."⁹⁰ Van Raalte's generation was pre-Kuyperian: Christian day schools were not yet integral to the Dutch Reformed faith, as they would be fifty years later among the Christian Reformed Church.

Van Raalte in 1869 reiterated his call for Christian elementary education. He declared: "I am astonished to find that people can expect a future of the Reformed Church without a training of the young by the clergymen." As chair of the classical education committee, the dominee in 1871 again publicly urged "every Christian citizen to use their influence to maintain the reading of the Bible in the schools."⁹¹

Two years before his death, in an article in *De Hope* about the Christian school movement in the Netherlands, Van Raalte called for similar schools in America "to raise and educate *Baptized Citizens* . . . in a positive Christian environment." He condemned "neutral schools" for teaching unbelief, like Darwinism, and declared Christian schools to be "essential." Christian parents should never "transfer to the government their calling to raise their children."⁹² Public schools were always "second best." By this time, however, the Classis of Holland had given up on Christian schools, preferring instead "to use their influence in our day schools, for obtaining competent and religious instructors, who have been brought up in our own church." Hope College did not graduate female teachers to staff elementary schools until the 1880s. Even with Christian teachers, Van Raalte remained skeptical. "To clothe [Holland's] Union School with the dignity of the church helps in the deception."⁹³

Van Raalte's vision for Christian education stemmed from his youth when—very likely—his father went against the grain to enroll him in the Wanneperveen Christian School. His convictions were strengthened at Ommen when he fought the mayor and King Willem I to establish a parochial school. Over forty years of ministry, Van Raalte maintained the ideal of Christian day schools and disdained

---

[90] De Vries and Boonstra, *Pillar Church*, 87-88; Dosker, *Van Raalte*, 184-94, trans. Dekker.

[91] Van Raalte to Phelps, 18 Nov. 1869, in *Envisioning Hope College*, 222-23; Van Raalte, "Opvoeding Neutraal Education," *De Hope*, 4 Mar. 1874, trans. Simone Kennedy, quoted in Kennedy, "Van Raalte and Parochial Schools," 194; Van Raalte, "Report by Committee for Schools and Education," *De Hope*, 28 Sept. 1871; Stegenga, *Anchor of Hope*, 38.

[92] Van Raalte made this point in "Education: Public Schools," *De Hope*, 4 Mar. 1874.

[93] Van Raalte's "Report by the Committee for School and Education for the Fall Session of the Classis of Holland" (*De Hope*, 28 Sept. 1872); Kennedy, *Commentary*, 11 Sept. 1872, 3:1705-7; Van Raalte to Phelps, 17 May 1873, in *Envisioning Hope College*, 314.

public schools, which were necessary but not preferable. The die was cast when he merged the Classis of Holland into the church in the East. This denomination after midcentury rejected Christian day schools as unpatriotic in the religious pluralism of the country. Even as public schools became more secular, the Reformed Church in America embraced them ever more ardently. The church and the family, in their view, had the chief responsibility to raise children in the fear of the Lord so they could be salt and light in public schools.

As a result, in Kennedy's words, "The true heirs of Van Raalte's original vision" were the hundreds of Christian day schools founded after 1880 by the Christian Reformed Church under the influence of Abraham Kuyper. Holland Christian Schools, established in 1901, fulfilled Van Raalte's vision. Their staff and curriculum are guided by Kuyper's famous quote: "There is not a square inch in the whole domain of our human existence over which Christ, who is Sovereign over all, does not cry, Mine!"[94]

---

[94] Kennedy, "Van Raalte and Parochial schools," 195.

CHAPTER 12

Land and Business: "God could have made me a capitalist."

In the Holland colony, Van Raalte was first and foremost a dominee. His main task was to conduct worship services and baptize, marry, nurture, and bury his congregants.[1] But the survival of the settlement depended on economic development, and the leader was increasingly drawn into worldly pursuits. His proclivity for business also dovetailed with his vision for social uplift in the Netherlands and in the Holland colony. He was a "social entrepreneur" and a real estate magnate, which he came by honestly. Brothers Petrus and Arend were Amsterdam merchants, and Benjamin de Moen, Van Raalte's father-in-law, was a Leiden landlord. Two brothers-in-law partnered with him in Ommen business: Dirk Blikman Kikkert, husband of Albertus's sister Johanna Bartha, was an Amsterdam ship broker, and Christina's full brother, Carel de Moen, was a Leiden surgeon and an obstetrician.[2]

---

[1] This chapter is based on Swierenga, "Albertus C. Van Raalte," and "Off the Pulpit."
[2] Bruins et al., *Albertus and Christina*, 193-94. Arend and Petrus married sisters born in Westzaan. Later, in 1840, the widower Petrus traveled to Albertus Christiaan's home in Ommen to die there. Sister Johanna Bartha Blikman Kikkert raised Petrus's only child in Amsterdam. I am indebted to Steve Vander Veen, "Holland founder was a 'social entrepreneur,'" *Holland Sentinel*, 1 Aug. 2021, for the term.

If Van Raalte had not aimed to followed his father into the Hervormde Kerk pastorate, he surely would have been a businessman. He had a dynamic view of money and expected to earn market rates of interest on his investments. "Profit" was not a dirty word to him. Beginning in Ommen and continuing in America until his last years, he was involved in various business ventures in manufacturing, milling, retailing, newspaper publishing, and especially real estate and mortgage lending. To maintain the lifestyle to which he was accustomed required that he be self-supporting. His parishioners had to provide for their own families, to buy land, work animals, and farm implements and build houses. They seldom contributed even half of the dominee's salary.

Some pious parishioners, however, considered it unseemly for their pastor to be so involved in off-the-pulpit projects, but as Elton Bruins argued, this was "absolutely crucial to the success of his pioneering endeavors."[3] Van Raalte explained to a colleague in the Netherlands: "We pastors have a unique position here, a personal calling owing to the special situation in which these newly formed people find themselves. We are not only counselors for spiritual affairs but for all affairs of life."[4]

Community needs were also pressing—a public school, a private academy (at Van Raalte's insistence), an impressive church edifice, roads and bridges, the vital harbor for economic development, and a local newspaper to meld the colonists. This infrastructure required tens of thousands of dollars, and the money had to come from local real estate taxes, state and federal government grants, and donors in the East. No wonder the city father became a master fundraiser and lobbyist for government grants of land and cash.

Land dealings

The success of the colony hinged on controlling the land. Speculators were already buying up strategic tracts around Black Lake, Van Raalte reported, but thousands of acres of federal and state government lands upriver were still available and cheap. This required hard cash, of which the Van Raalte party had precious little. As De Witt observed, they had "but small means in hand." Van Raalte agreed: "What I could not do if the association had $3,000." He soon raised the ante to $5,000. De Witt placed a notice in the *Christian Intelligencer* on the dominee's behalf.

[3] Bruins, "Funding His Vision," 53.
[4] Van Raalte to Helenius de Cock, 26 Sept. 1851, AGK.

As the means are not at hand to make the purchase in ready payments by Dr. Van Raalte, the inquiry is made whether persons among us possessing ample means would not advance capital for the purpose, say five thousand dollars, giving the assistance that it would be a safe and soon a profitable investment.[5]

Van Raalte devoted much of his time and energy in the first years to buying, financing, and titling land purchases. Obtaining clear titles, unencumbered with tax liens, squatters' claims, and faulty land surveys, was a challenge, especially to an immigrant with little knowledge of the complex American land system.

In January 1847, Ottawa County treasurer Pennoyer introduced Van Raalte to buying tax-delinquent properties for pennies on the dollar, and Van Raalte bought liens on hundreds of tracts of land for back taxes and penalties, which amounted to only a fraction of their true value. When owners failed to redeem by paying off the liens within the three-year grace period, which happened often, the state issued tax deeds to lien holders. But to have a fully warrantable title, holders of a "color of title" had to purchase a quitclaim from the original owner to "quiet the title," as it was said. Buying property at the tax auction was a controversial form of investment. Any process that wiped out property rights by legal fiat was emotionally laden, even though the tax lien investor was performing a valuable service to the county government by ensuring the timely payment of realty taxes, and losers were often nonresident "speculators" for whom locals had little sympathy.[6]

Congress lands

While in Detroit in late January 1847, Van Raalte made another unusual land purchase from squatters whose claims stretched along the upper reaches of the Black River, east of Holland. Under the Preemption Act of 1841, settlers who claimed land before the opening of public lands offices had a preferential right to claim up to 160 acres at $1.25 per acre and pay within a year after offices announced the start of public sales.[7] Van Raalte paid these squatters $1.25 per acre for their

---

[5] *Christian Intelligencer*, 11 Mar. 1847, reprinted in Lucas, *Dutch Immigrant Memoirs*, 1:35; De Witt to Scholte, 23 Feb. 1847, CCA.
[6] For the intricacies of buying at tax sales, see Swierenga, *Acres for Cents*. Hyma, *Van Raalte*, 214, incorrectly states that Van Raalte bought tax liens against land owned by his poor followers to "hold them in trust."
[7] For the Preemption Law and its workings, see Gates, *Public Land Law Development*, 219, 238-40.

quitclaim deeds, which gave him up to a year to enter the lands at the same price at the Federal Land Office in Ionia, the regional office for the western Lower Peninsula. In effect, he paid $2.50 per acre, half to extinguish the squatters' rights and half to the government. First buyers of public lands, known as original entrants, received patent titles, ostensibly signed by the president but actually dubbed by a treasury official.

Van Raalte boasted to his brother-in-law Brummelkamp in the Netherlands about his land purchases.

> Today I also got from other speculators [i.e., squatters] at the government price [$1.25 per acre] a stretch along both sides of the [Black] river about a half an hour in length [about 1.5 miles] and six or seven minutes [about .3 miles] in width. Then I will have a year to pay for it. Beyond this lies government land of which I will immediately secure as much as I can.

Measuring the size of the tract in minutes to pace it off speaks to the wilderness environment. Van Raalte correctly called the squatters speculators, although they operated on a small scale compared to wealthy easterners.[8]

Van Raalte returned to the Ionia office to enter thousands of additional acres at the Congress price. His entry in April 1847 of a 240-acre tract in the southern half of Section 29 (Township 5 North, Range 15 West) was the most significant. For three hundred dollars, he acquired the site of the village of Holland, which would become his goldmine.[9] He acquired many tracts at substantial discounts by paying with military bounty warrants purchased from land dealers like John Ball. Congress issued the land warrants to veterans for their service in the Mexican War and, retroactively, for service in the War of 1812. Land offices accepted this so-called land paper in lieu of specie (gold or silver coins) on most public lands. Congress made warrants assignable to third parties if veterans chose not to settle on the frontier themselves. Many sold their warrants to dealers at less than half the face value, and a market developed for this land paper. Depending on market forces, land warrants usually traded at discounts from 25 to 35 percent. Van

---

[8] Van Raalte to Brummelkamp, 30 Jan. 1847, in Brummelkamp, *Holland in Amerika*, English typescript, 21, 24.
[9] Swierenga, "Real Estate Sales."

John Ball, Grand Rapids
land agent, state representative
(JAH)

Raalte beat these prices by securing warrants from John Ball for as little as seventy-five cents per acre, a 40 percent discount.[10]

Van Raalte was the original entrant on 1,628 acres in Holland Township in 1847, which amounted to more than half (58 percent) of all federal land purchases that year. Jan Rabbers, the founder of the Groningen settlement, acquired 23 percent of Holland Township, with the rest purchased by twenty-one other buyers. Van Raalte's total was bested only by Jannes Van de Luyster, who purchased 1,680 acres in Zeeland Township. Van de Luyster's funds came from the sale of his extensive farm in old Zeeland for ƒ60,000 ($948,000 today). He platted the town of Zeeland and was the business leader in that colony, which was considerably larger than Holland in the first few years.[11]

Buying from "speculators"

Van Raalte's next step was to acquire key lands around Holland from three Eastern investors who had entered the land at the minimum

---

[10] Van Raalte to John Ball, 4 Oct. 1847, folder 435, no. 44, John Ball Papers; Hyma, *Van Raalte*, 163-64. For the operations of the land-warrant market and their use by investors, see Oberly, *Sixty Million Acres*, and Swierenga, *Pioneers and Profits*. The original owners of the tax title lands have not been investigated.

[11] Harms, "Fissures in the Fellowship,"157-58; Swierenga, "Population Statistics," in *Holland, Michigan*, 2:2289-90. The village of Zeeland was platted in the northern half of Section 19, Township 5 North, Range 14 West.

price when the Ionia Public Land Office first opened. The investors demanded double and triple their cost, but they offered generous credit terms—small down payments totaling only $800 and six-year mortgages at 7 percent per annum. The sellers were merchant Nathaniel Silsbee of Salem, Massachusetts; merchant Peter Schermerhorn of New York City; and insurance agent Courtland Palmer of New York City. Van Raalte, who had just returned to Detroit in late January 1847 after deciding on the Holland location, had no choice but to buy from these "speculators."[12] Labeling these investors as "speculators" shows that the dominee had quickly absorbed the frontier antipathy toward nonresident landholders.

Silsbee owned a key tract at the harbor. "I still must get [that land at] the head of the lake at river outlet," he told Brummelkamp. "All kinds of influence is being exerted to obtain these important areas cheaply. The owner is old and lives, I believe, in the State of Massachusetts and there is no doubt of our success." Van Raalte's confidence rested on the fact that Isaac Wyckoff had agreed to contact Silsbee through a mutual friend in Boston. The friend was to say that "Mr. Van Raalte is anxious to secure these lots" and wanted the first option to buy. Silsbee eventually agreed to sell, and nine months later, in September 1847, he sold the 260-acre tract for $923 ($34,300 today), or $3.55 per acre. Van Raalte agreed, believing that the property was well worth the price.[13] Also in September 1847, Van Raalte bought from Schermerhorn 320 acres for $810 ($30,000 today), or $2.53 per acre, with $200 down. This property lies south of today's Sixteenth Street and east of Fairbanks Avenue, covering the southern part of Pilgrim Home Cemetery and east to Waverly Avenue.[14] In November 1847, Van Raalte purchased from Palmer, on a land contract, 1,656 acres for $3,840 ($143,000 today), or $2.31 per acre. The deed included fifteen

[12] Van Raalte to Brummelkamp, 30 Jan. 1847, in *Holland in Amerika*, English typescript, 21.
[13] Ibid.; George Minot, Boston, to Nathaniel Silsbee, Salem, MA, MHA; Charles Noble, Monroe, MI, to Silsbee, 10 Apr. 1847, HMA; Van Raalte's account book with Nathaniel Silsbee for the tract, 1 Sept. 1847, HHA; "Dorpslands Dagboek," Apr. 1847-Dec. 1849; Hyma, *Van Raalte*, 164-65. Silsbee bought the 120-acre tract in 1836 at the Ionia Public Land Office. Today this tract includes Freedom Village senior center, Windmill Island, and the Federal District on East Eighth Street.
[14] Schermerhorn purchased 320 acres at the US Land Office at Bronson, MI, in 1836; Receipt, William Schermerhorn for Peter Schermerhorn from A. C. Van Raalte per George Young, 16 Sept. 1847; P. Schermerhorn to Henry D. Post, 2 Oct. 1848, HMA. Besides the cemetery, this tract today includes Holland Transplanters, Menards, and other businesses.

tracts in nine sections scattered across what would become Holland Township.[15]

The three private transactions totaled $5,573 ($207,400 today) plus thousands more in annual interest payments. This was a huge debt for the dominee to carry, and all the notes had to be paid in full in six years, by 1853. The notes called for increasing payments of principal and interest each year and a balloon payment at the end. Payment was back-loaded because Van Raalte was short of cash. He desperately needed credit terms. In these purchases, he acted on behalf of the board of trustees, which body was not incorporated and could not act in legal matters. The members also feared personal liability.

Van Raalte titled the lands jointly with his wife, and the couple bore the entire burden of meeting the terms of the mortgages. The down payments of $800 came from a $405 loan to the trustees by Jan Slag, a trustee himself, and the board provided the rest.[16] Van Raalte was pledged to provide clear titles at cost to all immigrants who had deposited money for land in America.[17] Hence, the chain of title in virtually every deed in Holland City and many in Holland Township carry Van Raalte's name at or near the top.

Van Raalte's many mortgages put him at risk. "Most perilous for me," he wrote De Moen, "is that all public land purchases and enterprises with the financial costs are mine to pay, [as well as] the debts incurred through that. I am burdened by that. Although it is opined that my duties are enviable, they are too much mixed with care and danger." Yet, he concluded, "I have been blessed in earthly means, and God has steadily given me abundance."[18] As explained below, when

---

[15] Palmer's father, William R. Palmer, and associates entered the various tracts at Bronson, MI, in 1836 and quitclaimed it to Courtland Palmer on 18 Nov. 1847, days before Van Raalte purchased it (Abstract of Title, Ottawa County Abstract & Title Co., book B, 437-40; book G, 425, Ottawa County Deed Registers). Hyma, not having the 11 Nov. 1847 deed in hand, mistakenly states that Van Raalte obtained "some 3,000 acres of land for about $7,000," and he signed a guarantee bond for $4,000, on which he would default if he did not pay $2,740 in five equal annual installments of $568 (Hyma, *Van Raalte*, 163). Palmer's deeds (Book B, 441, recorded 18 Nov. 1847, and Book G, 425, filed 8 Dec. 1853) list sixteen tracts, totaling 1,656 acres (not 3,000) for a price of $3,840. That the down payment was only $400 is stated in "Dorpslands Dagboek," 7 Nov. 1847. All deeds are in Swierenga, "Real Estate Sales." The US survey address of Holland Township is Township 5 North, Range 15 West.

[16] Swierenga, *Holland, Michigan*, 1:41, 72-73, 708.

[17] Van Raalte to Brummelkamp, 30 Jan. 1847, *Holland in Amerika*, English typescript, 15-16, 22; Pieters, *Dutch Settlement*, 56.

[18] Van Raalte to De Moen, 23 May 1851, trans. Nella Kennedy, ADC.

final payments on the mortgages came due in 1853, Van Raalte was in arrears and faced personal bankruptcy.

Michigan Internal Improvement lands

Internal Improvement lands were granted by Congress to the states to fund roads, canals, river improvements, and the like.[19] In fall 1847, Van Raalte learned from John Ball that the state of Michigan initially had received three hundred thousand acres of such lands, mostly in West Michigan, and they were coming up for sale. Governor Ransom had contracted with Ball to select these acres from the federal inventory of lands not yet entered at private entry at the Ionia Land Office. These lands included choice upland clay soils in Drenthe and Vriesland and Fillmore Township. All could be purchased at steep discounts by using Internal Improvement warrants, which "paper" could be purchased on the open market, like Military Bounty warrants. Dutch immigrants were eager for this choice farmland, but Van Raalte set an arbitrary limit of eighty acres to avoid greed. He did not, however, limit himself.

Van Raalte set off for the State Land Office at Marshall, walking to Allegan, taking the stagecoach to Kalamazoo and then the train to Marshall. He pushed himself to the limit but still missed the stage at Allegan. He borrowed a horse that proved so weak he had to walk beside it all the way to Kalamazoo. When Van Raalte finally reached Marshall after three harrowing days, he found prices had "terribly risen." "Worse," he wrote his wife, "speculators already took all the lands I had in mind." With the help of a sympathetic Marshall lawyer, Hovey K. Clark, Van Raalte learned that a key buyer was a Grand Rapids contractor on the Michigan Canal who had claimed the public lands as compensation for his work under the Internal Improvement land grant to the state of Michigan.[20]

Van Raalte persuaded Clark to accompany him to Grand Rapids, a two-day ride by rented carriage, to dicker with the man. Here they

---

[19] Gates, *Public Land Law Development*, 354-56, for Internal Improvement Land Grants and their workings.

[20] Van Raalte, Yellow Springs, to Mrs. C. J. Van Raalte, 2 Nov. 1847, trans. Dekker and Simone Kennedy; Van der Veen, "Life Reminiscences," 1:499. Hovey Kilburn Clark (1812-89) was a graduate of Philips Academy in Andover (MA), who married and practiced law in Allegan, Marshall, and after 1852, Detroit. He was a staunch Presbyterian, likely recommended by John Kellogg, who fit Van Raalte's bill as a trusted friend that went far out of his way to help the dominee. I am indebted to Earl Wm. Kennedy for information on Clark uncovered at Ancestry.com.

Hovey Kilburn Clark (1812-89), a Philips Academy, Andover (MA), graduate, who practiced law in Allegan, Marshall, and after 1852, Detroit. A friend of John Kellogg and a staunch Presbyterian, Clark fit Van Raalte's bill for trustworthiness and dedication.

found that the contractor was willing to sell, but he could not give a good title because the law required that the canal project be finished before titles could pass, which was at least four years away. With the intervention of "some very important people in Grand Rapids" (possibly John Ball), Van Raalte and Clark persuaded the contractor to allow the lands to revert to the state, "which meant that I could then buy them.... I have suffered through days full of worry," Van Raalte wrote his wife, "but I am thankful that God has saved our people from such destruction." The two men then returned to Marshall by way of Yellow Springs. Before heading back to Holland, Van Raalte went east to Detroit "to do business."

The entire trip took more than two weeks but gave Van Raalte ownership of ten valuable tracts in Holland Township totaling 744 acres. In May 1848, he returned to the Marshall State Land Office and bought 200 acres in Zeeland Township, and in April of 1849, he returned yet again and entered 365 acres in Holland and Laketown Townships. The twenty-three tracts he acquired at $1.25 per acre totaled 1,309 acres or $1,636 ($64,800 today). It was time and money well spent.[21]

[21] Van Raalte to Mrs. C. J. Van Raalte, 2 Nov. 1847. From 1 Feb. 1848 to 1 Jan. 1867, the Michigan State Land Office in Marshall issued Van Raalte twenty-three deeds totaling 1,309 acres, all in Ottawa County (Swierenga, "Real Estate Sales"). The state capitol moved to Lansing in 1847.

Indian lands

Van Raalte also kept an eye on Odawa lands around Old Wing Mission in Fillmore Township and on their sixteen-acre Landing on Black Lake. He assumed, correctly, that the natives would soon sell their lands and move north to get away from the swarming Dutch colonists. In September 1847, he asked Pennoyer, "How is it with the lands of the Indians? I wisch [sic] that they came for sale. When you can do something to get this ready, I would be very much obliged." Within six months, Van Raalte's wish was granted. Chief Peter Wakazoo decided to relocate to the region of Little Traverse Bay, and his band put their small farms up for sale. In May 1848, Van Raalte purchased forty acres from six Odawas, including Chief Wakazoo, for $226 ($8,700 today), or $5.65 per acre. This was more than quadruple the natives' original purchase price eight years earlier, and the improvements were minimal. The same month Van Raalte paid Wakazoo $86 ($3,300 today) for the chapel at the Landing, which he intended for newly arriving immigrants.[22]

City lots

After the village of Holland was platted, the board of trustees, under Van Raalte, took charge of selling nearly seven hundred lots, half with one-quarter down and three years to pay the remainder at 7 percent interest per annum. Lot prices were set as low as fifteen dollars at first, which barely covered the cost of surveying and clearing tress. Most deeds carried a stipulation barring on "said premises" the manufacture or sale of liquor and any "gaming, dancing, or theatrical performance."[23] The People's Assembly levied taxes on realty to pay for roads and bridges, schools, the Log Church, a fire brigade, the village bell, and other community needs.[24]

By 1849, account books of the assembly showed a deficit of $2,000 ($79,200 today) on lot sales of $2,800, mainly because of delinquent payments (see appendix, tables 12.1 and 12.2). The trustees feared being held liable and appealed to Van Raalte to assume all debts and

---

[22] Van Raalte to H. Pennoyer, Grand Haven, 22 Nov. 1847, HHA; Swierenga and Van Appledorn, *Old Wing Mission*, 47-48, 307-9, 318, 326.

[23] An example of this restriction is in Warrantee Deed, A. C. Van Raalte to John Van Vleck, 7 May 1857, Ottawa County Deed Register, Book M, 308-9; Van Raalte to John Ball, Grand Rapids, 9 Oct. 1850, folder 435, no. 44, John Ball Papers; Bruins, "Funding his Vision," 54-56.

[24] Village expenses, other than lots and lands, declined over time from $2,116 in 1847 to $397 in 1851; "Dorpslands Dagboek."

take ownership of lot sales. With some reluctance, Van Raalte accepted this huge responsibility. He realized full well the potential windfall if the lots rose in value as the town developed. "I figure that I could live on the income of the Village lots alone," he told Brummelkamp in 1852. Indeed, the lots became the foundation for his family's wealth. Perhaps unexpectedly, it also opened him up to increasing criticism for mixing his ministry with real estate dealings.[25]

Evaluation of land purchases

In the years from 1847 to 1852, Van Raalte bought some fourteen thousand acres for $14,000 in 154 separate transactions (see appendix, table 11.3). This totaled half-a-million dollars in today's currency. The range and sophistication of his purchases is truly astounding. He clearly received excellent coaching and personal assistance from key officials, such as county treasurer Henry Pennoyer and land dealer John Ball. Buying properties at tax auctions was risky, and using military land warrants required knowledge of congressional stipulations.[26]

When the federal census marshal in 1850 recorded the value of realty in Holland city and township, Van Raalte owned 30 percent more than the next wealthiest resident. The successful dominee shared his knowledge of the intricacies of investing in lands with Cornelius Van der Meulen in Zeeland and Seine Bolks in Overisel, who thereby augmented their meager salaries. Van der Meulen purchased more than one hundred tracts, many at delinquent tax auctions, mostly in Zeeland Township. Bolks bought eight tracts in Overisel and Fillmore Townships at the public land office in the first years. Both also made use of discounted military bounty warrants.[27]

[25] Van Raalte to Brummelkamp, 11 Sept. 1852 (quote), HMA; Swierenga, "Albertus C. Van Raalte," 295-97; Philip Phelps Scrapbook, 23 Nov. 1872, JAH; Van Raalte to Phelps, Feb. 1873; Phelps to Van Raalte, 29 Aug. 1873; lot sales account book, 1873-76 (HHA); Van Schelven, "Historical Sketch of Holland City and Colony," *Holland City News*, 26 Aug. 1876. All deeds are in Swierenga, "Real Estate Sales." Subsequent to the initial survey, Van Raalte platted new additions as Holland developed, which added more than four hundred lots. Van Raalte sold 842 lots during his lifetime and bequeathed another 268 lots to his heirs in 1875-76, bringing the total number of lots to 1,110.

[26] The acreage total is inflated because several tax-deeded tracts covered the same parcel for different years of delinquency, and seventeen tax-deed tracts were sold back to original owners within months of the purchase. By 1853 Van Raalte's list of lands in Holland Township assessed for taxes totaled only 1,400 acres, plus hundreds of village lots.

[27] Compiled from Ionia Public Land Office, Ottawa County Books of Original Entry; Ottawa County Deed Registers.

Sources of capital

At the outset of his land buying, Van Raalte developed a strategy that he explained to Brummelkamp.

I do not have enough money, but I pay a little, and the rest remains on the books until people come together more. And if I get into trouble, the people in America will help. I buy everything in my name. Then living among the people in the colony, I can give everybody his deed without trouble and get it registered in the county [courthouse], all of which will free the people of much trouble and expense.[28]

In short, Van Raalte counted on financial help from Reformed businessmen in the East. They realized that he handled land sales judiciously and with sound accounting, all of which gave Hollanders peace of mind. He had avoided the bitter title controversies faced by Henry Scholte in the Pella colony, who purchased eighteen thousand acres in his name and then failed to make timely accounts. Both leaders removed encumbrances on titles and provided warrantee deeds, rather than quitclaim deeds. But it required putting their financial futures at risk.[29]

Where did Van Raalte find the $14,000 ($554,700 today) for his land purchases? Private sellers, like Silsbee, Schermerhorn, and Palmer, took back mortgages, but federal land offices and county treasurers demanded payment in specie. So Van Raalte needed cash. Trustees provided $500, and Van Raalte borrowed another $2,600 locally; specifically, $200 from farmer-capitalist Jannes Van de Luyster, $700 from ship carpenters Jan Slag and son Harm, $400 from farmer Hendrik Hidding, and $300 from Judge John Kellogg of Allegan, for a grand total of $4,700.[30]

The total of Van Raalte's mortgages and loans was $6,400. With the $4,700 borrowed from friends, he had to raise only another $3000

[28] Van Raalte to Brummelkamp, 30 Jan. 1847, in Brummelkamp, *Holland in Amerika*, English typescript, 22.
[29] For Scholte's land dealings, see Lucas, *Netherlanders*, 190-91.
[30] All loans were at 7 percent interest, except the Wyckoff loan at 6 percent, "Dorpslands Dagboek," 16 Dec. 1849; Hyma, *Van Raalte*, 149, 151; Ottawa and Allegan County deed registers. The Wyckoff loan was paid off on 24 Sept. 1853. Hyma, *Van Raalte*, 162-65, gives a figure of $8,000 as the amount Van Raalte paid for his land purchases, but this is surely too low. Jannes Van de Luyster Account Book for 1847 lists loans to Van Raalte of $100 in June at 5 percent and $100 in Dec. at 7 percent (HMA).

to cover the $14,000 in land purchases. This was easily managed by land sales through 1849 of $5,100 ($197,000 today) (see appendix, table 12.4). He needed $500 for family travel costs and their frame house. Living expenses should have been covered by his pastor's salary of $600 ($21,000 today), but this was seldom paid.[31] In short, Van Raalte in the first eighteen months had sufficient cash for travel expenses, his home, and expenses for surveying, legal fees, and taxes.

How much money did Van Raalte carry with him from the Netherlands? Albert Hyma, the first biographer to have access to the Van Raalte Papers, asserted that the dominee carried $10,000 ($362,000 today) as his share in the Ommen pottery business. Said Hyma: "*We may presume* [italics added] that upon his departure for America, he sold his interest in the firm and used the capital ($10,000) for his great adventure."[32] The tip-off that this information is suspect is Hyma's use of the telltale words, "We may presume."[33]

I conclude that Hyma and other scholars who have accepted his $10,000 ($396,200 today) figure have greatly overestimated the size of Van Raalte's purse.[34] He likely carried little more than $3,000 ($109,000 today), with which he gained title to a treasure in lands and lots and thereby ensured the future of the entire colony. Over thirty years, almost $200,000 ($4 million today) in real estate passed through Van Raalte's hands, but he was highly leveraged in the early years, and the strain showed at times (see appendix, tables 12.3 and 12.4).

In Van Raalte's detailed record of sales, farmland near the village sold for $3 per acre in 1847, and three-acre village lots sold for $40. As the village grew and land values increased from normal development, Van Raalte pushed lot prices up to $45 in 1849, $48 in 1850, $70 in 1855, $120 in 1865, and $400 by 1874. Raw agricultural land by 1860 had nearly tripled in price, from $3 to $8 per acre, and surpassed $10 an acre by 1870. By then, the colony counted up to ten thousand

---

[31] Of Van Raalte's $600 annual salary, he received only $251 in 1852 and $240 in 1853 (minutes, First Holland, 22 Nov. 1853).
[32] Hyma, *Van Raalte*, 124.
[33] Bruins, "Funding His Vision," 53-54. Adding $2,000 from the Arnhem Emigration Society and Brummelkamp's gift brought Van Raalte's initial capital to $12,000, but he used only $700 of the $2,000 to buy land.
[34] De Graaf, "Een afgescheiden dominee," states: "There is reason to assume that, at his departure from the Netherlands, he had at his disposal $10,000" (8), and "We may agree with Dr. Hyma that he sold his shares in the brick factory before his departure to America and targeted their amount for his 'great adventure,' which yielded such precious fruit in America" (11).

Hollanders spread across five townships—Holland, Zeeland, and Olive in Ottawa County, and Overisel and Fillmore in Allegan County.

Van Raalte clearly understood the capitalist principle of "unearned increment"—an increase in the value of realty due to population growth and economic development, all without the labor or expenditure of the owner, except for paying annual realty taxes and occasional fees and commissions.[35] He expected in 1852 that city lots would "without doubt double their value in four years," and lots in a "small strip on the water's edge" were worth $250 each. "I am amazed," he admitted, with "the peculiar position in which I see myself as the owner of such really unimaginable wealth."[36] What he failed to realize was the burden over the years of paying annual realty taxes in hard cash. His annual tax bill quadrupled, from $146 ($5,700 today) in 1850 to $660 ($14,200) in 1868.[37] Nevertheless, within six years of founding the colony, his estate was the envy of many. His landed wealth grew while he slept, so to speak.

Colony store and ship

Ever the social entrepreneur, Van Raalte in 1847 enlisted the People's Assembly to spearhead two cooperatives, a colony store and a colony ship, the A. E. *Knickerbocker*.[38] Both aimed to squeeze out the middlemen and give the new settlement an economic leg up. The store would supply much-needed foodstuffs and merchandise, and the ship would fetch much-needed goods from Chicago and even New York and also transport fresh immigrants to the colony. Return voyages would deliver wood products. It would be a trifecta.

Jannes Van de Luyster and captains Ale Stegenga and Frederick Claussen of Singapore bought the one hundred ton, two-mast schooner in Chicago for eight hundred dollars, and Van de Luyster

---

[35] https://www.merriam-webster.com/dictionary/unearned increment.
[36] Van Raalte to Den Bleyker, 9 Jan. 1852; Den Bleyker Papers, trans. Nella Kennedy; Van Raalte to Brummelkamp, 11 Sept. 1852, HHA; Van Raalte to De Moen, 23 May 1851.
[37] "Dorpslands Dagboek"; tax receipts, Holland Township Treasurer's Office, 20 Jan. 1850, 15 Dec. 1852, 23 Jan. 1856, 8 Jan. 1869; Assessment of the Property of A. C. Van Raalte for 1853, Holland Township, Ottawa County, HHA.
[38] A. E. *Knickerbocker* (misnamed in histories as *E. A. Knickerbocker*) was built in Detroit in 1840, and after its sale in 1848 to a Milwaukee ship owner, it served Michigan ports until 1855, when it capsized in a gale ten miles off Port Washington, Wisconsin, and was abandoned to drift ashore and rot. The captain drowned, but two mates managed to swim to shore. https://www.wisconsinshipwrecks.org/Vessel/Details/4?region=MidLakeMichigan.

added money to buy goods for the store. Bernardus Grootenhuis, Van Raalte's assistant, agreed to manage the store with Jannes Van de Luyster Jr. Under Captain Stegenga, four young Dutchmen as mates, and buying agent Elias G. Young—a young man from First Reformed Church of Grand Rapids—the A. E. *Knickerbocker* on its maiden voyage sailed to New York City and Albany. There, agent Young bought dry goods, groceries, shoes, Yankee notions, children's toys, and many other articles for the store. When his cash ran out, Young charged the rest to "Dominee van Raalte and Company," a fictitious entity that the cleric later had to honor.[39]

The ambitious cooperative ran amok from the start. The harbor itself was a hindrance. A sandbar blocked the mouth, and the cargo had to be offloaded to scows in the lake and bark and cordwood loaded for the return trip to Chicago. The extra labor costs ate up any profit. The ship brought fresh immigrants from Buffalo, Milwaukee, and Chicago, but many passengers failed to pay their fares, reasoning that the ship was common property. The store, which stood on the corner of Seventh and River Streets, closed its doors within a year due to insufficient capital, high costs, and poor management. This proved the adage: "When everybody owns something, nobody owns it."[40]

The store's failure doomed the ship, and Van Raalte sold it to a Milwaukee shipper for four hundred dollars, half the purchase price, leaving Van de Luyster, the heaviest investor, strapped financially. Dashed hopes led to heated discussions about the decision of Van Raalte and his associates to adopt the "community of goods" principle. Van Raalte always had a soft spot in his heart for businesses with a social benefit, evidenced in the Scheveningen fishing boats and Ommen factories to employ poor Separatists. But the company store and ship was his last such venture. He had learned his lesson—*profit* is not a dirty word. In future investments, he demanded at least 7 percent interest and expected profits of up to 40 percent.

From social to economic entrepreneur

Making money in essential primary industries became Van Raalte's new investment plan. He laid out his thinking to Carel de Moen.

---

[39] Swierenga, *Holland, Michigan*, 1:706-7; Van der Veen, "Life Reminiscences," 1:495-96; Van Schelven, "Historical Sketches," *De Grondwet*, 8 June 1915.

[40] An adage of Milton Friedman, University of Chicago economist (https://www.dailysignal.com/2014/07/31/milton-friedmans-7-notable-quotes/).

> Although taken as a whole, we are a poor company of people, and the funds of even the well-to-do among us have dwindled away in supplying the thousands of needs of a new settlement as in bottomless pits.... Thousands of dollars could be invested with rich returns, and this is likely a sure thing. Yet we are taught, on the other hand, that it is not money or capital that helps us grow, but the caring, omniscient, Almighty hand does more than we can understand.[41]

In short, with God's blessing, he would make money.

Two years later, in 1851, Van Raalte expanded on his business philosophy in a letter penned to Helenius de Cock, another Netherlands confidant:

> Dealings, vocations, or trade opportunities, retail and wholesale, are not lacking here. At a glance, i.e., an experienced glance, one can find business everywhere—not just where one can make a living, but where, as Americans say, one can make money. Twenty-five years ago, nothing could be found around Lake Michigan except for a log cabin in a couple of places for the purpose of trading with the Indians. Now there is profit with the large cities and villages. The people who came there were generally people who began with nothing, or on credit, or with a couple of thousand dollars at most. They are capitalists now. It is a common occurrence that people become propertied in the course of eight to ten years. It is not considered important if one fails, for one begins with "A" again [i.e., one starts over again], and is granted credit soon.
>
> Among the capitalists, there are some who have gone bankrupt two or three times in fifteen years (even if they had begun with little or nothing, with everything on credit), and are wealthy after fifteen years. It is a strange country, incomprehensible to a European who knows nothing of growing along with the development of cities. And yet, that is key to why the new settlers in the West could come to prosperity so fast, even though they hardly possessed anything to start with. The flood of the influx of peoples brings value to the land in a short amount of time, and

---

[41] Van Raalte to De Moen, 11 Feb. 1849, published in *De toestand*, 6-7, trans. Nella Kennedy.

the land brings forth much in a short time, bringing about the necessity for all branches of trade, manufacturing, and others.[42]

What the dauntless dominee soon learned was how easily he would be facing bankruptcy and have to begin again with "A."

Colonial Mill

Van Raalte's first profit-making venture was a combined grain and saw mill. Colonists needed mills to grind wheat into flour and sawmills to rip lumber for frame houses to replace primitive log cabins. But they lacked capital and expertise. As a consequence, they were forced to buy flour and lumber from either Singapore (Saugatuck harbor), Allegan, or Grand Haven and carry the sacks of flour on their backs and the lumber either by oxcart or by water on rafts, sailboats, and scows.

In the summer of 1847, Van Raalte and Henry Post opened Colonial Mill, the first sawmill in the colony. James Forrester and other members of De Witt's Collegiate Church provided the funds with a $600 gift ($23,300 today), and the board of trustees under Van Raalte added $50 ($1,860 today). Alvan Benham, Benjamin Brist, and M. Gibbs, Americans in the area, built and operated the millrace and waterwheel on Van Raalte's land at the Zaagmolen Clearing along the Black River on present-day East Twenty-Fourth Street (today Van Raalte Farm Park). The water wheel powered three gangs of twelve to eighteen saws each, which by October were ripping four thousand board feet per day. This was enough, Van Raalte said, to provide "sufficient shelter for the coming winter." For the first time, Hollanders heard the toot-toot of the sawmill whistle, and it was all the sweeter because they no longer had to import lumber. Soon, however, the colony had a half dozen mills and competition cut into profits.[43]

Ash factory

The second Van Raalte-Post business was an ashery. Francis Denison of Kalamazoo, another Yankee supporter of the Dutch

---

[42] Van Raalte to Helenius de Cock, 26 Sept. 1851, AGK.
[43] Swierenga, *Holland, Michigan*, 1:761-62; De Witt, "Emigrants from Holland," *Christian Intelligencer*, 12 Aug. 1847; *Grand Rapids Eagle*, 2 Feb. 1849; Ottawa County Deed Register, Book E, 471; Moerdyke, "Pioneer Industries," box 4, Moerdyke Papers; Arthur A. Visscher, "Recollections [of Arend Visscher]," typescript, 1959, Visscher Family Papers; "Dorpslands Dagboek," 16 May 1848.

colony, urged Van Raalte to take advantage of ashes to manufacture potash (pearlash), or potassium carbonate, saleratus, or baking soda, and soap. "Procure as many Iron Kettles as you have men to use them," Denison advised. "I know of no other way in which you can clear up the farms and get a living from the labor of your men at the same time." Each wooded acre produced $6 ($223 today) worth of ash, and five or six men "could do all the work of making ashes to the value of $10,000 ($372,000 today) per annum. This would provide money to finish your saw mill and build houses and barns for those coming in this summer and fall."[44]

Van Raalte took heed, and in September 1847, he enlisted Post in an ash factory (Asch Fabriek) named Post & Co. Van Raalte, as the silent partner (i.e., "& Co."), provided $1,000 in capital. In June 1848, he added $1,300 ($45,000 today), making this factory a huge investment for the dominee. This first manufacturing plant in Holland stood on log pilings at the head of Black Lake, down the hill from Post's store on River Avenue at Eighth Street. The factory turned ashes into good quality hard soap, potash, and black salt for the New York and Chicago markets. Settlers up to eight miles away carried bundles of ashes on their backs to the factory. Potash was the first product the colonists produced for sale, and the few cents worth they brought to the factory was taken home in groceries from Post's store, which Jannes Van de Luyster Jr. managed, and his wife, Cornelia Van Malsen, clerked. The factory turned a profit, as Denison had predicted. An entry in the books of Post & Co. on July 1851 notes that the firm received $728.75 ($28,900 today) from Chicago for "pearl ashes." Despite a promising start, however, the ashery did not flourish, and the partners sold the indebted factory to George Colt of Williamsburg, New York, later of Kalamazoo. Post simply had too many irons in the fire.[45]

Post's store at this time doubled as the Black River post office, with Post's wife Anna as assistant. Willem Notting, who lived south of town, fetched the mail on his back from the Manlius (now New Richmond) post office twelve miles distant. His second wife, Jennigje, carried the sack the last three miles to Post's store. In 1851 Van Raalte

---

[44] Denison to Van Raalte, 15 May 1847, photocopy in Hyma, *Van Raalte*, 178.
[45] Ibid.; Cornelia Van Malsen Van de Luyster, 16 Nov., 16 Dec. 1847, to Jannes Van de Luyster Jr., 15 Dec. 1847, all in Yzenbaard, "'America' Letters," 54, 61; Van Raalte account book with Post & Co., 28 Sept., 25 Dec. 1847, 28 June 1848, 30 July 1851, HMA; De Witt, "Emigrants from Holland," *Christian Intelligencer*, 12 Aug., 28 Oct. 1847; Grand Rapids *Eagle*, 2 Feb., 6 July 1849, 8 Aug. 1850.

Land and Business 385

View of RIVER STREET.

River Avenue looking north from Ninth Street. Image from Lankheet City Plat of 1870, one year before the Holland fire. Only known prefire image. On the right (*front to back*) is Van der Veen's Hardware, Henry D. Post's General Store (later Model Drug), Jan Aling's brewery at Seventh Street (long building), City Four Mills (tall building), and American House Hotel (*in the distance*). On the left side (*front to back*) is Philip Pfanstiehl's residence, his Holland Hotel (now Reader's World), and Henry D. and Anna Post's house (*JAH*)

secured from the postmaster general in Washington an official Holland post office, which gave the village standing.[46]

Van der Sluis mill

In 1848 Van Raalte sold a lot at the foot of Fourth Street to Oswald Van der Sluis, who built a small steam sawmill with an upright saw, the first of its kind. Post acted as agent to buy the steam engine from an Ann Arbor manufacturer and the boilers from Detroit. In 1849 Van der Sluis and a partner added a gristmill to grind badly needed flour. This first flourmill eliminated the need to buy flour in distant cities or, in a pinch, to grind Indian corn for cornbread in coffee mills. But the steam engine proved to be inadequate, and the partners failed to

---

[46] *Holland City News*, 19 Jan. 1928; *De Hollander*, 29 May 1851; Swierenga, *Holland, Michigan*, 1:155.

make payments to Van Raalte on the mortgage for the lot. Van Raalte sued in 1851 and triggered a sheriff sale against the pair. The dominee cut Van der Sluis no slack, even though he was a parishioner. Business was business. Post tried without success to repair the neglected and decrepit mill, but all he could salvage was some of the machinery.[47]

Tannery

Tanning hides for leather was an ideal business because farmers raised cattle, and abundant hemlock bark yielded tannin. The region clearly had a comparative advantage in this type of enterprise, and tanneries were labor intensive and required little capital for machinery. Van Raalte sang the praises of tanneries: "Bark grows here in abundance; enormous profits are connected to it.... The market for leather is excellent.... One could as easily start twenty as one tannery." The dominee was spot on. Tanning became Holland's primary industry under Cappon & Bertsch, the first million-dollar company in Holland, which earned the title Leather City.[48]

In 1847 Van Raalte recruited Pieter Pfanstiehl to start the first tannery. P. F. Pfanstiehl & Co. hired Conrad Hoffman and Isaac Cappon, the latter a farmhand who had just arrived in the colony, to build the "log tannery" on two lots owned by Van Raalte in the Tannery Addition immediately to the west of Jan Slag's shipyard. Pfanstiehl brought to America $20,000 from the sale of his Parisian Shoe Shop at Arnhem and was assessing business opportunities in New York. Van Raalte convinced him to take advantage of the unlimited possibilities in Holland. A Mr. Knox came from Chicago early in 1848 with a party of men to instruct the Dutch how to peel and cure the bark.[49]

After four years, Pfanstiehl wanted to sell the tannery. Van Raalte promptly recruited I. (John) Kerler Jr., a Bavarian who had immigrated to Milwaukee in 1849. Van Raalte exuberantly described the twenty-eight-year-old as "a very knowledgeable man, has much experience, enjoyed an excellent education, has an amiable personality, and is well

[47] *De Hollander*, 18 Jan. 1851, 26 Jan., 6 Apr. 1853, 5 Dec. 1855; James F. Van der Sluis, "History of the Life of Mr. Oswald Van der Sluis and his wife Jacoba F.," HMA; Van der Veen, "Memories of Colonial Life."
[48] Van Raalte to Den Bleyker, 9 Jan., 21 Apr., 8 (quote), 23 May 1851, BHL; Van Raalte to Helenius der Cock, 26 Sept. (quote) 1851, AGK, trans. Boonstra and Nella Kennedy. For Holland's tanning industry, see Swierenga, *Holland, Michigan*, 1:790-800.
[49] Moerdyke, "A Brief History of A. A. Pfanstiehl," Moerdyke Papers; *Ottawa Register*, 5 Mar. 1861. Van Raalte's 1847 letter to Pfanstiehl in New York has been lost.

versed in various German philosophical principles, but is holding fast to God's revelation. I am very pleased with such a man and count him a great gift. I regard him highly." Van Raalte added $3,000 in fresh capital, and the firm became Kerler & Co. Kerler enlarged the plant and built two windmills, one to pump water and the other to turn grind bark.[50]

But once again, the partnership turned sour, despite the dominee's request to work harder and "avoid too hasty breaking up of the business." Kerler was served in Ottawa County Circuit Court in December 1853 for financial malfeasance. Was Van Raalte a poor judge of character? His partners who ran the businesses from day to day either lacked commitment, like Post, or they committed fraud, like Kerler. In any case, Van Raalte's favorable opinion turned sour. Kerler was "a man I'm afraid of," he confessed to Brummelkamp. "The time of the partnership is over, and I think as a result, I will lose my entire share and perhaps $1,000 besides." In late 1854, Van Raalte managed to recover $200 when another German, John Schurr, bought his interest and that of Kerler and continued the tannery as Schurr & Co.[51]

Den Bleyker Mill of Post & Co.

In 1851 Van Raalte took the biggest plunge on a combined lumber and gristmill, in partnership with Henry Post and Paulus Den Bleyker. Den Bleyker of Kalamazoo was the epitome of the kind of capitalist and entrepreneur Van Raalte had envisioned for developing the colony. Henry Lucas called Den Bleyker the first capitalist among the Dutch immigrants, and Albert Hyma dubbed him the "richest Hollander in Michigan." Den Bleyker, a Separatist, came to America in 1850 with $30,000 ($1.2 million today). Within months of his arrival, the dominee set to work mightily to lure the millionaire to Holland.[52]

Van Raalte had the instincts of a capitalist, but Den Bleyker had actual capital and a lot of it. He made his money draining the Eendracht

---

[50] *De Hollander*, 29 May 1851; Van Eyck, "Holland Tanneries," Van Eyck Papers; Van Raalte to J. S. Wilson, United States Land Commissioner, Washington, DC, 18 Jan. 1870, an appeal to quiet his original warranty title to the Colonial Mill and tannery property, which was being challenged by Scottish immigrant, George Lauder, who ran an art studio on Eighth Street.
[51] Van Raalte to Brummelkamp, 11 Sept. 1852, HHA; *De Hollander*, 1 Dec. 1853, 16 Nov. 1854.
[52] Van Raalte to Den Bleyker, 23 May 1851, BHL; "Dorpslands Dagboek," 27 Sept. 1848, 25 June 1849; Van der Veen, "Life Reminiscences," 1:510; Vander Velde, "Early Dutch Settlements in Michigan,"1.

Paulus Den Bleyker, Kalamazoo capitalist and Van Raalte business associate who reputedly became the "richest Hollander in Michigan" (*JAH*)

Polder on the Island of Texel and then selling the lands reclaimed from the Wadden Sea. When he reached Kalamazoo—a city not much bigger than Holland but with a Dutch contingent of four hundred—he saw unlimited opportunities to make money as a land developer. He purchased for $12,000 a 330-acre farm twelve miles from the city, with wheat fields ready for harvest, and another 180-acre farm on the edge of the city for an additional $12,000, this from Epaphroditus Ransom, ex-governor of Michigan and a Kalamazoo capitalist. The wealthy Dutchman platted part of the Ransom farm as Den Bleyker's Addition and expected the sale of lots to more than recoup his initial investment.[53]

When Ransom learned that Den Bleyker had another $20,000 ready for investment, he asked him to be a partner in a banking and land mortgage company, and he wrote Van Raalte to help him entice the newcomer. At this point, Den Bleyker asked Van Raalte, who knew Ransom and had found him trustworthy, for a character reference on the ex-governor. This placed Van Raalte in the happy position of go-between. He gave Den Bleyker a favorable reference of Ransom but could not let the opportunity pass to try to win Den Bleyker and his money for the Holland colony.[54]

---

[53] Lucas, *Netherlanders*, 280-84; Hyma, *Van Raalte*, 181-85, citing Den Bleyker Papers.
[54] Van Raalte to "Friend Bleker" (Paulus Den Bleyker), 23 Dec. 1850, BHL, trans. Simone Kennedy.

Van Raalte enlisted Cornelius Van der Meulen of the Zeeland church, where Den Bleyker's brother worshiped, and Rev. Hendrik Klyn of Graafschap, a friend of Den Bleyker from the Old Country, to write personal letters to him. Van der Meulen urged Den Bleyker to settle among his own people and benefit from the lower cost of living. Klyn warned him to be careful in dealing with strangers and quoted the scriptural injunction, "Behold, I send you out as sheep in the midst of wolves; so be wise as serpents and innocent as doves" (Matt. 10:16, KJV). Better to invest in wholly safe and profitable ventures with Hollanders.

Van Raalte reiterated the warning that Den Bleyker not get too involved financially with Americans who "scorn us as an uncivilized, dull, slow people" and might well take advantage of them as greenhorns. "Think: Opportunity makes the thief!!!" Ransom's risky banking venture offered Den Bleyker 10 percent, while he made 15 percent, keeping 5 percent of it as his salary, Van Raalte noted. "I want to give you that same 10 percent and will guarantee your interest and capital in real estate that is double its worth.... Begin business among Dutch folk he could trust and in a location with a great future." Continuing his sales pitch, Van Raalte declared that Holland was destined to become the distribution center of the Upper Great Lakes to Eastern markets. "I would want to start these with you," as either an active or a silent partner, Van Raalte added. "I can show you how this could be carried out." Specifically, Van Raalte suggested a double steam-driven sawmill and gristmill that would cost $2,000 and return 7 percent. Farmers who had to take their grain by oxteams two days' distance to get it ground "will shout for joy" to have a local mill.[55]

He then played the high notes on his keyboard:

> Perhaps you wonder at this language, not knowing my position. Yes, even I myself am frequently astonished at the position in which I find myself. Although I did come here with some capital, it never occurred to me that I would become involved in so many business matters. But I find that the Lord has wanted to bless me and [he] placed me uniquely as the possessor of large properties. Otherwise, I would not have been able to stand where I have stood in order to work on laying the foundations for these people. Especially because of these exceptional blessings and

---

[55] Van Raalte to Den Bleyker, 9 Jan. 1851, BHL, trans. Nella Kennedy (letter was marked "Strictly Confidential!!!!!"). I quote this letter at length because of its revealing insights about Van Raalte's business acumen and persuasive powers. See also, Van Raalte to Brummelkamp, 11 Sept. 1852, HHA.

many business interests, I can invest capital at a high rate of interest and give security by way of real estate. . . .

I shall now reveal, confidentially, something about this. At first, I traded in land for and in the name of the colony. But after all was said and done, no one wished to be involved anymore for fear of possible loss and other rationales. But this unreasonable foolishness actually became a blessing to me. . . . This people deserted me and broke contracts with me. At first, this was difficult, but now it is to my advantage. That is how it went with the village of Holland also.

And besides, I was very fortunate in the purchase of valuable lands. So that now, without having desired this, I own wonderful land along the water, besides thousands of acres of farmland, including strips of cultivated land and a good amount of natural meadowland and hayfields, as well as lime beds, all the land of the village of Holland, and three water power sources. Along with an Englishman [Homer E. Hudson], I began a tree nursery. Three years ago, I began, with another Englishman [Henry D. Post], a saleratus and potash factory in which soap and candles are also made. Another Hollander [actually a German, named Kerler] and I are in partnership in a tannery business, which is an excellent business; all that is made of leather will be made here. From this and that, you can see what my circumstances are and the basis on which I can talk to you about this.

I am convinced that you can enter into business here with pleasure and without danger, business that you could oversee, in which, under God's blessing, you can turn over capital and profit. . . . And if you choose to live here among Hollanders, you can live under the privileges and institutions of God's church. This is important above all, not only for the benefit of one's own temporal and spiritual prosperity, but also for that of his children. . . .

P.S. One more thing, I began with little capital, which always hinders enterprise. Moreover, in the beginning, there are always problems to be worked through. And yet, the profits were never less than 30% and 40%. With greater capital, interest is increased much more, and especially if you can double the capital. This can happen when the business affairs have developed more, and the money market becomes better. The tannery brings large profits, up to 80%. These percentages would be much higher if various businesses [would] work in combination. This is our plan and where it also naturally leads. This actually is the hidden art of American business, by which capital can be increased in a few years.

This frank letter, which appealed both to Den Bleyker's pocketbook and his Christian conscience, won him over, but he came to regret the decision. Van Raalte had downplayed the risks of investing on the American frontier, even in the tight Dutch colony among fellow believers.

In March 1851, Den Bleyker made the decision to move to Holland and invest in the project, taking up Van Raalte's promise to commit enough property to cover the investment. The dominee also provided the mill site along Black Lake with eighteen feet of water by its side. Post joined the firm as a partner for at least four years and agreed to supervise construction of the mills. He hired machinists to recover parts from the defunct Van der Sluis mill while he made a six-day trip to Chicago to contract for a powerful Gates & Co. steam engine. Den Bleyker provided $400 for the engine, plus $200 for travel expenses. With several millstones, Post & Co.'s gristmill went into operation in August, and the sawmill ripped lumber a few months later. The need for milling grain was great because colonists were raising wheat, and importing flour from other places was difficult and costly.[56]

Van Raalte purchased a fine house in town on Den Bleyker's behalf for $400, but Den Bleyker was cautious and delayed moving his family to Holland. Heavy spring rains washed out corn sprouts and sharply reduced the crop, so that, instead of making generous profits, the Den Bleyker Mill, as it was called, actually lost money. Then to his chagrin, Van Raalte wrote that he was unable to repay Den Bleyker's loan and cover the losses. Post & Co. had to deal with the financial fallout.

In November 1851, Van Raalte and Post cleared liens of $5,800 (owed to sixteen creditors), notably to the largest creditors, New Yorkers [Jonas C.] Heartt & Co. of Troy and George Colt of Williamsburg, by surrendering the property put up as collateral. It included five city lots and forty acres, together with their ash factory and its fixtures, a house and steam mill, six hundred bushels of ashes, fifteen thousand

---

[56] For this and the next paragraph, see Van Raalte to Den Bleyker, 28 Feb., 11, 18 Mar., 21 Apr., 3 June, 8, 22 Aug. 1851, BHL; Van Raalte to De Moen, 23 May 1851, JAH; Henry D. Post and Den Bleyker, agreement, 19 June 1851, HMA; *Grand River Times* (Grand Haven), 21 July 1852; *De Nederlander* (Kalamazoo), 20 Aug. 1852.

List of Van Raalte debtors in 1851 mill default (*HHA*)

pounds of black salts, 120 boxes of saleratus, a team of oxen and lumber wagon, and two hundred cords of wood. A few weeks later, Van Raalte indemnified Post by giving him nine mortgages on ten village lots, valued at $421. Van Raalte pegged his total losses in the venture at $3,000 ($119,000 today), likely the original purchase price of the forfeited lands.

Den Bleyker, meanwhile, continued to operate the mill. He advertised in October 1852 that the "flour grinding stones are now in excellent shape for sifting wheat, rye, and buckwheat. Everyone who has been here for grinding in the last 12 days has been very satisfied." In 1854 Den Bleyker sold the mill for $400. It was his first and last business venture in Holland, much to Van Raalte's keen disappointment.[57]

Mortgage troubles

Going bankrupt in the Post-Den Bleyker venture was a sobering experience for Van Raalte. He learned how easy it was to lose property put up as collateral. The loss weighed heavily on him and threatened the financial future of his family. "There is a storm brewing over my head," he confessed to Brummelkamp. His indebtedness in late 1852 was $4,000 ($158,500 today).[58] After this storm washed over him, he never invested in another business, except for several small ventures of Albertus, his oldest son and namesake. The early 1850s were dark years for Van Raalte and his family. Besides the financial hit, the conflict in the Classis of Holland over the Union of 1850 culminated in a church split, and the editor of his newspaper charged him with high-handed leadership.[59]

Worse of all, the financial setbacks impacted Van Raalte's preaching negatively. His elders believed it was necessary to warn: "The power of his preaching seems to have disappeared." They advised him to "Lay aside some other activities . . . in order to be more active within the congregation." The dominee admitted that his sermons were thin: "If I do not study, I cannot continue to preach longer than six weeks."[60]

On top of this, the three mortgages from Eastern investors were coming due in 1853, and Van Raalte did not have the money to pay off those loans. To safeguard his homestead, in early 1852, he deeded the

---

[57] Schedule A of Post & Co. indebtedness, dated 3 Nov. 1851, lists the sixteen creditors (photocopy in Hyma, *Van Raalte*, 150); Indenture between Post & Co. and Heartt & Co. and George Colt, executed 3 Nov. 1851, Ottawa County Deed Register, Book A, Miscellaneous Records, 22-25; Henry D. Post to Van Raalte, Bond, 13 Dec. 1851, HHA; Van Raalte to Brummelkamp, 11 Sept. 1852, HHA; *De Hollander*, 27 Oct., 1 Dec. 1852; Henry D. Post and George Post of NYC (Post & Co.) to George Colt, assignee of Henry D. Post and Van Raalte, "formerly doing business under the name of Post & Co.," Deed, $559, 16 Feb. 1854, Ottawa County Deed Register, Book G, 654-55, and Book H, 227-28. All deeds are in Swierenga, "Real Estate Sales." Theodore White of Grand Haven bought the Den Bleyker sawmill in 1853 for $4,200 and operated it successfully with partner Nicholas Vyn of Holland, under the name White, Vyn & Co. (*De Hollander*, 29 Apr. 1853); Lucas, *Netherlanders*, 284.

[58] Van Raalte to Brummelkamp, 11 Sept. 1852, HHA.

[59] Bruins, "Funding his Vision," 63-64; Bruins and Swierenga, *Family Quarrels*, 61-89.

[60] Minutes, First Holland, 28 Mar. 1853; *De Hope*, 21 Apr. 1880, quoting Van Raalte.

property for $1 to his five children.[61] Perhaps unwisely, he had spent $400 ($15,800 today) to enlarge the house. He owed the Silsbee estate $900 but had only $500 in hand. Van Raalte assured Silsbee's son, the executor: "I will surely pay you just as fast as possible. I hate debts.... This is a singular country," the dominee added. "We have enough to eat and still, to get money back [repaid], is next to impossible." True to his word, Van Raalte paid off the Silsbee mortgage within a year.[62]

Van Raalte was also behind on the Palmer land contract for $1,600. Fortunately, his New York benefactors, Schieffelin and Suydam, had purchased this contract. Suydam was Palmer's brother-in-law. Van Raalte appealed to his ministerial friends, Garretson and De Witt, to use their influence on Schieffelin to stay foreclosure. "I am willing to make every sacrifice to avoid this forced sale," Van Raalte implored Garretson. "It would hurt my position; it would be ruinous to my family... I beseech you to work and pray for me." In a follow-up letter a month later, Van Raalte detailed the wider implications of his predicament. If Schieffelin foreclosed, it would wipe out the titles of several immigrant families who had bought parts of Van Raalte's land behind his homestead and built houses. In a bit of melodrama, he said he would give up his home and farm for "these ruined families," despite the distress it would cause "my dear wife," but "it cannot make up their loss, it cannot heal the breach, it cannot cure the evil." Worse yet was the spiritual cost. "It will crush the hearts of the pious and strengthen the hands of the ungodly; the evil heart and Satan will make use of the ignorance of the many to undermine my influence as a minister of the Gospel."[63]

If Schieffelin could not make any concessions, Van Raalte as a last resort offered to come to New York, deeds in hand to Holland village lots, and Schieffelin could then "hunt up" some sixteen friends to buy them cheap at $100 apiece, and thereby cover the debt. "Dark clouds" were indeed "packing together" and threatening him.

[61] Foreseeing disaster, on 16 Feb. 1852, Van Raalte and his wife deeded for one dollar to their five children a forty-eight acre tract (Sec. 28, T5N Range 15West) that included the family homestead. The tract was apportioned as follows, with the price allocated from eldest to youngest: Albertus, 9.24 acres for $58.50; Benjamin, 9.76 acres for $48.50; Johanna Maria, 9.5 acres for $40.50; Dirk, 9.5 acres for $48.50; and Christina Catherina, 9.5 acres for $20.50. This transfer placed the homestead outside the reach of creditors.

[62] Van Raalte to Silsbee Executor, 19 Aug. 1851, quoted in Hyma, *Van Raalte*, 164-65 (quote 165); Van Raalte to Garretson, NY, 18 Apr. 1854, BDM.

[63] Van Raalte to Garretson, NYC, 22 June, 15 July 1853, BDM, for this and following paragraph.

The dominee found the lenders sympathetic to his cash squeeze and willing to give more time. Suydam and Schieffelin agreed to take interest only on Van Raalte's debt. "They have done a most noble act towards me," the dominee wrote Garretson. "Last summer, I was in great danger of a most ruinous destruction on account of a mortgage over a great deal of lands which I could not pay in time. They have taken the mortgage and did pay them to Mr. Palmer. May God reward them abundantly with temporal and spiritual blessings." A year later, Garretson offered Van Raalte financial help from mission board funds, but he declined "because my creditors, the brothers Suydam and Schieffelin, are very patient with me and are so patient to receive only the interest for the present."[64]

For mortgage payment to the two men, Van Raalte sent personal drafts (akin to modern checks) to De Witt, who cashed them at various merchants in New York, deposited the funds in a bank, and saw to it that the pair received their interest payments.[65] In 1857 Van Raalte gave Suydam and Schieffelin a new note on his eighty-acre farm as security for $874 still owed on the original loan, with interest of 7 percent per annum. In 1864 Van Raalte still owed the note plus interest, amounting to about $1,000 ($19,400 today). At this point, Schieffelin took back two new $500 mortgages bearing 7 percent interest, signed by Albertus and Christina, and he then assigned them to John J. Brower, treasurer of the General Synod of the Reformed Church. The $1,000 debt was now placed on the church books, and Van Raalte made annual interest payments to the denomination's treasurer until his death in 1876. His son Dirk, the designated successor, continued to pay interest and principal until the two $500 notes were finally paid off in 1885. So the Palmer mortgage of 1847 essentially evolved into a forty-year loan at 7 percent on the dominee's home and farm.[66]

---

[64] The legal description was the NE1/4 SW1/4 and NW1/4 SE1/4 Sec. 28 T5N R15W, 80 contiguous acres. Van Raalte to Garretson, 18 Apr., 10 May 1854, BDM.

[65] Mortgage Assignment, Courtland Palmer to James Suydam and Samuel B. Schieffelin, NY, 10 Mar. 1857, HHA.

[66] James Suydam et al. to Van Raalte, 10 Mar. 1857, Release of Mortgage, Ottawa County Deed Records, Book D, 17; Trustees of Nathaniel Silsbee, Salem, Essex County, Mass., to Van Raalte, Indenture Deed, 5 June 1855, Ottawa County Deed Records; Samuel B. Schieffelin to Van Raalte, 4 Apr. 1857; Van Raalte to Schieffelin, Mortgage Indentures, 10 Mar. 1857, 20 May 1864; Schieffelin to John B. Brower, Assignment of Mortgage, 20 May 1864; Schieffelin to Van Raalte, Satisfaction of [1857] Mortgage, 23 Aug. 1864; Van Raalte to Brower, 10 Oct. 1871, 31 Aug. 1874, 12 July 1875; Van Raalte to Schieffelin, by General Synod, Satisfaction of [1864] Mortgage, 5 Sept. 1872; mortgage payoff, General Synod to Albertus Van Raalte, 5 Sept. 1885. Copies of all legal documents and Schieffelin

Receipt for $500 interest payment on Schieffelin's Van Raalte's mortgages, August 28, 1865, signed by John J. Brower, treasurer of General Synod (JAH)

Business ventures with son Bertus

Admonition by the elders and the mill default dissuaded Van Raalte from new business ventures for six years, but then he plunged in again on behalf of his sons. These activities prove that he had the money to pay off the denominational loan, but he chose to pay the 7 percent interest and "let it ride." Capital on the frontier was worth far more than 7 percent.

In 1859 Van Raalte backed Albertus Christiaan, or Bertus, as he was known, in a tree nursery business. Bertus had inherited his father's entrepreneurial instincts but not his capabilities. The background is somewhat complicated. In late 1851 Van Raalte had purchased a half interest in a nursery that Homer Hudson had opened at the former Old Wing Mission on present-day East Fortieth Street. In the deal, he had obtained marketable fruit trees. The partners later sold the property to Isaac Fairbanks, the former agricultural agent at the mission, and Hudson opened an apple orchard on seventeen acres adjoining Van Raalte's property on East Sixteenth Street (both now part of Pilgrim Home Cemetery). In 1859 Van Raalte purchased Hudson's half interest in the orchard for $1,060 ($39,000 today), and Hudson busied himself founding Hudsonville.[67]

---

correspondence cited are in HHA. The Van Raalte bonds are noted in treasurer Brower's report for 1871-72 in *Acts and Proceedings*, 1872, 418. All deeds are in Swierenga, "Real Estate Sales."

[67] Swierenga and Van Appledorn, *Old Wing Mission*, 49, 351-51, 580; Indenture Deed for two tracts totaling 17 acres, Sec. 28 T5N R15W, from Homer E. and Clarinda Burt Hudson to Van Raalte, 19 Apr. 1859, Ottawa County Deed Register, Book O, 617, and Book P, 109; Van Raalte to Homer E. Hudson, Notes, 19 Apr. 1859, 18 Nov. 1865, and Deed Book P, 489, Deed Book E, 361; *De Hollander*, 29 Feb. 1860. Holland Nursery extended along the north side of East Sixteenth Street west from

Van Raalte's intent was to provide a business for Bertus, then twenty-two years of age, to support his new wife, Helena Hofman, even though the lavish wedding had stretched the dominee financially.[68] Bertus had big plans for the orchard venture. He wrote his father's friend, Philip Phelps, in New York, about buying "a power [engine?] and saw." Van Raalte told Phelps "Please let it drop because it is impossible for me to apply with his wishes; I am too much burdened." Bertus went ahead on his own and bought the engine in Grand Rapids. Van Raalte asked Phelps, who was coming to Holland as the principal of Holland Academy, to bring along a "saw with rigging" for the orchard. In 1862, Bertus purchased trimming knives to prune the trees. Van Raalte paid off the Hudson mortgage on the property in 1865.[69]

But Bertus also had other irons in the fire. He ran newspaper advertisements offering stud services for his pedigree Durham-Devonshire bull at his farm "at all times of the day." In August 1860, Van Raalte purchased for "my boys" (presumably Bertus and Ben) a threshing machine to do custom harvesting to augment orchard income. Grains would soon be ready for harvest. "Time is slipping away, and they ask me to step in," he wrote Phelps. "They are able to earn the amount in a short time. They have a new power [engine], and their sawing machine works well." The next year, Bertus lost a ship in Lake Michigan that he had purchased on credit.[70]

In 1863 Bertus partnered with Warren Wilder, a Grand Haven millwright, in a steam-powered lumber and shingle mill in Olive Township, under the company name Wilder & Van Raalte. Younger brother Ben called the decision "a silly thing," better to focus on the farm and orchard. Bertus might succeed if "he is lucky," but "I am sometimes afraid that he feels like a man standing on ice—a little unsteady. I personally do not like the mill business but, if it is handled right, a good living can be made at it." A year later, in March 1864, the dominee joined the firm. Each partner put up property and lands as collateral. Wilder was credited with $1,132, Bertus with $1,432, and Van

---

present-day Hoover Boulevard and Pilgrim Home Cemetery up to the Van Raalte grave plots.
[68] See ch. 10, under "A pleasant interlude."
[69] Van Raalte to Phelps, 8 Aug., 8 Sept. 1859, in Bruins and Schakel, *Envisioning Hope College*, 34n15, 47n19; ad in *De Hollander*, 24 Mar. 1859; Homer E. Hudson receipt stating Van Raalte's payment in full of $43.83 for principal and interest on his note, 18 Nov. 1865; Ben Van Raalte to parents, 11 Nov. 1862; Christine Van Raalte to Helena Van Raalte, Jan. 1863, all in HHA.
[70] Van Raalte to Phelps, 16, 19 Aug. 1860, JAH; Van Raalte to Giles Van de Wall, 29 June 1862, HMA.

Raalte with $1,480, for a total of $4,044, but capital stock was valued at $4,500 ($109,000 today), or $1,500 each ($36,300 today). Bertus raised $400 by selling 1,491 acres to his father. Wilder and Bertus Van Raalte pledged to "devote their whole time to the business." The dominee was responsible only "to put in his place a person (a Competent Bookkeeper) at his expense to be his representative in the business," renamed Wilder & Company.[71]

Less than four months later, the dominee bought out Wilder's interest for $1,700 ($30,200 today), $500 down and three years to pay the remainder at 10 percent interest, and Bertus was on his own. But his business acumen was questionable. Whether he made a go of the mill is doubtful. But Van Raalte cannot be faulted for providing his boys with business opportunities to give them a start as entrepreneurs, and he came out whole in the end. In 1867 and 1868, he sold the lumber mill and three building lots for $5,000 to Thomas Padgett of Rochelle, Illinois, director of the Port Sheldon Lumber Company. The small town that grew up around the millworks became Olive Township's administrative center.[72] The next year, Bertus ran off, leaving his family and businesses, never to be heard from again.

Serving two masters?

Financial pressures from Van Raalte's business affairs continued to consume him. His land holdings made him a wealthy man on paper, yet he complained of being "land poor." His money was tied up in unproductive land, and he had to raise specie (gold or coins) for annual tax payments. In 1860 he was by far the wealthiest man in Holland Township, which made him one of the few men subject to a temporary Civil War income tax in 1862. When the federal census marshal made his rounds in 1860 and recorded the value of real and personal property for each household, the land-rich Van Raalte topped the list at real estate valued at $14,800 and personalty at $1,300, for a total of $16,100 ($592,000 today). The dominee's $400 tax bill had doubled in 1862 to $800 ($29,400 today), due to the temporary income tax, "and

---

[71] Ben Van Raalte to father, 4 Feb. 1863, Albertus and Helena Van Raalte to Warren Wilder, Indenture Deed, 15 Mar. 1864, Deed Book Y, 127; Warren Wilder, Albertus C. Van Raalte, and Albertus Van Raalte, Partnership Contract, 16 Mar. 1864; A. C. Van Raalte to Warren and Olivia Wilder, 27 July 1864, Deed Book U, 307-8 and Book Y, 141; *De Hollander*, 29 Feb. 1860.

[72] Warren Wilder, Albertus C. Van Raalte, and Albertus Van Raalte, Agreement, 27 July 1864, HHA; Ben Van Raalte to father, 17 Nov., Dec. 1864, HMA; Swierenga, "Real Estate Sales," $1,000 on 1 June 1867, $4,000 26 Oct. 1868 (book 5, 65-71).

that on unproductive land," he lamented. "The boys are beginning to understand that it's a case of sink or swim."[73]

Van Raalte expressed his anxiety over his wealth as early as 1852 in a letter to Brummelkamp:

> I came here naked, but I have been able to live with a large family and was able to spend as one who had capital. But despite my continual resistance, yes, bitterness toward God and man, I find myself placed with possessions, which, if it pleased God, could make me a capitalist. And yet, they were thrown around my neck for my lack of trust and to kill me. They are possessions that the worldling by turns praises and envies, and still those same possessions seem to become my grace or my destruction because of the debts connected to this and from my position, at least to be for me a source of distressing cares. Often I ask Why? Why? Yet I have the root of all devilish evil in me and also the root of the desire to become rich. . . . Sometimes I say in impatience, let everything break up and go to pieces as it will. However, in a calmer moment, I see it is not without God's providence that I was placed in this important position.[74]

The tension between serving "God or mammon" (Matt. 6:24, KJV) hounded the dominee. In 1862 he confessed in a confidential letter to Giles Van de Wall that he felt like grain being ground between millstones.

> I am burdened with temporal difficulties that are great and that demand all of the time of a strong person. . . . On the one hand, I have to see to it that idle property yields a return, or I will have to sell it to pay the taxes. On the other hand, I say, "Is it proper for me to busy myself with worldly matters since I should devote myself to preaching the Gospel?" And still, I am responsible for the needs of my family. I am in a quandary. . . . I feel as if I have been placed between the upper and nether millstones. . . . [This] often leads me to say, "Is it not my duty to look for another field of labor, where I am not hampered by earthly difficulties?"[75]

---

[73] Federal Census of Holland City, 1870; Swierenga, *Dutch Households in U.S. Population Censuses*. Van Raalte had to pay $400 in 1862 under the new federal income tax law. Bruins, "Funding his Vision," 58.

[74] Van Raalte to Brummelkamp, 11 Sept. 1852, HHA.

[75] Van Raalte to Van de Wall, 29 June 1862, HMA, trans. Nella Kennedy.

These telling letters show that Van Raalte wrestled with his calling as a minister of the Gospel and his desire to enjoy a standard of living above that of most of his parishioners. He was torn between serving "two masters." Yet, he was the only university-educated man among thousands of immigrants, and this alone justified an upper middle-class lifestyle, according to his Old World standards.

More land

Although land dealings had complicated his life, Van Raalte could not resist buying more parcels, despite the debt the denomination still owed on his home. Between 1859 and 1874, Van Raalte purchased $10,000 ($187,000 today) in public lands, beginning with $3,500 of swamp land bought "for my boys." The federal government, from 1849 to 1860, serially donated to Michigan nearly twelve million acres, of which fourteen thousand lay in and around Holland, all to be drained and sold to fund harbor and river improvements, roads, and later railroads.[76] The Holland Harbor Board took charge of the lands.[77] In 1865, 1866, and 1867, the dominee also returned to the Ottawa County delinquent-tax auctions and snagged several dozen parcels, totaling fifteen hundred acres, for an average price of ten cents per acre (see appendix, table 12.3).[78]

A more complicated transaction took place in 1865 when Van Raalte paid Holland merchant Peter Pfanstiehl $2,160 ($40,400 today) for six tracts of swamp land totaling 1,440 acres, again "for my boys." To seal the deal, Pfanstiehl demanded two choice village lots in return, worth $290. Van Raalte sold several other city lots to raise more cash but not enough to pay off the Pfanstiehl contract. Within days, Van Raalte admitted that the "pledge of the Pfanstiehl lots drives me to a corner," and he implored the Hope College trustees to buy eight half-lots located adjacent to the campus for "professorial residences" at a price of $140 each. "This chance never comes back," he argued, "once the lots are sold

---

[76] Gates, *Public Land Law Development*, 321-27, for Swamp Land Acts and Michigan in particular.

[77] A. C. Van Raalte with Holland Harbor Board, Contract, 4 Feb. 1865, HHA. The first part of the purchase was made on 25 Nov. 1862 from John Roost, for $1,492 (Ottawa County Deed Register, Book W, 496). In 1867 Van Raalte still owed the Harbor Fund $2,000 for the lands. See "Statement of Debts and Credits of the Township of Holland . . . on the first day of April A.D. 1867," HMA. On 26 Nov. 1867, Van Raalte donated the lands back to the harbor board (book 5, 304).

[78] Swamp lands contract, Holland Harbor Board to Van Raalte, 4 Feb. 1864; receipt, Ottawa County treasurer, 2 Oct. 1865 for 1864 taxes; ibid., 9 Apr. 1866 for 1865 taxes; ibid., 4 Mar. 1867 for 1866 taxes; Van Raalte to Phelps, 7 Nov. 1865, VRI.

and occupied by a miserable mixture of houses of every description.... Is it possible in some way to secure them for the object?" The school trustees did not bail him out.[79]

His only recourse was to either sell more land or donate it. In 1867 he donated three city lots "to the public" and ninety acres to Hope College. He also donated fifty lots, valued at $1,325 ($27,300 today), as a wedding present to his daughter Christine who married William Gilmore. In 1869 he sold eleven lots at an average price of $265, and the $2,915 more than covered his real estate taxes that year of $660 ($14,200 today).[80]

Van Raalte was equally entrepreneurial minded when it came to higher education. Colleges, he said,

> produce the greatest indirect profits and benefits.... [They] make property values rise. They promote the growth of a community. They create markets and life. They attract capital and the best kind of inhabitants to such a place. Imagine for a moment of how much capital would this place have been deprived annually if the educational work of late years had not been promoted? What would our characters be worth? What would real estate prices be?[81]

How prescient this view was. Hope College has done that and much more for Holland.

After Van Raalte retired in 1867, he devoted even more time and energy to financial matters. His most profitable sale was to Michigan Lake Shore (later Pere Marquette) Railroad of forty-five choice lots alongside the college campus for a new depot and right-of-way. The price was $11,000 ($226,800 today), paid in railroad mortgage bonds, not cash. Van Raalte was inclined not to sell when the railroad first came calling, but Holland residents were caught up in a fevered campaign to bring rail service to town and had even voted to bond themselves for $16,000 to entice the company not to bypass the town. Thanks to Van Raalte, the train whistle was first heard in Holland in

---

[79] Peter F. Pfanstiehl and his wife Helena Mastenbroek to Albertus C. Van Raalte, Indenture Deed, 18 Oct. 1865, Ottawa County Deed Register, Book Z, 166; Van Raalte to Phelps, 7 Nov. 1865; JAH.
[80] Deeds, Van Raalte to Isaac Cappon, 21 Mar, 1864; Van Raalte to the Public, 29 Oct. 1867; Van Raalte and wife to Council of Hope College, 26 July, 26 Aug., 6 Sept. 1867, Ottawa County Deed Records, book 25, 232-35; city tax bill, 8 Jan. 1869, HHA; Van Raalte Lots account book, 1869, HHA; Van Raalte to Gilmore, 7 Mar. 1869, Ottawa County deed book, 10, 376.
[81] A. C. Van Raalte, NYC, to Benjamin Van Raalte, 13 Nov. 1869, HHA.

1870, twenty-three years after the colony's founding. The dominee and other dignitaries spoke enthusiastically at a commemoration marking the occasion. The dominee later donated many of the bonds to Hope College for female education, although he was so strapped for funds that he could not pay a $106 bill to a local storekeeper for two months.[82]

In 1873 another bout of illness led Van Raalte to put his "earthly affairs in order at the signs that my life is at an end." Selling and bequeathing his lands and lots became a priority. Over three decades, he had donated lots and lands worth in total $6,000 ($139,400 today). These included three acres for the Log Church site in 1847. Subsequently, he gave six lots to the Holland District School No. 1, seven lots to First Church, twenty-one lots for Holland Academy, four lots to Hope Church, five lots to Third Reformed Church, six lots and sixty rural acres to the Council of Hope College, five acres of his former orchard to Pilgrim Home Cemetery, and forty-two lots to the Classis of Holland to support foreign missions, a cause always dear to his heart.[83]

Over the same decades, he sold over five hundred rural tracts covering seven thousand acres, plus 842 town lots, totaling together $100,000 ($3.6 million today), with half concentrated in the six years before his death in 1876 (see appendix, table 12.4). The largest sale, for $10,000 ($285,000 today), three months before his death was to his son Dirk, for the purchase of the family homestead and farm, with the proviso that his two youngest daughters, Maria and Anna, could continue to live in the house until their marriages.[84]

Seven weeks before his death, on September 20, 1876, Van Raalte bequeathed equally to his six children and widowed daughter-in-law his remaining real estate of 268 city lots, valued at $400 each, worth $107,200 ($3.1 million today) total, and 1,246 rural acres, worth about $12 per acre, worth $15,000 ($428,000 today) total. Presumably, each heir also received cash and designated personal items. In today's

---

[82] Swierenga, "Albertus C. Van Raalte," 311-12; Swierenga, *Holland, Michigan*, 1:628-30; *Allegan Journal*, 21 June 1869; Van Raalte to Gerrit Van Schelven, 11 May 1871; Van Schelven to Van Raalte, 21 July 1871, HMA; Van Raalte to Phelps, 15 July 1869, in Bruins and Schakel, *Envisioning Hope College*, 197-98; *De Bazuin*, 15 July 1870 (www.delpher.nl, accessed June 2021).

[83] Minutes, Hope College Council, 19 Oct. 1867, JAH; Swierenga, "Albertus C. Van Raalte," table 2, 316, and table 4, 317; minutes, First Holland, 11 Dec. 1875, 26 Feb. 1876; *De Hollander*, 18 Aug. 1875; Swierenga, "Real Estate Sales."

[84] Compiled from 15 July 1871, book 14, 250-51; book 15, 140-41; book 29, 410, Ottawa County Deed Registers (Van Raalte deed to son Dirk); Swierenga, "Real Estate Sales."

dollars, the total landed bequest was worth $3.5 million, or $498,000, divided among the seven heirs. It was a handsome inheritance for PKs. Their father's decision in 1849 to risk taking ownership of city lots proved to be the foundation for the Van Raalte family wealth. It was a masterful stroke of good judgment.[85]

A proposed national bank

In his business activities, the biggest problem Van Raalte and his partners faced was the lack of capital for development, a ubiquitous problem on the American frontier. For manufacturing and trade to flourish, Holland needed a bank to issue reputable (rather than wildcat) bank notes, and for some time, the dominee considered chartering a bank under the aegis of the state banking act of 1857. Nathan Kenyon had opened the first private bank in Holland in 1856, and Kommer Schaddelee followed suit in 1871 with an exchange bank. Both accepted savings deposits, paid in currency on merchants' drafts and private bank notes submitted for exchange, and issued notes (paper money). But private bank notes lacked credibility and were worth no more than the reputation of the issuer. Van Raalte hoped to form a local bank that could tie in to the national banking system that Congress created in 1862.

The disastrous Holland Fire of October 8, 1871, prompted Van Raalte to put his bank plan into motion (ch. 15). The flames had spared his home, church, and college, but the entire business district and the residential heart of the city was lost. Holland could not be rebuilt without capital. "A bank institution I seek; the National is what we need," the dominee wrote Phelps. "I must go ahead or give up." He envisioned a bank capitalized at $100,000 ($2.5 million today) under the National Banking System created by Congress in 1862. Such banks were authorized to issue federal bank notes, dubbed "greenbacks," backed by the federal government. But the way to reach that goal was unclear. If Van Raalte sought help to obtain a charter from Americans in Grand Haven, such as US Senator Thomas White Ferry (1827-1896), the news would get out, Van Raalte feared, and "sharpers" and "society-enervating leeches or blood suckers" would try to take over.

---

[85] Calculated from Philip Phelps Scrapbook, 23 Nov. 1872; Van Raalte to P. Phelps, Feb. 1873; Phelps to Van Raalte, 29 Aug. 1873; lot sales account book, 1873-76; Gerrit Van Schelven, "Historical Sketch of Holland City and Colony," *Holland City News*, 26 Aug. 1876; Bruins, "Funding his Vision," 55.

As a capitalist himself, Van Raalte's foul depiction of investors was demeaning in the extreme, and his fears in any case were irrational.[86]

Van Raalte's "ripe plan" as he called it was actually brilliant. He offered to raise $8,000 in seed money by mortgaging his farmlands and to partner for up to $12,000 with Arent Geerlings, a "practical miller" whose mill and feed store were destroyed by the fire. With $20,000 ($500,000 today) in start-up capital, he and Geerlings could begin a small bank that might be able to attract capital from Dutch Reformed capitalists in New York. They would "take stock" in the bank by depositing government bonds they owned, from which they would continue to clip 6 percent coupons. With the bonds as collateral, the bank would engrave bank notes in multiples of the collateral and lend the notes to farmers and manufacturers. Such bank notes circulated just as paper currency does today. The notes would increase the local money supply and "bring business life back" after the fire. Hope College could also place its endowment monies in the bank at interest and borrow from it to erect buildings.[87]

The bank would operate out of Geerlings' rebuilt feed store in Holland and in his branch stores in outlying villages. Supplying feed and other necessities to farmers is "a safe and good business," Van Raalte reasoned, and the bank could piggyback on that cachet and expand into banking and investment services. "We could expect the first years more than barely to keep alive," but the business would expand "as fast as small deposits grow on the hands," Van Raalte told Phelps. "All my property is given to it, even self-preservation compels me. . . . Most sickening will be our situation without capital." Van Raalte then came to the bottom line: "If you could effect a loan for me of 20 m [thousand] on ample security on real estate, this would perhaps provide matters. They tell me life insurance companies are doing this sometimes."

Despite the dominee's desperate tone and the bleak situation facing the city, his appeal to Eastern friends went unheeded. No money for a charter bank in Holland was forthcoming, although relief funds for the townspeople did arrive. Hope College trustees also would not risk their endowment funds on such a venture. It was a missed

---

[86] Van Raalte to Phelps, 23 Oct., 267-70 (quote, 270), 8 Nov. 1871, in *Envisioning Hope College*; 283-84 (quote, 283); "Our Banking System," *Holland City News*, 26 Oct. 1872; Darlene Winter, "100 Years Ago Today," *Holland Sentinel*, 20 Dec. 1986; *Sheboygan Nieuwsbode*, 24 May 1871; Vande Water, "First Bank Was a Home"; Van Koevering, *Legends of the Dutch*, 475.

[87] Van Raalte to Phelps, 8 Nov. 1871, in *Envisioning Hope College*, 283-84.

opportunity for an ingenious plan, far ahead of most people of the day.[88]

The national financial panic in 1873, set off by wildcat banking, ended all hope for Van Raalte's bank project. But banker Nathan Kenyon, shortly before the Great Fire, had reorganized his private bank under the new Michigan bank law, with savings and commercial departments. In 1876, just before his death, Van Raalte had the satisfaction to see the enterprising Kenyon erect a three-story building for the bank on the southwest corner of River and Eighth Streets (now the site of Reader's World). Kenyon accomplished what Van Raalte could not.[89]

Promoter or businessman?

Apart from his land dealings, Van Raalte could be described as more of a promoter and fundraiser than a businessman. He raised tens of thousands of dollars in the East for the Holland colony, but his dabbling in factories and mills did not prove profitable. His primary purpose, however, was not to make a fortune but to ensure the success of the colony. His entrepreneurial mindset, capitalistic attitude toward money, and eagerness to take risks in various enterprises inevitably drew him into business life. Only his duties as a pastor restrained him from taking a more direct role—he could be a silent partner but not the person in charge.

Lots and lands lent themselves to Van Raalte's direct management since he could squeeze sales, legal work, and tax payments between pastoral duties. What value, one might ask, did he add to the community by such dealings? First, he assumed risks others were not willing or able to take, and he shielded immigrants from American land speculators. Second, he sold land on credit—which no government or other financial entity would do—at a time when cash was essential, and immigrants had very little of it. Third, he guaranteed titles by granting warrantee deeds that saved buyers from title problems. Fourth, he donated some seventy city lots and over one hundred acres

---

[88] Lucas, *Dutch Immigrant Memoirs*, 2:495; Van Raalte to Phelps, 8 Nov. 1871, in *Envisioning Hope College*, 283-84 (quotes); Vande Water, "Holland Had a State Bank in 1889"; "E. J. Harrington," *Holland City News*, 22 Dec. 1877. *Holland City News* (10 Aug. 1872) gave some credence to Van Raalte's efforts; it reported: "We learn that movements are being made toward establishing a National Bank in this city, and that it promises a success."

[89] *Sheboygan Nieuwsbode*, 24 May 1871; *Holland City News*, 4 Oct. 1873, 9 May 1874; Dunbar, *A History*, 231.

for churches, missions, schools, and various community projects, such as the first harbor lighthouse, a shipyard, and a flourmill.

His mental work, sorting through all the laws and bureaucracies, was worth more than any physical work he could have accomplished on a farm or in a factory. He rightfully and honorably profited from his economic endeavors, but he did not live a luxurious a life. His real estate dealings made him a fabulously wealthy man. Land in and around Holland gained value due to the rapid and steady development of the community. Van Raalte got in on the ground floor and parlayed a modest investment in land into a portfolio worth in excess of two million dollars in today's currency. Van Raalte became a rich man indeed. He could have shared the title of "wealthiest Hollander in Michigan" with Den Bleyker.

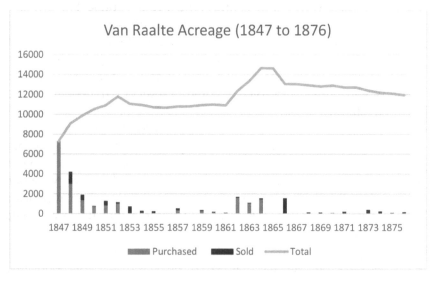

Van Raalte land dealings, both buying and selling, 1847-76 (*graph by Michael Douma*). See appendix, tables 12.1, 12.2, 12.3, and 12.4 for the actual dollar amounts.

CHAPTER 13

Newspaper Magnate, Political Leader, Civil War Patriot: More "worldly matters."

Dominee Van Raalte's life in the early 1850s had many setbacks, including near bankruptcy and a church schism, but nothing was more hurtful than attacks on his character in the newspaper he founded to bind the colony together. The venture did just the opposite and proved to be an unmitigated disaster. The bad press evolved into a political conflict over national policies on slavery, nativism, territorial expansion, and the Civil War. Van Raalte sparked controversy by switching party allegiance from the Democrats to the infant Republicans, but Dutch voters would not follow him for some years. The dominee insisted on his right as an America citizen, clergyman or not, to speak up on these issues, even to his detriment.[1]

Newspaper magnate

Van Raalte established the first newspaper in the colony and, indeed, all of Ottawa County. The seminal issue of *De Hollander*, a

---

[1] Kennedy, *Commentary*, 23 Apr. 1848, 1:11; 3 Apr. 1860, 2:933-34.

"The Hollander," January 4, 1851, the Dutch-language
Democratic newspaper in Holland from 1850 to 1895
(JAH)

weekly, appeared in September 1850.[2] As editor-in-chief, the dominee insisted on the right of prior censorship. He did not believe in the new-fangled idea of freedom of the press. This led to a running battle with the editor, which undermined comity in the community and drove the dominee to despair. Only the intervention of clerical colleagues and the heavy-handed consistorial discipline of the editor restored a measure of calm. The controversy raised questions about press censorship, the nature of governance in the colony, competition between churchmen and businessmen, relations between Holland and Zeeland, and especially the role of the colonial leader. It was a test of wills that revealed fissures within the colony and presaged trouble to come in both religious and political life.

Van Raalte took the lead in this new venture because he believed that the colony could not flourish without a newspaper. He arranged

---

[2] *The Hollander* masthead from 28 Dec. 1850 (first issue) to 2 May 1855 was in Dutch. From 16 May 1855 to 15 July 1857, the paper carried two mastheads, *The Hollander* for the English-language edition and *De Hollander* for the Dutch-language edition. Thereafter, the masthead read only *De Hollander*. I use *De Hollander* for all citations.

with Josiah Hawks and Elisha B. Bassett, owners and printers of the *Allegan Record*, a Democratic sheet, to begin a sister bilingual paper for the three thousand Dutch in the colony, with his business associate, Henry D. Post, as editor. To widen readership, the proprietors printed half the columns in English and half in Dutch. Van Raalte was responsible for the Dutch part, and Giles Van de Wall, a bilingual schoolmaster at Holland Academy from 1858 to 1861, was hired to translate Dutch-language news items and articles into readable English. The paper was titled in English, the *Democrat*, and the masthead carried a Democrat banner. This party had controlled the state of Michigan since territorial times, and all local Americans were Democrats.

The Allegan partners gave Van Raalte total editorial control and he, in turn, promised to line up subscribers among the colonists. He enlisted his fellow clerics in the effort at the October 1850 meeting of the Classis of Holland. "In unity there is strength," he declared, in the words of the Netherlands national emblem. They endorsed the new *Holland Weekly* and an "every family" subscription plan, which "urged the father of every family to take it and preserve it for the benefit of his children." Cornelius Van der Meulen in Zeeland, Seine Bolks in Overisel, and Koene Van der Schuur in Graafschap all agreed to serve as correspondents for their own churches and take responsibility for subscriptions.[3] Enlisting clerics, however, proved to be problematic.

Van Raalte laid out his rationale for the paper in a lengthy editorial in the first edition. Besides news from the Old Country, the paper would link settlements spread over fifty square miles and help immigrants become useful citizens by teaching the history and principles of American laws and institutions. It would also "profit the people, not only with religious articles but also with all kinds of necessary things," notably civic life and best practices in animal husbandry, cropping, and homemaking. The promo piece concluded with the promise to open the columns to anyone who has something to say "in the interest of the Holland people," or to express "differences of opinion." But writers bore a responsibility to show "love for truth" and not sow "discord." Did Van Raalte anticipate trouble?[4]

Starting a newspaper on the frontier was always risky, and the poverty of the Dutch immigrants made it all the more precarious. Van

[3] Van Raalte, "To the Hollanders," *De Hollander*, 30 Nov. 1850, HMA; Kennedy, *Commentary*, 30 Oct. 1850, 1:112; Lucas, *Netherlanders*, 132; *Grand Rapids Enquirer*, 18 Dec. 1850, as cited in Lucas, *Netherlanders*, 531-32.

[4] Van Raalte, "To the Hollanders," *De Hollander*, 30 Nov. 1850; minutes, First Holland, 5 Feb. 1852, trans. Buursma.

Raalte and his fellow clerics failed to deliver the promised subscriptions, and Hawks and Bassett began to carp at him. He complained to his consistory that the "many capricious actions" of Hawks "have greatly frustrated the actual purpose of the paper." Within a year, Hawks was ready to cut his losses. He sold the paper "cheaply" to Hermanus Doesburg and Giles Van de Wall, both members of Van Raalte's congregation. But neither man had money, so Van Raalte backed them as a silent partner. The pair were "greatly encouraged" by his offer to solicit capital from church friends in the East. Post resigned as editor within a year and founded the *Ottawa Register*, a paper solely for English readers. The *Register* shared offices with *De Hollander*, which then became a Dutch-language sheet.[5]

Van Raalte continued to demand full and exclusive control over the contents, including approving every article and letter to the editor prior to publication. Doesburg and Van de Wall agreed under pressure, but they soon had regrets. That the dominee demanded such tight oversight was not surprising, given his status in the highly stratified Dutch society where people of the "lesser sort" were required to show deference to those of the "better sort" by a doffing of the hat, a slight bowing of the knee, and other symbolic gestures of respect. The entire Dutch social system functioned within the rules of deference. As a university graduate and a Christian minister, Van Raalte expected deferential treatment and considered public criticism a personal affront to his honor.[6]

American political leaders, notably Thomas Jefferson, had demanded as much under the common law of seditious libel. They insisted that newspaper editors censor comments deemed too negative or hostile to their persons and policies. Jefferson and other top government officials often filed lawsuits for slander against critics who hit too hard. Editors were free, by Jefferson's reasoning, to publish the "truth" about government officials, but common law allowed aggrieved politicians to file suit for seditious libel. In court, however, one person's truth became another's falsehood. That was the rub.[7]

Van Raalte's demand for prior censorship went beyond the common law of prior restraint and was a recipe for disaster. It depended

---

[5] Swierenga, *Holland, Michigan*, 3:1660; "Holland Colony," *Allegan Record*, 14 Feb. 1859.
[6] This section draws on Swierenga, "Press Censorship."
[7] Levy, *Emergence of a Free Press*, 343-49; Levy, *Legacy of Suppression*, 297-308.

on continued cooperation between the managing partners, their submission of content to Van Raalte before setting type, and on his raising working capital in the East. Nothing went as planned. Doesburg and Van de Wall were at loggerheads over editorial policy. Their relationship "left something to be desired," Van Raalte noted wryly. Politics was the sore point. The upcoming 1852 presidential campaign was the first in which the Dutch were eligible to vote. *De Hollander* was a Democratic sheet—Doesburg's party—but Van de Wall held strong Whig views. For his part, the dominee was caught up not only in his busy life but also in other businesses, notably his milling business with Den Bleyker. He could not possibly find time to censor every issue before publication, and his partners for their part were negligent in sending him timely copy. Recognizing his part in the difficulties, Van Raalte gave up his share of the profits to his partners.[8]

By early 1852, Van de Wall believed his position was no longer tenable. Since he and Doesburg could not agree, he sold his interest to Doesburg and moved to Kalamazoo to begin a Dutch-language Whig paper, *De Netherlander*, which first appeared in May 1852.[9] Van Raalte assumed that his problems with the paper were over, but he was sorely mistaken. Doesburg and his teenage sons, Jacob and Otto, who helped in day-to-day operations, quickly took the paper, in the dominee's words, in an "independent direction, involving inappropriate principles . . . that would put in jeopardy the truth and good name of the community."[10]

In fact, Doesburg published anonymous articles with inflammatory titles, such as "De Paus en zijne Kardinalen" (The pope and his cardinals) and "Baasje Spelen" (Playing boss). Both criticized Van Raalte and his consistory for extending their ecclesiastical authority into secular affairs. The anonymous articles, later found to have come from the pen of Rev. Cornelius Van der Meulen, pastor of the Zeeland church, stung deeply and reverberated widely. The First Church minutes state clearly that "Rev. Van der Meulen in *De Hollander* has written about Rev. Van Raalte and his person in a covert way." These attacks on his character made his ministry "impossible," the offended dominee declared. "Attacking Rev. Van Raalte by presenting to the

---

[8] Minutes, First Holland, 7 Feb. 1852.
[9] Lucas, *Netherlanders*, 532, 543.
[10] Minutes, First Holland, 5 Feb., 1852, trans. Buursma. For the full story, see Swierenga, *Holland, Michigan*, 3:2150-57, and "Press Censorship," 171-82.

people in general, including those outside of our colony, a negative view of Van Raalte."[11]

Van Raalte decided to use the lever he controlled, namely, consistorial authority. He called Doesburg to a meeting with several consistory members, all city merchants and solid citizens. After admonishing the editor, the dominee reasserted his right to monitor the contents before publication, as originally agreed. Doesburg, in his defense, "pointed out the slovenliness and neglect of Rev. Van Raalte" and his failure to raise the promised support. Were it not for the editor's hard labors and that of his sons, Doesburg insisted, the paper would already have failed. Moreover, the dominee had in a "hateful way" made his sons "to be like servants," treating them with disrespect. That the sons were only fourteen and twelve years old doubtless gave Van Raalte reason to brush them off. Yet editors had to live by deadlines—censors did not. And editors had to pay the bills, even when benefactors had failed to do so.

The consistory cut Doesburg very little slack. Despite the dominee's "shortcomings," the editor had no "right to destroy the agreement." Doesburg reluctantly accepted the rebuke. Van Raalte also admitted his faults and promised to pay reparations and assume all debts in exchange for having exclusive authority once again. This agreement, however, was no better than previous ones. Van Raalte did not raise the operating capital, and Doesburg again went on the offensive, opening the pages, as Van Raalte claimed, to "any malcontent who wishes to set ablaze a fire of controversy." He complained bitterly about Doesburg's "misuse" of the paper and demanded an end to scurrilous personal attacks.

> The most recent articles make it clear that everything that is precious and good is at stake here. . . . Our good name in civic and ecclesiastical circles is scandalized. . . . This contributes to the devastation of pastoral and ecclesiastical rule, and the entire reason for our being here as a Christian people who proclaim the truth will be destroyed.

Unless Doesburg yielded, the dominee predicted "disastrous consequences," even to the point that he might be forced "to leave this place." To make his point, Van Raalte left his pulpit and went to

---

[11] Minutes, First Holland, 6, 22 Apr., 8, 21 May, 10 June (quote) 1852, trans. Buursma.

Kalamazoo for a time. The editor of the *Grand Rapids Argus* took great delight in washing Holland's dirty linen in its pages.[12]

The tiff with Doesburg was very untimely for Van Raalte. He had gone bankrupt in his business venture with Den Bleyker; the Classis of Holland was in the midst of a raging schism over the Union of 1850; his consistory had charged him with neglecting his pulpit, and the harbor project was stalling. Trouble assailed the dominee at every turn. By threatening to leave the colony in the lurch, he raised the ante and alarmed his consistory greatly. "The brothers are all in agreement that this weighty situation requires that the paper be returned to the influence of Rev. Van Raalte." And they agreed to go en masse to Doesburg to persuade him to yield. In return, the elders asked the dominee to allow Doesburg and his sons to continue to "earn their daily bread." Van Raalte reluctantly agreed.[13]

But the dominee did convene a special consistory meeting to discipline Doesburg. The question was: May a member slander others, particularly his pastor? "This is happening," Van Raalte cried, "because Mr. Doesburg is permitting filthy slander to appear in his newspaper." The consistory raised caution flags. Before anyone could be admonished, the anonymous writers must be identified.

> We must be extremely careful, particularly in times of confusion since many ordinary members are being led astray.... We do not wish to give the appearance of seeking to hinder the freedom of the press, nor do we wish to be accused of a party spirit. Nor do we wish to be accused of robbing a poor man of the opportunity to make a living. The latter must be particularly avoided, so that the situation is not made worse.

The consistory threaded the needle; it admonished Doesburg "in the capacity of friends," but did not proceed with formal church discipline.[14] At this lukewarm response, Van Raalte threatened to air the congregation's dirty linen in his annual report to General Synod and to bring the Doesburg affront to the Classis of Holland. We "have

---

[12] *Grand Rapids Argus*, 9 Mar. 1852; Van Hinte, *Netherlanders*, 241-42; Oswald Van der Sluis "To my dear Friend Hein" (Van der Haar); "Pope and His Cardinals," undated letter, published in *Sheboygan Nieuwsbode*, 9 Mar. (actually ca. 20 Apr.) 1852, trans. Moerdyke, Moerdyke Papers.
[13] Minutes, First Holland, 5 Feb. 1852.
[14] Ibid., 6 Apr. 1852, for this and next paragraph.

no objection to this," the consistory replied but advised that he "wait for the proper time and opportunity."[15]

The dominee plunged ahead anyway and assembled a "Greater Consistory" of sister churches to "seek advice concerning weighty matters," with Hermanus Doesburg in the dock and Rev. Bolks of the Grand Haven church in the chair. Attendees included Rev. Ypma of the Vriesland church and fifteen elders and deacons from four other churches—Holland, Drenthe, Overisel, and Graafschap. Tellingly, no representatives came from the Zeeland consistory, particularly its minister, Van der Meulen, who harbored grievances and was indeed the anonymous critic.[16]

Following the church order, Bolks asked first whether the Holland consistory had dealt with the matter officially. After the brothers gave an extensive recital of the facts, they had to admit that they "functioned exclusively as citizens" and not as consistory members. After noting this procedural misstep, the assembly still unanimously rebuked Doesburg for slandering office bearers, bringing "sorrow to God's children," and dishonoring the name of the Lord. He must name the offending writers, confess his sin before God and his congregation, and publish an apology in his paper. Otherwise, "It is the judgment of the assembly that he may not be permitted to come to the table of the Lord." Remarkably, classis short-circuited the discipline process by imposing the first step, barring Doesburg from the Lord's Supper, without his consistory first having voted officially and then asking permission of Classis to proceed with discipline. Classis also placed merchant Jan Binnekant under discipline for publishing a letter critical of Van Raalte. Rather than challenge the flawed classical procedure, both men willingly stood before the congregation to confess their sin of slander. Doesburg added tears of remorse to his confession and published an apology in his newspaper.[17]

Doesburg's public acts of contrition did not end the matter. Rumors circulated almost immediately that Rev. Ypma had coerced him and that the editor's words in church were "not genuine," because they did not jibe with his apology in the paper. This rumor riled Van

---

[15] Ibid., 22 Apr. 1852.

[16] Greater consistories were comprised of neighboring consistories. First Zeeland church minutes, in Rev. Van der Meulen's hand as clerk, contain no hint of this trouble.

[17] Minutes, First Holland, 8, 21 May 1852, for this and the next paragraph. Unfortunately, all the relevant issues of the *Hollander* surrounding this controversy were lost in the Holland Fire of 1871.

Raalte all the more. It "makes a mockery of the public confession of sin," he cried, and "places the labors of God's sincere office bearers in a bad light." Doesburg must stand before the congregation again and confess clearly so as to dispel all rumors. The dominee also warned the congregation that slandering Doesburg made them all equally guilty. No one may "speak against a brother who has made a tearful confession of sin," lest "confession of sin in God's congregation becomes a farce and a game." The "congregational misery" must end, or the body would become a "victim of anarchy."

The trouble that Van Raalte feared broke out when Doesburg came to church the next Sunday expecting to participate in Holy Communion, which quarterly celebration happened to fall on that day. The consistory had met with Doesburg the previous evening and accepted his confession as genuine. At that time, to celebrate the Lord's Table, communicants would sit around a long table in front of the sanctuary and pass the common cup. To guard the table from being desecrated by unworthy participants, an elder would stand at each end. According to Engbertus Van der Veen, an eyewitness, when Doesburg approached the table, an elder who had not attended the evening meeting "took him by the shoulders and requested him to leave the table, which caused a great commotion." Van der Veen continued: "Doesburg became very excited, stood up, and declared that he understood that on the day before all had been forgiven. Thereupon, the members of the consistory corroborated his statements; and peace was restored, whereupon Doesburg was permitted to sit down." "Needless to say," Jacob van Hinte noted wryly, for an incensed elder to manhandle a parishioner in front of the entire congregation "caused quite a tumult" and greatly embarrassed the dominee.[18]

The misery did not end there. Within days, Van der Meulen published another anonymous article in the *Hollander*, which in a "covert way . . . presented a negative view" of Van Raalte. The bad blood went back a year to the Holland Township caucus in the Zeeland church when delegates came to fisticuffs over offices and monies for roads, schools, and other projects. Van Raalte was inclined to overlook Van der Meulen's "attack," but several parishioners demanded that the consistory defend their pastor and "restore and maintain the good honor of his name." Van der Meulen "should be admonished and required publicly to confess in the above-mentioned paper of the error of his way." Failing this, the consistory should ask the classis to "deal with

---

[18] Van der Veen, "Life Reminiscences," 1:504; Van Hinte, *Netherlanders*, 447, 1060.

the matter . . . so that the wounds that the congregation has incurred may be healed." Van Raalte softened his stance and asked everyone "to bear patiently and respond in warm love." Van der Meulen, for his part, laid down his pen and ended his involvement with the newspaper.[19]

The bad blood between the two clerics ran deeper than money. It was reflected in the wide cultural differences between *de stad* and *de dorpen*. Personal issues of status and prestige were also at work. Van der Meulen's parents were poor, and he self-taught while working as a surveyor and building contractor. Gifted in mind and with an outgoing personality, he studied for the ministry under Scholte at Utrecht as a married man living in abject poverty. In contrast, Van Raalte's father was a university-trained pastor in the public church, and his son enjoyed the same high level of status and education.[20]

The gossip grapevine spread Van Raalte's troubles far and wide within a matter of weeks, notably via *De Sheboygan Nieuwsbode*, the widest-circulating, Dutch-language newspaper in America. Van Raalte was among its subscribers. Jacob Quintus, the Wisconsin editor, was mildly anticlerical and delighted in the chance to boost his circulation by spreading dirt about the *priesthood* in the flagship Dutch colony. He condemned the "degrading" decision of the Classis of Holland in declaring Doesburg's paper "heretical" (*kettersch*).[21]

One of Quintus's sources was Oswald Van der Sluis, the man Van Raalte had sued for not paying his debts on his failed mill. Van der Sluis, a keen observer, relished spreading the sordid details in a long letter to "my dear friend Hein" in Wisconsin, who happily shared the information with Quintus.[22] Van der Sluis's letter in the *Nieuwsbode* deserves quoting:

> Things are sad, very sad, here! You should know that Van Raalte, not two weeks ago, has informed his people that in these

---

[19] Minutes, First Holland, 10 June [*sic*, May] 1852.
[20] Lucas, *Netherlanders*, 120; Van der Meulen, *Ter nagedachtenis*, 10-11. Van der Meulen left Zeeland in 1859 to serve both the First Chicago and then the Second Grand Rapids churches. He died a few months before Van Raalte and was buried in Zeeland Cemetery.
[21] Krabbendam, "Cornelius van der Meulen," 315-32; editorial, *Sheboygan Nieuwsbode*, 9 Mar. 1852, trans. Moerdyke, HMA; Quintus to Van Raalte, 6 Mar. 1854, trans. Ten Hoor.
[22] O. D. Van der Sluis to "Dear Friend Hein," undated, but ca. 9 May 1852. H. Vander Ploeg gave a copy of the original to Gerrit Van Schelven on 16 May 1912, and Peter T. Moerdyke subsequently translated it into English. Only the English translation typescript survives in the Moerdyke Papers.

circumstances he can't preach anymore. He has absented himself and has gone off to Kalamazoo. The Consistory, not knowing what to do, decided to take Ypma into their arms. This person appears and, in alliance with Bolks, has so far succeeded that he convinced Doesburg . . . and he openly confesses that he was forced and pressed to publish these pieces. This confession is being contested by us, on the grounds of its being an untruth. Doesburg does not deny this, but he seeks to protect himself by stating that he did not make such a confession, although he really did (What, now, can one expect of such a man). . . . In the meantime, this is the fact; Doesburg has made the confession on the promise that the Consistory would bring the whole thing to an end. . . .

What do you think of our liberty? Isn't it worse than in the Netherlands? Will not the Pope and his Cardinals defend their rights just like all ecclesiastical States? I believe they will. And supposing this, we will soon have nothing left than the Roman Catholic faith, instead of a Reformed religion, so that we can obtain pardon for our sins (in their opinion) through *words, money, and influence*. . . . Vermeulen [Cornelius Van der Meulen] has made public confession at the Classis meeting that he is the author of the articles in *De Hollander*. They taunt him indirectly; they do not dare to go after him, for they do not challenge him. But if they do approach him, he intends to tear himself away from our Church's fellowship and possibly join the Scottish congregation. I dare not make a statement what the result will be. They should leave in peace. . . . Many often think to move, among whom I also belong, at least if the system now adopted will be maintained, that the *Church* is going to govern in civil matters.

Van der Sluis's missive overstated the case against Van Raalte and damaged Van der Meulen's reputation with the assertion that he had threatened schism, which was out of character for the mild-mannered pastor and is unsupported by the minutes of the Classis of Holland. The events of April 1852 clearly disturbed the peace in the Holland colony. The *Grand Rapids Argus* reported that "Van der Meulen seems by far the best liked of the two . . . as well on as off the pulpit." For Quintus to pass this put-down of Van Raalte to Hollanders across the Midwest showed that he shared Doesburg's disdain for the Holland dominee.[23]

[23] *Sheboygan Nieuwsbode*, 17 Feb. 1852, citing *Grand Rapids Argus*.

Van Raalte's troubles with *De Hollander* proved that his Old World outlook did not fare well in democratic America, with its wide-open society and frank public discourse. His demand for prior censorship was unreasonable in a frontier environment in which rival powerbrokers arose among preachers, teachers, businessmen, and politicians. The arrangement never worked as he had hoped, and the problems pushed him to the extremes of defiance and despair. Sometimes he took the offensive and forced his critics into silence. Other times he magnanimously turned the other cheek and accepted his lot as a leader with feet of clay. The pope of Holland showed that he was human after all.

Politics—prohibition and abolition

Van Raalte's struggle with Doesburg quickly degenerated into political infighting, first over prohibition and then abolition of slavery. The People's Assembly already in 1847 took a strong position against selling hard liquor, except for medicinal purposes. When Van Raalte took charge of all village lots, he proscribed distilling whiskey in every deed, but the Dutch had no problem with brewers and vintners.[24] Van Raalte's household accounts routinely listed beer by the keg, and Rev. Koene Van den Bosch of the Noordeloos Church had his own Bohemian beer stein. Wells were shallow and the water impure, so beer was a necessary beverage. Mina Van Raalte (Mrs. Peter) Oggel, when she was nursing her daughter, stopped drinking beer in hopes of increasing her milk supply. "I do not like beer, and you really gain weight with it," she added. But her husband ordered beer, nonetheless.[25]

Van Raalte never let up against whiskey and all other strong drink. He had Doesburg republish an article from a Dutch periodical that recounted a Pennsylvania town meeting where a pastor spoke in favor of selling strong drink, and a wife stood up and testified that her husband and five sons had died as drunkards. Her emotional speech moved hearts and brought tears and carried the day. The town board decided to no longer import liquor. "The only fit conduct for a Christian with regard to the curse of strong liquor is to abstain from any appearance of evil." Van Raalte added his postscript to Doesburg: "You will give me great pleasure to publish this piece." Doesburg did.[26]

[24] Swierenga, *Holland, Michigan*, 3:1675-78.
[25] Johanna Maria Wilhelmina Oggel to mother, 14 Nov. 1862; Pieters, *Dutch Settlement*, 155-56; *De Hollander*, 13 July 1853.
[26] *De Hollander*, 26 Oct. 1854, trans. Nella Kennedy.

Prohibition became personal in 1853 when the Michigan Whig Party put a referendum on the ballot to ban the manufacture and sale of alcoholic beverages and levy heavy fines for possession; even communion wine was proscribed. Hollanders in West Michigan were incensed; saloons could be closed but not the right to drink beer at home or serve communion wine at church. Dry laws were an infringement on personal and religious liberty, they insisted, and not a panacea for the nation's social and moral ills. Worse, the Dutch detected nativist overtones among proponents of the referendum. As a result, Holland voted down the proposal by a large majority of more than three to one and Zeeland by more than five to one. But the referendum passed handily statewide and by a slimmer 56 percent in Ottawa County, only to be overturned by the courts on a technicality.[27]

The Dutch vote against teetotalers brought nativist attacks down on their heads. "Dutch Cattle" was an epithet contemptuously hurled at the immigrants. A Michigan Whig charged that "not one single throb of patriotism" beat in the hearts of these immigrants. "Some tell me that many foreigners are intelligent; yes intelligent. Look at the Dutchman smoking his pipe, and if you can see a ray of intelligence in that dirty, idiotic face of his, show it to me."[28]

The stridently nativist Know Nothing (or American) Party captured many votes in the Midwest among Yankees who touted the slogan: "America for the Americans." Know Nothings also pushed a naturalization law that would have increased the residency requirement for immigrants from five to fourteen years. The effort failed, but the Dutch read the proposal as a personal assault.[29]

Van Raalte was so incensed by the Whig attacks on the Dutch that he personally went to the polling place in the November 1854 midterm elections and delivered an hour-and-a-quarter political speech, which was very uncharacteristic. When the results came in, he rejoiced that Holland Township had carried the Democrat ticket by forty-six votes. But Dutch dissatisfaction with the Democrat presidential vetoes of

---

[27] Van Hinte, *Netherlanders*, 239-40 (quote), 545; Dunbar, *A History*, 430; *De Hollander*, 7, 14 Sept., 1 Dec. 1853, 2, 23 Feb., 20 Apr., 14 Sept. 1854.

[28] *Grand Haven News*, 12 Sept. 1860, quoted in Wagenaar, "Early Political History," 27; Van Hinte, *Netherlanders*, 239; *De Grondwet*, 22 Mar. 1887 (quote), trans. Buursma. John Wilson may have had Germans more than Dutch in his line of fire because he made a reference to their love of "cabbage and lager beer." But Americans seldom differentiated between Germans and Hollanders (Deutsch and Dutch); all foreigners suffered from such stereotyping.

[29] Swierenga, "The Ethnic Voter."

public works was rising; their 100 percent vote of 1852 dropped to 64 percent in 1854. Yet, pastors like Van Raalte and his colleagues remained staunch Democrats.[30]

Prohibition and nativism kept the Dutch in the Democrat camp, despite their growing disappointment with the party's southern, proslavery stance, especially on the controversial issue of the fugitive slave law and the extension of slavery into Kansas, in violation of the Missouri Compromise of 1820. The Dutch had always opposed slavery, even before emigrating, but they had no firsthand experience with the institution, and slavery seemed a distant problem. Yet Van Raalte later preached a powerful sermon that condemned slavery in the strongest possible terms.[31]

During the 1856 presidential campaign, Doesburg clipped editorials from Scholte's Democratic *Pella Gazette*, which condemned "Know Nothing Abolition Republicanism."[32] In September Van Raalte opened his pulpit at First Church to Scholte, who visited Michigan for the first and only time. Scholte preached in the new sanctuary and spoke at a Democratic campaign rally in the schoolhouse where he was "received with much real enthusiasm." One attendee was not impressed. "He preached for us too but the people didn't like him. He was not as orthodox in his preaching as Van Raalte. The people here still cling to the old fashioned doctrine." Before returning to Iowa, Scholte also stumped among the Dutch in Zeeland, Grand Haven, Grand Rapids, and Kalamazoo. He got a hero's welcome everywhere, both for his role in leading the Secession of 1834 in the Netherlands and for his American political savvy. But as a clergyman, he took some brickbats for entering the domain of politics. Scholte's energetic speeches and Doesburg's sharp editorial pen held the Democrat vote in Holland steady at 64 percent in the 1856 presidential election.[33]

In the 1857 state elections, the Democratic Party of Kent and Ottawa Counties nominated Cornelius Van der Meulen to be a regent of the University of Michigan, which prompted their Republican

---

[30] "Democratic Victory in Holland!" *De Hollander*, 9 Nov. 1854; *Allegan Journal*, 23 May 1859; Cornelius Van Loo, "Zeeland Township and Village," in Lucas, *Dutch Immigrant Memoirs*, 1:246-47.

[31] A copy is preserved at BHL.

[32] Scholte editorials on "De Know Nothings," *De Hollander*, 25 Feb., 23 May 1855, 30 Apr., 4, 21 May, 27 Aug., 3 Sept. 1856; Doesburg, "Republican Consistency," *De Hollander*, 16 July 1856; *Allegan Journal*, 10 Sept. 1856.

[33] "Mr. Scholte's Visit to Holland," *De Hollander*, 9 July (quote), 12, 24 Sept. 1856; "Geesje Van der Haar-Visscher Diary," 13; Swierenga, *Holland, Michigan*, 2:1684-85; Lucas, *Netherlanders*, 552.

counterparts to nominate Van Raalte for the same position under its banner. Both parties hoped to snare the Dutch vote. The two ministerial colleagues sidestepped this crass use of their positions by withdrawing their nominations. Instead, they suggested educator John Van Vleck, who won easily with 2,400 votes, but Van Raalte and Van der Meulen still received 34 and 157 votes, respectively. Their wise withdrawal shielded them from political intrigue and relieved their parishioners from having to make a difficult choice. Van der Meulen remained active in Democratic Party gatherings and attended a rally in Chicago for US Senator Stephen Douglas of Illinois. Van Raalte's nomination by the state Republicans signaled the beginning of a political change of heart on his part.[34]

In the 1858 midterm election campaign, John Roost organized the first Republican meeting in Holland and recruited to the new national party more than a half dozen former Democratic leaders, many members of First Church. Van Raalte very likely supported the political realignment underway in Holland, but he was not yet emboldened to do so openly. The Dutch vote in the 1858 midterm elections climbed above 80 percent for the Democrats.[35]

Political cataclysm of 1859-60

The growing political cataclysm struck with full force in the Holland and Pella colonies in the summer of 1859 when both Van Raalte and Scholte openly switched party allegiances and joined the Republicans. Van Raalte, who might well have been a closet Republican since 1857, changed rather quietly, as befitting a minister of the Gospel, although none could doubt his newfound political convictions.[36]

---

[34] *Grand Rapids Argus*, 31 Mar., 14 Apr. 1857; *Grand Rapids Eagle*, 19, 27 Mar. 1857; *De Hollander*, 1, 15 Apr. 1857, 24 Oct. 1860; *Allegan Journal*, 23 Mar., 27 Apr. 1857. Van Vleck resigned in Oct. 1858 after only one meeting of the board (Hinsdale, *University of Michigan*, 186).

[35] *De Hollander*, 29 Apr. 1857, 7 Apr., 21 Oct. 1858, 14 Mar. 1860; *Allegan Journal*, 19 Apr. 1858; *Grand Rapids Eagle*, 6, 14 Oct. 1858.

[36] Swierenga, *Holland, Michigan*, 3:1683-93; Swierenga, "The Ethnic Voter," 38-40. There is no poll list or political party document to prove that Van Raalte became a Republican, but his close association and positive support of Lincoln's policies during the Civil War, and comments in letters of opponents such as George Steketee in 1867, all make it certain that Van Raalte indeed aligned himself with the Republicans (Wagenaar, "Early Political History," 57-59). Van Hinte noted that William O. Van Eyck personally told him in 1922 that, according to Van Eyck's father, editor of *De Hollander* during the Civil War years, "Van Raalte became a Republican, especially after he came to Detroit" (Van Hinte, *Netherlanders*, 1058n46); Dosker, *Van Raalte*, 229, trans. Dekker.

Henry P. Scholte (1803-1868), Pella's founder, land agent, notary, proprietor-editor of *Pella Gazette*, and political leader

Scholte, by contrast, defected from the Democratic Party in such dramatic fashion that his name appeared in Iowa newspapers statewide and far beyond. Scholte carried papers as a Marion County delegate to the state Democratic convention in Des Moines, but one day, before the opening, he showed up at the state Republican convention in the capitol city at the head of the Marion County delegation. The convention then chose Scholte as a delegate to the Republican national convention in Chicago, where he voted to nominate Abraham Lincoln for president, after his first choice, William Seward, fell short.[37]

Political activities at that time often degenerated into street theater. Dirk Vyn recalled that in the 1860 campaign, Republicans put up a flagpole on the west side of River Avenue at Eighth Street in front of Pfanstiehl's store, adorned with a twenty-five-foot party flag. Not to be outdone, the Democrats, led by Bernardus Ledeboer, a medical doctor, and Henry Post, erected their own pole, "larger and taller, and more beautiful," in the center of the intersection. On a Saturday night, high winds broke off the topmast of the Democratic pole, and it fell, knocking off a piece of the cornice of Bartje Van der Veen's hardware store. At this, the Republicans lowered their flag to half-mast "as an indication of mourning." This taunt, Vyn noted, "made the 'Demmies' boiling hot, after which a fist fight ensued."[38]

---

[37] Swierenga, "The Ethnic Voter."
[38] Dirk Vyn, "When Holland Was Democratic," *Holland City News*, 23 Feb., 6 Apr. 1911.

The political shenanigans reached Van Raalte's consistory room when the brothers practiced *censura morum*, "mutual censure," required prior to the quarterly celebration of the Lord's Supper. Each brother, in turn, declared "if they are able, in love and peace, to commune together." At the October 1860 meeting, however, two Democratic brothers stated that they were offended by two Republican brothers who had not "expressed more condemnation of certain music and torch lighting on the occasion of a recent Republican gathering." Presumably, the brothers reconciled. But the fact that political shenanigans on the streets affected the celebration of the sacrament in the church showed fraying social threads in the tight Dutch enclave.[39]

Party pros assumed that Van Raalte and Scholte would carry their followers into the Republican camp in the 1860 presidential election. After all, the immigrants still struggled with English and the nuances of American politics and would need dominees to explain ballot choices. Van Raalte, in the words of Van Hinte, "fired up popular enthusiasm; he saw in Lincoln the ideal American statesman. He could be found everywhere," Van Hinte continued, "on the streets, at meetings, in homes, at assemblies, near the rolling drums which were encouraging men to sign up—working for the Union." No one spoke out more strongly in support of Lincoln than Van Raalte, who "admired him with his whole heart."[40]

This activism brought criticism from some members of First Church. Democratic politico, Kommer Schaddelee, publicly accused the pastor of being a *knoeier*, a bungler, or cheat. Castigating the pastor in public was clearly unacceptable, even in the midst of an election campaign, but the consistory was reluctant to get involved. After considerable discussion, the brothers decided, "because of the profound political changes in which N. N. [Nomen Nescio, i.e., anonymous] and others are so deeply involved, there seems to be no purpose in pursuing the matter, lest both the pastor and consistory should become involved in affairs where they would rather not be." N. N. was Van Raalte himself, and he had to accept the decision to table the matter, much to his chagrin.[41]

In the Dutch Reformed Church in the East, however, Van Raalte's new political orientation was applauded. In 1858 both New

---

[39] Minutes, First Holland, 26 Oct. 1860, trans. Buursma.
[40] Van Schelven, "Michigan and the Holland Immigration of 1847," 72-96; Van Hinte, *Netherlanders*, 434.
[41] Minutes, First Holland, 16 Nov. 1858, 16 Apr. 1860, trans. Nella Kennedy; Dosker, *Van Raalte*, 228-29, trans. Dekker.

York University and Rutgers—the denominational college in New Brunswick—bestowed honorary doctor of divinity degree on him. Chancellor Isaac Ferris of New York University conferred the degree in recognition of his "earnest efforts in Christian education." The recipient received the unexpected news in deep humility. "I prefer the shade," he wrote Ferris, "and yet I ought to acknowledge thankfully the kindness of my Christian friends. . . . I value it highly and it is only by grace that I enjoy the esteem of God's people." From this time on, he was addressed formally as "Dr.," especially in the Netherlands, where he was the only cleric in Separatist circles during his lifetime with that degree, but always in the classical minutes as "Dr. A. C. Van Raalte" or "A. C. Van Raalte, D.D." Four years after Van Raalte's death, in 1880, Herman Bavinck earned his doctorate at Leiden University. The key word is *earned*; it was not bestowed. In the Holland colony, however, Van Raalte remained a dominee.[42]

Newspaper wars—*De Grondwet* versus *De Hollander*

Newspapers were the mouthpiece of political parties in the nineteenth century, and when Van Raalte joined the rising Republican Party, he realized that Holland needed a newspaper to counter Doesburg's Democratic sheet, especially with a presidential election looming. He enlisted Roost, founder of the Republican Party in Ottawa County, to help launch *De Grondwet* (the constitution) as a staunch party weekly.[43]

The inaugural issue of *De Grondwet*, with columns in both Dutch and English, hit the streets on April 30, 1860. Holland had arrived; it was now a two-newspaper town, with the rival editors critiquing each other's writings. The choice of *constitution* is significant. Although printed largely in the Dutch language, the paper sought an American identity, rather than an ethnic one. In editorial policy, Roost cloaked party principles with the mantle of the Constitution, thereby implying that Democrats disregarded the revered document. *De Hollander* continued to serve Democrat readers, but it played second fiddle to the *De Grondwet*, dubbed the Republican Bible, which soon had nine hundred subscribers in every Dutch settlement and became for seventy-five years the premier Dutch-language weekly in America.[44]

---

[42] Isaac Ferris, chancellor, to Van Raalte, 30 June 1858; Van Raalte's undated reply to Ferris, HHA; *Christian Intelligencer*, 8 July 1858; *De Bazuin*, 20 Aug. 1858, (www.delpher.nl, accessed June 2021).
[43] Swierenga, *Holland, Michigan*, 3:2157-71.
[44] Ibid., 3:2157; Van Hinte, *Netherlanders*, 446-48; Lucas, *Netherlanders*, 535.

The masthead of *De Grondwet* set off alarm bells for Doesburg, who launched Holland's first newspaper war with a sarcastic blast at the name *Constitution* as "hypocritical, simulated, sly, or a manipulation to attract the Dutch to their views." If the paper followed the radical Republican ideology, it would be anything but honoring the Constitution and upholding of Union. "Can it be called 'aiming for Union' if the North attacks the South?" he declared.[45]

Doesburg's strategy of labeling the Republican Party as radical worked for two national election cycles, 1860 and 1864. He painted Lincoln as an abolitionist whose election would destroy the Union because southerners would surely secede to safeguard slavery. Since the US Constitution protected slavery, a Lincoln presidency would constitute oath breaking. It would also link his administration with abolitionists who "served the antichrist." By labeling Democratic policies as Christian and Republican policies as anti-Christian, Doesburg was indirectly accusing Van Raalte, the spiritual leader of Holland, of allying with the devil. His support for the Union was merely Satan's "venom beautifully adorned." Such was hardball politics, Doesburg style.

To Doesburg's great satisfaction, and the consternation of Van Raalte and Republican leaders, a majority of voters in Holland and Zeeland supported the Democrat, Stephen Douglas, the Little Giant, not the real giant, the six-foot Honest Abe. Holland voted Democrat by 53 percent and Zeeland by 51 percent. Lincoln, however, carried the county, state, and nation. The war put Democrats on the defensive, and the party divided between Union supporters and Peace Democrats— those who favored peace at the expense of the Union. The 1864 election pitted the wartime president against General George McClellan, the commander Lincoln had fired for incompetence, who pledged to recognize the Confederacy in exchange for peace. McClellan, a Peace Democrat, or more derisively a "Copperhead" (poisonous snake), carried Holland by 58 percent. This vote was remarkable since more than four hundred Dutch soldiers—one in ten Holland residents—were putting their lives on the line in the Union army.[46] That the majority of Dutch voters in the city would endorse the candidate who would break up the Union testifies to the depth of the hurt inflicted on the Dutch

---

[45] "De Grondwet," *De Hollander*, 9 (quotes), 23 May 1860, trans. Simone Kennedy, for this and next paragraph.
[46] Ben Van Raalte wrote his father (11 Nov. 1864): "The *Hollander* was wrong when it reported that the Holland company was all Democrats. Thirty were for Lincoln, and nine for 'Mac,'" trans. Jalving, HMA.

in the mid-1850s by Whig and Republican nativists. It also shows that Van Raalte had no political coattails.

"Citizen first" in Civil War

When the South seceded from the Union and formed the Confederacy in 1861, Van Raalte wholeheartedly stood with Lincoln and the Union. He detested the "godless, cursed institution" of slavery but not enough to back abolitionism for its "rude, cruel, selfish, ungodly abolition-party spirit." Yet, he "could not bear the thought that our common Constitution of the United States should be a slavery-propagating instrument or our common government should foster slavery."[47] The dominee wanted to make an omelet without breaking any eggs.

But he did his best to keep the war out of his sermons. At the Classis of Holland meeting on April 12, 1861, five days after the declaration of war upon the Confederate shelling of Fort Sumter, Van Raalte by special request "mounted the pulpit and delivered to a large audience an earnest, probing, and instructive sermon about the Christ whom God has made to be our sanctification." He chose as his text I Corinthians 1:30 (KJV): "But of him are ye in Christ Jesus, who of God is made unto us wisdom, and righteousness, and sanctification, and redemption." The sermon is not extant, but it is unlikely that he mentioned the start of hostilities. His intent was to offer comfort and assurance.[48]

At Lincoln's first call for volunteers in 1861, Holland citizens raised $4,000 ($138,700 today) to pay 125 volunteers, fully 27 percent of the 459 men registered between eighteen and forty-five years of age. Thirty-seven local men enlisted, all but ten being Dutch immigrants. Nine men over age thirty were unmarried. When the president issued a second call for volunteers in July 1862, Van Raalte held a rally at First Church on Friday evening, August 15, 1862, to fill the local list. Defending the Union was so critical that he broke his rule not to bring politics into the pulpit.[49]

[47] Van Raalte, "Michigan Letter," 6 May 1862, in *Christian Intelligencer*, 22 May 1862.
[48] Kennedy, *Commentary*, 3:1014-15. All translations of classis minutes are either written or revised by Kennedy. The minutes of First Holland and Classis of Holland seldom mention the war, except for national days of fasting and prayer and Lincoln's assassination.
[49] Van Raalte to son Ben, 2, 9, 22 Mar., 6 June 1863; Kellogg to Van Raalte, 10 Mar. 1863, HMA; Edward J. Masselink, "Holland, Michigan, Residents in the Civil War," *Holland City News*, 30 Nov. 1961. See also, Jacobson, "Civil War Correspondence"; Jacobson et al., *Dutch Leader*, 101-37.

Henry Hidding was in the church that memorable evening and left the only known eyewitness account. "I remember entering the church, which was full of people, as soldiers had to be drafted, there not being enough volunteers," he recalled. After the dominee opened with a fervent prayer, he condemned the antiwar riots in New York City and urged young Hollanders to pick up weapons and fight. Kommer Schaddelee, a justice of the peace and church member, officially took the oaths as the men lined up. The meeting lasted into the evening until sixty-one young men had stepped forward as mothers and sweethearts wept. Girls presented each man with a flag bearing the motto: "The Lord is our banner." It was "a clean sweep of our boys," Van Raalte boasted, and "now all the married men are allowed to stay at home." Five more Holland men enlisted within the week, plus fifteen more from Zeeland, Grand Haven, and Grand Rapids, bringing the total to eighty-two. Filling the quota without a compulsory draft was a badge of honor for the Dutch. The three-year terms of the 1862 enlistees turned out to be for the duration of the war, which ended on April 9, 1865.[50]

Van Raalte was especially pleased that his sons Ben and Dirk volunteered, much to their mother's dismay. For months, she would not permit her boys to enlist. Her oldest son, Bertus, then married with two children, was spared from serving. In his patriotic speech, Van Raalte gave his blessing before the full house. "Here are my two sons. If they wish to go, I give them freedom to leave." He had written Brummelkamp earlier: "It doesn't do me any honor that not one of my sons has carried a weapon against treason and chaos." Ben was eager to fight and signed up, but Dirk, just eighteen and a student at Holland Academy, "has no desire or courage," his father lamented. Dirk signed up a week later and proved his father wrong. Their father's stark statement at their sendoff made a deep impression: "Remember, I would rather you come home dead than return a coward—a blemish on your generation and people."[51]

---

[50] Van Raalte to Phelps, 24 Aug. 1862, in Bruins and Schakel, *Envisioning Hope College*, 93-94; Henry Hidding, "The Ninth Street Church," *Holland City News*, 14 May 1912.

[51] Van Raalte to Brummelkamp, quoted in Dosker, *Van Raalte*, 229, trans. Dekker; Van Raalte to Van de Wall, 29 June 1862; Van Raalte to Christian Van der Veen, 20 Sept. 1862, all in HHA; *Allegan Journal*, 8 Sept. 1862; Rumohr-Voskuil and Bruins, "'Joyful Death'"; Van Raalte to son Ben, 14 Nov. 1859; McGeehan, *My Country and Cross*, 1 (quotes), see 90-91, for a complete list of Company I volunteers. A recent historical novel of Company I is Kuiper, *Through Many Dangers*.

Ben and Dirk Van Raalte in Civil War uniforms (*JAH*)

When the recruits boarded wagons for Kalamazoo to be mustered into Company I of the 25th Michigan Infantry, Hidding, one of the waggoneers of the "Holland Rangers," recalled the sad goodbyes, "for no one expected to see those again who were now leaving." Albertus and Christina accompanied their boys to Kalamazoo by carriage. "I am glad I went to see you off," his mother later wrote them. "Now my desire and prayer is that God may cover you and protect you and that He may give you courage and strength to serve him in your calling that he had laid on you." She closed, as any anguished Christian mother would, with a plea: "Now, dear and precious children, seek God, seek to prepare for that never-ending eternity. Pray much. He is a hearer of prayers."[52]

Geesje Van der Haar-Visscher captured the intense emotions of that week in her reminiscences. For her, everything turned on fervent prayer and Van Raalte's sermon on John 1:12 about receiving strength from God. She refused to allow her seventeen-year-old son to enlist,

---

[52] Hidding, "Ninth Street Church"; Christina Van Raalte, "Dear Children" (Ben and Dirk), Sept. 1862, HHA.

Lieve Kinderen,

Door des Heere goed ben ik in wel stand hier aan gekoome alles was wel. ik ben blyde dat gij ik uw Lieven heb weg ge bragt nu is myn wensch en Beede dat God uw Lieden mag dekken en bewaaren en dat hij uw moed en kragten mag schen ken om in uw roeping die God uw op de handen gelegt heeft hem te diene, Dirk als gij te huis komt en gij wilt hemden hebben dan moet gy het goed meede brengen dan sal ik ze maaken en ook 3 bonte sakdoeken en als B wil hebben dat ik ook voor hem hemd of onder broeken sal maaken dan moet gy het goed meede brengen en anders wil dan aan Jan oggel vragen of hij er is meede gaat naar pfyffer die zullen het wel voor uw laaten maaken, ik wil het zelven ook wel doen als dirk te huis komt en niet te gouw

C. J. Van Raalte

A rare letter of Christina Van Raalte to "Dear Children" (Ben and Dirk) in Kalamazoo, September 1862 (HHA)

and when her husband then determined to volunteer, she made him pledge to go only if other middle-aged married men also enlisted. They did not, so neither did he.

> Now the civil war broke out, and many of our young men volunteered to serve their country for right and freedom. Several Hollanders also volunteered, and they talked to our boy to get him to go too. He wanted to go. One evening, at a meeting at the town house, he signed up with the stipulation that he would have to get his parents' consent. I prayed about it. It seemed to me that God had not permitted any young man among the Israelites to go out to battle unless he was twenty. So my conscience would not let me give my consent. He wasn't even eighteen. So he stayed home, but the war continued. Many more had to go, either as volunteers or as draftees.
>
> Many married men also volunteered, and my husband now thought that it was also his duty to go. I couldn't see this and could not believe that such was God's will. We both prayed about it, and finally my husband said he was going to go if the others to whom he had spoken about it also went. I laid all my troubles before God and felt that if it had to be that my husband went, He would give me strength to let him go if he felt it was God's will.
>
> But things looked dark. Yes, I prayed that God might prevent his going if it wasn't His will. Oh, God comforted me in that dark time. When we went to church the next Sunday, Van Raalte's sermon was based on the words: "But as many as received him, to them gave he power to become the sons of God, even to them that believe on his name" [John 1:10 KJV]. The sermon comforted me. I might believe that I was a child of God and that all things would work together for good. Oh, now I could again give myself entirely to God, submitting to His will. But now look how good God was to us. On Monday evening, my husband went to sign up, but none of the others who were going to sign showed up. So the whole thing was dropped. Oh, how happy and grateful we were! We will never forget it. I had learned with David: "In my distress I called upon the LORD, and . . . He heard my cry" (Ps 18:6 KJV).

Van Raalte's political fervor for the war effort created a backlash, but he would not be cowed into silence. The fiery cleric sounded off at a consistory meeting. He "was a citizen before he was a minister," and he would not separate his political beliefs from his faith. He would continue to defend the Union and condemn American slavery, with its vile practice of "breeding men," a practice that is *absolutely* forbidden in the Bible." The consistory, knowing that the congregation was divided politically, did not discipline critics because of the "deep political happenings of the time."⁵³

The dominee admitted the disharmony in his 1862 "State of the Congregation" report, a regular component of the spring Classis of Holland meetings. "Holland says that the little piety striking the eye and the silence about the preciousness of Jesus betray that sweetness and the power of the secret prayer life is much lacking." In a confidential letter to Giles Van de Wall, Van Raalte frankly admitted: "It is impossible for me to continue my work amongst this dissension." Yet, the congregation was able to join in a prayer service on Thanksgiving Day in 1862, and they contributed copies of a denominational booklet for distribution to soldiers in the army.⁵⁴

Editor Doesburg opposed the war. His son Otto paid a substitute to serve in his stead, a legal way to avoid fighting, and his son Jacob volunteered the same evening as the Van Raalte boys, but after six months, he came home on a disability discharge. Ben Van Raalte scornfully accused him of "being homesick and in fear of bullets." Ben branded the Doesburg boys as cowards and condemned their father's anti-union editorials. "Doesburg is putting the fear of death into the hearts of the ignorant masses. They should burn his printing office. . . . He is no better than a Rebel. . . . If I may give advice, never give anyone any money in order to stay home. It would be better to perish."⁵⁵

The Van Raalte boys were bitter toward all the fellows who balked at serving, especially Hope College students. When Van Raalte asked Dirk to contribute some of his soldier's pay to the college, he replied forcefully:

> We are willing to shed our blood and suffer for our country, and those fellows are staying home to live off our money and mock us to boot. There is no way in which I will give them that opportunity . . . . The little money that we happen to earn, I can use myself too well. It would look a lot better if half of those students filled the

---

⁵³ Dosker, *Van Raalte*, 228, trans. Dekker; minutes, First Holland, 16 Nov. 1858, 4, 16 Apr. 1860, 18 Jan. 1861; Van Raalte to Phelps, 24 Aug. 1862, in *Envisioning Hope College*, 93-94.
⁵⁴ Kennedy, *Commentary*, 15 Oct. 1862, 2:1143; Van Raalte to Van de Wall, 29 June 1862; minutes, First Holland, 22 Dec. 1862, 30 Mar. 1863.
⁵⁵ Ben Van Raalte to father, 12 July 1864, HHA.

ranks here, rather than to stay home as cowards and wait until they get drafted.[56]

In late 1862, when the boys were stationed in Louisville, Kentucky—Dirk working as a hospital orderly and Ben in infantry training—their parents thought to visit them. "I think we will come to visit you together," his mother wrote, but they never did. Father Albertus sent Dirk a pocket-sized medical book to persuade him to consider that as a career. "You know that I am sort of a half-doctor, and therefore I can give you good counsel," he wrote. Consult the book when you see illnesses and medicines, and "you will learn in a single year an unbelievable great deal. The great secret to becoming a doctor is to stand at the bedside and observe the sick one." After the war, Dirk gave up any thought of doctoring for business and politics.[57]

Ben and Dirk survived many battles over the course of two years, but in August 1864, near Atlanta, Dirk took a musket ball in his right arm, and the shattered limb had to be amputated. When Ben, who was with Dirk at the hospital, reported the sad news in a letter home, Albertus immediately started south to bring his wounded son home. But the military stopped him at Nashville. "Those were dark days," he told Dirk in frustration, made worse dealing with "mosquitoes, lice, rats, and filthy service" south of the Ohio River. Ben had vengeance on his mind for Dirk's being maimed. He vowed to make any "poor Rebs who fall in to my hands ... pay for Dirk's arm." Whether he did or not remains a question. Dirk, as his father told Phelps, "carries an empty sleeve for the rest of his life."[58]

Letters from the brothers (Ben served until the end of the war) kept their father informed about their campaigns; he in turn passed the news on to Giles Van de Wall, serving the Reformed Church in Paarl, near Cape Town. The dominee applauded "our careful and peace-loving" president when he called for three hundred thousand more recruits after the capture of Vicksburg and New Orleans and

---

[56] Dirk Van Raalte to father, 20 Dec. 1862, HHA; also quoted in Krabbendam, *Freedom on the Horizon*, 307.
[57] Christina J. Van Raalte to Dirk, likely Oct. 1863; Van Raalte to son Dirk, 15 Sept. 1862 (quote), HHA.
[58] Ben to father, 29, 30 Aug., 16 Sept. (quote), 30 Sept. 1864; Van Raalte to Phelps, 29 Aug. 1864; Dirk to father, 23 Sept. 1864; Van Raalte to wife, 26 Sept. 1864, HMA; Swierenga, *Holland, Michigan*, 1:115-16; Van Hinte, *Netherlanders*, 433-34. The "sad news" that Van Raalte's youngest son lost his arm in battle was reported to Netherlands readers of *De Bazuin*, 14 Oct. 1864 (www.delpher.nl, accessed June 2021).

England's turning away from recognizing the Confederacy after the Emancipation Proclamation. Referring to the Union army, Van Raalte boasted: "A monster is being created here night and day. There will be no shortage of manpower.... Everything is in turmoil, but all turmoil must be subservient to God's will." Van Raalte likely had in mind the New York draft riots in 1863, which he described as lunacy.

> We have business enough to suppress the rebels in arms; and I hope that they may learn to deal with mobs too. Is the North crazy? Very well, the Lord will take care of the insane. He is never hindered nor helped in his grand majestic Forward March.

In terms of eschatology, the dominee was a postmillennialist; he believed that God ordained progress over national sins and woes in the coming millennium under Christ's reign.[59]

Ultimately, more than four hundred men from the Holland area served in the 25th Michigan regiment, all but a few as volunteers. More than half joined the infantry, but 120 were cavalry, forty-six mechanics and engineers, ten artillery, and one navy. The 415 Dutch soldiers comprised 42 percent of the 988 soldiers in the 25th Michigan. In battle casualties, the four suffered by Company I, an all-Dutch contingent of 122 men, or 3 percent, compared favorably with the thirty-five casualties in the 25th Michigan, or 4 percent. The greatest contrast was in deaths from disease. The 25th Michigan had 143 deaths at 14 percent, whereas Company I had only eleven deaths at 9 percent. Dutch cleanliness, moral living, respect for authority, and care with their equipment, especially rifles, paid off in lives saved. Colonel Orlando H. Moore, commander of the 25th Michigan, insisted that his men carry English-made Enfield rifles, accurate at 1,250 yards, instead of the standard American-made Springfield rifles with an effective range of only 300 yards, and his men fought frontier style, rather than in rigid British formations.[60]

Dominee Van Raalte's parishioners learned to "read" his demeanor as the war waxed and waned. "In his preaching and especially

---

[59] Van Raalte to Van de Wall, 29 June 1862, HMA; Van Raalte to Phelps, 7 Aug. 1863, in *Envisioning Hope College*, 102-3 (quote); Jacobson et al., *Dutch Leader*, 128.

[60] Stanley B. Burns, MD, "25th Michigan & Company I Casualty Rates as Compared to the Michigan Averages (unpublished essay). I am indebted to Kenneth E. Kolk, a Civil War historian, for the Dutch health data and to Joan Van Spronsen for the enrollment list at http://ottawa.migenweb.net/military/civilwar/CWDutch.html. See also for the list, *Holland City News*, 13 May 1909.

Giles Van de Wall (1828-1896), graduate of New Brunswick Seminary, teacher at Holland Academy (1858–61), and pastor of Cape Town Reformed Church (1862–95) (*JAH*)

in his prayers, the congregation could always hear a tone of triumph or defeat." Henry Hidding recalled that Van Raalte made it a practice before the "long prayer" at Sunday services to read "foxhole" letters from Holland boys, including Ben and Dirk, who often wrote "just before a battle and sometimes directly after a fight." Van Raalte wove these personal testimonies into his congregational prayers. With two sons in the war, he sometimes had to fight his emotions.[61]

In early 1863, Ben and Dirk, then fighting in the Kentucky campaign, were alarmed when their father became seriously ill from an undetermined affliction. His recovery relieved them, but weakness remained for months. Following Union victories in July at Gettysburg, Vicksburg, and Tebbs Bend, Kentucky, the dominee preached an "especially, serious, powerful, and fitting sermon" that pointed to the hand of God in all circumstances, in victories or in defeats. The sermon, based on 1 Samuel 14:12b (KJV): "For the LORD hath delivered them into our hand," recounted the glorious Israelite victory over the Philistines under King Saul's son Jonathan. Col. Moore's Company I suffered only one casualty at Tebbs Bend, prompting the dominee to declare: "We feel that God's hand did cover them."[62]

---

[61] Hidding, "Ninth Street Church"; Swierenga, *Holland, Michigan*, 1:115; Dosker, *Van Raalte*, 228-29, trans. Dekker.

[62] *De Grondwet*, 12 Aug. 1863, trans. Michael Douma, for this and the next two paragraphs; Kennedy, *Commentary*, 5 Sept. 1855, 1:511-12. Douma found this rare copy out of state, given that all back files were lost in the Holland Fire of 1871.

In the Prayer Day sermon, Van Raalte astonished his parishioners by recounting recent military campaigns as reasons for thankfulness, beginning with

> the glorious victory at Gettysburg, where the rebel invasion was stopped, and the north remained saved from immeasurable suffering and terror; the surrender without loss of blood of Vicksburg and Port Hudson, by which the Mississippi, the great artery of the West is returned to us; the victory and progress of [General William S.] Rosecrans; the capture of the guerilla chief John Morgan, and God's wonderful protection of our loved ones, who with about 200 men drove back and knocked down 2,000 to 4,000 rebel pirates, the demoralization of the rebel army of [General Braxton] Bragg and [General Joseph E.] Johnson; the complete frustration of the cunning and well-thought out rebel plans.

The dominee also addressed American slavery. Both defenders and supporters of the institution on biblical grounds "erred," he declared, by making the issue either political or religious. "Both are wrong." Modern slavery "was grounded upon breeding men and was therefore absolutely forbidden in the Bible, . . . [but] biblical slavery allowed none of the atrocities that are characteristic of our slavery." He abjured any of his descendants from ever supporting American slavery and condemned any who "should misuse God's word in defense of such a godless, cursed institution."

Marinus Hoogesteger, editor of *De Grondwet* and a member of First Church, concluded his report on the sermons with a ringing endorsement:

> Both sermons testified of the deep, serious loyalty and love of the Union and the many-sided political knowledge of the loved teacher and were given in a living and exciting manner. All true patriots, loyal citizens, and lovers of the Union and freedom were especially edified, encouraged, and inspired with new seriousness to once again pick up weapons and set forth on the "insuppressible fight."

General Ulysses S. Grant's victory at Vicksburg won the war in the West, and the 25th Michigan Infantry, with most of the Holland boys, including Ben and Dirk, was reassigned to General William T.

Sherman's March to the Sea in Georgia. Hearing of Grant's bloody Virginia campaign, Van Raalte called for a special day of prayer on Thanksgiving Day "because of the tragic circumstances of the Civil War." The offering was to send Christian books to "soldiers in the army."[63]

On Independence Day in 1864, Van Raalte preached on the topic: "A Day for Repentance and Prayer," based on Jeremiah 18:5-10, in which God is described as the potter and people as clay in His hands. His application was that "God holds almighty, sovereign power over a nation," and rules "with justice and mercy. . . . Our destiny depends on Him." The sermon made no mention of the war or that Peace Democrats wanted to concede to the Confederacy.[64]

At the news of General Robert E. Lee's surrender at Appomattox, Van Raalte exclaimed: "Thank God that's over." When the soldiers came home in the summer of 1865, he arranged an elaborate welcome celebration in Market Square (now Centennial Park), replete with an enormous cake, five feet tall, with a large American flag as the centerpiece, and platters of roasted baby pigs, each with an orange in its mouth. "When all had set down around the festive board and prayers had been said," the grateful dominee took a sword to cut the enormous cake to be doled out to the eagerly awaiting guests.[65]

But first Van Raalte gave a memorable address and ended by reciting the names of the thirty-two honored dead from the area, stating for each the birth date and place and date of death. Over half (18) were Dutch boys (56 percent), and fourteen were Americans and Native Peoples. The impression on the audience was overwhelming. "It was as though he drew a moving, bleeding panorama in which the entire war passed before the eyes of his listeners, and in which the dreadful cost of the war was depicted as if with the single stroke of a pen." All the fallen were buried in a soldiers' plot that Van Raalte had designated during the war. The Civil War Monument later erected on the site bears the name of each one.[66]

---

[63] Minutes, First Holland, 14 Jan., 22 Dec. 1862, 30 Mar. 1863.
[64] Van Raalte sermon, in Spykman, *Pioneer Preacher*, 100-105.
[65] *Holland City News*, 10 Sept. 1914, related by eyewitness Mrs. Anna Broadmore Walter of Kissimmee, FL.
[66] Dosker, *Van Raalte*, 230 (quote), trans. Dekker; Jacobson et al., *Dutch Leader*, 139; Vande Water, "Holland's First Decoration Day" (quote).

Lincoln's assassination leads to political reversal

On Friday, April 14, 1865, only days after the joyous news was received—"Lee has surrendered! We've won! The Union is saved!"— Confederate partisan John Wilkes Booth shot President Abraham Lincoln at Ford's Theater in Washington, DC. Lincoln died the next morning at 7:22 a.m. in the Petersen House across the street. The emotional impact was beyond words.

The news reached Holland on Sunday morning, and the sexton tolled the church bell at length to spread the stunning news. Van Raalte immediately dispatched messengers to the outlying villages in time for the afternoon worship services. The dastardly deed, which threatened the very survival of the Union, turned many Dutch Democrats into Republicans. Four days later, the Classis of Holland sponsored solemn worship services in First Church and Hope Church at noon to coincide with President Lincoln's funeral in the Capitol. Both sanctuaries, decked fully in black, were crowded.

The first speaker at First Church, Manly D. Howard, a Democrat, Episcopalian, and Freemason, "coldly" cast "insults" in a reprehensible address. Rev. John Karsten, a Reformed church missionary, then spoke briefly before Van Raalte mounted the pulpit and undid the wrong. As reported by editor Hoogesteger of *De Grondwet*, the dominee delivered a passionate speech. "Characterized by deep spirituality, pointing to a God who in all His deeds saved us by His omnipotence, he [Van Raalte] had the influence to bring back the chilled gathering to customary warmth." After brief remarks by Bernardus Ledeboer and the standard apostolic benediction, the assembly went home without adopting a resolution or any expression of public feeling. The Holland dominee saved the day.[67]

Nine-year-old Albert Pfanstiehl would remember the next Sunday at First Church for the rest of his life. Walking into the sanctuary, the congregation saw black crepe hanging everywhere, and the pulpit was "one black mass." But more drama was to come. Pfanstiehl later recalled that, during the congregational prayer, the dominee "began to choke with emotion, and suddenly buried his head in his hands and burst out sobbing." The entire congregation then "convulsed with

---

[67] *De Grondwet*, 17 Apr. 1865, as quoted in *De Bazuin*, 2 June 1865 (www.delpher.nl, accessed June 2021), trans. Earl Wm. Kennedy; Minutes, First Holland, 6 Feb. 1865; Swierenga, *Holland, Michigan*, 2:1692-95; Kennedy, *Commentary*, 19 Apr. 1865, 2:1276.

grief!... I cried as if my heart would break," Pfanstiehl added, and "felt as if some great catastrophe had come to overwhelm us all."[68]

Holland voted Democrat again in local races through the spring 1866 election but went Republican for the first time in the 1866 midterms in November, by the slimmest of margins—52 percent. Two years later, in the 1868 presidential election, Republican Ulysses S. Grant carried Holland by 58 percent. Veterans, all strongly Republican, finally felt vindicated.[69] Van Raalte's inability to carry Holland for the Republicans during the war is remarkable. His grip on leadership was clearly slipping; the immigrants' period of dependency had passed.

Van Raalte misfires in fighting city incorporation

Another sign of Van Raalte's waning influence was the incorporation of the city of Holland over his strenuous objections.[70] In March 1867, village leaders petitioned the state legislature to incorporate as a city, separate from Holland Township. Both sides of what would become a fierce political debate were backed by powerful personalities—the city by state representative Moses Hopkins, a native of Holland, and the township by Van Raalte, who objected to the city charter movement. Van Raalte believed that governance by township officials was quite adequate, and another layer of government would only increase his taxes. As the leading landowner, Van Raalte's annual tax bill was onerous. During the Civil War, he had to ask Ben and Dirk, his sons in the army, to help raise cash, saying that we must "pump or drown." He was land rich and cash poor. Ben even offered to contribute some of his soldier's pay to help with "tackses" (taxes). Daughter Christine, then sewing in Kalamazoo, asked her mother very delicately for money, fearing that "father's purse might be empty."[71]

Democratic politicos, George G. Steketee, Bernardus Ledeboer, and Kommer Schaddelee, launched the charter campaign by calling a

[68] Albert A. Pfanstiehl, Deal Beach, NJ, to "My dear Grandchildren Cody & Alfred," 16 Dec. 1919, letter no. 9, in "Letters to my Grandchildren, A. A. Pfanstiehl, 1919-1920," Pfanstiehl Family Papers.

[69] Van Eyck, "Old History on Sheriff-ship," and "Early Historical Data—Political," 3, Van Eyck Papers; *Grand Haven News*, 28 Nov. 1866; *De Hope*, 4 Apr. 1866; *Allegan Journal*, 23 Nov. 1868, clipping from the *Grand Rapids Eagle*; *Historical and Business Compendium of Ottawa County*, 88.

[70] This section is based on Swierenga, *Holland, Michigan*, 3:1694-96; Wagenaar, "Early Political History," 55-59; and Swierenga, "Changes and Complications."

[71] Ben Van Raalte to father, 21 Nov. 1862; Van Raalte to Giles Van de Wall, 29 June 1862, HMA; Christina Catharina Van Raalte to parents, 1 Dec. 1862 (quote); Ben Van Raalte to mother, 14 Aug. 1864, HHA.

Newspaper Magnate, Political Leader, Civil War Patriot 439

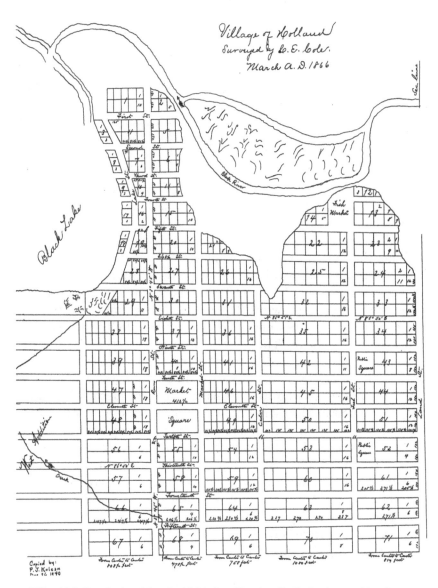

Third Holland plat, March 1866, by Charles E. Cole (copied by Peter J. Kolean, 26 Dec. 1940) (HMA). The city council adopted Cole's plat after checking it against the official 1847 plat. The city surveyor then established the grade for each street, and the street commissioners ordered the removal of trees and other obstructions.

citizens' meeting, which body named a commission to draft the charter. Proponents circulated petitions to determine the will of the public, one *for* and one *against*. This informal poll showed that residents were 54 percent in favor of incorporation and 46 percent opposed (140–120). Since the majority responded favorably, the charter committee submitted a charter to Representative Hopkins, who successfully steered the incorporation bill through both houses of the legislature.

For twenty years, Van Raalte had been accustomed to having his own way, but now he was losing his clout, not least because he was giving up his bully pulpit as founding pastor of First Church (ch. 14). Shifting politics was also a factor. Steketee said as much when he asserted that the main reason for setting off the city was to create a stronghold against the outlying villages, the "majority of which are Copper Heads." Opponents of incorporation, he added, are "Seven Eighths of them Cops."[72] With incorporation, the transformation of Holland from colony to city was complete.

When Van Raalte realized that he was in the minority on the charter issue, he asked that his home be left out of the city. His associate, Bernardus Grootenhuis, wrote Representative Hopkins to ask that the eastern city boundary be drawn to exclude Van Raalte's homestead and farm of eighty-plus acres. The parcel was mostly swamp land (i.e., Cedar Swamp), Grootenhuis claimed, probably with tongue in cheek, and "will never be fit for extension of the City or improvements." More important, "All the people who live in this quarter" are "decidedly against it." Van Raalte was clearly not the only one to oppose incorporation. Steketee urged Hopkins to ignore Grootenhuis's request. Van Raalte "has made him Self Rich [*sic*] out of us poor dutchmen and therefore it's no more than Right that he should help to bare [*sic*] the Expense of the city and in this way our taxes will be lower." This criticism was a bit unfair, for Van Raalte had only reluctantly agreed to take charge of selling lots in the village of Holland [73]

Democrat Gerrit Van Schelven, secretary of the committee on incorporation, agreed with Grootenhuis. As a concession to the father of the colony, Van Schelven asked Hopkins to "withdraw [Van Raalte's] farm from the City Territory. As [the] original proprietor and Settler of this place, we respected his claim & demand."[74] Hopkins agreed,

---

[72] *Allegan Journal*, 23 Nov. 1868.
[73] Grootenhuis to Hopkins, 1 Mar. 1867, Van Schelven Papers.
[74] Van Schelven to Hopkins, 2 Mar. 1867, Van Schelven Papers; Wagenaar, "Early Political History," 55-59.

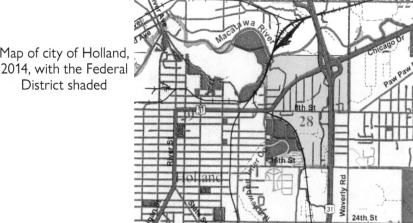

Map of city of Holland, 2014, with the Federal District shaded

and Van Raalte's homestead, known as the Federal District, remains outside of the city to this day.

The preamble to the charter reads:

> We, the people of the City of Holland, mindful of the ideals and labors of our fathers in founding and developing this community, grateful to Almighty God for the blessings of freedom, peace, health, safety, and desirous of further securing these blessings to ourselves and or posterity, do hereby ordain and establish this Charter for the City of Holland.

In the first city election, on April 1, 1867, Republican Isaac Cappon, co-owner of Cappon & Bertsch tannery, defeated Ledeboer, the Democrat warhorse, in a close race, which doubtless pleased Van Raalte. The first city council adopted the official seal, which portrayed a lion and crown in the center, surrounded by the phrases *Eendragt maakt magt* [Unity makes strength] and *God Zy Met Ons* [God be with us].[75] With Mayor Cappon in office, Van Raalte clearly played second fiddle in Holland. It was time for his new colonial venture in Virginia (ch. 15).

To lessen his city taxes, Van Raalte promptly deeded ninety acres to Hope College, sixty on the west side (Hope College Addition and Hope College Grounds) and thirty on the north (Female Academy Tract). But the three hundred city lots that remained in his inventory

---

[75] Holland City Records.

Holland city seal,
1867-present
(Herrick District Library)

were a tempting target for city council. The aldermen levied a special tax on lots of *non* residents that targeted Van Raalte directly. Steketee must have been pleased that Van Raalte had to pay after all.[76]

When the city incorporated, Holland Township lost almost half its tax base and its leading industries, businesses, and civic leaders. Money issues were foremost. It took four years to untangle the complicated financial issues between city and township. Both sides promised to do this amicably—they were, after all, friends and neighbors and fellow church members. But in the end, both hired legal counsel and bargained hard for every dollar as they pored over account books to determine the obligations of each entity. Complicating matters were two outstanding bond issues—Civil War Volunteer Bonds

---

[76] Van Raalte and wife to Council of Hope College, 26 July, 26 Aug., 6 Sept. 1867, Ottawa County Deed Records, book 25, 232-35. See also, "Certified Copy of Minutes of Board of Trustees of Hope College," 12 Oct. 1867. Keeping Van Raalte's home out of the city ultimately contributed to the home's destruction. Grand Rapids publisher William B. Eerdmans, who purchased the Van Raalte Papers, bought the house in hopes of making it the Van Raalte Research Center. But he failed to find a director fluent in Dutch and deeded the property to Hope College, who wanted the land for future development but had no use for the house, which stood vacant and was vandalized. Calls to the city police were met with the response: "It's not in the city, and we have no authority over there." In 1961 the college had the house torn down to make way for an athletic field (Bruins et al., *Albertus and Christina*, 31-62).

and Harbor Bonds—whose debt service was finally allocated between city and township based on population. The final settlement came less than two months before the Holland fire, which wiped out the work of the pioneer generation (ch. 15). Holland Township was unscathed and could help the city rebuild. In the aftermath, the bitterness over the charter and its aftermath was forgotten as friends and neighbors came together again in a common cause.

Van Raalte's life off the pulpit consumed him. He had his hand in everything: land dealings, business ventures, schools, the harbor, newspapers, and politics. In economic endeavors, he was more of a promoter and fundraiser than a businessman; as pastor, he was constrained from taking a more hands-on role. He raised vast sums in the East for colonial lands, Holland harbor, First Reformed Church, Holland Academy and Hope College, and various business ventures. His primary goal at the outset was to ensure the success of the colony, not to be a capitalist and accrue wealth. Yet his entrepreneurial mindset, capitalistic attitude toward money, and eagerness to take risks in various enterprises inevitably drew him into business life. When he could not lead, he drove, which led to charges that he "led people around by the nose." But the burdens of leadership weighed heavily on him, at times at the cost of his health and often to the detriment of his wife and children. He would be away for weeks at a time on fundraising trips, and his fundraising prowess was unmatched.[77] He truly deserves recognition and accolades not only as the founder of Holland but also a master colonizer.

---

[77] Letter of H. J. C., 3 Feb. 1849, printed in *De Grondwet*, 5 Mar. 1912 (quote); Bruins, "Funding his Vision," 55-57, lists the dominee's fundraising efforts.

CHAPTER 14

Retirement from First Church: "Ending a hurtful situation."

Before his tenth year in America, Van Raalte's health began to fail due to physical exhaustion and depression. His responsibilities were overwhelming, and the pressure led to missteps and shortcomings. The decision to join the Reformed Church in the East caused a church schism; demanding the right of press censorship damaged his reputation; near bankruptcy in the mill venture with Den Bleyker shook his business confidence; and most demoralizing of all, his consistory questioned his competence in the pulpit—his strong suit—and advised him to spend more time in study.

Swarming mosquitoes in the wetlands around Holland every summer caused Van Raalte to suffer another bout of malaria in 1858 that laid him up for eight days. "Now I am working again," he wrote Carel de Moen,

> and I must definitely eat quinine so that I can be up and around . . . with my weak and exhausted body. I have a worn-out body; I must have rest. All the doctors have told me this for the last three years. I understand it completely, but it is an insoluble riddle for me how to accomplish this. . . . My calling is very dear to me.

The dominee would willingly burn his candle at both ends to serve the Bride of Christ "in the midst of an apostate dark world."[1]

With Van Raalte at this low point physically, petty bickering broke out in the congregation when a member charged elder Teunis Keppel with false dealings in the purchase of a horse. One elder refused to shake hands with another brother because of gossip. And yet another elder resigned his office and left the church with a very public complaint against Van Raalte and his fellow elders for baptizing children of parents who had themselves been baptized as infants but had not made a public profession of faith. Following standard practice in the Dutch national church, Van Raalte baptized all children born into its bosom. His patience as clerk was taxed by having to write detailed minutes of these endless disputes. The immigrants were certainly "a peculiar people," he concluded.[2]

The dominee often dealt with despair by leaving town. In February 1859, he went to Pella for two months to fill a vacant pulpit. It was a welcome respite. In June he went to Albany with Peter Oggel as a delegate to General Synod. He returned to Holland, but after three months in the pulpit, he went back to New York in September for three more months of a second begging stint on behalf of the academy. While Van Raalte was canvassing in the East, Oggel accepted the First Pella call, which finally filled their pulpit after three fruitless years of calling. During Van Raalte's frequent absences, Peter Oggel, Giles Van de Wall, Adrian Zwemer, and Gerrit Nykerk filled in for him. Having such an abundant supply of young pastors to cover his pulpit, thanks to the academy, allowed Van Raalte to be away for weeks on end. The council of the academy applauded him for his successful fundraising trips, but his consistory less so, though they seldom complained publicly. If complaints were voiced, they were not recorded in the minutes since the dominee was the clerk until 1858.[3]

---

[1] Van Raalte to De Moen, 1 June 1858, trans. Ten Hoor, ADC.

[2] Minutes, First Holland, 1 Aug., 21 Sept., 25 Oct., 27 Dec. 1858, 4 Dec. 1860; Kennedy, *Commentary*, 13 Sept. 1854, 1:462-63; 3 Apr. 1860, 2:927-28; 17 Apr. 1861, 2:1050 (quote); Van de Wall to Garretson, 28 Dec. 1858, BDM; Gerrit Van Schelven, "Teunis Keppel obit.," *Holland City News*, 4 July 1896 ("peculiar people" quote attributed to Philip Phelps). In 1866 Van Raalte was apparently not practicing the half-way covenant. An elder urged him to change, but the consistory "put the item on the table for later consideration" (Van de Wall to Garretson, 13 Feb. 1866, BDM). It was never taken off the table.

[3] Minutes, First Holland, 18 Jan., 18 Feb., 19 Apr. 1859; Kennedy, *Commentary*, 2:851, 6-7 Apr. 1859. Van Raalte to son Ben, 14 Nov. 1859 (quote), HHA; *De Hollander*, 5, 15, 29 Dec. 1859. The Van de Wall family emigrated from Brummelkamp's Arnhem congregation in 1847.

In February 1860, when the dominee was finally back in his pulpit, a large crowd came and "hung on his every word," the newspaper reported. He had not lost his touch. The consistory, however, noticed that stress was wearing on him, and they gave him "some rest and relief" by temporarily discontinuing Wednesday evening preaching services. Instead, they asked him to give more time to family visitation.[4] At the same time, two of the dominee's children, Dirk and Mina, became seriously ill with bilious fever and dysentery.

On the Fourth of July, Van Raalte led a community Sunday school festival and gave one of the brief addresses, followed by Phelps, Christian Van der Veen, teacher Cornelius Doesburg, doctor Ledeboer, and merchant Henry Post. Between their remarks, the children sang Christian songs with gusto. It was a splendid way to mark the holiday.[5]

The glow, however, soon dimmed. Elder Benjamin H. Ploeg raised a "foul insane fury against hymns" in *De Hollander*, which created quite a "tempest." Van Raalte dubbed the paper, the "Lowlander," and lamented having to deal with "ignorance, sectarian spirits, and leaders full of ill-will, who know how to make use of the ignorance and prejudices of simple-minded but suspicious people." Van Raalte's family sang hymns around the piano in the parlor, and they were sung in Sunday school, but to avoid conflict, he never used them in worship services at First Church. In retirement, however, when the Classis of Holland in 1874 approved their use in worship, Van Raalte was present and voted with the majority, although his successor, Rev. Roelof Pieters, was opposed. This was another controversial issue on which Van Raalte had changed his mind.[6]

Ploeg then picked a second public fight after Van Raalte agreed to fixed, two-year terms for elders who, if willing and if re-elected, could serve consecutive terms ad infinitum. The dominee had agreed to fixed terms to quiet complaints about the consistory being under his thumb.

---

[4] Minutes, First Holland, 22 Sept., 24 Nov. (quote), 21 Dec. 1859, 10 Feb. 1860, 19 Oct. 1863, 1 Dec. 1865; "Reformed Protestant Dutch Church," *Allegan Journal*, 13 June 1859; *De Hollander*, 2 Feb. 1860 (quote, trans. Simone Kennedy).

[5] Van Raalte to Phelps, 14, 16, 19, 31 Aug., 24 Sept. 1860, in Bruins and Schakel, *Envisioning Hope College*, 58, 62, 64, 66, 74; *De Hollander*, 27 June 1960. Bilious fever, usually caused by malaria and dysentery, came by eating food infected with the bacteria Shigella, causing bloody diarrhea.

[6] *De Hollander*, 26 Jan., 13 June, 25 July, 8 Aug., 12 Sept. 1860, trans. Simone Kennedy, Ten Hoor; Van Raalte to Phelps, 14, 31 Aug. 1860, in *Envisioning Hope College*, 58-59, 66-69 (quotes, 59, 67). For the Ploeg-Oggel hymn controversy, see ibid., 371-86; *De Hollander*, 19 Sept. 1874; *Holland City News*, 12 Sept. 1874.

Ploeg held to the old policy—once an elder, always an elder, whether in or out of active service. This was at best a quibble over words. When the consistory moved to censure the "pesky" Ploeg, he and eleven cohorts bolted from the congregation. They "found so many faults and shortcomings . . . that they could no longer live in fellowship with the church." The exasperated pastor, in his congregational report to the Classis of Holland, called their departure "a reason for thanksgiving," since it promised to bring an end to the "disquieting disturbances." It was a case of good riddance to Ploeg's "slander and lies" against the Reformed Church. Classis sent a pastoral letter to the churches urging peace. Ploeg and some of these dissidents formed the nucleus of the True Holland Reformed Church (later Central Avenue Christian Reformed Church), founded in 1865.[7]

A young man in Van Raalte's congregation may have put his finger on the problem. Jacob Doesburg, son of the newspaper editor, in a letter to Christian Van der Veen, his former Holland Academy classmate, then studying at New Brunswick Theological Seminary, wrote: "His [Van Raalte's] preaching is very dull nowadays; it is as if he wants rather something else to do, Land Speculation, for instance. Excuse me, Chris, but it does seem strange to a good many persons who are able to track him." Besides, Doesburg continued, Van Raalte opposed a group that met at the academy building in 1860 to organize a "free English church" for those, including academy teachers, for whom Dutch was a foreign tongue. "His Ex[cellency] wants to force them to become Dutch Reformed & so broke up the plan & adjourned *sine die* [with no specified date to meet again]."[8] These negative comments hit home, but they must be seen in the light of the long-running feud between the Doesburg family and the dominee.

Near tragedies

Van Raalte nearly lost his home to fire in April 1860. The blaze that engulfed part of the city started from families boiling maple sap amid a rising storm, and, as the newspaper reported, a "terrible fire ensued." Flames spread fast at the tanneries, ship wharfs, and Plugger's steam mill on the west edge of the city. The clanging fire bell and steam

---

[7] Minutes, First Holland, 18 Jan. 1861; Swierenga, *Faithful Witness*, 4-6. Four *De Hollander* articles are reprinted in *Envisioning Hope College*, 317-84. On "pesky" Ploeg, see Kennedy, *Commentary*, 2:987, 2 Apr. 1856, 1:538-40, 2:987; and Sheeres, "Brother Ploeg," 15-16.

[8] Jacob O. Doesburg to Christian Van der Veen, 28 Mar. 1860, in Christian Van der Veen Papers, HMA.

whistle at the flour mill called young and old to fight the fire with pails of water, and they succeeded in extinguishing the flames. Fires also flared in Graafschap, Groningen, Overisel, and North Holland, in short, all around the city. The paper reported that the "the greatest danger" had occurred at Van Raalte's home and vicinity but houses and barns were saved by several men "full of courage and strength, . . . [but] all the wood for stoves and fence rails went up in smoke." Peter Oggel, who arrived from Pella amid the flames to marry Mina Van Raalte, relieved Van Raalte as guest preacher the following Sunday morning in First Church. Oggel chose as his text, Matthew 16:26a (KJV): "Verily I say unto you, there be some standing here which shall not taste of death." The congregation had mercifully been spared from any loss of life.[9]

Cape Town calling

The fire disaster fed Van Raalte's mood of despondency. He wanted a ministry away from Holland—anywhere—even worlds away. "I should like to preach in Asia, Africa, and Europe," he confided in Phelps:

> There is too much opposition to me here. . . . My influence is too much hated. By my struggling against ignorance, avarice, selfishness, and bringing them where they do not want to be, many are wounded and feel sour against me. . . . I see too much strife among the people on my account, the influence of my preaching is injured; they sin against God's gift of the ministry. Many good things are opposed on my account, and I have already too much time and strength wasted in defending myself. And now I reason thus: "you must withdraw a few years; opposition will cool down and energy will be developed, when their stumbling block and their abused prop is removed."[10]

The September meeting of the Classis of Holland appeared to provide a golden opportunity for Van Raalte when the brothers considered sending a "pioneer gospel minister" to extend God's kingdom

---

[9] *De Hollander*, 4 April 1860, trans. Nella Kennedy; *Excelsiora*, 5 May 1871. Van Raalte bought wood by the cord for home heating and cooking. In June 1860, a ship arrived with Van Raalte's order for twenty-six cords. A cord was a well-stacked pile measuring four feet high, eight feet wide, and four feet deep (*De Hollander*, 20 June 1860).

[10] Van Raalte to Garretson, 16 Apr. 1857, BDM; Van Raalte to Phelps, 31 Aug., 24 Sept. 1860, in *Envisioning Hope College*, 67-68, 72.

among the Zulus in South Africa, "if such a man was to be found who had both the will and suitability for this." Knowing the agenda beforehand, Van Raalte sought to get a leg up by sending a detailed letter to the Reformed mission in Cape Town, in which he expressed his deep interest to work under their auspices. "All my desires are stirred to preach in the destitute regions of Africa." But after laying the matter "before the Throne of God," he decided to wait upon classis. When the item came up, the erstwhile missionary immediately offered himself. The brothers, taken aback, asked him to state his motives. He gave three: first that his long-time leadership in the colony was "viewed in an unfavorable light," and leaving would end the discord. Second, by being commissioned by classis, "his hearty love for and emotional ties to the Holland Classis" would continue. And third, he had a need to labor "without restraints" and to "open the way for missionary work among God's church in Africa."[11]

The negative response stunned him. The body declared that it was

> unwilling to have Dr. Van Raalte removed from their midst and viewed the reasons that the reverend named as motive for this offer as not weighty enough to warrant sending the Doctor out to Africa. . . . His service and person are dear to the classis, and they absolutely could not decide to send him away out of their midst. Consequently, the proposal is not accepted.

The brothers believed that Van Raalte's call to missionary service was driven more by personal slights than a sincere call from God. After classis squelched his dream to minister to "native Africans," the dominee determined to solicit a call from his homeland. His desire to labor "without restraints" was naïve; no such place existed. Van Raalte expressed his unhappiness to Phelps: "Nobody could deny the flood of slander, suspicions, and opposition constantly going on, but they did refuse to send me." His final comment was an understatement: "The proposal did cause a great commotion."[12]

In truth, his real estate holdings alone required that he remain in Holland. His oldest son, Bertus, was unsuited to manage them, and the

---

[11] Kennedy, *Commentary*, 17 Sept. 1860, 2:980-83; Van Raalte to Phelps, 31 Aug. 1860, in *Envisioning Hope College*, 67-68. Van Raalte in 1858 mentioned the opening of China for missionaries. "We may look forward to God's great deeds for the furthering of Christ's kingdom. Let us pray with trust: 'Thy kingdom come'" (*De Bazuin*, 5 Nov. 1858, www.delpher.nl, accessed, June 2021), trans. Nella Kennedy.

[12] Kennedy, *Commentary*, 17 Sept. 1860, 2:983; Van Raalte to Phelps, 24 Sept. 1860, in *Envisioning Hope College*, 72.

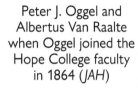

Peter J. Oggel and Albertus Van Raalte when Oggel joined the Hope College faculty in 1864 (JAH)

two younger boys were still in school. If he left the country, who would oversee his business—pay the taxes on his real estate and manage the paperwork of selling town lots and farmlands? His desire to serve in Africa was unrealistic in the extreme.

Albertus and Christina Van Raalte found solace by spending time in Pella in 1861 with newlyweds Peter and daughter Mina Oggel. It was the dominee's third visit to Pella, having been there in 1856 and 1859. This visit coincided with the Van Raaltes' twenty-fifth wedding anniversary, which Oggel marked with a lengthy poem full of endearing sentiments. Van Raalte tried to lift Oggel's heavy workload since he struggled with tuberculosis. Despite the burdens of office, Oggel was able to found a "well-furnished parochial school" in Pella.[13] Grandfather Albertus had the pleasure of bonding with his second grandson, Albertus Oggel. "Often I have little Albertus with me . . . and the little one runs around. He is a precious talker. I hope that God will use him as a preacher of the gospel." This little boy did not see his second birthday, but another grandson and namesake, Dirk's son,

---

[13] Dirk Van Raalte to father (Pella), 19 Feb. 1861; Peter Oggel, poem, 11 Mar. 1861, trans. Nella Kennedy, both in HHA; Kennedy, *Commentary*, 15 Oct. 1851, 1:204-5, 17 Apr. 1862, 2:1028; Bruins et al., *Albertus and Christina*, 100-104. In 1863 the Oggels returned to Holland where Peter accepted an appointment as divinity professor at Hope College and, in 1865, became editor of *De Hope*, the Reformed Church newspaper.

Albertus Christiaan, did become a preacher in the Reformed Church. How "glad," Van Raalte opined, "that my children are not at the other side of the ocean."[14]

Dreams of Zululand die hard

A year after rejecting Van Raalte, the Classis of Holland commissioned Van Raalte's understudy, Giles Van de Wall, to serve the Cape Town Reformed Church. Van Raalte, whose dreams died hard, penned a letter to his former student in Cape Town asking him if his congregation might sponsor a mission post among the Zulus. The response was more than disappointing: "It is doubtful whether he would be wanted by the Cape church." Yet the ardent missionary persisted: "My desire to be active . . . in a mission post in some corner of Zulu[land] has not diminished. What is the attitude of your people toward mission work? . . . How long does it take to learn the language well enough to get along?" Given the "height at which I am standing," at fifty years of age, "and my reputation in connection with the secession history in the Netherlands . . . I continually expect to receive a call from a congregation that desires to hear the truth." Unfortunately, no call came. He blamed the wider Reformed church. "How shamefully our Dutch nation has neglected work among the heathen in this noble central point in the middle of a pagan world." If only he could "bring the bread of life to Africa." No doubt he voiced this concern again as a delegate to General Synod in 1863.[15]

Not one to sit on his hands, Van Raalte asked Brummelkamp to obtain information about David Livingston, the Scottish medical missionary whose exploratory trek across the central and southern African continent inspired Christians everywhere. "Africa was always a painful and at the same time a precious, compelling field to me," Van Raalte confessed. To found such a mission, he wrote Brummelkamp, "would fulfill my dearest wishes, even if I should lose my life." He thought it preferable to work directly with Livingston's London Mission Society, which was contemplating supporting such a venture in lieu of the underfunded Board of Foreign Missions. Again, the classis crushed Van Raalte's hopes. Instead of him, they chose John H.

---

[14] Van Raalte to Phelps, 26 Dec. 1859, in *Envisioning Hope College*, 43 (quote), 73; Van Raalte to son Dirk, 7 Feb. 1861, HHA; Bruins et al., *Albertus and Christina*, 105; *De Hope*, 14 May 1866, in *Envisioning Hope College*, 416.

[15] Van Raalte to Van de Wall, 29 June 1862, HMA; Van Raalte to Brummelkamp, 22 May 1863, HHA. On Van de Wall and his appointment in Cape Town, see Kennedy, *Commentary*, 29-30 Sept., 1858, 2:802-3; 17 Sept. 1860, 2:980-81.

Karsten, a recent New Brunswick Seminary graduate, ordained for the work in a ceremony at First Church in June 1864. But Karsten, for want of funds, never went to Africa.[16]

Instead of Africa, Van Raalte might well have looked closer to home for another church to serve. Cornelius Van der Meulen, founding pastor of the First Zeeland Church, after twelve years, in 1859, accepted a call from the First Chicago church and then from the Second Grand Rapids church, where he retired in 1873. By serving three congregations, instead of one, Van der Meulen remained in harness longer, and his life and ministry were more harmonious.

Hope Church

With his dreams crushed, Van Raalte dutifully carried on at First Church. But he soon had to deal with the forces of Americanization as new English-speaking churches came on the scene and drew away younger families. In 1861 his Methodist friends, Isaac Fairbanks and George Harrington, managed to induce circuit-riding preachers to make Holland a regular stop on their itinerary, and the Methodist Episcopal Church had its start. It was the first English-speaking congregation in the Holland area.[17] The second English church was in the Reformed faith. Giles Van de Wall, fresh from finishing studies at New Brunswick Seminary, saw the pressing need for such worship among younger Hollanders and academy teachers, such as Rev. John Van Vleck. The two "Vans" began services in the chapel of the academy building (later Van Vleck Hall) in 1858. The next year, Phelps came in place of Van Vleck, and he and Van de Wall moved services to the First Church sanctuary on Sunday evenings.[18]

Van Raalte donated four lots (one acre) on West Tenth Street for the fledgling congregation, and Phelps, Van de Wall, and Henry Post began a subscription campaign for a building. In 1862 the trio organized Hope [Second Reformed] Church with ten families under the English-language Classis of Michigan. This was a natural fit and necessary, Van Raalte admitted, but "It must have a retarding influence on the Americanizing process of the immigrant churches,"

---

[16] Van Raalte to Brummelkamp, 22 May 1863, HHA; Kennedy, *Commentary*, 14 Oct. 1863, 2:1202, 23 June 1864, 3:1250-51; wikipedia.org/wiki/David_Livingstone, accessed 21 Sept. 2020.
[17] Miles, "Methodism in Holland," *First United Methodist Church Centennial History*, 1-51.
[18] These paragraphs rely on Parr, *Hope Church*, 10-37.

because it would draw away younger families with children.[19] He was correct. Hope Church began as a place for young families on the fast track to Americanization and retains its progressive character to the present. Only two Dutch immigrant families were among the charter members—Bernardus and Janna Grootenhuis and Bernardus and Alida Ledeboer. Ledeboer had practiced medicine in New York for more than a decade before coming to Holland and was fluent in English. The Grootenhuis family had temporarily resided in Algoma Township in Kent County, and their five children may have pushed for English-language worship.[20]

Missionary ship—"The keel that never kissed the sea"

In April 1864, at the height of the Civil War, Van Raalte and Phelps, a pair joined at the hip, jointly proposed to the Classis of Holland the appointment of a missionary professorship and the building of a three-hundred-ton ship to carry missionaries to far-flung fields. The first port of call, symbolically, would be Rotterdam or Amsterdam. The word went out, and a large crowd assembled at First Church to hear Phelps put flesh on the Lord's command to evangelize all peoples. Van Raalte and Peter Oggel, a theology professor at Hope College, "pressed its execution." The ship would undertake a "great work," buttressed with support from the East and even the Netherlands. Everyone agreed to press ahead. Van Raalte traveled to a meeting of the Classis of Wisconsin in Chicago to promote the mission.[21]

On June 24, a vast throng gathered with great fanfare at Black Lake for the keel-laying service, with Van Raalte as master of ceremonies. Prominent Dutch and American leaders spoke glowingly and offered emotive prayers, interspersed with the rousing singing of psalms and hymns, led by the academy choir. Despite a commendable zeal for missions, it was "the keel that never kissed the sea." Other pressing needs took precedence, enthusiasm faded, and donations dried up. The project to build the huge vessel was a pipe dream from the start. But 150 years later, Jacob E. Nyenhuis, placed the effort in perspective. "Although the missionary ship never set sail, nearly two hundred Hope graduates did sail as missionaries to all parts of the world during the next eight decades."[22]

[19] Van Raalte to Phelps, 19 Jan. 1861, in *Envisioning Hope College*, 81-82.
[20] Parr, *Hope Church*, 392-93.
[21] Minutes, Classis of Wisconsin, 14 Sept. 1864, art. 9.
[22] Zwemer, *Ship that Never Sailed*; Kennedy, *Commentary*, 20 Apr. 1854, 2:1232-34; 20

Retirement looms—"Old men have to learn to die by inches"

It seems odd that a man in his early fifties would talk about being "old and tired," but life expectancy was much shorter then, and people in their sixties were considered elderly. Van Raalte had burned the candle at both ends for many years, and his current congregation was huge. First Church in 1863 had grown to 870 souls, dispersed over a wide area, with 150 young people in catechism and 165 in Sunday school (see appendix, table 14.1, for membership stats by year). Dogged by ill health, Van Raalte was warned by his doctor to resign if "he did not wish to destroy himself." His son Ben, then fighting in the Civil War, concurred: "You should give up preaching altogether before it is too late." But preaching came easy for Van Raalte, and at age fifty-one, he was too young to stop. So he offered to continue in the pulpit if the consistory would relieve him of all other duties for a year. They agreed to cut his preaching to once on Sunday *for two months* and to reduce catechism teaching and all other administrative duties. His catechumens sent their "Beloved Teacher and Friend" impromptu poems, signed by forty-two "pupils and little friends," praying that "God may spare you for a long time."[23]

Van Raalte stopped attending consistory meetings for the next eighteen months, from March 1864 to December 1865, except for a June 1864 meeting, when he offered the radical proposal to either call a second pastor or split the congregation in two.[24] After five months of inaction, and given the pastor's "ongoing weakness and illness," the consistory in November 1864 dismissed the second-pastor idea on the flimsy grounds that "It would be very difficult to find a pastor who meets the requirements of the congregation." At the December congregational meeting, Van Raalte took the chair and reiterated his suggestion to divide the congregation, with each part having its own pastor. The congregation agreed by a vote of fifty-one to eighteen, a three-fourths majority. Van Raalte immediately had the members agree to a "free" nomination of a trio—that is, with nominations from

---

Sept. 1865, 2:1319; Van Raalte, "Het Zendeling-schip," *De Verzamelaar*, 1 June 1865; Nyenhuis, "A. C. Van Raalte," 328, citing Philip Tertius Phelps, *A Brief Biography of Rev. Philip Phelps, D.D., LL.D.* (n.p., 1941), 9.

[23] Minutes, First Holland, 30 Mar. 1863; Student Poems, 17, 18 Oct. 1863, trans. Ten Hoor, JAH; Christine Van Raalte to sister Mina Oggel, 16 May 1864, trans. Nella Kennedy, HHA; Ben Van Raalte to father, 24 Aug. 1864, trans. Nella Kennedy, HHA; De Vries, "Albertus C. Van Raalte," 12-18.

[24] Minutes, First Holland, 16 Nov. 1863. 13 Mar., 6 June, 19 Dec. 1864 (congregational meeting).

the floor, instead of by the consistory and selecting the three with the highest votes. This bypassed the consistory, which had continued to drag its feet.[25]

The congregation needed a bilingual pastor, able to preach fluently in Dutch and get along in English off the pulpit. But the free choice ended with two men serving in the Netherlands with no English language skills and prohibitive moving costs. The congregation also must buy or build a parsonage since Van Raalte had his own home. When the committee canvassed the members for pledges, they found "only minimal interest" and heard "many critical comments about the present pastor and consistory." Some were "completely unwilling," others were "extremely hesitant and uncertain," and yet others would make "some contribution" but not a generous pledge. The financial books showed more than $1,800 ($35,000 today) in unpaid obligations over the previous three years. Even the benevolent fund for the needs of the poor was short more than $200 ($3,900), and another canvass of the members failed to make up the shortfall. These shortages indicted the congregation on its weak spiritual condition.[26]

In three subsequent congregational meetings in the next weeks, attendance was so poor that "it was not possible to move forward with the election of a pastor." Barely one-third of the membership attended, and the meetings ended without a vote on the trios. A malaise was crippling the congregation.[27]

The situation confirmed that Van Raalte had overstayed his welcome. He should have sought a call much earlier. The frustrated pastor continued to boycott consistory meetings, even after he was asked to come and bring the membership books in order to compile membership data for the yearly report in the denominational yearbook. The dominee also stopped conducting Sunday evening Bible readings and bimonthly prayers services. To nudge him, the consistory offered three dollars per service "as a token of our gratitude for his concern for this congregation." But he found it "difficult to accept this task." The desultory behavior of his congregation convinced him that it was time to step down, "I am growing old, stiff, and dull," he told Phelps. "By keeping me in harness, I will be finished up, and soon obliged to retire. Old men have to learn to die by inches."[28]

---

[25] Ibid., 6 June, 21 Nov. 1864; 24 Nov. 1864 (congregational meetings).
[26] Ibid., 19 Dec. 1864, 23 Jan., 27 Feb. 1865 (congregational meetings).
[27] Minutes, First Holland, 9, 16 Jan. 1865.
[28] Ibid., 6, 20 Mar., 10 May, 13 Oct., 20 Nov. 1865.

At the December 1865 consistory meeting, Van Raalte "entered the meeting" to the surprise of everyone, and a wide-ranging discussion took place about the "condition of the congregation" and the "necessity for more spiritual labors." It quickly became evident that the pastor and consistory were not on the same page on splitting the congregation. To appease the dominee for not lessening his preaching and teaching duties, the consistory gave him a one hundred dollar bonus.[29]

Reincorporation of First Church

At this crucial juncture, First Church and all the congregations in the Classis of Holland updated their constitutions to take advantage of an 1863 Michigan statute that allowed trustees of ecclesiastical properties to reincorporate and thereby guarantee the property rights of the congregation against the denomination. In most Presbyterian denominations, the synod or general assembly held title to all church properties. The Reformed Church in America followed suit. Van Raalte provided his consistory with a Dutch translation of the new law, which guaranteed "the rights and the freedom of the congregation to handle their own financial affairs." Each one signed the law and thereby validated it for the congregation. This legal birthright had significant repercussions seventeen years later when the congregation in 1882 suffered a schism over Freemasonry (ch. 14).[30]

Clapper revival 1866

Throughout his ministry on both continents, Van Raalte had prayed for revival. He believed in the working of the Spirit, wherever He may move. God had answered Van Raalte's fervent prayers in 1858 when the New York revival reached Holland. In early 1866, Van Raalte witnessed a second season of revival. The revivalist was not the dominee, however, but the untutored stonemason Michael J. Clapper. He was a man short in stature like Van Raalte but with an acerbic personality that "hid a good disposition and a warm heart." Clapper

---

[29] Ibid., 1, 7 Dec. 1865, Van Raalte to Phelps, 19 Jan. 1861, 9 Mar. 1865, in Bruins and Schakel, *Envisioning Hope College*, 81-82, 122.

[30] Minutes, First Holland, 2 May, 26 Dec. 1865; Kennedy, *Commentary*, 15 Apr. 1863, 2:1151; 19 Apr. 19, 1865, 2:1282-83. The minority party, funded by the denomination, sued for ownership of the building in the Ottawa County Circuit Court, and upon losing, appealed to the Michigan Supreme Court, but the highest court affirmed the ruling of the lower court that the majority party owned the building. See Swierenga, *Holland, Michigan*, 1:218-21; De Vries and Boonstra, *Pillar Church*, 133-36.

hailed from the Reformed Church in New York and settled in Holland in 1859 where he helped Isaac Fairbanks and George Harrington found the Methodist Episcopal Church.[31]

In the dead of winter, 1865-66, with Van Raalte in the dumper, Clapper sensed he was "called of God to save Holland," and he would do so in the English language. His fiery style and free-grace Gospel first attracted cynical young people who had some fun at his expense. Preaching in shirt sleeves without a collar merited ridicule, to say the least. But the evangelist's earnest spirit and warmhearted manner soon won over the scoffers, and crowds grew, overflowing a room above a saloon, then the schoolhouse, and finally, the town hall. Clapper asked both Hope Church and First Church to use their sanctuaries, but Phelps and Van Raalte and their consistories refused. But then Van Raalte had second thoughts. When he shared this with his consistory, however, "chips flew." He challenged them:

> Are you blind to what is happening around us? ... Do you not see the hand of God in this? That he [Clapper] has something to tell us? Shall we resist the Spirit of God? When will the consistory of Holland learn to understand its duty? I should have had another consistory long ago!

This onslaught forced the brethren to relent and open the church to the revivalist.[32]

Then, "in an unexpected turn," practically the entire congregation followed the eccentric elder Clapper. Even students at Holland Academy and Hope College were enthusiastic about the awakening. Night after night, the staid Dutch stood up to give their testimonies and join in emotional singing of English hymns and Gospel songs. Clapper's favorite hymn, *Come, Ye Sinners, Poor and Needy*, led dozens to come forward and accept Jesus. "Every heart," Van Raalte observed, "seemed to be open to God's truth. The lips of God's children overflowed; the things of the world receded into the background; the house of God was full. . . . To make attendance easier, shops closed early, the saloons were empty, and the streets were deserted at night, but God's house was full. . . . The majority of God's children were quickened by it.

---

[31] Dosker, *Van Raalte*, 302, trans. Dekker. For a biographical sketch of Clapper, see Kennedy, *Commentary*, 18 Apr. 1866, 2:1351-53.

[32] Van Raalte report, *De Hope*, 3 May 1866, trans. Nella Kennedy; minutes, First Holland, 13 (quote), 20 Feb. 1866; De Vries and Boonstra, *Pillar Church*, 91-92 (quotes); Parr, *Hope Church*, 48-51.

Even the very elderly shared in the warming love of God's fire. Therefore, we are gladdened and praise God!" The baptism of an elderly Dutch couple was the talk of the town.

Van Raalte was truly flabbergasted. "Twenty years I have worked among this people, but where were the fruits? And now, God sends to us a Methodist to mow where we have sown; and such a Methodist! But I lay my hand on my mouth and worship."[33] Clapper brought Pentecost to Holland. He touched emotional cords in Dutch Reformed breasts that had lain dormant since the 1834 Afscheiding and the 1858 New York revival. Perhaps the revival also offered relief from the intense emotions of the Civil War and Lincoln's assassination.

The elders were in a quandary. Should they entrust the flock to Clapper's Arminian doctrines? The dominee and two elders decided to join with him and hopefully "regulate the matter, so that the offence might be removed." For a brief time, Clapper and Van Raalte led meetings together, but that "did not work out well." After "several unpleasant incidents," Van Raalte gave up. He and the elders then scheduled family visits with the newly inspired and encouraged them to be faithful members of First Church.[34]

In his 1866 report to the Classis of Holland, Van Raalte waxed eloquent over the "abundant outpouring of God's Spirit. . . . The old man and the young child, the mocker and the child of the covenant, the Pharisee and the publican have together called for and rejoiced in redeeming grace."[35] The spiritual renewal demanded a wholesome lifestyle. When a couple opened a theater in Holland, the consistory decried the "very worldly and tragic condition" and closed the communion table to any member who attended.[36] The demands of planting crops in April 1866 brought an end to the revival fires. Mundane tasks intruded. For the next twenty years, locals talked about the "extraordinary spiritual awakening . . . [as] a puzzle, an insoluble thing, in a way, for many human eyes."[37]

---

[33] De Vries and Boonstra, *Pillar Church*, 92 (quote).
[34] Minutes, First Holland, 20 Feb. 1866 (quote); Geert S. De Witt, "Experiences," *De Grondwet*, 25 June 1912, in Lucas, *Dutch Immigrant Memoirs*, 2:82.
[35] Minutes, First Holland, 3, 11 Apr. 1866, professions compiled in minutes, Feb.-June 1866; Kennedy, *Commentary*, Apr. 18, 1866, 3:1348, 1350 (quote). The number of families in First Church from April 1865 to 1867 increased from 190 to 250.
[36] Minutes, First Holland, 27 Mar., 11 Apr., 15 May, 5 June 1866; Kennedy, *Commentary*, 17 Apr. 1866, 3:1427.
[37] Quotes from Michael J. Clapper obit., *De Hope*, 22 Dec. 1886, trans. Nella Kennedy.

Netherlands homecoming as therapy

After the time of spiritual renewal, Albertus sensed that it was time to take Christina to the Netherlands for an extended stay. She suffered from tuberculosis and longed to see her family once more. "I crave such a change for Mrs. Van Raalte, it may restore her in a certain measure," he wrote Phelps. She "seems to be favorable affected by the proposed plan," but greatly fears being "tormented" by bedbugs on the boat. This fear did not lessen her eagerness to see her siblings and their families—sister Maria and Anthony Brummelkamp, brother Carel de Moen and wife Alexandrina, and brother-in-law Simon van Velzen, long a widower. The three men were employed at the Christian Separated Church Seminary at Kampen, Brummelkamp and Van Velzen as professors and De Moen as curator-treasurer.[38]

The dominee justified the trip as an appointed delegate of General Synod to attend the Amsterdam synod of the Christian Separated Church (Christelijke Afgescheiden Kerk). In late March 1866, the dominee shocked his consistory with the news that he and Christina were leaving shortly for the "enhancement of his, and even more, his wife's health." The brethren, stunned by the "hasty departure," reluctantly acquiesced and decided to celebrate the Lord's Supper "before the pastor leaves." His sermon, based on the Apostle Peter's benediction, "Grace unto you, and peace, be multiplied" (I Peter 1:2b, KJV), concluded by wishing the congregation "this blessing for you at my departure, in whatever circumstances." The trip was possible only because the "Lord opened the way" with a magnificent $500 gift ($9,600 today) from Samuel and James Schieffelin, his New York City friends. Wealthy in lands, the dominee lacked cash for the "sabbatical."[39]

Before departing, Christina again began spitting up blood, so Albertus took her to Grand Rapids to consult with Dr. Charles Shepherd, a New York-trained physician. Although the doctor could not cure her, he assured her that seeing her loved ones was better than any medicine. If nothing else, Shepherd proved to be an apt physician for recognizing her depression.[40] Albertus and Christina signed a power of attorney that gave middle son Dirk full authority to handle

---

[38] Van Raalte to Phelps, 26 Mar. 1866, in *Envisioning Hope College*, 141.
[39] Minutes, First Holland, 25 Feb., 6, 13 Mar., 11 Apr. 1866; Van Raalte sermon, 14 Apr. 1866, HHA.
[40] Van Raalte to Phelps, 5, 7, 10 Apr. 1866, in *Envisioning Hope College*, 145, 148, 150-51.

their financial affairs in the interim. Dirk had demonstrated greater business acumen than his older brother Bertus.

Van Raalte secured a passport from the state department (Christina could travel on his passport). He was age fifty-four and she fifty-one. His physical description on the passport revealed some aging since his military induction record at age twenty-one in 1832: his mouth was medium instead of small, his nose more prominent, and his hair color had changed from blonde to brown. He had shrunk a half inch, but at five feet, three inches, he stood only one inch below the average of Dutch males in 1840. In brief, he was a bit short, with blue eyes, a light complexion, and a large head seemingly out of proportion. He was clean shaven until he came to Holland where he sported a flowing beard and full mustache for the rest of his life, which compensated for a receding hairline.[41]

After the Schieffelin brothers donated travel funds, Phelps, who was fundraising in New York, obtained ship tickets and arranged for hotels for the Van Raaltes. The arduous journey to New York City took ten days, with frequent layovers for Christina to rest. She found it "too hard" even to leave home and was feverish on the stagecoach to Kalamazoo by way of Marshall, where daughter Christine was then living. En route on the New York Central Railroad, the couple stopped three days in Rochester, where Van Raalte preached. In Albany they stayed several days with Phelps' parents, Philip Sr. and Hannah. There Christina had another flare-up. In New York City, the couple stayed with Thomas De Witt and rested again for several days. This gave Van Raalte time to write his "Dearly Beloved Children" a whimsical letter recalling his first time in New York, twenty years earlier, in 1846, with his immigrant group, and how God had in His abundant grace allowed them to undertake the voyage and how much he treasured the "bonds of love" in the family. He signed the letter, "Your father who loves you."[42]

The couple boarded the Hamburg America Line SS *Teutonia*, "a fairly small and clean ship," which departed New York on April 28 and arrived at Southampton, England, on May 9 after a rough, twelve-day

---

[41] Power of attorney document, executed 10 Apr. 1866, and filed in Ottawa County Deed Register, 3 May 1866 (Book Y, pages 377-78); passport, notarized by Henry D. Post, 7 Apr. 1866, and signed by secretary of state William H. Seward, 14 Apr. 1866, HHA. Harinck, "'O, may the Lord,'" 77n35, gives the average height of Dutch males.

[42] Van Raalte to Phelps, 23 Apr. 1866, in *Envisioning Hope College*, 153; Van Raalte to dearly beloved children, 27 Apr. 1866, in ibid., 411-13.

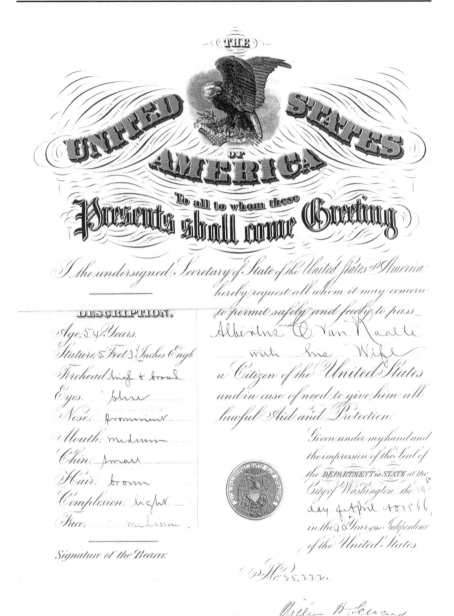

Van Raalte's US passport, 1866, with detailed physical description (*HHA*)

SS *Teutonia*, Hamburg America Line (*courtesy Norway Heritage Museum*)

crossing. "I was grinded to powder by that monster of Seasickness;" it was a "death struggle," Albertus wrote. But adrenaline and anticipation carried them along. Mercifully, steamships were four times faster than sailing ships, and *Teutonia* crossed thirty-three days sooner than the *Southerner* had in 1846. The Van Raaltes boarded an overnight train to cover the seventy miles to London, and then by carriage to the Dutch steamer *Fijenoord* for an overnight crossing of the English Channel. They stepped on Dutch soil at Rotterdam on May 11 and immediately caught a train for Kampen via Utrecht and Zwolle, arriving in the late afternoon for the longed-awaited reunion with the Brummelkamps.[43]

The cold rainy weather could not dampen the excitement and warm feelings of familiarity. "Everything comes back to me, and it makes me feel softhearted," Albertus wrote his children about the emotional reunions "with cherished family and friends in the Lord." He certainly spoke for their mother as well. "It is impossible to describe how great our joy was to meet each other again and stay together this whole time. . . . I saw the great joy on mother's face. . . . [It was] one of the most pleasant experiences imaginable." Young nephew Anthony Brummelkamp Jr. (called Anton) witnessed the reunion when the couple stepped out of an omnibus and came to the door. Anton caught Van Raalte's eyes, and in his own words, he saw

---

[43] Van Raalte to dearly beloved children, 14 May 1866, in ibid., 411-16.

a distinguished gentleman of small stature, in a long travel coat with large buttons and accompanied by a lone lady, his wife. Who can describe the surprise and joy of this reunion after twenty years of separation! It was Dr. Van Raalte with his wife, my mother's only surviving sister whom she pressed to her heart, with whom she had experienced the Secession and all the vicissitudes connected to it. And Van Raalte had been a brother and a friend of my father ever since his days at the university. On the first evening and in the subsequent days, there came no end to the stories about love and loss in the family of the leader of the emigration and among the emigrants, especially stories about the early years of the emigration.[44]

Van Raalte described the reunion from his perspective as a visitor:

On the other side of the street lives the Rev. van Velzen, and in the same street a couple of [houses] down the Rev. de Moen; some houses the other way were nephew S[imon] van Velzen [the only child of Simon and Johanna]. Quickly, we all assembled in the home of the Rev. Brummelkamp. We are all so joyful. To my surprise, all my dearly beloved friends were still strong as they were when I left. The Rev. Brummelkamp has turned gray but is healthier and stronger than before.... The Revs. van Velzen and de Moen are still the same.

Albertus had retained his brown hair, but his health could not compare with that of Anthony; the two, born three days apart in October 1811 were fifty-five years of age. Christina, despite being "much exhausted," found that being with her dear sister for nearly four months had a "very good influence" on her health. Van Raalte in gratitude wrote son Ben that her cough had improved a bit, and she had put on weight. But the respite proved to be brief. The first Sunday in Kampen, De Moen was slightly indisposed, so Van Raalte filled his pulpit and "poured out his heart in a fiery message."[45]

The ostensible purpose of the trip was for Van Raalte to address the synod in Amsterdam on May 30, 1866, on behalf of his denomina-

---

[44] Van Raalte to Phelps, 24 May 1866, in *Envisioning Hope College*, 155; Christina Van Raalte, "Dear Children!" 14 May 1866, in ibid., 413-15; Brummelkamp Jr., *Brummelkamp*, 504, quoted in English translation in Harinck, "'O, may the Lord,'" 75.

[45] *De Bazuin*, 18 May 1866 (quote) (www.delpher.nl, accessed June 2021, trans. Earl Wm. Kennedy).

Rev. Dr. Henry E. Dosker (1855-1926), Western Seminary professor and Van Raalte biographer who, at age eleven, had met the Van Raaltes in Kampen in 1866 (*JAH*)

tion. By then the Separatist body had doubled in membership to eighty thousand souls led by eighty ministers. It was a far cry from the first synod thirty years earlier, when delegates, meeting behind locked doors for fear of arrest, examined and ordained Albertus to the ministry. Now he returned as the honored American guest to a prominent building on one of the prestigious *grachten* (canals). After brother-in-law Van Velzen, who presided, welcomed Albertus with "heartfelt joy," the American conveyed "Christian greetings and good wishes" from the Classis of Holland. With strong emotions, Van Raalte noted how "refreshing for the soul" it was to renew ties of "love and fellowship" with friends who had together "suffered and struggled in times past." The "inspired and spontaneous words," which "emphasized again and again how this people were *oppressed* and *trampled*," moved the delegates "to tears." Delegates lingered until 1:30 in the morning and did not leave until singing the last verse of Psalm 72 and the *Avondzang* (evening song). It was the first highlight of the trip, with more to come.[46]

Van Raalte's mention of persecution in the 1830s was an implicit attempt to justify his act of deserting the fatherland. Many delegates could well remember the stinging critique he and Brummelkamp

---

[46] Brummelkamp Jr., *Brummelkamp*, 509; Kennedy, *Commentary*, 18 Apr. 1866, 2:1365; *Handelingen en verslagen*, 30 May-8 June 1866, trans. Ten Hoor; *Acts and Proceedings*, 1866, 44. Membership statistics by year and by province from 1856 to 1892 are in Te Velde, "Dutch Background," 94-97.

had leveled against the religious, social, and economic conditions in their 1846 *Landverhuizing* pamphlet. The delegates had borne the same afflictions, but remained loyal citizens who worked for the betterment of church and state.[47]

After trying to soften hearts, Van Raalte turned to the larger purpose: to win favor toward the American denomination in the fallout from the union of 1850 that was roiling immigrant churches. Surely the True Brothers' criticism of the Reformed Church had reached the ears of the "fathers and brethren" in the Old Country, and some of the latter were inclined to believe the former. The official communiqué, which Van Raalte had carefully drafted and the Classis of Holland and General Synod had approved, contained this key phrase: "We are and remain one in the Spirit with you, in devotion to the doctrine, discipline, and ministry of the Reformed Church." The American Reformed branch, in short, was orthodox in doctrine and life.

But these words did not reassure everyone. The minutes state that "Some brothers posed questions which he answered with great willingness and frankness." Why did the Classis of Holland join that church in 1850? Why did the secession of 1857 take place? Put on the defensive, Van Raalte reiterated that his adopted denomination was standing true to the Reformed Confessions. He blamed the 1857 secession on the cultural gap between Old and Young Dutch, and particularly on "certain elements" among the immigrants, such as the cantankerous Gysbert Haan. It was theological baggage from the fatherland and mere cultural differences with the Dutch church in the East that had caused the schism, not RPDC heterodoxy. The American dominee thus quieted doubts, and synod extended the right hand of fellowship to the American church.[48]

Douwe Van der Werp, who had immigrated to Holland after accepting a call from the Graafschap Church in Van Raalte's backyard, the strongest of the original four True churches in 1857, was highly critical of synod's endorsement. "Now they in the Netherlands have extended the hand of fellowship to Van Raalte and the Reformed Church, with all its heresies, which Van Raalte has camouflaged, and thereby condemned our secession." Feelings ran high in West Michigan,

---

[47] *De Hope*, 21 June 1866; Harinck, "'O, may the Lord.'"
[48] Van Raalte's speech, "Union with existing Dutch Reformed Church," undated, HHA; *Handelingen en verslagen*, art. 142; "Wat *De Bazuin* zegt," *De Hope*, 25 Oct. 1866.

and such questions did not die. They resurfaced again and again, even after Van Raalte's death (ch. 16). Van der Werp, it should be noted, belonged to the Gronings-Drents party of the Separatists, who stood against Van Raalte's Overijssels-Gelders party (ch. 2).[49]

The editor of the church periodical, *De Bazuin*, asked some hard questions after synod adjourned. "Are our ministers still allowed to accept calls from schismatic American congregations, and are our consistories still allowed to give attestations [membership papers] to these congregations?" The answer was yes, but Van Raalte had won a "resounding public relations triumph" judging from synod's response and a favorable Dutch press. But it was a pyrrhic victory. When, in the next few years, his denomination would waffle on the Freemasonry issue, the mother church in the Netherlands would throw its full support to the True Brothers, then renamed the Christian Reformed Church.[50]

During the week of synod in Amsterdam, Van Raalte preached on Sunday in the new church on the Keizersgracht that seated up to fifteen hundred people. Following his synod appearance, he preached in Zaandam and Putten. Most memorable were invitations to fill former pulpits in Genemuiden, Ommen, Zwolle, Utrecht, Kampen, and many other Separatist churches. It was an "unforgettable" Sunday when he stood before the large throng of worshipers in Brummelkamp's former congregation of Hattem, which he had often served before emigrating. Everywhere "people hung on his lips," reported the denominational voice, *De Bazuin*. Everywhere he was also addressed as Doctor, his honorary degree, in the socially conscious nation. At the Separatist seminary in Kampen, he participated in the annual examinations of students, some of whose parents he knew from years ago. When the faculty and students welcomed him by singing Psalm 129:8: "May the blessing of the Lord be upon you," it "filled his heart with thankfulness to see how God kept this trampled people by giving them numerous students and upholding their Servants, my former fellow fighters."[51]

---

[49] Van der Werp to Dirk Pieters Postma, Transvaal, South Africa, 30 Jan. 1867, quoted in Sheeres, *Son of Secession*, 141; *De Grondwet*, 30 Aug. 1881.

[50] Van Raalte report in *De Hope*, 12 July 1866, reprinted in *Envisioning Hope College*, 417-18; Harinck, "'O, may the Lord,'" 78-80. In 1869 the Christelijke Gereformeerde Kerk was formed in a merger of the Christelijke Afgescheiden Kerk (the former Christian Separated Church) and the smaller Gereformeerde Kerken onder 't Kruis (Kennedy, *Commentary*, 21 Apr. 1869, 3:1527-28).

[51] Harinck, "'O, may the Lord,'" 76, citing *De Bazuin*, 18 May, 14 Sept. 1866.

George Harinck, in his perceptive account of Van Raalte's 1866 visit, notes that the sectional riffs of the 1830s remained close to the surface. The pulpits opened to Van Raalte across the Netherlands were linked to the Overijssels-Gelders party of Brummelkamp, De Moen, and Henricus Beuker. Van Raalte did not receive a single invitation from churches identified with the Gronings-Drents party of Hendrik de Cock, Van Velzen, and Van der Werp. Van der Werp's True church at Graafschap had a year earlier given birth to a daughter church (now Central Avenue)—the first in the city of Holland since the 1857 secession and whose building stood within sight of Van Raalte's church. Van der Werp, as editor of the True church periodical, *De Wachter*, also used his pen to criticize Van Raalte's one-sided defense at synod of the Reformed Church. So the long arm of the Gronings-Drents factions of the Old Country continued to bedevil Van Raalte in Michigan.[52]

The Netherlands sabbatical, however, went from triumph to triumph for Van Raalte. The Fijnaart Hervormde Kerk consistory invited the renowned son of their beloved former pastor to fill his father's pulpit on a Sunday morning in late July. He received a hero's welcome. He could finally preach in his father's denomination, unimaginable thirty years earlier. In 1835 church authorities had refused to ordain him and then hounded him mercilessly as a Separatist preacher. Standing in his father's pulpit and visiting his father's grave in the adjacent cemetery was the highlight of his homecoming. People thronged from near and far to hear the famous American son of the church. Van Raalte later reflected on the day: "It was a great pleasure to see my father's place of prayer, fight, and struggle, to remember my earlier Ebenezers [places of struggle with God, like the patriarch Jacob], and to sow again in the field where my father had worked was my deepest wish and became my ultimate delight." The old adage, "Time heals all wounds," was true for orthodox congregations in the Bible Belt but not for this son of the national church. Van Raalte's negative attitude toward the Hervormde Kerk did not change; he described it in reports to Phelps in one word:

[52] For this and following paragraph, Harinck, "'O, may the Lord,'" 81-82; Te Velde, "Dutch Background," 85-98; Swierenga, "True Brothers." Henricus Beuker (1834-1900), born in Bentheim, Germany, trained at Kampen, served six congregations in the Gereformeerde Kerken in Nederland, then the Emlichheim congregation in his native Bentheim, before emigrating to the United States and serving two congregations in West Michigan before finishing his career as professor at Calvin Theological Seminary (1894-1900), where he died in harness (Harms, *Historical Directory*, 150; *Gereformeerde Kerken Nederland* directory, 197).

"Babel," meaning theologically confused, heterodox, and ungrounded. "Modern theology bans religion," he lamented.[53]

Two days after the Sunday service at Fijnaart, Van Raalte willingly accepted an offer from the sister church at nearby Willemstad to preach in a special Tuesday evening service. An evangelical periodical captured the spectacle.

> Today a totally unexpected worship service took place here... that was to the edification and awakening of many.... The attendance was unusually large, which the building could barely contain, with people having come from surrounding congregations.

In Van Raalte's words, "I could sow in large crowds, while praying and petitioning in silence, if God would use it to work in sinners' hearts."[54]

Van Raalte was at his best on his farewell Sunday in Kampen when he led the evening service in the Christelijke Gereformeerde Kerk before a thousand friends and admirers. The church pastor, Willem H. Gispen, was so impressed that he wished for a double portion of Van Raalte's spirit, channeling Elisha's final wish before Elijah's ascent in the fiery chariot. Gispen's description is vivid of Van Raalte's garb and oratory: "Without three-cornered hat, without long black coat, but with black tie [not traditional white] and stiff elevated collars, and a beard on his chin sometimes called a goatee. And then the manly, powerful, earnest, biblical word, without our preaching pattern of three parts with three times three subdivision." At the end of the service, Van Velzen stood up and gave a very friendly response to his brother-in-law, thereby healing a deep rift that had festered since 1846, when Van Raalte was about to depart for America (ch. 4).[55]

During most of the cold, wet summer days of 1866, the Van Raaltes enjoyed family reunions and social times, including a dinner in the home of Janke Wormser-Van der Veen, widow of the influential Amsterdam publisher, Johan A. Wormser, whose son, Johan Jr., then age twenty-one, almost fifty years later would write a full-length biography of Van Raalte. The elderly dominee made a positive impression on Junior.

---

[53] Reports of Van Raalte's daily activities, described in letters to Phelps, were published in *De Hope*, 12 (quote), 30 (quote) July; 16 (quote), 30 Aug. 1866 (reprinted in *Envisioning Hope College*, 417-18, 421-25).

[54] Van Raalte to Phelps, 30 July 1866; *De Heraut*, 31 July 1866 (www.delpher.nl, accessed, June 2021), trans. Earl Wm. Kennedy.

[55] *De Vrije Kerk*, 1 Feb. 1880 (www.delpher.nl, accessed June 2021).

Johan A. Wormser Jr. (1845-1916), who wrote *De Afgescheidenen van 1834 en hun nageslacht*

I can still see him at the table, short in stature, slightly but almost unnoticeably stooped, thin graying hair, wide forehead, bright blue eyes, tightly closed lips, cheerful but earnest in his speech; his entire countenance that of a man who thought clearly, responding without any hesitation at all, honest and headstrong in his actions, and persistent in following through.[56]

Henricus Beuker also had the pleasure to lodge the couple for several days at his home in Rotterdam. He found in the "little man ... a broad evangelical view, a steady will and a child-like faith. ... With great clarity of ideas and voice, he preached several times in my place, though he was suffering from a sore throat."[57]

The expatriate relished reliving the first thirty-five years of his life and connecting with colleagues and former students in the Old Country. "To tell you the truth," he admitted, "I enjoy it here. God gives me strength and energy, and in spite of all the traveling and preaching, I am becoming strong and fat." Nevertheless, he concluded that life in America was "far better" than the "old, densely populated countries" in Europe. The American citizen no longer had Dutch in the "very marrow" of his bones, although strings of the fatherland still tugged at his heart. Harinck aptly concluded: "Delight and love—was there a dissonance? Yes, there was."[58]

---

[56] The Wormser dinner is noted in Jansje Wüstenhoff-Wormser to Christina M. Budde-Stomp, 3 Oct. 1867, in *Iowa Letters*, 555; Wormser, *In twee werelddeelen*, 230; *De Bazuin*, 30 Nov. 1866 (www.delpher.nl, accessed June 2021).
[57] Henricus Beuker, "Dood van dr. A. C. van Raalte," *De Vrije Kerk*, 2 (1876), 608.
[58] Harinck, "'O, may the Lord,'" 83; Brummelkamp, "Van Raalte," 115.

En route home, the Van Raaltes were delayed at Antwerp by ship problems, and instead of a direct crossing to New York, they had to travel by ferry to Harwich, take the train via London back to Southampton, and then by steamship to Quebec, and lake steamer to Holland. The rerouting cost them an extra week. Back at home, Christina's health continued to decline, but she lived another five years in the glow of the fresh memories of being with loved ones.[59]

News about Pella especially disturbed the dominee. He learned that during his absence Douwe Van der Werp had gone to Pella for three weeks to organize a True congregation there with fifty members who had seceded from First Reformed Church, a body Van Raalte had organized; Peter Oggel had served as the first pastor (1860-63), and Egbert Winter, a graduate of Holland Academy, was then serving as the second pastor. Winter had often filled Van Raalte's pulpit in Holland when he was out of town, and in 1865 when the overworked dominee refused to mount the pulpit for months. The Pella schism was the ultimate slap in Van Raalte's face after his efforts in the Netherlands to undercut the True church and limit the impact of the schism in West Michigan a decade before.[60]

Freemasonry bedevils Van Raalte and First Church

Van Raalte stood firmly against Freemasonry his entire ministry, but neither he nor his consistory had to deal with this organization before 1866 when member Gerrit Van Schelven, a Civil War veteran, helped organize the first lodge in Holland as its secretary. The consistory discussed this serious matter and agreed unanimously that lodge members "should not be admitted to the Lord's Table." Van Raalte contacted the Second Grand Rapids consistory for guidance since that body was dealing with a baptized member who had joined the lodge. The Classis of Holland, which in 1861 had expressed its "inner aversion to every society and work that shuns the light," advised him to work with the wayward one so that he will "break with the society and get united to Christ."[61]

---

[59] Van Raalte to son Ben, 11 June 1866, 545, in *Iowa Letters*; *De Bazuin*, 21 Sept. 1866 (www.delpher.nl, accessed June 2021); Harinck, "'O, may the Lord,'" 87-88, provides a daily itinerary.

[60] *De Bazuin*, 21 Sept. 1866 (www.delpher.nl, accessed June 2021), summarizing a report in *De Grondwet* of 22 August about the Pella situation that greatly disturbed coeditors Brummelkamp and De Moen, Van Raalte's brothers-in-law. On Winter, see Van Raalte to Phelps, 9 Mar. 1865, in *Envisioning Hope College*, 122-23, and Kennedy, "The Summer of Dominie Winter's Discontent."

[61] Minutes, First Holland, 6 (quote). 13 Mar. 1866, Kennedy, *Commentary*, 17 Apr. 1861, 2:1041-43, 1045.

Van Schelven waffled on his Masonic membership status by telling his elder that he had broken fellowship with the lodge, which likely reopened the sacrament to him. Otherwise, he could worship at Hope Church, which was affiliated with the Classis of Michigan, not the Classis of Holland. Their consistory, Van Raalte complained, "seems to have no objection to receiving members of the Masonic Lodge into the fellowship of their congregation and admitting them to the table of the Lord." He penned a letter of protest on behalf of his consistory to their consistory, asking for "harmony on this subject." He posed the key question: "How can a Christian swear secrecy to a body of men, even if that body was as holy as the Church of God?"[62]

After "carefully" considering the letter, the Hope Church consistory replied: "The majority of us do not see the subject in the light that you do. To us, Free Masons seem like some other things, a matter about which Christians do and may conscientiously differ." The body did promise, for the sake of harmony, to try "to persuade these brethren to withdraw from their society." In any case, it was preferable "to receive such people into the Church on their giving evidence of conversion, and then teach them a better way."[63]

Van Raalte's consistory appreciated the irenic spirit but decided to take the issue to a higher level. They asked the Classis of Holland to protest to General Synod "against the acceptance of Freemasons as members of the church." The aim was to put Hope Church and others who shared its policy in the dock. Classis unanimously accepted the proposal and appointed Van Raalte to head a blue-ribbon committee to draw up a testimonial against Freemasonry for higher church bodies.[64]

Classis sent the document to General Synod 1867, which body voted overwhelmingly (89–19) to abstain from expressing an opinion on this subject. The five delegates from Holland and Wisconsin Classes—Van Raalte; Cornelius Van der Meulen, and his two sons, Jacob and John; and John Karsten—were among the nineteen nay votes. The next year, the classes of Holland and Wisconsin—the latter led by John Karsten of the Alto church—overtured General Synod 1868 again to condemn Freemasonry. The body decided by the same margin (82–18) to take no action, but they agreed to refer the issue to a committee

---

[62] Letter of First Holland, Jan. 1867, quoted in minutes, Hope Church, 13 Mar. 1867, trans. Nella Kennedy.
[63] The exchange is quoted in full in Parr, *Hope Church*, 55-57. The controversy is best covered by Boonstra, *Dutch Equation*; Bruins and Swierenga, *Family Quarrels*, 108-33.
[64] Kennedy, *Commentary*, 17 Apr. 1867, 3:1108-11.

for further consideration. This is the classic method of burying a problematic issue.[65]

Van Raalte believed so strongly in rooting out Freemasonry that, in November 1867, he traveled to Aurora, Illinois, northwest of Chicago, to attend a meeting of the National Christian Convention, a joint effort of Methodist, United Brethren, Presbyterian, Congregationalist, and Baptist denominations to oppose secret societies. The conferees heard former Freemasons describe the despotic, antirepublic threat to civil society and God's church posed by that society. According to Van Raalte's published report, the conferees agreed to oppose the lodge "in a united Christian way, by public meetings and discussion, and through the press." They planned for a national conference in Pittsburgh in 1868 to entreat God "to free the land from these secret societies." Van Raalte served on the national board, along with Wheaton College's first president, Jonathan Blanchard.[66]

In 1870 General Synod, in response to yet another missive from the Classis of Wisconsin, conceded that membership in the lodge was a "serious evil in the church," but it was not grounds for placing under discipline confessing members in good standing. To do so, synod declared, "would be to establish a new and unauthorized test of membership in the Christian church, and would interfere with consistorial prerogatives."[67]

After this defining statement by General Synod that condoned Freemasons as confessing members, Van Raalte reconsidered his previously strong condemnation and brought his thinking into line with denominational policy. He concluded that lodge membership was sinful only if "it led to a moral offense condemned in Scripture." The society, he averred, was merely a "childish secret," and the mutual aid it practiced was "commendable." Childish, yes, but sinful per

---

[65] Minutes, First Holland, 22 Oct., 20 Nov. 1866, 4 Feb., 12 Apr. 1867; *Acts and Proceedings*, 1868, 461-63; 1869, 551, 622; Bruins and Swierenga, *Family Quarrels*, 112-16; Kennedy, *Commentary*, 17 Apr. 1867, 3:1408-11, 1415, 1440; 15 Apr. 1868, 3:1475-76 (quote summarizing synod's response); 16 Sept. 1868, 3:1504-11; 21 Apr. 1869, 3:1519. Kennedy leaves Van Schelven's lodge membership ambiguous. Van Schelven later was able to transfer his baptized membership to the new Third Reformed Church, on condition that he resign his membership in the lodge. He supposedly capitulated but likely remained a Freemason until his death.

[66] Van Raalte report, Chicago, 2 Nov. 1867, in *De Hope*, 20 Nov. 1867, trans. Nella Kennedy; *De Bazuin*, 24 Apr. 1868 (www.delpher.nl, accessed July 2021).

[67] Kennedy, *Commentary*, 2 Apr. 1869, 3:1518-19; *Acts and Proceedings*, 1870, 96-97. On the RPDC position, see Kennedy, *Commentary*, 26 Sept. 1853, 1:390-91. For an erudite defense of General Synod, see Bruggink, "Extra-Canonical Tests."

se, no.[68] The dominee actually had little firsthand experience with this secret society since he had never ministered in western New York where the Anti-Masonic political party had emerged in the mid-1840s. He understood the lodge's humanist philosophy but not its undemocratic character and relationship with shopkeepers, businessmen, professionals, and even clerics, privileged by fellow brothers. Essentially, Van Raalte surrendered the biblical ground he had held over his entire ministry in hopes of preserving church unity. Loyalty to the church took precedence over his long antipathy to the lodge.

Van Raalte in 1873 reiterated his newfound acceptance of lodge members in the church. His successor at First Church, Rev. Roelof Pieters, and the consistory moved to excommunicate two members for joining the "sinful" lodge. This brought the ex-pastor to his feet, and he spoke at length. "Membership in the Freemasons is not, in itself an adequate reason to excommunicate a person. For that, there would need to be sins committed because of membership in the Freemasons, such as, breaking the moral law. Otherwise, Classis will never give its approval, and I, for one, will oppose such action as long as I can," he declared defiantly. When the issue reached classis, Van Raalte warned the brethren: "Do not make foolish decisions."[69]

At Van Raalte's insistence, the First Church consistory convened a special meeting together with representatives of the Classis of Holland to reconsider the matter. But after a long discussion, "No contra-argument could help in the differences between the chairman [Rev. Pieters] and the brother committee member [Rev. Van Raalte]. Hence, the discussion was closed without resolution." One Freemason recanted and transferred his baptized membership to Third Church, but the other did not and was excommunicated "in harmony with the previous decision." His wife then transferred her confessing membership to Hope Church, where her husband also presumably could freely worship. Van Raalte, now an aging parishioner, could no

---

[68] Bruins and Swierenga, *Family Quarrels*, 115-16; Bruins, *Americanization of a Congregation*, 32, quoting Dosker, *Van Raalte*, 301, trans. Dekker; Kennedy (ibid., 17 Apr. 1861, 2:1045) cites "The Story as Told by Gysbert Haan Himself," in *One Hundredth Anniversary, 1857-1957*, 7-8.

[69] Minutes, First Holland, 14 Mar., 25 Apr., 23 May, 8 Aug., 26 Sept., 13 Oct. 1873; Classis of Holland, 3-4 Sept. 1879, quoted in *De Hollander*, 23 Sept. 1879; Kommer Schaddelee, "Not Listening to the Timely Advice of the Late Rev. A. C. Van Raalte" (3-part article), *De Grondwet*, 5, 12, 19 Oct. 1886, trans. Buursma; Dosker, *Van Raalte*, 301.

longer dictate policy at First Church. Before Van Raalte's death in November 1876, the consistory put another member under discipline for the "sin of apostasy" for being a committed Freemason.[70]

Death spared Van Raalte from seeing the culmination of this issue. In 1880, because of great agitation in the immigrant churches, General Synod carefully revisited the Freemasonry matter and reaffirmed its stance, much to the dismay of the classes of Holland and Wisconsin. Two years later, in 1882, every congregation in the Midwest, including First Church, was rent by schism, and in the next two years, ten thousand members and a number of prominent pastors withdrew from the Reformed Church in America. Most joined what (after 1890) would be called the Christian Reformed Church whose congregations had banned lodge members from the beginning but officially by synodical decree in 1867. Witnessing this third major schism in 1882, after those of 1834 and 1857, would have torn Van Raalte's heart out. After the fallout, some who agreed with Van Raalte called up his ghost and quoted his defiant 1873 statement.[71]

The Freemasonry schism also caused a great discord within the Van Raalte family because Teunis Keppel, Mina's second husband, led the charge as president of the First Church consistory. He held the key that locked out the minority members who, as the continuing First Reformed Church, after a lengthy but failed court battle over the property, erected a new edifice on Ninth Street at Central Avenue, facing the majority members at the church with the pillars on Ninth Street at College Avenue. The Masonic troubles at First Church pushed out five of the seven Van Raalte siblings, and the "English" Hope Church pulled them in, except for Helena Van Raalte, who remained in the continuing First Reformed Church. Only Mina Van Raalte and her husband, Teunis Keppel, went with the seceding majority, who in 1884 asked to affiliate with what would soon be the Christian Reformed Church as the Ninth Street congregation.[72]

Ending a "hurtful situation"

Van Raalte's distress call for pulpit relief prompted several dozen members living on the southeastern county line (now Ottagon Street)

---

[70] Minutes, First Holland, 28 Apr., 15, 19 May, 11 Aug. 1874, 1 June 1875, 18 Apr., 2 May 1876.
[71] Bruins and Swierenga, *Family Quarrels*, 116-35; Boonstra, *Dutch Equation*, 19-28; Schaddelee, *De Grondwet*, 19 Oct. 1886.
[72] Bruins et al., *Albertus and Christina*, 71-79, 105-8.

to consider forming a congregation. Shortly before Van Raalte went overseas, these members met with him and elder Teunis Keppel and cited the problems of distance and overcrowding at First Church.

First Church had more serious problems than a lack of seating. The routine consistory report at the April 1867 classis on its spiritual condition exposed a schismatic spirit. Van Raalte was accused of being a "pusher of universal grace," neglectful of church discipline, and affiliated with a church that "no longer stands for the truth." These charges, he lamented, "give birth to groanings and should deeply humble us as a judgment on God's house." Much of these "deeply deplorable... abominations," he continued, were coming from preachers in the Netherlands who are "wholly unacquainted" with the "Christian churches in this land." The Gronings-Drents party, Van Raalte's old nemesis, had long arms, all strengthened by the Freemasonry issue.[73]

The old dominee was clearly at the end of his rope. At fifty-six years of age, and after twenty strenuous years as pastor of First Church, he absolutely must retire. He was well past the average male life expectancy in the 1870s of forty-three years. Classis recognized the situation and gave permission to form "out of the bosom of the congregation" two new congregations, one on the "town line" and one in the city, and to "give freedom for the calling of ministers." If only Van Raalte had sought a call in his naturalized nation, such as in Kalamazoo, Muskegon, or Pella, instead of looking to South Africa, he might have enjoyed another ten years of effective ministry.[74]

At the July 26, 1867, consistory meeting, Van Raalte opened with prayer and then dropped the bombshell—a lengthy statement that "flows out of a total conviction"—that change was needed. Apparently, the reluctance of the consistory to obtain an assistant, as Van Raalte had requested for months, dictated the need for a formal statement, which he first shared with the consistory and then with the entire congregation.

His statement, as summarized by the clerk, read in part:

> He finds himself compelled to make an end to this hurtful situation in which the congregation has for too long found itself in its relationship to him. Because of the manifold activities which he, through God's providence, is involved in, it has been impossible

---

[73] Kennedy, *Commentary*, 17 Apr. 1867, 3:1432-33.
[74] Minutes, First Holland, 4 Mar., 1, 12 Apr. 1867; Kennedy, *Commentary*, 17 Apr. 1867, 3:1408. https://www.statista.com.

for him, particularly now as his bodily strength is failing, to do for the church what he would dearly desire and which they also deserve to have.

Now that the congregation is to be divided, one would think that one part of the church will receive more profit from his labors, but that cannot happen, and as a consequence, new disappointments have arisen. The Rev. declares that for this reason, after mature reflection, he is forced for the welfare of the people that also this part of the congregation [First Church] must begin the process of calling a pastor. . . . In any event, a formal dissolution does not need to take place because there has never been a formal connection [the church had not called him in 1847]. . . . The only thing required is that each congregation should call a pastor in the normal fashion. . . . This will mean that the pastor [Van Raalte] will have opportunity to continue to utilize his time and strength on behalf of his people, without hindrances currently existing.[75]

The "hurtful situation" frankly characterized his two decades of ministry among often cantankerous parishioners who harped at his leadership, demanded 110 percent of his time, and seldom paid his full salary. The statement also hinted at the reluctance of the congregation to make the major changes of calling a new pastor and spawning daughter churches. The charter members of Ebenezer Reformed Church, the church on the county line, took the initiative and with the blessing of classis formally organized.[76]

Ebenezer Church did not relieve the pressure on First Church, which had grown to one thousand souls. The addition of a balcony in 1864 bought a few more years. Even the loss in 1865 of a few families to the Market Street (later Central Avenue) Christian Reformed Church did not alleviate the space problem. The seating shortage drove up bids at the annual pew auction, which drew bitter complaints. The best solution was to form another Dutch-speaking congregation in the city, as Van Raalte had recommended, and the membership agreed at its

---

[75] Minutes, First Holland, 26 July 1867. Van Raalte customarily referred to himself in the third person.

[76] Minutes, First Holland, 25 Feb., 6, 13, 27 Mar., 5 June 1866, 25 Feb. 1867; Kennedy, *Commentary*, 17 Apr. 1867, 3:1433; Ebenezer Reformed Church, *One Hundred Twenty-Fifth Anniversary, 1866-1991*; *Acts and Proceedings*, 1867, 209; *De Bazuin*, 15 Feb. 1867 (www.delpher.nl, accessed July 2021). Van Raalte preached at the dedication of the Ebenezer edifice and later at the ordination service of the first pastor, Arie C. Kuiper, a Pella elder he had recommended for the ministry.

December 1866 annual meeting. The consistory appointed elders Isaac Cappon and Jacob Labots to canvass the congregation, but they found few families willing to be the nucleus of the new church. Another knotty problem was financial. First Church still carried a building debt and would need to fund a parsonage, and the new city church would also need an edifice and a parsonage. First Church agreed to give the new church $1,000 ($19,200 today) or one-third of an estimated $3,000 for their building. They borrowed the remainder.[77]

The First Church consistory resolved the issue by drawing an arbitrary geographic line at Market Street (Central Avenue); members living west must join the proposed Third Church, and those living east may remain at First Church. The membership at a special congregational meeting in September 1867 reluctantly approved the unpopular plan. The result was a Dutch-speaking Reformed Church on both the east and west sides. A week later, Third Church was organized with ninety-seven charter members—267 souls. Many were faculty at Holland Academy and Hope College, which earned for Third Church a reputation as the college church. Hope [Second] Church, because of its name, was often mislabeled as the college church, but only one Hope Church charter member had a college affiliation—Margaret Jordan Phelps—and her four children. Rev. Phelps' membership was held by the classis, as is standard practice in the Reformed Church.[78]

In August 1867, under Van Raalte's guidance, First Church began the calling process, but not in the usual way. Instead of the consistory forming a trio, they left "the matter in God's providence and the free choice of the congregation." This required a lengthy voting process at the congregational meeting. First, every member suggested candidates, and then multiple ballots winnowed the slate to the three with the highest votes: Roelof Pieters at Alto, Wisconsin, a graduate of the Holland Academy who had formerly served the Drenthe church; Peter De Pree at the Pella Church; and Johannes H. Donner at the Christian Separated Church in Leiden, in the Netherlands. Donner, an able preacher, received the call. He was a Van Raalte protégé, having studied at the Arnhem seminary. The dominee's hand was in this "free" call, even to the point of raising the proffered salary by $200 to $1,000 annually. It would cost another $1,000 in overseas travel costs for Donner's large family. Worrisome was the fact that only two-thirds of the required members were present. Donner declined the call, as he

---

[77] Minutes, First Holland, 29 Nov., 4, 12, 18, 31 Dec. 1866.
[78] Bruins, *Americanization of a Congregation*, 9-10; Parr, *Hope Church*, 12-13.

had done with a call from the Pella church in 1859. Some members were doubtless relieved to be spared the extra expense.[79]

The consistory in late November 1867 formed a second trio of Pieters; Adrian Zwemer at South Holland, Illinois, who had previously served the Vriesland congregation; and Engelbert Christian Oggel (brother of Van Raalte's son-in-law), who had served the North Holland church and was editor of *De Hope*. Pieters received the call, but this time, fewer than half of the voting members attended, which suggested great disquietude in the body. Pieters sent another *bedank brief* (thanks, but no thanks) letter. Throughout these months of anticipation and disappointment, Van Raalte continued to lead the consistory and chair congregational meetings, but it was not going well. The December consistory meeting was his last, but he continued to preach in the morning service until early 1868 when he left on his scouting trip to found a new colony in the South (ch. 15).[80]

In January 1868, Van Raalte was distracted by a fire in the home of son Albertus and Helena on East Sixteenth Street that started in the roof and burned the house to the ground, leaving the family with only the clothes on their backs. Heating and cooking with wood made house fires all too common, but the house was quickly rebuilt. Two days after the fire, Van Raalte left on his southern exploration for a new colony. In late 1869, however, Bertus abandoned his pregnant wife and four children and was never heard from again. Whether the financial setback of the fire or business troubles (ch. 12) drove him over the edge is impossible to say, but he was somewhat impetuous. As the namesake of father and grandfather, his scandalous act was the "talk of the town."[81]

Since Helena was essentially a widow, the senior Van Raaltes took her and her children in. The timing was providential because Helena could help care for her ailing mother-in-law and cook and clean house for the dominee and Ben and Dirk, their two unmarried sons. In 1870 Van Raalte deeded the Sixteenth Street property to Helena and Bertus, should he return home, as everyone had fervently hoped. In late April 1871, Helena's house burned down again and was again rebuilt at the dominee's expense. On June 30, 1871, Christina died, and Helena

---

[79] Minutes, First Holland, 13, 22 Aug., 2, 11 Sept. 1867.
[80] Ibid., 26 (consistory), 28 (congregational) Nov., 4 (congregational), 23 Dec. 1867, 21 Feb., 24 Apr. 1868.
[81] *De Hope*, 15 Jan. 1868; Bruins et al., *Albertus and Christina*, 68-69; Van Raalte bill from Pauels, Van Putten & Co., Proprietors of Plugger Mills, 29 Nov. 1873, HHA.

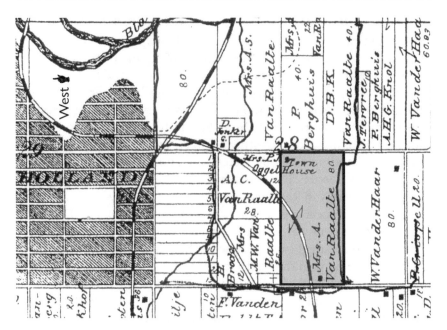

Eighty-acre farm of Helena (Mrs. Albertus) Van Raalte (shaded), bounded by present-day Eighth Street on the north, Sixteenth Street on the south, and Hoover Blvd. on the east, now bisected by the railroad and part of Pilgrim Home Cemetery. The Holland Town[ship] House occupied the far northwestern corner. *(1868 Holland Township plat)*

moved back to her own home. The dominee provided food for Helena and her five minor children. He was feeding an army. In 1873 his flour bill alone at Plugger Mills for sixteen hundred pounds over ten months totaled $95 ($2,400 today). This whopping bill was just for flour, not meat, vegetables, or other food, besides clothing, household expenses, and real estate taxes.[82]

Meanwhile, the calling process at First Church dragged on. In February 1868, the congregation approved a third trio, again using the free process. Days before the meeting, the elders learned that a local pastor had received a personal letter from Rev. Donner hinting that he might entertain a second call. With this encouraging news, the

---

[82] This 1871 fire is documented in *Excelsiora* (Hope College student newspaper), 5 June 1871. *De Hollander* and *De Grondwet* back files were lost in the Holland Fire of 8-9 Oct. 1871. *De Hope* made no mention of the house fire. Van Raalte donated the property, "except for the railroad right of way," to Mrs. Helena Van Raalte, on 16 Dec. 1871 (Swierenga, "Real Estate Sales," citing book 17, 119, Ottawa County deed registers).

members put him on the ballot and chose him by a large majority. This time, two-thirds of the voting members attended, up from fewer than half at the previous meeting. When Donner declined again, the consistory decided to pause in the calling process and wait "for some clear direction coming to us in the way of God's providence."[83]

In late April 1868, after Van Raalte had returned from a three-month Dixie scouting trip, the consistory, in desperate need of his leadership in the beleaguered calling process, offered to continue to pay his salary as long as the pulpit was vacant. The offer was couched in glowing terms. The minutes read: "This decision was taken out of the conviction that we have a responsibility, and at the same time, we will be giving a token of our esteem and love for the manifold services given to this and the other congregations of our colony." Why do parishioners wait to show appreciation to a dominee after he has left their pulpit?

In this case, the warm gesture had the desired effect. Van Raalte entered the May consistory meeting in progress and "assumed the chair." The brothers narrowed the list from eleven to two—Pieters and Oggel, in that order. It was not uncommon in those days to call the same minister more than once, sometimes even three times. The congregation, again in a free vote, elected the trio of Pieters, Oggel, and Van Raalte. The retired dominee immediately requested "not to be included in the vote," and the name of Rev. Johannes Brummelkamp (Van Raalte's nephew), of Tiel, Gelderland, was substituted. Two weeks later, the congregation gathered to vote on the trio, and Brummelkamp received the most votes, with Pieters a close second. Amazingly, one member insisted on voting for Van Raalte, who chaired the meeting.[84]

By January 1869, more than a year after the calling process had begun, Dominee Van Raalte was still deeply entwined in congregational affairs, including discipline cases, academy funding matters, and writing the letter of call to Johannes Brummelkamp, who also declined. In August the consistory settled on the fourth trio—Pieters, Oggel, and Hermanus Stobbelaar—with Pieters of Alto, Wisconsin, getting the call by a large majority. Pieters accepted and was installed in early 1869, fully fifteen months after Van Raalte had officially retired. Van Raalte was relieved, to say the least.[85]

---

[83] Minutes, First Holland, 13 Jan., 4, 21 Feb., 7 Apr. 1868.
[84] Ibid., 24 Apr., 14, 28 May, 28 July, 13 Aug. 1868.
[85] Ibid., 26 Nov. 1868, 1 Jan. 1869.

The decade from 1857 to 1867 was a difficult transition period for Van Raalte. Major issues came one after another—Freemasonry; a church secession; unsuccessful harbor projects; a failed parochial school; religious squabbles over hymns, infant baptism, and terms of consistory members; the stillborn missionary ship; a political revolution and Civil War; the city of Holland charter fight; his and Christina's declining health; family problems; and overstaying his pulpit at First Church. The troubles masked a generational transition. No longer was his leadership essential to survival, as in the early colonial years, and his authority and unilateral decisions were increasingly challenged by new leaders. The transition was a natural progression, but tensions were heightened by the dominee's involvement in local political, business, educational, and economic matters. Elton Bruins, who spent a lifetime studying Van Raalte, admitted that Van Raalte's role in community affairs by 1860 was "perhaps more than was right for him at this point."[86] Van Raalte himself had recognized this problem, but he found it impossible to pull back. He chose to "flee forward," as Netherlanders would say, setting aside old problems and taking on new ones. He was a born leader who could not lay down his burdens until life itself ebbed.

---

[86] Bruins and Schakel, *Envisioning Hope College*, 70.

CHAPTER 15

Ministry in Retirement: "May God give me strength."

At age fifty-six, Van Raalte in 1867 retired from the First Church pulpit because of ill health and exhaustion, but he hardly freed himself from active service. Visions of missions to build Christ's kingdom on earth drove him on. He planted another colony a thousand miles away, solicited endowment gifts as president of the Hope College council, and accepted church assignments in education and missions as far away as the frontier in Kansas. Instead of rest for the weary, he chose action, even in recognizing that his own health was deteriorating. He could not help himself; the traveling man could not slow down. But a year out of harness, he came down with

> rheumatic fevers in a horrible way; my whole system is terribly shaky. I never experienced it in such an unmitigated form. Life became a burden; if such spells must return, they will make me a perfect wreck.... But my hands are full, especially watching my wife, my anxieties increase, and yet I am hoping."[1]

---

[1] Van Raalte to Phelps, 30 Aug. 1870, in Bruins and Schakel, *Envisioning Hope College*, 259.

But the couple had returned from the Netherlands in 1866 to pursue his dream to plant a new colony in the South, even though Christina's health could not tolerate another move. So Van Raalte did recover and carry on.

Preaching and church planting

Van Raalte's lengthy sojourn abroad sparked anew his passion for missions, church planting, and fundraising for Hope College's endowment. In July 1867, before his retirement from First Church became a reality, on short notice, he wrote a sermon at the behest of the Classis of Holland for the National Day of Prayer for Crops and Industry that President Andrew Johnson had declared. That the nation would set aside a day for prayer impressed the dominee. "The humbling and public recognition of God by an entire nation is something uplifting," he declared. But he missed the school children at the Wednesday morning service and chastised their parents. "It is very damaging that parents send their children to school instead of taking them along to the house of prayer." Better to pray than to study for a day.[2]

In fall 1867 the Classis of Holland appointed Van Raalte chair of its new mission committee, and he gladly traveled to encourage congregations and fundraise for Hope at Fulton, Illinois; Forestville (Fillmore County), Minnesota; and Milwaukee and Racine, Wisconsin, preaching every Sunday along the way. In June 1868, he attended General Synod in New York, and in August, he traveled to churches in Fairview, Bushnell, and Pekin, Illinois, and raised more than $1,200 for the college endowment. A month later, he was in Virginia. No moss grew under Van Raalte's feet.[3]

He also found time to reach out to the six hundred non-Dutch residents of Holland. He held brief Sunday afternoon services in English in private homes. He could finally preach in English after twenty years in America, provided he kept his sermons short and simple. The services drew a Catholic family of ten, newcomers from Racine, Wisconsin, whose granddaughter later joined Hope Church because it was "better than no religion." In Van Raalte's lifetime, no Catholic worship took

---

[2] Van Raalte sermon draft, 17 Apr. 1867, trans. Nella Kennedy, HMA.
[3] Minutes, Fulton [IL] Reformed Church, 29 Sept. 1867; Van Raalte report to Peter Oggel, *De Hope*, 23 Oct. 1867, trans. Nella Kennedy; *De Hope*, 16 Oct. 1867 (quote); Van Raalte to Phelps, 14 Aug., 1868, in *Envisioning Hope College*, 184-88; *Holland City News*, 30 Nov. 1872.

place in Holland. The bitter wars of religion in Europe still resonated, and Reformed people did not readily welcome Catholics.[4]

Secession of 1857 revisited

In retirement, Van Raalte could not escape the continuing controversy of the Union of 1850 when Gysbert Haan, a leading antagonist, in 1871, published a lengthy apologia, *Stem van een belasterde* (Voice of one slandered) for the True Brothers. Haan levied charges of heterodoxy against the Reformed Church in America that Van Raalte in his 1866 address at the Amsterdam synod had declared to be confessionally orthodox. Van Raalte drafted a blistering response that slammed the "circuses" of slander of the "living dead brother De Haan [Haan]." He and his fellow critics

> made my heart and hands limp, and caused my soul to bleed and to cover my face with shame and embarrassment.... For me who vitally remembers the accumulated accusations of embezzlement and those against my sermons on blackmail of the last years of our settlement hardly needs to point out such persistent suspicions published in print.... O, should I now grieve as a retired man ... who stands ready at any instant to leave this circus.... It was ever and only the cold shoulder. Cold shoulder! I myself, the first departing minister, felt it as one feels trying on sleeves.

But this bitter lament of a man who sees his end should not be taken as his last word. His financial dealings were always honest and above board, and charges of cheating and blackmail are not supported by his extensive financial records.[5]

In the heart of his response, Van Raalte defended his joining the Christian Separated Church in 1836 after he was rejected for ministry by national church leaders. "I stand in a historic relationship that rejects breaking off from the Hervormde Kerk," he insisted. The provincial synod was "hostile to reconciliation, and I was given flatly

---

[4] Jacobson et al., *Dutch Leader*, 207, citing Maxine Hopkins Robbert's account from her father, in *Hope Church Historical Booklet*, 1982; Kennedy, *Concise History*, 309-13. Only three Catholic families lived in Holland in 1860 and six families in 1870. Later, more families dribbled in from Ireland, Germany, Poland, and the Netherlands. They met in homes for informal worship until 1883, when priests from Grand Rapids brought the sacraments. In 1903 St. Francis de Sales Church was organized (Swierenga, *Holland, Michigan*, 1:330-36).

[5] Haan, *Stem van een Belasterde*.

to understand that I would never be allowed to preach . . . [in] the church of my godly parents. . . . I commend her purpose and I believe in her mission." Thus, forced to be a Separatist, he became "a victim of stoning, quartering [soldiers], fines, and imprisonment." He continued: "No wonder, then, that we can be so sectarian and that our heart can be warmed if we here in the Reformed Church, recognizing the language of faith, thirst for spiritual life and struggle for orthodoxy." In short, Van Raalte made no apology for his irenic spirit and for his church affiliations. He blamed all his religious troubles on immigrants who brought "the same friction . . . by the Trojan horse in their own bosoms."[6]

He continued:

> If the unification with that church [in 1850] is judged to have been a false step, we bring that false step before the door of that large body, the Chr. Afgescheiden Geref. Kerk in the Netherlands. It is the fruit of her having closed her eyes to [us] and given [us] a cold shoulder.[7]

The American dominee was understandably frustrated that the Separatist church that had ordained him was siding with the Anti-Masonic True Brothers, but to blame them and not take any personal responsibility for this outcome reveals a man who was "tired, sick, cranky, and pessimistic." The energetic, optimistic pastor on two continents was no more. His signal contribution, the successful colony in West Michigan, had turned against him.[8]

Even Abraham Kuyper's newspaper, *De Standaard*, which embodied the principles of his Réveil hero, Groen van Prinsterer, failed to buoy Van Raalte's spirits. He warned Kuyper not to "expect too many subscribers from here because everybody is drowning in periodicals." The effort was praiseworthy, nonetheless. "Brother, God entrusts you with much. . . . I hope that the reality and the majesty of the things of God's kingdom may preserve your heart and make you happy and effective in your work." He closed with a word of personal advice.

---

[6] Van Raalte draft letter (1875), HHA. It can be assumed that he sent a rewritten copy and kept the draft.
[7] Van Raalte draft letter 1874 (?), HHA.
[8] The quote in *Envisioning Hope College*, 328, captures the spirit of Van Raalte's letter to Phelps of 17 May 1873, in which he expressed his anger that his church embraced public over Christian education, thus dashing his dream for parochial schools.

"Although I compliment you on your work, let me say this: don't work yourself to death, don't cripple yourself. Get enough sleep and take a vacation."[9] If Kuyper replied, the letter has been lost. But this comment proves the old adage: "It takes one to know one." Van Raalte to his detriment never lived by his own admonition.

In Dixie—Amelia Colony, Virginia[10]

When Van Raalte resigned as pastor of First Church, he claimed to need "surcease from strife within the church and the community." But he failed to seize it. He was a driven man who could not rest, even when his doctor, wife, and children urged him to take his ease and enjoy his five grandchildren. "I thirst after an opportunity to free myself of these annoyances," he confided to Phelps, "and to devote myself entirely to the Kingdom of God." That work turned out to be planting a colony in a small southern town more than eight hundred miles from Holland, in Amelia Court House, Virginia. Land was cheap there, as it had been in Holland two decades earlier, and the end of the Civil War saw a new wave of Dutch immigrants seeking low-priced land. "The future of Dutch emigration," he insisted, "rested on this work of mission," namely, to plant colonies with churches and Christian schools where fertile farmland awaits.[11]

But Van Raalte was torn. "It seems to me impossible to define the time of living at Holland or Virginia. Both call me, although the East seems to be the main field of labor. . . . I am somewhat dependent on my wife's choice."[12] Her health clearly dictated that he stay in Holland as the honored pioneer leader. Yet he decided otherwise, even at the expense of her health and wishes. Unfortunately, this had been a pattern throughout his married life, to make his wife play second fiddle to his own aspirations. The old gentleman with waning energy failed to see the obstacles that would ultimately make this venture a failure. He also forgot the clear and discerning advice in 1847 of Michigan congressman Charles Stuart, that "Southern states are

---

[9] Van Raalte to Abraham Kuiper (Kuyper), 4 July 1872, HHA. The paper was launched on April 1.
[10] The definitive history is Sheeres, *The Not-So-Promised Land*, which includes detailed genealogical information on virtually every family in the colony.
[11] Van Raalte, "Colonization and Education," *De Hope*, 13 Oct. 1869, trans. Simone Kennedy, HMA.
[12] Van Raalte to Phelps, 15 July 1869, in *Envisioning Hope College*, 197; Nyenhuis and Jacobson, *A Dream Fulfilled*, 87-88.

mortally unhealthful for the stranger," due to yellow fever, and they "are worse for growing wheat."[13]

Amelia was not on Van Raalte's radar when in early January 1868 he left on a three-month trip to Dixie to scout sites for a Dutch settlement in the war-ravaged region. He knew that the war's end would set off a greater immigration wave than in the 1840s. Farmland was cheap in the South, and immigrants from the homeland or already in America could take advantage of the opportunity. At this same time, Jan Vogel, a Civil War veteran, also realized that high land prices in the Holland colony indicated that the time was ripe to found a daughter colony. He chose Vogel Center in Missaukee County, 136 miles to the north, which was largely cut-over timberland ready for farming. This area grew slowly into a thriving Dutch community, Holland's first daughter colony. Van Raalte in his correspondence never mentioned this venture; his eyes looked south, not north or west, to his detriment.[14] He was enamored by the southern strategy that General Synod and the Classis of Holland had adopted, to do educational and missionary work among freedmen and demoralized southern whites.[15]

Van Raalte stopped first in Detroit to attend the State Convention of Christians, one of dozens of gatherings of that ecumenical organization to spark revival fires. The European counterpart was the Evangelical Alliance. The twelve hundred attendees at the "instructive, encouraging and love-provoking" Detroit assembly, as the dominee described the event, were shocked to learn that Michigan had only seventy thousand confessing Christians, leaving an "enormous number of people to live without the church." Van Raalte "spoke for an hour on prayer meetings," presumably drawing on his experiences in the New York City revival and the Clapper revival in his own church. He was clearly enthralled with ecumenical assemblies that pushed missionary outreach.[16]

The Dutch dominee was warmly welcomed at his next stop, Chattanooga, Tennessee, but he bemoaned the rigors of travel "in remote corners and unknown streets" and sleeping "on hard beds with

---

[13] Van Raalte to Brummelkamp, 30 Jan. 1847, in *Holland in Amerika*, English typescript, 8, 27.
[14] Lucas, *Netherlanders*, 1955, 300-303.
[15] *De Hope*, 8 Jan. 1868; Kennedy, *Commentary*, 4 Sept. 1867, 3:1457-58; 15 Apr. 1868, 3:1479-80.
[16] Van Raalte to Peter Oggel, 17 Jan. 1868, published in *De Hope*, 29 Jan. 1868; *De Hope*, 15 Jan. 1868 reports. For the Evangelical Alliance, see Kennedy, *Commentary*, 20 Sept. 1865, 2:1320; 18 Apr. 1866, 2:1343-44, 1366.

few covers." He happily found not "one single bedbug in this shabby town." Otherwise, he wrote daughter Mina Oggel, "Mother would have come down to help me remove them." As to the friendly people, "God will do whatever pleases Him with the South—with me and the South."[17] His reconnaissance took him to Ashville, North Carolina; Selma, Alabama; Charleston, South Carolina; and finally Norfolk, Virginia, where he found this Atlantic seaport to be most promising.

He returned in mid-April 1868, having logged more than three thousand miles, convinced, mistakenly, he later realized, that "Southerners are very eager for emigrants to come and persuasive in their invitation. They know and love the Dutch more than I thought.... I am often told: 'We greatly prefer Dutch and Scottish immigrants,'" over the hated Yankees. Given ex-slaves and bitter white politics, Van Raalte deemed it essential that the Dutch not be scattered, but "come together to form communities." Without delay, he recruited Berend Veneklasen, Evert Sprik, and William Brouwer to go to Virginia and scout for a good site.[18]

Within a month of his southern trip, Van Raalte was again on the train to New York to attend General Synod as a classical representative. On the agenda were several issues of great importance for Holland—a resolution on Freemasonry, another on Phelps' proposals to allow Hope College to open a theological school and become a university, and an endorsement of an ecumenical agency. Van Raalte lost on the first two issues and was especially embittered when synod tabled the proposal for a western seminary. "I do not like my position here," he told Phelps. In the eyes of synod, "The West is somewhat a region on the moon; it is all uphill business." In a follow-up letter, Van Raalte lamented: "We are left in the cold.... A great number here could be won for the western interest, but the managers [of synod] know how to kill it."[19]

By mid-June 1868, the Virginia scouting party returned with news that they had settled on a forty-five-hundred-acre site thirty-six miles southwest of Richmond, the state capitol, at Amelia Court House along the Appomattox River, which was for sale on credit terms for only twelve dollars per acre. Although Van Raalte, always harbor minded, preferred an area near Norfolk harbor, he wrote a report for *De*

[17] Van Raalte to Mina Oggel, 29 Jan. 1868, trans. Simone Kennedy, HHA.
[18] Sheeres, *The Not-So-Promised Land*, 10, citing *De Hope*, 1, 15, 29 Apr., 3 June 1868; Van Raalte to Peter and Mina Oggel, 15 Apr. 1868, published in *De Hope*, 29 Apr. 1868 (quote), trans. Simone Kennedy.
[19] *Acts and Proceedings*, 1868, 461, 463, 480-83; Van Raalte speech at Synod, June 1868, HHA; Van Raalte to Phelps, 5, 8, 10, 11 June 1868 (quotes), HHA.

Hope, titled "Southern Settlements" that urged Dutch immigrants and second-generation Hollanders to farm in Amelia County.

In typical booster fashion, Van Raalte wrote glowingly: "We want and desire to see the Dutch, their language and their churches flourish in this open and uncultivated region, with such a favorable climate, so rich in raw materials, and so near the Atlantic Ocean. The occasion is too good to let go."

Frisians would appreciate the great need for dairies and general farmers the red clay soil. But Van Raalte neglected to mention that the soil in the area was depleted by years of tobacco growing on slave plantations. Emigrants could take passage from Bremen, Amsterdam, or Rotterdam to Baltimore, disembark at Norfolk, and board the Richmond & Danville Railroad to Amelia via Richmond. Brummelkamp and several other pastors signed ads promoting Van Raalte's new colony. The dominee promised to reimburse emigrants for the train fare from Norfolk to Richmond.[20]

Immigrants from the Netherlands were Van Raalte's main target, and he recruited more than half of Amelia's sixty-five families from there. The remainder came from West Michigan and the Chicago area. That he convinced fifteen extended families, about eighty people, from Fillmore Township to follow him seems to belie Dosker's statement that local folks "had no faith" in his venture.[21]

Just when grandchildren were beginning to arrive, and the couple could enjoy the comforts of home and community, Christina had to move to the Amelia colony. No longer with the resilience of youth, she found that the relocation to salubrious climes failed to benefit her. The family with daughters Mary and Anna arrived in Amelia Court House in August 1869 to find a lack of decent housing. They temporarily rented a run-down farm with a dilapidated house, neither of which was appealing. Albertus happily purchased the 182-acre Court House properties, part of railroad lands for sale by Lewis E. Harvie, president of the Richmond & Danville Railroad and secretary of the Virginia Agricultural Society. The property contained a shabby house, a tavern, and other buildings.[22]

---

[20] Van Raalte, "Southern Settlements," 20 June 1868, in *De Hope*, 24 June, 21 Oct. 1868; *De Heraut*, 4 Dec. 1868, 12 Feb. 1869, www.delpher.nl (accessed June 2021).
[21] Sheeres, *Not-So-Promised Land*, xiii, 20-27; Dosker, *Van Raalte*, 290.
[22] Van Raalte to Phelps, 23 Sept. 1868, in *Envisioning Hope College*, 190-91; Deed, 30 Nov. 1869, John G. Jefferson and wife Aletia and Thomas T. Giles to A. C. Van Raalte, filed in Amelia County Courthouse. Sheeres, in *The Not-So-Promised Land*, 11-12, uncovers and documents Harvie as the seller. Lucas, *Netherlanders*, 309-10,

Amelia County, Virginia, Dutch settlements

Expecting the move to Virginia to be permanent, Van Raalte asked *De Hope* to inform readers that henceforth all correspondence to him should be addressed: "Care of General J. D. Imboden, corner of Main & 10th St., Richmond, Virginia." John D. Imboden, a lawyer and Democrat politician, was a former Confederate general, small-time slaveholder, and Freemason. Van Raalte ignored those negatives in the interest of establishing the colony.[23]

Van Raalte began worship services in various homes. "The first three Sundays, I preached for this small flock with much delight," he told Peter Oggel in a revealing letter. "I sensed the importance of this beginning for the future. It is such a meaningful matter to plant a church together with a settlement . . . [that] can save these stripped and depressed regions, and through them the population feels encouraged." Helping southern whites will also be a "powerful witness to the blacks," he added,

---

mistakenly states that Van Raalte purchased the property from Samuel Schieffelin, his wealthy New York friend.

[23] *De Hope*, 5 Aug. 1868. I am indebted to Earl Wm. Kennedy for this reference and for information on Imboden.

and encourage them to deal diligently with their time, to economize in household expenses, and form a close community because presently their religion does not benefit their life in society. Their religion is very passionate, and they often exhibit and make chaotic movements when worshiping. It is difficult to communicate sound beliefs and make them remember them. You find either impenetrable darkness or a religion that comes out in streams of words, which they themselves understand only partially, or are, at least, unable to communicate soundly.[24]

Christine Van Raalte Gilmore's critique was more specific:

Last night, Negroes held church services in the freight house at about seven o'clock. The freight house is right next to our place, so we got the full benefit. I never heard such a racket in all my life. Singing, laughing, praying, and screaming all at the same time. While the praying one would shout "Come in, Jesus," another would yell "Stand by my side, Hallelujah." Still another, "Come down by the railroad, Amen." "Bless man and woman and child." So it kept up the whole evening, and I can't describe it adequately.[25]

The Van Raaltes believed that blacks worshiped with wild abandon and held unsound beliefs.

The cultural gap was also wide, with southern whites, a "devastated people," who were friendlier than northerners but slovenly, uncouth, backward, and slow-paced in farming and work. Christine wrote brother Ben: "If you were to farm here, they would probably think that you were a wonder from heaven." They "take off their hats to a white person," just like peasants in the Netherlands doffed their hats to those of higher standing. The dominee described freedmen as "benevolent, friendly, fearful, . . . changeable, frivolous," easy going, and with "little domestic life. . . . I expect that they will unceasingly move south to the hot regions near the Gulf because they love to hunt and fish."[26]

---

[24] Van Raalte to Peter Oggel, 18 Sept. 1868, in *De Hope*, 30 Sept. 1868, trans. Simone Kennedy.
[25] Christine Gilmore to Ben Van Raalte, 31 May 1869, trans. Jalving, HHA.
[26] Van Raalte to Oggel, 6 Oct. 1868, trans. Simone Kennedy; Christine Van Raalte to brother Ben, 3 May 1869; Christina Van Raalte to brothers Ben and Dirk, 31 May 1869, all in HHA. These are her few letters to survive.

Surprisingly, the Van Raaltes after only three months, in October 1868, returned to Holland to spend the winter, before going back the next summer for what presumably would be the permanent move. In March 1869, Holland city council said goodbye with a resolution that expressed "deep regret for the removal of the founder of our City and Colony." The aldermen wished him well in his new venture and "cherished the hope that, although leaving his residence here, he will still retain his interest in the welfare and prosperity of his old home." Little did they, or he, know that they would soon be back. Van Raalte notarized son Dirk to manage his business affairs, and he charged his gardener to keep the garden and orchard. His frail health caused some misgivings. "I feel like an old man and walking is becoming very difficult for me. I miss my easy chair here," he confessed. Christina was bothered with rheumatism and night cramps and feared missing her children and grandchildren.[27]

The Van Raaltes were eager to return to Virginia because daughter Christine and her fiancé, William B. "Will" Gilmore, would join them and be married there by her father. Gilmore had accepted a call from the Mattoax Reformed Church as its missionary pastor under the auspices of the Classis of Holland. He also agreed to teach with Dr. Anson Du Bois in Amelia Institute, a preparatory school Van Raalte had established in the mold of Holland Academy. A native of Fairview, Illinois, Gilmore had taught five years at Holland Academy before completing the theological program at Hope College.[28] He expected to have equal billing at the institute with Du Bois who held an honorary doctorate from Union College. But Du Bois pulled rank, and Gilmore graciously accepted the lesser role. The third teacher was Mary (Maria) Van Raalte, the dominee's twenty-year-old daughter. None could speak Dutch, the language of the immigrant children, and the parochial school had to charge tuition, which immigrants could ill afford. So in 1870, the school had only fifty or sixty students. Du Bois left that summer for a pastorate, and Gilmore became the principal.[29]

[27] Power of Attorney, Albertus and Christina Van Raalte to Dirk D. K. Van Raalte, 31 Mar. 1869, Ottawa County Register of Deeds, book 2, 70-71; Resolution of Holland City Council, 25 Mar. 1869, HMA; Christine Van Raalte to brother Ben, 3 May 1869; Van Raalte to son Ben, 4 May 1869, both in HHA; Van Raalte letter in *Schenectady Evening Star*, 27 May 1869, reprinted in *Christian Intelligencer*, 10 June 1869.

[28] Bruins et al., *Albertus and Christina*, 148-49; Van Raalte to daughter Christina, 19 Oct. 1868; *Acts and Proceedings*, 1870, 104.

[29] Van Raalte to Phelps, 27 July 1870, in *Envisioning Hope College*, 253; Sheeres, *The Not-So-Promised Land*, 43-46; Gasero, *Historical Directory*, 113. Du Bois was the former secretary of Domestic Missions of the Reformed Church (1859-62).

William Brokaw Gilmore and Catharina (Christine) Van Raalte
(JAH)

Van Raalte married the Gilmores at Amelia Court House on July 14, 1869. Christine managed all the festivities; she was "a wonder in my eye," her father wrote. He gifted them with an astounding present—fifty building lots in the city of Holland, worth $15,000 ($336,500 today). The newlyweds honeymooned in the Appalachian Mountains. On their return to Virginia, Christine had to make do without a maid, much to her chagrin.[30]

A month before the wedding, Van Raalte made a quick trip to Philadelphia to attend General Synod, where the body elected him professor of evangelistic theology in the Theology Department of Hope College. The position was tailor made for the former seminary teacher, but he declined because of "insuperable reasons of situation and loss of strength." The situation was the pressing need to make the Amelia colony a success; the loss of strength came from "bowel, rheumatism troubles, and general disorder."[31]

By 1869 thirty-five families had settled at Amelia, the first of sixty-five families and fifteen single men who comprised the colony at its height. They spread across three settlements—Amelia Court House,

---

[30] Van Raalte to Phelps, 15 July 1869 (quote), HHA; Indenture, 15 Feb. 1870, Ottawa County Register of Deeds, book 10, 376.

[31] Van Raalte to Phelps, 12 June 1869, in *Envisioning Hope College*, 195; *Acts and Proceedings*, 1869, 647-48; 1870, 114-17; Wichers, *Century of Hope*, 65-67 (quote 66), 100.

Chula, and Mattoax—all within a nine-mile radius. Van Raalte's student, Seine Bolks, then serving the Zeeland congregation, agreed to organize the three congregations when he went east to raise money for the Hope College endowment.[32]

Gilmore served the Mattoax congregation of seventeen families with ninety-eight souls, and he assisted teaching elders in the smaller congregations at Amelia Court House (12 families with 57 souls) and Chula (12 families with 42 souls). Chula soon merged with Mattoax. These congregations in 1870 comprised forty-one families with 165 souls. That the True church did not plant a congregation in the colony dissuaded a number of families from settling there. Gilmore served at Mattoax for several years before returning to Holland to teach in the female academy of his alma mater. In 1885 the dwindling Mattoax and Amelia congregations, which had been transferred to the Classis of New York in 1873, merged into the Mattoax Presbyterian Church.[33]

From his first days in Virginia, Van Raalte raved about the colony, but he was also honest to point out problems—a region spoiled by slavery, with impoverished soils, a depressed economy, and stifling summer heat and humidity, albeit offset by mild winters and long growing seasons. "I rode my horse daily, and none of us were really bothered by the heat," he told Peter Oggel. In general, Van Raalte admitted:

> Slavery has spoiled this region, and the war impoverished everyone. On such large plantations are great lord's houses built, surrounded by Negro huts. Along the railroads, moreover, one sees little that can bear the name, little of what might be called farms. If conditions were different, there would be no need for new immigrants, and the land near railroads and cities could not be bought for $13 per acre.[34]

Van Raalte recruited settlers in three ways—letters and personal contacts; informative articles in *De Hope*, designed for clipping by

---

[32] Sheeres, *The Not-So-Promised Land*, 15; Van Raalte, "Colonization and Education," *De Hope*. 13 Oct. 1869, trans. Simone Kennedy, HMA; Kennedy, *Commentary*, 25 Aug. 1869, 3:1535-36.

[33] Sheeres, *The Not-So-Promised Land*, 52-62, makes a convincing case about the negative impact of denominational rivalry on the colony; Van Raalte, "Kolonizatie en Opvoeding," *De Hope*, 13 Oct. 1869.

[34] Van Raalte to Peter Oggel, 6 Oct. (quote) 1868, trans. Simone Kennedy, JAH; Van Raalte to J. G. ver Heulen, Netherlands, 3 Aug. 1869, trans. Seth Vander Werf, HMA.

editors of Dutch periodicals; and paid ads in Dutch newspapers.[35] Two letters to a prospective Netherlands family with twelve children are typical. "If you can begin something on your own, then I pray you, buy *little land and invest all possible money in milch cows*," Van Raalte advised. No wonder that fifty-two Frisian dairymen comprised three-quarters of the immigrant families. In all honesty, Van Raalte concluded, "as a Hollander and a Christian father," he would for the sake of the youth choose either Holland or Amelia. Both had Reformed churches and Christian schools, but Virginia's mild climate was preferable to Michigan's long, cold winters.[36]

The Bert De Haan family of four, along with thirty-six other families, fresh from the Netherlands, responded to the dominee's repeated urgings but found conditions far from rosy.

> Cannon balls were lying about, large buildings and homes in ruins, etc. There too were only a few white folks in that part of the country, mostly Negroes, who were overjoyed with their freedom. Naturally, food was scarce and prices high, and immigrant money was soon gone.

A major blow was a severe drought in 1870 that wiped out the harvest. This began a mass exodus of over-extended settlers who moved to other Dutch settlements, although some, like the De Haan family, returned to the homeland. After twelve years, however, the De Haans re-immigrated to Borculo, Michigan.[37]

Some who gave up had purchased, against Van Raalte's specific advice, far more land on mortgage than they could ever repay. One greedy immigrant paid $30,000 for 1,200 acres at $25 per acre, with $10,000 down and three years to pay $20,000 at 8 percent interest. "To make these payments," a young Peter Zuidema recalled years later,

> naturally proved as impossible as to fly to the moon on a wheelbarrow.... Some [who failed] ... vented their wrath on Dominie Van Raalte and, blaming him for their own mistakes, even threatened bodily harm. . . .The dissatisfied settlers raised so much ado about their disappointments that Dominie Van Raalte feared mob violence and went back to Holland.

[35] *Leeuwarder Courant*, 29 Jan. 1869.
[36] Van Raalte to J. J. Van Heulen, 3 Aug. 1869, 9 Mar. 1871, 3 Feb. 1873; Sheeres, *The Not-So-Promised Land*, 81-82.
[37] Emma (Mrs. Bert De Haan, nee Dykstra), 27 Feb. 1930; Sheeres, *The Not-So-Promised Land*, 19.

The dominee may have embellished the prospects of the area, but he was not responsible for greedy land buying and the disastrous drought that bankrupted farmers.[38] Unlike Zuidema, threats did not force Van Raalte to return to Holland. He never flinched from threats.

It was Christina who convinced Albertus to return to Holland before the end of the summer. Van Raalte wrote Phelps in early August 1869 that his wife's "mind is bend [sic] upon Michigan," and he needed to find money "somewhere" to return home.[39] Christina's health was the main reason; she could no longer care for her home and three adult children—Ben, Dirk, and Christine—without a housekeeper. Two other family concerns were also compelling. Peter Oggel, daughter Mina's husband, who was teaching at Hope College, was in the last stages of tuberculosis. And Helena Van Raalte needed a place to live with her five children since Bertus deserted them.[40] She would be Christina's helper. So after a mere three months in Amelia, they boarded the train back to Holland.[41]

The dominee was ready to take up his next challenge, the presidency of the Hope College council. To mark his return, merchant Aldert Plugger, a successful shipper and shipbuilder, named his new steel-hulled steamer, the *A. C. Van Raalte*. It was the first vessel in the Holland fleet to bear Van Raalte's name and the first to ply Lake Michigan waters under steam instead of sail.[42]

A year later, Van Raalte sold the Amelia Court House property that he had purchased in haste. Under duress to pay off the mortgage, he appealed to Schieffelin, who came to the rescue again, buying the property for $5,160 and making the dominee whole, much to his relief. The gracious Schieffelin told Gilmore, "I do not wish Dr. Van Raalte to have any responsibility or anxiety in the matter or be liable for one cent."[43] At the time, the dominee could not pay a $106 debt at the Van

---

[38] Peter Zuidema to Willard Wichers, 14 June 1941 (quote), Peter Zuidema Papers, HMA; "Peter Zuidema's Settlement in Virginia," in Lucas, *Dutch Immigrant Memoirs*, 2:292-93.
[39] Van Raalte to Phelps, early Aug. 1869, in Bruins and Schakel, *Envisioning Hope College*, 200.
[40] See ch. 14, under "Ending a 'hurtful situation.'"
[41] Van Raalte to Phelps, 10 Mar. 1870, in *Envisioning Hope College*, 243; Sheeres, *The Not-So-Promised Land*, 17; Bruins et al., *Albertus and Christina*, 68-69; Holland population census, June 1870.
[42] Swierenga, *Holland, Michigan*, 1:176, 714, 767-68; 2:1048-49.
[43] Gilmore to Van Raalte, 27 Mar. 1871; Schieffelin to Van Raalte, Indenture, 3 Apr. 1871; Schieffelin to Gilmore, 25 Mar. 1871, all in HHA.

Schelven store, and he pledged to pay interest on the bill and put up his home as collateral.[44]

In early August of 1871, five weeks after the death of his helpmeet in late June, Albertus as a widower returned to Virginia with daughter Mary (Maria), in hopes of salvaging his failing venture. On the way, the father-daughter pair arranged to meet at the Adams Hotel in Chicago with William Gilmore's sister Julia from Fairview, Illinois, son Ben's fiancé. (The couple wed a year later. This second Van Raalte-Gilmore marriage made family ties doubly strong and greatly pleased everyone). The threesome boarded a train in Chicago for Richmond and were warmly welcomed by Will and Christine Gilmore who had arranged lodging nearby with a Mr. Scott. The dominee enjoyed watching Christine's sixteen-month-old firstborn, Albertus Christiaan Van Raalte Gilmore, called Van, play all day with his little red wagon. Grandpa also had the company of his oldest grandson, eleven-year-old Albertus Christiaan Van Raalte, Bertus and Helena's oldest, who was spending a second summer in Amelia. So the widower spent his third sojourn in Amelia with two daughters and two grandsons.[45]

Van Raalte did what he could to alleviate a desperate economic situation in the Amelia colony. He and Phelps tapped the Hope College endowment for $2,100 to provide loans to the Mattoax Church and money for farmers to avoid foreclosure and buy seeds for spring planting. The Classis of Michigan also provided financial relief for fellow believers in the South. Van Raalte wrote Phelps in March 1871: "I thank God that I have been able to do something for the people of Amelia. The capital is safe enough, but it will increase your storm and hasten the crisis [at Hope College]." The tangible help allowed the settlers to hold on, as the Holland colonists had done in the desperate first years a quarter century before, but the deep problems could not be solved by words. The questionable loan, which proved to be unsafe, in the end cost Phelps the presidency of the college.[46]

Van Raalte's chief mistake in the Amelia misadventure was to go south instead of west, where choice farmland was available free under

---

[44] Van Raalte to Van Schelven, 11 May 1871, HMA.

[45] Julia G. Gilmore to parents and brothers in Fairview, IL, 5 Aug. 1871, letter owned by Cindy Van Orsdal Merwin, Weaverville, CA. Allie's undated letter from Amelia to his grandparents in Michigan was likely penned in mid-1870 since he mentions their illnesses and that his grandmother "is not worse" (Albertus C. Van Raalte to dear Grandpa, 26 Mar. 1870 [?], HHA).

[46] Sheeres, *The Not-So-Promised Land*, 35-37; Van Raalte to Phelps, 12 Mar. 1871, in *Envisioning Hope College*, 263-65.

the Homestead Law. Pella's first daughter colony, in 1869—the same year as the Amelia colony—was the successful Sioux County settlement in northwest Iowa, centered in Orange City, where Seine Bolks gave spiritual leadership.

Christina's health and final illness

Christina Van Raalte was often sick but not necessarily sickly. In fact, by the health standards of her time, she was sturdy and strong. She managed her household well, including cooking—then exclusively the women's domain—at which she excelled. She had learned during her months with Mary Otterson Kellogg and Arvilla Smith how to prepare strange American foods such as corn and squash in outdoor ovens. It was widely reported that she "showed many of the women a better method of baking bread." What exactly that method was is never stated. She shared her husband's passion for ministry and suffered along with him under persecution in the Netherlands and hardships and brickbats in the Holland colony.[47]

Christina Van Raalte was pregnant on average every other year, delivering eleven babies in nineteen years at a time when childbed fever was lethal to many women. Childhood diseases claimed the lives of four of their babies, but none in delivery. Although there is no mention of it in the sources, Christina likely hired midwives for the births in the Netherlands of the first six children—Albertus, Johanna, Ben, Christina Catharina, Dirk, and the second Christina Catharina. In the Holland colony, her "doctor" husband had to act the part in the deliveries of Maria Wilhelmina in 1848, the second Maria Wilhelmina (Mina) in 1850, and Anna Arendina Harking in 1853. For the deliveries of Anna Harking in 1855 and Anna Sophia in 1856, Christina likely had the services of Prientje (Mrs. Simon) Meerman Waling (1803-1867), the first known midwife to practice in Holland, who arrived from Noord-Brabant in 1854. A visitor that year found Christina to be a "noble Christian woman," but "how prostrate is her nervous system.... If she continues to bear children, I fear that this may carry her away sometime."[48]

---

[47] Dosker, *Van Raalte*, 89, English typescript, 36; Jacobson et al., *Dutch Leader*, 170-75; Van Hinte, *Netherlanders*, 224; Katherine Bratt, "Mrs. Van Raalte," *Young Calvinist* (Nov. 1947): 26-27.
[48] I am indebted to Janet Sjaarda Sheeres for information about midwife Waling. There are no extant Van Raalte letters that mention midwives, but Dutch women commonly used them.

In addition to childbearing, Christina suffered from chronic bronchial infections. As early the winter of 1851-52, Van Raalte confided to Garretson that she was "very sick and in great danger, but the Lord did have pity on me and did give her back." After a "prosperous confinement" in 1853 and the birth of Anna Arendina, she became "very sick and feeble" and was still ailing two months later when her husband returned from General Synod in New York. The baby brought joy but died before her first birthday. The bereft parents published a ten-stanza poem of lament in *De Hollander* for "our darling little child, Anna Arendina Harking, who God gave us for eleven months for our enjoyment. He is the Lord. May His name be praised."[49] Albertus and Christina, who lost four of eleven children to death, could never have imagined that less than 1 percent of their great-grandchildren would die in infancy or childhood.[50]

During the winter of 1854-55, Albertus again informed Garretson that Christina was "often sick, feeble, and suffering a great deal from a sore chest." The stove in the "log kitchen" in winter time was the culprit, he thought; it produced smoke from burning wood and dryness in the air. Fresh air would be good for her, Van Raalte opined, and once he asked his wealthy friend Den Bleyker whether he could occasionally borrow his buggy for an outing. Soon he could afford to buy his own buggy and cutter.[51]

The last child, daughter Anna Sophia, at one year of age in July 1857, became "severely" sick at almost the same age as Anna Arendina at her death in 1854. Christina reported this in a letter to her husband, who was begging for money in New York. She was "very much disappointed and rather discouraged on account of his long absence." Albertus received her letter in Poughkeepsie where he had just wangled a $100 donation from a woman. "My cup is mixed up with sweet and bitter," he confessed. A month later, the exhausted campaigner, on the advice of a doctor, "did hurry homeward" to find that the "gathering dark clouds were scattered by my save [sic] arrival." His own health was in jeopardy. He confessed: "I am able only to do half the work, and I

---

[49] Van Raalte to Garretson, 17 May, 22 June 1853, BDM; Death notice and poem in *De Hollander*, 9 Mar. 1854; Van Raalte Report, *De Bazuin*, 4 Apr. 1853; John N. Schultz to Garretson, 19 Sept. 1854, BDM; Bruins et al., *Albertus and Christina*, 65.

[50] Alison Gopnik, "A Modern Miracle: Child Survival," *Wall Street Journal*, 3-4 July 2021, C4.

[51] Van Raalte to Garretson, 10 Dec. 1851, 18 Apr. 1854, BDM; Van Raalte to Den Bleyker, 8 May 1851.

Christina Johanna De Moen Van Raalte in middle age, the only known photograph, likely taken by Holland photographer I. I. Barker, whose studio was above Engbertus Van der Veen's hardware store on Eighth Street (*courtesy Helena Winter*)

am trying new medicines and diet and live in hope. It is with me a slow business to get reconciled with this dying."[52]

After her tenth pregnancy in 1856, at age forty-three, Christina's health noticeably declined. Albertus at various times reported to Phelps she was "always exhausted and overworked and often unwell. . . . Not a day without a slow fever. . . . In bed a good part of the day. . . . I fear some hidden difficulty." In a letter to the Brummelkamps in 1862 Van Raalte speaks of Christina as "an easily fearful woman," who has "waves of fear and depression," although "through God's goodness [is] also often cheerful."[53]

Albertus was always deeply concerned about his wife's health, but this did not sway him from his calling, which took him to New York for long periods for synodical meetings and fundraising. Christina would only occasionally accompany him, such as on a trip to the East in 1854 when, "on account of her health," he gave her a break "from family care."[54] During frequent travels out of state, Van Raalte encouraged his children to "cheer up" their mother. In 1857 he begged Mina, the eldest daughter, "to step up efforts to make everything pleasant for Mother, to unburden [and] cheer her, to make sweeter the bitterness

[52] Van Raalte to Garretson, 27 July 1857, BDM.
[53] Van Raalte to Phelps, 26 Aug. 1857, 31 Aug. 1860, 17 July 1861, 9, 31 Mar. 1865, all *Envisioning Hope College*, 4, 66, 84, 123, 128; Van Raalte to Phelps, 29 Aug. 1863, HHA; Brummelkamp Jr., *Brummelkamp*, 229.
[54] Van Raalte to De Moen, 1 June 1858, trans. Ten Hoor, ADC.

A Carhart & Needham melodeon reed organ

of my absence."[55] Several times he reached out to Philip and Margaret Phelps to visit Christina to "cheer her up." He had earlier encouraged her to host the Phelps when they first visited Holland, and the couples became fast friends.[56] The children shared their father's worry about their mother. Their letters are sprinkled with phrases like "I hope that mother won't worry too much." When Dirk was wounded in the Civil War, he told his sister: "Tell mother not to worry, for he [Dirk] will get better." Christina's letters and postscripts, albeit infrequent, show that she reciprocated her children's tenderness. "Your mother is overcome by love," Van Raalte told Ben.[57]

The Van Raalte home had a piano by 1860 for Christina's enjoyment, and the girls all took lessons. In 1863 Albertus purchased a Carhart Improved Melodeon, a Reed or American Organ, that Christina and the girls played with foot-operated bellows that forced air past free reeds. It was the latest fad for upper middle-class families. A few bluenoses complained that young people overdid laughter, music, and other activities at the parsonage on Sunday evenings.[58]

---

[55] Van Raalte to daughter Wilhelmina, July 1857, HHA.

[56] Van Raalte to Phelps, 8 Sept, 2 Nov. 1859, in *Envisioning Hope College*, 20, 22; Van Raalte to wife, 26 Sept. 1864, 19 Oct. 1868, HHA.

[57] Dirk Van Raalte to mother, 25 July 1864; 23 Sept. 1864; 20 Nov. 1864; Ben to father, 29 Aug. 1864; Van Raalte to son Ben, summer 1866, HHA. For a thorough account, see Harinck, "'O, may the Lord.'"

[58] Christina Catharina Van Raalte to mother, 30 Jan. 1863; Gerrit Van Schelven, *De Grondwet*, 14 May 1912; Kennedy, "Twice Torn Asunder," 61. Henry Post's store on the northeast corner of River and Eighth Streets received a shipment of these popular organs, and Van Raalte was one of a half dozen leading families to acquire one (*De Hollander*, 29 Mar. 1866).

Piso's Cure for consumption, dating from the Civil War, a notorious quack nostrum of, at times, opium, morphine, marijuana, and alcohol

In the years following their Netherlands homecoming in 1866, tuberculosis caused Christina "lengthy and wasting suffering." Albertus had to rescind an offer to host their Detroit friend, Theodore Romeyn, because of his wife's "renewed sickness."[59] Even the "best medicine" of the "southern winds" of Virginia did not help, and she continued to spit up blood. She returned to the Amelia colony once more in the summer of 1869. Albertus turned to hard liquor and patent medicines to relieve her suffering and possibly his own. Holland druggist Heber Walsh provided liberal quantities of bourbon whiskey, cathartic pills (a laxative), quinine, castor oil, Holloway's Pills, Piso's Cure for Consumption, sulphuric morphine, and other opioids and nostrums.[60]

Christina died midmorning on June 30, 1871, with thanks to God on her lips for a fruitful marriage to a faithful husband and spiritual family head. On her deathbed, she confided to Albertus her gratitude for a husband with whom she was not ashamed to pray to God. She died a good death in her own bed, bathed in prayer. John Alberti, the city's first undertaker-livery located directly across Ninth Street from the church, likely prepared the body and supplied the hearse and carriages for the family.[61]

Her bereaved husband placed the following notice in *De Hope*:

Today CHRISTINA JOHANNA VAN RAALTE fell asleep in Jesus at the age of fifty-six years. For thirty-five years the faithful spouse for life, a gift of God of the undersigned
A. C. Van Raalte
Holland, Mich., June 30, 1871[62]

---

[59] Van Raalte to Phelps, 14 June 1866; Van Raalte to Theodore Romeyn, 4 Apr., 20 June 1867, HMA.
[60] Van Raalte to Phelps, 3 Aug. 1869; Van Raalte to son Ben 1866; Van Raalte to John H. Karsten, 28 Oct. 1870 (quote), trans. Simone Kennedy, HHA; Heber Walsh druggist bills, 10 Jan. 1872, 2 July 1873, HHA.
[61] Van Raalte to Phelps, 27 Oct. 1869, 30 Aug. 1870, in *Envisioning Hope College*, 201-5, 259; Dosker, *Van Raalte*, 293; Swierenga, *Holland, Michigan*, 2:1295-96. Another possibility is liveryman Jacobus Nibbelink, whose barn was on Ninth Street near Market Avenue, but he reportedly added undertaking in 1886 (ibid., 2:1298-99).
[62] *De Hope*, 6 July 1871.

Christina's funeral service at First Reformed Church on July 3, 1871, attracted a host of church members and community friends, as one would expect for Holland's First Lady. Christian Van der Veen, editor of *De Hope*, officiated at the funeral, as he would five years later for the dominee himself. He was a Van Raalte catechumen and protégé with impeccable credentials, including degrees from Rutgers College and New Brunswick Seminary. His florid eulogy portrayed Christina as an exemplary pastor's wife. "He was the ideal preacher, she the ideal wife—inseparable from him, true to him and bound to him in the best sense of the word; a woman who in the humblest and most natural manner presented herself as a helpmeet of the man whom we honored as God's servant. They belonged together."[63]

Another cleric who knew Christina personally was Henry Dosker, later a Western Seminary professor and Van Raalte biographer. As a Hope College student, he spent the years from 1873 to 1876 in Holland. He had already met the Van Raaltes as a preteen when they were in the Netherlands in 1866. Dosker lauded Christina as "an excellent wife for a preacher," who "deftly" took many burdens "from his shoulders by the hands of love." He continued: "She had a great influence over Van Raalte, and he took her judgment into consideration whenever decisions had to be made. She was a woman with a healthy outlook, a tender heart, inner spirituality and piety, a faithful companion and self-sacrificing mother." A pastor who filled Van Raalte's pulpit in more recent times described Christina as "a loving and elegant woman who faithfully supported her husband, devoted her life to the welfare of her children, and who cared deeply for all the parishioners."[64]

Albertus chose the following text for her gravestone (with no punctuation):[65]

Christina Johanna De Moen
Whom God gave as a life companion
to Albertus C. Van Raalte during 35 years
Born at Leiden The Netherlands Jan 30 1815
Slept in Jesus at Holland Mich June 30 1871

---

[63] Christian Van der Veen, "Mrs. Christina De Moen Van Raalte" (funeral sermon, 3 July 1871), HMA; Jacobson et al., *Dutch Leader*, 169.
[64] Dosker, *Van Raalte*, 235; De Vries and Boonstra, *Pillar Church* (quote in English translation), 102-3.
[65] Van Raalte purchased the stone for $50 ($1,250 today) from Grand Rapids Marble Works, A. E. Barr and H. W. Liesveld, 6 June 1872, HHA.

Forlorn husband

Losing his beloved Christina was a blow from which Albertus never fully recovered. "She was the sun in my home and the soul of the family. . . . She served me for the sake of the Lord and His kingdom! And the difficulties that she and I struggled through formed her and sanctified her." He found comfort from the fact that she was "able to leave this life with thanksgiving . . . and filled with God's caring love," as he told her brother Carel de Moen. Yet, he admitted, "I continuously feel that I need to get her advice." Dosker illustrated this by relating a poignant Van Raalte story. When visiting a dying parishioner, he whispered to her: "If you see my dear wife in heaven, and if saints still remember the earth, tell her that I always think about her, and that to be loosed [from this earthly life] and to be with Christ becomes more and more precious to me."[66] Van Raalte's hope in the resurrection sustained him in his grief. Words he had recently spoken over the open grave of Elizabeth (Mrs. Cornelius) Van der Meulen came to mind: "Corn must remain in the field a long time, endure much—rainstorms, rough winds, hailstorms, much bad weather, but through all this, it ripens for the granary where it is safe."[67]

Letters of condolence lifted the fresh widower and prompted reflections on her death. Albertus' touching letter to his colleague and friend, John Karsten, serving the Alto (WI) church, bears quoting at length:

> The emptiness and absence of her counsel, help and love is deeply felt. . . . During her last half year of illness, she was not free from this life. Then I saw in her a conflict and wrestling prayer day and night, for a will bent under God's will, which conflict I shall never forget. She compelled God; God had complied. It revives my heart, and it binds my heart most closely to her, and it causes me to praise God.
>
> For that reason, in the course of her blackest suffering, we enjoyed the sweetest moments of our life by day and by night. God

---

[66] Van Raalte to Phelps, 27 Oct. 1869, 30 Aug. 1870, in *Envisioning Hope College*, 201-5, 259; Dosker, *Van Raalte*, 239, quoted in English translation in De Vries and Boonstra, *Pillar Church*, 103; Dosker, *Van Raalte*, 293; Wormser, *In twee werelddeelen*, 230, trans. Ten Hoor; Van Raalte to De Moen and wife Alexandrina, 26 Jan. 1872, ADC, trans. Simone Kennedy; Van Raalte to daughter Christina Gilmore, Apr. 1875, HHA.

[67] Van der Meulen, *Ter Nagedachtenis*, 151 (quote), trans. Ten Hoor; Krabbendam, "Cornelius van der Meulen," 315-32.

was compassionate to us, notwithstanding her very frightening suffering.... In spite of her suffering, it was a thoughtful time. In the end she gave up her life thankfully. O! How full of joy she was when on one of her last days and the ease of speech had returned, she confided to me a God-praising review of all God's goodness during her lifetime....

She was so free and easy in surrendering us all that she became concerned that it might shock me, as though she seemed unconcerned about my being left behind. Therefore, she used the most emphatic words to reveal her love for me and her thanks to God for the fruit of our marriage and her joyful contentment and witness about my staying behind, so that I might still work a short while in the things of God's kingdom.... After such a long conversation, she herself ended with a childlike and trusting prayer and thanksgiving, and she said laughing: "See, when I accepted your marriage proposal, it was to possess a man in whose presence I need not be ashamed and with whom I could pray. Notice then how well God has heard and fulfilled my life's desire. And now how could I fail to love God for all these mercies!? So speaks my soul....

When I was by myself, asking an easy death for her, she called me inside and as usual she was sitting up. I fell into prayer for her, but having said little, I opened my eyes because I heard snuffling, and then I saw her with elevated eyes and hands that sunk down, and she was already dead. The Lord had formed and matured her for a place in the Father's house, the place prepared in his pleasure for his dear child, and my soul thanks God. And now I believe and pray for His grace to be able to empty that last cup in faith.[68]

Van Raalte's biographical sketch of Christina

Soon after her death, the bereft husband penned a biographical sketch of her life that doubled as her obituary. This significant document deserves extensive quoting.[69]

From her pious mother she received her early religious impressions and learned to seek the truth, which God made clear

---

[68] Van Raalte to John Karsten, 24 July 1871, trans. Ten Hoor.
[69] A. C. Van Raalte, "Biographical sketch of Christina Van Raalte," written soon after her death (July 1871), trans. Boonstra, HHA.

to her step by step and made a precious source of life during her adult blossoming. Thus she was formed for a world-renouncing life of struggle, meted out to her because she became joined as a life partner and help for one of those ministers who was involved in the formation of the Free Church in the Netherlands. She shared in the persecutions that arose from that. Motives of piety also prompted her to accept the marriage proposal because, according to her own witness on her deathbed, she had desired a spouse with whom she would not be ashamed to pray to God.... She suffered at the side of her husband—harassment in the home, disturbance of worship services, being robbed through fines for preaching, imprisonment of her husband—during these five years of struggling for freedom. In whatever hour of need and grief, her faith in God stood her in good stead, and in that same strength and flowering beauty, her thankfulness became evident.

Against all expectations, she was able for a few years to enjoy surprising peace and unforgettably sweet relationships in Ommen. However, the joining of the two schools brought her to Arnhem in 1844, to a brief fellowship with her only sister, M[aria] W. Brummelkamp. Because her husband was involved in the evolving movement for emigration, she received an unforgettable farewell on September 24, 1846—a prayerful and heart-rending departure on the Rhine boat to Rotterdam.

After many delaying, heavy storms, mother and her six-month-old baby arrived gratefully and safely in the month of November [in New York]. They enjoyed the first unforgettable Christian fellowship of Dr. De Witt and elder Forrester, and the hospitality of Dr. Wyckoff in Albany. The November freeze forced them to a temporary stay in Detroit, where they enjoyed God's loving care through the interest of Dr. Duffield, Dr. West, and lawyer Romein [Romeyn].

After enjoying three months of noble hospitality in the Christian home of Mr. and Mrs. Kellogg of Allegan, she wished to follow her spouse to the unbroken woods where only the frame of a house was ready for her. She especially wanted to go because she could no longer do without the Sabbath privileges in her mother tongue. Praying and singing, she moved in on one of the last days of May 1847. There she remained a silent, powerful support for the establishment of the settlement, which was dear to her heart, and of which she said gratefully while sick in bed: "God saved me and all mine whom I have brought here during nearly twenty-five years, and He showed me more of His help than I could expect." Her chest illness, somewhat slowed down by her ocean journey and meeting with her dear ones [in 1866], at last made her certain that her end was near. She looked back on her life with praise and blessed acknowledgement of God's grace, the answering of many prayers, and the Sabbath privileges so dear to her, and the fellowship with God's people. Full of thanksgiving for the prayed-for release and union with God's will, she committed the remaining ones in the Lord's hands. As she said herself during her death woes, she found refuge with the Lord and died in her Savior at ten thirty in the morning on June 30, 1871.

Van Raalte's final tribute highlights Christina's life and adds some details. She married out of "motives of piety" instilled by her pious mother. She suffered "great stress" during five years of religious persecution when her husband was jailed, and she had to harbor soldiers in her home. After the happy Ommen life, she experienced "surprising peace" and "sweet relationships" in Arnhem with the Brummelkamps. Clearly, she considered these pastorates the best years of her life.

Then she had to follow Albertus to America and suffer heartbreaking goodbyes with her beloved sister Maria. Heavy storms lengthened the ocean voyage for the young couple with baby Christine. Kindly Dutch and Yankee Christians welcomed and hosted them in Michigan. Albertus mentioned the Kelloggs, but curiously, not the Smiths, who had opened their large parlor with the fireplace for the Van Raaltes for seven weeks, from April 9 until the end of May. Even then, the Van Raalte's house was unfinished, but the welcome mat had worn out. Christina survived the ordeal of taming the wilderness and devoted herself to building the colony for almost twenty-four years. On her deathbed, she reflected on a life of praise, God's grace, answered prayers, and Christian fellowship and worship. It surely was a life well lived.[70]

"A happy Christian"—Christina's personality

Correspondence between husband and wife and comments of children and contemporaries, portray her as a woman with fortitude, deep feeling, and at times a happy disposition. Yet she was prone to worry and occasionally fell into depression. In a role reversal, she was

---

[70] Nyenhuis and Jacobson, *A Dream Fulfilled*, 88.

the one who cheered Albertus in her last days.[71] Geesje Van der Haar-Visscher, who knew Christina as a newlywed in Genemuiden and was a life-long confidant in Michigan, described her as "a happy Christian" who "always sang a great deal in days of health and sickness." Arvilla Smith, the missionary wife at Old Wing Mission, recalled that Christina taught her a "lesson that I shall never forget—that circumstances don't make us happy but the state of heart with God."[72] Her three-month sojourn in Allegan and at Old Wing Mission familiarized her with American foods and ways, which enabled her to teach the Dutch women how to cope on the frontier.[73]

Virtually no documents exist that speak ill of Christina, but there is one. In the correspondence of John Van Vleck, principal of the Holland Academy, dealing with a fairly insignificant dispute in 1859 with Van Raalte, we see a darker side of Christina and her daughters. They are described as unforgiving and as snubbing the Van Vlecks, which hurt the Van Vlecks deeply.[74] Christina could be intent on getting her way, as when she insisted on returning from Virginia, or when she refused to travel steerage on the lake steamer from Buffalo to Detroit in 1846. She also stood on privilege, but she was not too proud to clean Van Vleck Hall (and Van Vleck's quarters in it) and the new First Reformed Church. She chaired a committee to provide decorations for the sanctuary, including oil lamps on the walls, and promised to keep the church in "reasonable neatness and cleanliness," provided the consistory had a well dug to provide fresh water, which they did. The ladies earned kudos for "their excellent work and their ongoing concern for cleanliness."[75]

Mother Van Raalte was obviously loved by her family. Daughter Christine venerated her mother, "in whom she saw a thoroughly loving and earnest woman of fine manners." Christina's personality emerges in Albertus's letters. Her singing was an especially precious memory, notably amid the trials of 1847. As he noted a year after her death: "I thank God that my wife, without hesitation and with singing of psalms, occupied our unfinished house." He repeated the theme in an

---

[71] Van Raalte to De Moen, 20 Jan. 1872, ADC. See also, Rumohr-Voskuil and Bruins, "'Joyful Death.'"
[72] "Geesje Van der Haar-Visscher diary," English typescript, 32; Swierenga and Van Appledorn, *Old Wing Mission*, 464.
[73] Van Hinte, *Netherlanders*, 249.
[74] Kennedy, "Van Raalte and Parochial Schools," 193.
[75] Minutes, First Holland, 6 Oct. 1856, 15 Dec. 1857, 16 Nov. 1858, 20 Sept. (quote), 14 Oct. 1859; *De Hollander*, 13 Jan. 1858; Van Raalte to Den Bleyker, 8 May 1851.

emotional letter to son Dirk on his thirtieth birthday in 1874: "When I heard your mother singing at her work, I was glad because I then knew that everything went more easily, peacefully, and submissively. Then she was near unto God, and there were heavenly things in her heart."[76]

"Ideal wife and helpmeet" were the words spoken at Christina's funeral with admiration and love. "Every great man puts his work first, even before the woman he loves. And every great woman who loves her husband and her God would have it so, though it may mean suffering and deprivation," noted Marian M. Schoolland, the first female biographer of Van Raalte. Despite "delicate physical and emotional health," Christina was a capable and principled woman who survived the challenges of immigration and pioneering, which often fell the hardest on women. But Christina was no martyr; life in the parsonage was often pleasant and even opulent, at least by frontier standards.[77]

Aleida Pieters, daughter of Roelof Pieters, Van Raalte's successor in the First Church pulpit, who knew Christina personally, deserves the last word.

> Although Mrs. Van Raalte was brought up to a life of refinement, comfort, and ease, she adapted herself with remarkable skill and courage to the restricted means of a poor village preacher of a persecuted sect. With her charm and graciousness, she won the hearts of parishioners. . . . Through the years of hardship and privation that followed, she loyally stood by her husband because she believed in him and his cause.[78]

Christina was, after all, a Victorian, a proper, pious lady of fine manners.

Holland Fire of 1871—Van Raalte's finest hour

Barely three months after Christina's death, Van Raalte suffered another death—that of his city. A massive fire engulfed Holland during the night of Sunday, October 8-9, 1871. It was the worst disaster in the city's history. The million-dollar fire wiped out the progress of the first generation and shattered livelihoods, but only one life was lost out of twenty-four-hundred residents. The unspeakable tragedy required Van Raalte to step up again and heal broken spirits, including his own.

---

[76] Van Raalte to son Dirk, 27 Feb. 1874, HHA.
[77] Schoolland, *The Story*, 112. Jacobson et al., *Dutch Leader*, 170-73, offers a feminist perspective.
[78] Pieters, *Dutch Settlement*, 166.

Van Raalte was not in town during the fire. He was filling the pulpit in the First Muskegon Reformed Church that Sunday and was completely unaware of the disaster. Returning home Monday morning on the Michigan Lake Shore Railroad, he spotted fire and smoke as the train neared Holland, but he likely assumed it was simply farmers burning off stubble after the harvest. When the train was flagged down at the still-burning Black River trestle, he heard the unbelievable news: Holland was in ashes. *"Holland was, en is niet"* (Holland was, and is, no more) declared the headline of the first postfire newspaper. Passing through town, the dominee saw the "naked square, where once the city stood, filled with people digging for what was buried," while others milled about aimlessly in shock. "O, how my heart throbbed," he recalled "What a turn of events!"[79]

Holland's fire bell in the church belfry had sounded about three o'clock on Sunday afternoon as worship services were ending. The fire marshal came to church, and Rev. Pieters hastily dismissed the worshipers. The men rushed home to get shovels and join the fire brigade to battle the flames approaching from the Saugatuck area. The region was in a severe dry spell. Hope College had barely escaped a forest fire three days earlier, and firemen remained on high alert. On Saturday, near Saugatuck, it was reported: "Fires light up the heavens in all directions at night." Winds up to seventy-five miles per hour fanned the flames into an almost uncontrollable inferno. With no water available, the men had only sand to snuff out the flames.[80]

After midnight, the "fire monster" passed through Graafschap, unbelievably sparing the church on the hill, and reached Holland in the wee hours. In two hours, it reduced over three-quarters of the city to ashes, sparing only the southeast quadrant, including the small True Holland Reformed Church (now Central Avenue Christian Reformed Church), the majestic First Reformed Church (now Pillar Church), Union School, Hope College's Van Vleck Hall and *De Hope* printery, the city hall/fire station on East Eighth Street, and both railroad depots.

---

[79] Van Raalte, "Holland Disaster," *De Hope*, 12 Oct. 1871; *De Grondwet*, 27 Dec. 1910, 3 Nov. 1914; *Christian Intelligencer*, 8 Nov. 1871; Van Hinte, *Netherlanders*, 353 (quotes).

[80] *Holland City News*, 10 Oct. 1874; *Lake Shore Commercial*, 7 Oct. 1871 (quote). Accounts of the Holland fire: Van Raalte, "The Destruction of Holland City, Michigan," *Christian Intelligencer*, 8 Nov. 1871; Van Reken, *The Holland Fire*; Sara Michel's lucid popular history, *With This Inheritance*; Bruins, "Holocaust in Holland: 1871"; Jacobson et al., *Dutch Leader*, 183-93; Van den Dool, "Weather and the Fires of 1871"; Josias Meulendyke, "Memories of the Great Fire in Holland in 1871," *De Grondwet*, 8 Nov. 1921, trans. Nella Kennedy.

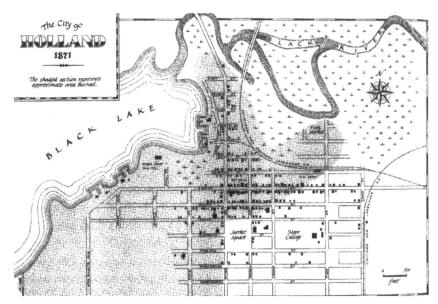

Area of Holland Fire, October 8-9, 1871
(courtesy Lumir Corporation, Holland)

Bible found in rubble after fire (HHA)

Stunned owners and workers survey the ruined Cappon & Bertsch tannery (now the Civic Center), with the loss estimated at $65,000 ($1.6 million today), not covered by insurance (Holland Sentinel, *Oct. 9, 2008*).

The survival of these buildings buoyed the spirits of the stricken townsfolk who had run for refuge into Black Lake. Flames consumed 243 homes—75 percent of the housing stock—leaving homeless three hundred families with thirteen hundred souls. Also lost were four of seven churches—Hope and Third Reformed, Methodist, and Episcopal—thirteen of fifteen factories, Cappon & Bertsch and City Mills, the entire business district—seventy-five shops and offices and all three hotels—and two of the three newspapers—*De Hollander* and *De Grondwet*. Only Black Lake and Black River stopped the flames, and Monday morning rain put out smoldering embers.[81]

Van Raalte was unaware of the fact that his home, safely nestled at the east edge of town, was swamped with people fleeing the flames. His family had to spring into action and provide water and comfort. The Van der Haar farm to the east, at present-day Holland Heights, also served as a relief station. Geesje described the horrendous night she had observed from her home just after midnight:

> We looked out of the windows to see whether we could see any fire, but the smoke was so dense that we could see nothing of

[81] Bruins, "Holocaust in Holland," 294; *Grand Haven Herald*, 17 Oct. 1871; *Holland City News*, 24 Feb. 1872; *De Grondwet*, 24 Oct. 1871 (printed on *Allegan Journal* presses) provided a detailed account.

the city. We feared for the worst for the city and prayed God for deliverance. Beyond the city, we could see the flames in the distance. The wind was so strong that we couldn't hear the fire bell, but at twelve o'clock, my husband and sons got up since it looked to us that matters were getting worse. They went back and alas, it was true. The west of the city was a mass of flames—the church [Third Reformed] which I had loved so much, many homes, stores, factories, hotels all became a prey of the sweeping flames within a short time. . . . The people all fled the burning city to Van Raalte's home, and to my brother and my husband's brother, who all lived on the other side of the city. On the way to town, my husband met Mr. [Engbertus] Van der Veen, who had always been a good friend of ours. He had lost everything—house, store, and all his merchandise. My husband asked him where his wife was, and he said she was at Van Raalte's.[82]

As newspaperman Gerrit Van Schelven remarked, "No one, unless he has been an eyewitness of such a scene, can conceive its terror or its awfulness." For the generations that lived through it, the fire was a seminal time; events thereafter were described as either before or after the fire. Most businessmen rebuilt their stores and shops, but the scourge inflicted that day left permanent anguish of heart and financial ruin.

Insurance

A rumor spread after the fire that the Dutch had refused on religious grounds to buy fire insurance on their homes and businesses or even to ring the city bell or fight the fire because it was Sunday. The Holland Relief Committee, formed a day after the fire by seventeen community leaders, including Van Raalte and Henry Post, denied these rumors forcefully, but unsuccessfully.[83] There was some truth to the report. The Dutch Separatists were wary of insurance and believed that God would guard them in times of storm. Many also had more pressing financial needs than paying insurance premiums. But reports of being underinsured were greatly exaggerated. Newspaperman Gerrit

---

[82] "Geesje Van der Haar-Visscher Diary," 34.
[83] A hastily published book by Goodspeed, *History of the Great Fires* (1871), reported that Holland's losses were more severe because of "a religious prejudice of the people against insurance" (p. 625), which was unsuccessfully refuted by the Holland Relief Committee statement, 14 Oct. 1871, published in *Lake Shore Commercial*, 21 Oct. 1871.

Van Schelven estimated insurance coverage at only $35,000. But a detailed damage survey by Henry Post, secretary of the Holland Relief Committee, found that seventeen insurance companies had written policies on Holland homes and businesses, and one-fifth of the losses were insured, a percentage only slightly below that of other cities hit by fire. Of total losses of $781,000, insurers paid $137,000—four times more than Van Schelven's estimate. The destroyed churches were valued at $21,500, with 28 percent of the losses covered by insurance.[84]

Van Raalte's homestead and barn were unscathed, but he still suffered "very heavy" losses, according to Julia Gilmore. He confessed to Phelps that the fire had left him pinched to provide for his family and to pay his $500 realty tax bill. "I am at a loss what to do." Since Van Raalte owned no buildings in the city, his losses were likely tied to his town lot mortgages that owners were unable to keep current because of losses of jobs and businesses. Also his hundreds of unsold lots were stripped of trees and thus reduced in value.[85]

Finances as well as religion played a deciding role in whether or not one was underinsured or entirely "naked." For the most part, businesses were insured, but individuals, except for a rich few, were not. Merchants, by and large, also had insurance for their homes. Although insurance monies covered only a quarter of the losses, the payouts did provide cash to rebuild. Homeowners learned a hard lesson, and many minds were changed regarding property insurance.

Relief aid

Because Chicago, coincidentally, had also been badly crippled by a fire at the same time, Holland had to look for relief from within the faith community and the state of Michigan. The Old Dutch graciously took pity on the Young Dutch. President Phelps, a native of Albany, went east to seek aid. Up and down the Hudson Valley and elsewhere, churches responded, and collections swelled to an astounding $40,000 ($1 million today). The *Christian Intelligencer* made a habit of listing contributors by name, which encouraged do-gooders to outshine one another. Even Separatist congregations in the Netherlands sent money

---

[84] *Holland City News*, 10 Oct. 1891, cites Van Schelven's estimate, but says $50,000 was insured. The actual amount insured is based on "List of Destroyed Property by Street." See also, George May, "Michigan Fires of 1871," unpublished paper, HMA.

[85] Julia Gilmore to Darius Gilmore, 23 Oct. 1871 (Cindy Van Orsdal Merwin, Weatherville, CA); Van Raalte to Phelps, 23 Oct. 1871.

by way of Abraham Kuyper's newspaper, *De Standaard*.[86] Van Raalte warned Phelps to ensure that church gifts were earmarked specifically for churches in Holland and not for general relief. Otherwise, the state of Michigan would follow policy and reduce public aid by the same amount.[87]

Van Raalte put his shoulder to the wheel. He traveled to western Illinois to solicit relief funds from Reformed congregations there. *Pella's Weekblad* appealed to readers to help "countrymen of the same Orange roots." Two weeks later, Van Raalte, whose hands Pella folks trusted, received a check for $1,050 ($26,300 today) from the Pella relief committee. "We are amazed to witness this flow of charitable contributions," Van Raalte noted in an editorial in *De Hope*.[88]

"God willed trial by fire, yet remember, God lives"

Van Raalte's focus was to encourage residents not to give up. "With our Dutch tenacity and our American experience, Holland will be rebuilt," he declared boldly. For many, faith provided a bulwark against despair. Thousands gathered for a mass meeting a day after the fire and resolved: "With God's help, we begin again with all our might." Van Raalte rallied the crowd by declaring confidently that God in His inscrutable wisdom had "willed trial by fire, yet remember, God lives!" In private, however, he confided to Phelps: "I see darkness and try to relieve myself by not to think more about the future." City aldermen, albeit in humble submission to God's providence over the "fire king [who] has devastated nearly our entire city," also pledged with spirits unbroken "to rebuild upon a more secure foundation." With Dutch determination and courage, they resolved to restore the city to a "relative position of honorable distinction with our sister cities of Michigan." Within two weeks, businessmen were rebuilding or reopening shops and stores in temporary buildings. Within six months, nearly fifty commercial buildings and one hundred houses had been built.[89] Hollanders were doers and did not wait for outside help.

[86] *Holland Sentinel*, 28 Jan. 1905; *Lakeshore Commercial*, 11 Nov. 1871; "Holocaust in Holland"; *Grand River Times* (Grand Haven), 12, 13 Oct. 1871; *De Hope*, 20 Oct. 1871; Van Raalte to Phelps, 2 Nov. 1871, in Bruins and Schakel, *Envisioning Hope College*, 277-78; *De Heraut*, 10, 17 Nov. 1871 (www.delpher.nl, accessed June 2021); Relief Committee receipts by Van Raalte, 2, 14 Nov., 4, 14 Dec. 1871, 29 Jan., 7, 28 Feb. 1872, HHA.

[87] Van Raalte to Phelps, 25 Oct. 1871, in *Envisioning Hope College*, 272-73.

[88] *Pella's Weekblad*, 21 Oct. 1871, trans. Douma; *De Hope*, 9 Nov. 1871.

[89] *De Hope*, 12 Oct. 1871 (quotes), 23 Nov. 1871; Van Raalte to Phelps, 27 Oct. 1871, in *Envisioning Hope College*, 274 (quote).

Roelof Pieters, Van Raalte's successor at First Church, on the first Sunday morning after the fire, gave up his pulpit to the "old doctor," for a "very instructive and sharply practical message." A worshipper, Josias Meulendyke, fifty years later harkened back to the message. "I do not recall the text and the content of the sermon, but the spirit of the old warrior impressed me." Like a prophet of old, Van Raalte thundered: "Oh, that godless Chicago! . . . But no, godly Holland is also covered in ash! That's something to think about." If the Chicago fire was the consequence of wickedness, as many seemed to think, the dominee asked his congregants to ponder why godly Holland had suffered the same fate.[90]

In later messages, Van Raalte emphasized thankfulness for lessons learned. He called the fire the "glowing edge of a dark cloud."

> A small house that should have been demolished long ago is now home to somebody who is more thankful to God for it than he ever was for the furnished rooms he lived in before they were destroyed in the fire. It is a miracle to him! Food tastes better now than in those days that you would go down to overflowing basements to take some for the next few days. I saw a mother and daughter clapping their hands of joy while leaving a saved home; their joy was caused by the arrival of a wagon full of saved possessions. The few remainders meant more to them than their riches of earlier days. With great joy and excitement people remember that night in which they had to flee for their lives. . . . That flood of fire, the blocked streets, the escape through waters and swamps, the land on fire all around them—all this a distant memory, and they kiss the great saving hand of God. . . . Our dark cloud glows on all sides with shining light! . . . Let us praise and worship Him because God glorifies His name![91]

The colony's founder was most grateful that his beloved college, "the crown and jewel of the Dutch," was spared from the flames. As chair of the classical committee for school and education, he extolled God in his 1872 report for the "almighty and gracious preservation [of] this educational work. . . . Instead of disruption, we enjoy surprising fruits of progress."[92]

[90] *De Grondwet*, 2 Jan. 1872; Josias Meulendyke, "Memories of the Great Fire."
[91] Van Raalte, "The Glowing Edge of a Dark Cloud," *De Hope*, 9 Nov. 1871, trans. Simone Kennedy.
[92] Van Raalte, article in *De Hope*, 7 Nov. 1871; Kennedy, *Commentary*, 11 Sep. 1872, 3:1704.

Eighth Street looking west from Cedar (later College) Avenue in 1875, showing a barber shop likely frequented by Van Raalte (*JAH*)

At a commemoration on the second anniversary of the blaze, Van Raalte preached on Jesus' parable of the ten servants in Luke 19:13 (RSV): "Trade with these till I come." He began:

> Seeing that your homes and goods have been restored, Congregation of Holland, I remind you of what Jesus says concerning all our possessions. They are a trust, indeed, they belong to Jesus himself. And we must be thoroughly convinced that our possessions, briefly held, must be placed in our Master's service. He is watching us.

The dominee had a way of challenging his people at every opportunity.[93]

Van Raalte's response to the fire was his finest hour. He helped the people deal with the question: "Is God punishing us for our sins?" Yes, said the dominee, and he called for repentance, but he also assured them of God's grace and lovingkindness. He went beyond spiritual counsel and raised money to rebuild factories and businesses. "Heart sickening will be our situation without capital," he wrote his confidant, Phillip Phelps.[94]

---

[93] Van Raalte sermon, "Commemoration of the Holland Fire," 19 Oct. 1873, in Spykman, *Pioneer Preacher*, 106-12.

[94] Van Raalte to Phelps, 8 Nov. 1871, in *Envisioning Hope College*, 273-74, 283-84 (quote).

Twenty-fifth anniversary celebration

A year after the fire, in September 1872, Holland celebrated its silver anniversary in both civic and church settings. The kick-off on the Fourth of July was a "day of thanksgiving and joy" sponsored by school districts and featuring the pioneers. Van Raalte agreed to be one of the speakers and write a newspaper announcement. Three weeks into the planning for the "good old fashioned" event, which was to include all the settlements, the Zeeland school board decided to stage a celebration for its own community.[95]

Van Raalte took great umbrage at Zeeland's insular attitude in a blistering letter to the Holland festival committee:

> I regard this splitting of the festival as an indignity and disgrace that consumes our people as a cancer. . . . I believe it is better to give up the gathering or festivities. Let Zeeland hold its festival and all who would join in it. I cannot celebrate the festival of a joint settlement this way. For me, the Christian character is missing.

He then asked to be excused from participating. "My hurt and antipathy is too deep. Neither can I lend my hand to those curse-deserving envious and angry ones who so continuously tear the body apart."[96] The Zeeland letter stirred the old pot of resentment that first surfaced in the raucous township caucus in 1851 when Holland's perceived haughtiness caused deep resentment in Zeeland, who considered itself an equal, if not a superior, settlement. The rivalry between the cities continued for generations, possibly even to the present day.

Holland civic celebration

After putting his stake in the ground, Van Raalte was persuaded to pull it out and lead Holland's celebration, which was rescheduled for September 17, 1872. The spirit of unity was broken without Zeeland, but the day was glorious nonetheless. Zeeland's founding pastor, Rev. Van der Meulen came from Grand Rapids to stand with his old friend Van Raalte.[97] The day was a holiday, with all stores and shops

---

[95] *Holland City News*, 8, 29 June 1872.
[96] Van Raalte to Teunis Keppel, 8 June 1872, HMA.
[97] Van Raalte and Van der Meulen, "Clarification" (*toelicting*), in *Handelingen en verslagen*; *De Hope*, 28 Aug. 1872; *Holland City News*, 21 Aug., 14 Sept. 1872.

closed and all general business suspended. The celebration was held in Rokus Kanters' "fine grove" a mile east of Holland on the road to New Groningen (now Paw Paw Drive).

At ten o'clock, the long procession made its way from the city square (Centennial Park today), led by the Holland city band, followed by two wagons. A team of horses pulled the first wagon with eleven ladies dressed in orange, representing each of the Dutch provinces. Two yoke of oxen pulled the second wagon with thirteen surviving pioneers dressed in character. The beasts were prodded with immense whips by pioneer ox masters Gerrit Havekate and Hein Van der Haar and their mongrel dogs. City and township officials, clergymen, and faculty followed in carriages. At the grove, ten honored guests were seated on a stage decorated with festoons and flags of the Netherlands and the United States, which signified the transformation of the Dutch into Americans. A vast crowd of two thousand sat under large shade trees.[98] Above the speakers' platform was a banner emblazoned with the words:

Nederland   *Eben Haëzer*   America
1847   1872
A. C. Van Raalte
Eendragt maakt magt

The Holland band opened the program with a rousing march, and Rev. Van der Meulen offered prayer. Then the congregation, led by Johannes Van Lente's choir, sang the 60th Psalm in the Dutch metrical version. Kommer Schaddelee, president for the day, introduced Dominee Van Raalte, the honored guest, who addressed the people in their native tongue "in a very eloquent and touching manner." He magnanimously overlooked the Zeeland snub and gave Van der Meulen his full due. His address stressed the positive—emigrating for freedom of church and school, crossing the fearful ocean, and receiving vital help from Americans in New York, Detroit, Allegan, and the Old Wing Mission. He named key people in each city, particularly General Robert Stuart of Michigan, who "first directed his attention to their present location." He ignored negative aspects—village rivalries, political divisions, religious schism, and challenges to his leadership as

---

[98] Van Raalte's "Ebenezer Speech," 17 Sept. 1872, in Lucas, *1847—Ebenezer—1947*, 21-36; also in Lucas, *Dutch Immigrant Memoirs*, 2:484-91; Dosker, *Van Raalte*, 306-7. For news reports, see "Twenty-Fifth Anniversary," *Holland City News*, 21 Sept. 1872; "The Hollanders," *Allegan Journal*, 5 Oct. 1872; "The Hollanders of Michigan," *Christian Intelligencer*, 24 Oct. 1872.

Netherlands royal coat of arms, 1815-1907

theocracy gave way to democracy. The handover of power in 1867 from minister to mayor marked the painful transition. All this was buried. It was a day to celebrate, not berate.[99]

Van Raalte focused his address on religious freedom, communal strength, and material blessings. "In truth, God had wrought great things for us! . . . In Michigan alone our churches already number twenty-six. Thirty-three ministers and fifteen school teachers have gone forth from our midst." In his mind, Holland had lived up to its reputation as "the home of the saints."[100] God had met every need and given beyond measure. In words that sang with satisfaction, Van Raalte boasted "Is there anyone who can visit our villages and townships, covered with the richest farmsteads, and not be astonished? . . . It is impossible to estimate the value of our ships, fisheries, mills, factories, and fruit farms. . . . We possess shipping lines and railway communications. In truth, God has wrought great things for us!" The Holland colony had become "simultaneously a market place, a harbor town, and an industrial center."[101]

---

[99] Van Hinte, *Netherlanders*, 343; Hyma, *Van Raalte*, 251.
[100] Lucas, *1847–Ebenezer–1947*, 29; *Holland Sentinel*, 11 Nov. 1935, quoted in 16 Nov. 1985 issue "On the Way to Today."
[101] Van Raalte, "Commemoration Address, 1872," 2:487; Lucas, *Netherlanders*, 253.

Rev. Cornelius Van der Meulen, pastor of First Zeeland (1847-59) and Second Grand Rapids (1861-73) Reformed Churches (*JAH*)

Van Raalte shared the stage with Isaac Fairbanks, Henry Post, Henry Pennoyer, and other Americans who had thrown in their lot with the Dutch. Post, Van Raalte's early business partner and family friend, in his address put hard numbers on progress. The Holland colony had fifteen thousand residents, and property values totaled $3.5 million ($87.5 million today). This was far too low, even taking account of the $1 million lost in the fire. Post estimated that the footprint of the colony covered ten townships across thirty-six square miles in Ottawa, Allegan, and Kent counties with twenty-five thousand residents. Holland was destined for prominence on the sunset coast of Lake Michigan. Van Raalte closed the celebration with a benediction.[102]

At the Zeeland celebration the next day, Van der Meulen's sparkling address recited the history of that settlement. He began with a gracious acknowledgement of Van Raalte's address. "I would feel free to rest content with what he said. His address applied to our entire settlement. *But each person also has special roots in his own location. For that reason I take the liberty here to discuss our history*" [italics added]. Zeeland would not be a cockboat in Holland's wake. Van der Meulen credited Van Raalte with leading the emigration by recalling a day in 1846 at Arnhem when he had objected to Van Raalte's decision to emigrate. The reply stuck with him: "You will not be able to stop this emigration any more than you can stop the Rhine in its course" (the Lower Rhine ran through Arnhem). To which Van der Meulen confessed: "That too, I soon realized, also came to be my judgment."[103]

---

[102] *Holland City News*, 21 Sept. 1872, *De Hope*, 9 Oct. 1872; *Allegan Journal*, 5 Oct. 1872; Van Raalte, "Prosperity of Colony in Michigan," 9 Nov. 1875, Moerdyke Papers.

[103] "Cornelius Van der Meulen's address at Zeeland," 18 Sept. 1872, in Lucas, *Dutch Immigrant Memoirs*, 1:180-89.

Ebenezer Memorial Fund

Eleven days after the Holland civic celebration came the apex event, the Ebenezer [Eben-Haëzer in Dutch] Memorial Thank Offering scheduled in all the churches on Sunday, September 29, 1872. The aim was to piggy-back on the colony's anniversary to raise $50,000 ($1.2 million today) as a permanent endowment for Hope College's Female Department (grammar school)—the "foundation of the whole institution," in Van Raalte's words. Van Raalte enlisted Van der Meulen to copublish a lengthy joint address in *De Hope* that thanked God for the "sweet freedom" that resulted from "rooting in this country" and the religious and secular benefactors who "like angels of God" had comforted the "strangers in a strange land."[104] A subscription list was opened in late August, and $12,000 came to hand in the first week. Van Raalte chose for the campaign the prophet Samuel's Hebrew word "Ebenezer" for the memorial stone he had erected to mark the stunning victory over the Philistines. "Ebenezer"—meaning "Hitherto hath the LORD helped us" (I Sam 7:12, KJV)—captured the immigrants' spirit of thanksgiving. "Self-sacrificing diligence" was the admonition, with the warning: "Do not come before the Lord empty-handed."[105]

All twenty-six congregations in Michigan dug deep and pledged $36,000, but the economic depression set off by bank failures in 1873 left many pledges unmet. Van Raalte, fearing that his life was ending, rushed to put his "earthly affairs in order" by donating to First Church, without prior permission, two lots and a forty-acre tract, all under mortgage contracts, with principal and interest payments earmarked for the Ebenezer fund. "I hope you will not think ill of me during my illness" for this bequest, he said sheepishly. It fulfills the "promises by me and mine to benefit the Eben-Haërzer thanksgiving memorial fund." He requested "urgently" that the consistory, as a "service of love," accept the mortgages and pursuant obligations of the three mortgagees. And they did.[106]

The churches of the Classis of Holland gave generously. Holland led with $11,000, followed by Zeeland with $2,800 and Overisel with $2,300. The eleven congregations together gave $22,000. This was

---

[104] Van Raalte and Van der Meulen, "Our Ebenezer Offering of Thanks," *De Hope*, 24, 31 July 1872, trans. Simone and Nella Kennedy.

[105] Lucas, *1847—Ebenezer—1947*; Van Raalte to Phelps, 15 July 1872, in *Envisioning Hope College*, 294-95; *Holland City News*, 21 Apr. 1872; Van Raalte and Van der Meulen, "Clarification," *De Hope*, 28 Aug. 1872, trans. Simone Kennedy; *De Hollander*, 6 Aug. 1873; Kennedy, *Commentary*, 11 Sept. 1872, 3:1707-8.

[106] Van Raalte to consistory of First Holland church, 6 Sept. 1873, HHA.

dwarfed by contributions from churches in the East that totaled $51,000 over ten years, from 1868 to 1878. The one-story female academy erected in 1869 had a second floor and library added in 1871.[107]

To fund an Ebenezer Thanksgiving Memorial plaque to be placed in the academy, Van Raalte donated $1,000 ($25,000 today) and son Dirk $100, and Van Raalte enlisted the three western classes (Holland, Michigan, and Wisconsin) to join the effort. Phelps in 1872 wanted to draw on the endowment to boost the academy, but Van Raalte called this a "plastering-over, a dishonesty." Phelps should go east to raise the additional monies. "This using up of the Endowment, an interest-bearing fund, weakens the Eben-Haëzer memorial fund," Van Raalte declared, and if Phelps desisted, "I prefer to resign." Phelps backed down, but he then drew on the endowment for faculty salaries in the Theological Department, another priority. Phelps' shirking of his duty to fundraise in the East, as Van Raalte had done at great personal sacrifice, led to the first serious rift between the dear friends.[108]

M. Cohen Stuart's 1873 visit to Holland

In late October 1873, Van Raalte hosted Rev. Martinus Cohen Stuart (1824-1878) and his wife for an intense five-day visit. The two had never met, but it was a prime opportunity to tout the colony. The famed Netherlands cleric, pastor of the prominent Rotterdam Remonstrant congregation, was a delegate to the Evangelical Alliance meeting in New York City. After which, the couple toured Dutch American settlements from New York to Iowa and Minnesota. Cohen Stuart later published a book about his travels.[109] His father belonged to a Jewish family and his mother to a Scots Presbyterian family. Their marriage hinged on his father's conversion to Christianity. Cohen Stuart was an outspoken critic of the modernism that had captured the Reformed (Hervormde) Church pastorate, as well as his own Remonstrant fraternity. This antimodernism and Alliance membership meshed with Van Raalte's views and made him doubly welcome, despite his Arminian theology.

---

[107] *De Hope*, 27 Aug. 1873; Indenture, Van Raalte to Consistory, First Holland church, 8 Apr., 6 Sept. 1873, JAH.

[108] Van Raalte to Christian Van der Veen, 23 Oct. 1872, HHA: Swierenga, "Stewardship of Resources," 1:516.

[109] For this section, see Cohen Stuart, *Zes Maanden in Amerika*, 1:300-323; *De Hollander*, 5 Nov. 1873; Van Raalte to Anthony Brummelkamp Jr., 26 Jan. 1874, HHA; *De Bazuin*, 7 Nov. 1873 (www.delpher.nl, accessed July 2021); Boonstra, "Martinus Cohen Stuart"; "Visit of Dr. M. Cohen Stuart, in 1873," box 8, Van Schelven Papers. Van Raalte's desire to "puff" his work in the homeland seemingly led him to overlook Cohen Stuart's position as a Remonstrant pastor.

A six-person committee, headed by Mayor Isaac Cappon, arranged for the significant visit since it was the first time a notable Netherlander came in person and acknowledged the Holland settlement. The couple arrived by train from Grand Rapids via Zeeland, where they stopped briefly to meet Rev. Van der Meulen, "the friendly old man with a ruddy face and a flourishing demeanor," who had recently retired there. The train pulled into the Holland station in a snowstorm, and Cohen Stuart observed "a man of more than middle aged run towards us with youthful speed and introduced himself as our host—Van Raalte." Continuing with first impressions, he observed that the man "demands attention," because although "small of stature," he "walks erect," and is "lively in all his movements." There is "something martial in his whole being. The alert and decisive gestures, the expression of determination in his small but vivid eyes, and the shape of his somewhat nervous mouth, the commanding and wrinkled forehead, the moustache and pointed beard, all give the expression of a pensioned general rather than a retired minister. This man does not know much about rest." It was an apt first-hand assessment.

The committee put up Cohen Stuart at the City Hotel on Eighth and Market Streets. The next morning, Rev. Pieters gave up his pulpit at First Church to the visitor, who in the afternoon preached in English in the college chapel and drew several members of the Market Street (Central Avenue) Church. In the evening, Cohen Stuart stood in Rev. Henry Uiterwyk's pulpit at Third Reformed Church. That these Dutch-born clerics, both graduates of New Brunswick Seminary, would open their pulpits to an Arminian is remarkable. Clearly, Old World theological distinctions were fading, and the free-will theology of the Second Great Awakening was making major inroads of the Reformed Church in the East.[110]

The next day, Van Raalte hitched his team to his open carriage, picked up local dignitaries, and drove through town to Black Lake. The still visible devastation of the "terrible" Holland fire two years earlier shocked the Netherlander. A small schooner festooned with a Dutch flag awaited the party for a sunset cruise of Black Lake to the harbor—Van Raalte's pride and joy—and then out onto Lake Michigan.

The next day, Van Raalte again took the visitor in his carriage for a twenty-five-mile tour of several outlying villages. At Zeeland, during the lunch break, Cohen Stuart preached to a large crowd. "Everything bespeaks of prosperity and abundance but without excessive luxury."

---

[110] Gasero, *Historical Directory*, 308, 402; Fabend, *Zion on the Hudson*, 214-16, 224-27.

Farm fences are "horse-high, bull-strong, and pig-tight," he added, paying farmers the ultimate compliment."[111] In the evening, Mayor Bernardus Ledeboer hosted the Hollander at a dinner with fifty notables that went past midnight. Van Raalte spoke and pointedly told his guest to report "to our kindred in the old fatherland what you found here; . . . a despised, disowned people, gotten rid of in the Netherlands; here they have developed into a Christian community." His visitor complied, but the story that caught the fancy of the Dutch press was that Van Raalte as host at the banquet served only water, not a drop of wine or beer, even for the toasts. How gauche![112]

After two days touring factories, mills, shops, and Van Vleck Hall, Van Raalte ended the whirlwind visit by taking his guests by train to Grand Haven, where he bid farewell after Cohen Stuart preached again. From there the couple traveled to Muskegon, then back to Overisel for a day, and on to Kalamazoo and Chicago. The Cohen Stuarts returned to New York by way of Amelia Court House, Virginia, where they spent a few days.

Cohen Stuart's assessment of Van Raalte is effusive. "The man with that decisive, restless, diligent nature is a pious, humble, loving Christian in the complete sense of the word, a warrior of his Savior and Lord, a character purified and sanctified through struggle and suffering. He is one of these people with whom one cannot associate without becoming richer in spirit and heart, in wisdom and love."[113] Hosting Cohen Stuart tested Van Raalte's stamina to the limit, but he enjoyed every minute of it, especially the opportunity to showcase his colony.

President, Council of Hope College

After his election as Hope College council president in June 1869, much of Van Raalte's focus turned to college business. The attractive stipend of $1,500 ($33,500 today) was almost twice his church salary. Although saying yes was an "absurdity," due to his "loss of strength," Van Raalte concluded: "I say at least try. Who knows if God may give me strength?" Despite the absurdity, he again became the money man to keep the college solvent and boost the endowment toward its overly ambitious $80,000 goal ($1.8 million today). He presided at council

---

[111] Van Hinte, *Netherlanders*, 337.
[112] *De Bazuin*, 29 Oct. 1880 (www.delpher.nl, accessed June 2021).
[113] Van Raalte to Phelps, 31 Oct. 1874, in Bruins and Schakel, *Envisioning Hope College*, 326-28.

meetings for six years, until late November 1875, a year before his death.[114] Phelps was the father of the college, but "the seed-thought of the institution lay in the heart of Dr. A. C. Van Raalte. He was the far-seeing man."[115]

Despite not feeling well, Van Raalte jumped right into the council presidency by joining President Phelps in June as a delegate to General Synod 1869, in Philadelphia, where they spoke on behalf of the college. In the fall, Van Raalte went to New York for six weeks to meet with benefactors Samuel Schieffelin and James Suydam. Schieffelin, an old friend who had saved the dominee from bankruptcy years earlier, donated $5,000 and advised him on how to deal with the crusty Suydam, who reluctantly gifted $10,000 to extinguish Hope College indebtedness. Suydam was encouraged by Van Raalte's report that Western churches had donated $3,000 for the college. Van Raalte himself donated thirty acres to the college and $4,000 ($99,700 today) for the primary and female "seminary." The money came from selling lots to Michigan Lake Shore Railroad for right of way and a depot.[116]

In 1871 the Hope College council allowed Freemasons to be members, contrary to the principles of the classes of Holland and Wisconsin. The First Church consistory, under Rev. Roelof Pieters, complained officially to the council about their stance. But they did not withhold financial support. Van Raalte, the council president, was in Virginia when the council's decision was made, but he doubtless concurred. On his return, sickness sapped his strength, and he was unable to attend council meetings for a time.[117]

In 1873 the ailing Van Raalte submitted his resignation as council president, but Phelps pressed him to stay on, and the council returned his letter. The indispensable man pled with the board to

---

[114] Swierenga, "Stewardship of Resources," 1:500-501; minutes, Hope College Council, 25 Oct. 1872, 16 June, 30 Nov. 1875, JAH; Phelps, Notice, 23 Nov. 1872, HHA.

[115] Bruins and Schakel so argue cogently in *Envisioning Hope College*, 197-99. See also, "School and College," *The Independent: Devoted to the Consideration of Politics, Social and Economic Tendencies, History, Literature, and the Arts* (1848-1921), 18 July 1895 (Michael Douma).

[116] Van Raalte to Phelps, 12 June, 15 July, 27, 29 Oct., 1, 4, 5, 6, 16, 18, 20 Nov. 1869, 28 Oct. 1873, in *Envisioning Hope College*, 195, 197, 201-17, 247, 317; Van Raalte (Jersey City, NJ) to daughter Mina Oggel, 18 Oct. 1869, HHA; minutes, Hope College Council, 7, 29 Mar. 1871, 13 Aug. 1873, JAH; Van Raalte Account book, 15 June 1871, 8 Apr. 1873, HHA.

[117] Minutes, First Holland, 25 Aug., 24 Nov. (congregational meeting) 1871; Van Raalte to Phelps, 5 Dec. 1871, in *Envisioning Hope College*, 288.

accept his resignation, due to "his injured and prostrate organs." They still refused, and he yielded. He was back in the chair by the April 1873 meeting. In June 1874, he resigned from the executive committee but continued to chair council meetings. In June 1875, he was re-elected as chair, but "many infirmities" caused him to miss meetings until his last hurrah in November 1875, when he declined a request to serve again as financial agent.[118] That year he addressed the graduating class with a sober reminder:

> The noblest privileges, beloved, are yours. . . . Your high calling also touches off the question: O Lord, what will grow out of this beginning? . . . Regard academic standing as a game, if you please. It is secondary, not primary. He who, in spite of sin, moves ahead in his life of perseverance proceeds with eyes aflame to give strong evidence that his heart is right with God.[119]

It was his last public address.

The Amelia loan of $2,100 from the college endowment in 1871 came home to roost in 1876, shortly after Van Raalte's death. He and Phelps had acted imprudently by not obtaining approval from the Hope College council. General Synod, in 1877, pushed by delegates in the East zealous to support Rutgers College, forced Phelps to resign, ostensibly for "mistaken financial management." Synod praised his theological soundness, "fidelity, and the long, untiring devotion" to the college. But only $100 of the $2,100 Amelia loan had been repaid.[120]

Besides the ill-advised loan from the college endowment, with $2,000 still outstanding, Phelps in 1869 had also tapped the endowment for $10,200 ($229,000 today) to buy 833 acres of Point Superior lands (now Waukazoo Woods subdivision) for a peach orchard to benefit the college. Van Raalte induced Suydam to donate $5,000 ($112,000 today) to buy the choice tract (now Marigold Lodge), in hopes that son Ben would take charge of the project. But Ben had his farm to operate. No peach trees were ever planted on the Point Superior land, despite the "peach craze" that would strike the lakeshore region in the

---

[118] Van Raalte to Council secretary A. T. Stewart, 25 Feb. 1873, JAH; Phelps to Van Raalte, 3 Mar. 1873; Van Raalte to Stewart, 14 Mar. 1873; Van Raalte to Council Executive Committee, 16 Mar. 1873; minutes, Hope College Council, 24 Apr. 1873, 23 June 1874, 10 June, 30 Nov. 1875, JAH.

[119] Van Raalte address, "Hope College 1875," in Spykman, *Pioneer Preacher*, 121-24.

[120] Van Raalte to Phelps, 5, 22, 23 Nov. 1869; A. C. Van Raalte to Benjamin Van Raalte, 13 Nov. 1869.

next decades.[121] Synod deemed the land purchase an "unprofitable investment." But Suydam Farm, as the tract was named, eventually became valuable recreational property on Black Lake. After thirty years, the college sold the tract for $27,700 ($692,700 today), almost triple the purchase price. The college came out smelling like a rose, and in the end, Phelps and Van Raalte were vindicated.[122]

Church work and missions

The dominee continued his church work in retirement but cut back on preaching assignments, except on special occasions, such as the installation of a pastor or the dedication of a church building. In 1871 Van Raalte served as the token western representative on General Synod's Centennial Memorial Commission, which raised $684,000 ($17.1 million today) to mark the 1771 break with the Classis of Amsterdam when the Reformed Church truly became an American institution.[123] In June 1872, the dominee gave a fitting farewell at the commissioning service of his protégé, Enne J. Heeren, a graduate of Hope's Theology Department. Heeren was the first missionary supported by the three western Dutch classes to be sent by the Board of Foreign Missions to serve overseas, in his case, in the Classis of Arcot in India.[124] If only Van Raalte could have done the same in South Africa. In November 1873, Van Raalte preached in First Church, where he worshiped regularly. His last time in that familiar pulpit was likely in late July 1874. In December of that year, he was able to deliver the address at the dedication of the new edifice of Third Reformed Church, rebuilt after the Holland fire. But in April 1875, he had to decline when First Church asked if he was able to provide pulpit supply for several months when Rev. Pieters traveled to the Netherlands on a denominational assignment. That month was also his last time at the Classis of Holland and serving as chair of the education, domestic missions, and nominations committees.[125]

---

[121] Swierenga, "Stewardship of Resources."
[122] Ibid., 1:507-11; Voskuil, "Vexed Question," 355-60.
[123] Kennedy, *Commentary*, 13 Sept. 1871, 3:1640; *Christian Intelligencer*, 12 Oct. 1871.
[124] Kennedy, *Commentary*, 3:1643-44.
[125] Van Raalte, "Farewell for Rev. Heeren," 16 June 1872, in Spykman, *Pioneer Preacher*, 113-17; *Holland City News*, 22 June 1872, 1 Aug. 1874; *De Hollander*, 2 Dec. 1874; minutes, First Holland, 20 Apr. 1875; Kennedy, *Commentary*, 7 April 1875, 3:1870. Heeren contracted a disease in India; he returned to the United States in 1877 and died in Pueblo, Colorado, in 1878.

The first years of his retirement were a whirlwind of activity, from founding the Amelia colony and Amelia Institute to marking Holland's silver anniversary to raising the Ebenezer Memorial endowment for the female seminary to the hectic visit of Cohen Stuart. These years before the flesh weakened were indeed full and challenging.

CHAPTER 16

Sunset of Life: "A quiet, joyous feeling."

In his autumn years, Dominee Van Raalte, a people-person, finally became the father and grandfather he had failed earlier to be. Never a loner, he thrived on companionship, even if only a dog. He seized on free time to write treatises on infant baptism and the secularization of public education, and preached a doctrinal sermon, uncharacteristically, on divine election. His wanderlust continued, with a winter holiday with the Gilmores in Illinois and a mission trip to frontier Kansas, Nebraska, and Iowa. A brief respite from chronic illnesses permitted him in 1875 to speak at major celebrations marking Memorial Day, the ten-year reunion of the 25th Michigan Volunteer Infantry Regiment, and the first Sabbath School convention held in Holland. Real estate sales gave him the money to bring his pioneer home up to the high standards of Mayor Cappon's Victorian mansion and other stately homes of the nouveau riche.

Wintering with the Gilmores in Illinois

Perhaps to recover and get away, Van Raalte decided to spend the winter of 1873-74 with Christine and Will Gilmore who were beginning a ten-year pastorate in the rural Spring Lake American Reformed Church in Manito, Illinois. Gilmore had been a missionary teacher and pastor in Amelia Court House for three years, from 1869 to 1872, and an instructor in the new Female Department of Hope College. He was not well received at Hope and stayed only a year. Van Raalte softened his disappointment by attributing Gilmore's resignation to reasons of health.[1]

Van Raalte traveled via St. Louis, a city with hundreds of Separatist immigrants, mostly Scholte followers who had not gone on to Pella. With no Reformed church after more than twenty-five years, Van Raalte found the St. Louis Dutch

> scattered among the Baptists, the Presbyterians, the Roman Catholics, the Darbyites, et cetera. They are alienated from each other. The "almost" Americans are ashamed of their nationality, and they avoid me.... I was considered a fox among the chickens.

This situation saddened him, but he lacked the energy to establish a church in the Gateway to the West.[2]

Over the Thanksgiving holiday at the Gilmores, Van Raalte came down with a debilitating cold and cough. This did not keep him from writing a congratulatory letter to Ben and Julia (Gilmore) Van Raalte on the birth of their first child, Julia Christina. Mother Julia was Will's younger sister. The birth served as a housewarming for Ben and Julia's new farmhouse on East Sixteenth Street, now Holland's Van Raalte Farm Park. Van Raalte also penned a reflective letter to Dirk on January 30, 1874. "Today is mother's birthday," he reminded Dirk. The thought led him to muse about her life in Heaven and his sense that he may "soon be there too.... Sometimes the thought of my approaching departure gives me a quiet, joyous feeling."[3]

Van Raalte's thoughts also turned heavenward because he had shortly before received a letter from Brummelkamp telling of his own wife Mietje's (Maria's) impending death, which occurred on December 21, 1873. Albertus's reply to Anthony, written before he received the death notice, is tender but somewhat awkward: "Tell her that her

---

[1] Julia Gilmore Van Raalte to brother Darius Gilmore, 21 May 1875 (Cindy Van Orsdal Merwin); Van Raalte to Brummelkamp, [early] Jan. 1874, HHA.
[2] Van Raalte to Anthony Brummelkamp Jr., 26 Jan. 1874, trans. unknown (HHA).
[3] Van Raalte to son Ben and wife Julia, 27 Nov. 1873; Van Raalte to son Dirk, 10, 30 Jan. (quote) 1874, HHA; *Holland City News*, 28 Feb. 1874; *Excelsiora* (Hope College student newspaper), 3 Apr. 1874; Kennedy, *Commentary*, 3 Apr. 1872, 3:1681.

passing away gives me joy; because she will soon be swallowed up in the wonderful acquaintance of Jesus." The words gushed out this way because the news "shattered my nerves," as he admitted to Anthony Jr., who posted the death notice. Mietje was the last sister to die, after Johanna van Velzen and Van Raalte's wife Christina. The news of Mietje's death led Van Raalte to reflect: "Now the three sisters, who have been our help and sweet trust during their lives, are joined again. Their labor is fulfilled. . . . I grant them to rest in peace together." He continued: "When God took my father away, on whom I concentrated my life completely, he gave me my dearest wife as a consolation." With her death, he added, "My house is empty."[4]

In the letter to Anthony, Albertus noted that, because of Will Gilmore's continued poor health, he was "busy preaching in English, unexpected and not willed. . . . Although the English language still acts as a stumbling block, oh, might the Lord's Spirit be glorified in the revelation of His most strong miracles." It truly was a wonder because Albertus had preached only in English in 1868 at informal services for Americans in Holland.[5]

Turning to Reformed theology

Back in Holland, with the rare luxury of leisure time, Van Raalte turned to Reformed theological subjects—election and infant baptism. The shift in focus likely stemmed from his being asked to substitute on occasion for Christian Van der Veen, the ailing editor of *De Hope*.[6] Van Raalte decided to preach on the "hidden counsel of God regarding election" in a sermon at the Spring Lake [Illinois] Reformed Church. This was the "hard" doctrine at the heart of the Reformed faith that left little room for free will, the side of the equation on which he had stood his entire ministry. Unfortunately, no copy of the sermon is extant. Albertus also wrote a theological treatise on infant baptism, the distinguishing Reformed sacrament rejected by Baptists and Mennonites but at the crux of the Abrahamic covenant of circumcision. The immediate purpose was to instruct Ben and Julia on their Christian duty concerning infant Julia. "Blessings cannot be received without responsibilities," he told the new parents. The handwritten treatise, written in English is titled: "Infant Baptism, presented to B. & J. Van Raalte from their father, A. C. Van Raalte, 1874."

[4] Van Raalte to Brummelkamp, Jan. 1874 (HHA).
[5] Ibid.
[6] *De Hope*, cited in *De Bazuin*, 22 Aug. 1873 (www.delpher.nl., accessed June 2021).

In the cover letter, grandfather Albertus stated his wider purpose: "That my children's children hereafter in generations may be lovers of the truth and faithful to the Church of their God on earth." He specifically asked Ben to make copies for his siblings—Helena, Dirk, Mina, and Anna. The essay follows closely the form for infant baptism in Reformed churches, except for extending the sacrament "to the children of the whole church family," whatever the spiritual status of parents. They must be dedicated to the Lord as heirs of the covenant promises. (Van Raalte never wavered from "volk" baptism.) A few weeks later, on Ben's thirty-fourth birthday, his father sent another sober letter warning him that his salvation was more important than developing a prosperous farm.[7]

Van Raalte also wrote a two-part article endorsing the Reformed weekly *De Hope*. He praised the paper awkwardly as "one of the most lesser gifts" for uniting the "Dutch emigration stream." The second longer essay a month later, "Concerning Neutral Education," condemned public schools for banning the Bible in favor of Darwinism. "To introduce ideas of Darwin in public schools would only disrupt the faith of these innocent children, who do not yet have a mature sense of judgment, a faith instilled in them by their parents or others." In short, Christian parents need Christian schools that raise and educate "*baptized citizens*," he declared, with his baptism treatise in mind. He had been educated in a Christian day school in Wanneperveen, founded such schools in Ommen and Holland, and held them close to his heart to his dying day.

That Van Raalte perceived the inroads of secularism in Holland High School already in the 1870s proves his perspicuity. He condemned public schools without Judeo-Christian values at a time when most Reformed families were quite satisfied with a veneer of Christianity. That Van Raalte had followed Groen van Prinsterer since the 1830s and subscribed to Kuyper's newspaper, *De Standaard*, in 1875, made him a Kuyperian a generation before Christian Reformed pastors in Holland had embraced Kuyperianism, even though their synod as early as 1870 had urged congregations to found Christian schools wherever possible.[8]

Van Raalte read the *De Standaard* "with much pleasure," he told

---

[7] Van Raalte, "Infant Baptism," 1874 (HHA); Van Raalte to son Ben and his wife Julia, 9 Mar., 5 May 1874 (Cindy Van Orsdal Merwin).

[8] *De Hope*, 18, 25 Feb. 1874; Van Raalte, "Opvoeding Neutraal Onderwijs" (Concerning neutral education), *De Hope*, 4 Mar. 1874 (quote), italics in original.

Anthony Brummelkamp Jr. On Kuyper rested his hope for reformation in the Dutch public church, noted the expatriate, who kept a sharp eye on religious developments in the Old Country. In fact, he had a warning for Kuyper: Beware state subsidies.

> Public opinion, influenced by the opposition, may decide that Dr. Kuyper has no longer any ecclesiastical influence. Nevertheless, the entire serious struggle and awakening in the Reformed Church is indirectly his work. Theological jealousy has done much harm. When he is chosen as a Member of Parliament, then the theological lords will calm down. Is not the doctor destined to defend the rights of the Reformed Church in the Parliament? I object strongly that modern theologians are going to occupy a lawful place in the church council and thus come into possession of our inheritance. The state subsidy is the root of this evil! Let the church be obligated to look after itself, and the confusion, or rather abnormal conjunction, will be dissolved. My heart sympathizes with the struggle.[9]

His ideal was free churches and free Christian schools, funded without a dollar of government money. He foresaw that Kuyper's model of state subsidies would eventually undermine Christian churches and schools. Far superior was the American model of member-funded churches and parent-controlled schools.

Being a grandfather

In retirement, Van Raalte was able to give more attention to his grandchildren, and he thought of them more often. With the Gilmores living in Illinois, he could bond with their son, his namesake, Albertus Christiaan Gilmore, nicknamed Raalte, and join in the boy's fourth birthday party. Second son William, "Willie," born in 1871, died before his first birthday in June 1872. And Margaret Anna was born in August 1873. Both boys were born in Amelia Court House, where their grandfather was also able to play and spend time with them. In a letter from Illinois to Dirk, Van Raalte's yet unmarried son, Van Raalte wrote: "Ben's baby is by now surely a pleasant child. I really would like to see her and I hope that may soon take place.... Greet Helena and her dear little children for me." When Dirk reported that he had sprained his ankle from his young, runaway horse, his father lamented: "Why

---

[9] Van Raalte to Anthony Brummelkamp Jr., 26 Jan. 1872, trans. unknown (HHA).

> **STATE OF MICHIGAN**
> **DOG LICENSE**
> **No. 184**
>
> **To Whom it may Concern:**
>
> I, *A. J. Hillebrands*, Clerk of the Township of *Holland*, DO HEREBY GRANT A LICENSE to *A. C. van Raalte* to keep a male dog: from *August 14* A. D. 1873, to April 1st, A. D. 1874, inclusive, Described as follows, to-wit:
> Color *White with black head*, Age *two months*, and name of dog *Rover*.
> Said License is granted in pursuance of the Statute in such case made and provided; for which there has been paid to me the sum of *One* dollar.
> Dated, *August 14* A. D. 1873.
>
> *A. J. Hillebrands*, TOWN CLERK.

Dog license for Van Raalte's puppy, Rover, August 14, 1873 (HHA)

may not I as your father share in the life and lot of my sons? What evil have I done?" He could have answered his own questions—stop taking distant mission trips. Back in Holland, the five children of Bertus and Helena were underfoot at the homestead, taking care of it, and relishing the newest addition to the family, the puppy Rover, a white-haired male with a distinctive black head, whom the dominee licensed for one dollar.[10]

Mission trip to Kansas

Ever a missionary at heart, Van Raalte in early 1870 wrote an open letter to the immigrant colony in Rotterdam (later Dispatch), Kansas, informing them that he had alerted the pastors of the Classis of Holland about the Kansas immigration and the need for financial help for the new congregations. He asked for local maps and about the distance from the nearest railroad station. Most important, he told the newcomers, was to lay a solid foundation of Christian elementary

---

[10] Van Raalte to son Dirk, 15 June 1874; dog license, 14 Aug. 1873, HHA.

and higher education. He urged them to set aside 160 acres to fund school buildings because "prominent gentlemen" in New York, such as the Schieffelin brothers, would give money for teachers. Van Raalte, as domestic mission chair of classis, brought this concern to the April 1870 meeting, warning the brethren that God willed them to "prevent the scattering of the seed of our congregations and of this emigration, which is put exclusively into our hands by God."[11]

Van Raalte was grateful that the denominational board was fully committed to gathering Dutch Reformed immigrants, scattered in "outposts across Minnesota, Kansas, Nebraska, Virginia, and Northern Iowa," and to planting churches "in the language of this country, as well as in our native tongue." The denomination, he declared, was "a blessing for our emigration stream and rescued it from dispersion, in spite of the hundreds of hours distance."[12]

In 1874 Van Raalte put legs on his Kansas campaign. He had hoped to go in 1873, but a "nervous debility" stopped him. He may have been infected by the Gilmore children, Raalte and Margaret, who were "quite sick." Then, in January 1874, while riding on a small streetcar, perhaps in Grand Rapids, he narrowly avoided injury when, in his words: "A heavy bay of runaway horses ran into the backside of the car where I was seated. The car was smashed, and I was astonished that my life was saved, apart from a bleeding ear and some scratches." In June his health allowed him to go west. He asked Phelps for his opinion.

> Would you conscientiously advise me to give myself to any business since I am a prey of a severe prostration of the nervous system, besides other serious disorders? Medical judgment calls it sure death, even they [the doctors] despair of my restoration if I remain where I am. And no wonder, because a conversation, yea, a walk, calmly, but farther than a mile, throws me in a fever.[13]

Given his general weakness, it was only an act of will that enabled him to make this last mission trip in the summer of 1874. And he almost had to turn back. In Nebraska, aboard the Union Pacific Railroad from Chicago, the elderly dominee took sick. But after

---

[11] Van Raalte to Dutch in Kansas, 10 Mar. 1870, published in *De Hope*, 7 Dec. 1904; Kennedy, *Commentary*, 6 Apr. 1870, 3:1552-53, 1561-62.

[12] Kennedy, *Commentary*, 14 Jan. 1873, 3:1716 (quote); Van Raalte to son Ben and wife Julia, 5 May 1874, HHA; minutes, Hope College Council, 26 May 1874, JAH.

[13] Van Raalte to Phelps, 31 May 1873, in *Envisioning Hope College*, 316. The runaway horses incident was reported, remarkably, only in the Netherlands church periodical, *De Bazuin*, 16 Jan. 1874 (www.delpher.nl, accessed June 2021).

Sod house on the western plains, model constructed for Sioux Center, Iowa's, 75th anniversary, July 1947 (Ebenezer 1847-1947 Centennial Souvenir)

"some remedies" (specifically, febrifuge, a fever reducer, like aspirin), he felt better and "risked going farther," specifically, ninety miles by stagecoach south to Manhattan in Smith County, midway across the northern border of Kansas.

The first sod houses he saw amazed him. "They have thick walls and are therefore much warmer than defective log cabins." He was hosted for almost a month in "a little sod house with a wooden floor and plastered walls. It is suitable alright," he told Dirk. The esteemed dominee was obviously not too proud for "pioneer living." His host family reported that the dominee "went out on his horse, crossing the prairies, visiting every one, encouraging everyone, pointing out the right way to live, and cherishing great expectations for Kansas." He preached catechism sermons every Sunday and urged the elders to begin catechism classes and start a church library. In his old age, he was reliving his youth as the itinerant preacher of Overijssel. He did double duty by collecting Ebenezer Fund contributions from "warm friends" in western churches for the Holland Academy endowment. "Cash was found everywhere," he gushed, and the endowment totals could possibly reach $104,000 ($2.8 million today).[14]

---

[14] Van Raalte to son Dirk, 1, 4, 15 June, 9 July 1874, HHA; Van Raalte letter from Kansas, *De Hope*, 7 Dec. 1904.

A. C. Van Raalte Church, Thule (Hull), South Dakota. The only sod church in the RCA, organized on October 8, 1886. The sixteen-by-thirty-foot sanctuary had whitewashed interior walls (HHA)

Van Raalte's most awful lament was that immigrants were scattering widely in search of free homesteads because transcontinental railroads owned alternate sections along their rights of way that sold for double the government minimum and more. This left gaps of virgin land. As a result, "The lack of schools and church benefits make many a person sick and faint hearted." Van Raalte preached both services for several Sundays and installed a consistory at Rotterdam, but the congregation had to wait six years for its first pastor. On his way home, Van Raalte stopped briefly at Holland, Nebraska, near Lincoln, where his student, Rev. Jan W. Te Winkel, served the young Reformed Church. The honored dominee then paid a brief visit to Orange City, Iowa, looking "fresh and healthy," according to the local newspaper, *De Volksvriend*. He was back in Holland by late July and mounted his old pulpit at First Church as guest preacher. The entire trip west, covering more than two thousand miles, pushed the elderly dominee to the limit of his endurance, but he managed it.[15]

[15] Van Raalte to son Dirk, 15 June 1874, HHA; Van Raalte to Phelps, 19 June 1874, in *Envisioning Hope College*, 323; *De Volksvriend*, 23 July 1874; *Holland City News*, 1 Aug. 1874.

Enlarging the homestead

Van Raalte's impressive home on Fairbanks Avenue was fit for a wealthy, landed dominee. But it could not compare with John Coatsworth's French Provincial-style mansion, erected in 1863, or Mayor Isaac Cappon's mansion, erected in 1873, facing each other on West Ninth Street across Washington Avenue. Van Raalte's home rivaled that of physician Geert Manting, erected in 1868, on the southeast corner of Michigan Avenue and Fortieth Street. Andries Steketee's two-story brick home, erected in 1851, on Old Groningen Road (Paw Paw Road) in Holland Township, surpassed Van Raalte's home in size but not in style.[16]

Van Raalte determined to bring his home up to the standards of these buildings. It was a form of keeping up with the Joneses. Over four years, from 1873 until the spring of 1876, six months before his death, Van Raalte directed the project to enlarge and upgrade his homestead. The entire first floor was covered in brick veneer, capped with a welcoming, wrap-around porch. Second and third floors were added, served by an elegant cherry wood staircase, leading to eight bedrooms on the second floor and the dominee's study on the entire third floor. The cellar floor was covered with cherrywood planks, and the tunnel to the barn/carriage house was lined with bricks. The expansion almost tripled the number of rooms, from seven to twenty. The widower and his two unmarried daughters, Mina and Anna, hardly needed more space. They were the only occupants after Christina died. Dirk was living with brother Ben and his wife Julia on their farm. Three years into the project, Van Raalte reported in 1875: "We are still in an open house. The roof has been laid and the glass put in partially, but the bricks have not been placed yet around the first floor. So we live in hope." He had expected the brick work to be finished by mid-November.[17]

The expansion was to benefit son Dirk, slated to purchase the now 120-acre homestead for $10,000 ($284,000 today). The transaction

---

[16] Swierenga, *Holland, Michigan*, 1:76, 148-49, 167, 710, 798. Steketee's home and shipping depot at the head of navigation on Black [Macatawa] River is the oldest immigrant home in the Holland area, located at 1811 112th Avenue. George Smith's home at Old Wing Mission on East Fortieth Street in Fillmore Township, dating from 1845, is the oldest home in the Holland area.

[17] *Holland City News*, 4 Apr. 1874; 12 June, 18 Dec. 1875; *Allegan Journal*, 31 Oct. 1874; Julia Gilmore Van Raalte to brother Darius Gilmore, 21 May 1875 (Cindy Van Orsdal Merwin); Van Raalte to daughter Christine Gilmore, 25 Oct. 1875 (Charles Vander Broek). The definitive history of the house is in Bruins et al., *Albertus and Christina*, ch 2.

Van Raalte homestead in later years, after additions, and before it was abandoned and razed in 1961. No photo is extant of the original house
(JAH)

occurred in August 1876, several months before his father's death. Dirk likely handled the details of the construction, although his father ordered and paid for all the materials. These included thirteen thousand bricks, seventy-five hundred board feet of pine and hemlock lumber and flooring, windows, doors, and hardware of all kinds. The many bills totaled $5,200 ($148,000 today). Only a wealthy man would undertake such a massive home improvement in a race against his life.[18]

Dirk, who became a prosperous merchant and Michigan state representative (1875-79), married Kate Ledeboer in 1880 and with her raised four children in the home.[19] Dirk's Civil War service, his obvious injury, and his famous last name made his quest for elective office a cinch. He and then his descendants lived in that home for seventy-one years, until 1947, when Dirk's grandson Dick sold the homestead to William B. Eerdmans Sr., at the behest of Albert Hyma. Hyma that same year had acquired from the family the Van Raalte Papers, including land and financial records, and used them to write the first biography of Van Raalte in English for the city's centennial celebration. Hyma induced Eerdmans to buy the collection in 1947 and create a Van Raalte Institute in the original Van Raalte home.

Eerdmans agreed and found a possible docent, the recently retired Jacob van Hinte, who in 1928 had published the first comprehensive

---

[18] Van Raalte receipts for building materials, 1872-76, HHA.
[19] Bruins et al., *Albertus and Christina*, 130.

history of Dutch immigration and settlement, *Nederlanders in Amerika*. Van Hinte, who was proficient in English, agreed to be the docent and to translate the Van Raalte Papers. Regrettably, he died unexpectedly, and Eerdmans' plans for the archives and historic house came to naught. So Eerdmans donated the house to Hope College with no strings attached. He assumed the college would preserve the historic house of the city's founder, but instead, the building, although loosely boarded up, was left to mischievous youth to explore and vandals to trash. In 1961 the college board of trustees had the building razed for an athletic field, to the consternation of the Tulip Time and tourist boards.[20]

Virtuoso orator

Van Raalte enjoyed an unexpected spurt of good health in 1875. He wrote his daughter, Christine Gilmore, in Spring Lake, Illinois: "My health is fine, not free from rheumatism and minor illness, but I could not have expected the way it is." This enabled him to put on paper several Heidelberg Catechism sermons he had often preached—Lord's Day 43, "The Ninth Commandment," and Lord's Day 31, "The Keys of the Kingdom." By request, he composed a brief history of Holland's founding. More important, he had the energy to speak at several large community events. The historical overview repeated themes in earlier writings: the "great religious awakening" in 1834 and subsequent persecution, the "sinking of the middle class" in the Netherlands, the emigration of congregations for religious and educational freedom and "wonderful self-government," the advantages of the Black Lake region, the rapid growth of the colony despite hardships, and the vast developments in the first quarter century—all "under God's guidance."[21]

Memorial Day 1875 address

Memorial Day celebrations in the 1870s resembled those of today, which proves the strength of the tradition. On May 31, 1875, the city band led a parade, followed by firemen with their pumpers, veterans, city aldermen, and the general public. At the cemetery, distinguished men spoke, and youths laid flowers on graves of fallen Civil War soldiers, all grouped at the west end of the cemetery. Van Raalte, a regular

---

[20] Ibid., 31-62, details the history of the Van Raalte home and papers. See also, Van Hinte, *Nederlanders*, introduction, xxxv-xliv; Ester et al., *American Diary*, 17-18.
[21] Van Raalte to daughter Christine Gilmore, 25 Oct. 1875 (Charles Vander Broek); Van Raalte, "History of the Founding of Holland" (in English), 9 Nov. 1875, HMA.

at the podium, spoke for the last time at the solemn annual event. Unfortunately, his address was not summarized in the newspaper or found among his personal papers. But his speech was likely a rehearsal of the address he would deliver at the Civil War memorial just four months later. Between these two events, the local newspaper reported in early July that he had made a quick trip to Pella "to fix up some church troubles there." This was his fourth time in Pella, but it was a shorter stay than his earlier visits. As the heart and soul of the classical missions committee, Van Raalte likely went of his own accord since the Classis of Holland had not directly delegated him. Classis, however, was concerned about a renegade pastor from the Netherlands who was ministering in vacant Pella-area churches.[22]

On his return, the dominee presided over a meeting of the Holland Cemetery Association, of which he was the long-time president, in a move to enlarge the burial ground on the east and the north, including Van Raalte's orchard. He also participated in two funerals at Third Reformed Church, together with their pastor, Henry Uiterwyk, his former catechumen. The first was for eleven-year-old William "Willie" Van der Veen, who died while playing at a shipyard. Willie's father, Engbertus, was a prominent merchant and brother of Rev. Christian Van der Veen, Van Raalte's close associate. The second funeral was for Frederik Van der Belt, a member of the 25th Michigan Infantry.[23]

25th Michigan Infantry reunion

On September 22, 1875, Van Raalte had a final opportunity to speak in a large public ceremony staged by the 25th Michigan Infantry regiment in Market Square (renamed Centennial Park in 1876). It was the birth on the tenth anniversary of Appomattox of the Albertus C. Van Raalte Post No. 262, Grand Army of the Republic, so named in his honor. His sons Ben and Dirk faced him, along with their comrades, with hundreds of local citizens filling in the rear.[24]

The dominee spoke in English—his second language—for this civic event. To avoid stumbling, he wrote out the speech and marked

---

[22] *Holland City News*, 3 July 1875; Van Raalte to Christian Van der Veen, 11 Aug. 1875, HHA; Kennedy, *Commentary*, 7 Apr. 1875, 3:1898-1902. The cleric was Arie G. Zigeler of Amsterdam.
[23] *De Hollander*, 2 June, 16 Aug. 1875, trans. Ten Hoor; *Holland City News*, 3, 17 July, 7 Aug. 1875.
[24] *De Hollander*, 25 Sept. 1875, trans. Simone Kennedy; *Holland City News*, 25 Nov., 11, 25 Dec. 1875; *Allegan Journal*, 25 Sept. 1875.

the main points on the left margin. Looking at the officers and soldiers of the renowned 25th Michigan, he said:

> We rejoice to receive you as our guests. We thank you for the honor to hold your reunion in our city. Your self-sacrifice for our country... in time of danger does deserve high appreciation in time of peace. Welcome, welcome then, beloved and honored 25th! Your presence thrills our hearts with the deepest emotions. We tasted the cup of bringing our beloved ones on the altar of our country. And yet, though there are among us tears and sorely bleeding hearts, yet how many are given back to us. You are all monuments of God's sparing mercy and love![25]

Addressing the vast crowd, he warned: "May none of us ever ungrateful forget it." Then pointing to First Church, he declared:

> There, that house of God, our place of prayer for you, while you fought our battles.... That memorable 4th of July on that Green River Bend [the famous battle of Tebbs Bend], posterity will remember. And that heroic stand, by which the threatening tidal wave of destruction over our northern regions was stayed [the battles of Gettysburg and Antietam], will receive its just dues as a most important link in our victory, securing the salvation of our invaluable union, and in deliverance from our African slavery, and the peace for our country.

Ever the evangelical preacher, Van Raalte closed with the prayer "that you may all earn that never fading crown in the higher battles under the Captain of our Salvation, Jesus Christ." It was a masterful moment that proved again the Dutch dominee's total allegiance to his adopted nation and his abhorrence of slavery. A banquet at Kenyon's Hall for four hundred comrades, wives, and invited guests topped off the day, with toasts by Michigan governor John J. Bagley, US Senator Thomas Ferry, and others. Another four hundred curious onlookers filled the balcony. The entire event was a grand success.

Sunday school convention address

The esteemed dominee's speaking engagements continued into the fall of 1875. In early October, Third Reformed Church, under

---

[25] Jacobson et al., *Dutch Leader*, 216 (quotes); and in Spykman, *Pioneer Preacher*, 141-42, for this and the next paragraph.

Henry Uiterwyk, hosted the First Holland Sabbath School convention, a two-day affair, for thirteen schools in the area. Elder Frans Van Driele of Second Grand Rapids Reformed Church spearheaded the event. The Reformed Church, under the influence of the 1801 Plan of Union of Presbyterian and Congregational churches and its interdenominational American Sunday School Union, formed its own Sabbath Union, with meatier Calvinistic lesson books.[26]

The Holland convention began with a review by Rev. Nicholas H. Dosker, the father of Van Driele's pastor Henry Dosker, on the origins and history of Sabbath schools. Teunis Keppel told of the first schools in the colony, and Uiterwyk spoke on "Sabbath Schools and Church" and Van Raalte on "Sabbath Schools and Family." Van Raalte called such schools "a blessed influence" and a way "to seek the lost," but without homes built on the "Cornerstone"—Jesus—the "scaffolding falls away." Again, he wrote his text in English. The evangelistic dominee had long been a strong advocate of Sunday school. Three years after founding the Log Church, he happily informed the Classis of Holland that a New York friend had given Sabbath school books for each congregation. "He pointed out how useful these would be for the children of the church." Written in English, these books hastened Americanization for the youth. Van Raalte's congregation in the early 1860s proudly reported 165 children in Sunday school. As public school curricula became more secular, Sunday schools became all the more necessary for studying the Bible.[27]

Losing a Christian warrior

In early 1876 Van Raalte began his final decline. In March he was reportedly "very low" with "many ailments" and "confined to his room." When he was unable to attend the May Classis of Holland meeting, the brethren prayed "that he may be spared for the church of God on earth and particularly for us." Albertus felt "slightly better" in the balmy spring weather, and the reprieve gave him the stamina on May 31 to perform an evening wedding at the residence of his daughter Mina, widow of Rev. Peter Oggel, to Teunis Keppel, a widower fifteen

---

[26] Van Raalte, "Sabbath School and Church," 5 Oct. 1873, in Spykman, *Pioneer Preacher*, 118-20; *Holland City News*, 9 Oct. 1875; Kennedy, *Commentary*, 30 Oct. 1850, 1:111-12. The young CRC strongly opposed Sunday schools, especially if they used Arminian-laced ASSU lessons, which led youth "astray" (ibid., 13 Sept. 1854, 1:453; 20 Aug. 1856, 1:624-25; 8 Apr. 1857, 2:710-11).

[27] *Holland City News*, 9 Oct. 1875; Kennedy, *Commentary*, 30 Oct. 1850, 1:111-12; 5 Apr. 1876, 3:1953-56; minutes, First Holland, 30 Mar. 1863.

Marriage certificate of Teunis J. Keppel and Johanna Maria "Mina" Van Raalte Oggel Keppel, May 31, 1876, last document in Van Raalte's handwriting (HHA)

years her senior with five grown children. Given the age difference, the marriage "caused considerable comment," but Mina, who had been a widow for six years, had an eleven-year-old daughter and no means of support. Keppel, a well-to-do merchant, gained a reputable wife and she a reputable husband to share twenty autumn years together. Van Raalte did not live to see Keppel lead First Church out of the denomination only six years later over the Freemasonry issue.[28]

In June the dominee sought relief from intense rheumatic pain by traveling out of state to Toledo, Ohio, and Buffalo, New York, to be examined by leading physicians. He returned home without relief in an "exhausted condition." Home remedies and patent medicines had to

---

[28] *Holland City News*, 18 Mar., 20, 26 May, 26 Aug. 1876; Pieters to Brummelkamp, *De Bazuin*, 11 Mar. 1876 (www.delpher.nl, accessed, June 2021); Kennedy, *Commentary*, 5 Apr. 1876, 3:1960-61; "Geesje Van der Haar-Visscher Diary," English typescript, 45 (quote).

Teunis and Mina Van Raalte Oggel Keppel
(courtesy John and Francis Van der Broek)

suffice from then on. In his final months, he ordered $30 ($853 today) in ointments, plasters, oils, and pills. On the nation's centennial, July 4, 1876, he wanted to attend the ceremony in person to dedicate Centennial Park, the refurbished Market Square, but could do so only in spirit. The concert band regaled the large crowd as the Stars and Stripes were unfurled atop a 130-foot pole in the center of the ellipse.[29]

Newspapers reported in August that the dominee was confined to bed with breathing difficulties, a "terrible sufferer" who "cannot recover." The death on August 23 of Cornelius Van der Meulen, the founding pastor of the Zeeland congregation, deepened the mood. In late August, it was "rumored on the street that he [Van Raalte] is failing and will not survive many days." In September he was "hopelessly ill," but he hung on through October, suffocating from congestion. "Oh," he said to daughter Mary, "if only I could rest my head on Mother's chest for a while, but I shall see her, child, and Jesus, I will see; have patience." According to a news reporter, the "dying dominee refused to spend his days in bed; he preferred to sit at the table fully dressed, still wearing his riding boots."[30]

---

[29] *Holland City News*, 10 June 1876; Swierenga, *Holland, Michigan*, 3:1909-10.
[30] *Holland City News*, 10, 12, 24 June, 5, 26 Aug., 7, 21 Oct. 1876; *Allegan Journal*, 5 Aug. 1876; "Ministerial Register," *The Independent*, 14 Sept. 1876; De Vries and Boonstra, *Pillar Church*, 106-9 (quote 107); Dosker, *Van Raalte*, 309 (quote), trans.

Geesje and husband Jan Visscher called on the dominee sometime in September and were mutually blessed.

> We were admitted by a daughter [Mary or Anna], and she went to announce to Van Raalte who was calling. We went to his bedroom, and he was glad to see us. He lay propped up in bed having a lot of pain and hardly able to speak. His daughter helped him from the bed to an easy chair. Now he seemed to be able to talk better and was quite cheerful. It was a sad experience for us to see a man who had been so forceful and dynamic and now so weak that he had to be helped like a child. We couldn't understand all he said, but he spoke about God's goodness and Jesus' love for sinners. He said he had never experienced so much of God's goodness as now. It was good to hear him say those things, and now he asked my husband to offer a prayer. We said goodbye to him but had the feeling that it was very likely the last time we would see him alive. He was so happy that we had called, as witnesses to a common faith, so he said.[31]

In his final months, Van Raalte found the energy to bequeath his real estate holdings, estimated to be valued at $122,152 ($3.5 million today), to his seven children and their spouses—$500,000 each in today's dollars (ch. 12). The deeds were recorded on September 20, 1876, but the distribution was likely done some weeks earlier.[32] This princely inheritance and farewell gift for the children perhaps was recompense for growing up in the parsonage with a preoccupied and often absent father.

The day before Van Raalte died, Rev. Pieters, his pastor and successor at First Church, found

> his eyes already broken, having lost appetite, limited in speech, trouble in breathing, yet he sat in his armchair at the table. He gave us still the clearest proofs, even in broken words, that his soul was at rest, and that he, as a lost, yet believing, sinner, surrendered himself in childlike trust to the arms of the all sufficient Redeemer.

Dekker; obits., "Dr. Van Raalte" and "Cornelius Van der Meulen," in *Christian Intelligencer*, 23, 30 Nov. 1876; "Dr. Van Raalte" obit., Brummelkamp, *De Bazuin*, 24 Nov. 1876 (www.delpher.nl, accessed June 2021). Van Raalte account with Heber Walsh, "Wholesale and Retail Druggist, 1 Jan. 1877, for Oct.-Nov. 1876, HHA.

[31] "Geesje Van der Haar-Visscher Diary," 46.
[32] Swierenga, "Real Estate Sales."

The "lost sinner" comment harkens back to Van Raalte's early ministry among the experiential Cross Followers (Kruisgezinden) in his congregations who were never fully convinced of Christ's mercy. Had he fallen back into that rejection of pure grace?[33]

On Monday, November 6, Van Raalte's last night on earth, he administered the Lord's Supper to his family and had evening prayers with daughters Mina and Anna, daughter-in-law Helena, and sons Ben and Dirk. Daughter Christine Gilmore did not arrive from Illinois in time to see her father alive. During the night, Van Raalte reflected humbly on his life. "I have done something with God's help, but it could have been so much more." Later, he spoke in Dutch: "Mijn bootje zwabbert nu op de schuimende golven; spoedig zal het in de haven zijn" (My little boat is now tossed about in the foaming waves; soon it will be in the harbor). He told his children in a faint, rasping voice: "Do not cry as I shut my eyes, you can be sure that I will rejoice in the hallelujahs before the throne."

At five o'clock in the morning, Van Raalte asked for something to eat but had to put it aside. The congestion was unbearable, and putting his hands on his chest, he said in a broken voice: "It churns so." A moment later, he asked for something to drink, and when son Dirk handed it to him, he said "Thank you." These were his last clear words. At 7:30 a.m., on November 7, 1876, he spoke an inaudible word to each of his children, smiled at them, and "pointing his fingers heavenward, he breathed his last." A disorder of the lungs had claimed his life, most likely tuberculosis, the disease that had had claimed Christina, her sister Johanna Van Velzen, Van Raalte's brother Petrus, his son-in-law Peter Oggel, John and Elizabeth Van Vleck, and so many other of his contemporaries. The dauntless dominee's battle with the last enemy was over, and his suffering mercifully ended. His mind was clear to the end.

"Dominee Van Raalte is Dead"

Van Raalte died a good death in his own bed surrounded by his loved ones, just like his beloved Christina who had breathed her last in the same bed five years earlier. "He died as he lived," Brummelkamp declared. "He has won much; his children and God's church have lost much. . . . How many were revived and strengthened by his mighty and gripping preaching and brought to the Lord will become evident

---

[33] Roelof Pieters, "In Memoriam of Dr. A. C. Van Raalte," *De Hope*, 15 Nov. 1876, trans. Nella Kennedy.

first in eternity." The sexton tolled the bell slowly, sixty-five times, Van Raalte's age, as was the custom, to alert the town to his death. Counting the tones gave everyone a strong clue that it was the dominee. The community was plunged into mourning for several weeks. "The blow, so long expected, had fallen."[34]

Local newspapers ran the story with all columns thickly lined in black ink, signifying mourning. *De Grondwet*, the newspaper Van Raalte had founded, captured the mood of the day:

> "Dominee Van Raalte is dead." Such was the message that passed from neighbor to neighbor in our community on the morning of election day. [November 7 was the fraught Tilden-Hays election.] Although it came in the moment when the attention of every citizen was absorbed by the commencement of the most exciting and perhaps the most political contest this nation ever witnessed, every voice was hushed, and every heart saddened, by the sound of a death knell amid the joy and excitement of festivity. . . . He takes the first place in our history as the organizer and pioneer of our settlement, and the founder of our religious and educational institutions.[35]

Of the four brothers-in-law who had first met at Leiden University in the early 1830s, Van Raalte, born in 1811, died first, at age sixty-five. Carel de Moen and Anthony Brummelkamp, who shared Van Raalte's birth year, lived to ages sixty-eight (1879) and seventy-seven (1888), respectively. Simon van Velzen, less than two years older than the others, lived to age eighty-six (1896). Van Raalte's decision to lead the emigration to America made his life far more stressful and may even have cut it short.

That the Dutch American patriot died on the morning of the contested 1876 election spared him the agony of living through four months of bitter controversy over the presidency. In a testimony to his reputation, his death quelled the tension in the community from the bitter campaign to end federal oversight of the former Confederacy. Democrat Samuel Tilden won the popular vote over Republican Rutherford B. Hayes by a thin margin of less than 255,000 of votes,

---

[34] Dosker, *Van Raalte*, 310 (quote), trans. Dekker; Brummelkamp, "Dr. Van Raalte," *De Bazuin*, 24 Nov. 1876 (www.delpher.nl, accessed June 2021), trans. Ten Hoor, Kampen Theological School; *De Hope*, 15 Nov. 1876, trans. Hero Bratt.

[35] *De Grondwet*, 14 Nov. 1876, trans. Nella Kennedy.

HOLLAND CITY NEWS.

SATURDAY, NOVEMBER 11, 1876.

"Dominie Van Raalte is Dead."

Such was the message which passed from neighbor to neighbor in our community on the morning of the election day. Although it came at the moment when the attention of every citizen was absorbed by the commencement of the most exciting and perhaps the most important political contest this nation has ever witnessed, every voice was hushed, and every heart was saddened, as by the sound of a death knell amid the joy and excitement of a great festivity.

He has passed from earth, and while his memory will be forever cherished by his kindred and his numerous friends, he takes the first place in our history as the organizer and pioneer of our settlement, and the founder of our religious and educational institutions. The results of his labors will ever be his noblest monument.

ALBERTUS CHRISTIAAN VAN RAALTE was born at Wanneperveen, Overijssel, Kingdom of the Netherlands, October 17th, 1811. He received his classical education at the University of Leyden, and after a course of theological study, entered the gospel ministry.

De Grondwet reporting Van Raalte's death, November 14, 1876 (JAH)

or .03 percent of the total votes cast, but Hayes ended on top with one more electoral vote than Tilden. Congressmen finally reached a deal—the presidency for Hayes in exchange for his pulling all federal troops out of the South, thereby leaving Southern Democrats free to resegregate blacks for what turned out to be ninety years. Van Raalte would likely have approved this deal, since survival of the Union was paramount in his mind.[36]

Funeral solemnities

It "rained resolutions" at Van Raalte's passing, starting with Mayor John Van Landegend's resolution, read at a hastily convened city council the same evening. It read:

> Gentlemen: Amid the multiplicity of duties devolving upon us during an important election, news has been communicated to me of the death of the Rev. A. C. Van Raalte at 7:30 this A.M. Dr. Van Raalte was the founder of this city and of this colony. His long and successful life among us, his energy and fortitude during the early settlement of this colony, his devotedness to the interests of this people, his charity, kindness and watchful care of those who with him left the "fatherland" for the greater freedom of this country, are records of an honorable life embalmed in history, and as successors and co-laborers with him, I deem it my duty, not without regrets, to convene this council, that appropriate measures be taken and resolutions adopted befitting the occasion.[37]

The mayor called for flags to fly at half staff, for schools, stores, and businesses to close the afternoon of the funeral, and for homes, businesses, and public buildings to be draped in mourning crepe. The city council praised the dominee as "an efficient instrument in the hands of Providence in securing happiness and a home to the hundreds that followed him." The college council praised the founder for calling the school "my anchor of hope for this people in the future." The theology faculty specifically recognized Van Raalte's efforts on behalf of Christian education. Classes at the college and preparatory school were canceled after Tuesday's sad news for the rest of the

---

[36] Dosker, *Van Raalte*, 312.
[37] City council resolution, 7 Nov. 1876, quoted in Hyma, *Van Raalte*, 252-53.

PROCLAMATION.

In accordance with the recommendation of the Common Council of this city made at their extra session on Wednesday last, and in token of respect to the memory of our deceased friend and father, Rev. A. C. Van Raalte, D. D. I, John Van Landegend, Mayor of the City of Holland, hereby request, that on the afternoon of next Friday, the 10th inst., it being the time designated for the funeral of the deceased, all business in this city be suspended; that the Public Schools be closed and that each citizen as he appreciates the past services of our departed leader, drape his respective residence or place of business in mourning.

Given under my hand, at the City of Holland, this 9th day of November, A. D. 1876.

JOHN VAN LANDEGEND, Mayor.

Common Council proclamation declaring a cessation of all business and schools during the Friday afternoon funeral of "our deceased friend and father, Rev A. C. Van Raalte" (HMA)

week.[38] Eulogies were also articulated in the Netherlands. Anthony Brummelkamp spoke of the great strength God had given "that short man" and the many talents that he had developed to the full.[39]

The day of the funeral, Friday, November 10, dawned with a clear blue sky, typical of Indian summer. Family and friends assembled first at the Van Raalte homestead, where the body had lain in state for several days in a beautifully carved oak casket. Rev. A. C. Kuyper of Ebenezer

---

[38] Common council resolution, 8 Nov. 1876, printed in *Holland City News*, 11 Nov. 1876; minutes, Hope College Council, 13 Nov 1876; Hope College theology faculty resolution, 8 Nov. 1876.

[39] Brummelkamp, "Dr. Albertus Christiaan van Raalte," 92.

First Reformed Church, decorated for the American Centennial in 1876, as it looked for Van Raalte's funeral. This is the oldest photograph of the sanctuary. Note the ladies' fans lying on the front rows (HHA)

Church led in prayer. Then the undertaker conveyed the corpse to First Church for the funeral service, with the casket set front and center. The pillared entrance was draped in crepe and also the pulpit and lamps.

Van Raalte's funeral with two thousand attendees was second only to the 1931 funeral, "fit for a president," of Holland attorney, Gerrit J. Diekema (1859-1930), US Ambassador to the Netherlands, congressman, city mayor, and political orator par excellence.[40] Since crowds were expected that would fill the large sanctuary twice over for Holland's first dominee, Rev. Pieters, and city leaders asked ex-mayor Isaac Cappon and alderman Leendert Kanters to handle funeral planning. The pair reserved seats for Hope College professors and board members, public school teachers and board members, city aldermen and township trustees, judges, newspaper editors, and other dignitaries, including US senator and acting vice president Thomas White Ferry of Grand Haven, and his brother, Grand Rapids mayor William Montague Ferry Jr. (1824-1906).

The dignitaries filled all the pews, to the consternation of ordinary people who had come from as far away as Grand Rapids and Grand Haven to "be ear- and eye-witnesses to the ceremony." A few could stand in the aisles and narthex, but most had to remain outside and hope to catch a few words through the open windows. Otto Doesburg, editor of the Democratic sheet, *De Hollander*, and son of Van Raalte's

---

[40] Swierenga, *Holland, Michigan*, 3:1730-33.

long-time nemesis, Hermanus Doesburg, published an anonymous complaint that seating arrangements amounted to "flagrant" class discrimination. Like so often in Van Raalte's life, even his funeral had some bad press.[41]

The service opened with a medieval Advent hymn, a favorite in the Van Raalte home: "Daar komt een schip, geladen tot aan het hoogste boord, draagt Gods Zoon vol genade, des Vaders eeuwig woord" (There comes a galley laden, carrying God's Son full of grace, the Father's eternal word). Pieters then offered prayer, and Henry Uiterwyk of Third Church read scripture, both in Dutch. Pieters continued in Dutch with a brief and touching description of the life of the deceased, based on II Kings 2:12 (KJV): "My father, my father, the chariots of Israel and the horsemen thereof," referencing Elijah, the greatest prophet of Israel, entering Heaven in chariots of fire.

Geesje Visscher recalled Pieters' message vividly:

> He emphasized how Van Raalte had lived among his people as a father and that he would be missed as a leader and advisor, also that he would live forever in the hearts of those who had become converted through his preaching or comforted by them. Then he mentioned how Van Raalte had fought for the establishment of a school for higher education, that we were now plucking the fruits of his efforts every year. He particularly noted how much Van Raalte had suffered during his illness and what a profound sense of unworthiness he experienced, always telling about the love of his dear Savior.[42]

College president Philip Phelps Jr., Van Raalte's closest friend, preached the funeral sermon in English, on II Samuel 3:38 (KJV), the words of King David: "Know ye not that there is a prince and a great man fallen this day in Israel?" Van der Haar-Visscher again recalled the gist of the message. Phelps praised his partner as

> a great man both in church life and civic life who had performed an inestimable amount of good in both fields. He also admonished the people to walk in his footsteps and never to forget him who had taught them so much and who had died with such an abundant faith in his God and Savior.

---

[41] "Funeral Solemnities," *De Hollander*, 15 Nov. 1876; "Dr. Van Raalte's Funeral," *Holland City News*, 18 Nov. 1876.
[42] "Geesje Van der Haar-Visscher Diary," 47.

John Alberti livery stable, Ninth Street (*HHA*)

Phelps closed the service in prayer after attendees sang Psalm 62:2, a favorite from the Dutch psalter that Van Raalte had requested: "Exalt, exalt the name of God; Sing, sing his royal fame abroad with fervent exaltation; . . . The Lord is our salvation" (1987 psalter versification).[43]

After the service, mourners passed the open casket for almost an hour "to view the remains of the highly honored man. . . . He hadn't changed any and lay in his coffin as if alive," recalled Geesje Visscher, who managed to find a seat in her sister's pew. Then the lid was closed, and pallbearers carried the coffin to the hearse, led by two aged Reformed Church pastors: Rev. Nicholas H. Dosker, Henry's father, of the Classis of Grand Haven, and Rev. A. C. Kuyper of the Classis of Holland; and six elders and deacons of First Reformed Church. Undertaker John Alberti likely prepared the body, as he had for Christina five years earlier, and supplied the hearse and carriages for the family. Other guests used their own carriages and buggies or rented them from Alberti or Jacobus Nibbelink and Hermanus Boone, the other liverymen in town.[44]

---

[43] Ibid., 40-41; *De Hope*, 15 Nov. 1876; *De Hollander*, 15 Nov. 1876, trans. Simone Kennedy; *Holland City News*, 18 Nov. 1876.

[44] *De Grondwet*, 14 Nov. 1876; "Geesje Van der Haar-Visscher Diary," 48; Swierenga, *Holland, Michigan*, 2:1294-97.

Jacobus Nibbelink livery hearse that carried Van Raalte's coffin to the cemetery. In 1886 Dirk Van Eenenaam, Zeeland liveryman, acquired the hearse, said to be the finest in the county. (*courtesy Hofman Museum, Beaverdam, MI*)

Lining up the stately procession was a challenge. The cortège counted seventy-six carriages, led by five vehicles with family members, followed on foot by the city council, pallbearers, consistory members, college faculty and students, dignitaries, old settlers and hundreds of inhabitants. Seventy-one carriages brought up the rear. The procession, which stretched for more than a mile, went east on Ninth Street to Fairbanks Avenue and then south to the cemetery. Passing Dr. Roelof Schouten's First Ward drugstore, mourners saw a large, translucent banner that he had tastefully created that featured Van Raalte's portrait trimmed neatly in black, framed with the phrase "Rest in Peace." The first carriages in the procession reached the cemetery before the last carriages left the church.[45]

At the committal service, Uiterwyk gave a brief but powerful message in Dutch before a large crowd. Rev. Cornelius Crispell, theology professor at Hope College, closed with prayer in English, and Rev. Pieters pronounced the blessing. Then the casket was lowered into the grave next to Van Raalte's dear wife Christina Johanna. "They belonged together," declared Rev. Christian Van der Veen in a

[45] *De Grondwet*, 14 Nov. 1876; Dosker, *Van Raalte*, 319.

fitting eulogy. Without her, life for Albertus had lost its color. Rense Joldersma, a student in the Preparatory School who had attended the services, spoke for all in the student newspaper *Excelsiora*: "We left the cemetery convinced that a great man had fallen." That the preachers alternated between Dutch and English speaks volumes about the Americanization of the West Michigan Dutch during Van Raalte's thirty years in America. Geesje Visscher added the last word: "There never has been a funeral here which will be remembered so long nor felt as deeply as that of Van Raalte. The church remained covered with crepe for six weeks." His truly was the funeral of the century.[46]

The gravestones of Albertus and Christina are engraved in English. The dominee's inscription reads just as written:

> Albertus C. Van Raalte by the Grace of God
> Minister of the Gospel
> Born in the parsonage at Wannet[sic, "p"]erveen,
> The Netherlands Oct. 18, 1811
> died Nov. 6, 1876 at Holland, Mich.

Albertus and Christina Van Raalte graves and historic marker, Pilgrim Home Cemetery. The inscriptions are in English, not Dutch. That the engraver misspelled Albertus's place of birth indicates the lost command by locals of the language and geography of the Netherlands.

---

[46] Christian Van der Veen, in Jacobson et al., *Dutch Leader*, 169; Rense H. Joldersma, *Excelsiora*, 12 Dec. 1876, JAH; "Geesje Van der Haar-Visscher Diary," 48.

On Holland's centennial in 1947, the state of Michigan placed an historical marker at the gravesite of Albertus C. Van Raalte. The inscription reads:

> Feb. 9, 1847. Today he speaks for us as he did to his followers on the twenty-fifth anniversary of his founding of our Holland Community in 1872: Behold, who follows us in this inheritance, we give it over to you with joy. But do not forget, we received it from God as a training school for eternity—a work place for God's kingdom. This shall prosper in your hands provided God and His kingdom remain as your precious portion in life.

Writing his own obituary

After Van Raalte's body was in the grave for several weeks, *De Hope*, the weekly of the western Reformed Church, published an obituary of "Dr. A. C. Van Raalte," written by "Anoki." This pseudonym is an Algonquin word meaning "origin" or "source." At the top of the page is a brief note, stating that it was written, presumably on the day of the funeral, by one who was "not able to cast a last glance on the well-known and beloved face." The author remained a mystery until Holland's semicentennial in 1897, when Professor Egbert Winter of Western Theological Seminary gave a speech, titled "Rev. Albertus Christiaan Van Raalte D.D.," in which he revealed that Van Raalte had written his own obituary for *De Hope*. As Winter phrased it: "There was charming simplicity and modesty in his obituary notice, *prepared by himself*" (italics mine).[47]

Van Raalte's obituary by his own hand reads:

> *In Memoriam*, First, Third, and Ebenezer church consistories issued a joint *Memoriam*, which was disseminated widely in the United States and the Netherlands. It read: The decease of our beloved shepherd, brother and father, is deeply mourned, for he was a man who, through natural disposition, extensive knowledge, principal conviction, firm will, and profound piety, possessed the quality as God's anointed to serve as a minister of the gospel, proponent of correct education, and as a leader of the people, all bringing about a great blessing.... We, although deeply mourning the loss, feel ourselves, nevertheless, compelled

---

[47] Egbert Winter, "Rev. Albertus Christian Van Raalte D.D.," 19 Aug. 1897, printed in Hope College *Anchor* (Oct. 1903): 202-9; and *Holland Sentinel*, 2 May 1911.

in humility to thank the Lord for all which, in God's grace, Rev. Van Raalte was able to be and to accomplish for us. We express our firm confidence that his remembrance will be holy and his influence blessed in the midst of the people he loved.[48]

The phrase "proponent of *correct* education" (italics added) reflects Van Raalte's commitment to *Christian* education until his last breath. But his influence faded fast in the Reformed Church he loved. As with most prominent people, his life and work was soon forgotten.

Pillar Church to this day has a memorial tablet in black marble mounted on the front wall of the sanctuary, planned by a committee funded by merchant Rokus Kanters who had gained national fame for his brush breakwaters, including those along Holland's channel and Chicago's waterfront. Alderman Kanters appreciated Van Raalte's commitment to the harbor and economic advancement. The tablet, which Kanters purchased in Chicago, was unveiled three years after Van Raalte's death, on April 23, 1879, in a very formal, midweek ceremony. The gathering sang a psalm; Rev. Pieters read scripture; Dr. Phelps offered prayer; perennial elder Harm Broek recalled incidents in the dominee's life beginning in 1835 in the Netherlands; son Dirk Van Raalte thanked the committee on behalf of the family; elder Teunis Keppel offered the closing prayer; they sang another psalm, and Pieters gave the benediction. A life-size portrait of Van Raalte, just completed by Holland photographer Benjamin P. Higgens, was hung next to the tablet. The plaque was affixed on the east side of the pulpit, next to the consistory pews. Hope College professors and students of theology occupied the pews to the west of the pulpit.[49]

The memorial plaque reads: "In Memoriam van Rev. A. C. Van Raalte, D.D. Eerste Leeraar dezer Gemeente, en Vader onzer Nederzetting. Een Dienstknecht des Heeren. Krachtig in Woorden en Werken, 1879" (In memory of Rev. A. C. Van Raalte, D.D., first minister of this congregation and father of our settlement. A servant of the Lord, mighty in words and deeds. 1879). The fitting memorial quoted Acts 7:22 (KJV), which describes Moses as a man "mighty in words and

---

[48] "In Memoriam," minutes, First Holland, 14 Nov. 1876; English translation in De Vries and Boonstra, *Pillar Church*, 109; *De Bazuin*, 12 Jan. 1877 (www.delpher.nl, accessed, June 2021).

[49] *De Grondwet*, 11, 18 Mar., 22, 29 Apr. 1879; Swierenga, *Holland, Michigan*, 1:712-13; 2:124-25; 3:1835-36, 1909. Kanters' carriage house on the ground floor of his home at 162 E. 8th St. housed Engine House No. 2 and later city hall (now an historic building). He served as mayor 1885-86.

Van Raalte memorial plaque,
in Pillar Church since 1879

in deeds." This memorial has kept the founding pastor's name before worshipers and visitors for more than 140 years.[50]

First Church very graciously designated the pew that the Van Raalte family had occupied since the 1856 dedication of the edifice as the "Van Raalte pew" for at least the next year. The "express desire" was that the pew be "used and occupied by the children of the reverend and honored founder and first pastor of the Church as long as any shall remain connected therewith or worship therein."[51] The family appreciated this kindly gesture, but few took advantage of it.

---

[50] *Holland City News*, 19 Jan. 1878. When the church remodel project was completed in 2020, the plaque was moved from the front wall of the sanctuary to the annex wall at the side entrance.

[51] Minutes, First Reformed, 12 Dec. 1876.

"Preacher's Kids"

As Christian parents in the fishbowl of the parsonage, Albertus and Christina had worked to raise their children in the faith. In a letter Van Raalte had written in 1857 to his children while in New York canvassing for funds for the academy building, he admonished: "Now, my children, fear God and hold his commandments before you, make the most of your time, and work with all your might. Do it prayerfully. . . . To achieve, you must in the first place fear God."

These were standard biblical admonitions, but Van Raalte added a stronger emotional twist. He mentioned the sad death of Teuntje Doesburg, a young woman in the New York church who had come down with a fever while ironing and died of a stroke minutes later.

> May this loud-speaking voice of God . . . bring you to the conviction that you must give your heart to the Savior and that you must not put off by deluding yourself that there is hope of a better opportunity in the future. . . . Do it yet this day, for death may also strike you as it did Teuntje.

He closed, saying, "Your father who loves you with all his heart."[52]

Rev. Thomas De Witt, who had visited Holland in 1859, praised Christina for "her intelligent and deep-toned piety" and observed that the household practiced well-ordered habits of devotion and religious instruction. But Van Raalte knew the habits had had little effect on Ben and Dirk. When Ben turned fourteen, his father pleaded with him to repent. "Turn, my child, to your God and seek his fellowship." On Ben's nineteenth birthday, his father wrote:

> Truly, Benjamin, you are neglecting your soul. You live as if you were going to live forever. You turn away from God and spiritual matters. . . . In God's name, my child, I pray of you, stop, do turn to God, and prostrate yourself before Him. . . . As I strike this cord, my father-heart is so moved that I pass by all other matters. I cannot write in any other way.

At Ben's twenty-ninth birthday, in 1869, his father again implored him to be reconciled to God and avoid being eternally damned. "Before I die, I so wish that I might hear from your lips that God is your refuge and joy; that Christ's atonement is dear to you and that you love Jesus."[53]

---

[52] Van Raalte to the children, 25 May 1857, trans. unknown, HHA.
[53] *Christian Intelligencer*, 22 Sept. 1859, 50; Van Raalte to son Ben, 14 Nov. 1859, 4 May

Dirk received similar admonitions. When Dirk was serving in the Civil War, Christina wrote him: "Dear Dirk, above all, seek the Lord. Yes, flee freely with all your sins to the atoning blood. Oh, dear Dirk, seek to be prepared for the hour of death." On Dirk's thirtieth birthday, in 1874, his father wrote an impassioned letter. "Your [spiritual] welfare concerns me deeply.... Dirk, do not halt between two opinions. I trust that you seek the Lord in secret, but also open your heart more tenderly to the tenderizing influences of God's Spirit and truth." Speaking from personal experience, Van Raalte told his young entrepreneur not to "think only of making money," because that path leads to "great ruin." Seek contentment in a "quiet, pleasant home life . . . where religion is the prop of one's life." He added: "Nothing would please me more than to see you obtain a God-fearing wife.... I have on occasion, to my great sorrow, heard you speak disparagingly of marriage because you have no home [of your own]." Van Raalte died two years later without seeing Dirk marry and join the church.[54]

Eventually, the parents' prayers were answered for all the children, except perhaps Bertus, the firstborn, for whom no fatherly admonition is extant. Helena Van Raalte and family and daughter Johanna Maria Wilhelmina (Mina) and second husband Teunis Keppel remained faithful members of First Church. Mina, Christina Catharina (Christine), and Anna Arendina had all made profession of faith as teenagers at First Church.

Hope Church welcomed the youngest five as confessing members after marriage—Dirk and Kate Ledeboer, Ben and Julia Gilmore, Maria and Gerrit Kollen, Anna and John Kleinheksel, and Christine Gilmore, after William's death in 1884. Christine was the first sibling to transfer to Hope Church in 1869, but her marriage that year to Rev. William Gilmore kept her elsewhere until he died. Maria and Gerrit Kollen joined Hope Church in 1879 and 1880, respectively, and Anna and John Kleinheksel transferred in 1882. At present, only one direct Van Raalte descendant is a member of Hope Church, and none are members of First Church, where the siblings had grown up.[55]

1869, HHA; Bruins et al., *Albertus and Christina*, 129-30.

[54] Christina Van Raalte to son Dirk, Sept. 1862, Van Raalte to son Dirk, 27 Feb. 1874, English typescript, trans. Herbert Brinks, HHA.

[55] Parr, *Hope Church*, app. C, 409-16, lists all the Van Raaltes at Hope Church, forty-eight total, over seven generations. Only five descendants were members in 2012. The others had either died or moved away. Just one was left in 2020. Two other direct descendants today live in Holland, a mother and daughter. The married daughter is expecting a baby this year, so that child will be the sole eighth-

Faithfulness to the Reformed faith among the Van Raalte children was rare in America, where most immigrants had also deserted their faith roots. From 1850 to 1880, up to two thirds of adult Dutch Reformed immigrants (35,000 of 50,000) either joined American denominations or discarded formal religious practice altogether. In 1880 the immigrant wing of the Reformed Church had 18,000 souls (baptized and confessing members), and the Christian Reformed Church had 12,300. Of these, nearly half were children born in America. Many adult members, of course, had died by 1880. In the diverse American religious environment, the joining of culture and faith, as the term "Dutch Reformed" implies, was problematic. The forces of Americanization were strong and not fully anticipated.[56]

The promise of American life

Before Van Raalte closed his eyes in death, he had taken satisfaction that his sons and daughters were enjoying the promise of America life. He had had the pleasure to marry three of his four daughters: the oldest, Christine, twice (to a clergyman and then a prominent businessmen); the second, Mary, to a minister; and the third, Anna, to a professor. The two sons became prominent businessmen. Ben built a Classical Revival-inspired farmhouse for his bride on his 160-acre farm on East Sixteenth Street. Besides raising grain crops and tending a peach orchard, Ben dealt in farm implements and horses and became a civic leader. In 1880 he moved the implement dealership to the center of Holland, on River Avenue and Ninth Street, and soon opened stores in Drenthe and Zeeland. Ben's annual sales in the mid-1880s reached $65,000 ($2 million today).

Dirk B. K. Van Raalte, the one-armed veteran, lived out his life in the family homestead and farm on Fairbanks Avenue. To the pleasure of his father, he entered politics in 1874 and gained fame as an ace political orator. In 1875 he parlayed a seat on the Ottawa County board of commissioners for a chair in the Michigan House of Representatives. He won a second term on the very day of his father's death, November 6, 1876. In 1880 he married Kate Ledeboer, a daughter of Bernardus, the

---

generation descendant. So three direct descendants, two sixth and one seventh generation, still live in Holland. The Van Raalte bloodline is nearly extinct. I am indebted to Judy (Mrs. William) Tanis Parr, Sara F. Simmons, and Charles Van den Broek for this information.

[56] Swierenga, "True Brothers," 72-73.

Van Raalte's sons (*l-r*) Albertus, Benjamin, Dirk B. K. (*JAH*)

Daughters (*l-r*) Christina Catharina (Christine), Maria Wilhelmina (Mary) Van Raalte Kollen, Anna Sophia Van Raalte Kleinheksel (Anna). There is no known photo of Johanna Maria Wilhelmina (Mina) as a young adult (*JAH*). Anna Van Raalte Kleinheksel photo (*courtesy Melissa Ramerez*)

leading medical doctor and politico in Holland. Dirk that year opened a boot and shoe store on Eighth Street, Holland's main shopping center, and later became a bank president, lumber wholesaler, and business magnate. With Ben and Dirk, apples did not fall far from the tree. But apples entirely missed Bertus, the firstborn, who proved to a major disappointment to the family.[57]

---

[57] Bruins et al., *Albertus and Christina*, 100-171; Swierenga, *Holland, Michigan*, 1:786-87, 2:1213, 1698, 3:1866.

Mina, widowed at age thirty-one, when Peter J. Oggel died in 1869, was left with a four-year-old daughter. Seven years later, in May 1876, she married veteran church elder Teunis Keppel, a merchant and Holland's "coal king" who built Keppel Village, served twenty years on the school board and was the city's first marshal. In her own right, Mina gained prominence in church, charity, and mission circles. After twenty years of marriage, Teunis died in 1896, and Mina succumbed to heart disease seven months later, in 1897, "after suffering a long time."[58]

Christine grew up in a Dutch-speaking family and mastered English in Holland Public School. She apprenticed as a seamstress for several years in Kalamazoo and then followed the three-year "ladies prep" program at Olivet College (1863-66) and married William Brokaw Gilmore, who was completing studies for the ministry at Hope College. The American Classis of Michigan ordained Gilmore to serve the Mattoax [VA] Reformed Church and Amelia Institute, where her father married the couple. In 1872 Gilmore returned to Holland to teach at Hope College. Unsuited for academia, he spent his remaining years serving American Reformed congregations in Spring Lake (Manito) and Havana, Illinois. Following his sudden death in 1884, Christine and her teenage son moved back to Holland, and in 1879, she was appointed "Lady Assistant and Matron," principal, actually, of Hope Preparatory [High] School and later dean of women at Hope College. She retired in 1909 after twenty years of counseling and lecturing. This remarkable, cultured woman, who inherited her father's religious zeal, forensic talents, and leadership qualities, set the mark high for Dutch immigrant women.[59]

Mary Van Raalte was living at home when her father died. Three years later, she married Gerrit J. Kollen, a professor at and later president of Hope College. The couple was the first to occupy the new president's home on campus, in 1895, with their twelve-year-old daughter. Hosting the president's home was a fitting role for the cofounder's daughter. She died in 1905 of tuberculosis, the same lingering ailment that had taken her mother's life.

---

[58] *Christian Intelligencer*, 3 May 1860; *De Hollander*, 11, 25 Apr. 1860; Swierenga, *Holland, Michigan*, 1:217-19; 2:1235, 1255-57; 3:1850-51; "Geesje Van der Haar-Visscher Diary," English typescript, 130 (quote), HMA. Bruins et al., *Albertus and Christina*, 100, cite the inaccurate Ottawa County marriage record, which states that Van der Meulen and Van de Wall did the honors.

[59] Bruins et al., *Albertus and Christina*, 147-58; Sinke, *Dutch Immigrant Women*, 200-204.

Anna Van Raalte, the youngest of the family, lived under the tutelage of Dirk and Kate Ledeboer Van Raalte until her marriage in 1884 to John H. Kleinheksel, another professor in Hope College, who served as vice president of the college under brother-in-law Gerrit Kollen. Anna before marriage had attended Hope College for several years. In marriage, she was a homemaker who raised four children. She died of pleurisy, a lung ailment that seemed to plague the Van Raalte and De Moen families.[60] So, all four daughters married well, to ministers, professors, and a business and civic leader.

Van Raalte's letters to his daughters and his wife indicate how he viewed the role of women. A woman should "spread around calm, love, peace and joy," and if insults come her way, she must counter them with "acquiescence and kindness."[61] The calling of a wife was to create a joyful family circle, to be a servant, to learn discipline, be a pious example, and "wipe away the worries from [her] husband's face."[62] Van Raalte and fellow clerics in 1858 drafted a "manifest" that urged mothers to manage their households well and enhance the "development of the social order." These documents display the Victorian dictum that women were the guardians and upholders of a civilized society.[63]

Van Raalte children and grandchildren, with city of residence

[1.i]   Albertus (15 Jan. 1837–??) and Helena Hoffman (also Hofman) (14 Aug. 1837–19 Sept. 1910), Holland
Albertus Christiaan (Allie) (12 Dec. 1859–17 June 1932) and Christina (Tia) Pfanstiehl (24 Dec. 1864–27 Feb. 1948), Holland
Christina Johanna (8 June 1861–14 Nov. 1921) and Jacob G. Van Putten (16 May 1859–9 Jan. 1909), Holland

---

[60] Bruins et al., *Albertus and Christina*, 159-61, 167-70. Besides Christina de Moen Van Raalte, tuberculosis took the lives of mother Wilhelmina Menzel de Moen, daughter Mary van Raalte Kollen, sister Johanna Maria de Moen van Velzen, and Van Raalte's brother Petrus.
[61] Van Raalte to daughter Christina Catharina, 19 Oct. 1868, HHA. Apparently, he also liked women's heads to be covered (Christina Catharina to parents, 20 Dec. 1862).
[62] Van Raalte to daughter Wilhelmina Van Raalte Oggel, Jan 1868, HHA.
[63] *De Hollander*, 21 Oct. 1858.

Anna Helena (17 Sept. 1862–14 May 1947) and
Bastian Dirk Keppel (16 Apr. 1862–5 July 1932), Holland
Carl "Karel" De Moen (3 June 1867–18 June 1896) and
Wilhelmina "Minnie" Vander Haar (3 Oct. 1870–22 Mar. 1956), Holland
Johanna Maria Wilhelmina "Minnie" (1 Jan. 1870–23 Feb. 1923), Holland

[2.ii] **Johanna Maria Wilhelmina "Mina" (19 Oct. 1838–22 Jan. 1897) and (first husband) Peter Jan Oggel (8 June 1829–13 Dec. 1869), Holland; (second husband) Teunis Jan Keppel (9 June 1823–27 June 1896), Holland**
Infant son (1861–1861), Holland
Christina Johanna (21 July 1862–19 Aug. 1864), Holland
Christina Johanna (25 Aug. 1865–13 Dec. 1911), Holland
Johannes Albertus (18 Aug. 1867–18 Apr. 1868), Holland

[3.iii] **Benjamin (8 May 1840–14 Aug. 1917) and (first wife) Julia Gilmore (27 Sept. 1841–10 Jan. 1911), Holland; (second wife) Abbie Connell (1862–14 July 1936), Muskegon**
Julia C. "Lu" (23 Nov 1873–28 Nov. 1952) and
Orlando Reimold (8 May 1873–12 Apr. 1962), Holland
Benjamin "Ben" Jr. (7 Feb. 1876–27 Sept. 1953) and
Adeline Huntley (5 May 1880–25 Apr. 1955), Holland

[iv] **Christina Catharina (12 Feb. 1842–24 May 1843), Genemuiden**

[4.v] **Dirk Blikman Kikkert (1 Mar. 1844–12 Feb. 1910) and Katherine "Kate" Ledeboer (1 Feb. 1852–11 June 1926), Holland**
Albertus Christiaan (29 Aug. 1889–30 Dec. 1944) and
Edna Dean Pillsbury (1 Sept. 1889–4 Dec. 1984), Pinehurst, NC
Dirk "Dick" Jr. (4 July 1891–5 Apr. 1964) and
Margret Elizabeth Hopson (26 June 1891–25 Oct. 1970), Holland

[5.vi] **Christina (also Christine) Catharina (30 Mar. 1846–12 Apr. 1933) and William Brokaw Gilmore (12 Apr. 1834–24 Apr. 1884), Holland**
Albertus C. Van Raalte "Raalte" (4 April 1870–24 Jan. 1955), Zeeland
William "Willie" (13 Sept. 1871–8 June 1872), Amelia Co., VA
Margaret Anna (27 Aug. 1873–21 Feb. 1879), Manito, IL
Frank Edwin (23 Jan. 1876–13 Feb. 1879), Manito, IL

[vii] **Maria Wilhelmina (16 Sept. 1848–2 Oct. 1849), Holland**

[6.viii] **Maria (Mary) Wilhelmina (14 Sept. 1850–16 Mar. 1905) and Gerrit Jan Kollen (9 Aug. 1843–5 Sept. 1915), Holland**
Estelle Marie (21 July 1886–30 July 1984) and
Jacob Carleton Pelgrim (9 June 1883–15 Apr. 1963), Florida

[ix] **Anna Arendina Harking (4 Apr. 1853–6 Mar. 1854), Holland**

[x] **Anna Harking (11 Mar. 1855–11 July 1855), Holland**

[7.xi] **Anna Sophia (27 July 1856–23 Feb. 1914) and John Kleinheksel (3 Mar. 1854–11 June 1916), Holland**
Paul Edwin (16 June 1885–31 Aug. 1956) and
Dorothy Gray (4 Sept. 1889–15 July 1969), Chicago
Anna Vera "Vera" (20 Feb. 1889–2 Feb. 1910), Holland
Frank De Moen (5 Apr. 1892–6 July 1973), and
(first wife) Helena (Helen) Pieters (14 Oct. 1892–30 Nov. 1934), Holland;
(second wife) Delia Ossewaarde (1883–12 Jan. 1955), Holland;
(third wife) Ruth Dunn (1 Dec. 1894–25 Jan. 1989), Allegan.
John Lewis (11 July 1896–30 Nov. 1963) and
Geraldine "Jerry" Maude Sauer (6 Aug. 1904–3 Feb. 1965), Kansas

Albertus and Christina honored in descendants' naming patterns

Albertus Christiaan Van Raalte III, "Allie"

Albertus Christiaan Van Raalte IV, Allie's son, stillborn
Albertus Christiaan Van Raalte (Dirk's son)
Christian Catharina (died at 15 months)
Christina Johanna (Mrs. Van Putten)
Christina Johanna Oggel
Albertus Christiaan Van Raalte Gilmore, "Raalte"
Albertus Christiaan Van Raalte, ordained minister (1914-25), RCA
Christine Ann Van Raalte (Mrs. Jeffrey Schaefer Smith)
Christine Cornelia Van Raalte (Mrs. Anthony Van Westenberg)

Source: Bruins et al., *Albertus and Christina.*

Celebrated or not

After his death, Van Raalte's name was sometimes celebrated and sometimes not. On Decoration Day, for many years, his grave was draped along with those of soldiers because the dominee "was their fatherly chaplain." But when the Classis of Holland in 1878 voted to raise funds in western churches to endow an Albertus C. Van Raalte Fund for a named chair in theology at Hope College, General Synod rejected the plan because of the college's "great indebtedness." Synod 1879 reaffirmed the negative decision, but averred that, if the western churches were able to raise the necessary monies, a future synod might approve. The chair was never funded.[64]

Another proposal that gained no traction was a suggestion by Ben Mulder, editor of *De Grondwet*, to replace the "ugly pole in the middle of our beautiful park" with a "statue of Dr. Van Raalte." That idea died aborning, only to be revived and again aborted in 1922 for the city's seventy-fifth anniversary. After another seventy-five years, in 1997, Holland's sesquicentennial, the vision became reality. The dominee's death was also marked at the city's golden (1897) and centennial (1947) celebrations.[65]

Holland's political leaders in 1878 proposed another honor: to create Van Raalte County by joining together four Ottawa County cities and townships—Holland and Zeeland cities and Holland and

---

[64] *Holland City News*, 2 June 1877; *Acts and Proceedings*, 1878, 118; 1879, 364. For the Theology Department controversy, see Voskuil, "Vexed Question," 341-70, esp. 360-61.

[65] Nyenhuis and Jacobson, *A Dream Fulfilled*; *Holland City News*, 11 Nov. 1926, 18 Mar. 1937. Hope College trustee Peter J. Huizenga and family financed the statue.

Zeeland Townships—and four Allegan County townships—Fillmore, Laketown, Manlius, and Saugatuck. These were the areas populated largely by the Dutch. Grand Haven and other northern townships in Ottawa County would be attached to Muskegon County. Editor Isaac Verwey of *De Grondwet* kept the realignment proposal alive for a decade, but it ultimately died for obvious political reasons. The Holland colony had some clout, but not enough to change boundaries in three counties and neuter Grand Haven as the county seat.[66]

Van Raalte's name became a marketing tool, as well as a political football. Barely two months after his death, furniture store magnate Hannes Meyer, advertised a new line of the "finest caskets ever offered for sale . . . like the handsome casket in which the remains of the late Dr. Van Raalte are reposing." Rev. Seine Bolks' adult son, Albert, an agricultural implement dealer, advertised Van Raalte "Chill Plows" (chill plows had semisteel or cast-iron shares and moldboards).[67]

The dominee's name also served as a lightning rod for criticism, to the point that Dirk Van Raalte, five years after his father's death, published in *De Grondwet* a request on behalf of the family to politely ask

> certain persons who lack both knowledge and sensitivity . . . [to] no longer make references to Van Raalte. We have too much respect and love for the sacrificial and frequently innervating labors bestowed on church and school to remain indifferent when, either indirectly or directly, groundless accusations are made against him. We believe that he has earned the right to a peaceful cessation of his labors.[68]

This family diktat stemmed primarily from the struggle in First Church over Freemasonry, which brought up the old issues of the 1850s, with Van Raalte in the lead role since the union of 1850, and Wyckoff's ill-advised promise that congregations were free to withdraw if they should be unhappy with the union. The Anti-Masonic majority, led by elder Teunis Keppel, harkened back to Wyckoff's promise and Van Raalte's lead role in the merger of the Classis of Holland with the Reformed Church. In 1882 the union caused a second schism, this time a major one, over the denomination's refusal to condemn Freemasonry. Van Raalte's name was dragged up again, but the critics had a point.

---

[66] *De Grondwet*, 2 May, 18 June 1878, 18 Dec. 1888, 2 Feb. 1889.
[67] *Holland City News*, 6 Jan. 1877; *De Hollander*, 15 Oct. 1878.
[68] Dirk Van Raalte statement, *De Grondwet*, 30 Aug. 1881.

As noted above, in retirement, the dominee had shifted his position on Freemasonry from blanket condemnation to reluctant acceptance.[69]

Freemasonry or not, the founder of Holland indeed deserved to rest in peace. Engbertus Van der Veen, who lived in Holland from the outset, at age eighty-seven, best captured Van Raalte's spirit in his reminiscences: "The principles to govern our life in a consecrated Christian commonwealth as laid down by our leaders were to educate the young, build seminaries and common schools, organize local government, establish factories, open navigation, construct a harbor, and build roads."[70]

Van Raalte rightfully could boast in his 1872 address: "Is there anyone who can visit our villages and townships, covered with the richest farmsteads, and not be astonished? It is impossible to estimate the value of our ships, fisheries, mills, factories, and fruit farms." But he did not let the occasion pass without reminding folks of the true source of their blessings.

> Our colonization efforts were based on religious principles; they drew their strength from God. So long as we remain permeated with this spirit, we will succeed. . . . May this inheritance be to you in all eternity the beloved spot in which you yourselves have learned to know God, where you have found your God. So be it![71]

The Holland colony, after twenty-five years, counted fifteen thousand inhabitants, spread across four hundred square miles in Ottawa and Allegan Counties. Twenty-six Reformed churches dotted the many villages, all served by the central city of Holland, with twenty-three hundred residents. The county tax assessor fixed the value of real and personal property at $3.5 million ($87 million today), which was far too low, even taking into account the $1 million lost in the fire a year earlier. It was a magnificent domain compared to the half dozen small settlements of 1847.[72]

---

[69] "Hoe zijn wij in de Reformed Church gekomen?" *De Hope*, 3 Aug. 1881, which included verbatim the Holland classis minutes of the April 1850 session, written in Van Raalte's hand (see Kennedy, *Commentary*, and his in-depth analysis, 1:98-99).

[70] Van der Veen, "Life Reminiscences," 1:501.

[71] Van Raalte, "Commemoration Address, 1872," 2:491.

[72] Van Raalte's 1872 Ebenezer address, "Eendragt maakt magt," in Lucas, *1847–Ebenezer–1947*, 21-30; non-Dutch percentage compiled from federal manuscript population census lists, Herrick District Library.

CHAPTER 17

Assessment and Evaluation: "Mighty in words and deeds."

Contemporaries and historians by the score have characterized Dominee Albertus C. Van Raalte variously as a modern Moses, a pope, Napoleon, a dictator, an emperor, a mighty pioneer leader, an American patriot, a statesman (like George Washington), a Jacksonian (like Andrew Jackson), a prophet (like Samuel and Elijah), and a Dutch pilgrim father. The very title *dominee* (lord) encompasses all of these designations. "Pilgrim father" is apt, with "father" in the Victorian sense of absolute head of his own household and also, in a sense, the greater household of the Holland colony. Van Raalte is described as a born leader, with an iron will, a true visionary, a guiding star, the soul of the colony, an aristocrat in bearing, a benefactor, and a counselor. Gerrit Van Schelven observed the dominee at first hand and concluded: "Dr. Van Raalte was THE leader of his people . . . and never evinced any longing to share it with anyone." Henry Dosker considered Van Raalte as *sui generis*—one of a kind. "No man stepped into his shoes; no one could fit into them."[1]

---

[1] Gerrit Van Schelven, Teunis Keppel obit., *Holland City News*, 4 July 1896; Dosker, *Van Raalte*, 261, trans. Dekker.

Other positive descriptors of Van Raalte are self-confident, forward looking, eager, earnest, energetic, humble, the "salt of the earth," sensitive, having unfailing endurance, entrepreneurial, with a magnetic personality, aglow with Eternal Truth, full of religious fervor, gifted with uncommon foresight, having fine mental endowment, resilient, persistent, resourceful, prompt to execute decisions, decisive, exhibiting extraordinary integrity, a man of tremendous courage, a man of power, a virtuoso orator, a towering preacher, full of natural eloquence, optimistic, confident in America's future, and as a *gutmensch* (Yiddish, a "good person," one with dignity and honor). Rev. Dirk Broek, a former catechumen, said his teacher had a strong will and indomitable courage, and his aristocratic bearing commanded respect. Though Van Raalte could criticize sharply, Broek noted, "He possessed a very sensitive heart." Negative descriptors are rare, but a few writers have portrayed Van Raalte as domineering, even violent at times, and prone to mistakes of judgment. Bernardus Grootenhuis, his faithful assistant, said the dominee "demonstrated a never-give-up and energetic character" that could be "somewhat arbitrary, intemperate, high-handed, as if he had dressed himself up in the livery of Dictator."[2]

Although many of the attributes are hyperbole, they do convey truth. Van Raalte had a domineering personality with an aristocratic demeanor, and he did take authoritarian actions. He did not take kindly to critics, dissenters, and rivals, and he would not take no for an answer. He did not share the phlegmatic character typical of the Dutch. Examples abound. When members of his Mastenbroek congregation seceded and formed their own church, he would not acquiesce and grant them the same right he had exercised to leave the national church. As a teacher and mentor of student preachers in Arnhem, he was so demanding and rigid that Brummelkamp, his brother-in-law and coprofessor, demanded that he lighten up and cut students some slack. When some church members in 1850 urged the dominee to wait to unite the Classis of Holland with the Reformed Protestant Dutch Church in New York, he plunged ahead anyway and suffered very negative consequences, even being charged with selling out for money. When in 1866 his ministerial colleagues refused to recommend him as a missionary teacher to the Zulus, he continued to press for the appointment behind their backs. When Holland residents in 1867 voted to charter the city, he stubbornly objected, and his homestead was ultimately left outside the city limits.

[2] Dosker, *Van Raalte*, 296; Van Hinte, *Netherlanders*, 362.

Van Raalte accomplished more in his life than most men of his time, as preacher, immigrant leader, community builder, and social entrepreneur. He was the undisputed leader of all Reformed Hollanders in the Midwest. Parishioners were captivated by his sermons and counseling; his colony became the engine for making West Michigan the Dutch center of North America, and his real estate dealings would have made him a millionaire in today's dollars. Most remarkably, he would have eschewed all accolades. In his mind, he faced more failures than successes. He experienced bitter church schisms in the Netherlands and in North America. His path to the ministry in the church of his birth was blocked unjustly by church authorities, but he refused to concede even minor points of church rules and regulations. He made the historic church name "Gereformeerde" a hill to die on. Polity, not doctrine, was his red line.

Van Raalte was unfairly castigated for selling the lots platted in Holland, which responsibility he had accepted at the urging of the community, but he had carried out the task openly and honestly. His business ventures in Ommen—clothed as jobs programs for harried Separatists—stumbled, and his silent partnerships in primary industries in the Holland colony were short lived or, like the Den Bleyker mill business, ended in near bankruptcy. At the same time, he lost a press war with the local newspaper editor. He learned to his chagrin that editors have a bigger bully pulpit than preachers. Also at that time, his consistory found his sermons weak. This was definitely a low point in his life. Then his followers voted against his expressed wishes in the 1860 and 1864 presidential elections, when survival of the Union was at stake. In 1866 he was emotionally burned out serving Holland's mother church and went to the Netherlands for a six-month sabbatical. On his return, he refused to attend consistory meetings for nearly a year until the brethren seriously searched for his successor.

With his successor in place, Van Raalte left Holland, presumably permanently, to found the sister Amelia, Virginia, colony, which, unlike the Holland colony, would fail dismally. He returned with his reputation severely damaged. Tragedies then drained him emotionally and sapped his strength. First was the disappearance of his firstborn son and namesake, Albertus, who at age thirty-two deserted his pregnant wife and four young children, never to be seen or heard from again. The "not knowing" made this a more grievous blow than the expected death from tuberculosis of Peter Oggel, his son-in-law and associate in ministry. Oggel was a kindred spirit, who walked in Van Raalte's footsteps, a path Van Raalte's three sons had avoided. Oggel served his second charge as founding pastor of First Reformed Church in Pella, the pulpit Van Raalte had declined, and then as theology professor at Hope College, another position Van Raalte had declined.[3]

His life companion and helpmeet died of tuberculosis in 1871, leaving a hole in his heart he could not fill. And three months later, the Holland fire destroyed the work of the pioneer generation. Van Raalte's words of encouragement in rebuilding efforts were said to be his finest hour, but the hard work had to be done by the victims. That same year, polemicists refought the 1857 church schism, and Van Raalte's name was again drawn through the mud.

His stupendous funeral and florid memorial resolutions should have cemented his reputation. These events were the talk of the town for a generation. The accolades were genuine, enthusiastic, and uniformly laudatory. But Van Raalte's day had passed. He was an old man resting on his laurels and no longer needed. The incorporation of the city in 1867 against his will was the handwriting on the wall. New leaders were in charge in Holland. The indispensable man was dispensable after all.

After his death, his name was again disparaged in the Freemasonry schism of 1882 at First Church. This compelled his children to publish a demand in the local press to let their father rest in peace. So embittered was the family that grandchildren, sixty-five years later, in 1947, as the city was planning its centennial, sold the Van Raalte Papers to Albert Hyma, who was writing the first English-language biography of Van Raalte. He had previously won the family's favor via a favorable lecture on their progenitor. The news of the sale jolted both Wynand Wichers and his nephew, Willard Wichers, who had established the Historical Trust Collection at the Holland Museum in 1937 and expected to snag the city founder's papers for the archives. Instead, Hyma took the papers to Ann Arbor and later sold them to Grand Rapids publisher William B. Eerdmans, who ultimately donated them to the Heritage Hall Archives at Calvin University. This was the final affront to Dominee Van Raalte. That disrespect, however, is being wiped away by the project, currently underway, to digitize Van Raalte's personal papers for world-wide access by scholars and the general public. A. C. Van Raalte will not be forgotten.

---

[3] Bruins et al., *Albertus and Christina*, 100-105.

World-and-life view

Van Raalte was part of the European religious awakening in the early nineteenth century that had both evangelical and pietist overtones. The Dutch Réveil was grounded in the Dutch Reformed faith, led by Willem Bilderdijk and Guillaume Groen van Prinsterer, defenders of the faith against the anti-Christian French Revolution. Van Raalte stood in that tradition and carried it to Michigan. He held to the Reformed Confessions and faithfully taught the beloved Heidelberg Catechism to youth and adults alike. He was also influenced by the Nadere [Later, or Second] Reformation of the seventeenth century, with its emphasis on piety and holiness. Van Raalte never escaped the tension between policy and practice. He tried to balance the two; his expositions emphasized doctrine and his applications urged pious living. But the Gospel he preached, to some theologians, set works over grace, piety over promise. Gordon Spykman, a student of his sermons, concluded that Van Raalte preached the Gospel in "parts—intellect over against emotions and will—rather than to the 'whole man.'"[4]

Van Raalte's mainly expository sermons minimized Reformed doctrine, but he did faithfully teach the Heidelberg Catechism to his congregation in the afternoon services and in the shorter compendium to youngsters. His catechism sermons in the early years were quite nontraditional. He preferred the Socratic teaching method he had learned from Brummelkamp that employed dialogue and discussion in a "highly interesting and instructive" manner. Besides the catechism, he upheld the Belgic Confession and Canons of Dort. In the early 1850s, Van Raalte urged Hermanus Doesburg, editor of *De Hollander*, to publish the Canons in a booklet, but Doesburg feared low sales. Hendrik Klyn seconded the request, and Doesburg asked the pastors to obtain subscriptions, but the matter came to naught. A bit later, one of Van Raalte's elders brought up the Canons when he asked an immigrant presenting his membership transfer paper (*attestatie*) if he agreed with this historic formulary.[5]

Although Van Raalte upheld Groen van Prinsterer's call for Christian education, he did not adopt his wider Reformed world-and-life view, which came to full expression under Abraham Kuyper later in the century. Van Raalte left the Netherlands long before Kuyper's day. The American dominee was a product of the nineteenth century.

---

[4] Spykman, *Pioneer Preacher*, 68-70, Engelsma, *van Velzen*, 143.
[5] Heideman, "Van Raalte," 270; *De Hollander*, 19 Jan. 1854; minutes, First Holland, 29 Apr. 1856.

He preached Christ as personal Savior and Lord but not that Christ ruled over "every square inch of creation." He never taught a Christian perspective in politics, journalism, business, and the arts and sciences. His purview was limited to personal behavior, not communal practice. The goal was to remain personally unspotted from the world, not to claim the culture for Christ.[6] He did not join the antislavery, temperance, or Anti-Masonic societies, push Sabbatarian laws, or prison reform, all part of the postmillennial crusades so common in Reformed circles of his day. He did join the Anti-Masonic societies and especially ecumenical crusades, like the Evangelical Alliance.

Church polity

In church polity, Van Raalte was a centrist. He grew up in a parsonage and aimed to walk in the steps of his father, a faithful pastor in the public church. At Leiden University, Albertus came under the influence of a coterie of seminarians who called for a return to biblical truth by rationalistic church leaders. The seminarians graduated, took pastorates, and worked for reform from within. But churchmen rejected all calls for change, and one by one, the young reformers were either expelled or withdrew.

Van Raalte never considered seceding, and he disapproved of De Cock's Secession of 1834. He was a loyal son of the church, like his father. But he had the misfortune of graduating last among the reformist seminarians. Church administrators deemed him guilty by association and would not recommend him for ordination unless he agreed with all the rules. "Preach as you please, but . . . obey the church laws," demanded Donker Curtius, but Albertus refused, in contrast to almost all the other Réveil reformers who remained in the church. This left him with the only option for fulfilling his calling, which was to join the Christian Separated Church. He became a secessionist unwillingly, not by conviction. He considered himself expelled. To describe his situation, he used the Dutch word *gescheiden* (separated), which is a weaker, more neutral form of the often pejorative word *afgescheidene* (being separated of). He and his cohorts considered the Separated Church to be a continuation of the historic Gereformeerde Kerk, which the Hervormde Kerk at the 1816 synod abandoned when they adopted a new church order in place of the foundational Dort document.

When the Seceded denomination divided into the less doctrinaire Overijssels-Gelders party and the more doctrinaire Gronings-Drents

---

[6] Spykman, *Pioneer Preacher*, 17.

party, Van Raalte and Brummelkamp led the former party, and their other brother-in-law, Simon van Velzen, led the latter party. This affiliation was consequential for Albertus's future direction both in the Netherlands and in America. The immediate repercussion of joining a free church was persecution by government and church officialdom, which deepened his disgust with the public church and eventually led to his immigration to America for religious, educational, and economic freedom for his family and followers. The long-term repercussion played out in America, since the contending factions brought the contentious issues with them in their luggage, so to speak.

In America, Van Raalte organized the Classis of Holland as a free church assembly, thus emulating the Christian Separated Church. But in 1850, he orchestrated the union with the Reformed Protestant Dutch Church in the East, which until 1793 had been affiliated with the Classis of Amsterdam of the Netherlands public church. The New York-based denomination was greatly influenced by the First and Second Great Awakening movements, which divided the body into a revivalist, pietist wing and a doctrinal, traditional wing. The colonial branch had so Americanized by 1771 that it cut off the Dutch mother church (an act finalized in 1793) and in 1867 dropped the word "Dutch" from its name, making it simply "Reformed Church in America."[7] This act signaled the change from a Dutch-speaking colonial church to an English-speaking American church.

By merging the Classis of Holland with this denomination in 1850, Van Raalte chose the fast track to Americanization for the immigrant congregations. This decision set both his course and that of the midwestern wing of the Reformed Church to the present day. The union of 1850 caused an immediate backlash in one Michigan congregation after another that hampered the dominee's ministry to the end. It also stymied his plans for Christian day schools since the American Reformed Church from the outset favored public education. This portended the failure of Christian elementary education in general in the colony but not at the high school and college levels in particular. Van Raalte carried to the grave his disappointment at not founding Christian day schools in Holland, something that Kuyperian immigrants in the Christian Reformed Church would accomplish in 1901.

Suffering through the second separation in Michigan in 1857 also changed Van Raalte's perspective on the Secession of 1834. The

---

[7] *Acts and Proceedings*, 1868, 458.

shoe was now on the other foot. The union of 1850 placed him on the side of the American counterpart to the Netherlands Reformed Church. Now the secession was against *his* church. Now he was on the side of church authorities, attesting to their orthodoxy and working to uphold their authority. Now as the leader of the immigrant congregations, he experienced the bitterness and anguish of secession again at first hand. In a sense, he had become the Dutch American Donker Curtius.

This fact sheds new light on his personal reflections in a lengthy 1862 letter to his nephew, Simon van Velzen Jr. The sticky question was the relationship of the Secession of 1834 to the Hervormde Kerk. In Van Raalte's words:

> If I could relive that struggle, with how much more determination, and with how much more courage, and with a louder voice, . . . I would not bend even a little under the pressure to create a new church organization and submit out of fear of disturbing the peace. . . . I would not now allow them to retain the hereditary title of the Gereformeerde Kerk, the Church of the Reformation.

As biographer Henry Dosker noted, Van Raalte lamented the fact that church authorities had closed his path to the pulpits of his father and was angered that they had "forced him into a separate organization and to accept a new name. In his heart, he never gave up the right to the title and the possessions of the Old Reformed Church."[8] In retrospect, Van Raalte at heart was not a Separatist. Rather, he would have stayed and fought to retain the name and rights of the Old Reformed Church.

In church governance, Van Raalte also followed Old Reformed polity that elevated the role of the pastor over the elders, instead of serving as one of the elders. Disregarding the Dort church order, Van Raalte handpicked his consistory, who served at will, term after term, without nominations by the membership. One such elder served forty years continuously. Van Raalte took too much responsibility in church affairs on his own shoulders. For the first decade and more, he was sometimes president but typically clerk of the consistory and the classis. He had a hand in every decision, which gave rise to complaints that he acted like a pope. He busied himself with general church work, business and land dealings, and community activities and left to the elders the mundane tasks of visiting families and calling on the sick and wayward. In 1860 church members were finally free to vote out

---

[8] Dosker, *Van Raalte*, 17-18, citing Van Raalte's April 1862 letter to Simon van Velzen Jr., in *Kompleete uitgave* (1863), 334, trans. Nella Kennedy.

entrenched men in favor of newcomers. At this, the minority became the majority. Van Raalte seemingly approved the change since he cried out in a rump consistory meeting: "Already twenty years I should have had a different consistory." But this was sour grapes; he had had the consistory he had chosen.[9]

Inconsistencies and contradictions

Few people live a life that is consistent in thought and action. Changing circumstances often dictate rethinking long-held opinions. Van Raalte had his inconsistencies. He rejected schism at all costs during his adult life but accepted ordination in a denomination born in schism and named "Separated." He could have followed Réveil leaders and worked for reform within the public church, and he could have served it with integrity and biblical preaching.

He emigrated for educational, as much as religious, freedom and the right to found Christian day schools. But in a major oversight, he did not recruit a Dutch Reformed schoolmaster, so he had to hire English-speaking Christian teachers. He personally took leadership of the Holland public school but failed to convince his own congregation of the biblical and cultural necessity for Christian day schools. His one attempt to establish a Christian elementary school in Holland failed.

He was firmly opposed to Freemasonry on biblical grounds—until retirement. Reformed Church synods refused to condemn this oath-bound, male club with a philosophy grounded in humanism. Then, for the sake of church unity, he went along and sacrificed his convictions about not serving two masters. If he had been the pastor of Holland's First Reformed Church in 1882, six years after his death, he would have opposed with all his might the majority decision to secede over Freemasonry and would have remained with the continuing congregation. In retirement, he also endorsed singing hymns in worship, a practice he had foresworn during his ministry.[10]

Van Raalte chose the Black Lake region for his colony because it was unsettled by whites, even though the lakeshore was densely wooded, mosquito infested, and unhealthy. That it was unsettled, however, offered a clean slate for a homogenous colony of Dutch

---

[9] Dosker, *Van Raalte*, 158-59; Wormser, *In twee werelddeelen*, 188-89; Van Hinte, *Netherlanders*, 362-63.

[10] Van Raalte endorsed singing hymns in worship, but Rev. Pieters was opposed, *De Hollander*, 16 Sept. 1874; Kennedy, *Commentary*, 1 April, 9 Nov. 1874, 3:1831-32, 1853-54.

Reformed believers. But Scholte's choice of rolling Iowa grasslands for his Pella colony was a better decision. He followers avoided a dying time, which befell many of Van Raalte's colonists. Van Raalte, in the beginning, did not deliver on his promises of prosperity.

Van Raalte's attitude toward Americans was also ambivalent. He relied on Kellogg, Harrington, and Fairbanks to establish the colony and entered business partnerships with Henry Post and Homer Hudson. Yet, in private correspondence with Paulus Den Bleyker, in 1852, Van Raalte castigated Americans and warned Den Bleyker not to trust them as business partners Yet, he went on to welcome American business and professional leaders to build the colony. By 1870 one-quarter of the population was non-Dutch, and by 1880, one-third was non-Dutch and included many other European nationalities. Practicality dictated diversity, cultural and religious, but the dominee never commented in print on the transition of Holland from a Dutch Reformed colony to the multiethnic city it had become by the time of his death.

The dominee's one and only return to the fatherland brought its own contradictions. He was eager to be back with family and friends, to revisit his old stomping grounds and savor the memories. He relished being honored with numerous preaching and speaking opportunities, even to be treated by old Separatists as an heroic returning son. But he found that both he and the land of his birth had changed; he could never really go home again. Continuing deformation in the national church that had persecuted him confirmed his earlier decision to join the Separatists. And the still largely agricultural economy could not compare with the modernizing American economy.

Albertus was devoted to his wife, but they both acknowledged that she played second fiddle to the Holland Academy and Hope College. He went to New York and New Jersey three times for several months to raise money for his precious schools. He accepted classical assignments to found churches in Illinois, Wisconsin, Iowa, and Kansas. He was a delegate to twelve meetings of the Particular and General Synods in New York, New Jersey, Pennsylvania, and Illinois. He was a pastor who had sacrificed his wife and children for ministry and fundraising. Already as the "apostle of Overijssel" in his first years of ministry, he was on the road for months at a time. His children grew up with an often absent father. Like the Apostle Paul, he should have remained unmarried. Brummelkamp and Van Velzen did not leave their wives— Christina's sisters—for extended periods.

Dominee Van Raalte preached publically and to his own children about revival and the need for a personal conversion, but only his oldest son and daughters had made professions of faith during his lifetime.[11] Ben and Dirk did not make public professions until long after their father's death, and that at the insistence of a confessing fiancé (Dirk) and wife (Ben). The Holy Spirit, who cannot be restrained, honored a father's fervent prayers, despite the negative effects of his frequent absences when his children were young. Mother Christina, who was always home, was able to bring up the girls in the faith.

The most anguished contradiction was the enterprising dominee's calling as minister of the Gospel and his desire to engage in business enterprises. As a man with independent means due to his wife's inheritance, he believed that he himself was responsible for initiating the economic life of the communities in which he ministered. In Holland, he partnered in mills, an ashery, a tannery, a saw and grain mill, harbor development, the colony store, and the colony ship. His major business, the millworks with Paulus Den Bleyker, ended in failure which nearly ruined him financially and sunk deep into his soul.

Van Raalte's decision to buy thousands of acres of land to ward off outside speculators was necessary initially to ensure the colony. But this required borrowing money to obtain key parcels, and one mortgage was still open at his death almost thirty years later. Even more crucial was the decision to take charge of the sale of Holland town lots. At his death, he still had more than five hundred virgin lots in his inventory. To pay real estate taxes in hard money was an annual challenge. Van Raalte was land rich and cash poor his entire life. Managing lands and lots was the tiger he had to ride all his days in America.

In personal ways, the dominee had his quirks. He would not allow hard liquor to be sold in taverns or from homes, but he purchased it regularly from druggists as "medicine." His beverage of choice was beer, and a pipe was his pacifier, as it was for many Dutch clergy. He did kick the habit later in life and also convinced Brummelkamp to do so. His student, Seine Bolks, never did quit, and lung problems caused his death at the ripe old age of eighty.[12]

---

[11] As related by Geesje Van der Haar-Visscher, "Van der Haar-Visscher diary," English typescript, 18, HMA.
[12] On Bolks, see Kennedy, *Commentary*, 3 Apr. 1872, 3:1675; "James De Pree's Rev. Seine Bolks," in Lucas, *Dutch Immigrant Memoirs*, 2:383. De Pree was Bolks's son-in-law.

Turning points

In retrospect, every life has pivot points where one makes choices that have lasting consequences. Van Raalte had a number of such turning points—his Luther-like stance against his synodical examiners, his immigration to America, his decision to unite the Classis of Holland with the Reformed Church in the East, his agreement to take control of Holland town lots, and the deeper issue of stinting on his ministerial calling to gain a competence. The dominee was a pastor by vocation and a colonial developer by avocation.

By nature, Van Raalte was dauntless, driven, restless, stubborn, and self-assured. In medical terms, he may have suffered from attention deficit hyperactivity disorder (ADHD), manifested by anxiety, impulsiveness, depression, frustration, mood swings, and fits of anger. As the youngest surviving son of the family, Albertus might have felt the need to prove himself. He once told some friends that, as a very small boy, he had climbed the spiral staircase of the steeple to the open tower of his father's church, where his mother alarmingly found him leaning out between the balustrades, fearing that he might lose his balance and fall to the ground. But his father stayed calm and coaxed him to climb down.[13]

As an adult, Van Raalte's best epithet is indispensable; he had to be the leader. He was a glutton for work and could not say no, to the point of mental and physical breakdown. Even after he retired under stress from the First Church pulpit, he sought an appointment as a missionary in Africa. Stymied at that, he planted a new colony in post-Civil War Virginia that proved to be a humiliating failure. Until his last years, he chaired the Hope College council and the Classis of Holland committees on education and missions, traveling as far as Kansas to visit new churches. His determination was legendary, but it did not match his strength.

Internecine apologists and critics

Clerics and historians continued to debate the merits or demerits of the union of 1850 and resulting schism of 1857, depending on their church affiliation. Reformed church apologists Dingeman Versteeg, Henry Dosker, Peter Moerdyke, Johan A. Wormser, William O. Van Eyck, and Aleida Pieters, among others, praised Van Raalte both for the union and his strong condemnation of the 1857 schism that followed.

---

[13] Incident related in Dosker, *Van Raalte*, 153.

Typical is Moerdyke's 1885 "Life and Labors" article. Moerdyke, an 1866 Hope College graduate, as a youth, sat under Van Raalte's preaching. Later, he taught at the college and then served the English-speaking First Reformed Churches in Grand Rapids and Chicago. Moerdyke's portrayal of Van Raalte is puffery and polemics in the extreme. His "pulpit was his throne." From it came the "authoritative, the aggressive, the uplifting, the soul-subduing, and the heart-bracing utterances of a veritable prophet of God." Moerdyke described the union as "most happy and beneficent," and the 1857 break was the work of "certain schismatic agitators, who appealed to ignorance, prejudices, and seceding tendencies contracted in the movements of 1834-35" to justify withdrawing from "the 'unsound' Reformed Dutch Church."[14]

Christian Reformed critics are equally emotive. Rev. Henry Beets praised Van Raalte as "a modern Moses," but justified the 1857 schism. Albert Hyma, the University of Michigan history professor, added an adverb—"truly a modern Moses." Yet Hyma castigated Van Raalte for the union decision. "What right did Van Raalte have to force through in such a hurry the act of union? Did he not know what the consequences of such a process would be for hundreds of thousands of persons in the future?" The dominee, in Hyma's opinion, held a "mistaken opinion" about the faith and practices of the American denomination. He knew in his heart "that a number of brethren in the East had become too lax in their interpretation of the Calvinist creed. But he remained a gentleman and favored charity over slander."[15]

Memory and myth

"The preacher," King Solomon, penned the proverb: "For the wise, like the fool, will not be long remembered; the days have already come when both have been forgotten" (Ecclesiastes 2:16a, KJV). Albertus C. Van Raalte, Holland's founder and leading cleric, was a wise man, but he too was soon forgotten, except as a mythical figure that bore little resemblance to the actual person. His name was invoked in church squabbles, in civic endeavors, and to promote ethnic pride. The local newspaper printed Van Raalte's iconic photo on the front page in 1926 and 1936 to mark the 50th and 60th anniversaries of his death, in 2011 to mark the 200th anniversary of his birth, and also for city anniversaries: the 50th in 1897, the 75th in 1922, the 100th in 1947, the 125th in 1972, and the 150th in 1997. And in 2022, the city's 175th

---

[14] Moerdyke, "Albertus C. Van Raalte," 1-9.
[15] Hyma, *Van Raalte*, 193, 206-7, 217, 255, 268, 272.

anniversary year, his photo may once again appear in print, as well as online. Tulip Time festivals have kept Van Raalte's name alive, and tour guides mention him when their trolley buses pass by Pillar Church and Hope College and stop at his statue in Centennial Park. But the historic Pillar Church sanctuary is the only living monument, since his homestead was razed.

Although Van Raalte was consumed by critics and failed ventures, Michael Douma has clearly noted that "Civic and business promoters... pietistic historians, and proud Dutch Americans remade the Dutch *dominee* into a symbol of ethnic pride. They turned a good man into a 'Great Man,' an energetic leader into a legend."[16] When pioneers died, their obituaries often mentioned that they had emigrated with Van Raalte. News editor Gerrit Van Schelven commemorated the semicentennial in 1897 by soliciting reminiscences from pioneers for news copy. These accounts usually portrayed Van Raalte positively. The local Grand Army of the Republic Post No. 262 adopted his name; city fathers named in his honor a boulevard-type street (Van Raalte Avenue) and a city park (Van Raalte Farm Park); school boards in the city and township named schools after him, and Hope College dedicated a classroom building as the A. C. Van Raalte Memorial Hall in 1903; this largest building on campus unfortunately burned to the ground in 1980.

In 1936 city fathers established Founder's Day every February 9, the day Van Raalte brought a small group of men to build the first log cabins. The Holland Museum opened on the second Founder's Day in 1937. Subsequent days celebrated "those hardy Dutch pioneers" who had set an example by the way "they met the challenge of their day." In 1947 Marvin Lindeman, an outspoken non-Dutch advertising executive, challenged city leaders with the question: "What do we want Holland to be?" Should it remain a cozy, homogeneous town, or a vibrant diverse, industrializing and expanding city? Their answer was the latter: "It's not up to Rev. Van Raalte; it's up to us." Thus, the dominee's name was purloined in the first "us versus them" moment in Holland.[17] Douma's conclusion is apt: Those who invoked Van Raalte's name "focused on his democratic, enlightened American side and marginalized his opponents as obstacles to progress. The

---

[16] Douma, "Memory and the Myth" (40 quote); Douma, "Writings about Van Raalte."
[17] Douma, "Memory and the Myth," 48; Lindeman, "A Non-Hollander"; Swierenga, *Holland, Michigan*, 2:1027, 1644-45, 3:1892, 2278-79.

Van Raalte statue in Centennial Park (*Lou Schakel*)

resulting image of Van Raalte tended to be sentimental, simplistic, and romantic."

Holland's sesquicentennial in 1997 put Van Raalte back on center stage in Centennial Park when Her Royal Highness Princess Margriet of the Netherlands Royal House unveiled a plaque in front of his statue amid solemn speeches and choral anthems. There he stands, just over five feet in real life, but nine-feet tall in bronze, thanks to a gift from the late Peter H. Huizenga, benefactor of the Van Raalte Institute, and the artistic guidance of Jacob E. Nyenhuis, Hope College provost emeritus, former director of the VRI, and founder and editor-in-chief of the Van Raalte Press. The model, based on a maquette designed by Leonard Crunelle for the seventy-fifth anniversary in 1922, portrays the dominee with his left hand firmly planted on a Bible placed atop a tree trunk. His right arm is raised with hands cupped in blessing, and his head is tilted slightly to the left so his eyes can gaze on both his church and college. He is now Holland's iconic founder.[18]

Holland Colony at Van Raalte's death, 1876

[18] See Nyenhuis and Jacobson, *A Dream Fulfilled*.

APPENDIX

Table 12.1. Village Board of Trustees Land Purchases, 1847-51

Year	$ Total	No. of Buys	Acres	Lots
1848	201	3	140	1

Table 12.2. Village Board of Trustees Land Sales, 1847-51

Year	$ Total	No. of Sales*	Acres	Lots
1847	1,810	35	0	38
1848	2,230	49	0	59
1849	548	12	0	68
1850	618	8	0	8
1851	563	3	80	1

* In twenty-one sales, the trustees accepted down payments and extended credit at 7 percent interest for several years. The subsequent payments of principal and interest are not included.

Table 12.3. Van Raalte Land Purchases, 1847-76

Year	$Total*	No. of Buys	Acres	Lots
1847	7,346	80	7,288	0
1848	2,536	41	3,010	0
1849	3,981	18	1,349	1
1850	103	5	720	0
1851	393	14	840	0
1852	35	13	1,024	0
1853	0	0	0	0
1854	50	1	83	0
1855	0	0	0	0
1857	0	0	0	0
1858	11	1	320	0
1859	1,180	2	17	2
1860	950	3	240	2
1861	660	3	120	1
1862	9	3	0	3
1863	910	3	1,582	0
1864	1,480	13	1,040	0
1865	2,160	12	1,440	0
1866	400	1	0	0
1867	540	2	0	2
1868	0	0	0	0
1869	0	0	0	0
1870	300	1	0	1
1871	1,100	2	80	1
1872	0	0	0	0
1873	0	0	0	0
1874	400	1	40	1
1875	0	0	0	0
1876	0	0	0	0
Total	**$24,504**	**219**	**19,193**	**14**

* Van Raalte bought some lands (especially in 1847) with small cash down

payments, and sellers took back mortgages for the remainder. The mortgage payments of principal and interest are not included.

Table 12.4. Van Raalte Land Sales, 1848-76

Year	$ Total*	No. of Sales	Acres	City Lots
1848	1,984	27	1,211	2
1849	2,158	20	563	14
1850	923	19	70	22
1851	2,558	26	454	36
1852	3,844	44	146	98
1853	1,511	18	730	18
1854	995	8	199	10
1855	2,540	18	234	17
1856	1,130	11	40	13
1857	2,619	19	212	36
1858	710	7	0	15
1859	750	6	110	5
1860	4,070	28	59	67
1861	2,559	18	80	20
1862	1,993	20	112	53
1863	2,440	25	70	32
1864	4,016	29	120	46
1865	4,866	25	40	30
1866	2,250	3	1,571	2
1867	10,701	32	16	66
1868	5,390	13	120	21
1869	4,485	12	105	15
1870	3,620	8	0	43
1871	16,567	17	192	92
1872	4,035	12	0	12
1873	3,630	9	350	12
1874	3,010	8	220	4
1875	5,075	13	80	16

Year				
1876	14,981	12	160	24
1877⁺	0	13		84
1878	240	1	0	1
Total	**$116,650**	**522#**	**7,264**	**926**

* These sums are the gross amount of land sales. On an unknown number of sales, Van Raalte accepted down payments and extended credit at interest for several years. The interest income is not included here.
⁺ Sold to heirs for "$1 and other considerations."
Excludes 70 lots and 13 acres donated for churches, schools, and so forth.

Table 14.1. Membership Statistics, First Reformed Church, Holland, 1850-76

Year	Families	Communicants	Souls
1851*	nr	278	624
1852	131	258	617
1853	141	280	669
1854	151	312	699
1855	149	316	737
1856	153	334	na
1857	158	346	na
1858	168	357	na
1859	151	321	na
1860	156	346	na
1861	160	355	na
1862	168	365	na
1863	179	369	na
1864	190	383	na
1865	201	455 (62 cf)	na
1866	250	486 (28 cf)	na
1867	nr		
1868	110	205 (8 cf)	na
1869	112	230	na
1870	117	241	na

1871	118	234	na
1872	119	236	na
1872	120	237	na
1873	129	260	na
1874	142	276	na
1875	142	276	na
1876	148	313	na

*	Report for previous year
cf	On confession of faith
na	Not available
nr	No report

Acts and Proceedings of the General Synod, 1851-1877

BIBLIOGRAPHY

Notes on sources

Albertus C. Van Raalte lived in the Netherlands thirty-five years and in the United States thirty years. He did not take any documents with him when he emigrated and could not make copies of outgoing letters in the era before typewriters and carbon paper, but he saved all incoming correspondence, and his correspondents saved his letters, which fortunately include letters sent to his wife and children. Van Raalte carefully kept real estate records, tax receipts, lists of lands and lots sold, and merchants' bills for goods and foodstuffs purchased on credit. He also made copies of important legal records.

Scholars are indebted to two men, Albert Hyma and Elton J. Bruins, for the rich corpus of the Albertus C. Van Raalte Collection in the Heritage Hall Archives in Calvin University Library and at the A. C. Van Raalte Institute in the Theil Research Center on the Hope College campus.

Hyma, late professor of history at the University of Michigan, purchased the original tranche of documents and business records from Van Raalte descendants in 1946. Bruins, late Blekkink Professor of Religion Emeritus at Hope College, spent fifty years collecting more than five thousand Van Raalte documents in archival collections in the United States and the Netherlands, including the rich archives of the Reformed Church in America at New Brunswick Theological Seminary in New Jersey. Mees te Velde, professor of church history at the Theological University of the Reformed Churches Liberated (Vrijgemaakt), Kampen, uncovered a number of Van Raalte letters.

Bruins also scoured periodicals and newspapers for articles and items by and about Van Raalte, most notably the weeklies: *Christian Intelligencer* (Reformed Church, NY), *De Bazuin* (Separatist weekly, Kampen), *De Hope* (Reformed Church, Holland), and the *Banner* (Christian Reformed Church, Grand Rapids). West Michigan newspapers yielded many rich items, notably *De Hollander* (1850-98, Holland) and *De Grondwet* (1860-1938, Holland). Unfortunately, many issues of *De Hollander* in the 1850s, and all of the *De Hollander* and *De Grondwet* issues in the 1860s, were lost in the Holland Fire of 1871. Newspapers in neighboring cities survived, including *Allegan Journal, De Nederlander, De Sheboygan Nieuwsbode, Detroit Daily Free Press, Detroit Daily Advertiser, Grand Haven Herald, Grand Haven News, Grand Rapids Argus, Grand River Eagle* (Grand Rapids), *Grand River Times* (Grand Haven), and *Ottawa* [Holland] *Register*, and they frequently contain Van Raalte items of interest.

Digitized copies of minutes of Netherlands Hervormde Kerken that Van Raalte served were consulted for Genemuiden, Ommen, and Velp/Arnhem, and also the minutes and acts of the provincial classes of Drenthe, Gelderland, Overijssel, and Zuid-Holland. The complete acts of the Christelijke Afgescheiden Kerken Synods of Amsterdam 1835, Utrecht 1837, Amsterdam 1840, and Amsterdam 1843 are published in *Handelingen en verslagen van de algemene synoden van de Christelijke Afgescheiden Kerk (1836-1869)*.

In the United States, the minutes of the Classis of Holland, organized on April 23, 1848, are published in English translation through June 30, 1876, in Earl Wm. Kennedy's *Commentary*. The minutes of First Reformed Church in Holland, from November 5, 1850, are available in their entirety at the Joint Archives of Holland. Prior to that date, from early 1848, church affairs were intermingled in the minutes of Volksvergadering, or People's Assembly, a copy of which is in the Joint Archives. William Buursma, with typing assistance from his wife Althea, translated into English the minutes from November 5, 1850, into the twentieth century, but the file is available only in typescript at the Joint Archives. For the minutes of the Christian Reformed Church, see *Minutes of the Christian Reformed Church, 1857-1870*, edited and annotated by Janet Sjaarda Sheeres.

Correspondence with government officials, such as the mayor of Ommen, the provincial governor of Overijssel, and King Willem II, are in Algemene Rijksarchief, The Hague. Some Van Raalte letters have been published, including nine with Scholte and one each with Johan A. Wormser and Johannes H. Donner in *Iowa Letters*. Other letters and documents relating to Van Raalte's ministry in the provinces of Gelderland and Overijssel are published in the multivolume books of Cornelis Smits and Jan Wesseling, cited in the bibliography.

Original entries at the Federal Land Office in Ionia, recorded in the "Original Entry" books in Ottawa and Allegan Counties, are located in the Recorder's Offices of the respective courthouses. The Recorder's Offices also contain deed registers and land mortgages, all of which have been digitized for ready access. Purchases at the Michigan State Land Office in Marshall, primarily of Swamp Lands and Internal Improvement Lands, are also recorded in the respective county deed registers. A listing of all Van Raalte deeds is given below.

There is no family portrait of the Van Raaltes. The customary twenty-fifth anniversary fell on March 11, 1861, when the family was settled comfortably in Holland, Michigan, before Ben and Dirk enlisted in the Civil War. The photographer shops on Eighth Street were all destroyed in the Holland Fire of 1871, but the family homestead did not burn. So, it is likely that no photo was taken. Only one photo of Christina Johanna exists (ch. 15), not dated, but estimated to be in the mid-to-late 1850s. There are several photos of Albertus at various ages, also not dated.

I. Archival Sources

Algemeen Rijksarchief, The Hague.
Algemeen Rijksarchief, Zuid-Holland.
Allegan County deed registers. Courthouse, Allegan, Michigan.
Archief de Cock, Gemeentearchief Kampen.
Archives and Documentation Center of the Reformed Churches, Liberated (Vrijgemaakt), Kampen (ADC).
Ball, John, Papers. Grand Rapids Public Library, Michigan.
Centraal Bureau voor Genealogie, The Hague.
Central College Archives, Pella, Iowa (CCA).

Den Bleyker Papers. Michigan Historical Collections. Bentley Historical Library, University of Michigan, Ann Arbor (BHL).
Fairbanks, Isaac, Papers. HMA.
Fijnaart Bevolkingsregister, 1830.
Georgetown Township Board. Record Book. Hudsonville, Michigan.
Graafschap CRC Minutes. Holland, Michigan.
Grand Rapids Public Library, Michigan.
Heritage Hall Archives for the Christian Reformed Church, Calvin Theological Seminary, and Calvin University, in the Hekman Library at Calvin University (HHA).
Herrick District Library. Holland, Michigan.
Het Archief van de Gereformeeerde Kerken, Amsterdam (AGK).
Historisch Centrum Overijssel, Zwolle.
Holland City Records. HMA.
Holland Harbor Board minutes. HMA.
Holland Museum Archives, Michigan (HMA).
Holland Township Board, Minutes. Michigan.
Leiden Regional Archives.
Moerdyke, P. T., Papers. HMA.
Ottawa County Deed Registers. Courthouse. Grand Haven, Michigan.
Pfanstiehl Family Papers. HMA.
Post Family Papers. HMA.
Post, Henry D., Papers. HMA.
Post, Hoyt G., Diary. HMA.
Puchinger, George, Papers. Protestant Documentation Center, Free University of Amsterdam.
RCA Archives. New Brunswick, New Jersey, and Grand Rapids, Michigan.
Te Velde, Mees, Collection. ADC.
Van der Veen, Christian, Papers. HMA.
Van Eyck, William O., Papers. HMA.
Van Raalte, A. C., Papers. See: https://digitalcommons.hope.edu/vrp.
Van Schelven Papers. HMA.
Visscher Family Papers. HMA.

II. Records of Churches, Classes, and Synods (published and unpublished)

Acts of the Particular Synod of Albany of the RPDC. Schenectady, 1850.
Acts and Proceedings of the General Synod of the RPDC [RCA], 1848-82.
Adres aan de Algemene Synode van het Nederlandsch Herv. Kerkgenootschap. Ommen: Egbertus ten Tooren, 1842. HHA.

Board of Domestic Missions of the RPDC. Annual Reports, Correspondence, 1850-76. Archives, New Brunswick, New Jersey.
Classis Holland Minutes, 1848-1858. RPDC [RCA]. Eerdmans, 1950.
Classis Nieuwleusen, Overijssel. Minutes, 1838-43.
"Dr. Albertus Christiaan van Raalte." In *Zalsmans Jaarboekje* (1874), 91-116.
First Reformed Church, Zeeland. Minutes, 1849-57.
Friesland Provincial Classis. Minutes, 1848.
General Synod Papers 1849-59. Archives, New Brunswick, New Jersey (microfilm, JAH).
Handelingen van de Opzieners der Gemeente Jesus Christi . . . . Den Haag, 1843.
Handelingen en verslagen van der Algemene Synoden van de Christelijke Afgescheidene Gereformeerde Kerk (1836-1869), met stukken betreffende de synode van 1843, bijlagen en registers. Den Hartog, 1984.
Handelingen van het Provinciale Vergadering Gelderland/Overijssel. Deventer, 1844.
Handelingen van het Provinciale Kerkbestuur van Zuid-Holland. 's Gravenhage, 1835-36. Algemene Rijksarchief. Province of Zuid-Holland.
Harms, Richard, H., "South Holland (Michigan) Presbyterian Church, Family Records, 1849-1867" (2008).
Honderd Veertig Jaar Gemeenten en Predikanten van de Gereformeerde Kerken in Nederland. Algemene Bureau van de Gereformeerde Kerken in Nederland. Druk Oosterbaan & Le Cointre, 1974.
Hope College catalogues, 1891-92.
Jaarboekje voor de Christelijk Afgescheidene Gereformeerde Kerk in Nederland. S. van Velzen Jr., 1856.
Kompleete uitgave van de officiëele stukken betreffende den uitgang uit het Nederl. Herv. Kerkgenootschap van de leeraren H. P. Scholte, A. Brummelkamp, S. van Velzen, G. F. Gezelle Meerburg, en Dr. A. C. Van Raalte. S. van Velzen Jr. Vol. 1, 1863; 2nd ed., G. Ph. Zalsman, 1884. Reprinted, Henricus Pieter Scholte, editor. ICG Testing, n.d.
Ommen Hervormde Kerk. Minutes, 1836-44.
Provincial Synod of Zuid-Holland. Minutes, 1835.
Sheeres, Janet Sjaarda, ed. and ann. *Minutes of the Christian Reformed Church, 1857-1870.* Transcribed and translated by Richard H. Harms. Eerdmans, 2013.
Van Deventer, J. Haz. *Jaarboekje voor de provincie Overijssel voor het jaar 1857.* Zwolle, 1857.

"Verkade's Dominees Memories." http://verkade.nu/dominees.nl/ dominees.php.
Verslag van de Vergadering van Opzieners, der Gemeente Jesu Christi gehouden den 6 en 7 Maart 1840, te Amsterdam. ('s-Gravenhage, 1840).
Wanneperveen Hervormde Kerk. Minutes, 1811-20.
Zalsmans Jaarboekje voor Kerk, School, en Zending in Nederland. J. H. Kok, 1874-86.

III. American Newspapers

Allegan Journal. Michigan, 1856-80.
Grand Rapids Argus. Michigan, 1852-57.
De Grondwet. Holland, Michigan, 1860-1900 (issues missing before 19 Dec. 1871).
De Hollander. Holland, Michigan, 1850-1900 (incomplete 1850s, missing 1860-71).
De Nederlander. Kalamazoo, Michigan, 1852.
De Sheboygan Nieuwsbode. Wisconsin, 1849-61.
Detroit Advertiser. Michigan, 1846-62.
Detroit Free Press. Michigan, 1847-48.
Grand Haven Herald. Michigan, 1869-78.
Grand Haven News. Michigan, 1858-69.
Grand [Rapids] *River Eagle.* Michigan, 1847-60.
Grand [Haven] *River Times.* Michigan, 1851-71.
Holland City News. Michigan, 1871-1970.
Kalamazoo Gazette. Michigan, 1847.
Lake Shore Commercial. Saugatuck, Michigan, 1871-77.
Ottawa Register. Holland, Michigan, 1857-61.
De Volksvriend. Orange City, Iowa, 1874, 1911.

Dutch Newspapers

Algemeen Handelsblad (Amsterdam), 1840-47.
Amsterdamsche Courant, 1797-98.
Arnhemsche Courant, 1845.
Delta, 1959.
Deventer Courant, 1842.
Groninger Courant, 1836, 1846.
Leeuwarder Courant, 1846, 1869.
Leydsche Courant, 1846-51.
Nieuw Kamper Dagblad, 6 Nov. 1876.
Noord-Brabander, 1837.

Opregte Haarlemsche Courant, 1833-45.
Overijsselsche Courant, 1841.
Provinciale Overijsselsche en Zwolsche Courant, 1845-47.
Rotterdamsche Courant, 1854.
De Saambinder, 1867.
Utrechtsche Provinciale en Stads-Courant, 1847-54.

IV. Church Periodicals

Banner, The. CRC weekly, 1900-2000.
De Bazuin. Amsterdam (Christelijke Gereformeerde Kerk), 1854-80.
Christian Intelligencer, The. RPDC, RCA weekly, 1846-77.
Excelsiora, The. Hope College student newspaper, 1853-76.
De Heraut, 1866-80.
De Hope. Hope College and Western Seminary faculty, 1866-84.
De Reformatie. Christelijke Afgescheiden Kerk weekly, 1840-46.
De Vrije Kerk, 1876-80.
De Verzamelaar, 1865.

V. Published Works

Aalders, M. J. *De komst van de toga: Een historisch onderzoek naar het verdwijnen van mantel en bef en de komst van de toga op de Nederlandse kansels, 1795-1989*. Eburon Uitgeverij, 2001.
Aay, Henk, and Peter Ester. "Jacob Van Hinte's Appraisal of Immigrant Leaders Hendrik Pieter Scholte and Albertus C. Van Raalte." In Nyenhuis and Harinck, *Enduring Legacy*, 297-321.
———. "Present from the Beginning: Reformed Dutch Day Schools in North America, 1638-2019." In *Dutch Reformed Education*, 3-38.
Bakker, W. *De Afgescheiden van 1834 en hun nageslacht*. J. H. Kok., 1984.
———, et al., eds. *De Afscheiding van 1834 en haar geschiedenis*. J. H. Kok, 1984.
Ballast, Daniel L. *Then, Now, Always, 1840 – 2004, Jesus Is Lord! The History of Central Reformed Church, 1840-2004*. Central Reformed Church, 2005.
Ball Powers, Kate. *Born to Wander: Autobiography of John Ball, 1794-1884*. Flora Ball Hopkins, 1925; reissued, Grand Rapids Historical Commission, 1994.
Barnhoorn. J. G. *Amicitia Christiana*. B. V. Uitgeverij De Banier, 2009.
Beets, Henry. *De Chr. Geref. Kerk in N. A: Zestig Jaren van Strijd en Zegen*. Grand Rapids Publishing Co., 1918.

———. *Life and Times of Jannes Van de Luyster: Founder of Zeeland, Michigan.* Zeeland Record Co., 1949.
Beuker, Gerrit Jan. "'The Area beyond Hamse and Hardenberg,' Van Raalte and Bentheim." In Nyenhuis and Harinck, *Enduring Legacy*, 23-42.
Biografisch Lexicon voor de geschiedenis van het Nederlandse Protestantisme. Uitgeverij Kok, 2000.
Bloemhof, Jacob, ed. *Wanneperveen 700 jaar: een bundel opstellen over heden en verladen.* Publikaties van de Ijsselakademie, 1984.
Blok, P. J. *Geschiedenis eener Hollandsche Stad.* Martinus Nijhoff, 1918.
Boekzaal der geleerde wereld, en tijdschrift voor de Protestantsche Kerken in het Koningrijk [sic] *der Nederlanden.* Amsterdam, 1793-1833.
Boonstra, Harry. "Martinus Cohen Stuart: Netherlander in Michigan." *Origins* 22, no. 2 (2004): 18-27.
Boot, C. *De kerk over de brug: 400 jaar Hervormde Gemeente Rijsoord.* Liebeek & Hooijmeijer, 1980.
Bos, David J. *Servants of the Kingdom: Professionalization among Ministers in the Nineteenth-Century Netherlands Reformed Church.* Brill, 2010. English translation of Bos, *In dienst van het Koninkrijk: Beroepsontwikkeling van hervormde predikanten in negentiende-eeuws Nederland.* Uitgeverij Bert Bakker, 1999.
Bos, Emo. *Souvereiniteit en Religie: Godsdienstvrijheid onder de eerste Oranjevorsten.* Verloren, 2009.
Bos, F. L., ed. *Archiefstukken betreffende de Afscheiding van 1834*, 4 vols. J. H. Kok, 1939-46.
———. *Kruisdominees: Figuren uit de Gereformeerde Kerk onder 't Kruis.* J. H. Kok, 1953.
Bosch, Roel A., and Freek Pereboom. "De Hervormde Kerk in de periode 1795-1840." In Pereboom et al., *'Van scheurmakers,'* 44-97.
Bouma, H. *Tot de prediking van het Woord des Geloofs.* Kampen Theological School, 1959.
Bouwman, Harm. *Der Crisis der jeugd: Eenige bladzijden uit de geschiedenis van de kerken der Afscheiding.* J. H. Kok, 1914; reissued, 1976.
Bratt, James D. *Abraham Kuyper: Modern Calvinist, Christian Democrat.* Eerdmans, 2013.
———. *Dutch Calvinism in Modern America: A History of a Conservative Subculture.* Eerdmans, 1984.
Bratt, John H., ed. *The Rise and Development of Calvinism.* Eerdmans, 1959.
Bredeweg, Dawn Bos. *The Rooster's Tail: An Informal History of Pillar Church, Holland, Michigan.* Clapbook Press, 2014.

Brienen, T., K. Exalto, J. van Gelderen, C. Graafland, and W. van 't Spijker, eds. *Nadere Reformatie, De beschrijving van haar voornaamste vertegenwoordigers*. Uitgeverij Boekencentrum, 1986.

Brinks, Herbert J. "Another Look at 1857." *Origins* 4, no. 1 (1986): 27-31.

———. "De Afscheiding: 1834-1984." *Origins* 2, no. 2 (1984): 24-26.

———. "Father Budding, 1810-1870." *Origins* 14, no. 2 (1986): 19-23.

———. "Religious Continuities in Europe and the New World." In Swierenga, *The Dutch in America*, 209-23.

———. "Church History via Kalamazoo, 1850-1860." *Origins* 16, no. 1 (1998): 36-42.

Bruggink, Donald J. "Extra-Canonical Tests for Church Membership and Ministry." In Nyenhuis, *A Goodly Heritage*, 50-54.

Bruins, Elton J. "Albertus Christiaan Van Raalte: Funding His Vision of a Christian Colony." In *The Dutch and Their Faith*, 53-63.

———. "Albertus C. Van Raalte: Leader of the Dutch Emigration to the United States, 1847-1867." *Origins* 19, no. 2 (2001): 4-11.

———. *The Americanization of a Congregation: A History of Third Reformed Church*. Eerdmans, 1970; 2nd ed. 1995.

———. "'An American Moses': Albertus C. Van Raalte as Immigrant Leader." In Harinck and Krabbendam, *Sharing the Reformed Tradition*, 19-34.

———, comp. "Bibliography on Van Raalte, Part 1: Works from 1975 to 2013." In Nyenhuis and Harinck, *Enduring Legacy*, 345-59.

———. "From Calvin to Van Raalte: The Rise and Development of the Reformed Tradition in the Netherlands, 1560-1900." In Klunder and Gasero, *Servant Gladly*, 89-103.

———. "Educational Endeavors of the Reformed Dutch Church, 1628-1866." *Reformed Review* 59, no. 2 (Winter 2005-6), 179-81.

———. "Holocaust in Holland: 1871." *Michigan History* 55 (Winter 1971): 289-304.

———. "Hope College: Its Origin and Development, 1851-2001." *Origins* 19, no. 1 (2001): 4-13.

———, and Karen G. Schakel. *Envisioning Hope College: Letters Written by Albertus C. Van Raalte to Philip Phelps Jr., 1857 to 1875*. Van Raalte Press; Eerdmans, 2011.

———, Karen G. Schakel, Sara Fredrickson Simmons, and Marie N. Zingle. *Albertus and Christina: The Van Raalte Family, Home and Roots*. Eerdmans, 2004.

———, and Robert P. Swierenga, *Family Quarrels in the Dutch Reformed Churches in the Nineteenth Century*. Eerdmans, 1999.

Brumm, James Hart, ed. *Tools for Understanding: Essays in Honor of Donald J. Bruggink*. Eerdmans, 2008.

Brummelkamp, A. "Dr. Albertus Christiaan van Raalte." In *Zalsmans Jaarboekje* (1877), 91-116.

——. *Holland in Amerika, of de Hollandsche Kolonisatie in den Staat Michigan*. J. W. Swain, 1847. An English translation by Gerrit Vander Zeil is available in HHA.

——. Report of Synod Amsterdam, 6-7 March 1840. Den Haag, 1840.

——. *Stemmen uit Noord-Amerika met Begeleidend Woord*. Amsterdam, 1847. Published in English as *Voices from North America*. Calvin College, 1992.

——, and Albertus C. Van Raalte. *Aan de Geloovigen in de Vereenigde Staten van Noord-Amerika*. Hoogkamer en Cie, 25 May 1846. Published in English in *Christian Intelligencer*, 15 Oct. 1846, and in Lucas, *Dutch Immigrant Memoirs*, 1:14-20.

——, and Albertus C. Van Raalte. *Landverhuizing, of waarom bevorderen wij de volksverhuizing en wel naar Noord Amerika en niet naar Java* (emigration, or why we promote the emigration of people to North America and not to Java), 3rd ed. Hoogkamer en Cie, 1846. An English translation typescript by John VerBrugge is in HHA.

——, Jan W. ten Bokkel, and A. C. Van Raalte. *Nog is er hulpe! Een woord aan al het Godvreezend volk*. Hoogkamer & Comp., 1844.

Brummelkamp, Anthony Jr. *Levensbeschrijving van wijlen Prof. A. Brummelkamp*. J. H. Kok, 1910.

Burgers, Herman. *De garoeda en de ooievaar: Indonesie van kolonie tot nationale staat*. Verhandelingen van het Koninklijk Instituut voor Taal-, Land- en Volkenkunde, 2010.

Capadose, Abraham. *Ernstig en biddend Woord aan de getrouwe Leraaren in de Hervormde Kerk in Nederland*. Amsterdam, 1835.

Classis Holland Minutes, 1848-1858. Eerdmans, 1950.

Cohen Stuart, Marten. *Zes Maanden in Amerika*, 2 vols. Haarlem, 1875.

Corwin, Edwin T. *A Digest of Synodical Legislation of the Reformed Church in America*. New York, 1906.

Da Costa, Isaac. *Bezwaren tegen den geest der eeuw*. L. Herdingh en Zoon, 1823.

De Clerk, Peter, comp. "Bibliography on Van Raalte, Part 2: Works from 1837 to 1975." In Nyenhuis and Harinck, *Enduring Legacy*, 361-405.

De Cock, Helenius. *Hendrik de Cock: Eerste Afgeschieden Predikant in Nederland, Beschouwde in Leven en Werkzaamheid*. S. Van Velzen Jr., 1860.

Deddens, D. et al., *Hendrik de Cock, Verzamelde Geschriften.* Vol. 2. Den Hartog, 1986.

De Graaf, W. "Een afgescheiden dominee als zakenman: Dr. A. C. van Raalte." *De Hoekstem: Tijdschrift voor Nederlands Kerkgescheidenis.* February 1983, 3-12.

———. "Een Monument der Afscheiding." In *Sola Gratia: Schets van de geschiedenis en de werkzaamheid van de Theologische Hogeschool der Gereformeerde Kerken in Nederland, 1854-1954.* J. H. Kok, 1954, 5-32.

De Haas, Johannes. *Gedenkt uw voorgangers.* Vijlbrief, 1984.

———. *Van Dominees en Gemeenten.* Speelman's Bookhouse, 1981.

De Jager, Jacob. "The History of Our Church." In *One Hundredth Anniversary, 1857-1957.*

De Jong, Gerald F. "The Controversy over Dropping the Word Dutch from the Name of the Reformed Church." *Reformed Review* 34 (Spring, 1981): 158-70.

De Jong, P. Y, and Nelson Kloosterman, eds. *The Reformation of 1834: Essays in Commemoration of the Act of Secession.* Pluim Publishing, 1984.

De Jonge, C. W. *Aan al mijne geliefde vrienden in Nederland.* Goes, 1848.

———. *Reglement der Zeeuwsche Vereeniging ter Verhuizing naar De Vereenigde Staten van Noord-Amerika* (1847).

De Kok, J. A. *Nederland op de breuklijn Rome-Reformatie.* Van Gorcum, 1964.

Demarest, David D. *History and Characteristics of the Reformed Protestant Dutch Church.* New York, 1856.

Den Herder, Jacob. "Brief History of the Township and Village of Zeeland." 1876 address. Trans. Nella Kennedy. Jacob Den Herder Papers, HMA.

Den Ouden, W. H. *Kerk onder patriottenbewind.* Uitgeverij Boekcentrum, 1994.

Den Uyl, Paul A. *The Holland Fire Department: The First Fifty Years, 1867-1916.* Holland, MI: 2008.

De Rijcke, D. *Huibert Jacobus Budding en Zijn Ring (1834-1839): Een bladzijde uit de geschiedenis van de Afscheiding in Zeeland.* J. C. & W. Altorffer, 1906.

De toestand der Hollandsche kolonisatie in den staat Michigan, Noord Amerika: Drie brieven aan C. C. de Moen door A. C. van Raalte, C. van der Meulen, en S. Bolks (The condition of the Dutch colonists in the state of Michigan, North America: three letters to C. C. De Moen, from A. C. Van Raalte, C. Van der Meulen, and S. Bolks). Hoogkamp, 1849. An English translation by Nella Kennedy is available at the VRI.

De Ruiter, J. *De Historie van 's-Heer Abtskerke*. Gemeente Borssele, 1993.
De Vries, Michael. "Albertus C. Van Raalte: A Look at the Autumn Years of His Life (1811-1876)." *Origins* 19, no. 2 (2001): 12-18.
———, and Harry Boonstra. *Pillar Church in the Van Raalte Era*. First Reformed Church, Holland, 2003.
Dosker, Henry E. *Levensschets van Rev. A. C. van Raalte, D.D. Een der vaders der 'Scheiding' in Nederland en stichter der Hollandsche Koloniën in den Staat Michigan, Noord Amerika, Uit oorspronkelijke bronnen Bewerkt*. Callenbach, 1893. This biography was published first in serial form in *De Hope* from 29 April 1891 through 8 June 1892. An English-language translation by Elizabeth Dekker is available at the VRI.
Douma, Michael J. *How Dutch Americans Stayed Dutch: An Historical Perspective on Ethnic Identities*. Amsterdam University Press, 2014.
———. "Memory and the Myth of Albertus C. Van Raalte: How Holland, Michigan, Remembers Its Founding Father." *Michigan Historical Review* 36, no. 2 (2010): 37-61.
———. "Rediscovering Van Raalte's Church History: Historical Consciousness at the Birth of Dutch American Religion." *Calvin Theological Journal* 49, no. 1 (2014): 5-24.
———. "Struggle against the Sand: The Development of the Harbor at Holland, Michigan, 1847-1881." *Inland Seas Journal* 61, no. 4 (2005): 282-93.
———. "Writings about Van Raalte: Historiography and Changing Views about the Dutch American Leader." In Nyenhuis and Harinck, *Enduring Legacy*, 279-95.
Dunbar, Willis F. *A History of the Wolverine State*. Eerdmans, 1965.
Ebenezer Reformed Church. *One Hundred Twenty-Fifth Anniversary, 1866-1991*. Holland, 1991.
Eglington, James. *Bavinck: A Critical Biography*. Baker, 2020.
Engelsma, David J., ed. *Always Reforming: Continuation of the Sixteenth-Century Reformation*. Reformed Free Publishing Association, 2009.
———. "Covenant Doctrine of the Fathers of the Secession." In Engelsma, *Always Reforming*, 100-136.
Engelsma, Joshua. *Watchman on the Walls of Zion: The Life and Influence of Simon van Velzen*. Reformed Free Publishing Association, 2021.
Envisioning Hope College. see Bruins and Karen G. Schakel.
Ester, Peter, Nella Kennedy, and Earl Wm. Kennedy, eds. *The American Diary of Jacob Van Hinte*. Van Raalte Press; Eerdmans, 2010.
Fabend, Firth Haring. "The Synod of Dort and the Persistence of Dutchness in Nineteenth-Century New York and New Jersey." *New York History* 77 (July 1996): 273-300.

———. *Zion on the Hudson: Dutch New York and New Jersey in the Age of Revivals*. Rutgers University Press, 2000.
Frederiks, Egbert. "Egbert Frederiks' Pioneer Memories." In Lucas, *Dutch Immigrant Memoirs*, 1:54-72.
Gasero, Russell L. *Historical Directory of the Reformed Church in America 1628-2000*. Eerdmans, 2001.
Gates, Paul W. *History of Public Land Law Development*. Government Printing Office, 1968.
Geschiedkundige herinneringen bij gelegenheid van de inwijding van het nieuwe gebouw voor de beide stichtingen, en van het drie honderdjarige bestaan van het Burgerweeshuis. W. P. van Stockum, 1869.
Goodspeed, E. J. *History of the Great Fires in Chicago and the West*. Chicago, 1871.
Griffiths, Richard T. *Industrial Retardation in the Netherlands, 1830-1850*. Martinus Nijhoff, 1979.
Groen van Prinsterer, Guilluame. *Ongeloof en Revolutie: Eene reeks van historische voorlezingen*. Leiden, 1847.
Gunning, J. H. *H. J. Budding: Leven en Arbeid*. 2nd ed. W. J. Van Nes, 1909.
Haan, Gysbert. *Stem van een Belasterde* (Voice of one slandered). Grand Rapids, MI, 1871.
Hambrick-Stowe, Charles E. *Charles G. Finney and the Spirit of American Evangelicalism*. Eerdmans, 1996.
Harinck. George. "Henry Dosker, between Albertus C. Van Raalte and Abraham Kuyper." *Origins* 19, no. 2 (2001): 34-41.
———, and Hans Krabbendam, eds. *Breaches and Bridges: Reformed Sub-Cultures in the Netherlands, Germany, and the United States*. VU Uitgeverij, 2000.
———, and Hans Krabbendam, eds. *Morsels in the Melting Pot*. Free University Press, 2006.
———, and Hans Krabbendam, eds. *Sharing the Reformed Tradition: The Dutch-North American Exchange, 1846-1996*. Free University Press, 1996.
———, and Lodewijk Winkler. "The Nineteenth Century." In Selderhuis, *Handbook of Dutch Church History*.
———. "'O, may the Lord give this country a mighty revival.' Van Raalte's Trip to the Netherlands in 1866." In Nyenhuis and Harinck, *Enduring Legacy*, 67-88.
Harms, Richard, comp. *Historical Directory of the Christian Reformed Church*. Historical Committee of the Christian Reformed Church in North America, 2004.

———, ed. *The Dutch Adapting in North America*. Calvin College, 2001.

———. "Fissures in the Fellowship: Dynamics of the Religious Divisions in the West Michigan 'Dutch Colony' during the 1850s." In Nyenhuis and Harinck, *Enduring Legacy*, 151-69.

———. "The Other Reformed: Dutch Presbyterians in Nineteenth-Century America." *Calvin Theological Journal* 42 (April 2007): 33-49.

Heideman, Eugene P. *Hendrik P. Scholte: His Legacy in the Netherlands and in America*. Van Raalte Press; Eerdmans, 2015.

———. "The Reverend Dr. Albertus C. Van Raalte, Preacher and Leader, as Reflected in His Sermons." In Nyenhuis and Harinck, *Enduring Legacy*, 261-78.

Hinsdale, Burke A. *History of the University of Michigan*. Ann Arbor, 1906.

Hope Church Historical booklet 1982: Our Time for Rededication. 1982.

House, Renee S., and John W. Coakley. *Patterns and Portraits: Women in the History of the Reformed Church in America*. Eerdmans, 1999.

Hulst, Lammert J. *Drie en zestig jaren prediker*. Eerdmans Sevensma Co., 1913.

Hyma, Albert. *Albertus C. Van Raalte and His Dutch Settlements in the United States*. Eerdmans, 1947.

———. "When the Dutch Came to Michigan," *Michigan Alumnus* 54 (1947).

Illustrated Historical Atlas of the Counties of Ottawa & Kent, Michigan. Beldon & Co. 1876.

Israel, Jonathan I. *The Dutch Republic: Its Rise, Greatness, and Fall, 1477-1806*. Clarendon Press, 1995.

Jacobson, Jeanne M. "Civil War Correspondence of Benjamin Van Raalte during the Atlanta Campaign. 'My opinion is that much will have to happen before this campaign is concluded. Whoever lives it will have much to tell.'" In Nyenhuis, *A Goodly Heritage*, 225-71.

———, Elton J. Bruins, and Larry Wagenaar, *Albertus C. Van Raalte: Dutch Leader and American Patriot*. Hope College, 1996.

Janssen, Allan. "A Perfect Agreement? The Theological Context of the Reformed Protestant Dutch Church in the First Half of the Nineteenth Century." In *Breaches and Bridges*, 49-60.

Kagchelland, A. and M. *Van Dompers en Verlichten*. Eburon, 2009.

Kamps, Marvin. *1834: Hendrik De Cock's Return to the True Church*. Reformed Free Publishing Association, 2014.

Keizer, G., ed. *De Afscheiding van 1834: Haar aanleiding, naar authentieke brieven en bescheiden Beschreven*. J. H. Kok, 1934.

Kennedy, Earl Wm. *A Commentary on the Minutes of the Classis of Holland, 1848-1876: A Detailed Record of Persons and Issues, Civil and Religious, in the Dutch Colony of Holland, Michigan*, 3 vols. Van Raalte Press, 2018.

———. "Richard Baxter: An English Fox in a Dutch Chicken Koop." In Nyenhuis, *A Goodly Heritage*, 121-61.

———. "The Summer of Dominie Winter's Discontent: Americanization of a Dutch Reformed Seceder." In Krabbendam and Wagenaar, *Dutch-American Experience*, 223-36.

———. "Van Raalte and Parochial Schools." In Nyenhuis and Harinck, *Enduring Legacy*, 171-95.

Kennedy, James C. *A Concise History of the Netherlands*. Cambridge University Press, 2018. In Dutch, *Een beknopte geschiedenis van Nederland*. Prometheus, 2017.

———, and Caroline J. Simon, *Can Hope Endure? A Historical Study in Christian Higher Education*. Eerdmans, 2005.

Kennedy, Nella. "Twice Torn Asunder: The Life of Christina Johanna De Moen Van Raalte." In Nyenhuis and Harinck, *Enduring Legacy*, 43-66.

———, Robert P. Swierenga, and Mary Risseeuw, eds. *Diverse Destinies: Dutch Kolonies in Wisconsin and the East*. Van Raalte Press, 2012.

Keppel, Ruth. *Trees to Tulips: Authentic Tales of the Pioneers of Holland, Michigan*. Privately published, 1947.

Kluit, M. Elizabeth. *Het protestantse Réveil in Nederland en daarbuiten 1815-1865*. H. J. Paris, 1970.

Klunder, Jack D., and Russell L. Gasero, eds. *Servant Gladly: Essays in Honor of John W. Beardslee III*. Eerdmans, 1989.

Konijnenburg, Jan. *Lessen over het Leeraars-ambt in de Christelijke Kerk*. G. T. van Paddenburg en Zoon, 1802.

Krabbendam, Hans, and Dirk Mouw. *Transatlantic Pieties: Dutch Clergy in Colonial America*. Eerdmans, 2013.

———. "Cornelius van der Meulen (1800-1876): Builder of a New Dutch American Colony." In *Transatlantic Pieties*, 315-32.

———. "The Education of Albertus C. Van Raalte as Preparation for his Role as Social Reformer." In Nyenhuis and Harinck, *Enduring Legacy*, 1-22.

———. "Emigration as Protest? Opinions about the Relation between Church and State as a Factor in the Dutch Emigration Movement." In Krabbendam and Wagenaar, *Dutch-American Experience*, 61-70.

———. *Freedom on the Horizon: Dutch Immigration to America, 1840-1960*. Eerdmans, 2010.

———, and Larry J. Wagenaar, eds. *The Dutch-American Experience: Essays in Honor of Robert P. Swierenga*. VU Uitgeverij, 2000.
Kraker, Herbert A. *Overisel, Michigan: The Formative Years of a God-Fearing Covenantal Community*. Privately published, 1983.
Kromminga, John H. *The Christian Reformed Church: A Study in Orthodoxy*. Baker Book House, 1949.
———. "What Happened in 1857." *Reformed Review* 27, no. 2 (1974), 112-18.
Kuiper, J. P. *Geschiedenis der wording en ontwikkeling van het Christelijk lager onderwijs in Nederland*. Bloomendaal, 1897.
Kuiper, P. M. *Through Many Dangers*, 2 vols. Reformed Free Publishing Association, 2021.
Lemmen, Loren. "The Early Church at Polkton, Michigan." *Origins* 12, no. 2 (1994): 39-42.
Levy, Leonard W. *Emergence of a Free Press*. Oxford, 1985.
———. *Legacy of Suppression: Freedom and Speech and Press in America*. Harvard University Press, 1960.
Ligterink, G. H. *De landverhuizers: Emigratie naar Noord-Amerika uit het Gelders-Westfaalse grensgebied tussen de jaren 1830-1850*. Walburg Pers, 1981.
Lindeman, Marvin. "A Non-Hollander Looks at Holland." *Michigan History* 37 (Dec. 1947), 405-16.
Lucas, Henry S., ed. *1847—Ebenezer—1947: Memorial Souvenir of the Centennial Commemoration of Dutch Immigration to the United States Held in Holland, Michigan, 13-16 August 1947*. Netherlands Information Bureau, 1947.
———. "Beginnings of Dutch Immigration." *Iowa Journal of History and Politics* 22 (Oct. 1924): 483-93.
———. *Dutch Immigrant Memoirs and Related Writings*, 2 vols. Van Gorcum, 1955; reprint, Eerdmans, 1997.
———. "Landverhuizing Memoriaal 1846." *Nederlands Archief voor Kerkgeschiedenis* 40 (1954): 101-11.
———. *Netherlanders in America: Dutch Immigration and Settlement to the United States and Canada, 1789-1950*. University of Michigan Press, 1955; reprint, Eerdmans, 1989.
Luidens, Donald A., Donald J. Bruggink, and Herman J. De Vries Jr., eds. *Dutch Reformed Education: Immigrant Legacies in North America*. Van Raalte Press, 2020.
Makkinga, Marten. "Bricks for Ommen Poor: Rev. A. C. Van Raalte: Nineteenth-Century Benefactor Died One Hundred Years Ago." *New Kamper Daily*. 6 Nov. 1876.

Mastenbroek, Fenna. *Zedelijke Verhalen uit den Bijbel, voor Vrouwen en Meisjes*. F. Holtkamp, 1822.
McGeehan, Albert H., ed. *My Country and Cross: The Civil War Letters of John Anthony Wilterdink, Company I, 25th Michigan Infantry*. Taylor Publishing, 1982.
Meints, Graydon M. "Eber Brock Ward: The Richest Man in Michigan." *Michigan History* (Nov./Dec. 2022), 41-45.
Michel, Sara. *With This Inheritance: Holland, Michigan—The Early Years*. Schreur Printing, 1996.
Miles, Fred T. "One Hundred Years of Methodism in Holland, Michigan." *First United Methodist Church Centennial History, 1861-1961*. Holland, MI, 1961.
Moerdyke, Peter. "Life and Times of Rev. Albertus C. Van Raalte. *Reformed Historical Magazine* 3 (Feb. 1895): 1-9.
Naamlyst der geenen welke hun hoop en verwagting, dat eene Constitutie op gronden van Een- en Ondeelbaarheid gebouwd . . . . Den Haag, ter 's Lands Drukkerij, 1798.
Nauta, Rein. "The Leadership of Albertus C. Van Raalte: Dynamics and Characteristics." In Nyenhuis and Harinck, *Enduring Legacy*, 107-23.
Noordeloos Christian Reformed Church, Centennial, 1857-1957. Holland, MI. 1957. HHA.
Nyenhuis, Jacob E., ed. *A Goodly Heritage: Essays in Honor of the Reverend Dr. Elton J. Bruins at Eighty*. Eerdmans, 2007.
———. "A. C. Van Raalte and his Eponymous Institute." In Nyenhuis and Harinck, *Enduring Legacy*, 323-42.
———, et alii. *Hope College at 150: Anchored in Faith, Educating for Leadership and Service in a Global Society*, 2 vols. Van Raalte Press, 2019.
———, and George Harinck, eds. *The Enduring Legacy of Albertus C. Van Raalte as Leader and Liaison*. Van Raalte Press; Eerdmans, 2014.
———, and Jeanne M. Jacobson. *A Dream Fulfilled: The Van Raalte Sculpture in Centennial Park*. Hope College, 1996.
———. "Striving for Excellence in the Academic Program." In Nyenhuis et alii, *Hope College at 150*, 1:21-135.
Oberly, James O. *Sixty Million Acres: American Veterans and the Public Lands before the Civil War*. Kent State University Press, 1990.
Oddens, Joris. "De Nederlandse revolutie in dorp en stad: Lokale geschiedschrijving over de patriots-Bataafse tijd, 1875 tot heden." *Tijdschrift voor geschiedenis* 130 (2017): 565-91.

One Hundredth Anniversary, 1857-1957, First Christian Reformed Church of Grand Rapids, Michigan. Grand Rapids, 1957.

One Hundredth Anniversary Historical Booklet, 1847-1947. First Reformed Church in Holland, Michigan, 1947.

Oostendorp, Lubbertus. *H. P. Scholte: Leader of the Secession of 1834 and Founder of Pella.* T. Wever, 1964.

Paasman, J. A. "Bestuurlijke en economische aspecten van 1813 tot omstreeks 1834." In Pereboom et al., *'Van scheurmakers,'* 25-43.

Parr, Judy Tanis. *Hope Church, Holland, Michigan: The First 150 Years, 1862-2012.* Holland, MI, 2012.

Pereboom, Freek, H. Hille, and Hemmo Reenders, eds. *'Van scheurmakers, onruststokers en geheime opruijers': De Afscheiding in Overijssel.* IJsselakademie, 1984.

Pieters, Albertus. "History of the First Reformed Church of Holland, Michigan, from the Time of Its Founding until 1882." In *One Hundredth Anniversary.*

Pieters, Aleida. *A Dutch Settlement in Michigan.* Eerdmans-Sevensma, 1923.

Posthumus, N. W. *De Geschiedenis van de Leidsche Lakenindustrie.* 3 vols. Martinus Nijhoff, 1939.

Potgieter, E. J. "Landverhuizing naar de Vereenigde Staten." In *De Gids*, 1855.

Prakke, H. J. *Drenthe in Michigan.* Eerdmans, 1983. English version of *Drenthe in Michigan: 'n Studie over het Drentse Aandeel in de Van Raalte-Trek van 1847.* Van Gorkum & Comp., 1948.

Pronk, Cornelius. *A Goodly Heritage: The Secession of 1834 and Its Impact on Reformed Churches in the Netherlands and North America.* Reformation Heritage Books, 2019.

Reenders, Hommo. "Albertus C. van Raalte als leider van Overijsselse Afgescheidenen, 1836-1846." In Pereboom et al., *'Van scheurmakers,'* 98-197. A typescript English translation of this lengthy chapter by Elisabeth "Ellie" Dekker is available at the VRI.

———. "Albertus C. Van Raalte: The Homo Oecumenicus among the Secession Leaders." *Calvin Theological Journal* 33 (Nov. 1998), 277-98.

Roelofs, Broek. "Hendrik Wormser (1810-1887)." *De Hoekstem: Tijdschrift voor Nederlandse Kerkgescheidenis* (1982), 57-65.

———. "Carel Godefroi de Moen (1811-1879)." *De Hoekstem, Tijdschrift voor Nederlands Kerkgescheidenis* (1981), 142-51.

Ruiter, A. *Op Weg . . . Anderhalve eeuw Gereformeerde Kerk Ommen.* Gereformeerde Kerk Ommen, 1986.

Rullmann, J. C. *De Afscheiding, in de Nederlandsch Hervormde Kerk der XIXe Eeuw*. J. H. Kok, 1930.

———. *De Strijd voor kerkherstel in de Nederlandsch Hervormde Kerk*. W. Kirchner, 1915.

———. *Een Nagel in de heilige Plaats: De Reformatie der Kerk in de XIX Eeuw*. Amsterdam, 1912.

———. *Ernst en Vrede: Het Leven van George Frans Gezelle Meerburg*. Bosch, 1919.

Rumohr-Voskuil, Karsten T., and Elton J. Bruins. "Is a 'Joyful Death' an Oxymoron? The Christina de Moen Van Raalte Story." In House and Coakley, *Patterns and Portraits*, 87-94.

Scheffer, Ivo. *A Short History of the Netherlands*. Allert de Lange, 1973.

Schelhaas, T. N. et al., eds. *De Afgescheidenen van 1834 en hun nageslacht*. Algemeen Secretariaat van de Gereformeerde Kerken in Nederland, Leusden. J. H. Kok, 1984.

Schoolland, Marian M. *The Story of Van Raalte*. Eerdmans, 1951.

Schotel, G. D. J. *Geschiedenis van den oorsprong, de invoering en de lotgevallen van den Heidelburgschen Catechismus*. Amsterdam, 1863.

Schram, P. L. "Raalte, Albertus Christiaan van." In *Biografisch Lexicon*, 1:270-72.

Selderhuis, Herman, ed. *Handbook of Dutch Church History*. Vandenhoeck & Ruprecht, 2015. English translation of *Handboek Nederlandse Kerkgeschiedenis*. Uitgeverij Kok, 2006.

Sheeres, Janet Sjaarda. "Brother Ploeg: A Searching Saint or a Burr under the Saddle?" *Origins* 29, no. 2 (2011): 12-19.

———. *The Not-So-Promised Land: The Dutch in Amelia County, Virginia, 1868-1880*. Eerdmans, 2013.

———. "Six Names; Six Stories: The People Who Helped Van Raalte Build the First Lodge in Holland, Michigan, in February 1847." *Origins* 22, no. 2 (Dec. 2004): 28-32.

———. *Son of Secession: Douwe J. Van der Werp*. Eerdmans, 2006.

———. "The Struggle for the Souls of the Children: The Effects of the Dutch Education Law of 1806 on the Emigration of 1847." In Swierenga et al., *Dutch in Urban America*, 38-47.

———. "'Zoo God het behaagt' (If it pleases God): Holland's Success Versus Amelia's Failure." In Nyenhuis and Harinck, *Enduring Legacy*, 89-105.

Sinke, Suzanne. *Dutch Immigrant Women in the United States, 1880-1920*. University of Illinois Press, 2002.

Sinnema, Donald. "The Origin of the Form of Subscription in the Dutch Reformed Tradition." *Calvin Theological Journal* 42, no. 2 (2007).
Smit, C.B.A. *Het Leiden Boek*. Waanders, 2010.
Smits, C[ornelis]. *De Afscheiding van 1834. Eerste Deel: Gorinchem en "Beneden Gelderland."* Vol. 1. J. P. van den Tol, 1971.
———. *De Afscheiding van 1834. Tweede Deel: Classis Dordrecht, C. A.* Vol. 2. J. P. van den Tol, 1974.
———. *De Afscheiding van 1834. Derde Deel: Documenten uit het archief ds. H. P. Scholte, bewaard te Pella, Iowa, U.S.A.* Vol. 3. J. P. van den Tol, 1977.
———. *De Afscheiding van 1834. Vierde Deel: Provincie Utrecht.* Vol. 4. J. P. van den Tol, 1980.
———. *De Afscheiding van 1834. Vijfde Deel: Documenten uit het archief ds. H. P. Scholte, bewaard te Pella, Iowa, U.S.A.* Vol. 5. J. P. van den Tol, 1982.
———. *De Afscheiding van 1834. Zesde Deel: Het Réveil en ds. H. P. Scholte, Correspondentie.* Vol. 6. J. P. van den Tol, 1984.
———. *De Afscheiding van 1834. Zevende Deel: Classes Rotterdam en Leiden.* Vol. 7. J. P. van den Tol, 1986.
Smitt, Walter W. *Is de verwerping van het Nederlandsch Hervormde Kerkbestuur al dan niet noodzakelijk geworden?* J. van Golverdinge, 1835.
Soepenberg, Jan-Henk. *Op ongebaande wegen: De Afscheiding in Amsterdam (1835) als landelijke proeftuin voor vrije kerken.* Uitgeverij Boekencentrum, 2017.
Souvenir History of Pella, Iowa. Booster Press, 1922.
Spykman, Gordon J. *Pioneer Preacher: Albertus Christiaan Van Raalte: A Study of His Sermon Notes.* Calvin College and Seminary Library, 1976.
———. "The Van Raalte Sermons." *Reformed Review* 30, no. 2 (1977), 95-102.
Stegenga, Preston J. *Anchor of Hope*. Eerdmans, 1943.
Stevenson, David. *Origins of Freemasonry*. Cambridge University Press, 1988.
Stokvis, Pieter R. P. *De Nederlandse Trek naar Amerika, 1846-1848.* Universitaire Pers Leiden, 1977.
Sweetman, Leonard. "Children of the Day; Not of the Night: The Background of the Afscheiding, 1834." *Origins* 19, no. 2 (2001): 27-33.
———, ed. *From Heart to Heart: Letters from the Rev. Albertus Christiaan Van Raalte to His Wife, Christina Johanna Van Raalte-De Moen, 1836-1847.* Heritage Hall Publications, 1997.
Swierenga, Robert P. *Acres for Cents: Delinquent Tax Auctions in Frontier Iowa.* Greenwood Press, 1976.

———. "Albertus C. Van Raalte as a Businessman." In Nyenhuis, *Goodly Heritage*, 281-317.

———. "'Better Prospects for Work:' Van Raalte's Holland Colony and its Connections to Grand Rapids." *Grand River Valley History* 15 (1998): 17-21.

———. "By the Sweat of our Brow: Economic Aspects of the Dutch Immigration to Michigan." In Swierenga, *For Food and Faith*, 1-29.

———. "Changes and Complications: Holland's 1867 Charter." Historical Society of Michigan *Chronicle* 42 (Summer 2019): 18-21.

———. "The Dutch." In Thernstrom, Stephen, ed. *Harvard Encyclopedia of American Ethnic Groups*, 284-95.

———, comp. *Dutch Emigrants to the United States, South Africa, South America, and Southeast Asia, 1835-1880: An Alphabetical Listing by Household Heads and Independent Persons*. Scholarly Resources, 1983.

———, comp. *Dutch Households in U.S. Population Censuses, 1850, 1860, 1870: An Alphabetical Listing by Family Heads and Singles*, 3 vols. Scholarly Resources, 1987.

———, comp. *Dutch Immigrants in U.S. Ship Passenger Manifests, 1820-1880: An Alphabetical Listing by Household heads and Independent Persons*, 2 vols. Scholarly Resources, 1983.

———. "Dutch Immigration in the Nineteenth Century, 1820-1877: A Quantitative Overview." *Indiana Social Studies Quarterly* 28 (Autumn 1975): 7-34.

———. "The Dutch Imprint on West Michigan." Historical Society of Michigan *Chronicle* 27 (Winter 2005): 18-22.

———. *The Dutch in America: Immigration, Settlement, and Cultural Change*. Rutgers University Press, 1985.

———, Donald Sinnema, and Hans Krabbendam, eds. *The Dutch in Urban America*. JAH, 2004.

———. "The Dutch in West Michigan: The Impact of a Contractual Community." *Grand River Valley History* 18 (2002): 18-27.

———. "The Dutch Transplanting in Michigan and the Midwest." Clarence M. Burton Memorial Lecture, 1985. Historical Society of Michigan, 1986.

———, ed. *Iowa Letters: Dutch Immigrants on the American Frontier*. Trans. by Walter Lagerwey. Eerdmans, 2004. First edition published as *Amsterdamse emigranten: onbekende brieven uit de prairies van Iowa, 1846-1873*. Edited by Johan Stellingwerff. Buijten & Schipperhein, 1976.

———. "The Ethnic Voter and the First Lincoln Election." *Civil War History* 11 (March 1965): 27-43.

———. "Exodus Netherlands, Promised Land America: Dutch Immigration and Settlement in the United States." In Northolt and Swierenga, *A Bilateral Bicentennial*, 127-47.

———. *Faithful Witness: A Sesquicentennial History of Central Avenue Christian Reformed Church, Holland, Michigan, 1865-2015*. Van Raalte Press, 2015.

———. *For Food and Faith: Dutch Immigration to America*. Holland Museum, 2000.

———. "Helping Hands: Old Dutch Aid Young Dutch." In Aay, Venema, and Voskuil, *Sharing Pasts*, 105-27.

———. *Holland, Michigan: From Dutch Colony to Dynamic City*, 3 vols. Van Raalte Press; Eerdmans, 2014.

———. "Local-Cosmopolitan Theory and Immigrant Religion: The Social Bases of the Antebellum Dutch Reformed Schism." *Journal of Social History* 14 (Fall 1980): 113-35.

———. "The New Immigration, 1840-1920." In Krabbendam et al., *Four Centuries of Dutch-American Relations, 1609-2009*, 295-306.

———, gen. ed. *Netherlanders in America: A Study of Emigration and Settlement in the Nineteenth and Twentieth Centuries in the United States of America*, 2 vols. Chief trans. Adriaan de Wit. Baker Book House, 1985.

———. "Off the Pulpit: Van Raalte as Community Leader." In Nyenhuis and Harinck, *Enduring Legacy*, 125-50.

———. *Pioneers and Profits: Land Speculation on the Iowa Frontier*. Iowa State University Press, 1968.

———. "'Pioneers for Jesus Christ': Dutch Protestant Colonization in North America as an Act of Faith." In Harinck and Krabbendam, *Sharing the Reformed Tradition*, 35-55.

———. "Press Censorship: Rev. Albertus C. Van Raalte and Hermanus Doesburg of *De Hollander*." In Swierenga, Nyenhuis, and Kennedy, *Dutch American Arts and Letters*, 171-82.

———. "Stewardship of Resources." In Nyenhuis *et alii*, *Hope College at 150*, 1:499-587.

———. "True Brothers: The Netherlandic Origins of the Christian Reformed Church in North America, 1857-1880." In Harinck and Krabbendam, *Breaches and Bridges*, 61-83.

———, "Van Raalte and Scholte: A Soured Relationship and Personal Rivalry." *Origins* 17, no. 1 (1999): 21-35. Also Wagenaar and Swierenga, *The Sesquicentennial of Dutch Immigration*, 29-45.

———. "Walls or Bridges: The Differing Acculturation Process in the Reformed and Christian Reformed Churches in North America." In Harinck and Krabbendam, *Morsels in the Melting Pot*, 33-42.

―――. and Hans Krabbendam. "Dutch Catholics and Protestants in Wisconsin: A Study in Contrasts and Similarities." In Kennedy, Swierenga, and Risseeuw, *Diverse Destinies*, 39-64.

―――, and William Van Appledorn, eds., *Old Wing Mission: Cultural Interchange as Chronicled by George and Arvilla Smith in their Work with Chief Wakazoo's Ottawa Band on the West Western Frontier*. Eerdmans, 2008.

Sytsma, William. *Our Blessed Heritage: Graafschap Christian Reformed Church, 1847-1997, 150 Years of Service*, 1997.

Tanis, Mark. *The Bell at Pillar Church: A Part of Holland's History*. Privately published, 2018.

Taylor, Lawrence J. *Dutchmen on the Bay: The Ethnohistory of a Contractual Community*. University of Pennsylvania Press, 1983.

Ten Zythoff, Gerrit. "The Americanization of Albertus C. Van Raalte: A Preliminary Inquiry." *Reformed Review* 77, no. 2 (1977): 77-82.

―――. *Sources of Secession: The Hervormde Kerk on the Eve of the Dutch Immigration to the Midwest*. Eerdmans, 1987.

Te Velde, Mees. *Anthony Brummelkamp, 1811-1888*. Uitgeverij De Vuurbaak, 1988.

―――. "The Dutch Background of the American Secession from the RCA in 1857." In Harinck and Krabbendam, *Breaches and Bridges*, 85-100.

―――. "The Ministerial Education of Albertus C. Van Raalte in Ommen (1839-1844) and Arnhem (1844-1846) and Its Significance for the Secession Churches." In Nyenhuis and Harinck, *Enduring Legacy*, 197-203.

Thernstrom, Stephen, ed. *Harvard Encyclopedia of American Ethnic Groups*. Harvard University Press, 1980.

Tris, Abraham C. *Sixty Years' Reminiscences*. Report Publishing Co., 1908.

Van Berkel, Klaas. *Universiteit van het Noorden: vier eeuwen academisch leven in Groningen: De Oude Universiteit 1614-1871*. Verloren, 2014.

Van Den Berg, J., et al., eds. *Aspecten van het Reveil-Opstellen ter gelegenheid van het vijftigjarig bestaan van de Stichting Het Reveil-Archief*. J. H. Kok, 1980.

Van den Broeke, Leon. "'Christ as Master Builder... me as a tool': Albertus C. Van Raalte and the Ecclesiastical Organization." In Nyenhuis and Harinck, *Enduring Legacy*, 241-60.

―――. *"Pope of the Classis"? The Leadership of Albertus C. Van Raalte in Dutch and American Classes*. Van Raalte Press, 2011.

Van den Dool, Huug. "Noordeloos on Two Continents." In Harms, *The Dutch Adapting*, 50-68.

―――. "Weather and the Fires of 1871." In Kennedy, Swierenga, and Risseeuw, *Diverse Destinies*, 129-41.

Van der Meulen, Jacob. *Opwekking tot het houden van eenen algemeenen Dank- Vast-, en Bidden* (An exhortation to hold a general day of thanksgiving, fasting, and prayer), 25 Feb. 1846. Hoogkamer & Comp., 1846.

———. *Ter Nagedachtenis van Rev. Cornelius Van der Meulen.* De Standaard Drukkerij, 1876.

Van der Veen, Engbertus. "Life Reminiscences" (1915). In Lucas, *Dutch Immigrant Memoirs*, 1: 489-514.

Vander Velde, Louis G. "Glimpses of the Early Dutch Settlements in Michigan." *Michigan Historical Collections, Bulletin*, no. 1. University of Michigan, 1927.

Van der Zwaag, W. *Réveil en afscheiding: negentiende-eeuwse kerkhistorie met bijzondere actualiteit.* Uitgeverij de Groot Goudriaan, 2006.

Vande Water, Randall P. *Holland: Happenings, Heroes, and Hot Shots. Illustrated Narratives of Memorable Moments*, 4 vols. Privately published 1994-97.

———. "Holland's First Decoration Day." In Vande Water, *Holland*, 3:115-18.

———. "First Bank Was a Home." In Vande Water, *Holland*, 3:26-29.

———. "First Election Held in 1849." In Vande Water, *Holland*, 2:19-21.

———. "Holland Had State Bank in 1889." In Vande Water, *Holland*, 2:62-64.

———. "Five Schooners Damaged in Storm." In Vande Water, *Holland*, 2:29-31.

———. "Holland Fairs Date Back to 1851." In Vande Water, *Holland*, 4:47-55.

Van Dijk, D. *De preektrant van de dominees in de kerken der Afscheiding in de jaaren 1834-1869.* Aalten, 1935.

Van Eyck, William C. *Landmarks of the Reformed Fathers, Or What Dr. Van Raalte's People Believed.* Reformed Press, 1922.

———. *The Union of 1850.* Eerdmans, 1950.

Van Gelderen, Jaap. *Frouwe Venema: Een verstandige vrouw.* Vereniging van Oud-Studenten van de Theologische Universiteit, 2001.

———. "Scheuring en Vereniging 1837-1869." In Bakker et al., *De Afscheiding van 1834 en haar geschiedenis*, 100-146.

———. *Simon van Velzen, Capita Selecta.* Vereniging van Oud-Studenten van de Theologische Universiteit, 1999.

Van Hinte, Jacob. *Netherlanders in America: A Study of Emigration and Settlement in the 19th and 20th Centuries in the United States of America* (Baker Book House, 1985). This is an English translation of *Nederlanders in Amerika: Een Studie over Landverhuizers en Volksplanting in de 19e en 20ste Eeuw in de Vereenigde Staten van Amerika*. 2 vols. P. Noordhoff, 1928.

Van Koetsveld, Cornelis Eliza. *Schetsen uit de pastorij te Mastland: Ernst en luim uit het leven van den Nederlandschen dorpsleeraar*. Van Nooten, 1843.

Van Koevering, Adrian. *Legends of the Dutch: The Story of the Mass Movement of Nineteenth Century Pilgrims*. Zeeland Record Co., 1960.

Van Maanen, R. C. J., ed. *De Geschiedenis van een Hollandse Stad, 1795-1896*. Stichting Geschiedsschrijving Leiden, 2009.

Van Malsen, A. *Achttal Brieven Mijner Kinderen uit de Kolonie Holland in Amerika*. Zwijndrecht, 1848. Published in English, John Yzenbaard, "'America' Letters from Holland."

Van Raalte, Albertus C. "Commemoration Address, 1872." In Lucas, *Dutch Immigrant Memoirs*, 2: 484-91.

Van Raalte, Albertus C., Anthony Brummelkamp, and Simon van Velzen. *Kerkelijk Handboekje, zijnde een kort uittreksel van de voornaamste acten der Nationale en Provinciale synoden betrekkelijk de zuiverheid der Leer, Rust der Kerk, enz...* N. Obbes 1841.

"Van Raalte and the Law." *Reformed Journal*. Jan. 1954.

Van Reken, Donald L. *The Holland Fire of October 8, 1871*. Privately published, 1982.

Van Schelven, Gerrit. "Historical Sketch of Holland City and Colony, July 4, 1876," 456-77, in Franklin Everett, *Memorials of the Grand River Valley*. Chicago Legal News Co., 1878, republished by Grand Rapids Historical Society, 1984.

———. "Michigan and the Holland Immigration of 1847." *Michigan History Magazine* 1 (Oct. 1917): 72-98.

Van Velzen, Simon. "The Apology of the Ecclesiastical Secession in the Netherlands, or, A Letter to Mr. G. Groen van Prinsterer Regarding His Opinions Concerning the Secession and the Secessionist." *Protestant Reformed Theological Journal* 45, no. 2 (April 2012): 30-67.

———. "Stem eens wachters op Zions muren." In Van Velzen Jr. *Kompleete*.

Van Velzen, Simon, Jr. *Kompleete uitgave van de officiëele stukken betreffende den uitgang uit het Nederl. Herv. Kerkgenootschap*, 2 vols. (1863). 2nd ed., G. Ph. Zalsman, 1884.

Van Zwaluwenburg, Reijer. "Reijer Van Zwaluwenburg's Life Sketch." In Lucas, *Dutch Immigrant Memoirs*, 1:411-28.

Veldman, Harry. *Hendrik de Cock, Afgescheiden en toch betrokken*. Cedrus Uitgeverij, 2004.

Verduin, Leonard. *Honor Your Mother: Christian Reformed Church Roots in the Secession of 1834*. CRC Publications, 1988.

Verhagen, J., Jr. *De geschiedenis der Christelijke Gereformeerde Kerk in Nederland*. Zalsman, 1886.

———. *Oude David*. 1889.

Verhave, Joh., and Jan P. Verhave "De Vaccinatiekwestie in het Réveil." In *Aspecten van het Réveil*. J. H. Kok, 1980, 230-54.

Versteeg, Dingeman. *Pelgrim-Vaders van het Westen*. C. M. Loomis & Co., 1886. An English translation typescript by William K. Reinsma is in HHA.

Voskuil, Dennis N. "Continuity and Change at Hope College and the Reformed Church in America." In Nyenhuis, et alii, *Hope College at 150*, 137-91.

———. "When East Meets West: Theological Education and the Unity of the Reformed Church in America." In Brumm, *Tools for Understanding*, 201-28.

———. "The Vexed Question: Hope College and Theological Education." In Nyenhuis, *A Goodly Heritage*, 341-70.

Vree, Jasper Azn. "The Dominating Theology within the Nederlands Hervormde Kerk after 1815 in Its Relation to the Secession of 1834." In Harinck and Krabbendam, *Breaches and Bridges*, 33-47.

———. "De Nederlandse Hervormde Kerk in de jaren voor de Afscheiding." In Bakker et al., *De Afscheiding van 1834 en haar geschiedenis*, 30-61.

Wagenaar, Larry J., ed. *The Dutch and Their Faith: Immigrant Religious Experience in the Nineteenth and Twentieth Centuries*. Hope College, 1992.

———, and Robert P. Swierenga, eds. *The Sesquicentennial of Dutch Immigration: 150 Years of Ethnic Heritage*. JAH, Hope College, 1997.

Warner, Gerko C. *Door het venster van Albertus Christiaan van Raalte: Het leven van de Afgescheiden Dominee op de kaart*. Heijink, 2011.

Weitkamp, J. "De vervolgingen." In Pereboom et al., *'Van scheurmakers,'* 198-309.

Wesseling, Jan. *De Afscheiding van 1834 in Overijssel: De Classis Zwolle*. Uitgeverij De Vuurbaak, 1984.

———. *De Afscheiding van 1834 in Overijssel, De Classes Holten/Ommen*. Uitgeverij De Vuurbaak, 1986.

———. *De Afscheiding van 1834 in Zeeland: De Beveland en Zeeuws-Vlanderen, 1834-69*, vol. 1. Uitgeverij De Vuurbaak, 1987.

———. *De Afscheiding van 1834 in Zeeland: Walcheren, Schouwen-Duiveland, Tholen, en Sint Philipsland, 1834-69*, vol. 2. Uitgeverij De Vuurbaak, 1989.

Wichers, Wynand. *Century of Hope, 1866-1966*. Eerdmans, 1968.
Wilson, Etta Smith. "Life and Work of the Late Rev. George N. Smith: A Pioneer Missionary." *Historical Collections, Michigan Pioneer and Historical Society*, 30 (1906), 190-212.
Wintle, Michael. *Pillars of Piety: Religion in the Netherlands in the Nineteenth Century*. Hull University Press, 1987.
Wormser, J. A. *Door kwaad gerucht en goed gerucht: Het leven van Hendrik Peter Scholte*. Bosch, 1915. An English-language typescript translation by William and Althea Buursma is available at the VRI.
———. *In twee werelddeelen: het leven van Albertus Christiaan van Raalte*. Bosch, 1915. An English-language typescript translation by Henry ten Hoor is available at the VRI.
———. *Karakter en Genade: Het Leven van Simon van Velzen*. Bosch, 1916. An English-language typescript translation by William and Althea Buursma is available at the VRI.
Wyckoff, Isaac N. "An Official Report on the Dutch Kolonie in Michigan, 1849." In Lucas, *Dutch Immigrant Memoirs and Related Writings*, 1: 449-57.
Yzenbaard, John. "'America' Letters from Holland." *Michigan History* 32 (March 1948), 37-65.
Zingle, Marie N. *The Story of the Woman's Literary Club, 1898-1989* (1989).
Zwemer, Samuel M. *The Ship that Never Sailed and the Keel that Never Kissed the Sea*. BDM, 1931.

VI. Unpublished Works/Monographs

Boer, Harry H. (with Barbara J. Boer). *God's Deacon: The Account of Johannes Van Haitsma and the Christian Reformed Church*. Holland, 2018.
Boonstra, Harry, *The Dutch Equation in the RCA Freemasonry Controversy, 1865-1885*. VRI, 2008.
Dorpslands Dagboek (village land diary), vol. 1 (1847-49); vol. 2 (1849-51). HMA.
Harms, Richard H., comp. "South Holland (Michigan) Presbyterian Church, Family Records, 1849-1867," 2008. HHA.
Lefever, Joel, comp. "List of Destroyed Property by Street [in Holland fire]." HMA.
Oggel, D. J. Jzn. "The History of the Oggel Family and Other Related Families." JAH.
Postma, Charles Henry, "Isaac Fairbanks: An American in a Dutch Community." Master's thesis. Ball State University, 1969.

Swierenga, Robert P., comp. "Real Estate Sales by Albertus C. Van Raalte and Christina Johanna Van Raalte, Grantors, as recorded in the Ottawa County Deed Register Books, 1847-1876." Ottawa County Courthouse, Michigan. July 2006.

Van der Haar-Visscher, Geesje. "Diary of Geesje Van der Haar-Visscher, 1820-1901." English typescript. Trans. Clarence L. Jalving, HMA

Van der Veen, Engbertus. "Memories of Colonial Life." Moerdyke Papers, HMA.

Verhave, Jan Peter. *Disease and Death among the Early Michigan Settlers in Holland, Michigan.* VRI, 2006.

Wagenaar, Larry. "The Early Political History of Holland, Michigan, 1847-1868." Master's thesis, Kent State University, 1992.

INDEX

à Brakel, Wilhelmus, 40, 146
A. C. *Van Raalte* (ship), 497
A. C. Van Raalte Church, Thule (Hull), SD: sod structure, *539*
A. C. Van Raalte Memorial Hall, 586
A. C. Van Raaltestraat (street in Ommen), 115
A. E. *Knickerbocker* (colony ship), 380-81, 581
Achterhoek region (Gelderland), 78, 165-66, 170, 172
Adams Hotel (Chicago), 498
Adams Road, 263
Africa. *See* Cape Town, South Africa; Zululand (Zulus), South Africa
African Americans, 262, 490-92, 552

Afscheiding of 1834. *See* Secession of 1834
agriculture, NL, xxi, 63, 67, 69, 115, 138, 156, 159-60, 164, 167-68, 170; and cultivation system, 168; and emigration, 170
agriculture, US: ACVR promotes, 229, 276-77, 390-91, 397-98, 488-90, 572; and Ben Van Raalte, 532, 534, 537, 564; and census of, xxii; cropping (crops), 156, 168, 240, 409, 463, 566; and dairy, 210, 496; failures, 276, 391; in Iowa, 214; in Michigan, 150, 164-65, 186, 193, 208-11, 220, 228, 240; and native peoples, 201, 211; and Prayer Days, 484; in Virginia, xxi, 442

ague (malaria), 236-37, 270, 445, 447n5
Albany, NY, 172, 188, 206n44, 213, 290, 344, 381, 446, 461. *See also* Second Reformed Church, Albany, NY; Particular Synod of Albany (NY)
Alberti, John, 503; livery stable, funeral, 504-5, 556
Albertus C. Van Raalte Post No. 262, GAR, 543, 586
alcohol, 238, 321, 503, distilling of, banned, 251, 418-19; and prohibition, 269, 420-22, 578
Algonquin language, 201, 559
Allegan County, MI, 195, 197, 199, 201, 207, 240n48, 380
Allegan Journal (newspaper), 276
Allegan Record (newspaper), 261n98, 409
Allegan, MI: and ACVR, 199, 200, 202-3, 207, 218-24, 228, 259-60, 374-75, 520; and Christina Van Raalte, 509; and circuit court, 321; and Detroit committee, 197, 205; and Elvira Langdon, 331; and farming, xxii; and merchants, 198, 256, 268, 378; and roads 250, 255-56; and supplies, 235, 383. *See also* Kellogg, John R.
Almelo (Overijssel), 95
Almkerk (Noord-Brabant), 49
alms, 161, 192; almshouses, 76; almsmen, 161
Alto, WI, xxi, 197; and Reformed Church, 150, 162, 472, 478, 481, 505
Ambt Ommen (Overijssel), 81

Amelia [VA] Court House, 487, 489-90, 494-95, 526, 532, 535; Dutch settlements map, *491*; and Reformed churches, 495-97
Amelia [VA] Institute, 493, 566
Amelia Colony (VA), 487-99, 575; and black people, 491-92; failure of, 498-99; and Hope College endowment, 499
American Bible Society, 248-49
American Classis of Michigan. *See* Classis of Michigan (RCA)
American Home Missionary Society, 200
American Sunday School Union, 545
American Tract Society, 248-49, 320
Americanization, 216, 280, 303, 453-54, 545, 558, 564; and ACVR, 278, 550, 570
Amsterdam (Noord-Holland), 150: ACVR's ordination in, 70, 72, and visits to, 74, 89, 134; and Blikman-Kikkert, 10, 138; and Classis of Amsterdam, 64, 529, 579, and Christian Separated Church, 72, 111, 113, 118, 120, 129, 149, persecution of, 84-85, 90-91; and Johan A. Wormser, xix, 169, 469; and newspapers, 168-69; and port, 454; and Scholte, 40, 136, 149; and Synod 1836, 69-71, 110-11, 129, 198, Synod 1840, 123-27, 129, 144, 148-49, Synod 1843, 128-29, 310, Synod 1866 and ACVR, 460, 464-65, 467, 485; and Singel,

137; and Van Raalte family, xvii, 3n3, 10, 22n49, 23, 74, 367; and Van Raalte-Harking marriage, 8-9, 207
Amsterdam Athenaeum, 40
Anti-Masonic political party, 474, 486, 571, 578. *See also* Freemasonry
Anti-Revolutionary Party, 31
Antwerp, Belgium, 471
Apeldoorn (Gelderland), 101, 148
apologetics: taught by ACVR, 39, 41, 147, 153
apostasy, 25, 31, 43, 70, 174, 475
Appomattox battlefield, 436, 543
Appomattox River (VA), 489
Aquinas, Thomas, 147
Arius (presbyter), 41
Arminian(ism), 289, 296, 298, 300, 459, 524, 525, 545n26
Arminius, Jacobus, 41, 298, 310
Army Corps of Engineers, 270, 275
Arnhem (Gelderland): ACVR, 58, 89, 157; and Brummelkamp, 128, 131, 153, 339, 447n4; and Christina Van Raalte, 507-8; and emigration 165, 167, 173, 522; society, 169-71, 185, 379n33; Hervormde Kerk Nederland; Israelite school, 153; Latin school, 112-13, 140; and Pfanstiehl, 386; visited by ACVR, 58, 89, 177; seminary, 133, 144, 149, 150-51, 153-56, 339, 478, 574; Separated Church, 131, 150, 152
Arnhem-Velp (Gelderland), 112-13, 118, 140, 157, 161, 175, 177
Ashville, NC, 489

Associate Reformed Church, MI, 292, 294
Atlantic Ocean, xvi, 181-82, 190, 489-90
Aurora, IL, 473
Austria, 162

Baambrugge (Noord-Holland), 122, 137
Baay, Gerrit, 162
Bagley, John J., 544
Bähler, Louis, 41
Balch, Nathaniel A., 195, 204-5
Ball, John, 195, 204-5, 207, 258, 370, *371*, 374-75
Baltimore, MD: as seaport, 176, 188, 214, 221, 232, 490
banks (banking), 195, 388, 395; buildings, 266; failures, 360, 523; Michigan charters, 405; national laws, 403-5; notes of, 186; officers, 565; wildcat, 186, 336
baptism: and ACVR, 88, 93, 253, 446, 531, 533-34; adult, 242, 459; and Christian education, 162-64; and De Cock, 47, 107, 534; and Dort rules, 104, 107; infant, 102; qualifications, 102, 107; and registers, 12, 15; and Separated Church, 107-8; and squabbles, 482; and *volk*, 107, 534
Baptist, 193, 473, 532-33
Barendregt, Hendrik, 197, 213-14
Barr, A. E., 504n65
Bassett, Elisha Bourne, 195, 205n41, 225, 242, 409-10
Batavian Republic, xxi, 4-5, 16, 39, 108

Batavus, Willem, xix
Bavinck, Herman, 424
Baxter, Richard, 296, 300
Bazuin, De (church periodical), 345, 467, 596
Beaverdam, MI, 234, 258
Beeckman, Lodewijk Justinus, 37
beer, 23, 251, 418-20, 526, 583. *See also* beverages
Beets, Henry, 585
Beidler, Frederick (Fred) P., 341
Belgian War of Independence, 28, 35-38, 159
Belgic Confession, 14, 17, 43, 126, 174, 577. *See also* Reformed Confessions
bell: village (city), 251, 314, 324, 515; and church, 316, 437; and fire, 448, 511, 514; and tolling at deaths, 550
Benham, Alvan, 383
Benjamin, Asher, 315
Bentheim (Fillmore Twp., MI), 234
Bentheim (Germany), Graafschap, xxii, 95, 129-30, 140, 233, 468n52; and ACVR, 132, 173
Bentheim [Germany] Hervormde Kerk, 95, 130, 140, 233
Bergen op Zoon (Noord-Brabant), 33; academy, 29
Beukenhorst, Jan Arend, 166-67
Beuker, Henricus, 468, 470
beverages: *boerenjongens*, 251; coffee, 152, 166, 231, 266, from corn, 235, 383; *jenever* (Dutch gin), 251; tea, 152, 166, 168, and kettle, 231, and visits, 108, 266, 271; wine, 526, and sacramental, 241, 419. *See also* beer
Bible: 130, 161, 163-64; attitude toward the, 308; burned in Holland fire, *512*; commentaries, 320; courses, 39, 147; preaching, 307; reading, 76, 117-18, 355, 364, 456; in schools, 359, 365, 534, 545; and slavery, 430, 435; and the Statenbijbel, 14, 240; studies, 69, 118, 153, 318
"Bible Belt" (NL), 1, 20, 297, 468; map of, *2*
bicentennial (ACVR's birth), xiii, xviii, 11n19
Biggekerke (Zeeland), 49, 64
Bilderdijk, Willem, 31-32, *33*, 40, 577
bilious fever, 447
Bingham, Kinsley, 274
Binnekant, Jan, 170, 178, 221, 230, 251, 254, 261, 271, 414
Black [Macatawa] River, 220, 225, 237, 258, 369, 383; bridging, 250, 254-55, 261-63, 291, 511; head of navigation, 291; and Holland fire, 513; and land values, 370; and mouth, 271; and south branch, 255; and watershed, 202, 207-8; and the Y, 233
Black Lake: and ACVR, 193, 203, 225, 230, 236, 454, 581; cruises, 525; and flatboats, 271; harbor, 270-72; head of, 219, 254, 384, 391; and Holland fire, 513-14; and lakefront property, 527; landing, 376; mouth, 208, 250, 271;

narrows 201; region, 207, 366, 542, 579; and speculators, 368; and Suydam farm, 529; watershed, 193, 202-3
black people, 262, 490-92, 552
Black River Band. *See* Odawa (Ottawa) band
Black River post office, 384
Blanchard, Jonathan, 473
Blendon, MI, 258
Blikman Kikkert, Dirk, 23, 137-38, 142, 151, 367; and Blikman Kikkert & Co., 139-40
Blikman Kikkert, Johanna Bartha (Van Raalte) (Mrs. Dirk), 13, 23, 136, 140, 142, 188, 367, 499
Bloemgracht No. 42 (street in Amsterdam), 72, 84
Board of Domestic Missions, RCA, 279, 281, 284, 289, 304, 336, 341, 529
Board of Education, RCA, 341, 347, 356, 358, 361
Board of Foreign Missions, RCA, 249, 452, 529
Board of School Inspectors (Ottawa County), 333, 531
Board of Trustees, Holland Colony, 253-54, 260, 373; land purchases, 589-90
Board of Trustees, Hope College, 401, 405, 542; and Female Department, 365
Boekzaal der geleerde wereld (periodical), 21
boerenjongens, 251. *See also* beverages
Boers, Mannes, 88
Boes, Jan H., 297

Bolks, Albert, 571
Bolks, Seine, *247*; and ACVR, 149, 150n17, 417; disciplined, 294n35; and Holland Academy, 351-52; and Hope College, 495; and land purchase, 377; leads emigration, xxii, 132n54, 234; and Orange City RCA, 499; and Overisel RCA, 246-47, 409; and Overijssels-Gelders party, 129; and pipe smoking, 583; and Plan of Union, 283, 414
Boone, Hermanus, 556
Booth, John Wilkes, 437
Borculo, MI, 496
Borger (Drenthe): map of, *133*
Borstius, Jacobus, 117
Boston, MA, 172, 180, 217, 232
Bostwick, Edmund B., 256
Bouwstraat (Ommen street), 87, 120
Bowes, John R., 271-72
Bragg, Braxton, 435
Brandt, Jan Daniël, 69
Bratt, James, 46
breweries, 385, 418
bridge(s), 250, 255, 262, 277, 366, 374; Black River, 254-55, 258, 291; North River Rd., 263; Paw Paw Rd., 220, 258; and rail, 342; Statesland [Adams] Rd., 262
Brinks, Herbert, 280
Brist, Benjamin, 383
Britton, William G., 205n41
Broek, Dirk, 574
Broek, Harm, 321, 560
Bronson, William, 261-62, 266
Brooklyn, NY, 274, 322, 344
Brooks, John A., 255

Brooks, John W., 195, 205
brothers' quarrels (Christelijke Afgescheiden Kerk), 101-34
Brouwer, John J. (Holland dentist), 294n35
Brouwer, L. Meijer, 17
Brouwer, Willem (tailor), 231
Brouwer, William, 489
Brower, John J. (RCA official), 395
Bruins, Elton J., 368, 482
Brummelkamp, Anthony, Jr., 152, 463, 533, 535
Brummelkamp, Anthony: 53, *179*, 196; and ACVR as "brother," 21, 40, 43, 57, 61, 72-75, 79, 89, 105, 140, 146, 157, 175, 177-79, 239, 460, 508, 582, as colleague, 70-71, 117, 143, 146-56, 298, 303, 416, as confidant, 298, 303, 370, 378, 387, 394, 399, 427, 452, 500, 532, as correspondent, 190, 193, 195-97, 213, 236, 339, 357, 372, 377, 490; apostle of Gelderland, 67, 77-78, 112; and Arnhem Emigration Society, 169-72; on baptism, 107-8; and Belgian revolt, 34-38; biography, xvii, 23, 49, 462; and Christian education, 119, 163-64; and Christian Separated Church, 101, 107, 110-11, 125-26; and church polity, 102, 124-26, 128-30, 468, 579; and clerical garb, 108-10; defrocked by state church, 49, 164-65; and doctrinal matters, 124, 130-32; on emigration, 141, 158-60, 165-69, 171-75, 178-79, 182, 339, 466, 507; and hymns, 61n73; and Leiden University, 29, 32-33, 40, 407; and ministerial teacher, 113, 143-44, 146-56, 175, 574, 577; and ministry, 67-68, 78, 81-83, 123; as pipe smoker, 23, 583; and Réveil, 32, 131; and Scholte, 125-27; and Secession of 1834, 43, 61, 64; and Van Velzen, 126-27
Brummelkamp, Johannes, 481
Brummelkamp, Maria Wilhelmina (Meitje) de Moen, *179*; Christina Johanna (sister), 74, 126, 151-52, 239, 460, 507-8; death, 532-34; inheritance, 136; marriage, 73, 75, 135; and Van Raalte family, 178-79
Brusse, Arend Jan, 173n43, 189
Brusse, Grada (Mrs. Jan), 173n43
Brusse, Jan, 172, 173n43
Budde, Diedrich A., 90-91
Budding, Huibertus J., *54*; and AVCR, 106, 114; and baptism, 107; deposed, 49, 52; dissention, 101-2, 149; emigration and return, 183; fines, 98; and garb, 108; and Gronings-Drents party, 129; and ministry in Zeeland, 67
Buffalo, NY, xxii, 188, 190, 225, 229, 232, 241, 381, 509, 546
Bunyan, John, 296
Burgerweeshuis, Leiden, 8
Burlington [IA] Reformed Church, 342
Bushnell [IL] Reformed Church, 484

Calhoun, John, 198
Calvin Theological Seminary, 302, 468n52
Calvin University, xvi, 576
Calvin, John, 47-48, 146-47, 307, 320
Calvinist, xiii, 6, 126, 131, 545; church, 63; doctrines (creeds), 48, 102, 585; Reformation, 297; and Scots-Irish, 292. *See also* Protestant Reformation
Campbell, Alexander, 320
Canons of Dort, 17, 47, 76, 124n31, 577. *See also* Reformed Confessions
Canton of Waadland (Switzerland), 98
Capadose, Abraham, 31-32, *33*, 57, 64, 76, 236
Cape Town, South Africa, 276, 433-34; and ACVR, 449-52
Cappon & Bertsch (tannery), 386, 441; damaged in Holland fire, *513*
Cappon, Isaac, 386, 441, 478, 525, 531, 540, 554
Carhart & Needham melodeon reed organ, *502*
Carley, William, 205n41
Carter, Artemus, 230
Cass, Lewis, 197, *198*, 266, 271
Castle Garden (NY), 186
catechism. *See* Heidelberg Catechism
Catholic church: attitudes toward, 209, 485; and emigration, xxii; in America, 209, 532; in the Netherlands, 35
caucus, political, 261-64, 415

Cecil, Richard, 320
Cedar Swamp, 220, 440
censura morum (Latin, mutual censure), 423
Centennial Memorial Commission, RCA (1871), 529
Centennial Park, 436, 520, 543, 547, 586; statue of ACVR, 586
centennials, Holland: 25th (1872), 585; 50th (1897), 309, 559, 585-87; 75th (1922), 568, 583, 586; 100th (1947), xvii, 541, 559, 570, 576, 585; 125th (1972), 585; 150th (1997), xx, 570, 585; 175th (2022), 585
Central Avenue CRC, 105, 280, 296n43, 297, 300, 303, 448, 468, 477-78, 511, 525
Centreville, MI, 282n7, 313
Chalmers, Thomas, 320
Charleston, SC, 489
Charnock, Stephen, 320
Chattanooga, TN, 488
Chicago, IL: and ACVR visits, 197, 312, 454, 498, 537-38; and Classis of Wisconsin, 454; and Dutch immigrants, xxii, 221, 280, 381, 490; fire (1871), 515-17; First RCA of, 304, 416n20, 421, 453, 586; harbor, xxii, 214, 380, 560; and Holland Academy, 347; as market center, xxii, 208, 210, 230, 275, 380-81, 384, 386, 391; and Particular Synod, 302, 342; as political center, 421-22; as rail hub, xv, 187, 214-15, 498, 526, 537
China: missions, 450n11
cholera, 28, 38-39, 45, 58, 175

Christelijke Afgescheiden Kerk (Christian Separated Church), 144-45, 149-50, 467n50; and ACVR, 69, 361, 485, 578-79; and Christelijke Gereformeerde Kerk (NL), 105n12, 303n59; illegal worship service, 78; synod of 1836, De Drie Fonteyn, 71, synod of 1866, 460, 464-69, 485-86; and CRC, 303; and divisions, 129-32; at Leiden, 77, 125, 135n62, 478; and RPDC, 297-98; and synods, 71, 101-34, 142; and Theological School Kampen, 460. *See also* individual congregations

Christelijke Gereformeerde Kerk (NL), 105n12, 110, 303n59

Christelijke Gereformeerde Kerk (US), 105n12, 303n59. *See also* Christian Reformed Church (US)

Christian education: and Van Raalte's convictions, 248, 329-30, 334, 363-66, 424, 486n8, 552, 560, 577; and emigration, 94, 99, 119, 163-64, 172, 175, 520-21; and father Van Raalte, 25; and Holland Academy, 341-48; and Pioneer School, 336-41; and Hope College, 348-53. *See also* parochial schools

Christian Intelligencer (Reformed Church weekly), 172-73, 176, 192, 261n98, 275-76, 312, 320, 350, 368, 515, 596

Christian Reformed Church (US), 132, 150, 215, 294; and ACVR, 585; and Christian education, 365-66; and Kuyperianism, 534, 579; and masonic lodges, 475; and membership (1880), 215, 564; and names, 303n59, 467; and Pillar Church, 475; and Secession of 1857, xviii, 280, 292, 295n39, 297, 302-3, 448, 477; and Sunday schools, 455; as True Brothers, 303, 466, 467, 485; and *volk* baptism, 108

Christian schools: in Amelia, 493; in Holland (MI), 358-63; in Ommen, 115, 117-19, 131, 142; in Wanneperveen, 14, 25, 534

Chula [VA] Reformed Church, 495

Chula, VA, 495

church discipline, 14, 63n79, 70, 104, 112, 114, 250, 289, 301, 314, 431, 482; abused, 294, 297; and ACVR, 476, of individuals, 297, 473, 475, 408-18; and RCA, 466

Church Order of Dort. *See* Dort

Cincinnati, OH, xxi

circus, 311, 321

citizenship, 14, 223, 260-62; and ACVR, 38, 265; and military service, 36, 104, 426-37; obligations of, 365; qualifications, 8, 261; and suffrage, 164, 186

City Mills (Holland), 513

civil code, French, xix, 54, 79, 81

civil registry, Netherlands, xiv, 10

Civil War Monument (Centennial Park), 436-37, 542-43
Civil War: and Company I ("Holland Boys"), 306, 428, 433-365, 455, 471, 487, 502-3, 536, 542, 563, 597, ("Holland Rangers"), 428; and ACVR, xviii, xxi, 414, 421n36, 422-23, 426-37, 542-43; draft, 427, 432, draft riots, 433; and federal income tax, 398, 438; and immigration, xxii, 173, 183, 487; and Lincoln's assassination, 459; neglected in church records, 426n48; Volunteer Bonds, 442-43; volunteers, 426-31. *See also* Twenty-Fifth Michigan Volunteer Infantry
Clapper, Michael J., 457-58; and revival, 488
Clarisse, Johannes J., 30, 41, *42*, 45, 58
Clark, Hovey Kilburn, 374, *375*
class distinctions, xv, xxii, 6, 55, 77, 161
Classis of Apeldoorn, 101
Classis of Amsterdam (NL): and RPDC, 61, 64, 529, 579
Classis of Arcot, India, 529
Classis of Drenthe, 154
Classis of Friesland, 154
Classis of Gelderland, 110, 113, 119, 150, 598
Classis of Grand Haven, 554
Classis of Groningen, 154
Classis of Holland (RCA), 246-48, 277, 279, 281-305, 311, 322, 325, 329, 366, 459; and ACVR: clash with H. Doesburg, 413-14, death of, 545-56, as synod delegate 465-66; and Civil War, 426-27, 431, 437; and education, 337-46, 355-58, 365-66, 570-71; and Freemasonry, 471-74, 476; and First Church reincorporation, 457; and hymns, 447-48; mission of, 402, 449-50, 452-54, 484-87, 488, 492-93, 523, 529, 536-37, 543-45; organized, 579; and Philip Phelps Jr., 478; and Union of 1850, 574-84
Classis of Michigan (RCA), 246, 281-82, 286, 305, 312n81, 453, 472, 498, 566
Classis of Middelstum, 47-48
Classis of New York (RCA), 176, 495
Classis of Ommen, 80, 101, 120, 151
Classis of Overijssel, 113, 148-49, 150, 155
Classis of Wisconsin (RCA), 302, 304n62, 312n81, 454, 472-73, 475, 527
Classis of Zuid-Holland, 42, 154
Classis of Zwolle, 79, 101, 105, 121
Claussen, Frederick, 380
Clay, Henry, 198
Cleveland, OH, xxi, 191, 280
Clymer, NY, xxi, 190
Coates, J. Saunders, 230
Coatsworth, John, 540
Cocksianen, 98
Coevorden (Drenthe), 133
coffee. *See* beverages
Cohen Stuart, Martinus, 524-26
coinage. *See* monetary units, NL

Cole, C. E., 439
Collegiate Reformed Church (New York), 176, 187-88, 315, 342-44, 383
Collendoorn, MI (East Saugatuck), 234
Colonial Mill, 383, 387n50
colony ship. See A. E. Knickerbocker
colony store, 380-81, 583
Colt, George, 384, 391
Colt, M. L., 195, 197
commissioners: highway (road), 255, 261, 269, 275n130; king's, 90; school, xiv; street, 439; board of (Ottawa County), 564
Committee on Education of the Reformed Church. See Reformed Protestant Dutch Church, Committee on Education
Communion. See Lord's Supper
Company I. See Civil War; Twenty-Fifth Michigan Volunteer Infantry
Comrie, Alexander, 40
Conant, Shubael, 195-96, *198*, 204-5
Confederate States of America, 426, 437, 489
Congregational Church, 192-93, 199-201, 204n41, 249, 306, 473, 545
Congress of Vienna, 35
Connell, Abbie (Mrs. Benjamin Van Raalte), 568
constables, 79, 85, 88, 92-93, 158, 251, 253. See also police

Constantine [MI] Reformed Church, 282n7, 305
Constantinian: idea of, 15
Constitution: American, 102, 265, 425; Arnhem Emigration Society, 170-71; Batavian Republic, 4; Napoleonic, 6; Netherlands: *1815*, 55, 90; *1848*, 119, 162n13, 172; Zeeland Emigration Society, 171n38
consumption. See tuberculosis
Continental System, 6
conventicle worship, 69, 103, 297, 302
Coopersville, MI, 300
Copper Heads, 440
Cranmer, Gilbert, 208
Crispell, Cornelius, 334, 557
crop failures. See agriculture: failures
Crosby, Tully, 180, *182*
Cross Followers. See Kruisgezinden
Cruden, Alexander, 320
Crunelle, Leonard, 588
Curtius, Hendrik H. Donker, 58, *59*, 61, 578, 580
custodian. See sexton

d'Aubigné, Jean-Henri Merle, 31, 320
Da Costa, Isaac, 31-32, *33*, 38, 76
Dalfsen [Overijssel] Separated Church, 85n47, 94, 110n25, 128
Dalman, Geert, 284
Dam, Hendrik, 300
Darby, John N., 128
Darwinism, 365, 534
De Bruijn, Adriaan, 147n11

De Cock, Helenius, 129, 287, *288*, 382
De Cock, Hendrik, 41, 146, 322n108; and ACVR, 61, 70, 578; biography, 46-47, 149; and clerical garb, 108; Cocksianen, 98; conversion, 46-48; and Dort Church Order, 103; and Genemuiden Separated Church, 68; and Groningen Separated Church, 149; and Gronings-Drents party, 280, 468; and infant baptism, 107; persecuted, 67; and royal recognition, 174; as Seceder leader, 101-4, 112, 145; and Secession of 1834, 46, 48-49, 81, and secession document, *50-52*; and Scholte, 125; as seminary teacher, 105n11, 106, 132, 144, 291, 297; and vaccination, 236; and Van Velzen, 123
De Cock, Isaac, 62
de dorpen (the villages), 263, 416
De Drie Fonteyne, 69, 71
De Graaf, W., 140-41
De Groot, Frans Breuhaus, *180*
De Groot, Petrus Hofstede, 14, 46, *47*, 307
De Haan, Bert, 496
De Haan, Tamme F., 129-30, 132, 144, 149, 151, 155
De Hope (newspaper), 451n13, 479
De Jong, Jacob, 69
De Klokkenberg (Ommen Christian School), 118n16
De Kruif, Hendrik, 182, 225n17

De Lange, Arie, 111n28
De Maas, Jasper, 112
De Moen & Co. (Ledeboerweg, Lemele), 135; brickworks, *136*
De Moen family, 13n22, 22-23, 72-77, 126, 142, 367-68; clerics, 77; siblings, 77; wealth, 76
De Moen, Agatha Sophia van Voss, 142, 178
De Moen, Alexandrina, 460
De Moen, Benjamin, 74, 76, 136, 367; and estate, 136n64
De Moen, Carel Godefroi, 75, 81, 129-30, *138*, 298, 460, 468, 505, 550, 568; and ACVR, 63, 74, 109, 125, 139, 142-43, 150n17, 155, 179, 282, 326, 373, 381-82, 445, 464, as business partner, 135-39, 367; and clerical garb, 109; death of, 550; as *De Bezuin* editor, 345n46, 471n60; and declined calls, 178; education of, 74-75, 369; and Den Ham Separated Church, 131, 209, 292; and Dort Church Order, 126; and Heemse Separated Church, 81; and inheritance, 135n62; and Kampen Separated Church, 464; and Ommen Separated Church, 142; ordained, 126, 149; and Overijssels-Gelders party, 129-30, 298, 468; as physician, 367; and sister Christina Van Raalte, 232, 259, 460, 505; and Scholte, 125
De Moen, Helena, 75
De Moen, Johanna Maria Wilhelmina, 74-76, 92, 126, 136, 152, 464, 533, 549

De Moen, Johannes Benjamin, 72, 74
De Moen, Maria Wilhelmina. *See* Brummelkamp, Maria Wilhelmina (Meitje) de Moen
De Netherlander (newspaper), 411
De Nieuwe Vlijt (tannery), 152
De Oratione Sacra, 307
De Pree, Peter, 478
De Putter, Marinus, 258
De Regt, Aaltje (Mrs. Reiner [Ryne]), 258
de stad (the town), 228, 263, 416, 443
De Tichelarij, *136*
De Vries, Hendrikus, 150n17
De Vries, Jan, 359
De Vries, Magdelene, 260
De Waal, Apolonius G., 155
De Wachter (newspaper), 468
De Weerd, Albert, 178
De Wit, Kees (Cornelius), 244
De Wit, Poppe Rykens, 145, 148, 150n17
De Witt, Thomas, 176, 187, *188*: and ACVR, 198n26, 233, 244, 368, 394-95, 461, 507; aids Holland colony, 274, 315, 336, 344, 383; assists immigrants, 176, 187-88, 192, 237, 281, and Netherlands Society, 205-6; and Vande Luyster, 206n44; visits Holland, 274n126, 317, 562
Decatur, IL, 166-67
Decoration Day, 532, 542-43
Dedemsvaart [Overijssel] Separated Church, 80, 94-95
deference, social, 8, 410
deism, 32

Delft (Zuid-Holland), 37
Democrat Party: and ACVR, 407, 418-26, 431; and Civil War, 407-8, 436-38; and congress, 271; and elections: *1852*, 265; *1860*, 425; *1864*, 425-26; *1868*, 438; *1876*, 550; and H. Doesburg, 420-26; and Jacksonian, 186, 197, 261, 265; and newspapers, 261n98, 269, 408-9, 411, 420, 556; and Peace Democrats, 436; and Scholte, 421-23; and slavery, 420; Southern, 552
Den Bleyker, Paulus, *388*, 406; as ACVR business partner, 259, 387-93, 411, 413, 445, 500, 575, 582-83
Den Ham (Overijssel), 63, 80-81, 88, 94-95, 120, 131, 209, 232
Den Herder, Jacob, 245
Den Hitzer (Zuid-Holland), 332
Denison, Francis, 383
Denison, William, 205n41
Den Lagen Oordt (street in Ommen), 114n4, 146
Des Moines, IA, xxii, 215, 422
Detroit Daily Advertiser (newspaper), 261n98, 276
Detroit Daily Free Press (newspaper), 261n98, 596
Detroit Free Democrat (newspaper), 261n98
Detroit, MI, xxi, 185, 187-88, 230, 236, 369, 385, 488, 503, 520; and ACVR, 230, 236, 375, 385, 431n36, 488, 503, 520; boosters, 197-99, 266; and A. E. *Knickerbocker*, 380n38; winter layover in, 190-93, 217-18,

225, 357, 372, 507, 509; and working committee, 203-7
Deventer (Overijssel), 88-89, 92, 94-95
dialects: Drents, 233; Fries, 233; Gronings, 233, 291; Low Franconian, 19; Low German, 233; Zeeuws, 19, 233, 291
Diekema, Gerrit J., 554
Dikkers, Jan, 81
diphtheria, 236
discipline (church): and ACVR, 76, 104, 112, 144, 250, 296n43, 481, 567; in Christian Separated Church, 14, 63n79; in First Holland RCA, 314, 408, 413-15, 431, 466; and Freemasonry, 473, 475-76; and True CRC, 290, 294, 301
diseases: bilious fever, 447; cholera, 28, 38-39, 45, 58, 175; diphtheria, 236; dysentery, 208, 238-39, 447; malaria (ague), 236-37, 270, 445, 447n5; neuralgia, 350; smallpox, 79, 211, 236, 270; typhus (typhoid), 157, 175, 236. See also tuberculosis (consumption)
Dispatch, KS, 536
District School No. 1. See Holland [City] District School No. 1
Dixie, 481
Doesburg, Cornelius, 363, 447
Doesburg, Hermanus, as editor, 410-11, 577; feuds with Van Raalte, 411-18, 425, 448, 555; and politics, 418, 420, 424-25, 431

Doesburg, Jacob, 411, 431, 448
Doesburg, Otto, 411, 431, 554
Doesburg, Teuntje, 562
Doeveren (Noord-Brabant), 49
dogmatics, 41, 146-47, 153
Donner, Johannes H., 167, 478, 480-81
Doorn (Utrecht), 30
Dordrecht (Zuid-Holland), 37, 102, 104-5, 110
Dorst, L. J., 28
Dort: Canons of, 75, 102, 124n31, 208; Church Order of, 15-16, 61, 102-4, 112, 115, 119, 123-32, 246, 248, 293, 297, 300, 301; Form of Subscription, 15-16, 70; Synod of, 31, 60, 111-12, 115, 124-25, 132, 147, 301
Dosker, Henry: and ACVR, xvii, 353n77; as ACVR biographer, xvii, xviii, 183-84, 279n1, 305, 309, 490, 504-5, 573, 580, 584; and Christina Johanna Van Raalte, 504; as pastor, 545, 556; as Western Seminary professor, 465
Dosker, Nicholas H., 45n42, 545, 556
Douglas, Stephen, 421, 425
d'Oultre, Countess Henriette (second wife of King Willem I), 38n24
Douma, Michael J., xviii, 434n62, 586
Drecht, 82
Drenthe, MI, 233, 248, 261, 262-63; churches, 282, 291-94, 414, 478; soils, 374; village of, 564; and West Drenthe (Statesland), 263

Drenthe, province of, xiv, xxii, 49, 154, 296; and ACVR, 94, *133*, 143, 289; and emigration, 123, 176, 291
Drogeham [Friesland] Hervormde Kerk, 49, 61, 74
Dros, Cornelis, 135, 139
Du Bois, Anson, 493
Duffield, George, 194-95, *198*, 204-5, 207, 507
Duin, Jacob, 297-98
Duke of Alva, 265
Dumont Road (Heath Twp., MI), 255
Dumont, John B., 225, 255
Dunn, Ruth (Mrs. Frank De Moen Kleinheksel), 569
Dunnewind, Egbert, 119, 225n17
Dunnink, Hendrik Egberts, 85; farmhouse, *86*
Dutch Calvinism. *See* Calvinist
Dutch Catholics. *See* Catholic church
Dutch monarchy, xiii, xix, 4; and ACVR, 71, 81, 85, 91; and Louis Napoleon, xix, 6; and Willem II (king), 98, 121, 161, 174, and ACVR, 224, 266; and Willem V (king), xix. *See also* Willem I, Willem III
Dutch New Yorkers, 172, 290. *See also* Yankees
Dutch Reformed Church (NL), xxi, 15. *See also* Hervormde Kerk Nederland
Dutch Reformed Church (US), 64, 249, 295, 424. *See also* Reformed Protestant Dutch Church (RPDC); Reformed Church in America (RCA)
Dutch Republic, 290
Dutch Road, 255-58; and the Half-Way House, *259*
Dutch War for Independence, 209, 265
dysentery, 208, 238-39, 447
dyspepsia, 325

East Saugatuck, MI, 234
East Williamson, NY, xxi, 190
Ebenezer [Eben-Haëzer] Memorial Fund, 523-24, 538; plaque, 524; thank offering, 524
Ebenezer Reformed Church (Holland, MI), 477
Ecclesiastical Manual (church order), 127
Edwards, Jonathan, 41, 320
Eendracht Polder (Texel), 387
Eerdmans, William B., Sr., xvi, 541-42, 576; and Van Raalte house, 442n76, 541
Effie (Van Raalte maid), 260
Egeling, Lucas, 56n61, 76, 77
Eighth Street, Holland, 219, 225, 228, 335, 384, 387n50, 422, 480, 501, 502n58, 511, 518, 571; post fire (1875), *518*
Eighty Years' War (1568-1648), 209, 265
Elbers, Lucas, 300
Eleventh Street, Holland, 351-52
Elliot, Charlotte, 323
Ely, Elisha, 218
Ely, Lydia Baxter (Mrs. Elisha), 218
Emancipation Proclamation, 433
Emigrants, The (Frans Breuhaus de Groot painting), *180*
emigration: aid societies, 170, 171n38, 176, 214, 379n33;

debate surrounding, 161, 165-66, 168-69, 171, 174, 177, 183, 511, 522, 537, 542, 550. *See also* immigration
Emmen (Drenthe), 133, 173
English Channel, 463
English language. *See* language: English
English people, 41, 158, 193, 219, 268, 277, 296, 390; confuse Dutch and Germans, 419n28. *See also* Yankee(s)
Enlightenment, xiii, xix, 3-4, 88
epaulette drones, 273
epithet(s), 80, 98, 327, 469, 584
Erie Canal, xxii, 187-89; boat, *189*; and route map, *189*
Eusebius Gate, 152
Evangelical Alliance, 488, 524, 578
Evangelische Gezangen (1807), 48
Excelsiora (Hope College newspaper), 480n82, 558

Fairbanks Avenue, Holland, 201, 228, 242, 372, 540, 557, 564
Fairbanks, Ann Woodruff, 199, 200, 201, 219
Fairbanks, Austin, 212
Fairbanks, Isaac: and AVCR, 219, *220*, 267, 331, 453, 522, 582; and family, 236; and Methodist Episcopal Church, 458; as justice of the peace, 201; and Odawa band, 212-13, 220, 228; and Old Wing Mission, 199-201, 208, 396
Fairview [IL], 493, 498; and Reformed Church, 484

Falconer, Cornelia, 335, 342, 359
family visitation (*huisbezoek*), 87, 94, 115, 248, 290, 300, 313, 447, 459
farming. *See* agriculture
farmland prices, xxi, 186, 371, 379, 388, 521
Faukelius, Herman, 118
Federal District (Holland city), 373n13, 441; and District School No. 4, 335
Felch, Alpheus, 272
female education, 354, 357-59, 402, 442, 495, 523-24, 527, 530, 532; and teachers, 332-33, 366
Fenn (Saugatuck builder), 228n22
Fennville, MI, 219
Ferris, Isaac, 424
Ferry, Thomas White, 196n23, 403, 544, 554
Ferry, William Montague, Jr., 195, 203, 554
Ferrysburg, MI, 203
Field, Mehetable, 230n25
Fijenoord (steamship), 463
Fijnaart (Noord-Brabant), 30; Hervormde Kerk, 20, 22, 29, 468-69
Fillmore Twp. (Allegan County, MI), 199, 208, 225, 234, 255, 374, 377, 380, 490; and Old Wing Mission, 201, 222n13, 376, 540n16. *See also* Odawa (Ottawa) band; Old Wing Mission
Fillmore, Millard, 272
financial depression: in the Netherlands, *1840s*: 6, 158,

160; in the United States: *1857*, 273, 361; *1873*, xx; *1893*, xxii, 521; *1930s*, 160
fines, of Seceders, xv, 55, 76, 79, 82, 85, 91, 94, 96-98, 111, 121, 158, 486, 507
Finney, Charles G., 31, 194n19, 310
firemen, 511, 542
fires, 287n18, 404, 448-50, 479; and preventatives, 250, 253, 376. *See also* Holland Fire of 1871
First Great Awakening, 401, 579
First Presbyterian Church, Detroit, 194-95, 198
First Presbyterian Church, Grand Haven, MI, 195, 203
First Presbyterian Church, Kalamazoo, 195, 198, 218, 232, 357
First Reformed [Pillar] Church, Holland, *318*; and ACVR: donates lots to, 523, funeral of, 554-57, pastorate of, xvii, 402, 440, 443, 523, 544, 581, and retirement, 445-53, 455-57, 475-84, 529, 539; and catechism, 366; and Clapper revival, 457-59; as college church, 478; consistory of, 246, 297, 235, 411, 556; and Christina Van Raalte's funeral, 505; and Cohen Stuart, 525; and discipline, 314, 408, 413-15, 431, 466, 473, 475-76; edifice, 314-18, sanctuary decorated for American Centennial, *554*; and Freemasonry, 471-75, 482, 572, 576; incorporation of, 248, *249*, 457; and Ladies Society, 316, 509; lawsuit for possession, 457n30; membership statistics of, 282n7, 317n96, 459n35, 592-93, table, 592; and missionary ship, 454; and politics, 421-23, 427, 437-38; and Roelof Pieters, 510, 517, 525, 548; Sunday school, 319, 447, 455; as tourist site, 586; and Van Raalte family, 475, 482, 563. *See also* Log Church, Holland
First Reformed Church, Chicago, 302, 585; Roseland, 304
First Reformed Church, Grand Rapids (First RPDC, name of, pre-1867), 195, 206, 381, 585
First Reformed Church, Kalamazoo, 232
First Reformed Church, Muskegon, 509
First Reformed Church, Pella, 340, 356, 469, 543, 576
First Reformed Church, Zeeland, 232, 239, 246, 248, 262, 290-91, 297, 389, 414, 416, 453, 495, 523; and ACVR, 409, 411, 547; and brawl, 263-64; membership, 282n7, 317n96; and Union of 1850, 284-85
Fisher, Henry, 230
flatboats, 230, 253, 271, 383
Flavel, John, 320
Floris, Lambert, 241
Fond du Lac, WI, 209, 304
Forestville [MN] Reformed Church, 484
Forrester, James, 383, 507

Fortieth Street, Holland, 201, 219, 396, 540
Fourth of July, 291, 436, 445, 517
Fourth Street, Holland, 385
Fox River Valley, WI, xxi, 209
France, 6-7, 35, 162; and French Civil Code, xix. *See also* French Revolution
Francken, Aegidius, 146
Franeker (Friesland), 176n51
Frederick II (king of Prussia), 4
Frederiks (Fredericks), Egbert, 173, 218, 225n17, 235, 240
Free Church (NL), 16, 28, 49, 65, 127, 174, 194, 507, 535, 579
Free Kirk Scots, 194
freedom of press, 408, 413
freedom of worship, 71, 80, 89, 91, 163, 174, 205, 240, 251, 521, 581
Freemasonry, 295-96; and ACVR, 296, 571-74, 581; and First Holland RCA, 471-76; and Hope College, 300; and RCA, 467, 527, 546, 571; and Secession of 1857, 295, 300, 301; and Van Raalte family, 475, 546-47, 571-72; and Van Schelven, 471-72, 473n65. *See also* Anti-Masonic political party
Frelinghuysen, Theodore, 336, 344
French Revolution, xiii, 32, 34; and Netherlands, xix-xx, 4, 6,- 8, 12, 29, 37, 39, 159, 577
Frenchman's Creek, 233
Friesland, province of, 145, 149; churches, 49, 94, 145, 233, 293; emigration, xxii, 173, 176, 233; and fines (Separatists), 98; and Van Velzen, 49, 61, 67, 74, 92, 123-24, 129-32
Fulton [IL] Reformed Church, 484
Fulton Street [NY] revival, 322

Gansoyen (Noord-Brabant), 49
garb (clerical vestments), 55, 81, 85, 108, *109*, 110, 126, 131-32, 134, 149, 467
Garretson, John, 289, 313, 326, 336, 337, 394, 395, 500
Geerlings, Arent, 404
Gelderland, province of: and Achterhoek, 172; and ACVR, xiv, 98, 109-10, 112, 119, 129, 132n55, 151-52, 154, 156, 482; and Brummelkamp, 67, 74, 78, 119, 129, 132n55, 151-52, 154; and churches, 3, 127, *132*, 155-56, 165; and emigration, 165-66, 173, 356; and fines (Seceders), 98; and Overijssels-Gelderse party, 132, 151, 155; and Wintersvijk, 165, 170
Gelok, Jan, 300
Genderen (Noord-Brabant), 49
Genemuiden [Overijssel] Separated Church, 67-69, 77-83, 92-94, 114, 134, 170, 176; and ACVR, 111-12, 114n4, 120, 122, returns, 467, and social work, 134; and clerical garb, 109-11; edifice on the Drecht River, 82; legal recognition of, 120-23; persecution of, 89, 95-97; and Vander Haar family,

509; and Van Raalte children, 141, 568
General Synod. *See* Reformed Protestant Dutch Church (RPDC); Reformed Church in America (RCA)
Geneva (Switzerland), 98; and psalms, 48; Réveil movement in, 31; Theological School, 146
Geneva, NY, 334
Georgetown Twp., MI, 255, 258
Georgia, 436
Gereformeerde Gemeenten (Reformed congregations), 105
Gereformeerde Kerken onder 't Kruis, 105n12, 467n50. *See also* Kruisgezinden
Gereformeerde: as historic name, 15, 55, 70; and controversy, 110-11, 121, 575, 578, 580
German(y), xxii, 162, 232; and emigration, 165-66, 187; and German Americans, 208, 387, 419n28; and German Catholics, 209, 485n4; and philosophies, 387; and travel guides, 214. *See also* Graafschap Bentheim (Germany); language: German
Germania Hotel (Albany, NY), 172
Gettysburg, PA, 434, 435
Gezelle Meerburg, George. *See* Meerburg, George
Gibbs, M., 383
Giles, Thomas T., 490n22
Gilmore, Albertus Christiaan Van Raalte (Raalte), 535, 537, 569
Gilmore, Christine Catharina Van Raalte (daughter), 492, 494, 497-98, 531, 542, 549, 563. *See also* Van Raalte, Christina (Christine) Catharina (daughter)
Gilmore, Frank Edwin, 568
Gilmore, Julia Christina, 498, 515, 532, 563
Gilmore, Margaret Anna, 535, 537, 569
Gilmore, William "Will" Brokaw, 352, 493, *494*, 495, 497-98, 401, 531, 533, 563, 566
Gilmore, William "Willie," 535, 569
Gispen, Willem H., 469
Goes (Zeeland), 160, 232
"Gouden Willempjes" (Dutch 2½-guilder coins), xxii, 164, 170, *171*
Graafschap [MI] church, 245-46, 248, 282n7, 287, 292, 297, 300, 389, 409, 414; and Secession of 1857, 284-85, 298-99; and Vander Werp, 105n11, *106*, 119, 466-68
Graafschap Bentheim (Germany). *See* Bentheim (Germany)
Graafschap, MI, 233; and 1871 fire, 449, 511
Graham, John D., 273
Grambergen (Gelderland), 135n62
Grand Army of the Republic, Post 262, 543, 586
Grand Central Railroad, 192

Grand Haven, MI: and ACVR, 240, 403-4; and bridge, 263; and Civil War, 427; as county seat, 202, 250, 261; court house, 203, 253, 321; early history of, 193, 207, 211-12, 526; and Ferry family, 195, 203, 204n41, 554; harbor, 221; and John Jacob Astor, 193; as market center, 383, 397; parochial school, 357n74; Reformed churches, 304, 414, 416n20, 420, 556; roads, 254-56

Grand Rapids Argus (newspaper), 413, 417

Grand Rapids Marble Works, 504n65

Grand Rapids, MI: and ACVR, xvi, 304, 374-75, 460, 504n65, 537; and Catholics, 485n4; and Civil War, 427; as commercial center, 256, 397; as Dutch center, xxi, 202, 280, 355; and Detroit committee, 204-5; and First RPDC, 195, 196n23, 206, 237, 246, 381, 585; and Hoyt Post, 270n112; and John Ball, 195, 204-5; and Mayor Wm. Ferry Jr., 554; and road link, 257; as transport center, xv, 214, 525; and Scholte, 420; and Secession of 1857, 300; and Second RPDC, 284, 295, 304, 416n20, 453, 471, 519, 522, 545; and Wm. B. Eerdmans, 442n76, 576

Grand River (MI), 199; watershed, 197, 202, 207

Grand River Eagle (newspaper), 273, 276

Grandville, MI, 250, 256, 258

Grant, Ulysses S., 435-36, 438

Gray, Dorothy (Mrs. Paul Edwin Kleinheksel), 589

Great [later, Grand Trunk] Western Railroad, 344

Great Depression. *See* financial depression: in the United States

Great Lakes, 208, 214, 256, 389

Great Western (steamship), *190*, 192

Greek language. *See* language: Greek

Greenleafton (MN), 150

Griffin, Henry, 261

Griggstown [NJ] Reformed Church, 345

Groen Van Prinsterer, Guilaume. *See* Van Prinsterer, Guilaume

Grondwet, De (newspaper), xvii, 424-25, 435-37, 480n82, 513; and ACVR death, 550-51

Groningen, MI, 221, 237, 239, 371, 449, 520, 540; churches, 282n7, 284-85, 290-91

Groningen, province of, xiv, xxii, 49; churches, 17, 46-52, 107, 111, 120, 126, 128, 182, 300; and De Cock, 46-52, 67, 144; and emigration, 163, 173, 176; University of, 3-4, 30

Gronings dialect, 291

Gronings-Drents party (Van Velzianen), 129-32, 130n47, 132n55, 144-45, 149-51, 154-55, 280, 284, 288, 298, 303, 310, 467-68, 476, 578

Grootenhuis, Bernardus, *285*; as ACVR's right-hand man, 192, 218, 237, 251, 381, 440, 574; family, 192, 219; and Holland work party, 218, 221; a founding family, 223, 225, 454

Grootenhuis, Janna, 218-19, 454

guilder. *See* monetary units, NL

Gun Plains, MI, 292

gymnasium (Latin school), 143; at Amsterdam, 40; at Bergen op Zoom, 29, 34; at Groningen, 3

Haaften (Gelderland), 3
Haak, Elizabeth, 74
Haan, Gysbert, 295, 297, *299*, 300, 302, 466, 485
Hackensack, NJ, 193
half-way covenant (infant baptism), 107n16, 446n2
Half-Way House, *259*
Hall, Samuel, 205n41
Hallerdyk, Arnoldus, 166-67
Hallum (Friesland), 233
Hamilton, MI, 255
harbor (Holland): 214, 230, 233, 265, 368, 521; board, 271-72, 275, 400; bonds, 443; as "cornerstone," 208, 525; land grant, 400; lighthouse, 406; mouth of, 236, 372; pier, 283; problems with, 217, 381, 482; project, 270-75, 413; promoted by ACVR, xiv, xxii, 176, 194, 276, 327, 413, 489, 560, 572, 583; surveys, 270-72
Hardenberg (Overijssel), 87
Harderwijk Academie, 30

Harinck, George, 468
Harking family, 1, 8-10, 12, 21-22, 72, 499
Harking, Arend, 8, 22
Harking, Cat[h]arina Christina (Mrs. Albertus Van Raalte), 1, 8-9, 12-13, 18, 21-22, 72, 91; children, 9-10, and wedding certificate, *9*
Harrington, Edward J., 221n10
Harrington, George S., 202, 219, *220*, 222, 224, 267, 453, 458, 582
Harrington, Margaret Van Alstyne, *220*, 222n13
Hartgerink, Alexander, 119, 166-67
Harvie, Lewis E., 490
Harwich (England), 471
Hasselt (Overijssel), 69
Hastings, Eurotas P., 195, 204-5
Hastings-on-Hudson, NY, 344
Hattem (Gelderland), 67-68; and ACVR, 94; and Brummelkamp, 49, 57, 74, 79, 89, 144, 150, 467; Hervormde Kerk, 49, 57, 74, 467
Havana [IL] American Reformed Church, 566
Havekate, Gerrit J., 255, 520
Hawkeye State, 208. *See also* Iowa
Hawks, Josiah, 409-10
Hayes, Rutherford B., 550, 552
Heath Township, Allegan County, MI, 255
Hebrew language. *See* language: Hebrew
Heemse (Overijssel), 80-81, 87, 120
Heeren, Enne J., 529

Heidelberg Catechism, 14, 17;
  and ACVR, 243, 297, 305-6,
  318-19, 331-32, 359, 455, 542,
  577; and books, 78, 117-18;
  and Christian schools, 119,
  353; controversies, 129, 290,
  295, 297, 300; lessons, 76, 87,
  117, 145, 153, 248, 259, 291.
  See also Reformed Confessions
Heideman, Eugene, 43n40, 305-6
Heidepark of Lemelerveld
  (Overijssel), 138
Heijningen (Noord-Brabant), 20
Heldring, Ottho, 134, 168, 276
Hellendoorn (Overijssel), 92-94,
  120, 131, 132n54, 234
Hellenthal, Johannes, 221n10
Hellevoetsluis (Zuid-Holland),
  178, 213, 221; and Separated
  Church, 178
Henry, Mathew, 320
Heritage Hall: archives, 576
Hervormde Kerk Nederland
  (HKN), xiii, xix, xx, 29, 39,
  40-43, 47, 107, 124, 146,
  176, 249, 316; and Abraham
  Kuyper, 535; and ACVR,
  40-43, 55-65, 131, 145, 368,
  468, 485, 580; and Bentheim
  church, 95; and Blikman
  Kikkert family, 140; and
  Brummelkamp, 74, 143; and
  Christelijke Gereformeerde
  Kerk, 65, 110; and clerical
  garb, 108; and doctrinal
  apostasy, 15-18, 110-11, 114,
  131, 174; and emigration,
  174-75, 363; and father Van
  Raalte pastorates, 1-22, 70,
  80, 368, 468; and Ministry
  of Religion, 111; and names,
  110; and National [General]
  Synod of 1816, 15-17, 56, 58,
  61, 64, 97, 578; and RCA,
  466-70; and RPDC, 282; and
  Réveil, 30-33; and Secession
  of 1834, 173-74, 580. See
  also Netherlands Reformed
  Church
Hesselink, Harmen Jan, 229
Het Kerkhof van Holland
  (cemetery), 239, 543
Hidding, Hendrik (Henry), 378
  427-28, 434
Higgens, Benjamin P., 560
High Prairie (Roseland, IL), xxi,
  304
Hillebrands, Anneus J., 266; ink
  drawings of, 237, 264, 265
Hodenpyl, Pieter, 205
Hoffman, Coenraad (Conrad),
  294, 386
Hofman, Anje, 324
Hofman, Gerrit Jan, 225n17
Hofman, Helena. See Van
  Raalte, Helena Hofman (Mrs.
  Albertus Christiaan)
Hofman, Klaas Jans, 324
Hofwijk House (Overijssel), 94
Hoksbergen, Derk, 104
holidays: festival (feast) days,
  129, 309; Christmas, 305; and
  controversy, 293; Easter, 293;
  Pentecost, 94, 112, 291, 293,
  323, 459; Thanksgiving, 293,
  431, 436, 532; working on, 112
Holland [City] District School
  No. 1, 305, 331, 333-34, 338,
  342, 358, 360, 362-63, 402. See
  also schools
Holland [NE] Reformed Church,
  539

Holland Academy: alumni, 358, 427, 448, 471, 478, 493; as ACVR's "second wife," 350, 443, 582; and church funding, 355-57, 361, 364, 538; and donated lots, 402; faculty: Gilmore, 493, Phelps, 348-55, 397, Van der Veen, 448, Van de Wall, 325n113, 409, 434; Van Vleck, 341-53, 509; and female education, 354, 357-58; students, xv, 317, 458; and Third Reformed Church, 478. *See also* Pioneer School

Holland anniversaries. *See* centennials, Holland

Holland Cemetery Association, 543

Holland city (colony): founding, 224-28, 573, 575; growth of, 232-34; and hard times, 235-40, deceased on oxcart, 237; naming of, 217-19; plats, 226, 227, 377n25, (1866) *439*, (2014) *441*; pioneers, 219n5, 221-23, 225n17, 519-20, 586; settlement maps, (1848) *234*, (1876) *588* (1871); seal, *442*; surveys (city), 225, *226*, *227*, 242, 255, 377n25, *439*; travel routes, 191

Holland city band, 510, 542

Holland Fire of 1871, 403, 443, 510-13; and ACVR, 516-18, and burned Bible, *512*; and damaged Cappon & Bertsch tannery, *512*; and insurance, 514-15; Relief Committee, 514-15

Holland First Church. *See* First Reformed [Pillar] Church, Holland

Holland harbor. *See* harbor (Holland)

Holland High School, 335-36, 360, 534, 573

Holland Museum, 576, 586

Holland Twp. School District No. 4., 335

Holland Twp.: ACVR's land in, 371-73, 375, 377n26, 393, 398; board of trustees, 261-62, 265-66, 272, 321; election, *265*; harbor board, 272-75, social policy, 321, caucuses, 261-676; and Holland fire, 443; organized, 253, 260, 331; politics, 260-67, 415, 419-20; population (1860), 336; school inspectors, 331, 335; separation from city, 270, 438-43

Holland, NE, 539

Hollander, De (newspaper): and ACVR, 312, 315, 323-24, 333, 346, 407-20, 447, 480n82, 554, 577; poem published in, 500; and Baxter book, 296; and editor H. Doesburg, 410-23; and politics, 424-26

Hollandsche Gereformeerde Kerk (US), 303n59. *See also* Christian Reformed Church (US)

Holy Communion. *See* Lord's Supper

homiletics, 39, 41, 146-47, 153

Hooldstraat (main street), Genemuiden (Overijssel), 68

Hoogesteger, Marinus, 435, 437

Hoogeveen [Drenthe] Christian Separated Church, 298, 300

Hoogeveen, Drenthe, 144, 148-50, 155

Hope [MI] Reformed Church: and Clapper revival, 458; as college church, 478; and Freemasonry, 472-75; as "English" church, 268n108, 475; and Lincoln memorial service, 432; and lots donated, 402; organized, 403-5; and Van Raalte family, 563
Hope College Addition, 441
Hope College, xv, xvi, xviii, 343, 404-5, 432, 458, 497, 526; and ACVR, 276, 357, 401, 443, 498, 554, 582, 584, 586, donates lots, 311, 401-2, 498, lectures, 307, as president of council, 483, 497; board of trustees, 400, 405, 542; and campus (1865), *354*; and Civil War, 431; and endowment, 498, 523, 528; and faculty, 478, 497, 504, 557, 560, 566-67, 588; and Female Department, 365, 532; and Freemasons, 527; and fundraising, 484, 495, 527; and gymnasium/chapel, *351*; and Oggel, 451n13, 454; and Phelps, 348-53, 487, 489, 511, 528; and RCA, 355-57; and theology program, 493-94, 570, 576; and Van Raalte house, 542; and Van Raalte Institute, 541, 588; and Van Vleck, 347-48, Hall, *354*
Hope Preparatory (High) School, 566
Hopkins, Moses, 438, 440
House of Orange, Netherlands, xix, 15, 36n20, 209, 266, 516; William of Orange, 265

Höveker, Henricus, 71n10, 90
Howard, Manly D., 437
Hoyt, Ova P., 195, 197, *198*, 204, 205n41, 207, 218, 331
Hudig & Blokhuizen (Rotterdam ship brokers), 175
Hudson Valley, NY, 515
Hudson, Homer E., 390, 396, 582
Hudsonville, MI, 258, 396
Huis van Verzekering, Zwolle, 90
huisbezoek. *See* family visitation (*huisbezoek*)
Huizenga, Peter H., 587
Hulst, Jan, 264, 293
Hyma, Albert, 183, 190, 379, 387, 541, 576, 585
hymns: and ACVR, 447, 581; and Brummelkamp, 61n73, and controversy, 48, 78, 290, 300, 447, 482, 581n10; and De Cock, 48; English, 458; and the *Evangelische Gezangen* (1807), 48; in worship, 129, 295, 325, 454

IJsselmuiden (Overijssel), 69
Illinois, xxii, 166-67, 484; and ACVR, 473, 516, 531-32, 535, 542, 549, 582; churches in, 303, 479, 484, 493, 533, 566; Dutch settlement in, 171, 207-8, 215
Illinois-Michigan Canal project, 193-94
Imboden, John D., 491
immigration: reasons for, 112, 119, 245, 251, 279, 329, 579; and "chain migration," 232; and the RCA, 281, 536; travel route map, *191*; waves, xx-xxi, 491; and women, 178-80, 510. *See also* emigration

Immink, Gerrit Jan, 92
Independence Day. *See* Fourth of July
Indian Village (Landing), 201
Indians, 194, 212, 220, 436; and Chief Wakazoo, 200, 208, 211; and corn, 210, 235, 385; and farming, 199, 201; as guides, 199; and Indian Rights movement, 212; lands of, 201, 213, 376; Odawa (Ottawa) band of, 193, 199, 200; and sugar making, 212; and trading, 382; trails of, 254; and white antipathy, 212, 213n58-59
inflation calculations, 403n85
inheritance, 135n62, 165, 186, 403, 535; and Christina Van Raalte, 120, 151, 583; and Van Raalte heirs, 548
insurance: agents, 372; and Holland fire (1871), 513-15; life, 404; property, 344
inter nos (informal pastor's gatherings), 288
Internal Improvement Land Grant of 1841, 255, 271-72; and Michigan, 374-75; and warrants, 258, 374. *See also* land policy
Ionia, MI, 207; and Public Land Office, 370, 372, 374
Iowa: agriculture, xix, 214; church planting in, by ACVR, 303, 342, 531, 537, 582; and Cohen Stuart, 524; politics, 422-23; Pella colony, xxi, xxii, 154n26, 162, 197, 206, 213-15, 232, 582; Sioux County, xxi, 240, 499; spurned by ACVR, 207-8. *See also* Pella, IA; Sioux County, IA
Israelite school (Arnhem), 153
Ithaca, NY, 302
itinerate(s): ACVR, xxii, 11, 84, 92, 95-96, 105, 113, 157, 254, 306, 538; preachers, 67, 74, 78, 145, 453
Itterbeek (County Bentheim), 95

Jackson, Andrew (US president), 266, 573
Jagers (riflemen), 36-37; and metric height measure, 37n23; in uniform, 36
James, John Angell, 320
janitor (sexton), 14, 17, 244, 316, 437, 550
Janssen, Jacobus D., 15
Java, Netherlands East Indies (Indonesia), 158, 167-68
Jefferson, Aletia (Mrs. John G.), 490n22
Jefferson, John G., 490n22
Jefferson, Thomas, 410
Jenison, Hiram, 258
Jenison, MI, 258
Johnson, Andrew, 484
Johnson, Joseph E., 435
Joldersma, Rense, 558
Joure (Friesland), 145

Kalamazoo Literary and Theological Institute, 334
Kalamazoo River, 219, 229-30, 255, 321; watershed, 202
Kalamazoo, MI, 55, 161, 239, 280, 331, 384, 420; and ACVR, 197-200, 207, 413, 417, 476; and

Christine Van Raalte, 354, 391, 438, 461, 566; churches, 178-79, 197, 232, 304, 357; and Civil War, 428; and Den Bleyker, 259, 301, 387-403; and Dutch, xxii, 195, 205, 218; as market center, 230, 254, 355, 383-84; newspapers, 409; and Ova Hoyt, 207; parochial school, 331, 355-57; rail station, xv, 187, *191*, 192, 197, 243, 335, 344-45, 374, 526; and Scholte, 420

Kampen (Overijssel), 104, 126, 463-65, 467, 469. *See also* Theological School Kampen

Kamper, Arend, 221n10

Kansas, xiv, 420, 483, 531, 536-39, 569, 582, 584

Kanters, Leendert, 554

Kanters, Rokus, 520, 560

Karsten, John H., 437, 452, 472, 505

Keith, Alexander, 320

Keizersgracht (Amsterdam), 467

Kellogg, John R., *198*; and ACVR, 99, 200, 202, 207, 219, 228, 37n20, 378, 507-8; and Detroit working committee, 195, 197-98, 205n41; aids Holland colony, 218-19, 222, 256, 582; and public service, 198; and West Michigan Society to Benefit the Indians, 202

Kellogg, Mary Otterson, 218, 499, 507-8

Kennedy, Earl Wm., 285-86, 289, 364, 366, 473n65

Kent County, MI, 256, 420, 454

Kenyon, Nathan, 403, 405

Kenyon's Hall, 544

Keokuk (IA), 342

Keppel, Anna Helena Van Raalte (Mrs. Bastian Dirk) (granddaughter), 568

Keppel, Bastian Dirk, 568

Keppel, Johanna Wilhelmina "Mina" Van Raalte (daughter) (Mrs. Peter J. Oggel, and Mrs. Teunis Keppel), 353-54, 357, 447, 449, 475, 501, 534, 540, 545, *547,* 549, 563, 566; and Keppel marriage certificate, *546*

Keppel, Teunis, *547,* and ACVR, 545-46, 563, 566; as elder, 313-14, 446, 475-76, 560, 571; and marriage certificate, *546*; as pioneer settler, 221-23, 545; and Van Raalte, Maria Wilhelmina (died in infancy), 569

Kerler, I. John, Jr., 386, 390, and Kerler & Co., 387

Kist, Nicolaas, 41-42, 45, 147

Kitto, John, 320

kleine luijden (lit. "little people"), 55, 161

Kleinheksel, Anna Vera "Vera" (granddaughter), 569

Kleinheksel, Frank De Moen (grandson), 569

Kleinheksel, John H., 563, 567

Kleinheksel, John Lewis (grandson), 569

Kleinheksel, Paul Edwin (grandson), 569

Kleinjan, Derk Jans, 114

Klokkenberg, De (school), 118n16

Klyn (Klijn), Hendrik G. 149,
  247, 300, 301, 304, 389, 577
Knickerbocker (ship), 378-81, 581
Knickerbocker: clerical garb,
  108, *109*; New York Dutch
  nickname, 205, 218, 290
Know Nothing (American)
  Party, 407, 419-20
Knox, Mr., 386
Koenen, H. J., 111
Kok, Frederik A., 127, 132, 144,
  151, 155
Kok, Harm, 218, 225n17
Kok, Wolter Alberts, *130*, 132,
  144, 148-49, 151, 155, 291,
  293, 298
Kolk, Kenneth E., 433n60
Kollen, Estelle Marie (Mrs.
  Jacob Carleton Pelgrim)
  (granddaughter), 569
Kollen, Gerrit Jan., 563, 566-67
Kollen, Maria (Mary)
  Wilhelmina Van Raalte (Mrs.
  Gerrit Jan Kollen), 239, 402,
  499, *565*
Kolvoord, Jan, 225n17, 235
Kolvoord, Lambertus, 235
Konijnenbelt, Martha, 87
Krabbendam, Hans, 161, 174
Krabshuis, Abraham, 296-97,
  300, 302
Kranz, Maria Hendrika (Mrs.
  Henry P. Scholte), 128,
  154n26, 214
Krom, Hermanus J., 29
Kromminga, John, 302
Kroon, Gerrit J., 242
Kruisgezinden (Cross Followers;
  Churches under the Cross),
  151, 467n50, 549; and schism,
  102, 104-6, 113-15, 134, 157

Kuiper, Arie C., 477n76
Kunk, William T., 345
Kuypenga, Klaas Pieters, 47
Kuyper, A. C., 553, 556
Kuyper, Abraham, 366, 486, 516,
  534-35, 577

La Crosse, WI, 197
Laarman, Geesje Schutte (Mrs.
  Jan), 218, 241
Laarman, Hendrik Jan, 241
Laarman, Jan, 218, 225n17, 241
Laarman, Widow, 218, 225n17
Labots, Jacob, 321, 478
Lake Erie, 191
Lake Huron, 190
Lake Macatawa. *See* Black Lake
Lake Michigan, 192, 202, 213-14,
  221, 497, 525
Laketown Twp. (Allegan County,
  MI), 375, 571
land policy: and ACVR, 251, 370-
  71, 376, 377, 379; and Federal
  Land Office, Ionia, 370, 372,
  374; and Homestead law, 499;
  and Land Ordinance of 1785,
  330; and land survey system,
  186, 193, 369, 373, 416; and
  Marshall Land Office, 374-76;
  and military bounty warrants,
  258, 374; and Swamp
  Land Acts, 400, 599; and
  survey(ing), 225, *226*, *227*, 242,
  255, 270-72, 377n26, *439*
land speculators, 196, 209, 213,
  368-74, 405, 583
Langdon, Elvira H., 239, 331-33
language: Algonquin, 201, 559;
  as barrier, 246, 282-83; and
  Dutch dialects, 223; formal
  Dutch, 34, 128, 146-47, 233,

268, in newspapers, 408-11, 416, 424-25, 456, 458, 490; English, 181, 207, 257, 533, 537, 543, 558, in books, 320, in schools, 331, 334, 337, 493, in worship, 176, 187, 246, 280, 282, 286, 302, 305, 339-40, 342, 357, 363, 453-54; German, 292; Greek, 5, 29, 144, 146-47, 153, 287, 305, 346; Hebrew, 5, 144, 146-47, 153, 348; Latin, 29, 34, 40, 45, 70, 74, 146-47, 289, 307, 334, 338, 344; and Latinized names, 3, 9; modern, 30, 205

Lankheet, Hermanus, 218, 225n17

Lasker, Fennegje, 180

Later [Nadere] Reformation, 40, 69, 104-5; Old Writers (17th century), 40, 47, 69, 83, 104-5, 130, 132; and books, 146

Latin school, 3, 74, 153

Lausanne (Switzerland), 98

lay preacher (*oefenaar*), 69, 78, 104, 128, 143, 145, 291; and Synod Utrecht, 102-3

Le Feburé, Johannes, 32, 40, 45, 72, 424, 550, 578

Leather City (Holland), 386

Ledeboer, Bernardus, 149, 422, 437-38, 441, 447, 454, 526, 564

Ledeboer, Katie Goetschius, 541, 563-64, 567, 583

Ledeboer, Lambertus, 101-2, 104, 149

Ledeboer., Alida, 454

Ledeboerweg (street) (Lemele, Ommen), 135-36

Lee, Robert E., 436

Leeuwarden (Friesland), 92, 123

Leiden (Zuid-Holland), 30, 33, 37, 72, 85; and cholera, 58, 175; and Christian school, 135n62; and De Moen family, 74-77, 319, 367, 548; economy, 75, 135; siege, 209, 265; and Van Raalte marriage, 72-73

Leiden [Zuid-Holland] Hervormde Kerk, 58, 77, 125, 135n62

Leiden [Zuid-Holland] Separated Church, 77, 135n62, 478

Leiden University, 4, 147, 424; and ACVR, 21-22, 28-46, 720, 127, 147, 162n13, 306, 550, 578; and University Hall, 35. *See also* Scholte club

Lemele (Lemelerveld) (Overijssel), 134-36, 138-40

Lemele-Archem Hervormde Kerk, 140

Lemelerveld (Overijssel), 135, 138, 140

Leuven (Belgium), 37

Leuze, Emanuel Gottlieb, 164

libel laws, 408-9

Liesveld, H. W., 504n65

Lincoln [NE] Reformed Church, 537

Lincoln, Abraham: and ACVR, 422-25, 434-37; assassination of, 437-38, 459; and Civil War, 424, 459; policies of, 421n36, 423; and Thanksgiving Day as holiday, 293

Lindeman, Marvin, 586

Lindeman, Sebilla Wilhelmina, 74

Lindermann, Helena, 74

Little Traverse Bay, 376

Little Water House (*het Waterhuisje*), 233
Littlejohn, Flavius T., 205n41, 255
Littlejohn, Silas F., 271
Livingston, David, 452
Livingston, Edward, 345
Log Church, Holland, *244*, 240-50, 268, 271, 293, 311, 317, 331, 376, 402, 545; South Holland, 292; Zeeland, 264-67
Lokkers' log cabin, *222*
London Conference (1830), 35
London Mission Society, 452
London, England, 463, 471
Long Island, NY, 344
Lord's Day, 129, 251, 297, 306, 317; sermons, 542. *See also* Sabbath observance
Lord's Supper, 87, 91-92, 94, 131, 353, 415, 423, 460, 549; and feast days, 293; regulation of, 107, 129, 295, 300, 364, 414, 459; and wine, 419
Louis Napoleon ("King of Holland"), xix, 6
Louisville, KY, 432
Low Prairie, xxii, 479
Lower Gelderland, 127
Lucas, Henry S., 387
Luther, Martin, 147
Lutheran Church (NL), 29, 32, 35, 74

Maatschappij tot Nut van 't Algemeen (Society for Public Welfare), 41-42
Macatawa River. *See* Black Lake
Mackinac Island, 193
Mackinaw, Straits of, 190, 207
Maksabe, Joseph, 228
malaria (ague), 236-37, 270, 445, 447n5
Manhattan, KS, 538
Manito [IL] American Reformed Church, 532-33, 566, 569
Manlius [New Richmond] post office, 384
Mansier, Jan, 23
Manson, Nathan, Jr., 224
Manting, Geert, 540
Maple Creek (Holland), 250
maple sugar making, 210, 212
Margriet, Princess (NL), 587
Marigold Lodge, 528
Marion County, IA, 422
Market Days: Holland, 275; Ommen (Overijssel), 116. *See also* agriculture, US
Market Square, 436, 543, 547. *See also* Centennial Park
Market Street CRC, 105, 280, 296n43, 297, 300, 303, 448, 468, 477-78, 511, 525
marriage, 81, 116, 152, 179, 286, 324, 402, 529; banns, 68n4; civil, 12, 16-17, 72, 75; interracial, 211; registers, 12, 15; religious, 15, 17, 69; of Van Raalte children, 546-47, 563, 567-69; Van Raalte-De Moen, 72-73, 75, 77, 80, 503, 506-7; Van Raalte-Harking, 8-10, 22-23; witnesses, 241-42
Marsh, Charles, 239
Marsh, Wells, 239
Marshall, MI, 205, 461; and State Land Office, 374-75
Martin, George, 266

Masonic Order (Masons). *See* Freemasonry

Mastenbroek [Overijssel] Separated Church, 67-69, 71, 77-83, 91-92, 94, 112, 114, 574. *See also* Genemuiden [Overijssel] Separated Church

Mattoax [VA] Presbyterian Church, 495

Mattoax [VA] Reformed Church, 455

McClellan, George, 425

McNeish, David, 305

medicine, 22, 40; and ACVR, 202, 237-38, 350, 432, 501; and hard liquor, 583; and patent, 236-37, 445, 503, 546; practice of, 74, 202, 237, 454, 460

Medina [MI] Reformed Church, 282n7

Meerburg, George F. Gezelle, 53; and the Almkerke church, 49, 67, 127, 183; and ACVR, 70, 72, 147n11, 149, 151; and baptism, 107; and garb, 108

melodeon (reed organ), 502

Memorial Day, 532, 542-43

Mennonites (Doopsgezinden), 145, 533

Mensink, Mannes, 150

Menzel, Carel Godfried, 72

Menzel, Christiaan Fredrich (Gottlieb), 74-75

Menzel, Johanna Maria Wilhelmina, 74-75

Menzel, Willem Fredrik, 72

Meppel (Overijssel), 94

Methodist Episcopal Church, 453, 458, 513

Methodists, 193, 200, 331, 473, 513; and Michael J. Clapper, 457-59

Mexican War, 167n26, 258, 370, 374. *See also* land policy

Meyer, Hannes, 571

Meyerink, Jantjen, 241

Michigan Central RR, 191, 195-96, 215, 218; and ACVR, xv, 577

Michigan Lake Shore RR, 511, 527; and mortgage bonds, 401; and Pere Marquette RR, xvii, 401

Michigan: banking, 407; boosters, 193-99; chosen, by ACVR, 110, 185-86, 209-11, by Vande Luyster, 232-33; and college charters, 352; as frontier Democrat stronghold, 265, 409; historic markers, 559; and Holland fire relief, 515-16; House of Representatives, 564; Indian Agency, 196n23, lands, 376; land grants, 255, 272, 374-75, 400, 401; as major Dutch region, xxi, 27, 277, 575; number of Christians in, 488, 508; poor reputation of, 236; and prohibition, 419-20; rejected by Scholte, 215-16; and land grants, 255, 272, 374-75, 400, 401; and State Land Office, Marshall, 374-75; Supreme Court, 457n30

Michmerhuizen, Hendrik Grijpmoet, 241

Middel, Harmen Hendriks, 154

Middelburg [Zeeland] Separated Church, 154

Middelstegracht, Leiden, 76
Middelstum Classis, 47-48
Middle Dutch Church (NYC), 176
Midwolda (Groningen), 145
military bounty warrants, 258, 374. *See also* land policy
mills (milling), 166, 264, 269, 276, 368, 383, 521, 526, 572, 583; coffee, 385; flour, 256, 383-85, 391, 513; saw, 210, 229-30, 256, 280, 391, 411, 481; water, 387
Milner, Joseph, 146
Milwaukee [WI] Reformed Church, 303-4, 484
Milwaukee, WI, xv, xxi, 190, 193, 280, 386; and ACVR, 185-86, 190, 197, 209, 303, 381; and Dutch settlers, 166-67, 170, 185, 192, 208, 381; markets, 210, port, 214
Ministry of Religion (NL), 111. *See also* Hervormde Kerk Nederland (HKN)
missions: and ACVR, xiii, xiv, 39, 301, 304-5, 312, 405, 483-84, 486-87, 529-30, 536-38, 574, 584, and China, 450n11, and South Africa, 449-52; and Classis of Holland (RCA), 402, 452-53, 493, 543; and Fairbanks, 201; and First Holland RCA, 248-49; and Mina Van Raalte Oggel, 566; and missionary ship, 454, 482; and RCA, 349, 437, 532; and George Smith, 200, 203, 212, 219-20, 245. *See also* Board of Domestic Missions;

Board of Foreign Missions; Old Wing Mission
Mississippi River, 197, 221, 342, 435; and riverboats, 213-14
Missouri Compromise of 1820, 420
Missouri, 208
Moerdyke, Peter, 296n43, 416n72, 584-85
Moes, Adrian, 229
Molenaar, Dirk, 57, *58*, 146
monetary units, NL (cent, florin, guilder, penningen, rijksdaalder, shillings, stuivers, willempjes), xxii, xxii, 13n23, 81-82, 98, 116, 118, 160, 164, 166, 170, *171*, 187
Montagne, Israel, 72
Moore, Orlando H., 433-34
Morse, Samuel F. B., 360
Mottville [MI] Reformed Church, 282n7
Mt. Baldhead (Saugatuck dune), 272
Mt. Pisgah (Holland dune), 272
Mulder, Ben, 570
Muntinghe, Herman, 46
Muscatine, IA, 342
Muskegon County, MI, 571
Muskegon, MI: and ACVR, 280, 476, 568; churches, 304, 511; and Cohen Stuart, 526; parochial school, 355, 357n74

Nadere Reformatie, 40, 69, 104-5, 577; Old Writers (17th century), 40, 47, 69, 83, 104-5, 130, 132, 146; and books, 146
Napoléon Bonaparte (Emperor of France), xiii-xx, *7*; and

Civil Registry, 12; and Code, 54-55, 79, 81; era of, 5, 12; and father Van Raalte, 8, 14; military conscription of, 12, 14; religious policy of, 6-7; trade policy of, 3; and United Provinces, 6
Napoléon Bonaparte, Lodewÿk, 6
Napoleonic Code, 54-55, 79, 81
Natelborg, Derk, 163
National [General] Synod Regulations (1816), 15-18, 35, 40, 48, 108; and ACVR, 56-61, 64, 122, 573; and father Van Raalte, 24
National Assembly (NL), 6
National Banking System, 403. *See also* banks (banking)
National Christian Convention, 473
National Day of Prayer for Crops and Industry, 485
Native Peoples. *See* Indians
nativism, 407, 419-20; and prohibition (alcohol), 269, 420-22, 578
Naturalization Law (1802), 419
Nauta, Rein: and ACVR hypothesis, 23n51
Nebraska, 531, 537, 539
Nederduitse Gereformeerde Kerk, 6, 10, *12*, 55, 70. *See also* Hervormde Kerk Nederland (HKN)
Nederlands Hervormde Kerk. *See* Hervormde Kerk Nederland (HKN)
Netherlander, De (newspaper), 411
Netherlands (NL): and ACVR homecoming, 464-70, 575; church affiliation, 215; and Christian education, 364-66, civil registry, 12; and class distinctions, 269, 289, 424, 492; economy, 158-63, 165-67, 172-73; and emigration, 165-67, 173-78, 183, 232, 490; and French conquest, xix-xx, 6-8, 12, 17, 54; monetary units, 13, 164; national motto, 214, 409; and Prussian invasion, 4; and religious unrest, 97-99, 106, 158-61, 240, 325, 449; royal coat of arms, *521*; royalty, xv, xxi, 6, 15-17, 22-25, 30-31, 35, 38, 54, 60, 223, 367, 587; Society for Public Welfare, 41-42; US ambassador, 554; and voting rights, 260-61
Netherlands East Indies, 167-68
Netherlands Reformed Church, xiii, xx, 1, 49, 63, 580. *See also* Hervormde Kerk Nederland (HKN)
Netherlands Society for the Protection of Immigrants from Holland, 205-6
neuralgia, 350
New Amsterdam, WI, xxi, 279
New Brunswick Theological Seminary (NJ), 195, 288, 302-3, 325n113, 337, 341, 348, 349, 448, 453, 504, 525, 596
New Groningen, MI, 291
New Jersey, 150, 582
New Orleans, LA, 188, 208, 213, 432
New Richmond (Manlius) MI, 219, 384

New Year's Day, 95, 202, 248; Eve, 199; and worship, 245
New York Central RR, xv, 461
New York City: and ACVR fundraising, 274, 322, 325, 335, 342, 344-45, 354, 359-60, 446, 500, 501, 562, 587, for medical treatment, 546, for RPDC synods, 282, 302, 424, 484, 489, 500, 501, 574, 587, to recruit settlers, 232-33; Anti-Masonic party, 474; Christian academy, 337; churches, 176, 187-88, 192, 259n92, 282, 304, 322, 335, 344, 545; and De Witt, 187-88, 206, 237, 317, 343; draft riots, 427, 433; as evangelical center, 249, 321, 457, 459, 488, 524, 579; as financial center, 274, 391, 395, 404; friends, 187-88, 197n, 206n44, 394, 520, 527, 545; harbor, 176, 180, 186, 188, 221, 232; immigrant aid, 172, 205, 520; markets, 196, 208, 229, 320, 380-81, 389, 397; as medical center, 454, 460; newspapers, 173, 261n98, 276; and Palmer, 372; and Phelps, 348, 461; as rail center, xxii, 186-87, 214, 344, 461; and Roost, 274; and Schermerhorn, 372; and Schieffelin family, 342, 394, 460, 536-37; and Suydam, 394; and Taylor, 333-34, 338, 340; and Van Raalte party, 186, 190, 192, 221, 290-91, 597; and Wyckoff, 187-88

New York University: honors ACVR, xiv, 423-24
New York, 213-14, 221, 579, 582; and Old Dutch, 290; and RPDC, 64, 219, 246, 282, 579. *See also* Christelijke Afgescheiden Kerk, and its particular and provincial synods; Hervormde Kerk Nederland (HKN); Reformed Church in America; Reformed Protestant Dutch Church
Newark, MI. *See* Saugatuck, MI
newspapers, xiv, 173, 261n98, 276, 405-16; rivalries among, 422-24
Newton, John, 320
Nibbelink, Jacobus, 503n61; livery hearse, 557
Nibbelink, Seth, 178
Nichols, S. D., 205n41
Nichols, William W., 326
Nieuwe Waterweg (New Waterway), 178n58
Nieuwe Zijds Achterburgwal, Amsterdam, 90
Nieuwleusen (Overijssel), 94
Nijlant, L., 80
Nijmegen (Gelderland), 118
Nijverdal (Overijssel), 134
Ninth Street, Holland: and Cappon House, 540; as commercial center, 564; and First RCA, 475; and Hope College, 311; and liveries, 503, *556*
Noordbarge (Drenthe), 176n51
Noord-Brabant, province of, 20, 29, 32, 49, 67, 499; Reformed churches, 122-23, 127, 129, 132, 225, 287

Noordeloos (Zuid-Holland), 297
Noordeloos, MI: colony, 233; creek, 233; Reformed Church, 167, 297-300, 418
Noord-Holland, province of, xxii, 67; Reformed churches, 129, 132
Norfolk, VA, 489-90
North Holland, MI, 167n26, 233; Reformed Church, 291, 297-98, 449, 479
North Reformed Protestant Dutch Church (NYC), 322
North Sea, 111-12, 178, 180, 388
Northport, MI, 212
Nortier, Mr. (paperhanger), 33
Norwegians, 270
Notting, Jennigje, 384
Notting, Macheldtje, 219, 236
Notting, Willem, 218, 225n17, 384
Nyenhuis, Jacob E., 454, 588
Nykerk, Gerrit, 446

Odawa (Ottawa) band, 193, 199, 200; and Chief Wakazoo, 200, 208, 211; and farming, 199, 201. *See also* Indians
Oggel House, 349
Oggel, Albertus Christian, 451-52
Oggel, Engelbert Christian, 330n4, 479
Oggel, J. P., 150
Oggel, Mina Van Raalte (Mrs. Peter). *See* Van Raalte, Maria (Mary) Wilhelmina (Mrs. Peter J. Oggel) (Mrs. Teunis Keppel)
Oggel, Peter J., and ACVR, 150, 330n4, 349, *451*, 481, 491, 495, 549; death of, 566, 575; and First Holland RCA, 446, 481; as fundraiser, 352, 446; and Grand Haven RCA, 304; as Hope College professor, 451n13, 454, 497; and Pella RCA, 449, 451, 471, 576; as synod delegate, 446. *See also* Van Raalte, Maria (Mary) Wilhelmina (Mrs. Peter J. Oggel) (Mrs. Teunis Keppel)
Ohio River, 176, 214, 221, 432; steamboats, 232
Ohio: and ACVR, 546; and Dutch settlers, xxi
Old Baldhead (Holland dune), 272, 365, 367-68, 379, 467, 507-8, 534, 575
Old Dutch Church (NY), 285, 290, 294, 297, 299, 301. *See also* Reformed Protestant Dutch Church
Old Dutch, 171, 187, 205, 209, 215, 274, 276, 288, 290, 515. *See also* Young Dutch
Old Groningen, *237, 264,* 290-91, 540
Old School Presbyterians, 194n19, 355
Old Wing Mission, 199-202, 219; and ACVR, 199, 200, 219, 376, 396, 520; and ague, 236; and mission home, *200*; and Odawa band, 200, 509
Old Writers (17th century), 40, 47, 69, 83, 104-5, 130, 132, 146; and books, 146
Oldemeyer, Hendrik, 225n17
Olive Twp., MI, 396-98
Olivet College, 354, 566

Ommen (Overijssel): and ACVR, 55, 81, 86-88, 91-95, 100, 109, 113, 131, 151-52, 307, 467, businesses, 134-35, 367-68, 379, 381, 575, family, 22, 23, parsonage and school, 115, razed, 114; Ambt, 81; factories, 134-41; Christian school, 117-19, 330, 365, 534; Classis of, 80, 120; market days, 116; mayor, 81, 88, 92; Oude Gereformeerde Kerk, 121; royal recognition of, 120-32; seminary, 144-50, 153, 155, 259, 304; Separated Church, 30-31, 63, 81, 86-89, 91-94, 104-5, 114, 116-18, 121, 128, 142, 191, and persecution, 88-89, and schism, 104-5; and Van Raalte family, 22-23, 141-42, 507-8. *See also* Christian education

Oostburg, WI, xxii, 292

Oostendorp, Lubbertus, 128

Oosterbeek (Gelderland), 170

Orange City, IA, xxi, 499, 539

Orange Free State (South Africa), 276

Orangists, the Netherlands, xix, 15, 36n20, 209, 266, 516; William of Orange, 265

Orphan House, 238, 332, 337, 339, 342, 360

Ossewaarde, Delia (Mrs. Frank De Moen Kleinheksel), 569

Otsego, MI, 200, 218, 222

Ottawa County, MI: and ACVR citizenship, 267, and delinquent tax auctions, 371, 400, and newspapers, 407; and agriculture, 229n23; board of school inspectors, 331, 335; board of supervisors, 260, 265; courthouse, 203; Circuit Court, 387, 457n30; and Holland city, 277; and Hollanders, 380; politics, 261-62, 419-20, 424; and officials, 195, 204, 254, 261, 266, 369, 387; realignment, 277, 570-71; roads, 254

Ottawa Register (newspaper), 269

Ottawa Township (Ottawa County), 260

Oude Gereformeerde Kerk, Ommen. *See* Ommen (Overijssel)

Oude Schrijvers. See Old Writers (17th century)

Overijssel, province of: ACVR as apostle of, xiv, xx, 67-99, 105-6, 112, 142, 145, 157, 254, 306, 538, 582, businesses, 134-42, fines, 58, as seminary professor, 143-52; agrarian economy of, xx, 67, 77, 156; and Bible Belt, 1; churches, xxii, 10, 68, 80, 91-92, 103, 112, 121, 128, 131-32, 149, 151-52, 209, 292, 234, 292-93; dialect, 19; and father Van Raalte, 1-19; governor, 13, 67, 78, 81; minister of internal affairs, 80; minister of religion, 13; Twente district of, 134; Zwolle, 150. *See also* provincial synods

Overijssels-Gelders party (Brummelkampianen), 129-

33, 132n55, 149, 280, 284, 300, 303, 467-68, 578-79
Overisel [MI] Reformed Church, 234, 246, 248, 282n7, 284-85, 377, 409, 414, 523
Overisel, MI, 250, 254, 449, 526; colony, 234, 260, 380; roads, 250, 255; township, 275, 377
Owen, John, 320

P. F. Pfanstiehl & Co., 386
Padgett, Thomas, 398
Palmer, Courtland, 372, 373n15, 378, 394-95
Palmer, William R., 373n15
Palmyra, NY, xxi
Parisian Shoe Shop, 386
Park Twp., MI, 260
parochial schools, 357n74; and ACVR, 356, 363-66, 482, 486; and Reformed churches: in Amelia (VA), 493, in Grand Haven, 357n74, in Grand Rapids, 355, in Holland, 318, 345, 356, 358, 360-63, in Kalamazoo, 355, 357, in Muskegon, 355, 357n74, in Pella (IA), 357n74, 358, 451, in Wanneperveen (NL), xx, 25; and Reformed Church Synod, 355-57; and Samuel Schieffelin, 355, 357
Particular Synod of Albany (NY), 286-87, 303, 312n81, 336, 351, 355
Particular Synod of Chicago, 302, 312n81, 342
Paterson, NJ, xxi, 280
Patriots: Netherlands faction, 4
Paw Paw Park, 233n30

Paw Paw Road (Drive), 220, 229, 233n30, 236, 258, 263, 540
Peace Democrats, 436
Pearce, John D., 205n41
peat: as fuel, 11, 139
Pekin [IL] Reformed Church, 484
Pelagius, 41, 239
Pelgrim, Jacob Carleton, 569
Pella Gazette (newspaper), 420, 422
Pella Weekblad (newspaper), 516
Pella, IA, 239; and ACVR, 342-44, 358, 360, 446, 451, 516, 543; as city of refuge, 162; and First Reformed Church, 342-434, 358, 449, 471, 476, 477n76, 478-79, 576; and parochial school, 357n74; and Scholte colony, xxi, xxii, 162, 206, 214-15, 421, 499, 532, 582; and Scholte lands, 378, 422; and True Reformed Church, 471. *See also* Iowa
penningen (pennies), 13
Pennoyer, Henry, 195, 203, *204*, 295n41, 240, 254, 369, 376, 377, 522
Pennsylvania RR, 214
Pennsylvania, 582
People's Assembly, 250, 254, 260, 270, 276, 331, 376, 380, 418
Pere Marquette RR, xvii, 401
persecution (religious), 67-69, 79-99
pew rental: Ommen, 116, 120; Holland, 245, 317, 477, 561
Pfanstiehl, Albert, 437
Pfanstiehl, Helena Mastenbroek, 401n79

Pfanstiehl, Pieter (Peter) F., 386, 400, 401n79
Phelps, Hannah, 461
Phelps, Margaret Jordan (Mrs. Philip), 478, 502
Phelps, Phillip, Jr., *349, 353*; and ACVR, as "begging" partners, 349-53, 453, 461, as confidant, 326, 346, 349, 397, 403-4, 432, 447, 449-50, 456, 458, 460-61, 468, 486n8, 487, 489, 515, 518, 537, 560, and falling out, 524, 528, funeral preacher, 555-56, 560, as Hope College cofounders, 349n54, 351-53, 498, 527-29; biography, 344, 348-49, 515; and Christina Johanna Van Raalte, 497, 501-2; and Holland Academy, 346-50, *349*; and Holland Fire, 515-16; and Hope College, xvii, 349, *351*, 489; and Hope RCA, 478; and missionary ship, 454
Philadelphia, PA, 322, 340, 494, 527
Philip II (king of Spain), 265
piano, 447, 502
Pierce, Franklin, 267
Pieters, Aleida, 510, 584
Pieters, Helena (Helen) (Mrs. Frank De Moen Kleinheksel), 569
Pieters, Roelof, as ACVR's pastor, 517, 528, and his funeral, 554-55, 557; and Cohen Stuart, 525; and First Holland RCA, 447, 478-79, 481-82, 510; and Freemasonry, 474, 527; and Holland Fire, 511, 517; and hymn controversy, 581n10; and Netherlands assignment, 529
Pieterskerk (Leiden), 33, 37, 45, 76
piety: and ACVR, 310, 313, 431, 559, 577, 586; American, 195, 205, 357, 579; and Christina Van Raalte, 504, 507-8, 562; as derisive, 98-99; and father Van Raalte, 21, 24; and Réveil, 307; and Separatists, 84, 144. *See also* Kruisgezinden; Old Writers (17th century)
Pigeon Creek, 253-54
Pilgrim Home Cemetery, 229, 239, 242, 250, 372, 373n14, 396, 402, 480; Dr. Van Raalte Drive, 250; and Van Raalte gravestone, *558*
pilgrims: compared to Dutch Separatists, 281, 283
Pillar Church. *See* First Reformed [Pillar] Church, Holland
Pillsbury, Edna Dean (Mrs. Albertus Christian Van Raalte), 568
pinks (fishing boats), 111-12, 135, 381
Pioneer School, Holland, *339*, 333-43, 360, 458
pipe smoking, 23-24, 246, 270, 419; and ACVR, 24, 82, 231, 583
Piso's Cure (consumption), *503*
Pitcher, E. P., 335
Pittsburgh, PA, 176, 232, 473
Plainwell, MI, 200
Plan of Union (1801), 201, 249, 545
Plasman, Dirk, 225n17

Ploeg, Benjamin H., 447-48
Plokker, Maarten, 111n28
Plugger Mills, 448, 479n81, 480
Plugger, Aldert, 314, 497
Pluiger, Johannes A., 56
Plymouth Brethren movement, 128
Plymouth Rock of Michigan (historic marker, Paw Paw Drive), 233n30
Point Superior (Black Lake), 528
police: in Michigan, 327, 442n76; in Netherlands, xiii, xiv, 55, 69, 80-81, 85, 90-91, 121, 158; *See also* constables
Polkton [MI] True Holland Reformed Church, 300
Pope and his Cardinals (phrase), 264, 411, 413n12, 417
Pope Pius VII, 7n12
Pope: and ACVR accusation, xiv, 108, 182, 264, 301, 327, 411, 417, 573, 580
Port Sheldon Lumber Company, 398
Port Sheldon, MI, 221, 254
Port Washington, WI, 380n38
Porter, Augustus S., 195, 204-5
Post & Co., 261n98, 268n, 384, 387, 391
post offices: Black River, 384; Holland, 266, 384-85; New Richmond, 384; Zeeland, 266
Post, Anna Coatsworth, 267, *268*, 269, 384
Post, Henry D., *267*-68, as ACVR business partner, 230, 268-70, 323, 383-86, 390-93, 409-10, 582, and friend, 239, 248, 262, 267-69, 323, 522; and attitudes on church decorum, 246, on Dutch folks, 260, on tobacco, 246; and Hope RCA, 453; as justice of peace, 248; as merchant, 251, 261, 447, 562n58; as public official, 261-63, 266, 269, 321, 331, 333-34, 422
Post, Hoyt G., 246, 248, 261-62, 266, 269-70
Postma, Dirk P., 304
potash (factory), 210, 273, 383-84, 391
potato(es): in the NL, 67, 166; blight and famine, 160-61, 182; in Michigan, 210, 221, 235, 270, 322
Potawatomi chief, 228
Potgieter, Everhardus Johannes, 164
Pottenbakkerij (former De Moen & Co. pottery), *137*
Poughkeepsie, NY, 287, 500
Prayer Day: for crops and industry, 484; Netherlands, 102, 160-61; United States, 305, 323, 435
predestination, doctrine of: anti, 17, 48, 124; pro, 124n31, 131, 301
Preemption Act of 1841, 369
Presbyterian Church, 197-98, 375, 457, 532; and ACVR, 193, 201, 209, 306, 473; and Associate Reformed Church, 292; and Michigan boosters, 209; and Old School/New School, 194, 355; and Plan of Union, 201, 249, 545; Scotch-Irish Church, 193-94,

292, 574; *United Presbyterian* (periodical), 320. *See also* individual congregations
Princeton Seminary, 192
profession of faith, 16, 325, 448, 565
prohibition (alcohol), 269, 420-22, 578
Protestant Reformation, 11, 16, 29, 147, 268, 297, 309, 357, 582. *See also* Calvinist
provincial classes: of Drenthe, 154; of Friesland, 154; of Gelderland, 110, 113, 119, 150, 154, 598; of Groningen, 154; of Overijssel, 113, 148-49, 150, 154; of Zuid-Holland, 42, 154
provincial synods, 101: Gelderland, 154, 598; Overijssel, 102, 110, 146, 154-55 298; Utrecht, 5, 30; Zuid-Holland: and rejection of ACVR, 55-65
Pultneyville (East Williamson), NY, xxi, 190
Puritans, in England, 158; in New England, 41, 217; writings of, 40, 322
Putten (Noord-Holland), 467

Quebec, 471
Queens College, xiv, xv. *See also* Rutgers College (University)
Quintus, Jacob, 416-17

Rabbers, Jan, 221, 290-91, 371
Rabbit River, MI, 255
Racine [WI] Reformed Church, 484
rafts, 230, 253, 271, 383

railroads: and ACVR, xv, 400, 401, 461, 480n, 511, 527, 536; depots, 511; entrepreneurs, 195; and immigrants, 186, 196, 490, 539; and Pella, xxii, 214-15. *See also* individual railroads
Randstad (Noord-Holland, Zuid-Holland, Utrecht), 129
Ransom, Epaphroditus, 207, 255, 271, 374, 388
rationalism: and the Enlightenment, xv, xxi, 40; and the National Assembly, 6; theological, 17, 30, 46, 56n61, 111, 162, 578
Ravenshorst, Elias, 136, 138
reading worship services, 145, 313. *See also* worship
Reddingius, G. Benthem, 17
reed organ, 502
Reenders, Hommo, 63, 78, 132
Reformatie, De (church periodical), 45, 102, 128, 161, 166, 171, 214
Reformed Church in America (name of, post-1867) (RCA), 132, 150, 466; and ACVR, 302, 464-65, 545, 560; and Christelijke Afgescheiden Kerk, 460, 464-67; and Christian schooling, 364; and Classis of Holland, 246-47, 571-72; clerics, 497, 539, 584; and De Witt, 187, 281; and Freemasonry, 475, 581; General Synods: *1868*, 472-73, 484, 488-89; *1869*, 494, 527; *1870*, 473-74; *1874*, 475; *1877*, 528-29; *1879*, 570, *1880*,

475; and Hervormde Kerk Nederland, 302, 558; and Hope College, 276, 342, 348-53; membership (1880), 215, 564, 854; and name change, 579; and Secession of 1857, 302-3; Sunday schools, 290, 319, 447, 455-56, 545; and Union of 1850, 281-301; and *volk* baptism, 108; and Wyckoff, 187, 280. *See also* Board of Domestic Missions; Board of Foreign Missions

Reformed Church under the Cross, 151, 467n50, 549; schism, 102, 104-6, 113-15, 134, 157

Reformed confessions, 17, 289; and ACVR, 153, 286, 289, 466, 577; and Form of Subscription, 15-16, 56; and Hendrik De Cock, 47; and Separatists, 107, 110, 146; and state church leaders, 17, 19, 41, 46-47. *See also* Belgic Confession; Canons of Dort; Heidelberg Catechism

Reformed doctrine(s), 5, 17-18, 43, 47-49, 112; and ACVR, 61, 70, 76, 124n31, 288, 313, 420, 466, 575, 577; and Dort, 60-61, 102, 147, 310; of election (predestination), 48, 58, 124, 130-31, 296, 298, 300, 301, 533; of grace, 21, 337; of human depravity, 280, of preservation of saints, 310

Reformed Protestant Dutch Church (name of, pre-1867) (RPDC), 108, 188, 193, 233, 246, 280, 292, 297-98, 525; ACVR as synod delegate of, 282, 302, 312, 336, 355-56, 358, 424, 466, 484, 489, 500, 574, 587; board of domestic missions, 281, 284, 287, 289, 304-5, 336, 361, 493; clerics, 451, 478; colleges, 340; committee of education, 337, 579; and dropping "Dutch," 284-5, 579; and Freemasonry, 295-96; General Synods: *1840*, 285; *1844*, 176; *1846*, 281; *1847*, 281; *1848*, 281; *1849*, 282; *1850*, 284-87, 290; *1853*, 340-42, 355, 500; *1857*, 302, 345-46, 358-59; *1858*, 326, 361, 446; *1863*, 351-52; *1865*, 460, 464; *1867*, 472; and Holland Academy, 355-56; and parochial schools, 355-57, 363-66; and Secession of 1834, 300, 303-4, 448, 466, 485; and Union of 1850, 289-90, 445, 574; and *volk* baptism, 108. *See also* Reformed Church in America; Particular Synod of Albany (NY); Particular Synod of Chicago

regional classes: of Apeldoorn, 101; of Middelstum, 47-48; of Ommen, 80, 101, 120, 151; of Zwolle, 79, 101, 105, 121

Remonstrants, 29, 41, 59, 524

Renswoude (Utrecht), 5-8, 12, 20, 30, 55

Republican Party: and ACVR, 407, 420-24; and elections: *1852*, 267; *1860*, 425; *1864*, 425-26; *1868*, 438; *1876*, 550; and Know Nothing (American)

Party, 407, 419-20; and newspapers, 424-25; and political revolution, 437-38; and Roost, 274, 424. *See also* Whig Party
Réveil, 28, 30-32, *33*, 64, 130-31, 134, 236; and Hague circle, 59
revivals: and ACVR, 310, 457-59, 488, 583; and Clapper, 457-59, 488; and New York City, 322-23, 459, 488; and RPDC, 172, 289, 579
revolutions of 1848, 162
Rhine River, 152, 165, 169, 507, 522
Richmond & Danville RR, 490
Richmond, MI, 215
Richmond, VA, 489-91, 498
Ridgeway [MI] Reformed Church, 282n7
rijksdaalder, 164, 170, *171*
Rijsoord (Zuid-Holland), 19, 29
Rijssen (Overijssel), 93-95, 148
road(s): NL, 11, 67, 95, 114; US, and AVCR, 213, 242-50, 276, 327, 368, 415, 572; Allegan, 255-56; early roads map (ca. 1850), *257*; Grand Haven, 254-55; Grandville (Dutch Road), 255-59; Holland colony, 186, 196, 210, 222n13, 229, 254-64, 269; and Indians, 219-20; and Pella (IA), 214-15; and People's Assembly, 376; and Zeeland, 258. *See also* bridge(s), Paw Paw Road
Robinson, John, 34
Rochester [NY] [Reformed] Church, 350
Rochester, NY, 189, 295, 310, 461
Rock Island, IL, 342

Roelevelt, Cornelis, 111n28
Roetman, Albert, 69
Romeyn, Anna, 194
Romeyn, Theodore, *198*; and ACVR, 194-95, 197, 203, 503; biography of, 193; and Detroit working committee, 204-7, 218, 507
Roost, John (Roest, Jan), *274*, and harbor bonds, 274, 400n77; as Republican leader, 421, 424
Rosecrans, William S., 435
Roseland, IL, xxi, 304
Rotterdam (Zuid-Holland), 470; churches, 111, 151, 524; as seaport, 172, 175-76, 178, 213-14, 232, 454, 463, 490, 507; and ship brokers, 175
Rotterdam, KS, 536, 539
Rouveen (Overijssel), 86, 293, 298
Royal House. *See* Dutch monarchy
royal recognition of churches, 55, 60n68, 102, 110-11, 114-15, 120-23, 142, 152, 161, 174
Rozendom, Hendrika Johanna, 242
Rutgers College (University), xv, 205, 336, 340, 345, 347, 351-53, 424, 504, 528
Rutherford, Samuel, 320
rye cropping, 160-61, 302

Sabbath observance, 167, 241; and ACVR, 64n79, 81, 116, 305; and Christian Separatists, 112; and Christina Van Raalte, 507-8; and Henry Post, 251; and King Willlem I, 25
salaries (stipends), 13, 80n34, 151, 153, 259, 284, 301, 478;

Index   663

and ACVR, 81, 112, 114, 125, 151, 153, 313-14, 368, 379, 477, 526; and Brummelkamp, 151; and C. Doesburg, 363, and Hendrik de Cock, 48, 77; and Taylor, 340, 346, 348; and Van Olinda, 362; and Veenhuizen, 146, 153

Sara Johanna ("Separatist pink" ship), 111

Sauer, Geraldine "Jerry" Maude (Mrs. John Lewis Kleinheksel), 569

Saugatuck, MI, 205, 229, 230n25, 511; harbor, 383; Mt. Baldhead, 272; Twp., 571

sawmills, 210, 244, 256, 291, 385, 391, 393n57; and Van Raalte, 383, 385-86, 389

Schaddelee, Kommer, 403, 423, 427, 438, 520

Schenectady, NY, 286, 290

Schepers, Jacob R., 290-92, 298, *299*

Schermerhorn, Peter, 372, 378

Scherpenisse (Zeeland), 10, 19-20, 29

Scheuer, Wilhelm, 78, 80

Scheveningen (Zuid-Holland): 111-12, 135, 381

Schiedam (Zuid-Holland), 144, 150-51

Schieffelin Brothers & Co. (NYC), 342

Schieffelin, Jacob, 342n39

Schieffelin, James L., 342, 460, 537

Schieffelin, Philip, 342, 537

Schieffelin, Samuel B., *343*; and ACVR, 394-95, 460-61, 491n22, 495, 497, and mortgage receipt, *396*; and Christian education, 344, 350, 352, 355-58, 537; and Holland colony benefactor, 342

schism. *See* Kruisgezinden; Secession of 1834; Secession of 1857

Schoemaker, Harm, 95

Scholte Church (Pella), 343

Scholte club, 40, 45, *53*, 56n61, 60, 64, 77n23. *See also* Leiden University

Scholte, Hendrik (Henry) P., *53*, *422*; and ACVR, 59-60, 69-70, 93, 111-12, 144, 153, 183, 218-22, as friends, xxi, 31, 91, 136, 420, as rivals, xxi, xxii, 183, 213-16, 221, 232-33, 343, 532; businesses, 40n32; career of, 32, 35-36, 65, 128-29, *420*; as Christian Separatist leader, 62, 64-65, 67, 69, deposed, 123-29, 137, 142; and church polity, 102-3, 105-10, 129-34, 174, 233; as Congregationalist, 102, 183, 343; as emigrant leader, 129, 161-62, 166-68, 171, 173-74, 176, 178, 183, 187, 197; and Hendrik de Cock, 47-49; and Java, 167-68, and military service, 34-35; as millennialist, 162; as newspaper editor, 166, 171, 214, 420; and politics, 420-24; and Pella colony, xxi, 214-15, 343, 532; and Réveil, 32; and royal recognition, 110-11, 120; as seminary professor, 144, 149, 153, 416; and student club, 28, 40-43, 45, *53*, 56n61,

59-60, 64, 77n23; training pastors, 144, 149, 232, 416; and Utrecht Christian Association for Emigration, 171, 214; and Utrecht Church Order, 71n10, 103, 125, 128; and wives, 128, 154n26, 214; and Zeelanders, 206n44, 232-33
Scholte, Sara Johanna, 111
School Law of 1806 (NL), 14
Schoolland, Marian M., 510
schools: 25, 67, 114, 131, 262, 330-36, 355, 357, 365, 368, 402, 566, 592; and ACVR, 327, 329-30, 364-66, 552, 579-81, in Amelia, 493; and language, 280; postsecondary, 348-53, 555; and RCA, 287, 486-87, 517; secondary, 336-48, 493; under Napoleon, xxii, 14; and Van Raalte children, 353-55. *See also* Christian schools; parochial schools
Schotsman, Nicolaas, 31
Schouten, Roelof, 557
Schrader, Jacobus, 315
Schultz, John, 313
Schurr, John, 387
Schuurman, Jan, 150n17
Scotch-Irish [Scotse] Church, 193-94, 292, 574
Scott, Winfield, 267
Seaman, Ezra C., 195, 204-5
Seaver, George A., 334-35
Secession of 1834, xiii, xiv, xvii, 16, 38, 46-52, 61n73, 63, 65, 77, 81, 106, 133, 143, 146, 175, 459; Act of, 50-52; and ACVR, 62-65, 132, 147, 420, 454, 464; and "fathers," 53-54, 144; and Hendrik de Cock, 48-52, 81; and Hervormde Kerk Nederland, 173-75; and social class, xv; and Van Raalte trek in Drenthe, *133*
Secession of 1857, 290-301, 468; condemned by ACVR, 301-3, 446, 466-67, 578, revisited, 485-87, 579-80
Second Great Awakening, 31, 289-90, 310, 525, 579
Second Reformed Church, Albany, NY, 172, 187, 348
Second Reformed Church, Grand Rapids, 545
secret societies. *See* Freemasonry
seditious libel, 410-11
Selma, AL, 489
semicentennial, Holland. *See* centennials, Holland
seminaries: at Arnhem, 113, 153-56, 339, 478; at Groningen, 132, 151, 155; at Holland Academy, 317, 325n114; at Hoogeveen (DR), 132n55, 144, 149, 151, 155; at Kampen (OV), 126, 147n10, 155-56, 175, 303, 345n46, 467, 468n52; at Ommen (OV), 113, 114n4, 142, 145-50; Princeton, 192; in United Kingdom, 34-35. *See also* Calvin Theological Seminary; New Brunswick Theological Seminary (NJ); Theological School Kampen; Western Theological Seminary, Holland
Seneca Falls [NY] Convention, 358
Separation, of church and state, 174

Separatist pinks, 111-12; at Scheveningen, 135, 381
Separatists of 1834. *See* Secession of 1834
sesquicentennial, Holland. *See* centennials
Seward, William, 422
sewing, 362, 440; machine, 352
sexton (*koster*), 14, 17, 244, 316, 437, 550
's Gravenhage (Zuid-Holland), 56-57, 59, 146, 168, 597
Sheboygan Nieuwsbode (newspaper), 259, 416
Sheboygan, WI, xxii, 183; county, 304
's-Heer Abtskerke (Zeeland), 18-19, 28
Shenick, Charles, 239, 283
Shepherd, Charles, 460
Sherburne, Harriet, 200
Sherman, William T., 435
's-Hertogenbosch (Den Bosch) (Noord-Brabant), 287
shipbrokers, 10, 73, 137, 175, 365
Shorno, Anton, 208
Silsbee, Nathaniel, 372, 378, 394
Singapore, MI, 230n25, 380, 383
Sioux County, IA, xxi, 240, 499. *See also* Iowa
Sixteenth Street, Holland: ACVR property, 228-29, 372, 396; Albertus and Helena farm, 477-78; Ben Van Raalte farm, 530, 562; and Log Church, 242
Slag, Harm, 378
Slag, Jan, 236, 373, 378, 386
Slaghuis, Abraham, 225n17
slavery, 280, 407, 418, 420, 425-26, 431, 435-36, 542; and abolition, 418, 420, 425-26; and Amelia colony, 495; and Van Raalte, 418-20, 426, 544, 578
Sleen (Drenthe), 133; map of, *290*
Sleyster, Roelof, 167, 172, 197
Sluiters, Hermanus H., 58, 61
smallpox, 79
Smijtegelt, Bernardus, 40
Smit, Frans, 225n17
Smit, Harm Jan, 292
Smit, Jansen, 88
Smit, Roelof, 263, 293-94, 298, *299*
Smith, Arvilla (Mrs. George), 199, *200*, 219, 224, 269, 499, 508-9
Smith, George N., 199, *200*, 202-3, 211-12, 219, 224, 228, 245; and family home, *201*, 504n16
Smith, Jeffrey Schaefer, 570
Smitt, Wolter W., 59, 104, *105*
smoking. *See* pipe smoking
Sneek (Friesland), 176n51
Socinianism, 32
sod house, *538*
Soetermeer, MI, 234, 258
soldiers (NL): and Belgian Revolt, 20, 29; Civil War, 426-27, 431, 433, 436-37, 542-44, 570; and Prussian invasion, 4; quartering of, xv, xvii, 79-89, 92-95
South Africa, xiii, 453, 531-55, 476, 529-31, 586; Cape Town, 276, 433-34; and slavery, 546
South Holland, IL, xxii, 479
South Holland, MI, 292, 294
South Holland, NL. *See* Zuid-Holland, province of

Southampton (England), 471
Southerner (schooner), 175, 180-82, 186, 213, 225, 463; ship model, *181*
Southworth, Ezra C., 205n41
speculators, land, 196, 209, 213, 368-74, 405, 583
Spring Lake American Reformed Church, Manito, IL, 532-33, 566, 569
Spykman, Gordon, 305-7, 309-10, 577
St. Clair [MI] Congregational Church, 192
St. Clair, MI, 218; river, 192; shipyard, 192
St. Joseph, MI, 192
St. Louis, MO, xxi, xxii, 176, 193, 197, 213-14, 221, 232, 280; and Dutch, 532
Stadskanaal (Groningen), 176n51
Standaard, De (Kuyper's newspaper), 486, 534
Staphorst (Drenthe), 263-64, 293, 298; consistory, 5, 293; immigrants from, 176n51, 233; mayor, 85-86, 89, 97; soldiers billeted at, 86
State Convention of Christians, 488
Statenbijbel (authorized Dutch Bible), 14, 146, 240
Statesland road, 263
steamboats, 126, 213-14, 232
Steenwijk (Overijssel), 94, 120, 128
Stegenga, Ale, 380
Stegeren (Overijssel), 95
Stegink, Jan Hendriks, 173
Steketee, Andries, 540

Steketee, George G., 438, 440, 442
Steketee, Jan, 232
Steuerwald, Johannes, 29
Stobbelaar, Hermanus, 481
Straw Hat Union, 8
Stuart, Charles, 271, 487
Stuart, Martinus Cohen, 524-26
Stuart, Robert, 193, *194*, 197, 208, 266
Sundag, Jan Barend, 130, 140, 233
Sunday school, 290; and ACVR address, 544-45; and CRC, 545; First Holland RCA, 319, 447, 455
Supranaturalism, 30n7
Suringar, Lucas, 41
Suydam Farm, 529
Suydam, James, 342, 344, 394-95, 527-28
swamps, 204, 213, 227, 254-55, 258, 517; Cedar Swamp, 220, 440; swamp lands, 400, 440, 597
Swedes, 270
Swierink, Annigje Van Raalte (Mrs. Rijnier) (Reinier, first wife), 3; Neeltje Van Raalte (second wife), 3n3
Swierink, Rijnier (Reinier), 3, 8
Swiss Réveil. *See* Réveil
Synod Amsterdam, Christian Separated Church: *1836*, 69-71, 110-11, 129, 198; *1840*, 108, 123-27, 129, 144, 148-49; *1843*, 128-29, 310; *1866*, 460, 464-65, 467, 485
Synod Groningen, Christian Separated Church: *1846*, 107, 126

Synod of Dort, 31, 60, 111-12, 115, 124-25, 132, 147, 301. *See also* Dort
Synod Utrecht, Christian Separated Church: *1837*, 102-10, 129, 134, 148
synods. *See* Christelijke Afgescheiden Kerk, and its particular and provincial synods; Hervormde Kerk Nederland; Reformed Church in America; Reformed Protestant Dutch Church
Syracuse, NY, 234

Taal, Matthijs, 111n28
tanneries, 152, 210, 386-87, 390, 441, 448, 513, 583
Tannery Addition (Holland), 386
Tannery Creek, 250
tax deeds, 369, 377n26
Taylor, Andrew B., 195, 202, 204, 295n41, *206*, 237, 346
Taylor, Anna, 333, 338
Taylor, Henry W., 205n41
Taylor, Hugh, 333-34
Taylor, Margaret, 333-34
Taylor, Walter T., 333, 337, *338*, 340-41
Te Roller, Derk, 358, *359*
Te Winkel, Jan W., 539
Tebbs Bend, KY, 434-35, 544
Teellinck, Willem, 40
Teessen, Anna Arendina Harking Van Raalte (sister) (Mrs. Johannes Teessen) 13, 23, 313, 499, 500, 563
Teessen, Johannes, 13, 23
temperance movement, 269, 420-22, 578

Ten Bokkel, Jan W., 118-19, 149, 150n17, 163
Ten Days' Campaign (Belgian Revolt), 37
Ten Tooren, Egbertus, bakery, *87*
Ten Zythoff, Gerrit, 61, 63
Tenth Street, Holland, 228, 316, 318, 333, 453
Ter Haar, Hein, 251
Terhorst, Johannes A., 286n16, 287n17
Ter Vree, Gerrit, 178
Teutonia (steamship), *463*
Texel (Noord-Holland), 388
The Hague, 56-57, 59, 146, 168, 597
Theological School Kampen, 126, 147n10, 155-56, 175, 303, 345n46, 460, 467, 468n52
Theological University of the Reformed Churches. *See* Theological School Kampen
theology. *See* Reformed confessions; Reformed doctrine(s)
Third Reformed Church, Holland, xvii, 473n65, 513-14, 525, 529, 543, 544-45
Tholen (Zeeland), 19
Thompson, John B., 345
Thompson, Oren C., 192
Thorbeke, Johan Rudolph, 162n13
Tichelarij, Lemele (Ommen), *136*
Tiel (Gelderland), 482
Tieleman, Adrien, 135n62
Tieleman, Casper, 135, 179
Tieleman, Wilhelmina, 179
Tieleman-Dros, Maria Elisabet, 135n62

Tilden, Samuel, 550, 552
Timmerman, Harm, 120
toga. *See* garb (clerical vestments)
Toledo, OH, 166, 546
Toonk, Johanna, 8
Transvaal (South Africa), 276
Tris, Abraham C., 146, 150
Trowbridge, Chester C., 195
Troy, NY, 188
True Brothers. *See* Christian Reformed Church (US)
True Holland Dutch Reformed Church (Holland), 105, 280, 296n43, 297, 300, 303, 448, 468, 477-78, 511, 525
True Holland Dutch Reformed Church (US). *See* Christian Reformed Church (US)
tuberculosis (consumption), 237, 347, 503; and ACVR, 549; and Annigje Van Raalte Swierink, 3n3; and Christina De Moen Van Raalte, 460, 503, 549, 567n60, 576; and Elizabeth Van Vleck, 346; and Johanna De Moen Van Velzen, 74, 92, 567n60, 576; and John Van Vleck, 346; and Mary Van Raalte Kollen, 567; and Peter J. Oggel, 451, 497, 575-76; and Petrus Van Raalte, 142; and Wilhelmina Menzel De Moen, 567
Twente district (Overijssel), 134
Twenty-Fifth Michigan Volunteer Infantry, 428, 431; and ACVR, 543-45; Company I, 432-36, 531, 543-44; reunion, 530. *See also* Civil War

Twenty-Fourth Street, Holland, 255, 383
typhus (typhoid), 157, 175, 236
Uelsen/Itterbeek (County Bentheim), 95
Uiterwyk, Henry, 525, 543, 545, 555, 557
Uithuizen (Groningen), 163
Ulberg, Tede, 284, 300
Ulrum [Groningen] Hervormde Kerk, 46-49; and Act of Secession (1834), 50-53; and Hendrik de Cock, 50-53, 61, 81
Union College (Schenectady, NY), 336, 348, 493
Union of 1850, 282-301, 413, 466; condemned by ACVR, 301-3; and Gysbert Haan, 295-97, 485; impact of, 303
Union Pacific RR, 537-38
Union School (Holland), 333, 366, 512
Unitarian(ism), 32
United Brethren, 473
United Kingdom of England and Ireland, 6
United Provincial Classes of Gelderland and Overijssel, 150-51
United Provincial Synod of Gelderland and Overijssel, 154, 596
United States coins (gold and silver), 186n3, 187, 370, 398
University of Groningen, 3, 46-47; and father Van Raalte, 3-4, 46; Groninger School, 46, 305; and Hendrik de Cock, 46
University of Leiden. *See* Leiden University

University of Michigan, xvi, xvii, 420, 585
University of Utrecht, 46-47, 307
US Centennial (1876), 547, 554, 586
Utrecht church order, 71n10, 103, 125, 127-28. *See also* Scholte Hendrik (Henry) P.
Utrecht Synod, Christian Separated Church (1837), 102-10, 129, 134, 148
Utrecht, province of, 5, 98, 137
Utrecht: and ACVR, 276, 463, 467; and Christian Association for Emigration, 171, 176, 214; and Christian Seceded Church of, 111, 120, 123, 127, 129-30, 134, 304; and father Van Raalte, 7, 30; and provincial synod, 5, 7, 30; and Scholte, 67, 71n10, 111, 125, 130, 144, 148, 173, 176, 416

vaccinations, 79, 236
Valley Twp., Allegan County, 255
Van Alstyne Harrington, Margaret (Mrs. George S.), *220*
Van Andel, Anna, 287
Van Anrooy, Johannes, 300
Van Assen, C. J., 39
Van Baalen, Henri W., 147n11
Van Dam, Adrianus, 227
Van de Luyster, Cornelia Van Malsen, 384
Van de Luyster, Jannes, 232, 261, 265, 371, 378, 380
Van de Luyster, Jannes, Jr., 150, 232n28, 245, 258, 295-96, 381, 384

Van de Meij, widow, 33
Van de Wall, Gilles, *434*; as ACVR confidant, 325, 363, 399, 431; and Cape Town RCA, 432, 452-53; family, 447; as newspaper editor, 410-11; as pastor, 325, 446; as teacher, 349, 409
Van den Boogard, Jan, 225n17
Van den Bosch, Koene, 298, *299*, 300, 418
Van den Broek, Theodorus, xxi
Van den Burg, Pieter, 264
Van den Dijk, Klaas, 111n28
Van der Brugghen, Justinus J. L., 118
Van der Haar, Elizabeth, 176
Van der Haar, Hein, 176, 221, 520
Van der Haar, Jannes, 79-80, 92
Van der Haar, Wilhelmina (Minnie) Van Raalte, 568
Van der Haar, Wouter, 176, 220, 221n10
Van der Haar-Visscher, Geesje (Grace), and ACVR, 101, 114, 555-56; and Christina Johanna Van Raalte, 269, 509; and emigration, 176-77; and Holland fire, 513; piety of, 68, 83, 240-41, 428
Van der Kemp, Carel, 64
Van der Linden, Hendrik Christian, 10
Van der Linden, Hendrik Cornelis, 23
Van der Linden, Johannes, 17
Van der Linden, Niescina Margaretha Anna (Van Raalte) (Mrs. Hendrik Christian), 10, 13, 23

Van der Meulen, Cornelius, *247*, *522*; and ACVR, 263, 389, 411-17, 519-23, recruited, xxi; as apostle of Zeeland, 160, 165; and Baxter book, 296; clerk of Holland Classis, 414n16; and Cohen Stuart, 525-26; and Den Bleyker, 389; and Ebenezer Memorial Fund, 523; death of, 416n20, 547; and emigration, 162, 232-33, 235, 522; and Freemasonry, 295; land dealings, 210, 377; as missionary pastor, 304; and Overijssels-Gelders party, 129; as pastor of Zeeland RPDC, 246, 263, 291, 317n96, 409, 411, 414, 453, 513, of First Chicago RPDC, 453, of Second Grand Rapids RPDC, 522, 525; and politics, 420-21; and Secession of 1857, 297; Scholte protégé, 127, 149, 232; and Union of 1850, 263; and Zeeland colony, 232, 235, 239, 258, 519-20, 522

Van der Meulen, Elizabeth (Mrs. Cornelius), 505

Van der Meulen, Jacob, 472

Van der Meulen, John, 472

Van der Palm, J. H., 15, 41

Van der Schuur, Koenraad (Koene) S., 292, 409

Van der Sluis, Oswald, 292, 385-86, 416-17

Van der Veen, Bartje, 422

Van der Veen, Christian, 241, 341, 447-48, 504, 533, 543, 557

Van der Veen, Engbertus, 212, 241, 244, 263-64, 316, 331, 415, 543, 572

Van der Veen, William, 543

Van der Werp, Douwe, 104, 105n11; *106*, 119, 466-68, 471

Van Dijk Mansier, Alberta Christina, 10, 25

Van Driele, Frans, 284, 545

Van Duren, Hendrik, 221n10

Van Elburg, E., 118

Van Eyck, Hendrik, 239

Van Eyck, William O., 203, 263, 584

Van Fasen, Jacoba, 260

Van Haitsma, Johannes, 300

Van Hall, Anne Maurits C., 83, *84*, 89, 111, 169

Van Hamelsveld, IJsbrand, 4n4

Van Hengel, Wessel A., 41-42, 45

Van Herwynen, Cornelis (Cornelius), 229, 260

Van Hinte, Jacob, 187n6, 193, 261, 277, 279, 415, 423, 541-42

Van Hogendorp, D., 41n36, 64

Van Hogendorp, Gijsbert Karel, xix

Van Hoorn, Paulus G., 72

Van IJsseldijk-Zeelt, Judith, 123n30, 137

Van Kampen, Jacob, 5

Van Landegend, John, 552

Van Leeuwen, Willem, 150, 154-55

Van Lente, Frederick J., 243

Van Lente, Johannes, 244, 520

Van Lippe-Biesterfeld, Margriet Francisca van Oranje-Nassau, 587

Van Lodenstein, Jodocus, 40

Van Maanen, C. F., 80, 84-85

Van Malsen, Cornelia, 232n28, 238, 245, 258
Van Malsen, Cornelis, 238, 240, 257-58
Van Nijevelt, Cornelis van Zuylen, 47, 59
Van Nouhuijs, H. G., 56
Van Nus, Johannes J. M. C., 239
Van Olinda, Marietta, 361, *362*
Van Os, Hendrik J., 229
Van Prinsterer, Guilaume Groen, 32, *33*, 61, 301; and ACVR, 39, 169, 174, 177, 329, 534, 577; and Anti-Revolutionary Party, 31, 111; as Réveil leader, 64, 486, 577
Van Putten, Christina Johanna Van Raalte (Mrs. Jacob) (daughter), 567
Van Putten, Jacob, 315
Van Raalte County, MI: proposed, 570-71
Van Raalte Farm Park, 586
Van Raalte Institute, 541, 588
Van Raalte Memorial Plaque, Pillar Church, 540-41
Van Raalte Papers, 541-42
Van Raalte Press, 588
Van Raalte School, 331, 402
Van Raalte, Albert(us) (father), character of, 24-25; children of, 9-10; death notice of, 20-21; life of, 1-2; marriage to Catrina Harking, 8-10, and wedding certificate, *9*; as pastor at Fijnaart, 20-22, at Groningen, 3-4, at Renswoude, 5, 8, at Rijsoord, 19, at Scherpenisse, 19, at 's-Heer Abtskerke, 18-19; salary of, 13

Van Raalte, Alberta Christina van Dijk Mansier (sister), 10, 25
Van Raalte, Albertus Christiaan (ACVR): *frontispiece*, 43, 53, 224, 247, 451; *Adres aan de Algemene Synode*, 63n79; advises settlers, 159, 208-11, 214, 236, 487-88; and alcohol: bans distilling, 251-52, 418-19, poem, *252*; and American agriculture, 277-79; as apostle of Overijssel, 84-94, and preaching tours, 94-95, and map, *96*; arrested at Den Ham, 88, imprisoned in Huis van Verzekering (Zwolle), *90*; and Arnhem Emigration Society, 169-71; and baptism, 107-8, 243, and handwritten register, *243*; and Belgian revolt, 36-38, exempt from service, 63n77; bias against Michigan, 196, 213-14; bicentennial of birth, xviii, 11n19; biography, xiii, xv, xix, xx, 27-30, 140-42, 157, 353-54, and change of given name, 12n21; and black people, 264, 352, 491-92; and board of trustees, 253-54; and business: failures, 217, 280, 312, 327, 394, *392*, 396, 407, 445, 527, 575, 583, with son, 396-98; and call to ministry, 38-39; and Calvinism, 577; candidacy exams, 43-46; and Cape Town, 549; as capitalist, 367-68, 372-91, anxiety about, 398-400, and failed mill venture, 392-93, and land dealings, 368-77,

acreage graph, *406*, table of purchases, 590, table of sales, 591-92; as silent partner, 98, 384-87; and catechism teaching, 241, 297, 303-4, 318-19, 331-32, 354n77, 453, 540, 575, and attendance record, *319*; character, 28-29, 573-76; children and grandchildren, 535-36, 567-70, and lands bequeathed, 377n25, 400-403; and choice of Michigan, 185-97, 201-11; and Christian education, 117-19, views of, 325-30, 357, 359-63, 486n8, primary, 359-63, secondary 335-37; and Christian Separated Church: factions, 129-34, polity, 100-102, synods, 102-3, 123-27, 184, 128-29; as church planter, xiv, xv, 95, 112, 187, 233, 281, 289, 303-5, 312, 342, 484, 487, 532, 537; citizenship (first papers), *223*, 224; and Civil War, 424-38, 543-45; and clerical garb, 108-10; and Cohen Stuart, 525-26; compared to colleagues, 64-65; criticized, as minister, 311-12, 225, 227, 377, 411, 448, 468, 498, as land dealer, 377, 440, as political activist, 423; as consistory president, 321-22; and Darwinism, 534; death of, 546-52, announced in *Holland City News, 551*, city proclamation, *553*, First Church sanctuary, *554*, hearse, *557*, gravestone, *558*; debtors list, *392*; descendants today, 563n55; and De Moen family, 72-73; and Den Bleyker partnership, 387-93; desk and chair, *309*; as doctor, 237-38, 432, 503; and dog license *536*; and Dort church order, 59, 62, 71, 103, 125, 577-60; and Ebenezer Fund, 523-54; and education: church, 117, 318-19, Sunday school, 228, 447, 455, 545-46; emigration of, 161-67, 171-73, 175-77, 182-83, farewell, 177-80, reasons, 158-61, 163-64; eulogies of, 559-61; fastidiousness of, 14; and feast days, 92, 129, 293, 305; final months of, 545-59; and fines, 93, 98; and friends, 27, 30-31, 37-38, 95, 378-79, 424, 465, 469, 553, 582, American, 193, 195n23, 197n26, 203, 207, 211, 262, 267-70, 276, 335, 453, in the East, 187, 315, 336, 354, 394-95, 404, 410, 460, Réveil men, 131, Phelps, 503, 524, Scholte, xxi, 70; and fundraising, xiv, 335, 342, 349-50, 354, 368, 405, 443, 562, 582, for harbor, 194, 271-74, for Holland Academy, 274, 322, 325-26, 336, 344-50, 354, 359-60, 446, 500, 501, for Hope College, 484, for Pillar church, 315; gymnasium diploma, *34*; and Gysbert Haan, 295-97; and height, 461; and historiography, xiv-xxii; and Holland Academy, 348, 580; and Holland incorporation, 438-43; as Hope College trustee, 526-29; homestead, *541*, heated with wood, 449n9, improved, 540-42, razed, 442n76; house and garden, 228-32; and hymns, 447, 481; and illness, 182, 402, 528-29, 542, 555, cold, 95, 350, 532, cholera, 28, 38-39, 45, 175, depression, 327, 350, dyspepsia, 325, dysentery, 210, 238, 240, 494, exhaustion, 202, 345-46, 350, 445-47, 464, 500, 501, 546, heart problems, 326, malaise, 445, 503, malaria, 236, neuralgia, 350, rheumatism, 93, 350, 431, 481, 494, 531, 538, 542, 546, sore throat, 91, 95, 105, 470, toothache, 326, 350, tuberculosis, 549, typhoid fever, 157, 175, 208, 537, 540, weakness, 434, 455, 537; inconsistencies of, 581-83; influence of, xxi, 110, 132, *133*, 277, 414, and failure, 437-38, 449, 560; Java rejected, 167-69; and Kruisgezinden schism, 104-6, 113-14, 134, 151, 157, 549; and Kuyper, 534-35; and lay preachers, 69, 78, 103, 143, 145, 148; at Leiden University, 33-34, 39-46, student photo, *44*, and Certificate in Theology, *44*; letter ordering lumber, *231*; letter to Brummelkamp Jr., 59n67; and Lord's Supper, 94, 131, 241-42, 423, 460, 549, regulation of, 107, 116, 124, 129, 295, 364, 415, 459, 549; and Ommen parsonage and school, *115*; marriage of, 72, and certificate, *73*; and Memorial Day address, 542-43; memorial plaque, *561*; and Michigan "boosters," 193-96, *198*, 204-7; and missions, 529-30, 536-39; and mortgage troubles, 373n15, 393-96; and national bank, 403-5; and native peoples, 211-13, lands of, 376; and Netherlands homecoming, 353, 460-71; as newspaper magnate, 407-11, and censorship, 411-12, and H. Doesburg conflict, 412-18; newspaper subscriptions, 261n98; obituary, 549-53; ocean crossings, 180-82, 460-62, 471; ordination, 69-71, rejected, 55-62; pastorates, 67-69, 77-84, 113-50, 244; and Pella RPDC, 342-44, 358, 360, 446, 479, 543; and People's Assembly, 250-54; and persecution, 67-69, 79-99; philanthropic businesses, 111-12, 134-40, 380-81, 583; and Ploeg, 447-48; as political activist, 418-24, 443; as promoter, 405-6; protagonists, 104-5, 299, 425, 447; retirement, 531; and Réveil, 30; and RPDC and RCA synod delegate, 312n81, 355n68; royal recognition of, 110-11, 120-23; on sacraments; 106-8; and salary, 122, 151, 153, 156, 314, 346,

361, 363, 368, 371, 379, 477-78, 481, 526; and Scholte, 40, 134, 178, 183, 233, 343, 420-22, breaks ranks with, 213-15; school inspector, 265n104, 312; scouting Holland site expenses, 204n40; and Secession of 1834, 301-3; and secularism, 124, 525-35; as seminary teacher, 143-50, 153-56; sermons, 305-11, and notes, *308*; and slavery, 418-20, 426, 544, 578; social life, 324-25; and state church, 62-64; statue (Centennial Park), *587*; theology of, 124n32, 577-78; trek in Drenthe, *133*; tributes, 570-72, 584-88; turning points, 584-85; and US passport, *462*; village trustee, 253-54, 260, 336, 373, 376, 383; village hand-drawn plat, 226; and Whig Party, 419-20; and women's education, 343, 358, and role, 567; zeal of, 454, 566. *See also* First Reformed [Pillar] Church, Holland

Van Raalte, Albertus Christiaan (Allie) (son of Bertus), 325, 498n45, 567, 569

Van Raalte, Albertus Christiaan (Bertus) (son), *324*, *565*; birth, 141; businesses, 396-98, children, 325, 536; and Civil War, 427; character, 497-98, 563, 565; desertion of family, 487, 497, 575; emigration of, 180; home lost in fire, 478; inheritance, 394n61; schooling, 358. *See also* Van Raalte, Helena Hofman (Mrs. Albertus Christiaan)

Van Raalte, Albertus Christian (son of Dirk B. K.) (cleric), 568, 570

Van Raalte, Anna Arendina Harking (Mrs. Johannes Teessen), 13, 23, 313, 499, 500, 563

Van Raalte, Anna Helena (granddaughter), 568

Van Raalte, Anna Sophia (daughter), 354, 402, 490, 499, 500, 534, 540, 549, 564, *565*, 567

Van Raalte, Arend (Arent) Johannes Christiaan (brother), 10, 13, 16, 22, *24*, 367

Van Raalte, Barteld Janz (ancestor), 2

Van Raalte, Barthus Cornelius Niesceüs, 10

Van Raalte, Bastian Dirk Keppel (grandson), 568

Van Raalte, Benjamin (son), *428*, 479, *565*, 568; birth, 141-42; businesses, 397, 528, 564; children, 535; and Civil War, 425n46, 427-28, 431-36, 438, 455, 543; emigration, 180; and farm, 492, 528, 540-41; and farmhouse, 532, 540; and father ACVR, 260, 533-34, and admonitions, 549, 562, 583; and Hope RCA, 563; and inheritance, 394n61; and Julia Gilmore, 498, 532; and mother Christiana, 464, 497, 499, 502

Van Raalte, Benjamin, Jr. (grandson), 562
Van Raalte, Carl De Moen (grandson), 568
Van Raalte, Catharina Alberta (sister), 22n49
Van Raalte, Catrina Catherina Harking (Mrs. Albertus) (mother), 1, 8-9, 12-13, 18, 21-22, 72, 91; children, 9-10, and wedding certificate, 9
Van Raalte, Christina (Chris) Johanna De Moen, painting 244, photograph, 501; biography, 566-68; and Brummelkamps, 152, 157, 178-79, 464; and childbirth, 141-42, 180, 239-40, 312-13, 325, 499; death of, 478, 499-504, 533, 549, 557, funeral, 504-5, grave stone, 558; family, 4, 78, 142, 358; hardships, 178-80, 189, 194, 219, 231-32; health, 259, 326, 460-61, 471, 482, 484, 490, 493, 497, 556; and household duties, 80, 257; and husband's affection, 92; inheritance, 76, 120, 136; letter to sons in Civil War, 429; and maids, 258-60; marriage, 72, 73; as mother, 428, 451, 487, 502, 562-63; and music, 502; as pastor's wife, 80, 113, 179-80, 189, 228, 242, 244, 314, 316, 353, 395, 490, 504, 508, 582; and persecution, 89, 92, 95; personality of, 230, 501, 504-5, 508-10, 562; social life, 259-60, 268-69; spiritual life, 310, 428, 583; upbringing, 74-78; and Van Velzens, 74; as wife, 310, 497, 503-8
Van Raalte, Christina (Christine) Catharina (daughter) (Mrs. William Gilmore and Mrs. Teunis Keppel), 494, 497, 565, 568-69; birth of, 141; career of: seamstress, 354, 438, 461, 566, Hope College matron, 566; emigration of, 180, 508; education of, 354, 359, 566; faith commitment of, 563; as Mrs. Gilmore, 492-94, 498, 531-32, 542, 549, 563-64; as Mrs. Keppel, 547, 564, 566, and marriage certificate, 546
Van Raalte, Christina (Tia) Pfanstiehl (granddaughter), 567
Van Raalte, Christina Catharina (II), 141, 499
Van Raalte, Christina Catherina (Christine or Chris) (sister) (died 15 months), 141
Van Raalte, Christina Johanna (granddaughter), 567
Van Raalte, Christine Ann (Mrs. Jeffrey Schaefer Smith), 570
Van Raalte, Christine Cornelia (Mrs. Anthony Van Westenberg), 570
Van Raalte, Dirk Blikman Kikkert (son), 428, 565; and businesses, 461, 524, 541, 556; and Civil War, 354, 427-36, 438, 502, 541,

543; education of, 355; and father's admonitions, 532, 534-35, 549, 560, 562-33, and inheritance, 394n61, power of attorney, 395, 460, 493; and Hope RCA, 563; marriage of, 567; and mother, 499, 502, 510; political career of, 422, 564; and purchase of Van Raalte homestead, 402, 540-41, *541*; as a youth, 141, 180, 260, 447, 479, 497

Van Raalte, Dirk, "Dick," Jr. (son of Dirk B. K.), 541; and Van Raalte homestead sale, 568

Van Raalte, Edna Dean Pillsbury (Mrs. Albertus Christiaan), 568

Van Raalte, Gerrit Jan Harking (died in infancy), 10

Van Raalte, Gerrit Rademaker, 10

Van Raalte, Helena Hofman (Mrs. Albertus Christiaan), *324*, 397, 475, 479-80, 498, 534, 536, 549, 563; and farm plat, *480*; and homestead, *541*

Van Raalte, Jan Harking, 10

Van Raalte, Joan Niescie, 10

Van Raalte, Johanna Arendina, 9

Van Raalte, Johanna Bartha (Blikman Kikkert), 13, 23, 136-38, 140-42, 151, 188, 367, 499

Van Raalte, Johanna Maria Wilhelmina "Minnie" (granddaughter), 239, 568

Van Raalte, Julia Gilmore (Mrs. Ben Van Raalte), 532-33, 540, 583

Van Raalte, Kate Ledeboer (Mrs. Dirk Blikman Kikkert), 541, 563-64, 567-68

Van Raalte, Maria (Mary) Wilhelmina (Mrs. Peter J. Oggel) (Mrs. Teunis Keppel), childhood, 239, 353, 402, 447, 499; education, 357, 359; death, 499; and parents, 489, 501, 534, 547-48; marriage to P. J. Oggel, 349, 354, 418, 449, 451, 497; marriage to Keppel, 475, *547*, 563-64, 566, and marriage certificate, *546*; as teacher, 490, 493, 498, 540, 549, *565*

Van Raalte, Maria Wilhelmina (died in infancy), 569

Van Raalte, Neeltje (Mrs. Rijnier Swierink), 3, 8

Van Raalte, Niescina Margaretha Anna (sister), 10, 13, 23

Van Raalte, Petrus (Peter) Johannes Alberti (brother), 9-10, 13, 16, 22, 23n51, 142, 367, 549, 567n60

Van Raalte, Petrus Alberti (brother, died in infancy), 9

Van Raalte, Pieter (maternal grandfather), 2-3, 8, 10

Van Raalte, Roelof Barth Niesceüs, 10

Van Raaltestraat (Ommen), 146

Van Rechteren, Jacob Hendrik Graaf, 78-81, 85-86

Van Rees, Hendrik, 79

Van Roosenburg, Abraham J. Twent, 32

Van Schelven, Gerrit, 199, 277, 440, 471-72, 473n65, 514, 573, 586

Van Slochteren, 60

Van Spronsen, Joan, 433n60
Van Velzen, Johanna Maria (Naatje) de Moen (Mrs. Simon), 74-76, 92, 126, 136, 152, 464, 533, 549
Van Velzen, Simon, 53; and ACVR, 40, 61, 67, 71-74, 126-27, 134, 142, 151, 157, 174, 460, 464-65, 469, 550, 579; and Belgian revolt, 35-38; and Christian Separated Church, 70-71, 84-85, 97, 101-8, 147, 174, 183; and Dort church order, 128-34; and fines, 98; and Gronings-Drents party, 129-32, 288, 468, 579; as Kampen professor, 345n46, 460; as Leiden University student, 30, 32, 40-41; and Luther moment, 62n75; longevity of, 550; marriage of Johanna Christiana, 73-75, 152, 460, 550, 582; as pastor, 49, 61-62, 66-67, 74, 132, 145; and Secession of 1834, 62; and Scholte, 123-34; and state church, 64-65; and wife's inheritance, 135n62
Van Velzen, Simon, Jr., 60-63, 74, 464, 580
Van Vleck Hall, Hope College, 274, 346, *348*, 350, 509, 511, 526
Van Vleck, Elizabeth (nee Falconer), 335, 342, 549
Van Vleck, John, *347*; and ACVR, 345-48; and Pioneer Academy, 335, 341-42, 347-48, 353-54, 359, 421, 453, 509, 549
Van Voss, Johanna Alida, 74

Van Westenberg, Anthony, 570
Van Zwaluwenburg, Hendrikje, 358, 361
Varkensstraat (Arnhem), 152
Varkevisser, P., 112
Varsen, Ambt Ommen (Overijssel), 81
Varsenerdijk (street in Ommen), 135, 137
Vecht River, 93, 95
Veenhuizen, Albertus Bernardus, 146-47, 150n17, 153, 156
Veenstra, IJsbrand Jans, 145, 148
Velp (Gelderland): and Separated Church, 112, 151-54, 156, 161, 167, 170, 175, 177
Veneklasen, Berend, 489
Verbeek, Jannemieke, 259
Versteeg, Dingeman, 584
Verwey, Isaac, 571
Vicksburg, MS, 432, 434-36
Victorian culture, 510, 526, 540, 567, 573
Vinke, Jacobus "Koos", 251, 269-70
Vinke, Wilhelmina, 270
Vinkemulder, Hendrik, 300
Virginia, xxi, 436, 527, 584; Agricultural Society, 490
Visscher, Evert Jans, 176
Visscher, Geesje, 548, 555-56, 558
Visscher, Jan Jans, 176
Visscher, Jan, 548
Vogel Center, Missaukee County, MI, 488
Vogel, Jan, 488
volkskerk: and baptism, 107, 534
Volksvergadering, 250, 254, 260, 270, 276, 331, 376, 380, 418
Volksvriend, De (newspaper), 539

Voorne Canal, 178
voorzanger (foresinger), 28
Vree, Jasper, 18, 62n75, 63
Vriesland, MI, 261, 374; churches, 248, 263, 282n7, 284-85, 295-97, 414, 479; and colony, 233
Vrieze, Jannes, 176
Vriezenveen [Overijssel] Separated Church, 122
Vyn, Dirk, 422

Wakazoo, Chief Peter, 376
Wakker, Gerrit, 325-26
Walling, Prientje (Mrs. Simon), 499
Walling, Simon Meerman, 499
Walsh, Heber, 503
Walter, Anna Broadmore, 436n65
Wanneperveen (Overijssel), 19; and ACVR, 12-13, 28-29; Hervormde Kerk, 16-17, 24; Nederduitse Gereformeerde Kerk, 12; and parochial school, 14-15, 25, 365, 534; pastorate of father Van Raalte, 10-15, 18, 20; public school, 14; and Van Raalte family, 3n3
War of 1812, 370
Ward, Eber Brock, 190, *192*
Ware Hollandsche Gereformeerde Kerk (US), 303n59. See also Christian Reformed Church (US)
Washington, George (US president), 573
Waterman, Israël, 153
Waupun, WI, 167, 197

Waverly Ave., Holland, 219-20, 228-29, 372
Waverly Stone, 268
Webster., Daniel, 198
Webster's Elementary Speller, 320, 331, 334
well-meant offer of the Gospel, 124, 130, 310. See also Reformed doctrine(s)
West Drenthe, MI, 263
West Michigan Society to Benefit the Indians, 200
West, Dr., 507
Western Theological Seminary, Holland, 303, 348, 351, 353; and ACVR, 337, 465, 489, 504, 559
Westveer, James, 248
wheat (buckwheat), 159, 235, 383, 392; cropping, 388, 391-92; milling, 392
Wheaton College, 473
Whig Party, 205, 267, 411, 426, 459; and ACVR, 419-20
whiskey. See alcohol
White, Thomas W., 205n41
Whitefield, George, 41
Wichers, Willard, 576
Wichers, Wynand, 576
Wildeboer, Klaas Marinus, 145, 148, 151, 259
Wilder & Company, 398
Wilder, Warren, 397-98; and ACVR, 397
Wildervank (Groningen), 145
Wilhelminastraat (street), Velp (Gelderland), 152

Willem Frederik (stadtholder). See Willem I

Willem I (king, prince of Orange-Nassau, grand duke of Luxembourg): *17*; abdicates throne, 159; and ACVR, 25, 34-35, 37, 71, 81, 114, 121-23, 142, 365; authoritarian rule of, xiii, xix, 54-55, 58, 60; and Belgian Revolution, 34-38; and Christian school policy, 365; and church polity, 15-16, 58, 108; and Cultivation System, 168; and Réveil, 30-32, 61, 168; and royal recognition, 110-11, 114, 120-23, 142; second marriage (Countess Henriette d'Oultre), 38n24; and Van Velzen, 84-85

Willem II (king), 98, 121, 161, 174; and ACVR, 224, 266

Willem III (king), 110n25

Willem of Orange (Willem the Silent), 265

Willem V (stadholder, king), xix, 4-5

Willemstad Hervormde Kerk (Zeeland), 29, 469

Wilpshaar, Albertus, 139

Wilson, Etta Smith, 211

Wilson, John, 419n28

wine. See beverages

Winter, Egbert, 471, 559

Winterswijk (Gelderland), 165, 170

Wisconsin, xxii, 416; and ACVR, 187, 192, 196-97, 203-4, 207-8, 213, 582; Catholics, 209n50; churches, 150, 303, 312; Dutch, 170-71, 215

Witherspoon, William, 194-95

Woertink-Gerrits, Hendrikje, barn, *93*

Wolterink, Hendrik, 115

Woodruff, Henry S., 200, 228

Woodruff, Milton, 228

worldliness, 87, 116, 280, 364

Wormser, Andries, 140

Wormser, Hendrik, 131

Wormser, Johan A., *169*, 469, 584

Wormser, Johan A., Jr., xvii, xviii, 123n29, 132n54, 140, 183, 469, *470*

Wormser-Van der Veen, Janke, 469

worship, 129, 293; Christmas, 293, sermon, 305; controversy, 305; and conventicles, 69, 78-79, 103, 115; disrespected, 116-17, on Ascension Day (1837), 92; festival (feast) days, 92, 129, 293, 305; freedom of, 80, 164, 174, 191, 240, 251; and hymns, 129, 293, 323, 445, 447, 452, 581; Prayer Day, 305, 435; reading services, 145, 313; regulated, 48, 52, 54, 61n73, 81-82, 85, 120-21; restricted, 158; Second Pentecost, 112; Thanksgiving, 293, 431, 436, 532

Wubben, Frederik Ebbinge, 85, 89

Wyckoff, Isaac N., *188*; and ACVR, 193, 197n26, 206-7, 372, 378n30, 501; aids emigrants, 187-88, 336; aids Holland colony, 271, 274, 344; as pastor Second Albany RPDC, 172, 187, 348; and

Union of 1850, 281-86, 295, 571

Yankee(s), 208, 268n108, 383, 419, 489, 508; Dutch, 188, 209; Methodists, 200, 331; notions, 381. *See also* English people
Yellow Springs, MI, 375
Young Dutch, 187, 205, 222n, 281, 290, 446, 515. *See also* Old Dutch
Young, Elias G., 381
Young, George, *195*, 205n41, 206
Ypma, Marten, xxii, 233, 246, *247*, 263, 283, 293, 339, 414, 417

Zaagmolen Clearing, 383
Zaandam (Noord-Holland), 467
Zagers, Evert, 173, 218, 225n17
Zahn, Theodor, 318
Zeeland Reformed Church. *See* First Reformed Church, Zeeland
Zeeland, MI: cemetery, 416n20; Cohen Stuart visit to, 525-26; colony of, 165, 229, 233; and caucus brawl, 263-64; and Dutch Road, 250, 255-56, 258, 263; and harbor, 275; and Holland fire relief, 523; and land purchases, 375, 377; and merchants, 258; and naturalization, 261; politics, 420, 425; and prohibition, 419; rivalry with Holland, 262-64, 408, 411, 414-15, 519-20; semicentennial, 522-23; taxes, 275; township, 260, 262, 265, 267, 380, 570-71; and Union of 1850, 284-85, 414; village platted, 371
Zeeland, province of, xxii, 18-19, 28-29, 49, 67; and ACVR, 131-32, 151; and Bible belt, 1, 102, 104; and Christian Separated Church, 54, 67, 129, 151, 154, 165; and emigration, 170-73, 189, 196, 206n, 232-33, 239, association 171n38; and father Van Raalte's ministry, 18-19, 28-29
Zeeuws dialect, 291
Zoetermeer, MI, 233
Zuid Beveland (Zeeland), 18-19
Zuidema, Peter, 496
Zuidenveld (Drenthe), 132
Zuid-Holland, province of, 18-19, 67, 98, 127, 129; and emigration, 173, 214, 234, 297, 298, 332, 363; and fines, 98; provincial church board, 42; provincial classes, 154, 596; provincial synod, 55; and Scholte, 67, 127; synod, 55
Zululand (Zulus), South Africa, xvi, 449-50, 452, 574
Zwartsluis (Overijssel), 1
Zweedijk, Adriaan, 146-47
Zwemer House (Hope College), *339*
Zwemer, Adrian, 339, 446, 479
Zwolle (Overijssel): and ACVR, 463, 467; classis, 79, 101, 105, 122; and government officials, 14, 112, 139; and lay preachers, 59, 78, 104-5; prison, 89, *90*; as provincial capital, 150; provincial synod, 146, 298
Zwolle [Overijssel] Separated Church, 104, 213

Made in United States
Troutdale, OR
10/22/2024